POLICE
IN AMERICA

TASK FORCE REPORT

The Police

The President's Commission
on Law Enforcement and
Administration of Justice

ARNO PRESS & THE NEW YORK TIMES
NEW YORK, 1971

Reprint Edition 1971 by Arno Press Inc.

Reprinted from a copy in
The Pennsylvania State Library

LC# 73-154585
ISBN 0-405-03383-4

Police In America
ISBN for complete set: 0-405-03360-5
See last pages of this volume for titles.

Manufactured in the United States of America

TASK FORCE REPORT: THE POLICE

Task Force on the Police

THE PRESIDENT'S COMMISSION ON LAW ENFORCEMENT AND
ADMINISTRATION OF JUSTICE

U.S. Government Printing Office, Washington : 1967.
For sale by the Superintendent of Documents, U.S. Government Printing Office, Washington, D.C. 20402. Price $1.50.
Copies of the Commission's general report, "The Challenge of Crime in a Free Society," can be purchased from the Superintendent of Documents for $2.25.
Copies of other task force reports and other supporting materials can also be purchased.

FOREWORD

In February of this year the President's Commission on Law Enforcement and Administration of Justice issued its General Report: *The Challenge of Crime in a Free Society*. As noted in the Foreword to that Report, the Commission's work was a joint undertaking, involving the collaboration of Federal, State, local, and private agencies and groups, hundreds of expert consultants and advisers, and the Commission's own staff. Chapter 4 of that Report made findings and recommendations relating to the problems facing the Nation's police.

This volume, the Task Force Report on the Police, embodies the research and analysis of the staff and consultants to the Commission which underlie those findings and recommendations, and in many instances it elaborates on them. Preliminary drafts of most of the materials in the volume have been distributed to the entire Commission and discussed generally at Commission meetings, although more detailed discussions and intensive review have been the responsibility of a panel of five Commission members attached to this Task Force. While individual members of the panel have reservations on some points covered in this volume but not reflected in the Commission's General Report, this volume as a whole has the general endorsement of the panel. The organization of the Commission and the Task Forces is described in the General Report at pages 311–312.

Three chapters of this volume were prepared by Commission consultants after extensive consultation with Commission staff. Chapter 2, "Law Enforcement: The Police Role," was prepared by Profs. Frank Remington and Herman Goldstein of the University of Wisconsin College of Law at Madison. Chapter 4, "Coordination and Consolidation of Police Service," was the work of the Public Administration Service of Chicago, Ill., and Chapter 9, "The Community's Role in Law Enforcement," was written by Patricia M. Wald, former Commissioner of the President's Commission on Crime in the District of Columbia.

Among the Research Studies to be published shortly by the Commission will be a number of field studies, conducted by consultants to the Commission, which will have bearing on various aspects of police operations.

The Commission is deeply grateful for the talent and dedication of its staff and for the unstinting assistance and advice of consultants, advisers, and collaborating agencies whose efforts are reflected in this volume.

NICHOLAS DEB. KATZENBACH
Chairman

THE COMMISSION

Nicholas deB. Katzenbach, *Chairman*

Genevieve Blatt
Charles D. Breitel
Kingman Brewster
Garrett H. Byrne
Thomas J. Cahill*
Otis Chandler*
Leon Jaworski
Thomas C. Lynch
Ross L. Malone*

James B. Parsons
Lewis F. Powell, Jr.
William P. Rogers
Robert G. Storey
Julia D. Stuart
Robert F. Wagner*
Herbert Wechsler
Whitney M. Young, Jr.*
Luther W. Youngdahl

*Police Task Force panel members.

THE STAFF

Executive Director:

James Vorenberg

Deputy Director:

Henry S. Ruth, Jr.

Associate Directors:

Gene S. Muehleisen‡
Elmer K. Nelson, Jr.
Lloyd E. Ohlin
Arthur Rosett

Assistant Directors:

David B. Burnham
Bruce J. Terris‡
Samuel G. Chapman (*Police*)‡
Howard Ohmart (*Corrections*)
Vincent O'Leary (*Corrections*)
Charles H. Rogovin (*Organized Crime*)

Director of Science and Technology:

Alfred Blumstein

William Caldwell
Weston R. Campbell, Jr.
Gerald M. Caplan
Roland Chilton
Joseph G. J. Connolly
Virginia N. Crawford
Elizabeth Bartholet DuBois
Paul B. Duruz‡
Robert L. Emrich
Floyd Feeney
Victor Gioscia
Sheldon Krantz‡
Anthony Lapham
John L. McCausland
Sheila Ann Mulvihill
Albert W. Overby, Jr.
Nick Pappas
John F. Quinn‡
Robert Rice
Gordon D. Rowe‡
Susan Freeman Schapiro
Gerald Stern
Thelma C. Stevens
Keith Stubblefield
Martin Timin
G. Joseph Vining
Richardson White, Jr.

‡Staff members devoting primary attention to the work of the Police Task Force.

CONSULTANTS

Richard H. Blum, Professor, Stanford University, Stanford, Calif.
Allen P. Bristow, Associate Professor, Department of Police Science and Administration, California State College at Los Angeles, Los Angeles, Calif.
William P. Brown, Professor, State University of New York, Albany, N.Y.
James E. Carnahan, Associate Professor, Department of Police Science and Administration, California State College at Los Angeles, Los Angeles, Calif.
Edward V. Comber, Project Director, Criminal Justice Information Systems Design Study, California Department of Justice, Sacramento, Calif.
J. Shane Creamer, First Assistant U.S. Attorney, Philadelphia, Pa.
William F. Danielson, Director of Personnel, City of Berkeley, Calif.
Harry Diamond, Associate Professor, Department of Police Science and Administration, California State College at Los Angeles, Los Angeles, Calif.
George D. Eastman, Headquarters Representative, Public Administration Service, Chicago, Ill.
John Fabbri, Chief of Police, South San Francisco, Calif.
Edward A. Farris, Professor of Police Science, New Mexico State University, University Park, N. Mex.
James L. Fyke, Field Representative, Public Administration Service, Chicago, Ill.
Raymond Galvin, Assistant Professor, School of Police Administration and Public Safety, Michigan State University, East Lansing, Mich.
A. C. Germann, Professor, Department of Criminology, California State College at Long Beach, Long Beach, Calif.
Herman Goldstein, Professor, University of Wisconsin Law School, Madison, Wis.
G. Douglas Gourley, Professor and Chairman, Department of Police Science and Administration, California State College at Los Angeles, Los Angeles, Calif.
John Guidici, Captain, Oakland Police Department, Oakland, Calif.
Richard O. Hankey, Professor, Department of Police Science and Administration, California State College at Los Angeles, Los Angeles, Calif.
William H. Hewitt, Associate Professor and Chairman, Department of Police Science, State University of New York, Farmingdale, N.Y.
Roy E. Holladay, Chief of Police, Fort Collins, Colo.
Norman C. Kassoff, Supervisor, Police Training Unit, International Association of Chiefs of Police, Washington, D.C.

Joseph Kimble, Chief of Police, San Carlos, Calif.
Richard Laskin, Associate Professor, Department of Political and Social Science, Illinois Institute of Technology, Chicago, Ill.
B. Earl Lewis, Foothill College, Los Altos Hills, Calif.
G. Stephen Lloyd, Field Representative, Public Administration Service, Chicago, Ill.
Joseph D. Lohman, Dean, School of Criminology, University of California, Berkeley, Calif.
Lawrence S. Margolis, Special Assistant U.S. Attorney for the District of Columbia, Department of Justice.
Gordon E. Misner, Visiting Associate Professor, School of Criminology, University of California, Berkeley, Calif.
Richard A. Myren, Dean, School of Criminal Justice, State University of New York, Albany, N.Y.
David L. Norrgard, Field Representative, Public Administration Service, Chicago, Ill.
George W. O'Connor, Director, Professional Standards Division, International Association of Chiefs of Police, Washington, D.C.
Bruce T. Olson, Police Administration Specialist, Institute for Community Development and Services, Michigan State University, East Lansing, Mich.
J. Kinney O'Rourke, Executive Director, Massachusetts League of Cities and Towns, Boston, Mass.
Margaret G. Oslund, Department of Political and Social Science, Illinois Institute of Technology, Chicago, Ill.
Wesley A. Pomeroy, Undersheriff, San Mateo County Sheriff's Police Department, San Mateo, Calif.
Norman E. Pomrenke, Assistant Director, Institute of Government, University of North Carolina, Chapel Hill, N.C.
Louis Radelet, Professor, School of Police Administration and Public Safety, Michigan State University, East Lansing, Mich.
Leonard E. Reisman, President, John Jay College of Criminal Justice, The City University of New York, New York, N.Y.
Gerald Robin, Office of National Analysts, Philadelphia, Pa.
Jewell L. Ross, Captain (retired), Berkeley Police Department, Berkeley, Calif.
James D. Stinchcomb, Supervisor, Police Education Unit, International Association of Chiefs of Police, Washington, D.C.
Patricia M. Wald, Commissioner, President's Commission on Crime in the District of Columbia.
John B. Williams, Associate Professor, Department of Police Science and Administration, California State College at Los Angeles, Los Angeles, Calif.

ADVISERS

Claude Abercrombie, Jr., Sheriff, Douglas County, Douglasville, Ga.
Charles R. Adrian, Professor and Chairman, Department of Political Science, University of California, Riverside, Calif.
Douglas W. Ayres, City Manager, Salem, Oreg.
David A. Booth, Associate Professor, Department of Political Science, University of Kentucky, Lexington, Ky.
C. Beverly Brily, Mayor, Nashville, Tenn.
Thomas Brownfield, Special Agent Supervisor, FBI, Department of Justice.
Robert L. Carter, General Counsel, National Association for the Advancement of Colored People, New York, N.Y.
Joseph Casper, Assistant Director, FBI, Department of Justice.
George E. Causey, Deputy Chief, Metropolitan Police Department, Washington, D.C.
Ben Clark, Sheriff, Riverside County, Calif.
Donald E. Clark, Sheriff, Multnomah County, Portland, Oreg.
James Cotter, Inspector in Charge, FBI National Academy, FBI, Department of Justice.
John Creer, County Commissioner, Salt Lake City, Utah.
Thompson S. Crockett, Professor of Police Science, St. Petersburg Junior College, St. Petersburg, Fla.
Louis R. Damiani, Chairman, Legislative Committee, National Office of the Fraternal Order of Police, Philadelphia, Pa.
Jerome Daunt, Chief, Uniform Crime Reporting Section, FBI, Department of Justice.
C. D. deLoach, Assistant to the Director, FBI, Department of Justice.
Leonard J. Duhl, Special Assistant to the Secretary of the Department of Housing and Urban Development, Washington, D.C.
Woodrow W. Dumas, Mayor, East Baton Rouge, La.
Edward L. Epting, Sergeant, San Francisco Police Department, San Francisco, Calif.
Paul E. Estaver, Dissemination Officer, Office of Law Enforcement Assistance, Department of Justice.
Rev. Walter E. Fauntroy, Director, Washington Bureau Office, Southern Christian Leadership Conference, Washington, D.C.
Thomas F. Fitzpatrick, Director, Bureau of Special Services and Intelligence, San Francisco Police Department, San Francisco, Calif.
Arthur Q. Funn, General Counsel, National Urban League, Inc., New York, N.Y.
Charles R. Gain, Deputy Chief, Oakland Police Department, Oakland, Calif.
Robert R. J. Gallati, Director, New York State Intelligence and Identification System, Albany, N.Y.
Bernard Garmire, Chief of Police, Tucson, Ariz.
Peter F. Hagen, Inspector, Los Angeles Police Department, Los Angeles, Calif.
William Harpole, Sheriff, Oktibbeha County, Starkville, Miss.
Patrick Healy, Executive Director, National League of Cities, Washington, D.C.
William W. Hermann, Police Consultant, Rand Corp., University of Southern California, Los Angeles, Calif.
James C. Herron, Captain, Philadelphia Police Department, Philadelphia, Pa.
Roderic C. Hill, Lieutenant General, Adjutant General, California National Guard, Sacramento, Calif.
William Hollowell, Sheriff, Sunflower County, Indianola, Miss.
John E. Ingersoll, Chief of Police, Charlotte, N.C.
Adolph C. Jacobsmeyer, Major, St. Louis Police Department, St. Louis, Mo.
John J. Jemilo, Deputy Assistant Director, Office of Law Enforcement Assistance, Department of Justice.
Herbert T. Jenkins, Chief of Police, Atlanta, Ga.
Mark E. Keane, City Manager, Tucson, Ariz.
John T. Kelly, Deputy Chief of Police, Chicago, Ill.
Hubert O. Kemp, Chief of Police, Nashville-Davidson County, Tenn.
Harold Light, Assistant Special Agent in Charge at Quantico, Va., FBI, Washington, D.C.
Floyd Mann, Former Superintendent, Alabama Highway Patrol, Chambers County Sheriff's Office, Langdale, Ala.
Daniel H. Margolis, Attorney, Washington, D.C.
Robert E. McCann, Director of Training, Chicago Police Department, Chicago, Ill.
William P. McCarthy, Inspector, New York Police Department, New York, N.Y.
Roy McLaren, Director, Field Operations Division, International Association of Chiefs of Police, Washington, D.C.
Karl A. Menninger, M.D., Chief of Staff, The Menninger Foundation, Topeka, Kans.
Raymond M. Momboisse, Deputy Attorney General, California Department of Justice, Sacramento, Calif.

William Mooney, Special Agent Supervisor, FBI, Department of Justice.
Patrick V. Murphy, Assistant Director, Office of Law Enforcement Assistance, Department of Justice.
John F. Nichols, District Inspector, Detroit Police Department, Detroit, Mich.
Joseph D. Nicol, Superintendent, Illinois Bureau of Criminal Identification and Investigation, Joliet, Ill.
Harvard Norred, Chief of Police, Gwinnept County, Lawrenceville, Ga.
Peter J. Pitchess, Sheriff, Los Angeles County, Los Angeles, Calif.
George H. Puddy, Executive Officer, California Police Officers' Standards and Training Commission, Sacramento, Calif.
Thomas Reddin, Chief, Los Angeles Police Department, Los Angeles, Calif.
Rudy Sanfillippo, Task Force Director, Joint Commission on Correctional Manpower and Training, Washington, D.C.
Lloyd G. Sealy, Assistant Chief Inspector, New York Police Department, New York, N.Y.
Carleton F. Sharpe, City Manager, Kansas City, Mo.
Daniel J. Sharpe, Inspector, Rochester Police Department, Rochester, N.Y.
Robert Sheehan, Professor, Department of Law Enforcement Administration, Northeastern University, Boston, Mass.
R. Dean Smith, Director, Research and Development Division, International Association of Chiefs of Police, Washington, D.C.
Charles L. Southward, Brigadier General, Assistant Chief for Army National Guard, U.S. National Guard Bureau, Washington, D.C.
Daniel Stringer, Sheriff, Cherokee County, Canton, Ga.
Quinn Tamm, Executive Director, International Association of Chiefs of Police, Washington, D.C.
Carl C. Turner, Major General, Provost Marshal General, Department of the Army, Washington, D.C.
William Veeder, City Manager, Charlotte, N.C.
Nelson A. Watson, Project Director, Research and Development Division, International Association of Chiefs of Police, Washington, D.C.
Leon H. Weaver, Professor, School of Police Administration and Public Safety, Michigan State University, East Lansing, Mich.
James Q. Wilson, Associate Professor of Government, Director, Joint Center for Urban Studies of Massachusetts Institute of Technology and Harvard University, Cambridge, Mass.
Minor Keith Wilson, Assistant Chief of Police, Chicago Police Department, Chicago, Ill.
O. W. Wilson, Superintendent, Chicago Police Department, Chicago, Ill.
Orrell A. York, Executive Director, Municipal Police Training Council, Albany, N.Y.

SUPPORTING STAFF AND SERVICES

Secretarial and Clerical

James A. Adkins	Conchita A. Brown	Doris T. Farmer	Patricia A. Lanham
Doris J. Bacon	Scennie M. Brown	Ann Felegy	Joan E. Peterson
Margaret Beale	Suzanne L. Carpenter	Mary Fox	Evelene Richards
Mary G. Bergbom	Barbara A. Casassa	Carol A. Hambleton	Lee E. Salerno
Margaret R. Bickford	Sally M. Chopko	Rosalind M. Humphries	Shelia M. Sheahan
Nancy B. Bradley	Willie Copeland	Nancy Hunt	Nancy Strebe
Rita Louise Brooke	Catherine Cyrus	Betty C. Irby	Margaret Triplett
	Mary Frances Factory	Barbara J. Jones	

SUPPORTING SERVICES

INDEX

Edward T. Johnson & Associates, Washington, D.C.

COPY EDITING

Katherine M. Hanna
James O'Bryan

CONTENTS

	Page
CHAPTER 1 INTRODUCTION	**1**
History of the Police	3
Profile of the Police	7
CHAPTER 2 LAW ENFORCEMENT POLICY: THE POLICE ROLE	**13**
The Range of Problems Confronting the Police	13
The Police Response	14
Police Attitude Toward Their Role in the Development of Law Enforcement Policies	16
The Need To Recognize the Police as an Administrative Agency With Important Policymaking Responsibility	18
Current Police Practices in Need of Administrative Policy Formulation	21
The Policy Formulation Process	25
Internal Controls	28
External Controls	30
Implications for Police Leadership, Personnel, Training, and Organization	35
Conclusion	38
Attachment A: Policy Statement	38
CHAPTER 3 POLICE ORGANIZATION, MANAGEMENT AND OPERATIONS	**42**
Introduction	42
Developing Police Leadership	44
Improving Organization	45
Administrative and Staff Support Personnel and Units	48
Utilizing Field Personnel More Effectively	51
Applying Technology to Police Service	57
State Role in Providing Consultant Assistance	61
Conclusion	61

	Page
Appendix: The Police Legal Advisor	63

CHAPTER 4 COORDINATION AND CONSOLIDATION OF POLICE SERVICE 68

Introduction	68
General Findings and Conclusions	71
Coordination and Consolidation of Staff Services	73
Coordination and Consolidation of Auxiliary Services	82
Coordination and Consolidation of Selected Field Services	93
Police Service and Jurisdictional Consolidation	98
Obstacles to Coordination and Consolidation	109
Appendix A: Jail Contract Agreement—City of Oakland and Alameda County	113
Appendix B: Police Cooperation Agreement—Cities of Allentown, Bethlehem, and Easton, Pennsylvania	114
Appendix C: Number of Full-Time and Part-Time Police Officers in Cook County, Illinois	115
Appendix D: Arguments for and Against Unification of the 13 Police Departments in the Metropolitan Toronto Area Into a Metropolitan Police Department	116
Appendix E: Method of Determining Cost for Contract Law Enforcement Services in Los Angeles County	117
Appendix F: Interlocal Cooperation Act	118

CHAPTER 5 POLICE PERSONNEL 120

The Police Task: Its Challenge and Diversity	120
The Need to Improve Personnel Assignments	121
Needed Qualities and the Selection Process	125
Attracting Personnel	133
Career Development	137
Minimum Statewide Standards for Selection, Screening, and Training	142

	Page
CHAPTER 6 THE POLICE AND THE COMMUNITY	**144**
The Scope of the Problem	144
Police Programs Directly Related To Community Relations	149
Personnel	163
Police Field Practices	178
Ensuring Fairness	193
Conclusion	205
CHAPTER 7 POLICE INTEGRITY	**208**
The Need for Ethical Conduct	208
Patterns of Dishonesty	208
The Background of the Problem	210
Maintaining Police Integrity	212
Private Police	215
CHAPTER 8 IMPLEMENTATION THROUGH STATE COMMISSIONS ON POLICE STANDARDS	**216**
Role of Police Standards Commissions	216
State Standards	216
Recommendations for Organization and Operation of State Commissions	218
The IACP Model Police Standards Council Act	218
The Continuing Role of State Commissions	219
Appendix A: Model Police Standards Council Act	219
CHAPTER 9 THE COMMUNITY'S ROLE IN LAW ENFORCEMENT	**221**
Citizen Precautions Against Crime	221
Education in Crime Prevention	222
Citizen Aid to Law Enforcement	223
Citizen Resources for Crime Prevention	224
Community Planning Against Crime	225
Legislation and Federal Action To Compel Crime Prevention	226
Citizen Crime Commissions	228
Conclusion	228

TABLE OF RECOMMENDATIONS

This Table of Recommendations is reprinted from the General Report of the Commission, "The Challenge of Crime in a Free Society." It lists the Commission's recommendations on the police and shows where in this volume each is treated in more detail.

COMMUNITY RELATIONS

Establish community relations units in departments serving substantial minority population.............. 150–156
Establish citizen advisory committees in minority-group neighborhoods.............................. 156–159
Recruit more minority-group officers.. 167–171
Emphasize community relations in training and operations... 175–178
Provide adequate procedures for processing citizen grievances against all public officials................ 194–197

PERSONNEL

Divide functions and personnel entry and promotion lines among three kinds of officers................ 122–124
Assess manpower needs and provide more personnel if required.. 133–134
Recruit more actively, especially on college campuses and in inner cities.............................. 136–137
Increase police salaries, especially maximums, to competitive levels................................... 134–135
Consider police salaries apart from those of other municipal departments............................. 135
Set as goal requirement of baccalaureate degree for general enforcement officers....................... 126
Require immediately baccalaureate degrees for supervisory positions................................... 127
Improve screening of candidates to determine character and fitness.................................... 128–130
Modify inflexible physical, age, and residence recruitment requirements............................... 130–132
Stress ability in promotion... 141–142
Encourage lateral entry to specialist and supervisory positions.. 142
Require minimum of 400 hours of training... 137–139
Improve training methods and broaden coverage of nontechnical background subjects................. 139
Require 1-week yearly minimum of intensive inservice training and encourge continued education...... 139–140
Require 12–18 months' probation and evaluation of recruits... 132–133
Establish police standards commissions.. 142

ORGANIZATION AND OPERATIONS

Develop and enunciate policy guidelines for exercises of law enforcement discretion.................. 21–27
Clarify by statute authority of police to stop persons for questioning................................. 183–186
Include police formally in community planning... 225–226
Provide State assistance for management surveys... 63–67
Employ legal advisers... 50–51
Strengthen central staff control... 48–50
Create administrative boards of key ranking personnel in larger departments......................... 25–28
Establish strong internal investigation units in all departments to maintain police integrity........... 50, 214
Experiment with team policing combining patrol and investigative duties............................. 53
Adopt policy limiting use of firearms by officers.. 189–190

POOLING OF RESOURCES AND SERVICES

Provide areawide communications and records coordination.. 82–88
Pool and coordinate crime laboratories.. 90–92
Assist smaller departments in major investigations.. 93–97
Explore pooling or consolidation of law enforcement in all counties or metropolitan areas............ 98–112

Chapter 1

Introduction

The police—some 420,000 people working for approximately 40,000 separate agencies that spend more than $2½ billion a year—are the part of the criminal justice system that is in direct daily contact both with crime and with the public. The entire system—courts and corrections as well as the police—is charged with enforcing the law and maintaining order. What is distinctive about the responsibility of the police is that they are charged with performing these functions where all eyes are upon them and where the going is roughest, on the street. Since this is a time of increasing crime, increasing social unrest and increasing public sensitivity to both, it is a time when police work is peculiarly important, complicated, conspicuous, and delicate.

Because the police have the responsibility for dealing with crime hour by hour, where, when and as it occurs, there is a tendency on the part of the public, and often of the police themselves, to think of crime control almost exclusively in terms of police work. One response to the recent increases in the volume of crime has been the charge that the police lack the competence or the will to keep crime within bounds. A far more common one has been the assertion that the police could keep crime within bounds if only the appellate courts, or civilian review boards, or corrupt politicians, or an uncooperative public allowed them to. "Take the handcuffs off our police" is a cry familiar to everyone.

The fact is, of course, that even under the most favorable circumstances the ability of the police to act against crime is limited. The police did not create and cannot resolve the social conditions that stimulate crime. They did not start and cannot stop the convulsive social changes that are taking place in America. They do not enact the laws that they are required to enforce, nor do they dispose of the criminals they arrest. The police are only one part of the criminal justice system; the criminal justice system is only one part of the government; and the government is only one part of society. Insofar as crime is a social phenomenon, crime prevention is the responsibility of every part of society. The criminal process is limited to case by case operations, one criminal or one crime at a time. Some "handcuffs" on the police are irremovable. It is with that plain fact in mind that this volume, whose purpose is to propose ways in which the police can increase their effectiveness, must be read.

The volume also should be read with an understanding of what the police actually do to combat crime. This is a subject that is often neglected, with the result that public expectations of the police and prescriptions for improving police work are unrealistic. The heart of the police effort against crime is patrol—moving on foot or by vehicle around an assigned area, stopping to check buildings, to survey possible incidents, to question suspicious persons, or simply to converse with residents who may provide intelligence as to occurrences in the neighborhood.

The object of patrol is to disperse policemen in a way that will eliminate or reduce the opportunity for misconduct and to increase the likelihood that a criminal will be apprehended while he is committing a crime or immediately thereafter. The strong likelihood of apprehension will presumably have a strong deterrent effect on potential criminals. The fact of apprehension can lead to the rehabilitation of a criminal, or at least to his removal for a time from the opportunity to break the law.

When patrol fails to prevent a crime or apprehend a criminal, the police must resort to investigation. Some investigation is carried out by patrolmen, but the principal responsibility rests with detectives. Investigation aims at identifying offenders through questioning victims, suspects, witnesses and others, through confronting arrested suspects with victims or witnesses, through photographs or, less frequently, through fingerprints or other laboratory analysis of evidence found at crime scenes.

When the number of square blocks—or in some cases square miles—of city each policeman must patrol is considered in conjunction with the many ways, times and places that crimes occur, the severe limitations upon the effectiveness of patrol and investigation are placed in dramatic focus. Such consideration will also suggest why crime rates often appear to fluctuate with relatively little correlation to what the police do.

The rate of apprehension of offenders in property crimes is extremely low—approximately 22 percent of those reported. The police have greater success with violent crimes—approximately 59 percent of those reported. In large part this is because more victims of violent crimes know or can identify their assailants. The ability of a victim or witness to identify the criminal is the factor responsible for solving a large percentage of the crimes that are solved.

To say that the police have a limited ability to prevent crime is not to criticize the police. The police, more than anybody, are frustrated by the wide gap between the task they are expected to perform and the methods at their disposal to perform it.

Seen from the perspective of history, the anomalies of regarding the police as solely responsible for crime control become evident. In the preindustrial age, village societies were closely integrated. Everyone knew everyone else's affairs and character; the laws and rules of society were generally familiar and were identical with the moral and ethical precepts taught by parents, schoolmasters, and the church. If not by the clergy and the village elders, the peace was kept, more or less informally, by law magistrates (usually local squires) and constables.

These in the beginning were merely the magistrates' agents, literally "citizens on duty"—the ablebodied men of the community serving in turn.[1] Not until the 19th century did policing even have a distinct name.[2] Until then it would have been largely impossible to distinguish between informal peacekeeping and the formal system of law enforcement and criminal justice. The real outlaws—murderers, highwaymen and their ilk—were handled mostly by the military when normal procedures for crime control were unsuccessful.

The greatly increased complexities of society and its laws today only make more important the kind of unofficial peacekeeping that Jane Jacobs has called the "intricate, almost unconscious, network of voluntary controls and standards among the people themselves."[3] In communities and neighborhoods where the other instrumentalities of society whose success bears directly on controlling crime have failed—families, schools, job markets, and welfare agencies—the police must handle an enormously increased volume of offenses, both serious and petty.

It is when it attempts to solve problems that arise from the community's social and economic failures that policing is least effective and most frustrating. For, while charged with deterrence, the police can do little to prevent crime in the broader sense of removing its causes. On the whole, they must accept society as it is—a society in which parents fail to raise their children as law-abiding citizens, in which schools fail to educate them to assume adult roles, and in which the economy is not geared to provide them with jobs. The most eminent of modern police administrators, August Vollmer, once said: "I have spent my life enforcing the laws. It is a stupid procedure and has not, nor will it ever solve the problem unless it is supplemented by preventive measures."[4]

The difficulties and inherent limitations of law enforcement are seldom appreciated by the public when it considers what the police can do, and reacts to what they do. Americans are a people used to entrusting the solution of their social ills to specialists, and to expecting results from the institutions those specialists devise. They have entrusted the problems of crime to the police, forgetting that they still operate with many of the limitations of constables of years past, even though today's citizens are no longer villagers.

The adjustment of conceptions of what can be expected of the police is particularly difficult for people who are themselves law-abiding and who live in a law-abiding community. For them the phenomenon of crime seems far simpler than in fact it is. The voluntary controls of society work well for them and, since they have no desire to violate the criminal law, their supposition is that crime must be a choice between right and wrong for all men, and that more effective policing alone can determine this choice. Thus public concern about crime is typically translated into demands for more law enforcement, and often into making the police scapegoats for a crime problem they did not create and do not have the resources to solve.

No one, of course, is more sensitive to demands for more law enforcement than the police themselves. They see the menace of crime most directly, and their lives are dominated by their professional task. In addition, they have encouraged and share the idea that they are inherently more capable of controlling crime then analysis has thus far shown them to be. In part, this conception derives from the efforts of modern police leaders to secure support and respect as professionals with a specialized ability capable of effective exercise apart from political control. And naturally enough the police, like men in all occupations, tend to view problems in terms of their own function and to have particular faith in their own skills to resolve them.

The police are fully aware of many of the restrictions that are placed upon them, and protest some of them. Their reaction is intensified by a general and often justified feeling that the very public that is responsible for these limits on effectiveness at the same time demands greater success in law enforcement. A leading police training text, for example, states:[5]

> Many police executives are frustrated today, because of the heavy pressures brought to bear upon them and their agencies to eliminate crime and delinquency hazards and to successfully solve cases. . . . Instead of pressuring legislative representatives for changes in the law, many citizens pressure their chief of police. And much such pressure is without knowledge of the law and its limitations, its restrictive interpretations by the courts, and its scope.

In its more extreme forms this reaction has had serious consequences. It has intensified police sensitivity to criticism and to contacts or controls that imply criticism. It has evoked frequent suspicion and bitterness toward those sections of the public seen as responsible for police limitations: politicians, courts, civil libertarians. In combination this sensitivity, suspicion, and bitterness has become in itself a significant limitation on police effectiveness.

In a sense, this entire volume is a discussion of how the police can either overcome or more effectively work within the limitations upon them. Many of those limitations are functions of the way the police are organized and managed; they, probably, are the easiest to surmount. Chapter 3 examines the organizational and operational problems of individual departments. Chapter 4 discusses ways in which two or more departments can improve their service by coordinating or pooling their activities and resources. Chapter 8 discusses "State Commissions on Police Standards."

Most police departments are plagued by a shortage of resources of all kinds: skilled personnel, money, modern scientific and technological equipment. Chapter 3 touches on equipment, a subject that is discussed in detail in the report of the task force on science and technology. Chapter 5 considers in great detail the many ways in which better educated and more skilled men and women

---

[1] Michael Banton, "The Police in the Community," (London: Tavistock Publications, 1964), p. 5.
[2] Charles Reith, "The Blind Eye of History," (London: Faber and Faber Limited, 1952), p. 9.
[3] Jane Jacobs, "The Death and Life of Great American Cities," (New York: Random House, 1961), p. 32.
[4] August Vollmer, "Community Coordination," March–April, 1939, as quoted in V. A. Leonard, "Police Organization and Management," 2d ed., (Brooklyn: The Foundation Press, Inc., 1964), p. 246.
[5] A. C. Germann, Frank D. Day, and Robert R. J. Gallati, "Introduction to Law Enforcement," (Springfield: Charles C. Thomas, 1966), p. 32.

can be attracted to police work and how, once attracted, they can be trained to perform their difficult tasks. Securing more money for the police is essential and is, of course, the responsibility of local, State, and Federal government and, ultimately, of the public. Chapter 13 of the Commission's "General Report" discusses this subject.

Public hostility and indifference are among the most perplexing problems the police face. Chapter 6 is devoted to the timely subject of police-community relations, and chapter 9 proposes a number of ways in which individual citizens and their organizations can help the police. The discussion of police policymaking in chapter 2 is also immediately relevant to public attitudes toward the police, as is the discussion of police integrity in chapter 7.

The limitations on police work that in recent years have aroused the most controversy are those imposed by court decisions about such subjects as interrogation, surveillance, and search and seizure. This subject is discussed in chapter 4 of the "General Report." In addition, chapter 2 of this volume proposes ways in which the police can, in the future, make sure that their interests are presented clearly and fully to appellate courts reviewing police actions.

Finally, a theme that runs through this entire volume is the extent to which police work is limited by a lack of precise knowledge about crime and the means of controlling it. Almost every chapter demonstrates, indeed documents, the urgent need for research into every aspect of police work by the police and by scholars working with the police. As the "General Report" stated, and as cannot be too often repeated, "The greatest need is the need to know."

HISTORY OF THE POLICE

The face of America has changed since colonial days from a collection of predominantly rural and independent jurisdictions to an industrialized urban nation. Yet in several respects law enforcement has not kept pace with this change. As America has grown and policing has become correspondingly complex, the existing law enforcement system has not always been altered to meet the needs of a mechanized and metropolitan society.

Over the years, the proliferation of independent and, for the most part, local policing units has led to an overlapping of responsibilities and a duplication of effort, causing problems in police administration and in the coordination of efforts to apprehend criminals. America is a nation of small, decentralized police forces.

Other problems have plagued the police over the years. Forces have lacked an adequate number of sufficiently qualified personnel. Unattractive salaries and working conditions, and a general lack of public support have hindered police development. And the need for harmonious police-community relations has been a persistent problem, one which, unfortunately, has not been widely recognized until recently. Community relations problems are nothing new; they have existed since American cities were divided into subsocieties by virtue of different ensuing waves of immigrants from western, and later eastern, Europe, who started settling in urban centers before the turn of this century.

To understand better the prevailing problems that police agencies face today, it is helpful to examine their development in England as well as in the United States; for there are many weaknesses in the existing system that stem from practices developed in the rural colonies and from the colonial philosophy of law enforcement.

EARLY HISTORY OF ENGLISH LAW ENFORCEMENT

France and other continental countries maintained professional police forces of a sort as early as the 17th century. But England, fearing the oppression these forces had brought about in many of the continental countries, did not begin to create police organizations until the 19th century. Moreover, England, in its early history, did not maintain a permanent army of paid soldiers that could enforce criminal laws when not engaged in guarding the country's borders against invaders. The cost of developing a force specifically for peace-keeping duties was believed to be too high for the royal purse. Private citizens could do the job cheaper, if given a few shillings reward for arrests. This simple law enforcement expedient, which had begun with Alfred the Great (870–901), can be recognized as the forerunner of American police agencies.

Primarily, the system encouraged mutual responsibility among local citizen's associations, which were pledged to maintain law and order;[6] it was called the "mutual pledge" system. Every man was responsible not only for his own actions but also for those of his neighbors. It was each citizen's duty to raise the "hue and cry" when a crime was committed, to collect his neighbors and to pursue a criminal who fled from the district. If such a group failed to apprehend a lawbreaker, all were fined by the Crown.

The Crown placed this mutual responsibility for group police action upon 10-family groups. Each of these was known as a "tithing." From the tithing, there subsequently developed the "hundred" comprised of 10 tithings. From this developed the first real police officer—the constable.[7] He was appointed by a local nobleman and placed in charge of the weapons and equipment of each hundred.

Soon, the "hundreds" were grouped to form a "shire," a geographical area equivalent to a country.[8] A "shire-reeve"—lineal antecedent of tens of thousands of sheriffs to come—thus came into being, appointed by the Crown to supervise each county. The constable's breadth of authority remained limited to his original "hundred." The shire-reeve was responsible to the local nobleman in ensuring that the citizens enforced the law effectively. From his original supervisory post, the sheriff soon branched out to take part in the pursuit and apprehension of lawbreakers.

It was during the reign of Edward I (1272–1307), that the first official police forces were created in the large towns of England. These were called the "watch and

---

[6] J. Daniel Devlin, "Police Procedure, Administration and Organization" (London: Butterworth & Co., 1966), p. 3.

[7] Supra, note 5 at p. 49.
[8] Ibid.

ward," and were responsible for protecting property against fire, guarding the gates, and arresting those who committed offenses between sunset and daybreak. At the same time the constable became the primary law enforcement officer in all towns throughout England.

In 1326, to supplement the "shire-reeve" mutual pledge system, Edward II created the office of justice of the peace. The justices, originally noblemen, were appointed by the Crown to assist the sheriff in policing the county. This led in time to their taking on local judicial functions, in line with the primary duty of keeping the peace in their separate jurisdictions.

The constable, who retained the responsibility of serving as a major official within the pledge system, meanwhile gained in importance. He became an assistant to the justice, responsible for supervising the night watchmen, inquiring into offenses, serving summonses, executing warrants, and taking charge of prisoners.[9] It was here that the formal separation between judge and police officer developed.

As law enforcement increasingly became the responsibility of the central government in 14th century England, the justice, as the appointee of the King, exercised a greater degree of control over the locally appointed constables. By the end of the century the constable no longer functioned independently as an official of the pledge system. Rather, he was obliged to serve the justice. This essentially set the justice-constable patterns for the next 500 years. The "justice [remained] the superior, the constable the inferior, conservator of the peace"[10] until the second quarter of the 19th century.

Meanwhile, over these years, the local pledge system continued to decline. Community support languished. And with considerable reason.[11]

What was everybody's business became nobody's duty and the citizens who were bound by law to take their turn at police work gradually evaded personal police service by paying others to do the work for them. In theory constables were appointed annually, but in fact their work was done by deputies or substitutes who so acted year after year, being paid to do so by the constables. These early paid police officers did not rank high in popular estimation as indicated in contemporary references. They were usually ill-paid and ignorant men, often too old to be in any sense efficient.

But as the local pledge system was declining, innovations in policing were cropping up in the emerging cities of the 17th and 18th centuries. Those first law enforcement officers were increasingly assisted by a paid nightwatch force. Although these nominally were responsible for guarding the cities against thieves and vandals, apparently they were not effective. Reportedly they did little more than roam the streets at night, periodically calling out the condition of the weather, the hour, and the fact that "all was well."

INDUSTRIALIZATION IN ENGLAND

While England remained essentially a rural country, the dominance of the justice of the peace in law enforcement machinery aroused little formal opposition. But with the advent of the Industrial Revolution at the end of the 1700's families by the thousands began traveling to factory towns to find work. Inevitably, as the cities grew, established patterns of life changed and unprecedented social disorder resulted. Law enforcement became a much more complex enterprise.

Government and citizens alike responded to this need for better law enforcement. A number of fragmented civic associations, such as the Bow Street Horse and Foot Patrol, were formed to police the streets and highways leading out of London and the Government passed statutes creating public offices, later to be known as police offices. Each of these housed three paid justices of the peace, who were authorized to employ six paid constables. These new posts thus helped to centralize law enforcement operations within a small area.

By the beginning of the 19th century nine police offices had been established within the metropolitan area of London, but there was little apparent effort to coordinate their independent law enforcement activities. This was reportedly due to the fact that each office refused to communicate with another for fear that the other might take credit for detecting and apprehending an offender.

In London especially, these weaknesses combined to make the police forces seemingly powerless to combat crime. Highwaymen on the road, thieves lurking in the cities, daily bank robberies, juvenile delinquency—all presented major law enforcement problems.[12] However, out of this difficult situation emerged a unique remedy to discourage thieves from attacking citizens; in the early 1800's gaslights were introduced on the streets of London.

Many of the experiments in law enforcement before 1820 failed "because no scheme could reconcile the freedom of action of individuals with the security of person and property."[13] In 1822, Sir Robert Peel, England's new Home Secretary, contended that, while better policing could not eliminate crime, the poor quality of police contributed to social disorder. Seven years later he introduced and guided through Parliament an "Act for Improving the Police In and Near the Metropolis." This led to the first organized British metropolitan police force. Structured along the lines of a military unit, the force of 1,000 was the first one to wear a definite uniform. The men were commanded by two magistrates, later called commissioners, who were given administrative but not judicial duties. Ultimately, the responsibility for equipping, paying, maintaining, and to a certain degree supervising the "bobbies," as they later became known, was vested in the Home Secretary. Because he was made accountable to the Parliament "for the exercise of his authority over the Metropolitan police, it could [thus] be said that the new force was under the ultimate control of a democratically elected Parliament."[14]

Availability of competent manpower, then as today, became an immediate problem. It was difficult to recruit suitable men to serve in the "new police," for the salaries were poor and the commissioners selective. And

---

[9] Supra, note 6 at p. 6.
[10] Royal Commission on the Police, "Royal Commission on the Police 1962, Final Report" (London: Her Majesty's Stationery Office), p. 12.
[11] Supra, note 6 at p. 7.

[12] Supra, note 5 at p. 59.
[13] Supra, note 6 at p. 10.
[14] Supra, note 6 at p. 16.

there were other harassments. Parliament objected to appropriating Government funds to maintain a police force. The radicals were afraid of tyranny. The aristocracy, though willing to accept the protection of such a force, was disgruntled because the commissioners refused to abide by the traditional rules of patronage in making appointments.

Nevertheless, the London metropolitan police proved so effective in suppressing crime and apprehending criminals that within 5 years the provinces, which were experiencing increasing crime problems and violent riots, asked London for policing help.[15] Shortly after, Parliament enacted a series of police reform bills. Among them, one empowered justices of the peace in 1839 to establish police forces in the counties; and in 1856 another required every borough and county to have a police force.

As regular police forces developed, the justices of the peace voluntarily relinquished their law enforcement duties and confined themselves to deciding questions of law. Before this change occurred, the police had served as the agents of the powerful justices and had consequently used the justices' authority to carry on investigation of those in custody. When the justices relinquished their law enforcement powers, the legislature gave no consideration as to what, if any, investigative responsibilities should be transferred to the police. As a result, the statutes for law enforcement officers that remain on the books today contain little recognition of the broad discretion that police continue to exercise.[16]

LAW ENFORCEMENT IN THE AMERICAN COLONIES

American colonists in the 17th and 18th centuries naturally brought to America the law enforcement structure with which they were familiar in England. The transfer of the offices of constable and sheriff to rural American areas—which included most colonial territory—was accomplished with little change in structure of the offices. Drawing upon the pattern of the mutual pledge system, the constable was made responsible for law enforcement in towns, while the sheriff took charge of policing the counties. The Crown-appointed Governors bestowed these offices on large landowners who were loyal to the King. After the revolution, sheriffs and constables tended to be selected by popular elections, patronage then being on the wane.

In many colonial cities the colonists adopted the British constabulary-nightwatch system. As early as 1636 Boston had nightwatchmen, in addition to a military guard. New York and Philadelphia soon developed a similar nightwatch system. The New York nightwatchmen were known as the "Rattlewatch," because they carried rattles on their rounds to remind those who needed reminding of their watchful presence.

URBANIZATION IN THE UNITED STATES

As American towns grew in size and population during the first half of the 19th century, the constable was unable to cope with the increasing disorder. As in England years before, lawlessness became more prevalent:[17]

New York City was alleged to be the most crime-ridden city in the world, with Philadelphia, Baltimore and Cincinnati not far behind. . . . Gangs of youthful rowdies in the larger cities . . . threatened to destroy the American reputation for respect for law. . . . Before their boisterous demonstrations the crude police forces of the day were often helpless.

Again, as in England, many American cities began to develop organized metropolitan police forces of their own. Philadelphia was one of the first. In 1833 a wealthy philanthropist left a will that provided for the financing of a competent police force in Philadelphia. Stimulated by this contribution, the city government passed an ordinance providing for a 24-man police force to work by day and 120 nightwatchmen. The force was unfortunately shortlived, for the ordinance was repealed less than 2 years later.

In 1838, Boston created a day police force to supplement the nightwatch, and other cities soon followed its lead. Crime, cities were finding, was no respecter of daylight. There were certain inherent difficulties, however, in these early two-shift police systems. Keen rivalries existed between the day and night shifts, and separate administrations supervised each shift. Recognizing the evils of separate police forces, the New York Legislature passed a law in 1844 that authorized creating the first unified day and night police, thus abolishing its nightwatch system. Ten years later Boston consolidated its nightwatch with the day police.

Following the New York model, other cities developed their own unified police forces during the next decade. By the 1870's the Nation's largest cities had full-time police forces. And by early 1900's there were few cities of consequence without such unified forces. These forces gradually came under the control of a chief or commissioner, often appointed by the mayor, sometimes with the consent of the city council and sometimes elected by the people.

These first formal police forces in American cities were faced with many of the problems that police continue to confront today. Police officers became the objects of disrespect. The need for larger staffs required the police to compromise personnel standards in order to fill the ranks. And police salaries were among the lowest in local government service, a factor which precluded attracting sufficient numbers of high standard candidates. It is small wonder that the police were not respected, were not notably successful, and were not known for their vitality and progressiveness. Moreover, the police mission in the mid-1800's precluded any brilliance:[18]

The aim of the police departments was merely to keep a city superficially clean and to keep everything quiet that [was] likely to arouse public [ire].

Many of the problems that troubled these first organized metropolitan police forces can perhaps be traced to a single root—political control. As one authority has explained:[19]

Rotation in office enjoyed so much popular favor that police posts of both high and low degree were constantly changing

---

[15] Christopher Hibbert, "The Roots of Evil." (London: Weidenfield and Nicolson, 1963), pp. 125–128.
[16] Edward J. Barrett, Jr., "Police Practices and the Law—From Arrest to Release or Charge " California Law Review, March 1962, 50: 17-18.
[17] Arthur Charles Cole, "The Irrepressible Conflict, 1859–1865," A History of American Life in 12 Volumes, vol. VIII, Arthur M. Schlesinger, Sr., and Dixon Ryan Fox, editors (New York: The MacMillan Co., 1934), pp. 154–155.
[18] Arthur M. Schlesinger, Sr., "The Rise of the City, 1878–1898," A History of American Life in 12 Volumes, vol. X, Arthur M. Schlesinger, Sr., and Dixon Ryan Fox, editor (New York: The MacMillan Co., 1934), p. 115.
[19] Bruce Smith, Sr., "Police Systems in the United States" (2d rev. ed., New York: Harper and Bros., 1960), pp. 105–106.

hands, with political fixers determining the price and conditions of each change . . . The whole police question simply churned about in the public mind and eventually became identified with the corruption and degradation of the city politics and local governments of the period.

In an attempt to alleviate these problems, responsible leaders created police administrative boards to replace the control exercised over police affairs by mayors or city councils. These boards were given the responsibility of appointing police administrators and managing police affairs. Unfortunately, this attempt to cure political meddling was unsuccessful, perhaps because the judges, lawyers, and local businessmen who comprised the administrative boards were inexpert in dealing with the broad problems of the police.

Another attempt was made at police reform during the close of the 19th century. Noting that poor policing tended to occur mainly in urban areas, the State legislatures, which were dominated by rural legislators, required that police administrators be appointed by authority of the State. Thus State control became an alternative to local control of law enforcement. This move brought little success, for many problems had not been anticipated: [20]

For one thing, the theory of state control . . . was not uniformly applied. It was primarily directed at the larger cities, by legislatures seeking to [perpetuate] rural domination in public affairs.

In spite of increased state control, the large city continued to pay for its police service, and police costs rose. One reason was that police boards were not even indirectly responsible to the local taxpaying public which they served. In cases where the State and city governments were not allied politically, friction increased. It increased further when the State-appointed administrator instituted policy out of harmony with the views of the majority of the city population. It was not until the first decades of the 20th century that cities regained control of police forces in all but a few cases.[21]

After these sincere attempts at reform during the last half of the 19th century, police forces grew in size and expanded in function. However, there was very little analysis of the changes in society that made expansion necessary nor of the effect such changes would work upon the role of the police. Civil service proved helpful, spreading to local police agencies and alleviating some of the more serious problems of political interference. The concept of merit employment, which some reformers had been proposing, was embraced by some forces.

One of the most notable police advancements of the 1900's was the advent of police training schools, even though on a somewhat modest basis. In the early 1900's, the new policeman learned chiefly in the school of experience:[22]

. . . Thus, for the most part the average American city depends almost entirely for the training of its police recruits upon such casual instruction as older officials may be able and willing to give.

In numerous areas, however, it was not until the 1940's and notably in the 1950's that police departments established and, in many cases, greatly expanded their recruit training programs.

STATE AND FEDERAL LAW ENFORCEMENT AGENCIES

Although a State police force, known as the "Texas Rangers," was organized in 1835 to supplement Texas' military forces, modern State police organizations did not emerge until the turn of the century. In 1905, the Governor of Pennsylvania, in the absence of an effective sheriff-constable system, created the first State force. Its initial purpose was to cope with a public dispute between labor and management. Soon such continuing factors as the inadequacy of local policing by constables and sheriffs and the inability or unwillingness of city police forces to pursue lawbreakers beyond their jurisdictional limits convinced State legislatures of the need for Statewide police forces.[23]

The majority of State departments were established shortly after World War I to deal with the increasing problem of auto traffic and the accompanying wave of car thefts. Today all States except Hawaii have some form of State law enforcement body. While some State agencies are restricted to the functions of enforcing traffic laws and protecting life and property on the highways, others have been given general policing authority in criminal matters throughout the State.

The role of the Federal Government in law enforcement has developed in a sporadic and highly specialized manner. Federal law enforcement actually started in 1789, when the Revenue Cutter Service was established to help prevent smuggling. In 1836, Congress authorized the Postmaster General to pay salaries to agents who would investigate infringements involving postal matters. Among the more important law enforcement responsibilities later recognized by Congress were internal revenue investigation and narcotics control. Congress authorized a force of 25 detectives in 1868 and increased the number in 1915. In 1924, J. Edgar Hoover organized the Federal Bureau of Investigation in the Justice Department.[24]

With the expansion of interstate movement of people and goods, and Federal involvement in all aspects of life, the responsibilities of Federal agencies have increased significantly within the last few years. These Federal agencies are responsible to departments of the National Government. The Treasury Department's Secret Service is, for example, charged with the protection of the President and with investigating counterfeiting and forgery of Federal documents. Civilian departmental agencies, with the sole exception of the FBI, function under civil service regulations.[25]

The manpower and jurisdiction of the FBI have increased greatly since its establishment. Some of the statutes that have been responsible for this expansion are the National Stolen Property Act, the Federal Kidnapping Act, the Hobbs Act (extortion), the Fugitive Felon Act, the White Slave Act, the National Bank Robbery Act,

---

[20] Id. at p. 186.
[21] Id. at pp. 186–187. State control of urban police continues to exist in certain cities in Missouri, Maryland, Massachusetts, Maine, and New Hampshire.
[22] Elmer D. Graper, "American Police Administration" (New York: The MacMillan Co., 1921), pp. 109–110.
[23] Supra, note 19 at pp. 147–150.
[24] Supra, note 5 at pp. 67–68.
[25] John Coatman, "Police" (London: The Oxford University Press 1959), p. 50.

Federal interstate gambling laws, and the Dyer Act. The last brings within the FBI's jurisdiction automobiles stolen and taken across the border of a State. Recent passage of strong Federal legislation has enhanced the FBI's role in the enforcement of civil rights.

MODERNIZATION

Serious study of police reform in America began in 1919. The problems exposed then and those faced by police agencies today are similar in many respects. For example, in 1931 the Wickersham Commission noted that the average police chief's term of office was too short, and that his responsibility to political officials made his position insecure. The Commission also felt that there was a lack of competent, efficient, and honest patrolmen. It said that no intensive effort was being made to educate, train, and discipline prospective officers, or to eliminate those shown to be incompetent. The Wickersham Commission found that with perhaps 2 exceptions, police forces in cities above 300,000 population had neither an adequate communications system nor the equipment necessary to enforce the law effectively. It said that the police task was made much more difficult by the excessively rapid growth of our cities in the past half century, and by the tendency of different ethnic groups to retain their language and customs in large cities. Finally, the Commission said, there were too many duties cast upon each officer and patrolman.[26] The Missouri Crime Commission reported that in a typical American city the police were expected to be familiar with and enforce 30,000 Federal, State, or local enactments![27]

Despite the complexity of these problems, many hopeful improvements have occurred in the past few decades. Some cities, counties, and States have taken great strides in streamlining their operations through reorganization and increased use of technology and the use of modern techniques to detect and apprehend criminal offenders. Others are on the threshold of modernization. But many departments remain static. And it is these that obviously constitute a burden on the machinery of justice, and are detrimental to the process of achieving a truly professional police service.

PROFILE OF THE POLICE

To understand many of the analyses and recommendations in this volume, it is helpful to have as background information a profile of law enforcement organization, manpower, and expenditures in the United States today. The statistical data, which are summarized in table 1, are explained in this section. Much of the same information will be expanded in later chapters as different aspects of policing are discussed in greater depth.

NUMBER OF POLICE AGENCIES, DISTRIBUTION, AND LINES OF RESPONSIBILITY

There are today in the United States 40,000 separate agencies responsible for enforcing laws on the Federal, State, and local levels of government. But law enforcement agencies are not evenly distributed among these three levels, for the function is primarily a concern of local government. There are only 50 law enforcement agencies on the Federal level of government and 200 departments on the State level. The remaining 39,750 agencies are dispersed throughout the many counties, cities, towns, and villages that form our local governments.[28]

If we look at a breakdown of the numbers of local agencies, it is again apparent that distribution tends toward the local unit, for only 3,050 agencies are located in counties and 3,700 in cities. The great majority of police forces—33,000—are distributed throughout boroughs, towns, and villages.

Because the concept of local autonomy in enforcing laws has prevailed throughout our history and because the many local policing agencies have held firmly to their traditional jurisdictional authority, responsibility for maintaining public order is today extremely decentralized. This decentralization is further accentuated by the fact that a police officer's responsibility for enforcing law is usually confined to a single jurisdiction.

The problems caused by decentralization are many, particularly where a number of police agencies exist within a radius of a few miles. Jurisdictional barriers are often erected between these agencies; maintaining ade-

Table 1.—A Profile of Federal, State, and Local Law Enforcement Agencies

	Agencies	Full-time personnel				Dollars spent					Percent average annual ncrease, 1955–65
	Number in 1965	Number in 1955	Number in 1965	Percent of total in 1965	Percent average annual increase, 1955–65	Total in millions, 1955	Total in millions, 1965	Per capita expenditure, 1955	Per capita expenditure, 1965	Percent of dollars 1965	
Federal	50	22,000	23,000	6.2	0.5	129	220	$0.78	$1.26	8.5	7.7
State	200	22,000	40,000	10.8	8.2	139	315	.84	1.79	12.2	12.7
Local	39,750	229,000	308,000	83.0	3.4	1,091	2,051	6.60	11.25	79.3	8.8
Total	40,000	273,000	371,000	100.0	3.6	1,359	2,586	8.22	14.20	100.0	9.0
Percent increase			35.9				90.3		72.7		

SOURCE: Memorandum from Michael S. March, Assistant Chief of Education, Manpower and Science Division. U.S. Bureau of the Budget, May 11, 1966.

[26] National Commission on Law Observance and Enforcement, "Report on the Police," (Washington: U.S. Government Printing Office, 1931), pp. 5–7.
[27] Preston William Slossom, "The Great Crusade and After, 1914–1929," A History of American Life in 12 Volumes, vol. XII, Arthur M. Schlesinger, Sr., and Dixon Ryan Fox, editors (New York: The MacMillan Co., 1931), p. 102.
[28] Supra, note 5 at p. 153.

quate communication is difficult, and obtaining assistance from several adjacent agencies when needed becomes a complex operation.

The problems of decentralization have been overcome in part either by creating county, State, and Federal agencies or by increasing the responsibility of existing ones. These agencies have tended in many areas of the country to supplement and coordinate the work of local police agencies.

The 50 Federal law enforcement agencies have directed their efforts mainly to enforcing national laws dealing with interstate violations or with such specific Federal violations as theft of Federal property, postal violations, and counterfeiting U.S. currency, or with enforcing such Federal statutes as those that control the import and sale of narcotics. The duties and activities of these agencies have been defined by Congress through a series of statutes passed over a number of years. It is because of America's strong tradition of local autonomy that the Federal Government has not become extensively involved in local law enforcement.

The States have the primary constitutional responsibility for maintaining order within their boundaries, and all of the States have exercised this authority by enacting broad criminal codes. But because local police departments have traditionally maintained law and order within their jurisdictions and because thousands of violations occur daily in all parts of States, the responsibility for preventing crime has been delegated by States to the local governments in which the violations occur.

Through legislation each State has defined the scope of police responsibility among its many agencies—the State police; county sheriffs; and city, township, borough, and village police. The States have not only divided the responsibility for enforcing law among these various agencies, but they have also determined the extent to which each agency may exercise its power. In addition, State legislatures have passed statutes setting the bounds of civil and criminal liability for police officers who overstep their authority.

On the State level of government the State police are the major law enforcement agents. Their primary responsibility is to enforce some State laws, to patrol highways, and to regulate traffic. They also provide services as needed to local police such as maintaining a State system of criminal identification, conducting police training programs or providing a State communications system. Some States, in addition, have created specialized agencies to enforce particular regulations, such as conservation or alcoholic beverage control laws.

At the county level of government, the sheriff is the primary law enforcement officer. He is an elected official, whose term usually spans from 2 to 4 years and whose jurisdictional responsibility primarily covers unincorporated portions of each county. His functions include keeping the peace, executing civil and criminal process, patrolling the area, maintaining the county jail, preserving order in county courts, and enforcing court orders. The sheriff as a rule performs only restricted law enforcement functions in incorporated areas within a county, and then usually only when the city requests his participation in such activities as patrol or investigation.

In suburban townships and municipalities, police officers are vested with broad law enforcement authority and perform functions similar to those of city police. In rural areas, where most of the 18,000 townships of America are located, police officers usually confine their activities to a limited range of ministerial and traffic duties. In the absence of a local police agency, the local unit of government relies upon the services of the sheriff or State police for law enforcement assistance. These duties may include patrol, investigation, or enforcement of traffic regulations.

Two additional types of police agencies operate on the local level of government. One is the police special service district, created to protect residents or industry in unincorporated portions of urban areas. But few of the Nation's 19,000 special service districts actually provide police service. Most have been created to provide fire protection, street lighting, drainage, and sewage treatment.[29] The second type is the force whose mission is highly specialized. Such forces may be established to protect parks, housing developments, ports, toll roads, and subways. But neither these forces nor police in special service districts have had significant impact on American police administration.

PERSONNEL

There were 420,000 full- and part-time law enforcement officers and civilians employed by police agencies in 1966. The majority of these persons—371,000—were full-time employees, and 11 percent, or approximately 46,000, were civilians. In 1965 there was an overall ratio of 1.7 police officers to every 1,000 persons.[30] (Tables 2 and 3 show police manpower and population ratios.) The total number of police employees at the local level of government has been increasing at an average annual rate of 3.5 percent over the past 8 years.[31]

Twenty-three thousand of the full-time officers serve at the Federal level of government, and 40,000 at the State level. The remaining 308,000 officers—or 83 percent of the total—are divided among the many county and local police agencies.

Table 2.—Full-Time Local Police Manpower Per 1,000 Population

	Police officers and civilians	Police officers only	Range in different geographical divisions
Cities over 250,000	2.6	2.3	1.5 to 4.1
Cities of—			
100,000 to 250,000	1.7	1.5	1.3 to 2.5
50,000 to 100,000	1.5	1.4	1.2 to 1.9
25,000 to 50,000	1.5	1.3	1.1 to 1.7
10,000 to 25,000	1.4	1.3	1.2 to 1.7
Cities under 10,000	1.4	1.3	1.2 to 1.9
Total	1.9	1.7	1.1 to 4.1

SOURCE: Federal Bureau of Investigation, U.S. Department of Justice, "Uniform Crime Reports, 1965" (Washington: U.S. Government Printing Office, 1966), p. 148–51. These data include civilian employees.

---

[29] Committee for Economic Development, "Modernizing Local Government" (New York: Committe for Economic Development, July 1966), p. 32.
[30] Federal Bureau of Investigation, U.S. Department of Justice, "Uniform Crime Reports, 1965" (Washington: U.S. Government Printing Office, 1966), p. 32.
[31] Memorandum from Michael S. March, Assistant Chief of Education, Manpower and Science Division, U.S. Bureau of the Budget, May 11, 1966, table 4.

Table 3.—Full-Time Local Police Manpower By Character of Jurisdiction

	Population served	Number of agencies reporting	Number of police employees	Average number of employees per 1,000 population
City police	109,633,000	3,613	212,883	1.9
Suburban police [1]	40,251,000	1,770	55,040	1.4
County sheriffs	32,357,000	1,154	32,159	1.0

[1] Agencies and population represented in suburban area are also included in other city groups.

SOURCE: Federal Bureau of Investigation, U.S. Department of Justice, "Uniform Crime Reports, 1965" (Washington: U.S. Government Printing Office, 1966), p. 149.

Of the 308,000 police officers serving on the county and local level of government, about 197,500 enforcement officers are distributed among the 39,695 agencies with jurisdictions in county or local areas. These include:
  3,645 cities of under 250,000 population,
  3,050 counties, and
  33,000 townships, boroughs, villages, and special districts.
The remaining 110,500 police personnel are divided among the 55 agencies enforcing law in the 55 cities of the United States of a population over 250,000.[32]
The number of personnel in local police agencies also varies to a considerable degree among locales. On the county level of government the 3,050 sheriff's offices range from a one-man force in Putnam County, Ga., to a 5,515-man force in Los Angeles County, Calif. The average number of police officers serving on the county level is small; only about 200 counties of the 3,050 in the United States have a sheriff's staff of more than 50 officers.[33]
In the local police forces below the county level of government the size of a force may vary from the 1- to 5-man force in the many boroughs and towns of the United States to the mammoth 28,671-member New York City police force.
Even within the radius of a major city, police forces have extraordinary range in size. Chicago, for example, has a total force of 11,745 civilians and officers. Within Cook and DuPage Counties, which encompass much of metropolitan Chicago, there are only 2,187 full-time officers enforcing the law among the 119 municipalities (other than Chicago) located there. One community in Cook County controls crime with only 1 full-time officer, assisted by a part-time complement of 26 people.[34]

AVAILABILITY OF MANPOWER

Due to the great difficulties of attracting capable personnel, almost all large police departments in the United States are substantially below their authorized strength. In 1965 a survey of about 300 police departments—including nearly all of the large city departments—showed that 65.5 percent of the forces polled were below authorized strength. The average force was 5 percent below its quota; the average large-city force was 10 percent below standard capacity.[35]
The difficulties in filling quotas are increased by a low rate of eligibility among police applicants. In 1961 a survey indicated that the acceptance rate dropped from 29.9 percent in 1956 to 22.3 percent in 1961. (See table 4.) An even further rate reduction is suggested by recent experiences in two large metropolitan areas. In 1965, Washington, D.C., was able to hire less than 10 percent of people applying.[36] Los Angeles reported that only 2.8 percent of police applicants were accepted, and 4.9 percent of applicants for the county sheriff's police were hired.[37]

Table 4.—Applicant Success Rates—Regional Replies—1956–61

Region	1956			1961		
	Applicants	Eligible	A.S.R. percent	Applicants	Eligible	A.S.R. percent
New England	2,934	992	33.8	2,107	700	33.2
Middle Atlantic	22,094	7,707	34.8	19,967	5,863	29.4
East North Central	7,111	1,211	17.0	5,939	879	14.8
West North Central	1,538	522	33.9	2,641	577	21.8
South Atlantic	5,518	1,580	28.6	4,851	1,125	23.2
East South Central	973	427	43.9	1,014	480	47.3
West South Central	1,881	689	36.6	3,066	764	24.9
Mountain	1,077	344	31.9	3,016	622	20.6
Pacific	7,887	1,795	22.8	13,018	1,420	10.9
Total	51,013	15,267	29.9	55,619	12,430	22.3

SOURCE: George W. O'Conner, "Survey of Selection Methods" (Washington: International Association of Chiefs of Police, 1962), table 33.

Manpower problems are also caused by turnover in personnel. Each year an average of 5 percent of a police department's force leaves the police service. In the next 10 years, as the mass of police officers recruited just after World War II reaches retirement age, many departments will face severe recruiting needs. For example, 41 percent of the existing Los Angeles Police Department [38] and 10 percent of the 83-man force in Joliet, Ill., will be eligible to retire in 1967.[39]
The present need for manpower and the anticipated rate of turnover both indicate that over 50,000 new police officers will be required in 1967 alone.

CHARACTERISTICS OF PERSONNEL

In 1960 the census showed that the median age of male local law enforcement personnel was as follows: [40]

	Years of age
Police and detectives	37.6
Marshals and constables	50.5
Sheriffs and bailiffs	45.4

A cross section of the age distribution of male and female police officers and detectives is seen in table 5.

[32] International City Managers' Association, "The Municipal Year Book 1966" (Chicago: International City Managers' Association), pp. 444–445.
[33] Conversation with Ferris E. Lucas, Executive Director, National Sheriffs' Association, Washington, D.C., Oct. 31, 1966.
[34] Information received from the Illinois Police Association, Elmwood Park, Ill.
[35] Raymond L. Bancroft, "Municipal Law Enforcement, 1966," (Nation's Cities: Washington, Feb. 1966), p. 16.
[36] The President's Commission on Crime in the District of Columbia, "A Report on the President's Commission on Crime in the District of Columbia" (Washington: U.S. Government Printing Office, 1966), p. 17.
[37] American Trial Lawyers Association, "Crime and Its Causes in Los Angeles" (Lancaster, Pa.: Golden West Publishing Co., 1966), pp. 7–8.
[38] Wall Street Journal, Apr. 5, 1966, p. 1, col. 5.
[39] Herald-News, Joliet, Ill., July 15, 1966, sec. 1, p. 1, cols. 5–7.
[40] U.S. Department of Commerce, Bureau of the Census, "U.S. Census of Population: 1960. Subject Reports. Occupational Characteristics," Final Report PC(2)-7A (Washington: U.S. Government Printing Office, 1963), table 6, p. 79.

Table 5.—Employed Public Police and Detective Personnel, by Age and Sex, 1960

Age range	15-17	18-19	20-24	25-29	30-34	35-44	45-54	55-59	60-64	65-69	70-74	75+	Total
Number of employees:													
Male	41	163	12,381	36,733	46,117	71,389	38,633	10,518	6,805	2,840	1,130	728	227,478
Female	0	40	364	695	881	2,077	1,179	221	60	19	20	0	5,556
Total	41	203	12,745	37,428	46,998	73,466	39,812	10,739	6,865	2,859	1,150	728	233,034

SOURCE: U.S. Department of Commerce, Bureau of the Census, "U.S. Census of Population: 1960. Subject Reports. Occupational Characteristics," Final Report PC(2)-7A (Washington: U.S. Government Printing Office, 1963), table 6, pp. 79, 89.

The median educational level of police officers has risen slightly in this decade. Figures released by the U.S. Department of Health, Education, and Welfare set the median at 12.4 years of education in 1966, a slight rise from the 12.2 level reported by the Bureau of the Census in 1960. A recent national survey of 6,300 police officers indicated that approximately 24 percent of patrolmen and 31 percent of top-level department administrators had attended college.[41]

Police personnel are predominately Caucasian. The 1960 census showed that only 3.5 percent of law enforcement employees throughout the Nation were non-Caucasian. A study by the Civil Rights Commission in 1962 revealed that only one-fifth of 1 percent of State police officers were Negro. Of the 36 Negroes serving as State police officers in the Nation, 24 were employed in Illinois.[42] The same Civil Rights Commission survey polled 271 sheriffs' offices and found that in 1962 there was a Negro-white employment ratio of 1 to 20 on the county level of government.

Some cities have recently recruited a substantial number of Negro officers. In Washington, D.C., for example, Negro employment in the past few years has increased from 14 to 19 percent of the police force, and in Chicago it has increased from 9 to 20 percent of the force.[43] And a notable event occurred in the South in January 1967 when Lucius D. Amerson was sworn in as sheriff of Macon County, Ala. Amerson became the first Negro sheriff in a Southern jurisdiction since Reconstruction.

EMPLOYMENT REQUIREMENTS

More than 70 percent of the Nation's police departments have set the high school diploma level as an educational requirement for employment. About one-fourth of the agencies require no more than some degree of elementary education.[44] Most large cities and counties maintain a high school education or its equivalent as a minimum standard, and at least 22 departments have raised their standard to require college credit. But 21 of these are located in California.

Physical requirements for police employment are rigid. The minimum standards usually require that a recruit be between the ages of 21 and 35, have nearly perfect vision, weigh between 150 and 250 pounds, and be at least 5 feet 8 or 9 inches tall. Many departments only recruit people who have lived within the police jurisdiction for a given period of time before employment. The requirement for preservice residency may vary from 6 months to 5 years. In 1965 more than two-thirds of local law enforcement officers throughout the United States were born in the State in which they were employed.

Almost all local police departments require that an applicant take written intelligence tests. But these tests are in no way standard, and many are ineffective for purposes of measuring educational achievement or personal capability for service. In 1961 a survey showed that only about 15 percent of the local agencies screened their candidates for emotional fitness as a routine procedure.[45] The National League of Cities, which sampled police departments in 1965, indicated that only 27 percent of the agencies responding conducted some kind of psychiatric evaluation of applicants.

POLICE COMPENSATION

In the past 30 years, police salaries have risen, and the number of hours worked in a week have been reduced. The 40-hour week is now standard in the majority of agencies. In small communities median salaries for patrolmen have risen from a figure of approximately $1,600 in 1937 to $4,600 in 1966. Maximum salaries rose from a 1938 figure of $1,800 to a 1966 figure of $5,500. In larger cities during these same years median beginning salaries for patrolmen, which had been $1,900, rose to $5,300. At the same time median maximum salaries rose from $2,400 to about $6,600. Compensation for chief administrators on a nationwide scale in 1938 ranged from $1,980 to $12,500 per annum.[46] In 1965 it had risen to a range of $3,600 to $35,000.[47]

The above compensation figures do not include retirement, health, and other benefits accrued by public police employees.

POLICE TRAINING

Classroom training for recruits is a relatively new concept in American policing. During the early years of this century, experience on the job was the most prevalent method for learning police skills.[48] In the last few years, however, there has been a marked trend toward formal training programs for recruits. Of the 1,352 cities responding to a 1965 survey, 84 percent of city police forces reported formal, in-service training for police officers.[49]

In 1965, a survey of law enforcement agencies showed that 4,000 agencies had appointed over 16,000 new police

---

[41] Institute for Community Development and Services, Michigan State University, "Police Training in the Detroit Metropolitan Region: Recommendations for a Regional Approach" (draft submitted to the Metropolitan Fund, Inc., of Detroit, 1966), table 25, p. 70.
[42] U.S. Commission on Civil Rights, "Administration of Justice, 1963" (staff report, draft submitted 1963), pp. 13–16.
[43] Ibid.
[44] George W. O'Connor, "Survey of Selection Methods" (Washington: International Association of Chiefs of Police, 1962), table 15.
[45] Id. at table 19.
[46] International City Managers' Association, "The Municipal Year Book 1939" (Chicago: International City Managers' Association), p. 424.
[47] Supra, note 32 at p. 434.
[48] Supra, note 22 at p. 110.
[49] Supra, note 32 at p. 437.

officers between July 1964 and June 1965.[50] The extent of the recruit training programs provided by these agencies is reflected in table 6. A 1966 survey indicated that 97 percent of the 269 agencies responding had formal training programs that ranged from 1 to 12 weeks.[51]

While almost 100 percent of the police departments in cities over 250,000 in population conduct their own recruit training programs, many of the smaller departments either have limited training programs or none at all. Some departments, which do not have their own training programs, use the training facilities of other local, State, and Federal agencies.[52]

EXPENDITURES FOR LAW ENFORCEMENT

As table 1 shows, law enforcement services cost the Nation slightly in excess of $2.5 billion in 1965. Approximately $2 billion of this sum was allocated to local law enforcement agencies. The remainder was divided between State agencies, which received $315 million, and Federal agencies, which obtained $220 million.

The bulk of money for law enforcement is spent on salaries. At the local level a police department may spend between 85 and 90 percent of its budget for this purpose.[53]

Like other services, the cost of policing has increased in the past few years. For example, since 1955, numbers of police personnel have increased about 36 percent and expenditures have soared 90 percent. The cost increase is primarily linked to the expense of salaries and equipment. If the present average increase in expenditures of almost 10 percent per year continues, law enforcement costs will total almost $5.5 billion by 1975—more than double the 1965 figure.

Clearly, law enforcement is competing for tax dollars with a large number of other social services provided by all levels of government, for police agencies over the past 65 years have received a declining percentage of increasing total government expenditures. In 1902, for example, police agencies were allotted 4.9 percent of total governmental fiscal outlay. In 1962 this figure had declined to 3.5 percent.[54] The percentage of governmental allotments to law enforcement continues to decline even though the cost of enforcing the law has risen from $8.22 per capita in 1955 to $13.52 per capita in 1964.[55]

The costs of policing are highest in large urban areas. As depicted in table 7, the per capita policing costs in a city of over 1 million people are almost twice the cost of police activity in cities of between 200,000 and 300,000 population. Furthermore, the relative cost rate in the largest cities is more than triple that of cities having fewer than a 50,000 resident population.

The trend toward greater per capita expenditure in large urban areas is not a phenomenon unique to law enforcement. It demonstrates that the complex way of life found in large, populated cities today costs more than the relatively simple life of small towns. As expenditures for education, public welfare, and public housing increase, so do police budgets. A comparison between governmental expenditures in urban and nonurban areas is presented in table 8.

SPECIAL URBAN PROBLEMS

The relative urban-rural crime rate has been the subject of much statistical study in recent years. As crime rates have increased throughout the United States, the rate in cities has continued to be substantially higher than in less populous areas. For example, the FBI's "Uniform Crime Reports, 1965" indicates that the rate for robbery in urban areas was 88.6 per hundred thousand population, as compared to a rate of 9.9 in rural areas.[56] The urban rate of aggravated assault was 127.7 per hundred thousand population as compared to a rural rate of 58.3—more than double. Similarly, the urban rate for burglary was 732.7 per hundred thousand population as compared to a rural rate of 308.4. And the urban rate for larceny of $50 and over was 492.0 per hundred thousand population, while the rural rate was 176.2.[57]

In addition to the greater incidence of serious crime, urban police face rising rates for other types of crimes. The increase of petty crimes, for example, is much more severe in cities than in nonurban areas. The problem of drunkenness has caused a major drain on police time in

Table 6.—Percent of Departments Providing Recruit Training by Program Length, 1965

Population group	Weeks of training									
	Less than 1	1	2	3	4	5	6	7	8	More than 8
Over 1,000,000	100.0	100.0	100.0	100.0	100.0	100.0	100.0	100.0	80.0	60.0
500,000 to 1,000,000	100.0	100.0	100.0	80.0	80.0	80.0	70.0	70.0	70.0	60.0
250,000 to 500,000	100.0	88.0	84.0	84.0	84.0	80.0	68.0	52.0	52.0	40.0
100,000 to 250,000	100.9	97.7	85.3	77.5	67.4	58.4	46.0	34.8	24.7	14.6
50,000 to 100,000	100.0	91.0	76.1	64.0	53.4	43.9	29.2	12.6	10.5	4.7
25,000 to 50,000	100.0	81.6	69.5	53.5	42.9	34.1	23.8	3.7	6.2	4.5
10,000 to 25,000	100.0	74.2	61.5	48.3	38.6	29.3	21.0	7.6	6.0	2.9
5,000 to 10,000	100.0	63.3	49.4	33.9	26.1	21.3	15.3	5.7	3.8	1.6
Under 5,000	100.0	48.6	39.0	25.3	18.0	14.7	9.6	2.3	1.5	1.0
Percent of agencies	100.0	68.3	56.0	42.0	33.4	27.7	19.0	8.1	6.0	3.5
Percent of total officers	100.0	87.6	76.6	69.0	63.1	57.9	49.5	41.0	34.7	25.9
Number of total officers	16,169	14,178	12,399	11,162	10,203	9,352	8,011	6,632	5,619	4,199

SOURCE: International Association of Chiefs of Police, "Police Training," report submitted to the President's Commission on Law Enforcement and Administration of Justice Washington, D.C., 1966.

[50] International Association of Chiefs of Police, "Police Training," report submitted to the President's Commission on Law Enforcement and Administration of Justice, Washington, D.C., 1966.
[51] Supra, note 35 at p. 20.
[52] Supra, note 50.
[53] Supra, note 27 at p. 443.
[54] U.S. Department of Commerce. Bureau of the Census of Governments: 1962, vol. VI, no. 4, "Historical Statistics on Government Finances and Employment" (Washington): U.S. Government Printing Office, 1964) table 1.
[55] Supra, note 31, table 2.
[56] Supra, note 30 at pp. 94-95.
[57] Ibid.

Table 7.—General Services and Police Expenditures Per Capita by City Population, 1963–64 [1]

	City population					
	50,000 and less	50,000 to 100,000	100,000 to 200,000	200,000 to 300,000	300,000 to 400,000	500,000 to 1,000,00	1,000,000 and over

City per capita expenditure on:							
General services	73.23	119.11	137.93	135.12	133.97	178.74	248.12
Police	8.74	12.19	12.78	13.92	14.82	19.21	27.31

[1] Source: U.S. Department of Commerce, Bureau of the Census, Government Finances in 1963–64, table 4, p. 22.

Table 8.—Per Capita Local Government Expenditure Patterns Within and Outside Metropolitan Areas in the United States, 1962

	Within SMSA's [1]	Outside SMSA's	United States
Total	267.05	199.68	242.96
Education	97.29	95.29	96.57
Highways	18.46	22.85	20.03
Public welfare	16.13	9.78	13.86
Police protection	12.59	5.28	9.98
Fire protection	7.79	2.91	6.05
Sewerage	8.44	3.98	6.85
Housing and urban renewal	8.69	1.61	6.16
Parks and recreation	6.43	1.77	4.77

[1] Standard Metropolitan Statistical Areas.

SOURCE: Advisory Commission on Intergovernmental Relations, "Metropolitan Social and Economic Disparities: Implications for Intergovernmental Relations in Central Cities and Suburbs," "Report" A–25, Jan. 1965, p. 51.

Table 9.—Mean Per Capita Expenditure of Cities on Police Services, 1951

City type	Number of cities	Mean per capita expenditure
Major resort city	5	$11.36
Core city of major metropolitan area	77	7.33
Industrial suburb	68	7.17
High-income residential suburb	34	6.39
Low-income residential suburb	68	5.72
Core city of minor metropolitan area	106	5.56
Independent city	137	4.95
Mean for 462 cities		6.04

SOURCE: Ruth L. Mace, "Municipal Cost-Revenue Research in the United States," Institute of Government, University of North Carolina, 1961, p. 164, computed from data in U.S. Department of Commerce, Washington Bureau of the Census, "Compendium of City Government Finances in 1951," pp. 44–61.

large cities, while in the small town the problem is likely to be handled quickly and informally in the relatively few cases where it comes to police attention. Major metropolitan areas also face increasing incidents of juvenile delinquency, fed by social conditions in the city. Finally, the complex city problem of daily traffic snarls requires police regulation and control different in degree from that required in small towns.

The changing makeup of urban population is another factor in explaining the increasing cost of police services today. Table 9 shows the per capita expenditures for policing in different types of urban areas.

Each large urban sprawl has one major section that serves as the commercial hub. Generally, the number of residents in this hub is relatively few in comparison to the surrounding area. During the day the middle and upper classes travel to the central area for business purposes, sometimes increasing the population enormously. Although Detroit's resident population, for example, had decreased 9.7 percent between 1950 and 1960, its weekday population had approximately doubled. The Detroit police force was, therefore, required to add 133 personnel, an increase of 2.8 percent, to serve a city whose population was decreasing.[58] Similar considerations apply to resort cities whose populations increase severalfold during the seasonal influx of tourists.

[58] Samuel G. Chapman, "Police Manpower and Population Changes in Michigan Communities of 10,000 or More Population, 1950–60" (East Lansing, Mich.: Institute for Community Development and Services, Michigan State University, 1961), pp. 8–9.

Chapter 2

Law Enforcement Policy: The Police Role

Law enforcement has always been a difficult task. It is especially difficult in a society such as ours that has so heterogeneous and mobile a population; that has so prosperous an economy; that has so high a degree of urbanization, with its accompanying congestion and anonymity; and that places so high a value on individual freedom, upon equality under the law, and upon local control over the police power.

The current widespread concern with crime and violence, particularly in large cities, commands a rethinking of the function of the police in American society. It calls for a reassessment of the kinds of resources and support that the police need to respond more adequately to the demands that we make upon them.

In this effort to look at the police function, the term "police" is used to refer to all persons having law enforcement responsibility, but major emphasis is upon the departments and the police officers, particularly patrolmen, who have responsibility in the large urban areas for dealing with the wide range of social and behavioral problems that are of primary concern today.

THE RANGE OF PROBLEMS CONFRONTING THE POLICE

While each person has a somewhat different impression of the nature of the police function, based primarily upon his personal experiences and contacts with police officers, there is a widespread popular conception of the police, supported by news and entertainment media. Through these, the police have come to be viewed as a body of men continually engaged in the exciting, dangerous, and competitive enterprise of apprehending and prosecuting criminals. Emphasis upon this one aspect of police functioning has led to a tendency on the part of both the public and the police to underestimate the range and complexity of the total police task.

A police officer assigned to patrol duties in a large city is typically confronted with at most a few serious crimes in the course of a single tour of duty. He tends to view such involvement, particularly if there is some degree of danger, as constituting real police work. But it is apparent that he spends considerably more time keeping order, settling disputes, finding missing children, and helping drunks than he does in responding to criminal conduct which is serious enough to call for arrest, prosecution, and conviction. This does not mean that serious crime is unimportant to the policeman. Quite the contrary is true. But it does mean that he performs a wide range of other functions which are of a highly complex nature and which often involve difficult social, behavioral and political problems.

Individual misbehavior with which the police must deal, for example, ranges from that of the highly dangerous, assaultive sex offender to that of the petty thief or common drunk. Organized criminal activity varies from that affecting a large segment of a community, such as the "policy" or "numbers" rackets, to the two-party agreement between a burglar and the person buying his stolen property. The peace-keeping function of the police requires that they deal with human conflicts ranging from large-scale rioting to disputes between husbands and their wives. Laws enacted to preserve order within a community require the police to perform a variety of tasks, from enforcing traffic regulations to assuring that dogs, peddlers, and various businesses have their proper licenses. And, in addition, the police are called upon to provide certain emergency services which their availability and skills qualify them to fulfill—services largely unrelated to crime or potential crime situations.

It is generally assumed that police have a preventive and protective role as well. Thus, for example, the police endeavor, through such activities as patrol, to lessen opportunities for the commission of crimes; they initiate programs to reduce the racial tensions that exist in the ghettos of large cities; they conduct educational programs to promote safe driving and prevent accidents. Police are expected to afford protection to individuals who are likely to be victimized or are in some other way prey to harm—the down-and-out drunk, the mentally ill, or the naive patrons of vice activity who may be subjecting themselves to the risk of robbery or worse. Moreover, they are expected to preserve the right of free speech—even when that speech is intensely antagonistic and likely to incite opposition.

To fulfill their obligations, the police are given formal authority to invoke the criminal process—to arrest, to prosecute, and to seek a conviction. But making use of this traditional process is much more complex than is commonly assumed, due to the infinite complications that distinguish separate incidents. The police must make important judgments about what conduct is in fact criminal; about the allocation of scarce resources; and about the gravity of each individual incident and the proper steps that should be taken.

When the police are dealing with highly dangerous conduct, for example, they are expected to arrest the offender, and participate in his prosecution in order to insure correctional treatment. But when the conduct is not considered particularly dangerous as, for example, in the case of the common drunk, police may conclude—given the volume of cases—that it is not worth the effort to invoke the full criminal process. Often the police will simply pick up the drunk, detain him overnight, and release him when sober.

Domestic disputes account for a high percentage of the total number of incidents to which the police are summoned. They generally occur late at night and result in a call for the police because an assault has taken place, because there is the potential for violence, because the neighbors are disturbed, or simply because a low income couple has no other source of help in arbitrating marital conflicts. Given the nature of such disputes, the formal system of arrest, prosecution, and conviction is rarely an appropriate means for dealing with them. In the absence of likely alternatives to police involvement, police officers are left with the responsibility for dealing with such situations without being adequately equipped to do so.

When criminal activity involves a "willing buyer" and a "willing seller," a somewhat different pattern of problems is present. Widespread community support for some forms of gambling activity or an ambivalent community attitude toward some forms of sexual conduct require that a police agency decide what constitutes an appropriate level of enforcement. In the absence of a complainant, police must determine the amount of resources and the investigative procedures that they should employ to discover criminal offenses.

Because a high percentage of crimes is committed by juveniles, police are frequently called upon to deal with the youthful offender. In spite of this, there remains uncertainty as to the proper role of the police in the juvenile process. In practice most incidents involving juveniles are disposed of by the police without referral to a social worker or a judge, and consequently what police do is of great significance.

Finally, police must respond to the conflicts that arise out of what has been termed the "social revolution." It is difficult, in policing such situations, to distinguish between legitimate and illegitimate group behavior and to balance the value of free expression against the risk of public disorder. The lines which must be drawn are difficult to determine and call for policy decisions quite different from those made in traditional crimes like burglary.

It has been argued that many of the complex problems of the criminal process could be solved by more narrowly defining the police function. If drunkenness were dealt with by medically qualified people, for example, police would not have to contend with the habitual drunk. If family problems were handled by social work agencies, police would not have to deal with the many domestic and juvenile matters which now confront them. If the substantive criminal law were revised, police would not be confronted with the difficult decisions resulting from broad prohibitions against narcotics, gambling, prostitution, and homosexual activity. And if increased efforts were made to solve some of the social ills that give rise to criminality, the police could be relieved of many of their crime prevention functions.

But little effective action has been taken to develop the kind of resources required by the adoption of any of these alternatives. Some courts have recently held that it is unconstitutional to treat habitual drunkenness as a criminal offense. Presumably, this means that the police should no longer be concerned with public drunkenness, although it is possible that the police might be involved through a process which is medically rather than criminally oriented. But the test of such decisions is in whether they result in a more adequate and humane method of dealing with drunks rather than in their conformity with principle. Because few efforts have been made to develop alternatives to police involvement, the consequence of police not taking action is that drunks would be left to lie where they fall.

Proposals to relieve the police of what are essentially social services have also been lacking in their consideration of the relationship of such services to the incidence of more serious crimes. Domestic disturbances, for example, often culminate in a serious assault or a homicide. The down-and-out drunk is almost a certain victim of a theft if he is left to lie on the street and has any article of value on him. The streetwalking prostitute may, in one sense, be primarily a social problem, but many streetwalkers engage regularly in arranging the robbery of their patrons as a supplement to their income.

It might be desirable for agencies other than the police to provide community services that bear no relationship to crime or potential crime situations. But the failure of such agencies to develop and the relationship between the social problems in question and the incidence of crime suggest that the police are likely to remain, for some time, as the only 24-hour-a-day, 7-day-a-week agency that is spread over an entire city in a way which makes it possible for them to respond quickly to incidents of this kind.

If, as seems apparent, continued reliance is to be placed upon law enforcement agencies for meeting the wide range of functions that now comprise their task, it is important that attention be turned to the manner in which they perform those functions.

THE POLICE RESPONSE

To urge recognition of the fact that the police task covers a wide range of activities and that it is highly complex is not to maintain that the police adequately fulfill all of their functions. It is obviously difficult and often impossible for police officers to respond in an appropriate manner to the numerous incidents called to their attention. They are under constant pressure, especially in highly congested areas, to handle a volume of cases that is beyond their capacity—forcing them to develop "short-cut" responses to run-of-the-mill situations. They lack adequate training with respect to some of the more complex social problems. And there has been little effort to provide individual officers with the guidelines which they require if they are expected to make more effective and judicious decisions in disposing of the incidents which come to their attention. In the absence of adequate resources, training, and guidance, the tendency is for individual police officers to attempt to meet largely by improvisation the varied demands made upon them.

Some indication of the manner in which this is achieved can be gathered from the following account of an observer who accompanied two police officers functioning in a congested urban area during a tour of duty that began in the early evening hours:

After receiving routine instructions at the rollcall held at the precinct station, Officers Jones and Smith located the car to which they were assigned and started out for the area in which they would spend their tour of duty. While enroute, the officers received instructions from the dispatcher to handle a fight in an alley. Upon arrival, they found a group of young men surrounded by their parents, wives, and children.

One of the young men, A, had a couple of knives in his hand. While the knives were within legal limits, Officer Smith took them (and later disposed of them in a refuse container). Another of the young men, B, stood by his mother. The third, C, stood by A, from whom the knives had been taken.

The mother of B was the complainant. She claimed that C had attacked her son with a knife and she demanded that C be arrested and jailed. C readily admitted he had been fighting with B, but he claimed that he had just tried to protect A. C had been drinking and was very belligerent. He indicated a readiness to take on anyone and everyone, including the police. He kept shouting and was obviously antagonizing the officers.

A attempted to explain the situation. He stated that he had been the one originally fighting B and that C had merely come to his aid. B concurred in this account of what had taken place, though he did not reflect very much concern as the supposed victim of the attack.

A's mother-in-law interrupted at this time to claim that A was innocent; that the fight was B's fault. B's mother did not stand for this accusation and entered the fray.

The confusion spread. Other police officers, in the meantime, had arrived at the scene and the number of observers had grown. Officers Jones and Smith decided to take the participants to the precinct station where conditions would make it possible to make a more orderly inquiry.

At the station, the families and participants were separated and talked with individually. The mother of B insisted on signing a complaint against C and A, but finally relented as to A when he promised not to allow C to come to his apartment.

C was then formally arrested and charged with disorderly conduct. A and B were sent home with their wives and mothers. By charging C with disorderly conduct rather than a more serious crime, the officers observed that they were saving themselves some paperwork. They felt that their action in letting the mother sign a complaint against the "loudmouthed" C had served to pacify her.

After filling out the arrest reports on C, Officers Jones and Smith notified the dispatcher that they were available and resumed patrolling. But in several minutes they were dispatched to another beat to handle a domestic situation.

A young Indian girl met them at the door. There obviously had been a fight; the place was a shambles. Furniture was broken, food was on the floor, and beer cans were scattered everywhere. The girl gave an explanation to which the police officers were very much accustomed—her husband had gotten drunk, had become angry, and had gone on the "warpath." When she told the officers that her husband had been behaving in this manner for 5 years, any sympathy which they had for the girl disappeared. They explained that they were not in a position to do anything for her since her husband was not there. They advised her to go to court to obtain either a warrant for his arrest or to arrange for the issuance of a peace bond.

Upon reporting back in service with the dispatcher, Smith and Jones were assigned a domestic problem involving a couple who had been married for 27 years. The couple had only recently begun to have trouble getting along. But when the difficulty started, it was serious. The wife had been attacked by the husband a week previously and had suffered a concussion. She was now back from the hospital and wanted her husband locked up. The woman led the officers to the apartment, but the husband had, in the interval, left. They then went through the ritual of telling the wife the procedure by which she could obtain a warrant or a peace bond. They also told her to call back if she had any more trouble.

After this call, there was a short lull in activity, during which the officers patrolled the southeast corner of their assigned area. They were then told to see a complainant at a designated address.

The complainant, it turned out, was a landlord. One of his tenants had a child who had been bothering other tenants. The mother had been told to quiet the child down, but she apparently had not done so. In addition, the mother was behind in the rent. The landlord had attempted to serve her with an eviction notice but had not been able to find her at home.

The mother was at work at a lounge and the landlord asked the officers to serve the eviction notice on her there. The officers explained that they would not be able to do so since the lounge was outside the district to which they were assigned. The landlord countered this by contending that he had been a friend of the police and that he had helped them in the past. He also stressed that he was a taxpayer. Officer Jones reacted by requesting the dispatcher to assign a police officer to meet the landlord at the lounge and help him in serving the notice. The officers, in this manner, disposed of the incident.

Smith and Jones were next dispatched to investigate a noisy party. When they arrived at the scene, they found the party was going "full blast." They knocked and when the door was answered, Officer Smith asked for the host. He told the person who then came to the door that someone had complained and that they would have to "hold the noise down." The host and others who were listening in readily agreed. When Officer Jones notified the dispatcher that the first party had been quieted, the men were dispatched to another.

The officers could not find the second party and could hear no loud noise at the address which had been given. Officer Jones requested the apartment number from the dispatcher. Both officers then went to the apartment. When the hostess came to the door, Officer Smith told her that someone had complained about a loud party. He told her that while the party seemed quiet enough at the moment, she should be careful because she evidently had some touchy neighbors.

Smith and Jones stopped for a coke before placing themselves back in service. While they were parked, Officer Jones spotted a "downer" in the doorway of the office occupied by the city council member representing the area. They called for a patrol wagon. They then went over to the drunk, awakened him, and asked him some questions. He had been sleeping and eating wherever he could, having slept the previous night in a "flophouse" downtown. When the wagon arrived, the "downer" was placed in it and taken to jail.

When the officers reported back in service, they were immediately assigned to a juvenile disturbance at a hotdog stand. They did not rush to the scene, since they had been there numerous times in the past.

The owner of the hotdog stand would not force the youths to leave, letting them stand about until the whole parking area was congested. He would then call the police. Smith and Jones dispersed the crowd. One youth started to resist but moved on when Officer Jones threatened him with jail.

The officers informed the dispatcher that they had handled the problem at the hotdog stand and then resumed patrol. They had traveled several blocks from the hotdog stand when they observed a driver run a red light. The officers gave chase and pulled the vehicle over to the side of the street. The motorist, it was revealed, had just returned from Vietnam and Officer Smith felt that he deserved a break. He released him with a suggestion that he be more careful. While Officer Smith was talking to the veteran, Officer Jones spotted a fight between two youths. He ran over, broke it up, and talked to the combatants. He sent them on their way with a warning.

The officers requested permission from the dispatcher to take time out to eat, but he responded by sending them back to the first party that they had quieted.

A great deal of damage had been done by the time they arrived. The youths had gotten drunk and loud. They had created a disturbance when the party broke up and the manager of the building had called the police. The officers advised the manager to exercise more care in deciding upon the people to whom she rented her apartments. Since the persons causing the disturbance had already gone, there was nothing else that the officers could do; they departed.

They again asked permission to take time for food, but were instead dispatched to the scene of a stabbing. They hurried to the location, which turned out to be a new portable public swimming pool.

There were three persons present—two lifeguards and a watchman. One of the lifeguards had been knifed. He was placed in the police car and officers started off for the nearest hospital. Enroute, the victim told the officers that a man had tried to go swimming in the pool after it had been closed for the night. When the lifeguard attempted to stop the intruder, he was stabbed during the scuffle. The other lifeguard called the police. At the hospital, the officers made out their reports while the victim received medical care. They later returned to the scene but found no additional information or people who would assist in the identification of the assailant. The reports were turned in for attention by the detectives.

The officers then, without asking, took their meal break, after which they reported that they had completed their work on the stabbing. They were dispatched to a party disturbance. Upon arriving at the scene, they encountered a young fellow walking out of the building carrying a can of beer.

He was stopped and questioned about the party. Officer Smith told him that "this is not Kentucky" and drinking on the street is not allowed. The fellow agreed to take the officer up to the party. When he turned to lead the way, Officer Jones observed a knife in the youth's back pocket. He took the knife away. There was not much going on at the party. Those present were admonished to keep it quiet.

Back on patrol, the officers cruised for a short period. It was soon quitting time, so they headed in the direction of the precinct station. As they turned a corner, Officer Smith saw a couple of fellows drinking on the street, but rather than get involved at this time, nothing was done.

This day in the life of Officers Jones and Smith reflects the broad and varied demands for police service, the pressures under which it is provided, and the informal and improvised responses which tend to develop. While neither articulated nor officially recognized, common responses obviously tend to develop in frequently recurring situations.

A new police officer quickly learns these responses through his associations with more seasoned officers. The fact that a response is routine does not mean that it is satisfactory. To the contrary, many routine responses are applied on the basis of indefensible and improper criteria. But once developed, the routine response is generally immune to critical reevaluation unless a crisis situation should arise. Because of their informal character, such responses tend not to be influenced by developments in police training. And, because they consist of the accumulated experiences of frontline officers, they tend to take on a vitality which continues even without the active support of the higher echelon of police administration.

Unique situations do arise, usually where the frequency of a given kind of incident is small, for which there is no routine response. Unless time permits him to confer with his sergeant, the individual officer is left to respond without any form of guidance. Under such circumstances, the decision of the individual officer will reflect his own personal values and opinions about people and about group behavior.

Improvement in the capacity of law enforcement agencies to perform the essential and highly sensitive functions that comprise the total police task requires a willingness on the part of the public and the police to take several bold steps.

There must, in the first place, be a more widespread recognition on the part of the citizenry and the police of both the range and the complexity of the problems which the police confront. Secondly, there must be a willingness on the part of the police to respond to these problems by the careful development and articulation of policies and practices which are subject to continuing reevaluation in the light of changing social conditions.

POLICE ATTITUDE TOWARD THEIR ROLE IN THE DEVELOPMENT OF LAW ENFORCEMENT POLICIES

The absence of carefully developed policies to guide police officers in handling the wide variety of situations which they confront is in sharp contrast to the efforts taken to provide detailed guidance for other aspects of police operations.

Like all military and semimilitary organizations, a police agency is governed in its internal management by a large number of standard operating procedures. Elaborate regulations exist dealing with such varied phases of an agency's internal operations as the receipt of complaints from citizens, the keeping of records, and the transportation of nonpolice personnel in police vehicles. Established procedures govern such matters as the replacement of vehicles, uniforms, and ammunition. Police agencies also have established policies with respect to certain public service functions, but these usually do not involve important criminal law issues. There are policies, for example, which provide guidance in determining whether to transport a person requiring emergency medical assistance, in deciding whether to take a stray dog into custody, and relating to the inspection of the premises of a vacationing resident.

Progressive police agencies have developed sophisticated methods for establishing procedures in these areas, methods which call for analyzing the basic problems, weighing the desirability of various alternative solutions, and then developing and adopting criteria to serve as a basis for the decisions of operating personnel.

In contrast, there have been only occasional efforts to make use of a deliberative planning process to develop policies to guide and control police officers in dealing with the wide variety of situations that require the exercise of some form of police authority.

One of the most adequate statements of enforcement policy was produced in New York State in conjunction with the enactment in 1964 of the new "stop and frisk" law. Police and prosecuting officials recognized that this newly legislated authority to stop and question persons short of arrest and to subject them to a frisk was vulnerable to attack on constitutional grounds, and they were aware that opposition to its passage would result in its implementation being closely watched.

It was for these reasons that the New York City Police Department and the District Attorney's Office joined with other law enforcement agencies throughout the state to publish a set of guidelines for operating personnel prior to the date on which the new law became effective.[1] Five pages of specific requirements, limitations, prohibitions, and examples were used to elaborate upon the legislation which itself is contained in two relatively brief paragraphs. Emphasis was not placed upon defining the law so much as it was upon urging the police to exercise restraint and to act well within the outer limits of their prescribed authority.

In the area of traffic enforcement, a number of jurisdictions have developed "tolerance policies" which establish the point above the speed limit at which officers are to warn a motorist or issue a summons to him, and also provide criteria for making similar decisions with regard to other types of motor vehicle violations. Such policies are most frequently found in State police organizations, reflecting a need for providing guidelines for the isolated officer who cannot frequently consult with his supervisor or with fellow officers. They also reflect an organizational response to the demands for fairness and uniformity voiced by the cross-section of citizens who commit traffic violations—a group with the capability of insisting upon consistency in law enforcement.

There also have been some efforts on the part of police agencies to formulate policies relating to the disposition of juvenile offenders. This has, for the most part, consisted of an attempt to develop criteria to serve as a basis for deciding whether to release a juvenile offender to his parents, refer him to a social agency, or process him through the juvenile court.

Significant as these efforts are, they deal with but a small portion of the total police responsibility.

There are a number of factors which account for the general failure of police to develop policies for dealing with crime and potential crime situations, in contrast to their willingness to do so for issues of internal management of the department.

In the first place, devising procedures for handling routine matters of internal management can be done with relative certainty and assurance that the decision will not be a subject of major debate in the community. Few people are concerned about these issues. To the extent that there is public interest, police seem confident of the propriety of their making policy decisions and of their ability to defend decisions that are made. In contrast, procedures for frisking suspects in high crime areas, for dispersing crowds which gather, and for deciding who is to be arrested inevitably involve difficult and sensitive questions of public policy.

Many police administrators are caught in a conflict between their desire for effective, aggressive police action and the requirements of law and propriety. Direct confrontation of policy issues would inevitably require the police administrator to face the fact that some police practices, although considered effective, do not conform to constitutional, legislative, or judicial standards. By adopting a "let sleeping dogs lie" approach, the administrator avoids a direct confrontation and thus is able to support "effective" practices without having to decide whether they meet the requirements of law.

The police administrator has greater control over management questions than he does over the criminal justice process, responsibility for which he shares with the legislature, the courts, the prosecutor, and other agencies. The fact that the courts in particular have assumed increasing responsibility for control in this area has resulted in a prevalent attitude by police administrators that criminal justice policy decisions are not their concern. As a consequence, neither police training nor research has been directed toward these basic policy questions.

The reluctance of the police administrator to deal explicitly with important enforcement policies is reflected in a common administrative attitude toward "tolerance limits" developed in the traffic field which are usually maintained with a high degree of official secrecy. The reluctance to publicize "tolerance limits" reflects several factors: (1) a concern that the administrative action which they reflect would be criticized as a perversion of legislative intent—a concern which gives rise to the basic issue of the propriety of police policymaking; (2) a fear that publication would lead to a public debate as to what constitutes an appropriate tolerance and would lead to arguments between the officer and the offender in a given case—a concern which relates to the willingness of police to be held publicly accountable for the policy decisions which they make; (3) a concern that the existence of such a document might be used as a basis for litigation in those situations in which an officer chooses to enforce the be free to deviate from their own policy in an individual case without having to justify such deviation; and (4) a fear that widespread awareness of the existence of such tolerances would result in drivers adjusting their behavior, utilizing the established tolerances rather than the posted and published laws as their guides.

In contrast, police agencies that have formulated policies relating to juvenile offenders have generally made their policies public. The frankness with which discretion is acknowledged in the handling of juveniles is ap-

---

[1] See Attachment A, a Policy Statement on the New York "Stop-and-Frisk" and "Knock, Knock" Laws Prepared by New York State Combined Council of Law Enforcement Officials, June 1, 1964, appearing at the end of this chapter.

parently attributable to (1) general recognition that it is both necessary and desirable for police to handle a large number of juvenile cases at the police level without referring them to the courts, an assumption less common with respect to adults; (2) a feeling that the juvenile process is in the "best interests" of the child while the adult process is punitively oriented—thus the sort of flexibility considered appropriate in dealing with the juvenile may be thought of as a denial of equal protection as it pertains to the adult offender; and (3) the usual existence of a specially trained group of juvenile police officers to whom the decisionmaking function is delegated.

The various factors that have been cited, taken together, account for the absence of a tradition for policymaking in most aspects of police functioning that relate to crime and potential crime situations. As a result, individual officers continue to depend primarily upon routine responses and upon their individual judgment when functioning in these areas. And critical problems which the police confront do not receive the kind of attention which they require.

THE NEED TO RECOGNIZE THE POLICE AS AN ADMINISTRATIVE AGENCY WITH IMPORTANT POLICYMAKING RESPONSIBILITY

There are two alternative ways in which police can respond to the difficult problems currently confronting them:

(1) The first is to continue, as has been true in the past, with police making important decisions, but doing so by a process which can fairly be described as "unarticulated improvisation." This is a comfortable approach, requiring neither the police nor the community to face squarely the difficult social issues which are involved, at least until a crisis—like the current "social revolution"—necessitates drastic change.

(2) The second alternative is to recognize the importance of the administrative policymaking function of police and to take appropriate steps to make this a process which is systematic, intelligent, articulate, and responsive to external controls appropriate in a democratic society; a process which anticipates social problems and adapts to meet them before a crisis situation arises.

Of the two, the latter is not only preferable; it is essential if major progress in policing is to be made, particularly in the large, congested urban areas.

To assert the importance of the police playing an important role in the development of law enforcement policies in no way detracts from the importance of the legislature, the appellate and trial judiciary, or the prosecutor.

There is undoubted need for greater legislative attention to the important issues of the criminal law. Major improvement can be made by thorough revision and codification of the substantive law, following the lead of some of the States and the American Law Institute's Model Penal Code. There is need and opportunity to go further and to deal with some of the borderline types of criminal conduct which have either been ignored or dealt with inadequately in the revisions which have taken place. Major improvement can also be made by careful legislative attention to some of the basic and important questions involved in criminal procedure and administration. However, the opportunity for careful legislative attention to this field is complicated by appellate judicial opinions announcing increasingly specific rules of constitutional, procedural due process.

However great the legislative contribution may be, experience demonstrates that legislatures can never deal specifically with the wide variety of social and behavioral problems which confront police. Legislation was inadequate to deal in detail with regulation of the economy during the depression of the 1930's. As a consequence, there was a great increase in the number of economic regulatory agencies and in the importance of the administrative process. The administrative agency has survived as an essential vehicle for the introduction of needed flexibility and expertise in the economic regulatory process.

Certainly there is no reason to expect that legislatures can be more effective with respect to the work of police than they were with respect to the task of the economic regulatory agency. The "administrative process" and administrative flexibility, expertise, and, most important, administrative responsibility are as necessary and as appropriate with respect to the regulation of deviant social behavior as they are with respect to other governmental regulatory activity. This seems perfectly obvious. Yet the common assumption has been that the police task is ministerial, this perhaps reflecting an assumption that administrative flexibility and "the rule of law" are inconsistent. This assumption seems invalid. The exercise of administrative discretion with appropriate legislative guidance and subject to appropriate review and control is likely to be more protective of basic rights than the routine, uncritical application by police of rules of law which are often necessarily vague or overgeneralized in their language.

The judiciary has played and will undoubtedly continue to play an important role in the determination of what are proper law enforcement practices. It is a proper and traditional function of courts to listen to complaints from citizens alleging abuse of power by governmental agencies. And, through their interpretation of the Constitution, courts have defined the limitations upon the proper exercise of governmental power.

How specifically courts become involved with detailed law enforcement practices in the future may well depend upon how willing legislatures and police are themselves to assume the responsibility for defining appropriate practices and insuring conformity with them. However, no matter how specifically judicial review may deal with enforcement practices, it cannot be an adequate substitute for responsible police administrative policymaking. Judicial review is limited, for the most part, to cases which "go to court," and many important and sensitive police practices used in maintaining public order and settling minor disputes are seldom reflected in court proceedings. In addition, judicial review is most effective if it relates to carefully developed administrative policies rather than to the sporadic actions of individual police officers.

The prosecutor has an important responsibility in the development of appropriate law enforcement policies. But there are practical reasons why his involvement cannot adequately substitute for a commitment by police to the importance of their participating, in a major way, in the policymaking process. Usually the prosecutor, particularly in the large urban areas, confines his principal attention to cases in which there is a desire to prosecute or to issues which are important to the political life of the community. He seldom, for example, becomes involved in the development of a policy for settling domestic disturbances or dealing with the down-and-out drunk or streetwalking prostitute.

The problems which confront law enforcement today are sufficiently important and sufficiently complex to require the participation of the prosecutor, the legislature, and trial and appellate courts. But it is essential to realize that they require as well the mature participation of police, as a responsible administrative agency, in the development and implementation of enforcement policies. Some of the advantages to be gained by such participation are worth describing in some detail.

THE MAINTENANCE OF ADMINISTRATIVE FLEXIBILITY

The problems confronting police are such that it seems both necessary and desirable that police be given some flexibility to adapt law enforcement practices to changing social conditions. Giving police flexibility is not new. Police have had a great deal of flexibility in the past, but this has been as a result primarily of legislative default rather than deliberate, overt legislative choice. A traditional legislative response to difficult issues has been either to deal with them by an overly generalized statute as is the case with respect to gambling, or not to deal with the issue at all which has been the case, until recently at least, with respect to stopping and questioning suspects.

The practical consequence has been to leave police with broad flexibility, but the delegation of responsibility has been at best implicit and police have not taken it as a mandate to develop and articulate proper enforcement policies. Partly as a consequence of this, the trend has recently been pretty clearly in the direction of increasingly specific rules to govern police conduct. This is certainly the effect, for example, of the *Miranda* case. This trend is inspired in large part by a prevalent assumption that police are unwilling or unable to develop proper policies and to conform their practices to those policies.

In some situations, control by specific judicial or legislative rule may be workable. Where this is the case there is opportunity for major legislative contribution through carefully drafted code provisions which clearly and adequately prescribe proper police practice. In other situations, however, highly specific rules may result in an inflexibility which makes the system unable to react adequately to complex and changing conditions. For example, police have had broad flexibility in dealing with the domestic disturbance—the fight between husband and wife—which, in the large city, often results in a call to police. These disturbances occur in such widely varied circumstances and there are such varied ways of dealing with them, that it would be both difficult and unwise to try to specify the police response by categorical legislative treatment. Under present conditions, there seems obvious merit in allowing police flexibility in dealing with the domestic disturbance provided that this flexibility is not abused. The development by police of proper policies for dealing with the domestic disturbance and a demonstrated willingness to adhere to those policies would aid greatly in maintaining the desired flexibility.

A SOUND BASIS FOR THE EXERCISE OF DISCRETION

The results of efforts on the part of individual police officers, under current practice, to improvise their response to many of the situations they confront are often surprisingly good considering the absence of systematic planning: disputes are resolved; persons are disarmed; people not in control of their capacities are protected; and many are spared what, under some circumstances, would appear to be the undue harshness of the criminal process. But there are numerous situations in which mere volume and the lack of guidance result in an officer disposing of incidents less satisfactorily because of the ease with which the matter can be disposed of, the officer's personal attitudes toward the victim or the complainant, or his guess as to what form of disposition will most please his immediate supervisor. Similarly, command officers and entire departments will often respond to situations in a manner primarily dictated by the pressures exerted by the community, rather than by careful assessment of the competing values involved.

Proper and consistent exercise of discretion in a large organization, like a police department, will not result from the individual judgment of individual police officers in individual cases. Whatever the need for the exercise of judgment by an individual officer may be, certainly the development of overall law enforcement policies must be made at the departmental level and communicated to individual officers. This is necessary if the issues are to be adequately defined and adequately researched and if discretion is to be exercised consistently throughout the department.

ACKNOWLEDGMENT OF THE "RISK FACTOR" INVOLVED IN POLICING

Numerous factors contribute to the defensive posture commonly assumed by the police. Among them is an awareness on their part that members of the public will often question their exercise of discretion in a case in which subsequent developments focus attention upon an officer's decision. A police officer may, for example, locate one underage youth in a group of young people engaged in a drinking party. The fact that he is only under age by one month may influence the officer to release him with a warning. However, if subsequently the released youth becomes involved in a serious accident, the fact that he was released earlier in the evening will often result in the officer being castigated by his superior because he has no publicly acknowledged right to exercise discretion, although all agree that it is both necessary and desirable that he do so.

Given the range of responsibilities which the police have, they cannot be held to a system of decisionmaking which involves no risk-taking—any more than can psychiatrists in deciding whether to release a person who has attempted suicide or parole board members in voting upon the release of an inmate. The formulation of policy and its articulation to the public would, over a period of time, begin to educate the public into recognizing that the police must not only exercise discretion, but must assume a risk in doing so. Prior statements which "put the community on notice" with regard to police functioning in various areas would afford some relief from the current dilemma in which, in the absence of such policy formulations, the police are both subject to ridicule for not exercising discretion and subject to condemnation for making such judgments when they do not work out.

A MEANS FOR UTILIZING POLICE EXPERTISE

Many actions which the police officer takes are based upon the knowledge and experience which he has accumulated in his years of service. For example, an officer may, in deciding whether a situation is a suspicious one, reach a judgment quite different from that which would be reached by an inexperienced layman or even an experienced trial judge. An officer may have the ability to recognize the smell of narcotics or the sound of a press used in printing illegal numbers or policy tickets. Yet there has been little effort made to capitalize upon police experience or to attempt to assess its reliability: to distinguish accurate inferences from inaccurate ones; or to systematize experience so that it can be effectively communicated through police training to new police officers and to others, like judges, when the propriety of police action is challenged.

MORE EFFECTIVE ADMINISTRATIVE CONTROL OVER POLICE BEHAVIOR

Lacking a formulated policy and thus a preannounced basis for internal disciplinary action, the police administrator is hesitant to impose sanctions upon the individual police officer who acts improperly but whose conduct does not violate the law or departmental regulations.

The police administrator finds himself caught in a conflict between his desire to be responsive to a citizen who has reason to complain about a policeman's behavior and his fear of the reaction of his force to seemingly arbitrary discipline where there is no clear breach of a preannounced standard of proper conduct.

This reluctance to characterize an officer's conduct as unwise is increased when the administrator feels that to do so will result in either the officer or the municipality being sued for damages. The administrator, therefore, may be placed in the position of defending a given action as legal, and thus seemingly "proper," even though it reflected poor judgment on the part of an officer. To minimize the chance of similar situations in the future, the administrator may urge his subordinates to use "common sense," but this is not very effective unless he is able to indicate more clearly what "common sense" is in the wide variety of situations confronted by the police officer.

Formulated administrative policies to which police officers are required to adhere would provide a basis for disciplining those who violate them and would serve also in a positive way to inform members of a force what is expected of them. Progress in elevating the quality of law enforcement is much more likely to come about as a result of trying to induce conformity to standards prescribed by department policy than by relying solely upon those minimal "legal" standards which must be adhered to to avoid civil liability or to avoid having important evidence suppressed in a criminal prosecution.

THE IMPROVEMENT OF RECRUIT AND INSERVICE TRAINING PROGRAMS

Recruit training in police agencies is most often inadequate because the instruction bears little relationship to what is expected of the officer when he goes to work in the field. In the absence of recorded and analyzed formulations of police experience, the instructor usually is left only with the formal definition of police authority, and this is often communicated to the trainee by reading statutory definitions to him. Procedures for dealing with crime and potential crime situations are thus typically taught in doctrinaire fashion. Laws are read on the assumption that they are to be fully enforced. With this kind of formal training, the new officer finds that he has to acquire a knowledge of all the patterns of accommodations and modifications from the more experienced officers with whom he is initially assigned. As he becomes aware of the impracticality and lack of realism in much of what he learned, he may begin to question the validity of all aspects of his formal training.

The obvious need is for training related to the important problems which the officer will face in the field, training which will not only inform him of the limits of his formal authority but will also inform him of the department's judgment as to what is the most desirable administrative practice to follow in the implementation of his formal authority.

This kind of training has an additional advantage. If adequately done it ought also to serve as one important way of raising the basic enforcement issues requiring attention. Thus training can serve to improve the process by which administrative policies are developed and the adequately developed policies will, in turn, make training more effective.

A BASIS FOR THE PROFESSIONALIZATION OF THE POLICE

It is now commonplace to refer to practically any effort that is aimed at improving law enforcement as contributing toward the professionalization of the police.

Thus, improved training, the application of the computer to police work, the adoption of a code of ethics, and increased salaries have all, at one time or another, been cited as contributing toward police professionalization.

Certainly, there is much that police do today that would not, under any definition, be viewed as constituting professional work. Directing traffic at a street intersection or enforcing parking restrictions requires stamina, but little knowledge of the social structure of the community. In sharp contrast, however, the beat patrolman assigned to police a congested, high crime area is called upon to make highly sophisticated judgments having a major impact upon the lives of the individuals involved. Such judgments are not mechanical in nature. They are every bit as complicated as the decisions made by any of the behaviorial scientists and in many instances are more difficult because they must be made under the pressure of the immediate circumstances.

Adequate development of administrative policies for dealing with complex social and behavioral problems will require the maximum use of police experience, research, and experimentation. The effort to systematize experience and to test its validity by research is one important mark of a profession. Another, also implicit in the development of proper administrative policy, is adherence to values more basic than those required in the interest of efficiency. These relate to the place of police and law enforcement in a democratic society.

The utilization of experience, research, experimentation, and the effort to define the proper role of police in our society would constitute a more adequate basis for the development of a true profession.

INVOLVING THE POLICE IN THE IMPROVEMENT OF THE SYSTEM OF LAW ENFORCEMENT

Decisions relating to the enforcement function have traditionally been made for the police by others. The police have typically not been consulted when changes were contemplated in the substantive or procedural criminal law, despite the fact they clearly have more experience in dealing with some of the basic issues than anyone else. The reason that they have not been consulted is probably because they have not been considered qualified to deal with the complicated questions involved. But it probably is also true that police lack this skill precisely because they have not been involved in the making of important decisions in the past.

Today there is a strong commitment to the involvement of minority groups, young people and the poor in decisions about their future in the view they will respond most affirmatively if they have a feeling of participation in the initial decision. The same need is apparent in relation to police. They too are more likely to want to conform and have an ability to conform if they are part of the process for making important decisions affecting criminal justice administration.

CURRENT POLICE PRACTICES IN NEED OF ADMINISTRATIVE POLICY FORMULATION

Most practices currently used by police to deal with crime or potential crime situations give rise to important and sensitive policy questions of a kind that can and should be dealt with carefully and systematically by a law enforcement agency. Illustrative of these are the decision as to whether or not to make an arrest; the decision to use or not use certain methods of detection or investigation such as surveillance, field interrogation, or search; the decision to release rather than prosecute some guilty persons who have been arrested; the effort to keep public order by breaking up crowds and ordering people to keep moving; the settlement of minor disputes by the use of various formal or informal devices; and the effort to protect the right of free expression for individuals or groups who wish to express views unpopular to the majority of people in the community.

There are other aspects of the police function which also raise important policy questions. The ones listed are, however, adequate to illustrate the difficulty of the issues and the importance of police developing and articulating policies for dealing with them. They are discussed in some detail to give an indication of the kinds of questions which can and should be addressed in re-evaluating current practice and developing adequate policies for the future.

THE DECISION WHETHER TO INVOKE THE CRIMINAL PROCESS

Whether a criminal prosecution is initiated against an individual depends, in most instances, upon a police judgment. Theoretically, this judgment is based upon the statutory definition of the crime, but it is abundantly clear that there are many situations in which a violation has in fact occurred and is known to the police, but where there is no effort by the police to make an arrest. Among the factors accounting for this exercise of discretion are the volume of violations, the limited resources of the police, the overgeneralization of legislative enactments defining criminal conduct, and the various local pressures reflecting community values and attitudes.

Social gambling affords a good example of the dilemma which police face. In most jurisdictions, all forms of gambling are illegal. Yet it is apparent that legislatures neither intend nor expect that such statutes be fully enforced. The consequence is that police are left with the responsibility for developing an enforcement policy for the particular community. The policy of a department may, for example, be clear, albeit unwritten, with regard to games of chance at church carnivals. They may be permitted because of their charitable nature. But, in the same community, the police response to gambling in a private home may vary with the circumstances of the individual case.

Usually there is no written policy but rather an informal policy which may reflect factors such as: Is there a complainant and, if so, is he adversely affected by the gambling activity? Is the gambling the prime purpose in a group's getting together, or is it incidental to some other activity or pastime, such as a bridge game? Is the activity organized? Do the participants know each other? Were they steered to the location for purposes of engaging in gambling, or is the assemblage a get-together of old friends? Is the gambling for small stakes? Is there a profit separate from winnings being realized by the individual hosting the activity or by any one of the individuals present?

It is not clear that the existence of any one of these factors will necessarily result in an arrest. Usually police will take action when there is an insistent complainant or when there is evidence that the gambling activity is commercial in nature. The difficulty is that the employment of such criteria by individual officers may lead to disparity in practice and even where practice is consistent may involve basic policy questions which are not raised and thus not considered and resolved. Complaints may originate from neighbors who are disturbed by the noise from the gambling or from wives who are either concerned over the monetary losses of their spouses or resent their absence from home. Should a police agency allow itself to be "used" under such conditions? Is a pattern of enforcement which takes action only when there is an insistent complainant a desirable one?

The tests used in practice to determine whether the game is "commercial" rather than "social" also raise important policy questions which have not been resolved. Social gambling in a ghetto area takes on a different form than does social gambling in a middle-class neighborhood. A number of men commonly get together in a private apartment, placing comparatively small bets on a dice game. When the police investigate such get-togethers, they typically find that the participants cannot identify each other; the gambling is therefore viewed as not "social" and thus properly subject to enforcement. Yet, considering the pattern of life in a ghetto area, is there any reason to characterize such behavior as more reprehensible than that engaged in by a group of men involved in a poker game for some financial stakes at a local country club? Under present practice, the participants in the dice game will generally be arrested, searched, transported to a lockup, detained overnight, and brought before a judge the following morning. For the police, the net effect of such actions seems obvious; relationships with the residents of a ghetto area, which are typically very strained, are further aggravated.

The police action with regard to the dice game in the ghetto area is often in response to complaints from ghetto residents who are disturbed by the game. It is also a response to the general police concern, based on prior experiences, that the dice game in such areas frequently ends in a fight, sometimes resulting in a homicide. Intervention by the police is viewed as serving a crime prevention function. But neither of these aspects, i.e., the attitude of the community or the relationship of the dice game to more serious crime, is studied and evaluated. As a consequence the current police practice gives the appearance of improper class and racial discrimination.

The police handling of aggravated assaults raises issues of a different character. These offenses come to police attention more routinely because they frequently occur in public; the victim or witnesses seek out the police; there is a desire for police intervention before more harm is done; or simply because the victim desires police assistance in acquiring medical aid. But while the perpetrator is known to the victim in a high percentage of the cases, there frequently is no arrest or, if an arrest is made, it is followed by release by the police without prosecution. This is especially true in the ghetto areas of large urban centers, due, according to police, primarily to an unwillingness on the part of the victim to cooperate.

The failure to make an arrest for a serious assault is especially common if the parties involved are related or close friends. Police, based upon their experience, feel that there will be an unwillingness on the part of the victim to assist in establishing the identity of the assailant, in attending showups, in viewing photographs, or even in answering questions truthfully. Even if the victim cooperates at the investigation stage, the police assume from their experience that the willingness to cooperate will disappear at the time of trial when the victim will refuse to testify and may even express a desire that the assaultive husband or acquaintance be set free.

It would be possible for police to achieve some success in assault cases by resort to the subpoena in order to compel the victim to testify. But this procedure is seldom used. Given the high volume of cases and the competing demands upon a police agency, the path of least resistance is to acquiesce to the desires of the victim. The position is often rationalized on the grounds that the injured party was the only person harmed and that the community as a whole was not affected by the crime. These cases can be written off statistically as clearances, which is viewed as an index of police efficiency, and thus the most immediate administrative pressure is satisfied.

There is serious question about the relationship between current police practice in ghetto assault cases, on the one hand, and the amount of crime and community attitudes toward police, on the other hand. If the criminal justice process does deter, why will it not deter assaultive behavior in the ghetto area?

To what degree does police tolerance of assaultive conduct result in the formulation of negative attitudes on the part of ghetto residents toward law and order in general? What is the impact upon the residents of a ghetto when an attack by a ghetto resident upon a person residing outside the ghetto results in a vigorous prosecution?

Today these and other basic policy questions which can be raised are not dealt with by the police. Their practice continues to be informal, and, as a consequence, may very well serve to complicate rather than solve important social problems. Were the police to review their current practices, they might well conclude, for example, that so far as assaults are concerned, it is desirable to base police decisions to arrest on such criteria as the nature of the assault, the seriousness of the injury, and the prior record of the assailant.

THE SELECTION OF INVESTIGATIVE METHODS

Although there has been increasing attention given by legislatures and particularly by courts to the propriety of current police detection and investigative methods, there remain many areas in which the determination as to the investigative technique to be used is left for the police. Neither legislatures nor courts have been much involved, for example, with the propriety of police use of "undercover" or "infiltration" techniques, surveillance, or the employment of methods intended to afford an opportunity for an alleged offender to commit a crime in a manner that will make evidence of his offense available to the police.

On the other hand, some police investigative practices, like search for physical evidence, have been subject to increasingly close judicial scrutiny.

If the present trend continues, it is not at all unlikely that current investigative practices thought by police to be proper and effective will be held to be unconstitutional or subject to increasingly specific rules. This has occurred with respect to in-custody interrogation which is now specifically controlled by the *Miranda* decision. Whether this will happen with respect to other police practices will depend in large measure upon whether police can develop policies which differentiate the proper from the improper use of the particular investigative practice and develop the capacity to see to it that improper methods are not used as a matter of informal departmental policy or by individual officers out of either ignorance or excessive zeal.

Field interrogation is illustrative of an important police investigative technique which may or may not survive attack. Police have generally argued that the right to stop and question people is essential, especially when persons are observed in an area in which a crime has just been committed.

But, with several exceptions, there has been little effort to provide individual officers with carefully developed guidelines to assure that such interrogation is sparingly and carefully employed under conditions that justify its use.

The use of field interrogation as an investigative technique is complicated by the fact that it is a part of the total preventive patrol program which represents a current response of police in large cities to the demand that the "streets be made safe." Preventive patrol often involves aggressive action on the part of the police in stopping persons using the streets in high-crime areas and in making searches of both persons and vehicles. The purpose is not only to talk with individuals who may be suspected of having recently committed crimes but, more broadly, to find and confiscate dangerous weapons and to create an atmosphere of police omnipresence which will dissuade persons from attempting to commit crimes because of the likelihood of their being detected and apprehended.

It is probably true that an aggressive program of preventive patrol does reduce the amount of crime on the street, although there has been no careful effort to measure the effectiveness of this technique. It is also apparent, however, that aggressive preventive patrol contributes to the antagonism of minority groups whose members are subjected to it. A basic issue, never dealt with explicitly by police, is whether, even solely from a law enforcement point of view, the gain in enforcement outweighs the cost of community alienation.

The continuation of field interrogation as a police investigative technique depends upon a police willingness to develop policies which carefully distinguish field interrogation from clearly illegal street practices and to take administrative steps to demonstrate that a proper field interrogation program can be carried out without it leading also to indiscriminate stopping and searching of persons on the street. As yet, police have failed to make this kind of demonstration, and thus today field interrogation as a police investigative technique remains in jeopardy.

THE DECISION NOT TO PROSECUTE INDIVIDUALS WHO HAVE BEEN ARRESTED

While it is the practice in some States to take all arrested individuals before a judge, it is standard procedure in others for the police to release some individuals prior to their scheduled court appearance. Drunks are often given their freedom when they are sober. Juveniles are often released after consultation with parents or a social service agency. And in large urban areas, narcotic addicts and minor peddlers are often released with a grant of immunity in exchange for information leading to the arrest of more serious violators.

Where it is the practice to release some drunks without charging them, eligibility for release tends to be based upon such factors as appearance, dress, reputation, place of residence, and family ties. The process is generally intended to separate the common drunk from the intoxicated person who "knows better," but, in the judgment of the police, simply had "one too many." Whether this kind of distinction adequately serves an enforcement or social welfare objective is not entirely clear. Certainly police, who are daily confronted with the problem of the drunk, ought to give continuing attention to whether defensible criteria are being employed. Perhaps more important, they ought to lend support to and participate in an effort to develop ways of dealing with the alcoholic which are more sensible than the current arrest and release programs.

In some communities meaningful criteria have been formulated as a basis for the police decision as to whether a juvenile offender should be released to his parents, referred to a social agency, or brought before the juvenile court. In other communities, however, such decisions continue to be made without an articulated basis and often reflect indefensible criteria such as the color of the child, his attitude toward the police, or the status of the parents in the community.

The practice of releasing some narcotic addicts and minor peddlers in exchange for information or cooperation raises complex issues. Persons involved in narcotics control assume that the investigation of narcotics traffic requires the accumulation of knowledge from those who are involved and that convictions depend upon the help of informants who are given immunity in return for cooperation. Certainly this is a practice also in need of continuing evaluation to determine whether the gain really justifies the costs which are involved.

THE ISSUANCE OF ORDERS TO INDIVIDUALS REGARDING THEIR MOVEMENTS, ACTIVITIES, AND WHEREABOUTS

The public, whether as pedestrians or motorists, generally recognizes the authority of the police to direct their movements in traffic. But there are many other situations in which police regularly tell people what to do under circumstances where police authority is less clear. Police order people to "keep the noise down" or to stop quarreling—usually in response to a complaint from a neighbor. They frequently direct a husband to stay away from his wife with whom he has had a fight. They order a young child found on the streets at night to go home. Troublesome "characters" are ordered to stay out of a given area. Persons who congregate on street corners are often told to disperse.

Police generally assume that congregating on a street corner is likely to give rise to disorderly conduct. This is especially true if such assembling takes place outside of taverns; if those who assemble are intoxicated to varying degrees; and if there is heavy pedestrian traffic which is likely to be blocked by the congregating group. The police response is to order the persons to "move on"—thus presumably minimizing the risk of a group disturbance. This response tends to become standard operating procedure applied to all groups that congregate on sidewalks and street corners, without regard to the varying character of the groups. In some cultural groups, for example, congregating on the streets is the most common form of socializing. In some congested areas of a city, the corner is used because of the absence of adequate public recreational facilities. For police to respond to these groups in the same manner as they respond to an intoxicated group outside a tavern may not serve a real enforcement objective. It may, instead, strain the relationship between the police and the residents of areas where the street corner is the place of social and recreational activity.

The practice of ordering people to "move on" is one which has major implications and one which warrants more careful use. Confronting the question of proper policy in dealing with congregating groups would afford police an opportunity to give attention to why groups congregate; to distinguish those congregations which create risk of serious disorder from those which do not; and to relate police work with other community programs designed to create positive social and recreational opportunities for persons who now lack these opportunities.

THE SETTLING OF DISPUTES

A substantial amount of the on-duty time of police officers is devoted to the handling of minor disputes between neighbors; between landlords and their tenants; between merchants and their customers; between taxicab drivers and their riders; and between husbands and wives. Relatively little importance is attached to the handling of such matters by police administrators, particularly in large urban areas. The patrolman who responds to the disturbance usually either informs the parties of their right to initiate a prosecution; undertakes to effect a resolution of the dispute by ordering the parties to leave each other alone (advising the drunk husband to go to the movies, for example); or uses some other form of on-the-scene counseling. The method used depends largely upon the attitude of the individual officer.

Important policy questions are raised by the police handling of all disputes and particularly by police handling of domestic disturbances. Yet, there has not been a systematic effort to measure the results of the alternative methods which police use or to develop more adequate referral resources (to social agencies, for example) which might, if they existed, provide a basis for a positive police program for dealing with disputes like the domestic disturbance. In an effort to develop adequate policies to guide the actions of the individual patrolman, police should learn how often disturbances are caused by families who are the subject of police intervention on a repetitive basis; how often the husband or wife does swear out a complaint; the disposition of such cases and their impact upon the likelihood of future disturbances; the number of serious assaults or homicides which result from domestic disturbances and whether these follow a pattern which will enable the patrolman to identify a potentially dangerous situation; and the kinds of cases which can be referred, with positive results, to existing community resources for dealing with family problems.

Through the process of careful evaluation of existing practices, police can acquire a competence which should enable them to develop more adequate methods of followup work in the domestic disturbance case, thus giving the emergency intervention of the individual officer more meaning and perhaps in the long run reducing the heavy burden on police who deal with this type of recurring social problem.

THE PROTECTION OF THE RIGHT TO FREE EXPRESSION

None of the functions which police perform so illustrates the sensitive and unique role of the police in a democratic society as that involved in the safeguarding of the constitutional rights of free speech and assembly. Police frequently find themselves in situations where they are called upon to provide adequate protection for a speaker or demonstrating group that wishes to exercise the right to express opinions, however unpopular their opinions may be and however hostile their audience.

Many urban police have not developed and formulated policies to guide police action in such situations. Although the issues involved in recent demonstrations reflect many factors which are beyond police control, it is nonetheless a fact that the manner in which police respond to demonstrations will determine, in large measure, whether violence will break out and, if it does, the degree to which the resulting conflict will escalate and spread.

The problem is particularly difficult because of the fact that police officers may themselves identify more with maintaining order in their community, particularly to prevent disorder created by outsiders, than they do with their basic responsibility to preserve the right of free expression of social and political views. Thus, the officer assigned to a white neighborhood may view a Negro march through the neighborhood in favor of open housing as both a threat to public order in his district and also a threat to the values of the people in the neighborhood on whose support he depends in his day-to-day work.

In rural areas or small cities, the population may be relatively homogeneous, and thus the police officer can be responsive to the local citizens without this producing conflict for him. But the large urban areas today are made up of communities which differ in economic, racial, religious, and other characteristics. The officer who protects the right of free expression of ideas may find himself protecting an attack upon the segment of the community with which he identifies.

Adequate and consistent response by police in the highly tense situations which arise in some political and social demonstrations obviously requires a careful effort to work out in advance those policies which will govern their actions. Development of policies must be coupled with an effort to communicate them to individual officers in a way which will give each officer a basis for identifying with the protection of freedom of expression as an important enforcement objective. In addition, an effort must be made to articulate such policies to the affected community so that the public understands the reasoning behind police actions. This, in itself, can serve to lessen the likelihood of major disorders.

THE POLICY FORMULATION PROCESS

The formulation of policies is a difficult undertaking. For police officials who have not previously been called upon to fulfill the function, the task requires the development of a systematic process by which important issues are identified, studied, and resolved. The police are, of course, in a position to benefit in this effort from the experiences of other administrative agencies that are, in varying degrees, committed to developing guidelines covering their respective operations.

IDENTIFICATION

Police attention is currently drawn to problem areas only when crises arise. The recent civil rights disorders, for example, have resulted in a reexamination of police practices in some jurisdictions. There are obvious limitations in examining operating practices under the kinds of pressures generated by such crises. It would be preferable for the police to make use of a number of alternative methods by which issues can be dealt with before they reach crisis proportions.

One method of identifying important issues is by the analysis of routine complaints that are received. While there are dangers in relying on complaints as an adequate index of discontent with police actions because of the reluctance of large segments of the population to file complaints, they nevertheless often reveal patterns of police action which at least suggest the need for inquiry.

Another method of identifying important issues is by observation of field procedures. The size and semimilitary nature of large police organizations often result in those at the top of the agency having a quite different concept of prevailing practices than actually exists at the operating level. Absent an opportunity for occasional involvement at the operating level, administrative and supervisory personnel tend to discuss practices and resolve problems while quite oblivious to what is happening on the streets.

A third method of identifying important issues is by analysis of court decisions. Recurring problems become apparent to the trial judge, but typically are not communicated to the police. Motions to suppress evidence may, for example, be routinely granted because of the procedure used by the police in acquiring the evidence. Systematic review of these cases would disclose to the police administrator patterns of field practices which ought to be reevaluated.

Many operating police officers are themselves conscious of the need for addressing particular problems, but the semimilitary nature of the police agency tends to stifle the initiation of suggestions or the calling of attention to major problems by persons occupying the lower ranks of the organization. One means for overcoming this is through an effective in-service training program. Experienced officers, placed in a classroom setting which takes them out of the chain-of-command, can be encouraged to discuss the relationship between existing policies and apparent needs in the field. Training instructors ought to encourage such discussions and to communicate the field problems to those who are in a position to correct them.

STUDY AND RESEARCH

Systematic study of a problem requires that the police develop a research methodology that equips them to clarify issues; to identify alternatives; to obtain relevant facts; and to analyze these facts in an effort to develop a basis for the formulation of a departmental policy.

Research methods must be devised to produce accurate understanding of current practices and, so far as it is measurable, their impact upon crime and the community. Adequate evaluation of existing practices may require the collection of a substantial amount of data not now gathered. Study of alternative practices may be aided by a willingness to engage in experimentation and demonstration projects.

Developing adequate research in a police department will require some specialization. It has, in recent years, become common for a police agency to establish a "planning and research" unit and to assign a number of police

Formulation and Execution of Police Policy

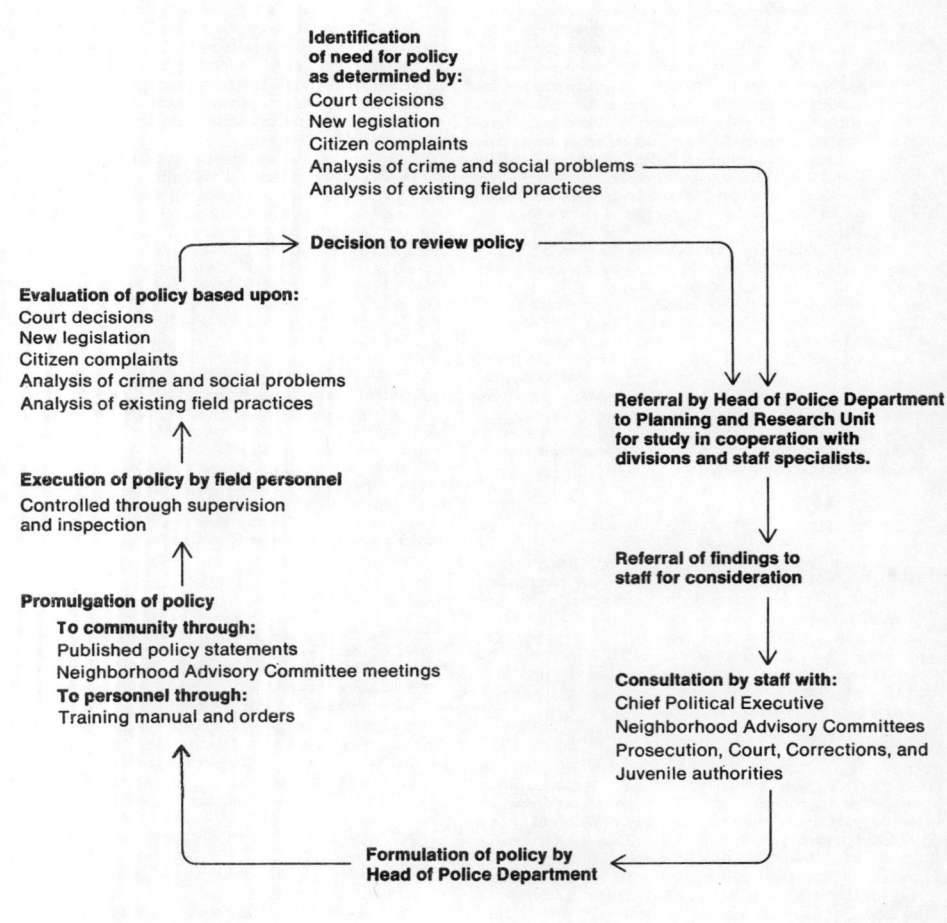

personnel to such a unit. But their function, until now, has focused almost exclusively upon the analysis and improvement of internal operating and managerial procedures, such as the deployment of manpower, the evaluation of equipment, and the streamlining of clerical procedures. The responsibility of these units should be expanded to include the continual review of practices and formulation of policies relating to the crime control and crime prevention functions of the police.

In the creation of a research staff an effort should be made both to utilize the rich and untapped knowledge of experienced police officers and also the knowledge and techniques of a substantial proportion of his own time, by gist; a criminologist capable of relating the existing body of knowledge regarding criminal behavior to law enforcement practices; and a lawyer trained to recognize and deal with the basic legal issues which police confront today.

Essential is a strong commitment on the part of the police administrator to the importance of research. He must give meaning to this commitment through the devotion of a substantial proportion of his own time, by providing for adequate staffing, and by closely relating the function of the research unit to other aspects of departmental operations.

CONSULTATION BOTH WITHIN AND OUTSIDE
THE POLICE AGENCY

The final stages in the formulative steps of the policymaking process should consist of achieving agreement on the part of the command staff of the agency and those outside the agency whose approval may be necessary or desirable.

Consideration by the command staff of policy proposals affords an opportunity to weigh the practicality of what is being advocated; to consider ramifications that a new policy might have throughout an agency, and to crystallize opinions and hammer out compromises. The process serves as a means for focusing the attention of operating personnel upon important issues that they might otherwise tend to ignore under the pressure of their daily tasks. Participation also should serve to elicit a commitment on the part of the command personnel to support the policies which are adopted.

Because many important police practices are of concern to other criminal justice agencies, particularly the prosecutor, trial judge, and correctional officer, it would be desirable to discuss proposed policies with these agencies.

ARTICULATION, PUBLICATION, AND DISSEMINATION

The major challenge in the formulation of policy is to deal adequately with the complex problem involved and to do so in terms that are clear, sufficiently precise, and meaningful to the officer at the operating level whose job it will be to implement it. Police agencies stand to gain from exploration of existing methods and from experimentation with new methods for more effectively communicating written policy to operating personnel.

Most police agencies already have available to them the mechanical means for disseminating administrative directions. They are variously referred to as general orders, memoranda, or bulletins. Existing procedures could easily accommodate the series of publications likely to result from reducing operating policies to paper.

Emphasis on methods for disseminating and communicating policies reflects the assumption that openness, affording an opportunity for public criticism, is of major importance as a protection against the arbitrary exercise of governmental powers. It follows that policies of administrative agencies, including those of the police, ought not to be kept secret except in those exceptional cases in which confidentiality is necessary in order to maintain their effectiveness.

TRAINING

However successful a draftsman may be in building clarity and preciseness into a policy statement, dependence cannot be placed upon the written word in order to achieve effective implementation. Opportunities must be afforded for officers at the lowest level in the organization to ask questions and, more importantly, to gain a full understanding of how the policy came about and why it is important that it be implemented. An officer who knows why a policy is adopted is more likely to comply with it and, to the extent that he identifies with the new policy, is more likely to work toward its successful implementation.

If adequate policies exist, they can best be communicated to the individual officer by a problem approach to training rather than the more traditional lecture form of police training. The problem approach, if done well, serves to test whether the training staff understands the important situations encountered in the field and whether existing policies are adequately responsive to these situations.

REVIEW

Flexibility is one of the major objectives in the formulation of policy, both as a means for enabling a department to adjust its operating practices and, at a lower level, as a means for affording individual officers functioning within departmental policies an opportunity to adapt to the varied circumstances they confront. The desirable degree of flexibility for both the department and for the individual officer is not static, but rather changes from time to time. A decision as to what constitutes proper guidelines for the police must, therefore, be subject to frequent review to assure that adequate room is allowed for the exercise of an officer's judgment, but to assure as well that the guidelines are not so broad as to encourage or allow for the making of arbitrary decisions.

In addition, experimentation with a given policy over a period of time is likely to result in experience which will make possible a more comprehensive review of the basic problem than was possible at the time the policy was first formulated.

INTERNAL CONTROLS

It is in the nature of an administrative organization that the establishment of policies to guide the exercise of discretion by individuals is not enough. There is need also for the development of methods for assuring compliance. This requires a system of administrative controls to be applied within an agency.

METHODS OF INTERNAL CONTROL

An analysis of patterns of deviations from appropriate policy standards indicates that such deviations usually fall into three general categories: situations in which an officer violates departmental regulations or policies; situations in which an officer's behavior is considered improper, but does not constitute a violation of existing departmental policy; and situations in which an officer's behavior is clearly illegal or improper, but is consistent with the routine practice of the particular agency and is generally condoned by its administration.

(1) There are a limited number of situations today in which police administrators have issued policy statements to control police conduct. These tend to mirror the requirements of appellate cases as, for example, policies to implement the specific interrogation requirements of the *Miranda* case. Field studies conducted by the Commission indicate that such policies, promulgated at the top of the agency, are often disregarded in practice. Occasionally situations may arise in which a failure to adhere to existing policy becomes a source of embarrassment to the top echelons of the police agency, as, for example, if a failure to give the warnings required by the *Miranda* case were to prevent the conviction of a serious criminal in a highly publicized case.

The fact that administrative policy for dealing with crime or potential crime situations does not have a very significant impact upon the actions of individual officers appears to be primarily attributable to two factors: the ambivalent attitude which often accompanies the pronouncement of a policy implementing a decision like *Miranda,* and competing influences brought to bear by subordinate command staff who are subject to more immediate pressures from the community they serve.

Top police officials have been quite outspoken in registering their opposition to recent decisions of the U.S. Supreme Court. Personnel within an agency are fully aware of the public pronouncements of their superiors. They recognize that an order which purports to urge compliance with a recent decision is necessitated by the decision and is reluctantly issued by their superior. Without a special effort on the part of the administrator to distinguish between his right to enter into public debate over the wisdom of court decisions and the need for compliance with court decisions, it is likely that departmental policies which simply mirror the requirements of an appellate decision will be largely disregarded.

A somewhat similar situation exists when operating personnel believe that a change in departmental policy reflects a somewhat reluctant effort on the part of the administration to appease some community group that has made a complaint against the department.

In current practice, such departmental policy as exists is but one of a number of competing considerations that influence police actions at the operating level. Tremendous pressures are generated upon the various command levels in a large police agency by community groups—pressures from which such personnel cannot be easily isolated. The desire on the part of a supervisory officer or precinct commander to satisfy a prominent citizen, to meet the demands of a community group on whose support his continued effectiveness and acceptance depend, to obtain favorable publicity, or simply to satisfy his most immediate superior may override any desire he may have to adhere to established policy. Subordinates, in turn, have their eye upon their superior rather than upon formal pronouncements which come to them in written form. The extent to which they conform with policy formulated at the top levels will be determined, in large measure, by the spirit and tone in which it is communicated to them by their more immediate superiors. Each of the many levels of supervision in a large agency, therefore, constitutes a point at which policies may be diluted or ignored.

(2) An entirely different set of problems is raised when an individual officer acts in a manner which none of his superiors would condone, but there is no formulated policy to serve as a basis for discipline or condemnation.

The problems are complicated by the peculiar nature of the police function. Officers are usually spread out about an entire city. They do not have the opportunity for immediate consultation with superior officers when called upon to take action. The danger of mass disorder is always present, and the need for quick decisions often requires that the officer take some form of action before he has the opportunity to acquire all of the facts. It is, therefore, difficult for the police administrator to hold an individual police officer to the same standard one would hold a person who had an opportunity to consult and to think about the matter before acting.

The actions of individual police officers are not easily subject to review. Contacts between police officers and citizens are often contentious, tending to evoke an emotional response on the part of both the officer and the citizen. They occur at times and in locations where others are not present. And an informal code among police officers, which bands individual officers together for mutual support when challenged from the outside, silences fellow police officers who may be the only witnesses to an incident. As a consequence the typical complaint will consist of an assertion of wrongdoing on the part of a citizen and a denial by the officer. There usually is no available basis for corroborating either story. The consequence of continually disbelieving the officer would obviously mean a loss of morale. Hence, the tendency in such cases is for the police administrator to accept the officer's version unless there is some reason to believe the officer is being untruthful.

(3) The most complicated situations that arise in current practice are those in which the actions of an officer

are clearly illegal or improper but are consistent with prevailing practices of a department. Such practices are commonly found in the police agencies serving large urban areas, where the practices constitute part of the informal response which the police have developed for dealing with problems of a recurring nature. It is, for example, common for police officers to search the interior of a vehicle without legal grounds in high crime-rate areas. It is similarly common for police to search gamblers or arrest known prostitutes without adequate grounds. Since such actions are generally encouraged by superior officers, it is inconceivable that the officer would be administratively criticized or disciplined upon the filing of a complaint. Nevertheless, complaints tend to be processed administratively in the same way as complaints alleging a violation by an officer of administrative policy. As a consequence, the complaint procedure does not serve as a vehicle to challenge and cause a reconsideration of policies which are sanctioned by the department even though not articulated.

PROPOSED IMPROVEMENTS IN METHODS
OF INTERNAL CONTROL

Some of the problems of achieving control over the conduct of individual police officers would be simplified if there were a commitment by the police administrator to a systematic policy-formulation process. This would require specific attention to present unarticulated policies which are clearly illegal and as a consequence would create administrative pressure to reject them or develop alternatives rather than assume the indefensible position of formally adopting illegal practices as official departmental policy. The development of adequate policy statements would afford the individual police officers greater guidance with respect to important decisions like the use of force, and the decision to arrest or to search.

But the mere adoption of administrative policies will not alone achieve compliance. This will require "good administration," that is, the use of the whole array of devices commonly employed in public administration to achieve conformity. These include, but are not limited to, the setting of individual responsibility, the establishment of systems of accountability, the designing of procedures for checking and reporting on performance, and the establishment of methods for taking corrective action.

The police administrator currently achieves a high degree of conformity on the part of officers to standards governing such matters as the form of dress, the method of completing reports, and the procedures for processing of citizen complaints. Sleeping on duty, leaving one's place of assignment without authorization, or failing to meet one's financial obligations are all situations against which supervisory personnel currently take effective action.

The success of internal controls as applied to such matters appears to be dependent upon two major factors: (1) the attitude and commitment of the head of the agency to the policies being enforced and (2) the degree to which individual officers and especially supervisory officers have a desire to conform.

The average police administrator, for example, has no ambivalence over accepting responsibility for the physical appearance of his men. He does not wait to act until complaints are received from a third party. He undertakes, instead, by a variety of administrative techniques, to produce a desire in his subordinates to conform. This desire may reflect an agreement by the subordinates with the policy. Or it may reflect respect for their superior, a lack of interest one way or the other, or a fear of punishment or reprisal. Whatever the reason, the officer in a sort of "state of command" does what he is told rather than follow a course of his own choosing.

In sharp contrast, the police administrator is typically ambivalent over the responsibility he has for controlling the activities of his force in the exercise of discretionary power in dealing with crime or potential crime situations. While he views the physical appearance of his men as his concern, he often sees the methods by which the law is enforced as involving matters which are the primary responsibility of others outside the police establishment. This deference may, in part, be attributable to the sharing of responsibilities with other agencies—particularly the courts. Unlike internal matters over which the police administrator has complete control, much of what the police do relating to crime and criminals is dependent for approval upon the decisions of nonpolice agencies.

Strengthening of administrative control requires the creation of the same sense of personal responsibility on the part of the police administrator for the implementation of proper law enforcement policies as he presently has for implementing policies relating to internal matters.

This will require that the administrator be given the education, training, and resources necessary to fulfill the role. It requires also a change in what is expected of police administrators by the public and by those occupying key positions in other agencies in the criminal justice system. Police officials cannot be expected to develop a sense of responsibility, if they are treated like ministerial officers, and excluded from important policy-making decisions, such as those regarding the revision of substantive and procedural laws.

Also required is the development of a professional identification which can serve police officers as a frame of reference within which they can see the importance of their conforming to appropriate law enforcement policies. Blind obedience to orders, such as is currently elicited for some aspects of police operations, is limited in both its value and desirability to functions of a purely administrative nature. Personnel called upon to deal with complex problems of human behavior and expected to make decisions on the basis of professionally developed criteria must, themselves, have some form of professional identification as a common basis from which to function.

Professional identification has, for example, been a major element in the rapid development of what are now some of our more highly regarded correctional systems. With training and education in social casework as a prerequisite to employment, operating personnel function from a framework for decision-making which is consistent with and supportive of departmental policies. The whole administrative process is facilitated because both administrators and field personnel are on the same "wave length," talking the same language and supporting the same values.

A somewhat similar development is essential in the police field. Individual police officers must be provided with the training and education which will give them a professional identification consistent with the police role in a free society. Such training and education will equip them to understand the policies of their superiors; make them receptive to efforts to make law enforcement both fair and effective; and enable the officer to take appropriate action in the unpredictable situations not dealt with by even the best efforts at policy formulation.

EXTERNAL CONTROLS

The operations of the police, like the operations of any other administrative agency that exercises governmental authority, must be subject to effective legislative, executive, and judicial review and control. This is important when the police are called upon to carry out specific legislative, executive, or judicial mandates. It is doubly important in areas in which the police are left with discretion to develop their own policies within broad legislatively or judicially fixed limits.

METHODS OF EXTERNAL CONTROL

While there is a very strong formal commitment to local control of law enforcement in this country, the actual means for exerting control has become quite obscure. To whom is a police agency responsible? By what means may citizens influence its functioning?

By City Councils and Mayors. Ultimate control, in local government, is normally exerted through the ballot box. But efforts to protect the police from partisan political influence have, in many jurisdictions, made the police immune from the local election processes. Early efforts to assure popular control of the police did include provisions in some cities for the chief of police to be elected. In others, the police were made responsible to the local legislative body. It became quickly apparent, however, that such direct control led to a pattern of incompetence, lax enforcement, and the improper use of police authority. Elected office holders dictated the appointment and assignment of personnel, exchanged immunity from enforcement for political favors, and, in some cities, made use of the police to assist in the winning of elections.

In more recent times there has been a continuing effort to compromise the need for popular control with the need for a degree of operating independence in order to avoid the undesirable practices that have generally resulted from direct political control. Election and city council supervision of the police function gradually gave way to the establishment of administrative boards, variously constituted, in an effort to assure both independence and some semblance of civilian control.

These organizational patterns have, in turn, often led to an obscuring of responsibilities, resulting in a swing back to more direct control in the form of a movement for the appointment of a single executive, directly answerable to the elected mayor or, more recently, to a city manager who in turn is responsible to a city council. Variations of each of these arrangements, including some attempts at State control, continue to this day, with periodic shifting from one organizational pattern to another in response to a community's conclusion that its police force has too much or too little independence.

The record of involvement by elected officials in police operations, to the detriment of both the efficiency and effectiveness of the police establishment, has had a lasting and somewhat negative impact on the lines of control between the citizenry and the police. In cities in which the desire to isolate the police from political interference led to the adoption of special organizational patterns, the change in some instances has had the effect of making the police impervious to citizen demands of a legitimate nature. Although the organizational structure provides for direct control, the results have nevertheless been somewhat similar even in those cities in which the police administrator is directly responsible to an elected mayor.

Fear of being accused of political interference and an awareness of the sensitive nature of the police task have often resulted in the mayor abdicating all responsibility for police operations by granting complete autonomy to his police department. Indeed, the mayors of several of the largest cities, considering police department autonomy to be a virtue, have campaigned for reelection on a platform stressing the independence which they have granted to their police agencies. A mayor's apprehensions are created by his knowledge that any action on his part affecting the police, no matter how legitimate, may be characterized as political or partisan interference. The consequence is that we are now in a period of uncertainty as to the best relationship between police and the city government, the issue aggravated by the situation of unrest in large urban areas.

By Prosecutors. The prosecutor, State's attorney, or district attorney is designated as the chief law enforcement officer under the statutes of some States. However, despite this designation he is not generally conceived of in this country as having overall responsibility for the supervision of the police. His interest in police operations is usually limited to those cases likely to result in a criminal prosecution, thereby excluding the non-prosecution-oriented activites that constitute so high a percentage of the total police effort.

Practices vary significantly from one jurisdiction to another as to the degree of involvement on the part of the prosecutor in the review of police procedures and actions in those cases in which the police objective is prosecution. While some cases are subject to review prior to the effecting of an arrest, the vast majority of arrests by municipal police officers are made prior to consultation with the prosecutor. Some prosecutors establish procedures for the review of all arrests prior to their presentation in court, while others do not become involved until the initial hearing is begun before a magistrate. Systematic review of all cases prior to their presentation in court tends to result in the adoption of standards that are informally and sometimes formally communicated to the police agency. Police practices may be criticized or changes suggested, but such criticism and suggestions are not generally viewed as a form of control. Rather, they are seen as being primarily motivated by a desire on the part of the prosecutor to facilitate his task in the review and prosecution of cases. Where there is no prior review, the staff of the prosecutor in large cities often routinely presents in court cases in which the practices by the police were clearly illegal, apparently feeling no responsibility for reacting to the police practice, either in the form of a refusal to prosecute or in the form of a communication through appropriate superiors to the administration of the police force.

In general, instructions or guidelines issued by the prosecutor relating to procedures for the prosecution of criminal cases will be accepted and followed by the police, particularly if the prosecutor is viewed by the police as seriously interested in the effective presentation of the case in court. But neither the police nor the prosecutor assume that the prosecutor has the responsibility either to stimulate or to participate in the development of administrative policies to control the wide range of police practices.

By the Judiciary. In many jurisdictions the trial judge has acted as a sort of chief administrative officer of the criminal justice system, using his power to dismiss cases as a method of controlling the use of the criminal process. But except in those cases in which his action relates to the admissibility of evidence, this has been done largely on an informal basis and has tended to be haphazard, often reflecting primarily the personal values of the individual trial judge.

In contrast, the function of the trial judge in excluding evidence which he determines to have been illegally obtained places him very explicitly in the role of controlling police practices. However, trial judges have not viewed this role as making them responsible for developing appropriate police policies. Many trial judges, for example, when asked if they would explain their decision to the police, indicate that they have no more responsibility for explaining decisions to police than they have with regard to private litigants. When asked whether they would suggest to the police proper ways of acquiring evidence in the future, some judges assert that it would be unethical for them to do so unless they also "coached" the defense.

Occasionally a judge will grant a motion to suppress evidence in order to dismiss a case he feels should not be prosecuted because the violation is too minor or for some other reason. Use of a motion to suppress evidence in this manner serves to confuse the standards that are supposed to guide the police, and has a destructive effect upon police morale.

Most often, the process of judicial review is seen as a decision about the propriety of the actions of the individual officer rather than a review of departmental administrative policy. Judges seldom ask for and, as a consequence, are not informed as to whether there is a current administrative policy. And, if there is one, they seldom ask whether the officer's conduct in the particular case conformed to or deviated from the policy. As a result, police are not encouraged to articulate and defend their policy; the decision of the trial judge is not even communicated to the police administrator; and the prevailing police practice often continues unaffected by the decision of the trial judge.

The effectiveness of trial court review is further complicated in courts of more than a single judge by the disparity of their views about the propriety or desirability of given police practices. Ordinarily the prosecution has no opportunity to appeal adverse decisions. And where appeals are allowed, prosecutors seldom view them as a way of resolving conflict between trial judge rulings. As a result police often tend to ignore all of the decisions, rationalizing that it is impossible to conform to conflicting mandates. While increasing attention has been given to minimizing sentencing disparity through such devices as sentencing institutes, designed to minimize disparity, no similar attention has been given to disparity in the supervision of police practices.

Finally, the effectiveness of the exclusionary rule is limited by the fact that it deals only with police practices leading up to prosecution. Many highly sensitive and important practices are confined to the street and are not reflected in prosecuted cases.

Civil Liability of the Police Officer. One much discussed method of controlling police practice is to impose financial liability upon the governmental unit as well as the police officer who exceeds his authority. A somewhat similar approach is provided for under the Federal Civil Rights Act.

The effect of the threat of possible civil liability upon police policy is not very great. In the first place, plaintiffs are seldom able to sustain a successful lawsuit because of the expense and the fact that juries are not likely to have compassion for a guilty, even if abused, plaintiff. Insurance is also now available along with other protective methods that insulate the individual officer from financial loss.

The attitude of the police administrator is to try to protect his man or the municipality from civil liability even though he may privately be critical of the actions of the officer. Usually legal counsel will instruct the police administrator to suspend departmental disciplinary proceedings because they might prejudice the litigation.

Even in the unusual case where an individual is able successfully to gain a money judgment in an action brought against a police officer or governmental unit, this does not cause a reevaluation of departmental policy or practice.

In general, it seems apparent that civil litigation is an awkward method of stimulating proper law enforcement policy. At most, it can furnish relief for the victim of clearly improper practices. To hold the individual officer liable in damages as a way of achieving systematic reevaluation of police practices seems neither realistic nor desirable.

By Citizen Complaint. Complaints alleging police misconduct may relate to an isolated incident involving the actions of a specific officer or may relate to a formal or informal practice generally prevailing throughout a department. However, the citizen complaint process, like the civil action, is typically limited, in its effect, to the specific case which is subjected to review. Experience has shown that most complaints come not from the ghetto areas where there may be most question about police practice, but rather from middle income areas where an articulate citizen becomes irate over the actions of an officer which deviate from prevailing police practice in his neighborhood.

Most attention in recent years has focused upon the means for investigating such complaints, with public discussion concentrated upon the relative merits of internal departmental procedures versus those established by a form of citizen complaint board functioning in whole or in part outside the department. Whatever the method for conducting an investigation, there is no evidence that the complaint procedure has generally served as a significant vehicle for the critical evaluation of existing police practices and the development of more adequate departmental policies.

PROPOSED IMPROVEMENTS IN METHODS OF EXTERNAL CONTROL

The primary need is for the development of methods of external control which will serve as inducements for police to articulate important law enforcement policies and to be willing to have them known, discussed, and changed if change is desirable. There is obviously no single way of accomplishing this.

The task is complicated by the fact that popular, majority control over police policy cannot be relied upon alone. Often the greatest pressure for the use of improper police practices comes from the majority of articulate citizens who demand that "effective" steps be taken to solve a particular crime, to make the streets safe, or to reverse what is often seen as the trend toward an increase of lawlessness.

Effective response to crime is obviously a proper concern of police. But it is also apparent that police policy must strive to achieve objectives like consistency, fairness, tolerance of minority views, and other values inherent in a democratic society.

The creation of an institutional framework to encourage the development and implementation of law enforcement policies which are effective and also consistent with democratic values is obviously difficult. To achieve this requires a basic rethinking of the relationship between the police and legislatures, courts, prosecutors, local government officials, and the community as a whole.

The Legislature. Adequate external control over police policymaking requires first an explicit recognition of the necessity and desirability of police operating as an administrative policymaking agency of government. One, and perhaps the best, way to accomplish this is through legislative action which will delegate an explicit policymaking responsibility to police in areas not preempted by legislative or judicial action. Often it is neither feasible nor desirable for the legislature to prescribe a specific police practice; there is a need for administrative variation, innovation, and experimentation within limits set by the general legislative purpose and such legislative criteria as are provided to guide and control the exercise of discretion.

Legislative recognition of the propriety of police policymaking should encourage the development of means to develop enforcement policies and their subjection to adequate external control. It should also encourage flexibility and innovation in law enforcement while at the same time providing some guidance to police policy-making through the prescription of appropriate legislative standards or criteria.

Judicial Review of Police Policymaking. Given explicit legislative recognition of police policymaking, it ought to be possible to develop effective methods of judicial review which will not only serve to minimize the risk of improper police practices but will also serve to encourage the development, articulation, defense, and, if necessary, revision of police policies.

If there is legislative acknowledgment of the propriety of police policymaking, it would seem to follow that it would be appropriate for a person, with proper standing, to challenge existing policy, formal or informal, on the ground that it is inconsistent with general legislative policy. Where there is challenge, courts would have an opportunity to require the law enforcement agency to articulate its policy and to defend it, and, if the challenge is successful, to change the policy.

It is possible and certainly desirable to modify the current system of judicial control and to make it consistent with and, in fact, supportive of the objective of proper police policymaking. To accomplish this would require some basic changes in judicial practice:

(*a*) When a trial judge is confronted with a motion to suppress, he, and the appellate court which reviews the case, should request a showing of whether the conduct of the officer in the particular case did or did not conform to existing departmental policy. If not, the granting of such a motion would not require a reevaluation of departmental policy. However, it ought to cause the police administrator to ask whether a prosecution should, as a matter of police policy, be brought when the officer violated departmental policy in getting the evidence.

If departmental policy were followed, the judge would be given an opportunity to consider the action of the individual officer in the light of the overall departmental judgment as to what is proper policy. Hopefully, a judge would be reluctant to upset a departmental policy without giving the police administrator an opportunity to defend the reasons for the policy, including, where relevant, any police expertise which might bear upon the reasonableness of the policy. To do this will slow down the proceedings, will take judicial time and effort, but if judicial review of police policy is worthwhile at all, it would seem that it is worth doing properly.

(b) Trial judges in multijudge courts should develop appropriate formal or informal means to avoid disparity between individual trial judges in their decisions about the propriety of police policy. The Sentencing Council, created in the Eastern District of Michigan to minimize judicial disparity in sentencing, would seem to be a helpful model. This council uses a panel of judges to consider what is an appropriate sentence rather than leaving the decision entirely to a single judge. The panel serves to balance any substantially different views of individual judges, and results in a more consistent judicial standard. Again, this involves cost in judicial time.

(c) It seems obvious that judicial decisions, whenever possible, ought to be effectively communicated to the police department whose policy was an issue. Yet it is common in current practice for the police administrator to have to rely primarily upon the newspaper as a source of information about judicial decisions, even those involving an officer of his own department. One way of achieving effective communication might be through making the police officer commonly assigned by departments to regular duty in the courtroom responsible for reporting significant decisions to the police administrator. This would require a highly qualified, legally trained, court officer. In addition, trial judges would have to be willing to explain their decisions at least orally, if not in writing.

(d) If the exclusionary rule is to be a principal vehicle for influencing police policy (as distinguished from disciplining an individual officer who acts improperly) then it seems apparent that the appellate process must be accessible to the prosecution as well as the defense so that inconsistent or apparently erroneous trial court decisions can be challenged. It is nonetheless often urged that allowing appeal in a particular case is unfair to the particular defendant. Moreover, where the authority to appeal does exist, prosecutors often limit appeals to cases involving serious crimes rather than systematically appealing all cases in which an important law enforcement policy is affected.

Other Forms of External Control Over Police Policymaking. Even with carefully drafted legislation and a more adequate system of judicial review, there will still be wide areas of police practice which give rise to very important issues which must be resolved by administrative action without specific legislative or judicial guidance. This is particularly true with regard to the wide range of police contacts with citizens on the street, contacts which usually do not result in criminal prosecution but which do have a major impact upon public order and upon the relationship between police and the community. It is very important that these practices be the subject of careful administrative policymaking and be subject to appropriate methods of external control.

It has been said that one of the major current challenges to our system of governmental control is to devise appropriate methods for safeguarding the exercise of discretionary power by governmental agencies in situations where judicial review is not feasible or not desirable.

Because there is no "best" answer to the question of control over the exercise of discretionary power, it seems obviously desirable to encourage a multifaceted approach, stressing innnovation and experimentation, with the hope that, in the process, enough will one day be learned to afford an adequate basis for deciding what methods are best.

The basic need can be stated briefly, though at some risk of oversimplification. It is for giving police policymaking greater visibility, so that the problems and current police solutions are known to the community; to devise methods of involving members of the community in discussion of the propriety of the policies; and to develop in police a willingness to see this process as inherent in a democratic society and as an appropriate way of developing policies which are both effective and supported by the community.

There are some worthwhile alternatives which can be identified:

The Involvement of the Mayor or City Council in Policymaking. It may be helpful, in the long-range interest of law enforcement, to involve local officials in the process of developing enforcement policies, particularly those which have an impact upon a broad segment of the community. If, for example, a police agency is to adopt a policy to govern individual officers in deciding what to do with the down-and-out drunk, it would seem appropriate and helpful to report that policy to the mayor and city council in order to see whether there is opposition from the elected representatives. Where the issue is significant enough, a public hearing may serve to give an indication of the community response to the particular policy being proposed. Although this involvement of city government may give rise to concern over "political influence," the risk of improper influence is minimized by the fact that the involvement is open to view. The vice of political influence of an earlier day was that it tended to be of a personal nature and was secretive.

The Involvement of the Prosecutor and Trial Judiciary. Where a police policy deals with an issue such as investigative practices, which have impact upon the arrest, prosecution, and conviction of offenders, it would seem desirable to involve those other criminal justice agencies which also have policymaking responsibility.

This will require, in practice, a greater interest by the prosecutor who often today conceives of his role as limited to the trial and appeal of criminal cases rather than the development of enforcement policies which anticipate many of the issues before they arise in a litigated case.

The participation of the trial judge on an informal basis in policymaking raises more difficult questions. In theory, the judge is the neutral official not involved until an issue is properly raised in the course of the judicial process. In fact, some trial judges do act as if they are the administrative head of the criminal justice system in a particular community, and do deliberately try to influence policy with regard to when arrests are to be made, who is to be prosecuted, when charges are to be reduced, and other matters which vitally affect law enforcement.

Citizen Involvement in Policymaking. In some areas of governmental activity, there is increasing utilization of citizen advisory committees as a way of involving members of the community in the policymaking process. In some cases, the group may be advisory only, the governmental agency being free to accept or reject its advice. In other instances, the group is official and policies are cleared through the committee as a regular part of the policymaking process. The advantages of both methods are that they serve as an inducement for the police administrator to articulate important policies, to formulate them, and to subject them to discussion in the advisory group. How effective this is depends upon the willingness of the group and the police administrator to confront the basic law enforcement policy issues rather than being preoccupied with the much easier questions of the mechanics of running the department. Where there is a commitment to exploring basic enforcement policy questions, the citizens' advisory group or policymaking board has the advantage of involving the community in the decision-making process, thus giving a broader base than would otherwise exist for the acceptance and support of enforcement policies.

Official or Unofficial Inquiry Into Police Practices. In some other countries of the world there is a greater commitment to continuing inquiry into governmental activity designed to learn and assess what is going on. Thus, in England a royal commission has, on several occasions, been used as a vehicle for helpful inquiry into the state of police practice there. In other countries, especially in Scandinavia, there has been reliance upon the ombudsman, not only as a way of handling complaints, but also as a vehicle for continuing official inquiry into governmental practice, including the practices of police.

There has been less tradition for systematic, official inquiry into governmental practice in this country. Where there has been inquiry into police practice, it has commonly been precipitated by a crisis, has been directed toward finding incompetence or corruption, and, whatever the specific finding, has failed to give attention to the basic law enforcement issues involved.

It would be helpful to have systematic legislative inquiry into important police practices at the local, state, and federal level. If devoted to an effort to learn what the existing practices are and to give the police an inducement to articulate their policies and a forum for explaining and justifying them, the process of legislative inquiry can have a positive impact upon the long-range development of the police as a responsible policymaking agency. To achieve this objective, the short run price which police would have to pay in criticism and controversy would be well worth it.

Unofficial studies of law enforcement practices can also be helpful. For example, a bar association may make an important contribution by the maintenance of a standing committee which has as its mandate a continuing concern with important law enforcement policies. The police field would, in the long run, be aided by the critical, but at the same time sympathetic, interest of the organized bar.

There is also need for greater involvement of universities and especially social science research into the basic problems which confront police. Continuing university interest is itself a form of inducement to confront some of the basic policy questions; and by reporting and critically evaluating current law enforcement practices research can serve as a method of review and control in the same way that law review comment has served this function with regard to the appellate judicial process. Greater involvement of the university would also serve as a basis for the development of badly needed social science courses which deal adequately with the tasks confronting police and the role which police play in our society. This in turn should increase the number of educated and articulate citizens who are knowledgeable about and interested in the important problems of law enforcement and who thus hopefully will constitute a support for proper police policies.

Establishing Communication With the Inarticulate Segments of the Community. One of the most important ways of asserting appropriate control over police practice is to have an informed and articulate community which will be intolerant of improper police practice. A difficulty in the law enforcement field is that the groups which receive most police attention are largely inarticulate, and no formal system for the expression of views will be utilized by the groups. There is need, therefore, for development within the minority community of the capacity and willingness to communicate views and dissatisfactions to the police.

Fulfillment of this need would not only be in the interests of the community, but is desirable from the police standpoint. If the minority community could better articulate its needs, a more balanced community support for the role that the professional police administrator sees himself as filling in a democratic society would be provided. A stronger minority voice would also serve to offset some of the pressures brought to bear upon the police to adopt policies and engage in practices that are of questionable nature.

Secondly, the police have a very practical reason for wanting to be informed about what is bothering the residents of an area. However narrow a focus a police administrator may assume with regard to the development of the police function, it seems apparent that if he is to take seriously his responsibility for preventing outbreaks of violence in his community, he must undertake programs which will keep him informed of the basis for unrest.

There has been substantial progress toward meeting this need through the establishment of a wide range of police-community relations programs. The success of these is in large measure dependent on the degree to which they serve as a vehicle for enabling the otherwise unorganized citizenry to make themselves heard. It seems apparent that programs which rely primarily upon contact with well established and organized interest groups, while of value in their own right, do not serve to meet the kind of needs that are most critical. Properly developed, police-community programs afford an opportunity for police to take the initiative in soliciting the kind of insight into their own operations and the way they affect a community, which should in turn contribute to the development of more adequate police policies.

Total dependence obviously cannot be placed upon the police to assist the minority community in articulating its needs. Indeed, the lack of sensitivity to the problem on the part of the police in some jurisdictions may place the entire burden on other methods, such as the development of community action programs and neighborhood law offices. Services of this kind, which are becoming increasingly available, are likely to bring demands upon the various governmental agencies, including demands that the police review some of their policies for dealing with problems encountered in the ghetto area. A sensitive police administrator ought to recognize that such groups can contribute to a process of development and continuing evaluation of important law enforcement policies.

IMPLICATIONS FOR POLICE LEADERSHIP, PERSONNEL, TRAINING, AND ORGANIZATION

Achievement of an important policymaking role for police will require major changes in police leadership, personnel, training, and organization. These changes are described in detail in chapter 5, but the relevancy of the need for change as it relates to policy-making is briefly discussed below.

Asserting that there is need for change does not mean that current leadership is not capable, but it does mean that the traditional attitude of the police leadership toward their own function will have to be altered. There will obviously have to be a commitment to the importance of police playing this kind of role and a willingness to have police policies the subject of community interest, discussion, and debate.

There is also need for police personnel adequate to develop and articulate policy and for individual officers who can apply general departmental policies in the difficult and sensitive situations in which police find themselves, particularly in the congested urban areas. Large police departments will have to take on some of the organizational characteristics of traditionally recognized regulatory agencies, staffed to engage in on-going research and policy development. Training will have to reflect the importance of trying to deal in an adequate way with the function of the police officer in sensitive situations, like his on-the-street encounters in high crime areas, and do so in a way which supports his professional identification, including a willingness to conform to rules devised by courts and other nonpolice agencies.

LEADERSHIP

Police administrators, in the past, have been primarily selected on the basis of their demonstrated technical skill in the apprehension of criminal offenders. This tendency has apparently been supported by the fact that appointing authorities share the common impression that the apprehension and prosecution of criminals constitutes the major aspect of the law enforcement task.

Investigative skill by itself is obviously an inadequate criterion by which to evaluate and select persons to head police agencies. As has been noted, there is much more to the police task. For example, there is no reason to believe that the abilities required of a good detective relate sufficiently to the talent and skill required to be an administrator capable of leading a police agency which has a major policymaking responsibility.

The current need for police administrators to effectively handle the broad range of social issues with which they must deal makes obsolete the narrow standards for selection which have been utilized in the past. The need today is for a police administrator who is much more of a generalist rather than a person possessing narrow technical skills. He must have a sound grasp of the unique function of the police in a democratic society. He must support values which often are in conflict with the most immediate goals of arrest and successful prosecution. He must have the ability to relate police functioning to the functioning of the other agencies in the criminal justice system; to analyze and resolve complex issues relating to the exercise of police authority; to direct his subordinates in a manner which will elicit their compliance with the policies he establishes; and, in the process, to be especially sensitive to legitimate community demands and interests.

Such leadership is not likely to develop on its own. If it is to emerge from within the police establishment, means must be designed to afford police officers having the basic intellectual capacity with the opportunity to acquire a broad college-level education. Promotions in rank must be based more directly upon the degree to which officers possess the abilities required of the police administrator, rather than upon measures of seniority or technical knowledge.

The monolithic structure of police agencies must be altered to enable greater freedom of movement on the part of supervisory personnel between and among agencies. It is essential that appointing authorities be afforded the opportunity to select the best available person to head a police force; they ought not to feel any inhibition in recruiting their leadership from outside their own police agency. The current tradition of limiting appointments to persons employed within an agency has served to reduce the caliber of police leadership to a low common denominator. Selection practices should instead serve to encourage a steady flow of the most competent leaders into police agencies, thereby serving to lift the overall quality of law enforcement throughout the country. Such a change is also essential if competent police officers are to be afforded a broader basis for the development of their careers than is typically available in a single police agency. Freedom of movement is an important characteristic of a profession. Creation of more opportunities for such movement is thus needed in the development of professional status for police officers.

If means are not devised to meet the need for more effectively identifying and developing leadership from within the police field, it is likely that the increasing need for competent leadership will lead to the appointment of individuals without prior law enforcement experience to head police agencies. To the degree that such a tendency is viewed by police as undesirable, it may serve as an impetus to them to make the changes essential to the development of leadership from within their ranks.

SELECTION OF PERSONNEL

Until recently, the dominant concern in the screening of applicants for the job of a police officer has been to assure that they met the rigid physical standards that were established. Such standards are still applied in many jurisdictions, despite the fact that they do not bear directly on the most difficult problems faced by the police officer today. Emphasis upon physical strength and aggressiveness reflects the popular image of what the police do rather than a careful analysis of job requirements.

There has been a failure to stress important characteristics which relate directly to the ability of an officer to perform the police function well, namely, intelligence and emotional stability. The adequate performance of the complex task given the patrolman in highly congested urban areas requires a great deal of talent. Perhaps this is not so with respect to some police functions like enforcement of parking and traffic regulations. This suggests that there may be need for job classifications which will reflect the different needs.

Certainly, many of the duties required of patrolmen and supervisory officers in urban areas require a person of above average intelligence and a high degree of emotional stability. This is necessary if the officer is to function adequately in an organization which assumes policymaking responsibility, and which leaves to the individual officer sufficient flexibility to make appropriate decisions under the varying and complex circumstances which characterize crime and threats to public order today.

There is need for careful reassessment of the assumption that the highly aggressive individual makes the best police officer. If, as it appears, there is need for mediation and conciliation more often than there is need for the use of force or the making of an arrest, it would seem to follow that the emphasis should be placed upon getting officers who are able to understand the problems of the community and who relate well to its members. This would increase their ability to participate effectively in the solution of the social and behavioral problems which confront the police officer.

There is need for educated police officers. Certainly a liberal education should be a prerequisite for those police officers who aspire to positions of leadership in the police service. Encouraging the educated young man to enter the field of law enforcement is increasingly important. Most intelligent, well-adjusted high school graduates now go on to college. Unless law enforcement attracts individuals from this group, it will be forced to recruit from among those who lack either the ability or the ambition to further their education.

Ways exist of attracting the college qualified high school graduate. Very effective methods, such as the work study program, have been developed in other fields like corrections. Basically these programs consist of the person being sent to college as part of his job. There is no reason why these kinds of programs cannot be adapted to the law enforcement field. But police leadership must be willing to take the view that it is essential to have educated police officers; that education is relevant to the major problems of the field; and, therefore, that support should be given to programs which create an opportunity for recruiting the college educated person or offering the college qualified person an opportunity after he joins the police force, through a work-study or similar program. Certainly police departments cannot perform as responsible policymaking agencies of government unless they can successfully recruit, inspire, and retain their share of intelligent, educated young persons.

TRAINING

While considerable progress has been made in recent years in the development of training programs for police officers, the total training effort in this country, when related to the complexity of the law enforcement task, is grossly inadequate.

Many smaller jurisdictions continue to put men to work as police officers without giving them any formal instruction as to their duties. Training in numerous departments consists primarily of assigning a new man to work with a senior officer. More formal efforts to provide instruction are often of a very amateur quality. Some agencies put together a string of speakers who talk on subjects which represent their special interests, but with no real effort either to relate the talks to each other or to assure comprehensive treatment of the areas that ought to be covered. Others depend for their training upon special programs. One or two men are typically selected to attend national or regional institutes, often concerned with but a single aspect of police work, these ranging in duration from one day to several months.

Large cities do have their own training programs and facilities for both recruits and officers with years of experience. But even these established programs are limited in their effectiveness by inadequacies in course offerings, staff and facilities, and by the tendency on the part of administrators to resolve the competing pressures for manpower by restricting the amount of time allocated for instruction.

While current police training programs are better than what has existed in the past, they nevertheless continue to be a somewhat fragmented, sporadic, and rather inadequate response to the training needs of the field in a day when police are confronted with some of the most perplexing social and behavioral problems we have ever known.

For there to be basic improvement, it is essential that the legitimacy of the training needs be recognized. There ought not to be any hesitation or reluctance on the part of police administrators or the public to support police training. It should be viewed as a vital and indispensable process in equipping a police officer to perform highly sensitive and complex functions. It ought also to be recognized as a continuing need. Training cannot be accomplished by occasional and improvised programs. Rather there is need for established programs, qualified staffs, and adequate physical facilities.

Course offerings must be revised. Police officers should be given a much more solid foundation in the fundamental principles of democratic government and the society in which we live. They should be provided with sufficient background on the growth of democratic institutions to enable them to understand and appreciate the complexity of the law enforcement task and the challenge inherent in its fulfillment.

Training programs should be designed to elicit a commitment on the part of a police officer to the importance of fairness as well as effectiveness in the exercise of his authority. He must be provided with much more than has traditionally been provided in the way of guidance to assist him in the exercise of his discretion. He should be provided with a basis for understanding the various forms of deviant behavior with which he must deal. And he should be acquainted with the various alternatives and resources that are available to him, in addition to the criminal process, for dealing with the infinite variety of situations which he is likely to confront in his daily work.

This kind of training is beyond the capacity of the police officer, no matter how experienced, who is drawn from a force and temporarily assigned to the training function. There is an obvious need for more adequate staffing of training operations and new and better training materials. In the case of small departments, achievement of this objective will require a statewide effort or some other form of cooperative endeavor by which agencies can pool their resources to support a single training program.

ORGANIZATION

Efforts to improve the organization of law enforcement, both within an agency and on an areawide basis, have been influenced primarily by a desire to achieve a greater degree of operating efficiency. Within police agencies, the trend has been toward centralization designed to facilitate the control of the chief executive, to make more efficient and more flexible use of manpower, and to enable the development of expertise through specialization.

These same objectives account for many proposals that have been made to consolidate police agencies on a metropolitan or county basis, but there has been much less movement in this direction, due primarily to the high value which Americans place upon the control, at least in theory, of their local police forces.

The need for creating a sufficiently broad base to support the kind of leadership required if the police are to fulfill their policymaking function is another reason supporting the current trend toward centralization and consolidation. But it is, at the same time, increasingly clear that one of the other major needs in law enforcement is to establish closer relationships and more direct lines of contact between the police and the citizenry. One can only speculate on the degree to which current antagonism toward the police is due to too great an emphasis having been placed upon the desire to achieve operating efficiency, characterized as it has been by the move toward centralization which has resulted in a degree of detachment by the police from the communities they serve.

This suggests that a pattern of organization must be devised to balance more adequately the need for centralization, which is a very compelling need for the administrator, with the necessity for having a form of organization that facilitates contacts with the community. The concept of community service officers described in chapter 5 is one way of achieving a better balance; another is the organization of the British police which has been designed to achieve such a balance. Training programs, for example, are established and administered by the Home Office for the entire country; regional crime squads have been created to work on crime problems that cut across jurisdictional boundaries; the special services of Scotland Yard are available to police agencies outside of London that require assistance in the investigation of major crimes; and a program of amalgamations has served to combine the resources of small police forces into larger units. But, at the same time, a continual effort is being made within this framework to assure a direct relationship between police officers and citizens. Thus, for example, the police in several urban areas are currently running experiments in which a police officer takes up residence in the area he serves, thereby establishing the same kind of relationship between the officer and the neighborhood as exists in rural areas where the constable is the resident officer. The situation in this country is probably more complex than that which exists in Britain, and therefore calls not only for careful examination of the British experience, but for much more in the way of experimentation in meeting specific needs.

Insofar as police policymaking is concerned, it seems clear that the police agencies serving our major cities are sufficiently large and have sufficient resources to develop their own capacity to fulfill their policymaking role. For smaller agencies, the need should serve as a stimulus for development of new patterns of cooperation or for the creation of a unit within a state agency, such as the office of the attorney general, that would develop the capacity to assist the administrators of the smaller agencies in meeting their policymaking function.

CONCLUSION

Certainly there is a real need for basic improvement in law enforcement. To assert this is not to be unfairly critical of those who now devote themselves to a police career. Major responsibility for current inadequacies lies with the community as a whole which has made large and complex demands upon the police and has failed to furnish to police the resources necessary to adequately discharge their task.

However, some of the fault lies also with police leadership which has found it more convenient to leave major policies ambiguous and invisible rather than risking discussion and controversy; has mirrored the public's conception of the good police officer as an aggressive crime fighter despite the fact that police spend much of their time dealing with sensitive social problems which are aggravated rather than solved by aggressiveness; and, as a consequence, has been content with a process of drift rather than with direct confrontation of major law enforcement problems in America today.

The need can be stated very briefly, though at the obvious risk of oversimplification:

(1) There is need to recognize the variety of functions which police perform today, particularly in the large urban community. The demands upon police are likely to increase in number and complexity rather than decrease.

(2) Important and complex social, behavioral, and political problems can adequately be dealt with by American government only if there is room for administrative variation, innovation, and experimentation of a kind presently lacking in the police field.

(3) To deal adequately with current law enforcement needs requires an explicit acknowledgment that police are one of the most important governmental administrative agencies in existence today. It requires also that major changes be made to equip police to develop appropriate administrative policies and a willingness and capacity to conform with these policies.

ATTACHMENT A: POLICY STATEMENT

TO: All Law Enforcement Officers in New York State
FROM: New York State Combined Council of Law Enforcement Officials, June 1, 1964

Re: The "Stop-and-Frisk" and "Knock, Knock" Laws

Two new statutes, with major impact on police authority, become effective in New York State on July 1, 1964.

These laws, if properly utilized, can be of considerable aid in safeguarding our communities. Their passage resulted in part from the combined strenuous efforts expended by New York State's various law enforcement agencies. As is the case with all other law enforcement powers, whether or not these sorely needed enactments will withstand the attacks that will be made upon their constitutionality, and will stand as laws upon the books of this State, will depend in large measure upon the fashion in which they are carried out. They should be enforced with full recognition that their purposes are to protect the community, while simultaneously protecting and treating fairly all persons in it.

Every law enforcement officer in the State of New York has the responsibility of seeing to it that the powers conferred by these new statutes are used to further those purposes for which they were enacted. Some guidelines for law enforcement conduct pursuant to these statutes are set forth here.

I. The "Stop-and-Frisk" Law

The new statute, which becomes section 180–a of the code of criminal procedure, provides as follows:

§ 180–a. Temporary questioning of persons in public places; search for weapons.

1. A police officer may stop any person abroad in a public place whom he reasonably suspects is committing, has committed or is about to commit a felony or any of the crimes specified in section five hundred fifty-two of this chapter, and may demand of him his name, address and an explanation of his actions.

2. When a police officer has stopped a person for questioning pursuant to this section and reasonably suspects that he is in danger of life or limb, he may search such person for a dangerous weapon. If the police officer finds such a weapon or any other thing the possession of which may constitute a crime, he may take and keep it until the completion of the questioning, at which time he shall either return it, if lawfully possessed, or arrest such person.

A. General principles:

1. The new law does not permit an officer to stop just any passer-by and search him, nor does it allow the search of any person merely because he has a criminal record.

2. The new law does not permit the stopping and searching of any person found in the vicinity of a crime scene, merely because he happens to be there.

3. The new law does not dispense with the need for adequate observation and investigation, depending upon all the circumstances, before a stop is made.
4. No officer should stop anyone, under the new law, unless he is prepared to explain with particularity his reasons for stopping such person.
5. No officer should stop anyone, under the new law, unless the crime he reasonably suspects is a felony or one of those misdemeanors listed in section 552 of the code of criminal procedure.
6. When a person is stopped under the new law, the officer—if not in uniform—must properly and promptly identify himself to the person stopped.
7. Not everyone stopped may be searched; searches are only permitted when the officer reasonably suspects he is in danger.
8. The right to stop provided in the new law in no way changes the previously existing authority of an officer to make an arrest without an arrest warrant, as provided by section 177 of the code of criminal procedure. The new rights to stop and to search, as defined in the new statute, are separate and distinct from the established right to arrest, as provided by existing law, and to make a complete search incident to such arrest.
9. Whether or not an arrest follows a stopping under the new law, whenever any force is used in stopping the suspect, or whenever any frisk or search is made, a written report shall be made to the officer's superior officer. A proposed form for such report will be provided.

B. The right to "stop."

1. "stop":
The new statute gives the officer the right to stop a person under the indicated circumstances. If the suspect refuses to stop, the officer may use reasonable force, but only by use of his body, arms and legs. He may not make use of a weapon or nightstick in any fashion. (Of course, if there is an assault on the officer or other circumstances to justify an arrest, the officer may use necessary force to effect that arrest.)

2. "abroad in a public place":
a. For the purposes of practical enforcement procedures, this phrase is viewed as being restricted to public highways and streets, beaches and parks (to include outdoor facilities open to the public although privately owned) depots, stations, and public transportation facilities.
b. For the purposes of practical enforcement procedures, this phrase is viewed as not including the public portion of private buildings such as hotel lobbies, moving picture theaters, licensed premises, etc.

c. Definitions of the words "public place" as found in other laws, such as those dealing with disorderly conduct, are not to be substituted for the strict definition of "abroad in a public place" as outlined above.

3. "whom he reasonably suspects":
a. The words "reasonably suspects" are not to be lightly regarded; they are not just an incidental phrase; they have real meaning. "Reasonable suspicion" is clearly more than "mere suspicion." At the same time it is something less than "reasonable ground for believing" that a crime is being committed, as is necessary for an arrest.
b. No precise definition of "reasonably suspects" can be provided, other than that it is such a combination of factors as would merit the sound and objective suspicions of a properly alert law enforcement officer, performing his sworn duties. Among the factors to be considered in determining whether or not there is "reasonable suspicion" are

i. The demeanor of the suspect.
ii. The gait and manner of the suspect.
iii. Any knowledge the officer may have of the suspect's background or character.
iv. Whether the suspect is carrying anything, and what he is carrying.
v. The manner in which the suspect is dressed, including bulges in clothing—when when considered in light of all of the other factors.
vi. The time of the day or night the suspect is observed.
vii. Any overheard conversation of the suspect.
viii. The particular streets and areas involved.
ix. Any information received from third persons, whether they are known or unknown.
x. Whether the suspect is consorting with others whose conduct is "reasonably suspect."
xi. The suspect's proximity to known criminal conduct.
(This listing is not meant to be all inclusive)

c. "Reasonable suspicion" of any crime at all does not afford a basis for stopping under the new bill; there must be reasonable suspicion that the suspect is committing, has committed, or is about to commit either any felony or one of those misdemeanors enumerated in section 552 of the code of criminal procedure. (These misdemeanors are weapons crimes, burglar's tools, receiving stolen property, unlawful entry, escape, impairing, carnal abuse, indecent exposure, obscenity and other indecency provisions, sodomy, rape, narcotics, amphetamines, and hypodermic needles.) Suspicion of disorderly conduct, an offense, is not for the purpose of practical enforcement procedures a basis for stopping.

C. The right to "question."

1. No questions are to be asked until the officer has, either by being in uniform or by showing his shield and stating he is a police officer, identified himself.
2. Promptly thereafter, the suspect should be questioned (and "frisked", when appropriate) in the immediate area in which he was stopped.
3. Should the suspect refuse to answer the officer's questions, the officer cannot compel an answer and should not attempt to do so. The suspect's refusal to answer shall not be considered as an element by the officer in determining whether or not there is a basis for an arrest.
4. In ascertaining "his name" from the suspect, the officer may request to see verification of his identity, but a person shall not be compelled to produce such verification.
5. If the suspect does answer, and his answers appear to be false or unsatisfactory, the officer may question further. Answers of this nature may serve as an element in determining whether a basis for arrest exists. (But if an officer determines that an answer is "unsatisfactory" and relies upon this in part to sustain his arrest, he should be able to explain with particularity the manner in which it is "unsatisfactory.")

D. The right to "search."

1. Clearly no right to search exists unless there is a right to stop.
2. Nor is a search lawful in every case in which a right to stop exists. A search is only justified under the new law when the officer reasonably suspects he is in danger. This claim is not to be used as a pretext for obtaining evidence. In instances in which evidence is produced as a result of search, the superior officers, the prosecutors, and—it is anticipated—the courts, will scrutinize particularly closely all the circumstances relied upon for justifying the stopping and searching.
3. No search is appropriate unless the officer "reasonably suspects that he is in danger." Among the factors that may be considered in determining whether to search are:

   a. Nature of the suspected crime, and whether it involved the use of a weapon or violence.
   b. The presence or absence of assistance to the officer, and the number of suspects being stopped.
   c. The time of the day or night.
   d. Prior knowledge of the suspect's record and reputation.
   e. The sex of the suspect.
   f. The demeanor and seeming agility of the suspect, and whether his clothes so bulge as to be indicative of concealed weapons.
   (This listing is not meant to be all inclusive)

4. Initially, once the determination has been made that the officer may be in danger, all that is necessary is a frisk—an external feeling of clothing—such as would reveal a weapon of immediate danger to the officer.
5. A search of the suspect's clothing and pockets should not be made unless something is felt by this frisk—such as a hard object that feels as if it may be a weapon. In such event, the officer may search that portion of the suspect's clothing to uncover the article that was felt.
6. If the suspect is carrying an object such as a handbag, suitcase, sack, etc. which may conceal a weapon, the officer should not open that item, but should see that it is placed out of reach of the suspect so that its presence will not represent any immediate danger to the officer.

E. An example:

An example may help to illustrate. Assume that a mugging has just occurred. The officer questions the victim. She says that her pocket book was taken and she gives a description of the suspect stating, among other things, that he is about six feet tall and was wearing a brown leather windbreaker. While the victim is receiving medical treatment, the officer starts a search of the area. He sees a man hurrying down a dark street. The man's hand is clutching at a bulge under his brown windbreaker, and he glances back at the officer repeatedly. The suspect meets the description of the perpetrator except for one discrepancy—he is only five feet tall.

The officer does not have reasonable grounds to arrest the suspect for his description is clearly inconsistent with the victim's estimate of the perpetrator's height. However, from the officer's experience he realizes that victims of crime, in an excited condition, often give descriptions which are not correct in every detail. Although he lacks reasonable grounds to make an arrest, from all of the circumstances the officer "reasonably suspects" that the man he has spotted has committed the crime. Under the new law, the officer may stop this person, and may ask for his identification and an explanation of his actions. And because the crime involved violence and the suspect's windbreaker seems to conceal unnatural bulges, a frisk may be in order.

II. THE "KNOCK, KNOCK" LAW

The new statute amends section 799 of the code of criminal procedure, which will read as follows:

§ 799. Officer may break open door or window to execute warrant. The officer may break open an outer or inner door or window of a building, or any part of the building, or any thing therein, to execute the warrant, (a) if, after notice of his authority and purpose, he be refused admittance, or (b) without notice of his authority and purpose, if the judge, justice or magistrate issuing the warrant has inserted a direction therein that the officer executing it shall not be required to give such notice. The judge, justice and magistrate may so direct only upon proof under oath, to his satisfaction that the property sought may be easily and quickly destroyed or disposed of, or that danger to the life or limb of the officer or another may result, if such notice were to be given.

A. General principles:

1. Seeking to dispense with the usual notice requirements when executing search warrants should be the exception, not the rule. Stereotyped forms should not be prepared that might encourage too ready use of this extraordinary procedure. When it is to be used, it should be upon carefully drafted papers.

2. The facts relied upon as indicating that "the property sought may be easily and quickly destroyed or disposed of, or that danger to the life or limb of the officer or another may result if such notice were to be given" should be spelled out in detail in the affidavits.

3. Every application for this type of search warrant should have the endorsement or approval of a superior officer, who must be satisfied that the case is of sufficient significance to justify this procedure, and that the danger or risk of destruction is soundly anticipated.

4. When it is permitted, unannounced entry should be made with the least disruption possible. Often a passkey or the help of a superintendent may assist an officer to enter the premises with a minimum of disturbance. Every action possible should be taken to allay the fears of the occupants of the premises, or others, which may be occasioned by an unannounced entering.

5. Copies of all affidavits and court orders should be filed in the office or command of the executing officer. A proposed form will be provided for reporting the execution of all search warrants.

These instructions were prepared by the New York State Combined Council of Law Enforcement Officials, and unanimously recommended by that Council for adoption by all law enforcement agencies in the State of New York.

The Combined Council consists of:
  The New York State Association of Chiefs of Police
  The New York State District Attorneys' Association
  The New York State Sheriffs' Association
  The Police Conference of the State of New York
  The Temporary State Commission of Investigation
  The Waterfront Commission of New York Harbor
  The Grand Jury Association of New York County
  The Attorney General of the State of New York

This Training Bulletin is distributed by the New York State Municipal Police Training Council for the information of and use by law enforcement officers throughout the State. Additional copies may be obtained from:

Municipal Police Training Council
Office for Local Government
155 Washington Avenue
Albany, New York 12210

Chapter 3

Police Organization, Management and Operations

INTRODUCTION

Significant strides have been made during recent years in the organization of police departments, the management of personnel, and operational procedures. Excellent municipal police departments have been created in many urban centers. Each year, more forces abandon antiquated methods, reorganize internally, and initiate new techniques for general supervision and improved day-to-day operations. Progress has not been limited to urban forces. Several sheriffs' departments have succeeded in modernizing their departments, and now provide better protection in urban fringe areas and the nearby inhabited countryside.

Among the recommendations of the Wickersham Commission 36 years ago was one that State police forces be established to provide protection for rural areas. In 1931 there were but 21 such forces.[1] Today, 49 of the 50 States have organized State police or highway patrols, Hawaii being the exception.

In 1931, Wickersham noted that the fractionalization of law enforcement agencies and their lack of coordination were seriously affecting the fight against crime:[2]

> The multitude of police forces in any State and the varying standards of organization and service have contributed immeasurably to the general low grade of police performance in this country. The independence which police forces display toward each other and the absence of any central force which requires either a uniform or a minimum standard of service leave the way open for the profitable operation of criminals in an area where protection is often ineffectual at the best, generally only partial, and too frequently wholly absent.

As described in detail in chapter 4, some jurisdictions have recognized these deficiencies and are taking steps to counter them by consolidating police forces or pooling common resources. For example, in Nashville, Davidson County, Tenn., the police service previously provided by numerous departments has been consolidated into one central law enforcement agency.

In Salt Lake County, Utah, and Pierce County, Wash., city and county police departments are housed in one facility, and pool several common resources. Other jurisdictions, such as Suffolk and Nassau Counties, N.Y.; Marion County, Oreg.; St. Louis County, Mo.; and Dekalb County, Ga., are devising practical plans designed to result in partial consolidation.

Some smaller communities, noting the limitations of maintaining their own police forces, have contracted with larger agencies to have them assume their policing needs. These include 62 California municipalities that have contracted for policing with 21 separate county sheriff departments; 46 Connecticut towns that by contract have a resident State police trooper; 7 cities and villages policed by the St. Louis County, Mo., police; and the unincorporated portions of Fulton County, Ga., which are policed by the Atlanta Police Department.

States are playing an increasing role in improving local police service. For example, State-level agencies in Illinois, California, and Kansas upon request provide local law enforcement forces with crime scene and laboratory analyses. The New York State intelligence and identification system spans that State, and the California Department of Justice operates the bureau of criminal identification and investigation which houses criminal records and modus operandi data on a statewide basis. Several States, including Connecticut, Rhode Island, Oregon, and Illinois provide police training for the personnel of small departments. Further, many States are now playing an active role in upgrading the preparedness of law enforcement personnel within their boundaries. To date, 23 States have programs to improve the quality of police training.

At the national level, the Federal Bureau of Investigation has since 1924 assisted local law enforcement in such important areas as fingerprint identification and training, and since 1935 in laboratory analysis of physical evidence. This assistance has had significant impact on local response to crime. Further, representatives of other Federal agencies such as the various investigative agencies within the Treasury Department and the Post Office Department work closely with State and local officials in facing common problems which have assumed area, regional, or interstate scope.

Improvement has been far from universal, however. America is still unrivaled in the number and range of quality of its police agencies; advances in technology have not as yet been widely adapted for police use, and many police departments are still plagued by poor organizational structures:[3]

> [Considering the 40,000 separate departments in this Nation] * * * the vast majority of American police agencies

---

[1] National Commission on Law Observance and Enforcement, "Report on the Police" (Washington: U.S. Government Printing Office, 1931), p. 125.
[2] Ibid, at p. 124.

[3] Bruce Smith, "Police Systems in the United States" (2d rev. ed., New York: Harper & Bros., 1960), p. 209.

continue to function according to patterns laid down several generations ago.

Since traditional police practices have at best been only modestly successful in deterring criminal behavior and in apprehending offenders, it is obvious that blind adherence to tradition will not do. Also, traditional organizational structures and operational procedures have detracted from the attractiveness of police work. This is one reason for the rising resignation rates in our Nation's police departments, and for the increasing difficulty many departments have had in recruiting adequate numbers of personnel. Other than such factors as low pay and financial insecurity, these problems are caused by procedures which stifle initiative, and, in some departments, by poor direction and control, by confused responsibility, and by improper grouping of duties. Even though these conditions are apparent, there is only slight evidence that the departments most in need of reorganization are taking steps in that direction.

EXISTING ORGANIZATIONAL AND OPERATIONAL PATTERNS

To assist in evaluating the present state of American police organization, management, and operations, the Commission staff:

☐ Conferred with expert advisory panels;
☐ Sought guidance from 250 police leaders and representatives from professional bodies;
☐ Reviewed police literature and textbooks;
☐ Reviewed police consultant surveys of 75 police departments;
☐ Reviewed a comprehensive study of police organization and management which was prepared by California State College at Los Angeles for the U.S. Department of Justice; and
☐ Reviewed responses to a letter sent to 2,100 police agencies by the Attorney General requesting information on effective procedures.

Advisory Panels. Discussions of the advisory panels—four in number—were of a comprehensive nature. Participants included police chiefs, sheriffs, mayors, a county commissioner, city managers, political scientists, police consultants, and professors of police science. These panels met between December 1965 and March 1966 in San Francisco, Los Angeles, Chicago, and Washington, D.C. They discussed the present state of police organization and allied problems, and sought to identify the greatest needs of police administration.

Review of Literature and Consultant Surveys. Over the years an impressive body of knowledge about police organization, management, and operations has been assembled in police consultant reports. One of the most complete collections of such literature is housed in the International Association of Chiefs of Police library in Washington, D.C. The Commission staff took the opportunity to review in detail over 75 survey reports, some prepared as early as 1926 and others as recently as the fall of 1966. Most of them were products of such organizations as the International Association of Chiefs of Police; the Public Administration Service of Chicago; Michigan State University's Institute for Community Development and Services; the Institute of Public Administration in New York City; the Harvard Law School; and the University of Iowa Institute of Public Affairs.

Others were products of such experts as August Vollmer; Bruce Smith, Sr. and Jr.; Esther and George Eastman; Donald S. Leonard; Mayor John Lindsay's Police Task Force; and Donal E. J. MacNamara. Departments that were surveyed ranged in numerical strength from one full-time officer as in Norton Township [Muskegon], Mich., to forces many hundreds strong as in Baltimore, Boston, Washington, D.C., Pittsburgh, Seattle, and New Orleans.

The California State College at Los Angeles Study. The report prepared by the police science department faculty of the California State College at Los Angeles was based on a study conducted between May and August 1966 of American police organization and management. Underwritten by a research grant from the Office of Law Enforcement Assistance, it was completed in the fall of 1966. During this study, 6 researchers (all of whom at one time were police officers) consulted with 155 police chiefs and sheriffs and 259 personnel of midmanagement rank in 277 different law enforcement agencies at State, county, and local levels of government. The college staff also reviewed 41 different police consultant surveys, 195 different police texts and pamphlets, and 226 articles appearing in police journals.

Survey of Effective Field Operations. Also available to the Commission's staff were the responses received by then Attorney General Nicholas deB. Katzenbach, Chairman of the National Crime Commission, to an inquiry concerning the effectiveness of field operations, which he had directed to police forces serving cities of 10,000 or more inhabitants; to sheriffs with forces of 50 or more sworn members; to 49 State police and highway patrol forces; and to professors supervising the Nation's 125 police science college, university, and junior college police education programs.

The inquiry expressed the National Crime Commission's interest in "* * * learning of specific police field procedures which effectively meet and reduce crime." It also asked that forces report their techniques for preventing and solving crime and for support data. Responses to the Attorney General's letter were received from 414 forces located in 47 States, and from 33 colleges, universities, and junior colleges. Some of the responses were further enlarged upon through personal staff contact with certain police officials and observation of some procedures.

FINDINGS AND RECOMMENDATIONS

The Commission's studies enabled it to identify a number of generally prevalent deficiencies in police organization, management and operations, and suggested to it the means for correcting those deficiencies. This chapter will discuss these findings and recommendations in some detail. First, however, it is important to point out that putting the recommendations into effect will not be easy. It will require a fundamental change in attitude on the part of many police administrators and local officials. It will require spending considerable sums of money. In the police world, as anywhere, significant reform requires imagination, labor and sacrifice.

In summary, the Commission has found:

☐ Many departments lack qualified leadership. Police chiefs and personnel in middle management ranks should be required to have sufficient education and training to enable them to administer the complex affairs of a police force, and should receive salaries sufficient to attract and retain top administrators.

☐ Many departments are not organized in accordance with well-established principles of modern business management. They should be reorganized in accordance with such of those principles as best apply to the police, and those principles themselves should be periodically reexamined in the light of the changing nature of the police role.

☐ Many departments resist change, fail to determine shortcomings of existing practice and procedures through research and analysis, and are reluctant to experiment with alternative methods of solving problems. The police service must encourage, indeed put a premium on, innovation, research and analysis, self-criticism and experimentation.

☐ Many departments lack trained personnel in such fields as research and planning, law, business administration and computer analysis. Specialist units, staffed by sufficient personnel trained in a variety of disciplines, should be utilized to plan and project programs, evaluate and streamline procedures, improve management and administration, engage in special operations and establish methods for maximizing the use of personnel. In-house legal advice must be made available to medium-sized and large police forces on a full-time basis.

☐ Many departments fail to deploy and utilize personnel efficiently. Police administrators should study such matters as (a) the basis for deploying uniformed personnel; (b) the use of one- or two-man motor patrol; (c) whether or not, and for what purposes, men should be assigned to foot patrol, and whether men so assigned should serve alone or in pairs; (d) the feasibility of "team policing"; (e) the extent to which civilians can be used in staff and clerical work; (f) the extent to which such police activities as jailing, communications, records, and laboratories can be "pooled" with other departments or assumed by other governmental units.

☐ Many departments have not adequately applied technological advances that would be beneficial to law enforcement. Regional information storage and retrieval systems, communications and command-control systems, and radio-frequency-channel sharing concepts must be adapted to the police service.

☐ Finally, States, through their commissions on police standards or other appropriate agencies, should provide financial and technical assistance to departments to conduct surveys and make recommendations to improve police organization, management, and operations.

DEVELOPING POLICE LEADERSHIP

As long ago as 1921, there was recognition that the uneven development of American police organization appeared to be caused, more than by any other factor, by the lack of trained and intelligent leadership.[4] Ten years later the Wickersham Commission concurred, noting that uniformed and unimaginative leadership was a major contributing cause to existing weaknesses in police organization and management. The Wickersham Commission report said:[5]

Not infrequently the chief is wholly incompetent to discharge the onerous duties of his position. He may lack experience, executive ability, character, integrity, or the confidence of his force, or all of them put together.

In the years following the Wickersham report, some progress has been made in upgrading the level of police leadership. Even so, the overall need for infusing police departments throughout the nation with well-trained, educated, and able administrators is still clear. For example, a 1964 study disclosed that only 33.6 percent of America's police administrators had attended college, and of these only 9.2 percent possessed one or more college degrees.[6] Unfortunately, as a rule, procedures for selecting police administrators have changed little during the past 25 years. One police executive in 1966 describes the traditional road to the top:[7]

The time-honored, uninspired path of promotion sees an administrator fish-laddering his way up through the ranks without being prepared in anything more than a "by chance" manner for the new and difficult responsibilities of successive commands. The consequence is that many of today's police commanding officers are simply promoted policemen, not professional administrators carefully prepared for demanding roles in the complex enterprise that is the hallmark of contemporary police work.

The reason this condition is so prevalent is not hard to find. With few exceptions, police departments have not set minimum standards of education and achievement for administrators and middle managers, and do not offer training in administration, management and supervision to candidates for, or appointees to, such jobs. The Committee for Economic Development has pointed out:[8]

* * * young employees contemplating careers as professional administrators should receive additional training in basic administrative techniques such as those used in budget preparation and administration, organizational techniques, space and

---

[4] Raymond B. Fosdick, "American Police Systems" (New York: The Century Co., 1921), p. 215.
[5] Supra, note 1 at p. 3.
[6] George W. O'Connor and Nelson A. Watson, "Juvenile Delinquency and Youth Crime: The Police Role" (Washington: International Association of Chiefs of Police, 1964), p. 79.
[7] Samuel G. Chapman, "Developing Personnel Leadership," "The Police Chief," March 1966, 33: 24.
[8] Committee for Economic Development, "Modernizing Local Government" (New York: Committee for Economic Development, July 1966). p. 52.

manpower studies, and procedural analysis. Local units without enough recruits each year to conduct their own on-the-job programs should use contract systems with universities, professional associations, or other governments.

Beyond training for new employees, there is pressing need for continuous development of persons in responsible positions. A program of continuing education and midcareer development—with universities and professional associations—is crucial to effective administration in all local governments. Universities should accept responsibility for provision of such programs, and federal grants-in-aid for them would yield large returns at small cost compared with potential benefits. Universities should also develop or strengthen schools of public administration to play positive roles in training students for technical and managerial responsibility in governments.

The subject of standards and training is discussed in further detail in chapter 5. Lateral mobility among police forces, without loss of such fringe benefits as retirement credits, is another means for increasing the numbers of qualified police middle and executive managers as well as permitting competent civilians a career opportunity in police staff work. And there will never be more than token lateral police mobility without a system of transferable retirement credits. These concepts also are discussed in chapter 5. The issue of lateral mobility was posed by prominent police authority Frank Kreml at the 1965 International Association of Chiefs of Police meeting: [9]

Why should a department be denied access to fresh outside executive talent of proven ability? What is there about the management of police resources that causes it to be different, in this respect, from all other professions? Why, only in the police field, are the managerial skills not regarded as transferable?

Other means of developing personnel, once they achieve mid-management and executive levels, is to rotate them among the various command positions within a force or temporarily exchange key personnel with other law enforcement agencies or even with nonpolice governmental agencies. Command-level personnel should be exposed to new, diverse experiences as a practical means of instilling broader executive vision, and removing narrow, parochial thinking.

Exchange and rotation programs are not without precedent in the police world. A few forces have as a matter of practice rotated their command level personnel internally for several years. And one department, the Multnomah County Police, exchanged a police lieutenant for a Lancashire, England, Constabulary police inspector (a rank equivalent with lieutenant) for a 6-month period in 1966.[10] And in the summer, 1966, a police science college professor served the sheriff as visiting chief-in-residence. Programs such as these should be experimented with by other law enforcement agencies.

Finally, to insure that individual departments establish appropriate qualifications for executive positions, each State should assume responsibility for establishing minimum educational and training standards for such positions. The concept of minimum statewide standards is fully discussed in chapter 8 of this volume.

IMPROVING ORGANIZATION

Although some forces have long been recognized as being well-organized and progressively managed, far too many of America's city and county forces have serious organizational deficiencies. In fact, many police forces appear to have evolved over the years without conscious plan. These forces are characterized by diffusion of authority, confused responsibility, lack of strong lines of direction and control, and improper grouping of functions. An example of one such department is seen in figure 1. This force of over 300 men was reported by a consultant as having:

* * * serious deficiencies of internal communications, coordination, supervision, and direction of effort and control.
This general dissipation of personnel resources—the scattering of specialized work units about the Department without the essential bond of control and direction to hold each such unit to the main objectives of the organization—has reduced the ability of the Department to function as an organized group. The ultimate result is a reduction in the efficiency of the total effort.

With virtually no exception, other consultant reports found serious weaknesses in forces that were surveyed. For example, one consultant noted the following organizational and management defects in a force having more than 450 personnel:

Sound management practices apparently are not understood nor used by administrative and command personnel * * * Planning and research are not utilized * * * to resolve present problems of organization, personnel deployment, performance inadequacies * * * nor to prepare programs, procedures, and policies for strengthening the [department]. Career development programs have not been formulated. Staff inspection as a control device is not known * * * and therefore not used.

Another consultant body reported these findings in a force of about 3,000 persons:

The Department suffers from a deficient organizational structure which contributes to poor management. These weaknesses make it difficult for the Department leadership to exercise full control over the entire police operation; the chain of command is confused and supervision is erratic. The excessive decentralization of the Department's operations into 14 precincts adds to these problems. One of the important consequences of poor organization and management is the diversion of police personnel to specialized or administrative assignments, thus unduly curtailing the number of men available for the street operations of the Patrol Division.

That the Nation's small police forces are also not free of organizational and management problems is confirmed in a consultant report which noted the following conditions in a 10-man force:

It may be said unequivocally that the department has no organization pattern * * * The chief * * * has had [no] training in police administration, command, or supervision * * * [T]he chief's desk duties have created an unfavorable situation in which proper administrative and command precepts are not followed and in which field supervision and training is nonexistent.

---

[9] Franklin M. Kreml, "The Role of Colleges and Universities in Police Management," "The Police Yearbook, 1966" (Washington: International Association of Chiefs of Police, 1965), p. 36.

[10] For a detailed description of the exchange program see: John P. deB. Kennard, "An Account of an Exchange Visit to the United States and Canada" (Lancashire, England: The Lancashire County Police, December 1966), 27 pp.

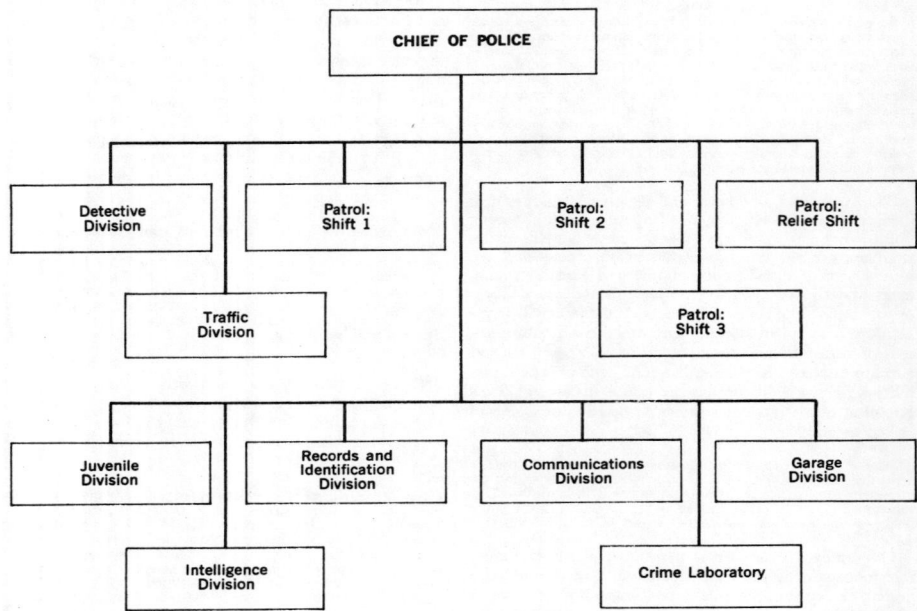

Figure 1.—An Example of a Poorly Organized Municipal Police Department

There is little justification for American police forces not to be well organized. Available for the asking since the turn of the century has been a large and authoritative general body of guidance in public administration. And for some 30 years there have been adaptations of this to police management prepared by such knowledgeable police authorities as O. W. Wilson and V. A. Leonard, and the International City Managers' Association.[11]

The crux of the problem seems to be that relatively few police forces have taken advantage of this valuable compilation of organization and management principles. This is the more regrettable in view of successes achieved by the departments that have utilized them.

Almost all highly regarded police practitioners, public officials, management consultants and university faculty members agree that an essential need in police organization and management is for all police departments, preferably with the assistance of recognized consultants, to examine their internal organizations in order to determine whether:

☐ The force's work is apportioned among the various individuals and units according to a logical plan.
☐ Lines of authority and responsibility are made as definite and direct as possible.
☐ The number of subordinates who can be effectively supervised by one officer is not exceeded.
☐ There is "unity of command" throughout the organization.
☐ Responsibility, once placed, is accompanied by commensurate authority, and that once delegated, the user is held to account for the use he makes of it.
☐ The efforts of the organizational units and of their component members are coordinated so that all will be directed harmoniously toward the accomplishment of the police purpose. The components thus coordinated will enable the organization to function as a well-integrated unit.[12]

Police department objectives can be achieved more easily, efficiently, and satisfactorily when these principles

---

[11] See O. W. Wilson, "Police Administration" (2d ed., New York: McGraw-Hill, 1963), 528 pp.; V. A. Leonard, "Police Organization and Management" (2d ed., Brooklyn: The Foundation Press, Inc., 1964), 459 pp.; "Municipal Police Administration" (5th ed., Chicago: International City Managers' Association, 1961), 545 pp.; and R. Dean Smith, "Organization," "The Police Chief," June 1962, 29: 10-34, 44. Forerunners to the above include: Leonhard Felix Fuld, "Police Administration: A Critical Study of Police Organizations in the United States and Abroad" (New York: G. O. Putnam & Son, 1909), 551 pp.; Elmer D. Graper, "American Police Administration" (New York: The MacMillan Co., 1921), 357 pp.; Raymond B. Fosdick, "American Police Systems" (New York: The Century Co., 1921), 408 pp.; and "Municipal Police Administration" (1st ed., Chicago: International City Managers' Association, 1938), 441 pp.
[12] For a more comprehensive treatment of these six principles see: O. W. Wilson, "Police Administration" (2d ed., New York: McGraw-Hill Co., 1963), pp. 34-36; and the International City Managers' Association, "Municipal Police Administration" (5th ed., Chicago: International City Managers' Association, 1961), pp. 44-45. Sixth ed., in preparation for publication by 1968.

Figure 2.—One Form of a Well Organized Municipal Police Department

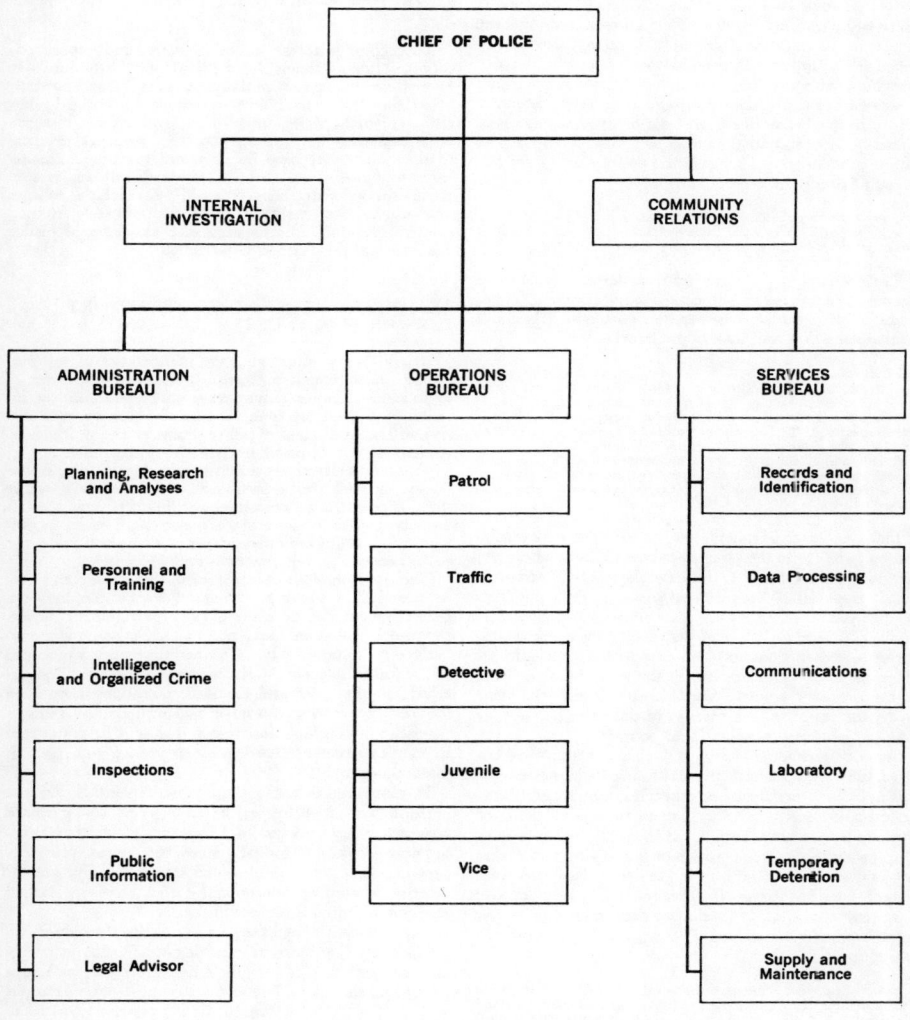

have been applied. Figure 2 shows one form of a well organized police force. Its structure coincides with the requirements noted above.

Even though there is considerable knowledge about police organization, insufficient experimentation and reassessment of traditional principles is taking place in the police service today. In general, too many police departments appear unwilling to abandon outmoded concepts, to work in close collaboration with community agencies (especially social service agencies), or to encourage personnel to show initiative or offer suggestions. This prevailing attitude must change if the police are to meet the changing conditions of police service:[13]

> Every activity of police administration will require new ideas effectively put into practice to meet new conditions. This is particularly true within the area of police management. * * *

Unfortunately, the police and academic worlds have not yet collaborated to induce necessary change. There seems to be a schism between the two, which includes mutual suspicion and lack of confidence:[14]

> Large police departments * * * are for the most part secretive about the internal life of the force. Almost anyone who undertakes research on police administration in a big city quickly discovers the extent to which he is held in suspicion and treated circumspectly * * * But the commitment to secrecy far exceeds what normal prudence would seem to dictate. Secrecy in fact is * * * one of the most important ways by which policemen defend themselves against the presumed hostility of civilians. An outsider is considered * * * to be antipolice until he is proved otherwise.

Many police departments do not have the expertise to recognize their shortcomings or to correct them when they are recognized. Most do not have the financial resources to pay the costs of organization surveys, and some cities are not interested in reform even when it is desperately needed. These are some of the reasons for the wide disparity in the effectiveness and efficiency of law enforcement agencies. Citizens within the same State, or even within the same county, do not always receive the same quality of police service because of differences in agency management and in operational policies.

Some departments and local governments have recognized their own limitations in assessing their police service, and have engaged outside consultant assistance to perform this task. But the costs of surveys by qualified consultants are often considered by public officials to be simply another financial burden on already over-extended city budgets. Such an attitude seems shortsighted since a comprehensive survey, if implemented, is likely to lead to a wiser allocation of funds and personnel. As Mayor John Lindsay's New York Police Task Force stated in its report:[15]

> * * * Police departments must be subjected to an unrestricted and unstinting review of long-standing traditions, attitudes, and practices * * * the experience of revitalized police departments in other cities as well as of other governmental and private organizations will be highly instructive to this inquiry. An effective means of tapping this expertise is through the temporary employment of individuals from outside the department. These outside experts could provide the commissioner with fresh insights and also act as a training mechanism for those in the department.

To encourage research, development, and experimentation, it seems timely for Federal and State funds to be made available to stimulate such activity, and partially offset the costs which must otherwise be borne by law enforcement agencies, universities, and private research organizations. For example, certain agencies external to the police may help improve organization, management and operations through research and analyses in collaboration with the police. These include colleges and universities, research institutes, privately funded foundations, and research arms of State criminal justice agencies and the Federal Government.

ADMINISTRATIVE AND STAFF SUPPORT PERSONNEL AND UNITS

In addition to improving the competence of top and middle management and applying known principles of organization, police departments must establish special units whose function is the continual planning, administration and assessment of police practices and procedures. A chief of police, particularly as his force grows larger, cannot alone effectively administer a department, devise policy, or evaluate performance. He needs supporting staff, administrative personnel and management specialists who can supervise and train personnel, assist in policymaking, fulfill administrative functions, and assess the soundness of existing practices and procedures.

These personnel must be sufficient in numbers and they need not all be sworn members. For example, before a police budget can be utilized as a management device, personnel skilled in fiscal matters must be assigned to budgetary responsibility. In medium- and large-sized police forces, lawyers should be available to provide legal advice to the chief and his staff. Training should be handled by persons who have backgrounds and skills in education. Planning and research should be conducted by men or women trained in social science and research methodology.

In many forces today these functions either are not performed at all or are performed by persons who do not possess the necessary qualifications to perform them well. Support services historically have been weak primarily because many police chiefs feel compelled to give greater priority to staffing operational rather than specialized service and administrative positions.

Often, city managers or city councils discourage increasing staff support by asserting that crime is fought in the streets, not in the office, and therefore, staff support units should be cut to a minimum. For example, in 1964 the 283-man Fresno, Calif., police force had to discontinue its personnel, planning, and training division

---

[13] International City Managers' Association, "Municipal Police Administration" (5th ed., Chicago: International City Managers' Association, 1961), p. 515.
[14] James Q. Wilson, "The Police and Their Problems: A Theory," "Public Policy," 12: 207–8, 1963.
[15] Law Enforcement Task Force, "Report to Mayor-Elect John V. Lindsay" (New York: 1965), pp. 3–4.

because of a major budget cutback.¹⁶ The 250-man Multnomah County, Oreg., police department has but 1 man each assigned to such key special units as training, staff inspections, and planning and research. This circumstance has existed since the units were created in 1963 despite annual requests for additional qualified staff to make the units truly productive.¹⁷

The fields in which staff experts are most badly needed by most departments are training and education, as discussed in chapter 5; police-community relations, as discussed in chapter 6; planning, research and analysis; staff inspection; internal investigation; the law; and the search of crime scenes and the analysis of the evidence thereby obtained. To the extent that this last activity involves the setting up of crime laboratories, which are beyond the resources of all but the largest departments, it is discussed in chapter 4.

PLANNING, RESEARCH AND ANALYSIS

A police force cannot be effective if it is administered on a day-to-day or crisis-to-crisis basis. It needs plans: contingency plans about, for example, how to handle a visit by the President or how to capture an armed desperado holed up in an apartment; operational plans about how to deploy men in various neighborhoods at various times of day or how to deal with the problem of apartment burglaries; long-range plans about improving the quality of personnel, installing new equipment or controlling widespread vice activities; budgetary plans, community-relations plans, technological plans, plans of many other kinds. It needs not only to develop new plans but to review continually the operation of plans already in effect and to amend them or discard them when necessary. To do this kind of planning to best advantage, a department must first engage in research and analysis. Crime trends, long range and short range, must be studied, as well as the social conditions associated with them. Experimental projects must be devised to test novel police techniques on a limited scale and under controlled conditions. Such departments as Chicago, St. Louis, and Los Angeles already have good-sized, expertly staffed research, analysis and planning units, but even in those places, it can be said, the enormous possibilities of this kind of police staff work are still largely unexplored.

A department's planning and research unit should:

☐ Review and analyze periodically all department plans and suggest, either directly to the heads of operating divisions or to the police chief, the modernization and improvement of their plans.
☐ Develop plans having departmentwide application.
☐ Analyze the operations of plans to ascertain their suitability; when a new plan is placed in operation, discuss its weaknesses with operating and clerical personnel to effect needed improvements in it.
☐ Prepare statistical and other reports of police department activities, needs, and objectives.

☐ Pepare the annual budget and extend project fiscal and manpower requirements for up to 5 years.
☐ Engage in crime and traffic analyses and supply data and patterns to operating divisions.

STAFF INSPECTION

Only a few American police forces use staff inspection as a management control process. Yet staff inspection is an essential component of modern police organization and management.

Staff inspection is a process outside the normal lines of authority and responsibility. It is detailed observation and analysis of a line or service unit designed to inform the chief of police of the performance of the unit. Staff inspection is a standard military practice and is used in one way or another by several Federal agencies. It is also a cornerstone of good police practice in many progressive police forces.

Consultants recognize the concept as important to the the police. For example, in its comprehensive survey of the Baltimore police in 1965, the International Association of Chiefs of Police said: ¹⁸

> In all organizations there is need for a system of quality control. This is usually accomplished by line supervisors, by direct observation and supervision, and by report-review. When the organization is large and decentralized there is a need for a further examination of procedures to insure that the policies of the top administrator are being followed with precision and uniformity. This can most effectively be accomplished by the creation of a staff inspection unit.

It must be clearly understood that the staff inspection concept differs substantially from the casual daily examination of process and personnel reasonably expected of all supervisors. The staff inspection unit should look at a broader picture and seek to insure, among other things:

☐ That accurate records are maintained without inefficient and unnecessary duplication.
☐ That sworn personnel are properly deployed and not wasted on menial, clerical tasks.
☐ That manpower is deployed on the basis of analysis of need.
☐ That supervisory and command personnel operate within the framework of announced policy declarations, and adhere to objectives.
☐ That line and service units are coordinated.
☐ That policies, procedures, and regulations are carried out in the spirit for which they were designed.
☐ That policies, procedures, and regulations are adequate to attain the desired results.
☐ That resources at the force's disposal, both personnel and material, are utilized to the fullest extent and that resources are adequate to carry out the mission of the department.

Findings and recommendations should be forwarded through channels to the chief. After staff discussion, they may be sent to the planning and research unit for further study and the preparation of appropriate policy

---

¹⁶ International Association of Chiefs of Police, "A Survey of the Police Department of Fresno, California" (Washington: International Association of Chiefs of Police, May 1965), p. 71.
¹⁷ Interview with Donald E. Clark, sheriff of Multnomah County, Portland, Oreg., Dec. 21, 1966.

¹⁸ International Association of Chiefs of Police, "A Survey of the Police Department of Baltimore, Maryland" (Washington: International Association of Chiefs of Police, 1965), p. 52.

or procedures; forwarded to the internal investigations unit for action; or assigned to the training unit for additional in-service and recruit instruction. In any event, staff inspection should have a salutary effect on personnel since it seeks to counteract the inherent weaknesses of a self-inspection process.

INTERNAL INVESTIGATION

All large police departments should maintain an internal investigation unit whose purpose is to investigate all alleged breaches of police integrity and complaints, official or anonymous, made against members of a department.[19] The function of an internal investigation unit has been described by the International Association of Chiefs of Police as follows:[20]

* * * all complaints and breaches of discipline must be thoroughly investigated and reported to administrators through channels. Responsibility and authority for investigations is placed with the internal investigation division. Other subunits of the department are required to cooperate with these investigations. The order insures that penalties imposed for breaches of discipline are fair and equitable.

Over and above its role in the investigation of complaints and the supervision of discipline by line units, the internal investigation division should constantly and critically examine all areas of police action which represent hazards to the integrity of the department. Misconduct must be discovered at its earliest stages and prompt action taken to correct unsatisfactory conditions.

The key to an effective internal investigation unit is an impartial and fairminded staff. Properly staffed and supervised, an internal investigation unit affords protection both to the public and to the department. By exposing complaints made maliciously, it can in appropriate cases vindicate an unjustly accused officer. By investigating all complaints fully and objectively, it will serve to assure the public that harassment, undue use of force, or other police misconduct will not be tolerated.

Most of the existing internal investigation units operate by the case method—tracking down and bringing to book individual officers who misbehave. However, they should also serve in a deterrent or preventive capacity. This means identifying the problems that cause police misconduct and the neighborhoods or situations in which such misconduct is most likely to occur; devising procedures that will help solve the problems; patrolling and scrutinizing the neighborhoods; and keeping track of situations. Ways must be found to rid police mores of the pervasive feeling that an allegation of misconduct against one officer is an attack upon the entire police force, and that to report a corrupt fellow officer is a detriment, rather than a benefit, to the department. Finally, an internal investigation unit should be responsible to a department's chief and to him alone. By these means it should be possible to bring police misconduct to a minimum. The role of internal investigation in preventing corruption is discussed in chapter 7.

THE POLICE LEGAL ADVISOR

An addition to the police management team that seems well suited to forces of about 250 men or more is the police legal advisor. He should be a part of the department's administrative bureau staff so that he will be near the chief as well as near those engaged in training, discipline, internal investigation, crime analyses, and similar activities.

The need for continuing legal advice within a department has long been recognized by authorities on police operations, and should now be evident to everyone in view of the great interest in police practices the courts are now evincing. For example, even though Superintendent O. W. Wilson of Chicago wrote in 1962 of a need for a "legal unit" to furnish "advice to staff and field personnel" and to survey "departmental orders and practices in the light of actual or proposed changes" in the law, a 1965 nationwide survey of police departments conducted by the National League of Cities revealed that only 14 of the 276 departments responding employed lawyers, and of these, 6 were only part-time advisors.[21]

Many municipal governments do not appear to realize the importance of legally trained personnel in law enforcement. Given the wide range of duties to which a legal advisor can apply his special training, this omission is a serious one. A legal advisor could perform many services with his special skills. He could help with training and continuing education, police planning, community relations, legislative drafting and lobbying and departmental legal problems, and could advise on problems arising out of specific cases. And legal skills are especially relevant to police policy planning and liaison with prosecutors.

The legal advisor's role in policy planning is linked to the fact that total enforcement of the law is neither practical nor desirable; discretion in the enforcement of the law must be exercised. Generally, the police have been hesitant to articulate or record for either internal use or public information the criteria upon which enforcement decisions are made. The difficulty is that although wide areas of flexibility are now left to police agencies without general legislative or judicial policy guidance, police have not assumed it to be their responsibility to develop and articulate their own policies. As a result, important policy decisions affecting such problem areas as undercover investigations, informants, and drunkenness offenders are seldom brought to light. It is here, in the development of policies—particularly those arising from the necessity for selective enforcement—that the legal adviser can provide substantial assistance to troubled police executives.

Very few prosecutor's offices endeavor systematically to provide legal counsel to the police.[22] Save for those few departments which employ legal advisors, most police forces receive only sporadic counsel from the prosecutor's office or from individual prosecutors who have developed a special relationship with certain squads or officers. As the American Bar Foundation researchers noted:[23]

* * * While private counsel representing a business client would believe it to be of the utmost importance to consult fully with his client, prosecutors commonly proceed on the assumption that the police need not be consulted. A prosecutor who understood the problems of the police * * * could better decide what

---

[19] This unit's importance in assuring that police field practices are executed in line with policy and in countering police corruption is described in chapters 6 and 7.
[20] Supra, note 18 at p. 136.
[21] O. W. Wilson, "Police Planning" (2d ed., Springfield, Ill.: Charles C. Thomas, 1962), p. 11; O. W. Wilson, "Police Administration" (2d ed., New York: McGraw-Hill, 1963), p. 60; and Raymond L. Bancroft, "Municipal Law Enforcement, 1966," "Nation's Cities," 4: 24. February 1966.

[22] Conversation with California Attorney General Thomas C. Lynch and Chief of Police Thomas J. Cahill, Jan. 11, 1966, in Washington. These men note a few model cities, such as San Francisco, where each of the police department's specialized investigative squads has an assigned prosecutor, and where the police also have two lawyers on the force.
[23] Wayne R. LaFave, "Arrest: The Decision to Take a Suspect Into Custody" (New York: Little, Brown & Co., 1965), p. 516.

issues are in greatest need of clarification * * *. [Commonly] communications between the prosecutor and the police chief [are virtually] nonexistent.

A legal advisor could be a civilian employee, or a policeman, or a prosecutor. If he is a member of the city attorney's or district attorney's staff, he could be assigned to the force either on a rotating or permanent basis. It does seem, however, that a civilian advisor (rather than a police officer-lawyer) would be preferable in most cases; a civilian is likely to be more sensitive to the nuances and needs of other agencies, particularly governmental agencies such as welfare, education, and housing, which should coordinate their efforts more closely with law enforcement. The legal adviser would also be essential to review pending legislative proposals for the force as well as proposals drafted by nonpolice agencies whose provisions, if passed, would bear on the police.

It is impossible to calculate the number of legal advisors now needed by police agencies. An estimate of manpower needs will depend upon the duties the legal adviser will perform, which will of course, vary from department to department. For the very large departments, a legal advisory unit consisting of from 5 to 10 lawyers may be needed to meet minimum needs. For other departments one individual may be able to service the entire agency. In smaller communities, particularly suburban ones whose police force is far below 250 personnel, it may be necessary to obtain a part-time lawyer, or to share the services of one lawyer among several departments. Viewing the needs of departments for police legal advisors nationwide, approximately 250–400 attorneys knowledgeable in criminal law, administrative law, and police science seem needed on a full-time basis to meet minimum requirements.

The law schools of Northwestern University and the University of Wisconsin now have programs to train people in law enforcement legal processes. These programs alone cannot train enough people, but they do provide models for other schools to study and emulate. Private foundation and government grants to support programs for providing departments with police legal advisors would be an important step toward more just and more effective law enforcement. A more detailed discussion of the need for police legal advisors is given in a staff report, attached as appendix A to this chapter.

SEARCHING THE CRIME SCENE

The comments of Justice Goldberg, speaking for the majority of the Supreme Court in *Escobedo* v. *Illinois*, should have alerted public officials and the police throughout the country to the necessity of more adequate police crime scene searching and painstaking laboratory review: [24]

> We have learned the lesson of history, ancient and modern, that a system of criminal law enforcement which comes to depend on the "confession" will, in the long run, be less reliable than a system which depends on extrinsic evidence independently secured through skillful investigation.

More and more, the solution of major crimes will hinge upon the discovery at crime scenes and subsequent scientific laboratory analysis of latent fingerprints, weapons, footprints, hairs, fibers, blood, and similar traces. As a result, departments must train and devote greater numbers of men to searching crime scenes for physical evidence.

While forces are aware of the need to search crime scenes for physical evidence, few seem prepared to do so on a broad scale for want of adequate manpower. For example, the following summary shows by shift the small number of personnel assigned as evidence technicians in 1965 in four cities: [25]

City	Number of sworn members	Evidence technicians by shift			Total serious crimes, 1965
		Day	Evening	Night	
Buffalo	1,349	2	1	1	9,833
Cleveland	2,014	2	2	2	16,697
Omaha	403	1	1	1	5,752
Honolulu	818	1	2	0	9,281

In addition to limited manpower, forces lack equipment and training for evidence technicians. Every force, regardless of size, should devise an adequate system suited to local needs so that crime scenes are fully searched. Furthermore, the staff and facilities of the crime laboratory should be bolstered to accommodate what may be a dramatic increase in workload. This is so whether the laboratory is State, regionally, or locally administered.

Each department should keep a statistical check on the assignments of evidence technicians so that an index of need for their services may be established. With such an index, a force may be able to distribute them better according to the demonstrated demand for their services both by location and hours of the day.

UTILIZING FIELD PERSONNEL MORE EFFECTIVELY

Many American police forces do not utilize their available field personnel effectively. The most significant weakness appears to be the failure of departments to distribute patrol officers in accordance with the actual need for their presence. Other weaknesses, present to varying degrees in various forces, include too great reliance on foot patrol without providing officers with either modern communications or mobility; the extensive use of two-man motor patrol; detectives deployed in pairs; loose and insufficient patrol and detective supervision, and a lack of unity at the field level among investigators; outmoded report preparation systems; and the assignment of too many diverse tasks to police field officers. These weaknesses are outward signs of the failure of many police departments to develop field assignments on the basis of systematic evaluation of street needs.

---

[24] *Escobedo v. Illinois*, 378 U.S. 478, 488 (1964).
[25] Police Department of Kansas City, Mo., "1966 Survey of Municipal Police Departments (Cities of 300,000 to 1,000,000 Population, 1960 Census)" (Kansas City, Mo., Police Department, 1966), p. 22. Data on serious crime is sourced in U.S. Department of Justice, Federal Bureau of Investigation, "Uniform Crime Reports, 1965" (Washington: U.S. Government Printing Office, 1966), p. 176.

At least seven steps must be taken to assure that police departments derive maximum utilization from field personnel:

- ☐ Distributing available field officers according to need for their services.
- ☐ Improving supervision of the field force.
- ☐ Improving coordination of effort among field personnel.
- ☐ Improving patrol techniques by critically analyzing the need for foot patrol and two-man motor patrols. Unless there is found extraordinary personnel hazards of more than an occasional nature, uniformed personnel should be deployed singly.
- ☐ Deploying investigators singly unless there is an unusual series of cases which demands that two or more men be assigned jointly.
- ☐ Modernizing report preparation and duplicating techniques.
- ☐ Relieving police officers of certain routine menial tasks.

PROPORTIONAL DISTRIBUTION OF PATROLS AND SATURATION TECHNIQUES

Efforts must be made to schedule police patrol at the times when, and places where, crimes are most likely to occur. This concept is known as proportional distribution of the patrol force. It involves measuring the relative need for police patrol services, and distributing personnel to beats on the basis of a crime variation index derived from data collected over an extended period.

Proportional distribution was conceived as early as 1909, when Chief August Vollmer assigned the Berkeley, Calif., patrol force (which then was bicycle-mounted and in 1911 became autoborne) to two 12-hour shifts and to beats which were laid out in accordance with the number of calls anticipated in each part of the city. Some men worked very large beats and some patrolled areas far smaller, where "action" was more localized. Following Vollmer's move, Elmer Graper and Raymond Fosdick elaborated on the distribution concept. This in turn led to further sophistications of it by Bruce Smith and O. W. Wilson, and to its implementation by several police forces. Today in dozens of cities patrols are distributed according to the best available need-for-patrol formulas.[26] The success inherent in distributing uniformed personnel in accordance with the need for their services was noted in the "Missouri Crime Survey" in 1926 in language that seems valid today although infrequently heeded: [27]

* * * several forces are faced with the fact that under their present scheme of distribution, uniformed patrols are inadequate in number. Rising police costs render personnel increases both inexpedient and undesirable. But this survey shows that the effect of a substantial increase can be secured if outworn schemes of distribution are abandoned, and the patrol force distributed and administered not according to conditions which existed a generation ago, but in line with conditions existing today.

The concept of proportional distribution of manpower is essentially sound although not necessarily fully developed, and every force of more than a few men could advantageously be allocated on a need-for-service basis. Several departments with computer capacity have commenced a continuous statistical assessment of patrol workloads and deployment. The St. Louis police are actively engaged in implementing a program that not only will predict the police field problems for the forthcoming tour of duty but will also monitor the crime picture as it emerges, and adjust the predictions as changes develop. Although this is a highly sophisticated application and is practical for only a few departments, any agency can engage in continuing manual reassessment of patrol areas through record analysis.

Saturation is another method which makes fullest use of available operational personnel. This is accomplished by assigning additional men to patrol areas that, according to available statistics, require greater-than-usual patrol coverage. Given the manpower, a chief may assign some men to a fourth shift, which overlaps two of the present shifts (i.e., serves from 7 p.m. to 3 a.m. as has been done in Toledo, Phoenix, San Diego, and Birmingham); form a tactical patrol unit as Savannah, Ga., and Berkeley have done; or pay off-duty personnel overtime to work a regular day off as is done in Washington, D.C. The purpose of each of these operations is to saturate high crime areas with officers when there is need for greater coverage and when the use of more men would not aggravate, but would help resolve, the conditions.[28]

IMPROVING SUPERVISION

The fact that uniformed personnel operate throughout a city at all hours of the day and night sometimes prevents the desired level of supervisory control. Accordingly, opportunities for personnel to engage in minor delinquencies, and to bestow or receive special favors, are always present. The whole scheme of patrol is such that supervisors are challenged to stimulate initiative and individual judgment. The relationship between organization, management, and full utilization of personnel and supervision is well stated in the District of Columbia Crime Commission's report to the President: [29]

Closely related to organizational and management deficiencies is the poor quality of supervision which is pervasive through the Department. The inadequacies in supervision can be attributed to the following factors: Too few supervisors at some levels, a failure to use a supervisory probation period, a lack of in-service supervisory training, inadequate transportation available to supervisors, unclear Department policies and procedures, and a failure to define supervisory responsibilities or to perform adequate line inspection. As a consequence, there is "excessive familiarity with subordinates and lack of bearing" and a "frequent loss of respect for the supervisor and administrator." These conclusions have been confirmed by the comments of many police officers to Commission representatives. Officers have repeatedly complained of the inadequacy of supervision and the

---

[26] A comprehensive discussion of distribution of police strength, applicable to the interests of both small and large forces, may be found in Samuel G. Chapman, "Police Patrol Readings" (Springfield, Ill.: Charles C. Thomas, 1964), pp. 171–233. Pages 234–276 describe the team policing concept which has had some limited application in Great Britain.
[27] "The Missouri Crime Survey" (New York: The MacMillan Co., 1926), pp. 46–47.

[28] See chapter 6 for a discussion of the kinds of problems in which the use of saturation patrol may be subject to question.
[29] The President's Commission on Crime in the District of Columbia, "A Report on the President's Commission on Crime in the District of Columbia" (Washington: U.S. Government Printing Office, 1966), p. 9.

lack of encouragement and support by high-ranking officers. Such attitudes reflect a low state of morale which cannot help detracting from police efficiency.

Viewed from any aspect, supervising a widely dispersed field team constitutes a difficult problem. In Denver, newspaperman Mort Stern vividly described the events that led to the burglary indictments in 1960. He showed that when field personnel are free-lance operators and lack sufficient supervision, they are susceptible to special temptations: [30]

The rule book forbids [delinquent acts]. But it isn't enforced. It's winked at, at all levels.

A force must provide a sufficient number of supervisors at the first command level—that of sergeant—to control adequately and direct all police activities and assure the maximum utilization of personnel. These supervisors should spend most of their time in the field, providing personnel supervision, leadership, training, and incentives, and checking on conditions throughout the city to insure that proper and immediate police action is taken. Supervisors should be charged with inducing men to apply themselves, and should also be notified of and dispatched to all incidents that might reflect discredit on the police department or on an individual officer. The additional supervisory role of police agents will be described in the next section of this chapter.

IMPROVING PATROL-DETECTIVE DIVISION COORDINATION

In almost all large police departments there is a considerable amount of organizational fragmentation. Traditionally and almost universally, patrol and investigative forces have separate lines of command and tend to be isolated from one another; often they keep separate sets of records; frequently they work different shifts or are based in different places so that there is a minimum of contact between patrolmen and detectives. In addition, investigators are more often than not divided at both headquarters and precinct levels into squads—vice, robbery, burglary, fraud, homicide, and so forth—that may themselves keep separate records, use separate informants and remain more or less isolated from each other in other ways.

At both the staff and the field levels, this overseparation of functions, or overspecialization, can have undesirable results. When intelligence is not centralized and coordinated, staff planning for the purpose of either apprehending specific criminals, or solving crime problems such as, for example, an outbreak of burglaries in some neighborhood, is almost impossible. When lines of command are kept rigidly separate, it is difficult to bring the full resources of a department to bear on crime solution. Also considerable conflict exists in many forces between uniformed branch officers and the detective division. An early report of the problem is found in the 1926 "Missouri Crime Survey": [31]

The ancient rivalry between the uniformed and plainclothes forces has a substantial basis. It arises from the fact that in a given case the patrolman is often the first to risk life and limb. With the arrival of detectives, however, he is automatically displaced. The plainclothes operative takes command of the situation, and the patrolman returns to his beat. This condition inspires a natural resentment, which sometimes leads to a series of retaliatory acts by the two branches. In the maneuvers which follow, the public functions of these officers are lost sight of. Their energies are directed at causing each other confusion, discomfort, and discouragement.

A 1962 consultant report shows that this issue is still current: [32]

The lack of coordination between detective and uniformed divisions leads to duplication of effort, unarticulated field work, and the loss of some cases, and the missing of arrests which might otherwise be made.

The most promising means of overcoming this problem is to combine the patrol and detective field forces under a common supervisor.

The agent-officer-community service officer recommendation made in chapter 4 of the "General Report" and discussed further in chapter 5 of this volume has not only the improvement of the quality of police personnel as its objective, but also a change in the way the police work in the field. The concept, which might be called "team policing," is that police work, including patrol and criminal investigation, in a given number of city blocks should be under unified command. A "field supervisor" would have under his command a team of agents, officers, and community service officers. The team would meet at the beginning of a tour of duty and receive a briefing on the current situation in the neighborhood—what crimes were unsolved, what suspects were wanted for questioning, what kinds of stolen goods to look out for, what situations were potentially troublesome and so forth. On this basis the members would be assigned to specific areas or duties. If conditions warranted it, agents might be assigned to patrol, and wear uniforms or plainclothes. Officers might be assigned to investigation. Community service officers might be delegated to help either. In specific investigations or incidents, agents would be given authority over the actions of CSO's and officers. If the conditions in the area changed during the tour, if a major crime was committed or a major disorder erupted, the assignments would be promptly changed by the field supervisor.

Obviously, this proposal does not envision the abandonment of special duties or special squads. An agent serving as a narcotics, juvenile, or community-relations specialist, for example, would almost always cover a territory policed by several teams, and would be moved into other work only in emergencies. There would still be a need for squads of officers with special knowledge of certain kinds of crime.

IMPROVING PATROL TECHNIQUES

Patrol may be executed in a host of ways. The time-honored fashion is on foot, but the mass-produced motor vehicle has brought auto and motorcycle patrol into

---

[30] "The Denver Post," Oct. 8, 1961, as reprinted in Samuel G. Chapman, "Police Patrol Readings" (Springfield, Ill.: Charles C. Thomas, 1964), p. 49.
[31] Supra, note 27 at p. 49.

[32] Public Administration Service of Chicago, "Police and Fire Services in Meriden, Connecticut" (Chicago: Public Administration Service, 1962), p. 36.

prominence. More recently, some forces, including the Michigan State Police, Los Angeles County Sheriff's Police, and the California Highway Patrol, have integrated fixed wing aircraft and helicopters into their field forces. Of course, where large bodies of water or rivers must be patrolled, appropriate marine equipment must be used. Other forces, including many park police agencies, continue to use horses, solo motorcycles, four-wheel-drive vehicles, and bicycles for patrol as needs dictate.

Selecting the patrol method best suited to protect a city and derive at the same time maximum usefulness from personnel challenges administrators. There has been little research in this area, consequently hard facts are lacking about the practices that really are most effective. Decisions governing a force's patrol methods are, unfortunately, usually linked solely to tradition.

Foot Patrol. Many of the Nation's forces have some uniformed personnel assigned to patrol on foot. Without question, there are certain areas in some cities that require the kind of intimate, personal, police-citizen contact and police presence which only patrol on foot affords. However, in many cities, especially small ones, there is less and less justification for full-time foot patrolmen.

That there is no "standard" for foot patrol duty is clear when one studies the 1966 foot patrol deployment pattern in 37 American cities of between 300,000 and 1 million population. Of these, all but Forth Worth, Memphis, St. Paul, and San Diego had some personnel assigned to walking beats. But among cities having foot patrol beats, the total beats on each shift varied greatly, ranging from 2 in Birmingham and Phoenix, and 3 in Dallas, Kansas City, Oklahoma City, and Omaha, to 185 in Boston, 212 in Pittsburgh, and 434 in Baltimore.[33]

A decision to use foot patrols should be made only after careful analysis, since it is a highly expensive form of coverage, geographically restrictive in nature, and can be wasteful of manpower. Without transportation at hand, it provides extremely inflexible and rigid close patrol for specifically limited geographical areas and does not permit the ready reassignment of the personnel to surrounding locations when and where police services may be specifically requested.[34] Moreover, close supervision of foot patrolmen has proven very difficult.

The essence of the problem was well stated in the District of Columbia Crime Commission report: [35]

> The Department's continued reliance on foot patrol is an inefficient and outdated utilization of manpower resources * * * Leading police authorities are in general agreement that, with few exceptions, foot patrol is not the most efficient method of patrol * * * Of course, officers should be assigned walking beats in particular commercial and high-crime areas where the need can be demonstrated. As long as the Department uses foot patrol as the primary method of patrol, however, available economies will not be realized and the city will not be provided the best possible police service.

Putting the Officer "Back on the Beat." The most significant weakness in American motor patrol operations today is the general lack of contact with citizens except when an officer has responded to a call. Forced to stay near the car's radio, waiting an assignment, most patrol officers have few opportunities to develop closer relationships with persons living in the district.

There is considerable merit in "getting the policeman back on the beat" in high crime rate areas. But this can be accomplished without depriving an officer of the many advantages of radio-equipped vehicles. For example, motor patrol officers should be equipped with very small transistorized portable police radio transmitting-receiving equipment. Small, compact portable radio devices would greatly expand the operational radii of motorized personnel by permitting them to engage in extensive foot patrol and to range well away from their vehicles at any hour of the day or night without sacrificing contact with headquarters. Police forces serving Oakland; Berkeley; Meriden, Conn.; and Kalamazoo, Mich., reported they had patrolmen so equipped. As discussed below, chapter 11 of Commission's General Report recommends Federal support to develop such equipment to be available at reasonable prices.

Chiefs may also wish to equip their footmen with motor scooters, which can be parked unobtrusively and with ease almost anywhere. New York City; Washington, D.C.; New Rochelle; North Bergen, N.J.; and Newport, R.I., have so equipped some of their footmen and report the system to be working satisfactorily. Smaller forces, which feel they must assign some men to foot patrol, should carefully consider the motor scooter-radio equipment concept to insure full availability of these men and their mobility.

Whether equipped with portable radios, motor scooters or standard police vehicles, patrolmen should be considered as foot officers who possess vehicles available nearby for quick, nonfatiguing transportation from one point to another. It is while out of their cars on foot that motorized patrol officers can serve very effectively as the "eyes and ears" of the police department and yet be subject to immediate recall and assignment. Consequently, by distributing the patrol force on a basis of need, and providing close supervision to its operation, the Nation's policemen will, in fact, be "on the beat" providing protection and accessibility for America's citizens.

One- and Two-Man Motor Patrol. There has been a discernible pattern away from the exclusive use of two-man cars in American cities, and a distinct movement toward the far greater use of one-man patrols as is shown in table 1. This trend lends support to those police authorities who believe that local police problems can be most immediately met by covering a city with motorized one-man patrol units, rather than by a system of less intensive patrolling caused by an exclusive pattern of two-man units. The District of Columbia Crime Commission presents this concept in its report: [36]

> Conspicuous patrol, conveying a sense of police omnipresence, is best effected by a highly mobilized force, with considerable emphasis on one-man cars. The Commission endorses the Department's recent experimental efforts in this direction and recommends an accelerated program to increase the number of one-man cars.

---

[33] Supra, note 25; col. 61, table 5, p. 22.
[34] Police chiefs will find a Chicago Police Department staff report on foot patrol utilization very helpful in assessments of their cities' needs for footmen. This appears in Samuel G. Chapman, "Police Patrol Readings" (Springfield, Ill.: Charles C. Thomas, 1964), pp. 105–110.
[35] Supra, note 29 at p. 53.
[36] Ibid.

Table 1.—Manning of Police Patrol Cars in Cities Over 10,000 Population

Population group	Number cities reporting motorized patrol			Cities using 2-man patrol cars only					
	1946	1954	1964	1946		1954		1964	
				Number	Percent	Number	Percent	Number	Percent
Over 500,000	13	18	20	8	61.5	9	50.0	4	20.0
250,000–500,000	21	21	31	10	47.6	5	23.8	2	6.0
100,000–250,000	52	63	75	30	57.7	24	38.1	3	4.0
50,000–100,000	90	120	160	48	53.3	43	35.8	14	9.0
25,000–50,000	171	260	320	69	40.4	63	24.2	13	4.0
10,000–25,000	493	518	728	140	28.4	89	17.2	32	4.0
All over 10,000	840	1,000	1,334	305	36.3	233	23.3	68	5.0

Population group	Cities using 1- and 2-man patrol cars						Cities using 1-man patrol cars only					
	1946		1954		1964		1946		1954		1964	
	Number	Percent	Number	Percent	Number	Percent	Number	Percent	Number	Percent	Number	Percent
Over 500,000	5	38.5	9	50.0	15	75.0	0	0	0	0	1	5.0
250,000–500,000	10	47.6	14	66.7	25	81.0	1	4.8	2	9.5	4	13.0
100,000–250,000	19	36.5	33	52.4	59	79.0	3	5.8	6	9.5	13	17.0
50,000–100,000	35	38.9	66	55.0	102	64.0	7	7.8	11	9.2	44	27.0
25,000–50,000	77	45.0	147	56.5	171	53.0	25	14.6	50	19.3	136	43.0
10,000–25,000	238	48.3	300	57.9	342	47.0	115	23.3	129	24.9	354	49.0
All over 10,000	384	45.7	569	56.9	714	54.0	151	18.0	198	19.8	552	41.0

Source: "The Municipal Yearbook, 1947," p. 385; 1955, p. 411; and 1965, p. 426 (Chicago: International City Managers' Association).

Another consultant supports the view that one-man units should be the rule wherever possible:[37]

The more men and more cars that are visible on the streets, the greater is the potential for preventing crime. A heavy blanket of conspicuous patrol at all times and in all parts of the city tends to suppress violations of the law. The most economical manner of providing this heavy blanket of patrol is by using one-man cars when and where they are feasible.

Almost all cities have long forsaken the practice of having two patrolmen walk a beat together. For the same reasons it seems generally undesirable and unnecessary to have two men in a car. One-man operations permit more intensive patrol of a city with a like number of officers, prevent partners from spending much of their time aimlessly conversing with each other, and contribute to the safety of the individual officers by compelling each officer to give his undivided attention to his duties. One-man cars allow rapid assignment of more vehicles from more directions as another means of combatting crime.

Conditions which justify the use of two-man patrol cars are similar to those which dictate the assignment of two-man teams to patrol duty on foot. Such conditions include those of too many incidents for one man to handle in a physically limited, densely populated area; a high frequency of circumstances in which officers are likely to be assaulted; and the high prospect of raucous misbehavior that can only be prevented by the concerted action of two or more officers. Such decisions must be made locally and, whatever the deployment practice, forces should periodically reevaluate their one- and two-

man districts to be sure of the wisdom of their decisions. For example, in its 1965 survey of the Baltimore police, the International Association of Chiefs of Police recommended a broad pattern of one-man motor patrol with some two-man units. In addition, the consultant very properly urged:[38]

After some experience (6 months to a year) with the new distribution, workload and the incidents that seem to justify two-man cars may be reevaluated with changes made in staffing as appropriate. Workload varies in many ways, and annual study is needed. Of course, a particular event such as an assault against an officer cannot be predicted to the day, hour, and location, but the likelihood of such events can be predicted reasonably well, provided the data base is current and is a valid sample, if not the total, of all events.

IMPROVING INVESTIGATOR DEPLOYMENT

The same deployment principles should apply to headquarters-based plainsclothes investigative personnel. Several cities, both large and small, routinely deploy detectives in twos and sometimes threes! Since the bulk of a department's investigative work is routine, the widespread use of investigative teams is an unnecessary waste of manpower. In many departments today, including such Federal agencies as the FBI and Secret Service, investigative personnel primarily work alone. This should be the practice in all departments. A basic pattern of one-man plainclothes investigations, with exceptions as conditions indicate, would have the effect of increasing the effective manpower of those detective divisions in which two-man teams are presently the rule.

---

[37] International Association of Chiefs of Police, "A Survey of the Police Department of Youngstown, Ohio" (Washington: International Association of Chiefs of Police, June 1964), p. 89.

[38] Supra, note 18, at p. 93.

Some American forces have a formally established detective rank whose incumbents have tenure and, other than for gross misconduct, cannot be removed from plainclothes status. Such a practice is basically unsound and overprotective. Plainclothes investigative positions should be filled by appointments of worthy police officers who would serve for indefinite duration. Such appointment latitude is significant for several reasons, the most important being the urgency of maintaining the vitality of a force by having some especially challenging assignments open to men who seem ready to assume greater responsibility.

Chiefs of police should take full advantage of their power to make occasional changes of personnel assignments at the patrol and investigative levels of execution. In some cities, the chief is free to do so, uninhibited by civil service restriction as to classification of detectives in a special rank complete with special pay and tenure. But where civil service precludes the chief from assigning men to plainclothes status at his discretion, he is unduly hindered and the system should be changed. The lateral transfer of men from any unit of a department to another should be the sole prerogative of the chief.

REPORT PREPARATION AND DUPLICATION

There are two other means by which the police may maximize the field time of personnel. One is to give uniformed police officers the means to prepare reports while in the field so that they need not go to headquarters or to the precinct for this purpose.

The extent of street contact hours lost to report writing at headquarters in some forces is notable. For example, in one large city, departmental procedure requires a police car team to return to the district station and prepare a report after handling almost any type of incident. Then the team returns to its prescribed patrol area. In another large city an average of 14 percent of a police officer's time is spent writing reports.

If patrol officers, investigators, and other field personnel are to be fully utilized, a force should consider implementing a system whereby reports may be dictated without requiring personnel to leave their patrol area. The same is necessary to free detectives from countless hours they are required to spend at their typewriters. One way to accomplish this is to install dictation equipment either in each vehicle or at headquarters so that an officer or detective may "call" his report onto a tape. Clerical employees could then transcribe reports and the officer could quickly resume his field duties. Many forces, including Wichita Falls, Tex.; Tulsa, Okla.; Stockton, Calif.; New Bedford, Mass.; and the Adams County, Colo., Sheriff's Police are so equipped.

Some forces report that they require their uniformed personnel to handwrite reports in the field on preprepared master forms suitable for subsequent offset duplication at headquarters. These include Los Angeles, Oakland, Chattanooga, and Moline, Ill.

Whether officers dictate reports while in the field or handwrite them, the means by which adequate copies of such reports are prepared and distributed at headquarters affects the optimum utilization of clerical personnel. Many small forces still find that typewritten carbon copies satisfy their distribution requirements. Larger forces, however, often require more copies than can be prepared on a typewriter, and hence have integrated various dry copy processes into their records procedures.

ROUTINE TASKS

Another means for making better use of police officers is to relieve them of many less important tasks so that they may attend to matters criminal and preventive in nature. The real issue here centers around the role of the police and the problem of overextending available personnel. August Vollmer noted the problem in 1929: [39]

* * * Protecting lives and property and preserving the peace of a community is a huge task. Apparently it is believed to be an unimportant and small responsibility, and the legislative bodies continue to heap innumerable duties upon the police, until they are loaded to the breaking point.

The problem was noted long before Chief Vollmer's lament. For example, in 1866, the president of the Board of Commissioners of the Detroit Police Department reported to the Common Council: [40]

* * * for the last year the force has been compelled to perform an excessive amount of service, the present police establishment is not deemed sufficiently large. The force should be large enough, without being overworked, to afford protection to life and property equally throughout the city.

Related problems arise when towns and cities grow in population; the police are assigned to a broader range of tasks, and become especially involved in a host of noncriminal functions.

The police workload increases each year. Discussions with police officials and a review of several forces' annual reports over the 11-year span of 1955–65 confirm the trend. The gross workload for three cities reflected in Table 2 provides an example of this trend: [41]

Table 2.—Number of Cases

City	1955	1960	1965	Percent increase 1965 over 1955
Atlanta	383,171	514,599	778,353	103.1
Denver	332,352	381,797	466,581	40.4
Philadelphia	1,123,477	1,319,611	1,567,088	39.5

Increasing caseloads compel that sworn officers be relieved of responsibility for minor tasks. Methods for accomplishing this end are described in chapter 5.

---

[39] August Vollmer, "The Police in Chicago" as published in the "Illinois Crime Survey" (Chicago: Association of Criminal Justice, 1929), p. 366.
[40] "First Annual Report to the Board of Commissioners of Metropolitan Police of the City of Detroit" (Detroit: Daily Post Printing House, April 1866), p. 6.
[41] Telephone conversations with Superintendent Beerman, Services Division, Atlanta Police Department; Captain Smith, Records, Identification, and Communications, Denver Police Department; and Lieutenant Powers, Director of Research and Planning, Philadelphia Police Department, Dec. 5–16, 1966.

APPLYING TECHNOLOGY TO POLICE SERVICE

Only token progress has been made in introducing technology into the police world. Some police departments, mainly the largest ones, have taken solid steps alone or in collaboration with nearby forces toward applying advances in science and technology to law enforcement. They have done so in spite of the costliness of equipment. Laudably, those large forces that have installed information storage and retrieval and communications systems have invited smaller forces to draw on the larger departments' facilities once the systems become operative.

Nevertheless, a majority of our Nation's police departments are constrained by limited funds and a few by lack of appreciation of the role of technology in law enforcement. Los Angeles Police Chief Thomas Reddin reported at the National Symposium on Science and Criminal Justice that [42]

> Research should be a program of discovery and design, not merely patching the dike. * * * This nation's "knowledge explosion" has so far left law enforcement untouched. * * *

The Commission's Science and Technology Task Force has completed preliminary investigations of four specific areas in which there is promise of a major scientific contribution to law enforcement.

First, the task force determined that modern information systems can greatly assist the police in identifying persons as currently wanted; provide the basis of studies whose goal is to better deploy police personnel and analyze community crime patterns; and provide the basis for both short and long range research. This includes the outline of a national information system, but not the detailed design of the system.

Second, the task force has outlined a new command and control system with which to improve a police agency's field operations by enabling men to be more quickly dispatched to those calls which by their nature may escalate into grave disorder or where suspects are still on the crime scene or in the vicinity. The system is based on the premise that too much time elapses between the time a call for service comes in from the public and the moment cars are dispatched under present dispatching-command-control techniques. Valuable minutes can be saved.

Third, the task force has attacked the problems of police radio-frequency usage and has shown how a dramatic reduction in radio frequency congestion may be made.

Fourth, the task force has proposed a research and development program for law enforcement.

THE NEED FOR INFORMATION

It is readily evident that many criminal justice problems result from the lack of complete and timely information. For example, a police officer does not know whether an arrested suspect is wanted for a more serious crime elsewhere. There are other such information problems, characterized by the inaccessibility of stored information. Government and industry have made extensive use of computer technology to solve related problems in such diverse fields as continental air defense, production scheduling, airline reservations, and corporate management. Some police agencies already use or have ordered computers.

The technical development potentially most profoundly affecting criminal justice operations is the advent of computer-based information systems. Some pioneering installations have been or in the immediate future will be established at the city, county, State, and National levels. These include the St. Louis, Chicago, and New York Police Departments, the inter-county "Police Information Network" (PIN) of Alameda County (Calif.), the State police systems of California, Pennsylvania, and New York and statewide criminal justice information systems of California and New York. The FBI is now operating a National Crime Information Center (NCIC) providing 15 police terminals around the Nation with on-line computer-based information on wanted persons, stolen vehicles, and stolen property.

A greatly expanded development of computer-based information systems is one concrete step that would make a dramatic impact on the police service. Such systems can aid the police in the following functions:

☐ *Police patrol.*—Enabling a police officer to check the identification of people and property against a central "wanted" file in a few minutes.
☐ *Crime investigation.*—Providing a police officer or investigative agent with supporting information files such as crime patterns, modus operandi, criminal associates and personal appearance and, hopefully in the future, matching latent fingerprints from a crime scene against a central fingerprint file. The latter process, when it is developed, would constitute a major breakthrough in the war on crime.
☐ *Manpower deployment.*—Altering police deployment in response to changing patterns of crime on an hourly or daily basis.
☐ *Individual protection.*—Completing arrest records to include court disposition, presenting a fairer picture to the police and judges.
☐ *Federal, State, and local budgeting.*—Collecting uniform statistics on agency operations and workloads, providing a basis for estimating personnel needs and for optimum allocation of men and dollars.

The Science and Technology Task Force volume contains a full discussion of the need for integrated information systems to which all criminal justice agencies can contribute.

COMMUNICATIONS, COMMAND, AND CONTROL

The scientific community has more to offer the modern police organization than the prospect of information

---

[42] Thomas Reddin, "Police Weapons for the Space Age," "The Police Chief," November 1966, 33: 10–17. Chief Reddin's article suggests several police enterprises which may be broadly influenced through science, technology, and research.

storage and retrieval networks and data for research. It holds promise for improving a department's ability to operate more efficiently in the field as well by modernizing the traditional radio dispatching system in large departments. The main purpose of modernizing the dispatching function is to reduce the total time it takes an officer to reach an incident from the time a call for assistance is received.

The question of what deters people from criminal acts is very complex, and one about which little is known. Basic to deterrence is the assumption that to increase the threat of apprehension raises the risk in committing the crime, and so reduces the likelihood of the crime being committed. Projecting that threat of apprehension is a primary objective of police field operations. Improving the apprehension capability itself is one approach to raising the threat thereof.

The apprehension process can be viewed as a sequence of actions taken in response to the commission of crime. These are shown schematically in Figure 3 and listed below:

- ☐ The crime is detected—
    - (a) By police on patrol.
    - (b) By an alarm device.
    - (c) By a victim or another citizen.
- ☐ In the latter two cases, information about the crime is communicated to the police, usually by telephone.
- ☐ An appropriate police response (e.g., choosing a patrol car to send to the scene) is selected; this is part of the "command and control" function.
- ☐ The assignment, or "dispatch order," is communicated to the patrol force, usually by voice radio.
- ☐ The appropriate patrol cars travel to the crime scene.
- ☐ A search is conducted for the perpetrator of the crime:
    - (a) A "hot" search at the crime scene.
    - (b) A "warm" search in the general vicinity of the crime.
    - (c) A "cold" investigative search by officers or plainclothes investigators.
- ☐ Throughout the search, suspects appear and have to be checked out.
- ☐ If the search is successful, a suspect is captured and evidence to support a charge is assembled.

Throughout this process, there are many opportunities for technological contributions: Better alarms, more accessible telephones to help the public reach the police, up-to-date police personnel status boards, more reliable radios, faster vehicles, nonlethal weapons, and modern crime laboratories.

Selecting the best of these technological aids from among the many possibilities requires information on the conditions that make apprehension likely.

To examine the question of what factors give rise to apprehension, Commission consultants conducted a preliminary survey of over 4,700 calls for service to a very large city police department. Over the period of the survey for 2 police divisions, all calls to the police communications center, all actions reported by the police patrol, all crimes reported, and all eventual arrests were studied. In the survey, there were 1,905 crimes examined, of which 482 (25 percent) resulted in arrests or other clearances. Of these, 70 percent involved arrests, 90 percent of which were made by the patrol force. More than half the arrests were made within eight hours of the crime, many at or near the crime scene, and almost two-thirds of the arrests were made within the first week after the crime. If a suspect is neither known to the victim nor arrested at the scene of the crime, the chances of ever arresting him are very slim. Of the 482 cleared cases, 63 percent involved "named suspects." In the 1,556 cases without named suspects, only 181 (or 12 percent) were solved later by arrest.[43]

Common sense suggests, and the data from the survey seem to confirm, that response time—the speed with which police can arrive at a crime scene—is important to apprehension. But to establish firmly the relationship between response time and apprehension rate, further studies are necessary. The limited research already conducted, however, supports the conclusion that a greater expenditure of funds is warranted to mount a concerted effort to reduce the total response time in the apprehension process.

The technology of communications and police command and control have developed markedly in recent years, and they can help provide better information faster both to reduce the field response time and to improve the quality of the response. The vital links in the apprehension process are the information-transfer functions indicated in figure 3.

Apprehension Process Figure 3

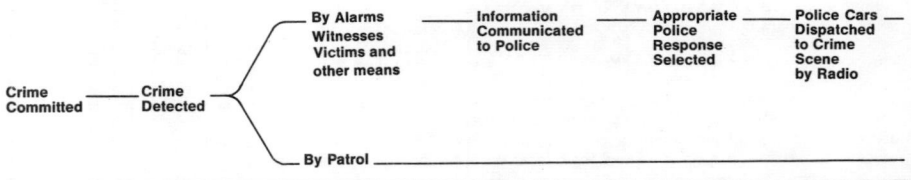

---

[43] For a detailed description of this study see chapter 2 and Appendix B of the Science and Technology Task Force volume.

The Police Communications Center. The police communications center is the link that connects the citizen in trouble to the police officers who will respond. Its role has increased as the telephone has become the more common access means to police, and as more and more police officers are equipped with radios.

Considering that the communications center is the nerve center controlling the minute-by-minute deployment of the police force, it has received surprisingly little attention. It is often squeezed into a spare corner of police headquarters, frequently under the command of a sergeant or a patrolman, and usually operated with obsolete and poorly designed equipment, and in accordance with procedures that have tended to evolve by chance rather than through careful design.

An important question is what constitutes the optimum division of functions within a communications center. Few, if any, communications centers are organized in the same fashion. In some, mostly those of small forces, the same person serves as the complaint clerk and dispatcher; as forces become larger, the functions are separated. Some centers in turn have a dispatcher handling only part of a city. Other centers have a more desirable arrangement wherein dispatchers handle calls for the whole city.

The advantages and disadvantages of the various possible patterns should be experimentally assessed, both by measurements in operating centers and under laboratory control in a simulation laboratory. In this manner, standard and emergency plans and procedures can be tested, doctrine and decision rules evaluated, and training and experience can be provided police personnel under simulated extreme conditions.

Computer-Assisted Command and Control. The above modifications could surely lead to some immediate improvement. However, needed even more urgently than short-range improvements is a basic reexamination of the entire police command and control function taking full account of the promising new technological opportunities offered by computers and communications links. The review should not begin with the new technology, however. It should begin by considering questions of when, where, and how to use the police patrol force, and how to respond to various types of routine and emergency situations. It should examine on paper and by experiment the extent to which preventive patrol really deters crime, the manner in which forces should be allocated by time and by geography, optimum patrol tactics, appropriate conditions for conspicuousness and for covertness, how to respond to riots, and many other related questions. The patrol operation will then be able to benefit markedly from computer assistance—much more than if the current procedures were merely automated.

It is possible at this stage to describe only the general outlines of a computer-assisted command and control system. In such a system, a properly applied computer could reduce control-center response time significantly—from about 90 seconds under optimum conditions to about 30 seconds. For example, in a computer-aided command and control system, telephone calls to the police would still be answered by a complaint clerk, or "controller." He would enter the type of incident, the address, and a priority code into a keyboard connected to a computer. The controller can specify any additional requirements, whether a one- or two-man car should be sent, whether two, three, or more vehicles should respond, or any other requirement posed by the situation. The rest is then automatic.

The computer maintains records of street-address locations and the location and availability of each patrol car. From these it finds the closest car to respond to the call. It prepares a dispatching order which is automatically sent to the selected car as a computer-generated voice message, or by a digital data link such as teletype. If the patrol officer does not acknowledge the message within, say, 10 seconds, a second car can be sent on the call. The control orders the status of the patrol cars, events in progress, and other basic control information can also be generated by the computer and displayed to dispatching command officers who can always countermand the computer-originated orders if required. Having "override" capability, they can concentrate on the unusual while the computer deals with the routine.

Since the field response time depends strongly on the car's distance from the call, automatic electronic car location devices could be tied directly to the computer so that it could dispatch the closest car. Analysis shows that extreme precision is not essential, and that knowing position within a radius of about one-quarter mile would ordinarily be adequate.

With such a computer-assisted command and control system, many new possibilities are presented for the deployment of the patrol force. As the crime pattern in the city changes hour-by-hour, the patrol force could be redeployed to respond to it. As parts of the city are

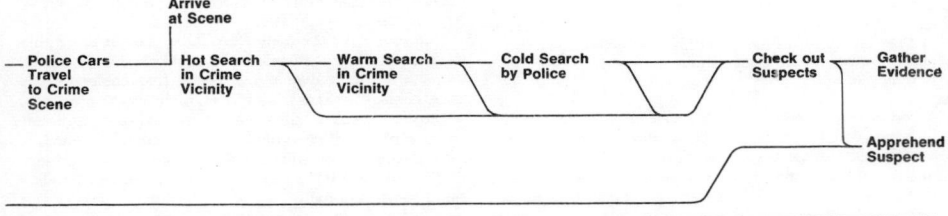

stripped of patrolmen by called-for-services, other units could be assigned as back-up. Under a riot or other emergency situation, contingency plans could be programmed so that the appropriate units are deployed to the emergency, and adequate backup maintained.

An advantage of the modern command-control system is its option that all the information stored in the computer on the locations of various kinds of calls is available when needed for complete analysis of the operations of the department. This study could be conducted daily or every few hours.

Mobile Radio Equipment. Communications must be maintained with police officers, even when they leave their cars, as well as with foot patrolmen. It is noted above that police officials are interested in securing small portable radios so that patrolmen can call for assistance in any emergency and so that more effective use can be made of the entire police force.

Miniaturized transceivers for the officer away from his car and for the foot patrolman would have similar features. Both will require base stations—the car for one and probably the precinct structure or other public buildings such as a firehouse for the other. Large-scale production economies can produce a miniaturized unit at a low cost (perhaps under $150). To assure a market warranting such production, the Commission has recommended in chapter 11 of its General Report that the Federal Government should assume leadership in initiating these two programs and should assume responsibility for guaranteeing the sale of the first production lot of perhaps 20,000 units.

A modest standardization program of car radios is possible and would add flexibility to a police department's choice of radio suppliers. Gross standardization of size, mounting brackets, receptacles and control heads can be accomplished immediately, and should go far toward making it possible to use the products of different manufacturers interchangeably. More detailed standardization of electronic equipment is less obviously useful for it may serve to inhibit the manufacturers from improving their product. Certain obvious electronic features which involve system compatibility—such as selective codes—should be standardized as early as practicable.

Digital data links to and from the police car can remove a large part of the normal voice traffic and also provide a paper copy of the message to the car. The link can be a minimal system for routine messages or a more complete teletype system. While digital links may save band-width, the need for redundant transmissions to eliminate teletype errors may substantially reduce much of that saving. Further investigation of the error characteristics of mobile digital links in a city environment is required.

Standardized Computer Code and Formats. Finally, it is essential to develop a standardized computer code and formats, fingerprint classifications, and other such uniform systems and "language" to assure national consistency of procedure when mutual support is required.

Once developed, these uniform systems must be implemented, and media for dissemination must be developed. Without a standard computer code and formats, computers and systems will be unable to "talk" with each other and systems will be correspondingly weakened for lack of direct, immediate communication ability.

OVERCOMING RADIO SPECTRUM LIMITATIONS

Radio-spectrum congestion and frequency compatibility seriously hamper police radio communications. For example, although 50 police cars are considered normal radio-channel capacity, New York City until recently had to control over 100 cars with 1 radio channel, and relied on the telephone to relieve its radio congestion. In the Chicago area, 38 separate cities with 350 patrol cars must all share one frequency. This congestion results in excessive delays and underutilization of the police force while patrol officers or dispatchers try to gain the air. In emergency situations, such as riots, storms, major conflagrations, aircraft disasters, and so forth where mutual support is required, neighboring police departments are unable to maintain communications because their radios operate on different frequencies.

To overcome the problems of radio-spectrum congestion and frequency incompatibility, the implementation of frequency-sharing concepts through the development of larger, more efficient police mobile radio networks should be encouraged. The larger number of small, independent, overlapping, and inefficient systems should be reduced through voluntary sharing. In this way, each user, when its demand peaks, can utilize the others' slack capacity, a basic concept common in telephone and electric-power networks. For instance, if two police departments each use their private channels 50 percent of the time, then each finds a busy signal half the time. If they were to share their channels, a user would find both channels busy about 35 percent of the time. If four such users were to group together, then all channels would be busy less than 20 percent of the time. Any peak-sharing advantages are in addition to these.

Two distinct trends must be set in motion to encourage such sharing. First, the relationship between the Federal Communications Commission and the police and other public safety band users must be restructured so that the Federal Communications Commission no longer receives piecemeal individual requests from the ultimate public safety user. Rather, coordinated requests must come through governmental entities which represent reasonably large areas and populations.

The core cities themselves are large enough to be able to develop efficient mobile radio networks for their own use, sharing their own public safety frequencies to balance the peak loads as school buses, highway maintenance, police, etc., peak at different times. With the gradual creation of coordinated networks, the Federal Communications Commission will be in a position to require projection of future needs so that radio spectrum can be allocated more rationally.

The second trend to be set in motion for more efficient use of the mobile radio spectrum requires greater use of switchable radio channels and of multichannel trunks. Generally, addressing will have to be accomplished by selective address coding rather than, as at present, by frequency. Selective coding minimizes the present system's inflexible dependence on frequency, but enables the individual user agency to retain its independence while using the system. It is evident that usage of these techniques will increase the cost of the mobile radio network. Basically, the networks will be less wasteful of radio spectrum, more flexible in use, but more costly to implement than the many small individual networks now existing. Federal Government encouragement in the form of financial support appears essential.

Finally, frequency space is available within the VHF–TV band between TV stations and within the underloaded UHF–TV band. One TV channel can provide over 100 radio channels. The Federal Communications Commission should consider allocating portions of the TV spectrum to land-mobile use from which the police should receive a significant share. This would represent a small loss (2 percent for 1 channel in UHF) to the TV community.

OPERATIONS RESEARCH

It might seem that the most important contribution that science and technology could make to public safety would be to develop equipment for law enforcement with the same degree of ingenuity that it has demonstrated in a great variety of human needs. But advanced "hardware" is only one aspect of the promise that science and technology hold for the police. One of the most promising contributions, yet one most obscure by present standards of adoption, is that which involves operations research.

As an important mechanism for innovation within police agencies, it is urged that police departments of 1,000 or more employees establish an operations research group comprising professionally trained scientists, mathematicians and engineers, including at least one person with a broad statistics background, and at least one with electronics competence. There are today about 37 State, county, and local forces of 1,000 or more personnel.

An operations research group once formed would study the organization of the department, provide technical guidance to the department management, analyze operations, and assess the effects of all experimentation within the department. Such groups, which have proven extremely effective in industry, the Federal Government, and the military, should prove to be a significant force for experimentation and innovation. The group need not be large; depending upon the size of the force, it may include up to about seven professionals. The dollar investment for thus significantly improving the effectiveness of over 1,000 men is small compared to that of most other operations of this sort and size.

STATE ROLE IN PROVIDING CONSULTANT ASSISTANCE

Legislative bodies, city managers, mayors, and chiefs should seek consultant assistance in reviewing the organization of forces. This will lead toward police force modernization across the nation. Individual States have a key role to play in inducing improvements. Most of the organization, management, and operational suggestions presented in this chapter could be implemented locally if States were to create commissions on police standards to upgrade county and local police effectiveness through surveys and inspections. In order to overcome management and operational weaknesses, these commissions should be given certain powers and responsibilities:

☐ Authority to increase police effectiveness through surveys and inspections;
☐ Authority to see that physical resources common to a given area are jointly pooled;
☐ Authority to provide financial assistance to jurisdictions which comply with established standards;
☐ Responsibility for encouraging research in police organization, management, and operations and the publication and dissemination of such research.

The formation of commissions with power to survey the organization and management practices of police agencies, which is more fully described in chapter 8 of this volume, focuses attention on the State government as the catalyst for improving local law enforcement. Periodic surveys of the organization, management, personnel standards, and operations of all law enforcement agencies by recognized consulting experts are of such importance that each department should be so surveyed at least once every 5 years. Moreover, other State funds should not be made available to local departments unless they show good faith in their intent to implement survey recommendations which are clearly necessary and feasible.

CONCLUSION

Law enforcement cannot remain static and still serve the public adequately. Progress will require change in many of the time-honored ways in which numerous police officials have habitually functioned. Progress will also require an infusion of more promising police recruits, an openmindedness and daring previously unknown on the part of many police administrators, and financial and public support of higher order than that heretofore afforded the police. And progress will require time and personal commitment by public and police officials alike. The present state of police organization in the United

States remains essentially similar to the way it was when summarized in 1962: [44]

* * * about 40,000 police jurisdictions and approximately 300,000 police officers conform to no fixed or definable standard of organization, structure, public responsibility, or general efficiency. Among them are some of the best law enforcement agencies that have been developed anywhere in the world, at any level of government. Others are in the process of changing over from antiquated methods and are now embracing new techniques for popular control, general supervision, and improved day-to-day functioning. Included also are a considerable number of agencies that have failed to show any sign of renaissance and seem bypassed by constructive impulses that have brought development and progress to the first two groups. These last police forces constitute a burden on the entire machinery of justice and are detrimental to the process of achieving a professional police service held in esteem by the citizens of the nation.

The task of police executives is becoming more difficult each year, particularly as forces become numerically larger. For example, police management in the 28,671-man New York City Police Department is as demanding as supervising a vast industrial or manufacturing corporation, managing an airline or railroad, or commanding a military division. In fact, it seems that police administration is essentially similar in principle to managing any complex nonpolice enterprise. One writer asserted: [45]

* * * Study of scores of police reorganization surveys makes abundantly clear that there are few if any principles of police administration which are not at the same time principles of business, military, and general public administration.

Inducing America's police chiefs to implement proven organizational principles intended to streamline their forces and accommodate innovations is an important step forward in the war on crime. Without internal reorganization, police forces can only become larger, more inefficient likenesses of their present structure, and offer scant hope of furnishing better police service. All that such forces can promise is a steady commitment to mediocrity, drastically rising expenses over an indefinite period of time, and growing frustration among personnel. Excepting some departments from his statement, one writer thus capsulized the state of police organization and the feeling within the ranks in 1960: [46]

* * * Typical police organization in 1960 cannot or will not utilize top brain power. Young policemen who are "too intelligent" do not remain with the police force. If they do, they all too frequently get into trouble. They become frustrated sowers of seeds of discontent. These men obviously do not fit into the general pattern of police organization in 1960.

Legislative and nonpolice administrative officials including mayors and city managers must take at least some responsibility for the current organizational condition of many police forces. These officials may induce change and modernization by demanding it, supporting modernization programs fiscally, and defending change designed to result in streamlining government citywide.

And the public must shoulder some responsibility, too. They can cause elected officials to initiate police as well as citywide governmental reforms.

Any city may have an outstanding police department—but only if it really wants one and is willing to pay for it. The public, through sustained demand for improved law enforcement, may also influence the quantitative and qualitative levels of police service. The late Chief William H. Parker wrote: [47]

Despite the most aggressive and enlightened leadership, law enforcement cannot rise above the level set by the electorate. *A condition precedent to the establishment of efficient, professional law enforcement in a community is a desire and a demand on the part of the residents for that type of service.*

---

[44] Samuel G. Chapman, "The Police Heritage in England and America: A Developmental Survey" (East Lansing, Mich.: Michigan State University Institute for Community Development and Services, 1962), p. 30.
[45] Donal E. J. MacNamara, "American Police Administration at Mid-Century," "Public Administration Review," summer 1950, p. 188.
[46] Richard A. Myren, "A Crisis in Police Management," "The Journal of Criminal Law, Criminology and Police Science," March–April 1960, p. 600.
[47] William H. Parker, "The Police Challenge in Our Great Cities," "The Annals," January 1954, p. 6.

Appendix

THE POLICE LEGAL ADVISOR

In recent years the criminal law has become increasingly complex. The appellate courts have dramatically enlarged their supervision over law enforcement agencies in opinions that reflect a heightened concern with the detail and routine of policing.[1] These opinions have narrowed the range of police behavior and demanded more refined judgments at the earliest stages of an investigation. More and more, these initial judgments—especially regarding admissions, confessions, and searches—serve to determine the ultimate disposition of the case. A mistaken conclusion by a patrolman, usually the first officer on the scene, is often irremediable, dooming an entire investigation, particularly if the error invokes one of the exclusionary rules. The short story is that today cases are "harder to make."

A necessary response, now more than ever before, is police departments and policemen that are better trained in the law and more sensitive to current judicial pronouncements. Such sensitivity will mean that the enormous power and responsibility entrusted to the police will be exercised more discriminatingly and effectively. Cases will be more expertly screened, and those cases which ultimately go forward will have a sounder evidentiary foundation.

A major instrument for insuring this increased effectiveness is the introduction of lawyers into the law enforcement process, particularly in the areas of planning and investigation. Even the best policeman and the best police administrator will, at times, need the advice of a lawyer who is knowledgeable in administrative and criminal law. In fact, the better the officer and the department, the more sensitive they will be to the complexity of the law, and the more likely to test their judgments against those of the legal advisor.

Many police executives and police studies have recognized the value of a legal advisor unit. As long ago as 1934, a study of police administration in Boston recommended that "a staff of lawyers be included in the police organization."[2] Nearly 30 years later, Chicago Police Superintendent O. W. Wilson reemphasized the need for a legal unit to furnish advice to staff and field personnel and to survey departmental orders and practices in the light of actual or proposed changes in the law.[3] Most recently, the Report of the President's Commission on Crime in the District of Columbia called for a permanent legal advisor for the Metropolian Police Department.[4]

Despite these repeated expressions of need, few departments today employ legal advisors. A recent, nationwide survey of police departments conducted by the National League of Cities revealed that only 14 of 276 respondents employed lawyers, and of these, six were part-time employees.[5] The Commission's own research, particularly in the study of municipal court systems in Baltimore, Detroit, Denver, and the District of Columbia, supports the view that police legal services today are inadequate at best and often nonexistent. The fact is that with few exceptions State and municipal governments have not recognized the importance of staffing law enforcement agencies with law-trained personnel.

DUTIES OF THE LEGAL ADVISOR

It is neither possible nor desirable to blueprint here the precise functions a legal advisor or legal unit should perform. These will necessarily vary from department to department. It is useful, however, to provide a catalog of the types of duties that a lawyer is especially capable of performing. These include: training and continuing education; policy planning; liaison with the legislature and the community; liaison with prosecution and courts; civil suits against individual officers; and problems arising out of specific investigations. From this catalog, individual police agencies can provide for assignments that best reflect their own special needs.

TRAINING AND CONTINUING EDUCATION

The legal advisor could assume a large, perhaps a primary, role in recruit and inservice training; or he could

---

[1] One appellate court even made findings on the permissible length of an undercover narcotics investigation, concluding that the officer remained "undercover" too long. *Ross v. United States*, 349 F. 2d 210 (D.C. Cir. 1965). The dissent criticized the majority for undertaking to "supervise the police in their conduct of an investigation." Id. at 126.
[2] Harrison, "Police Administration in Boston" (Survey Crime and Criminal Justice in Boston, vol. III, Cambridge: Harvard University Press, 1934).
[3] O. W. Wilson, "Police Planning," 11 (2 ed. 1962); cf. Wilson, "Police Administration," 60 (2 ed. 1963).
[4] Report of the President's Commission on Crime in the District of Columbia 173–174 (1966). See also the remarks of former New York Police Commissioner Michael J. Murphy, "Courts Must Be Told What Laws Needed To Halt Crime Trend," American Trial Lawyers 17 (December-January 1965–1966): "The police * * * need competent advice as to how best to proceed to protect the rights of all" and "this professional assistance is not usually available."
[5] Full-time attorneys: Boston, New York, Syracuse, Memphis, San Antonio, Kansas City, Missouri, and Portland, Oreg. Part-time assistance: New Haven, Ann Arbor, Tampa, Scotts Bluff, Nebr., and Odina, Minn. Oklahoma City employs both a full-time and a part-time legal advisor.
Chief Hilton Geer of the Oklahoma City Police comments that "the value of policemen-lawyers has been so amply demonstrated that this department waives the usual rules to permit officers to attend law school by preferred shift assignments." (Letter to the author, Mar. 17, 1966.)
Since the survey was taken, several other departments have retained legal advisors.

limit himself to preparing specific aids such as an annotated manual on the criminal code or rollcall training bulletins on recent judicial decisions and legislative enactments. In addition, he could prepare materials on courtroom procedures, including brief explanations of the most frequently encountered rules of evidence, and courtroom manners and decorum.

More generally, a need exists to anticipate trends in the law and develop operating procedures to cope with them. By alerting officers to current trends, it may be possible to initiate innovative administrative procedures that will ward off overly restrictive court decisions.

In performing these various training tasks, the legal advisor can help line officers achieve a better understanding of their complex role in society. For example, in attempting to understand judical decisions, most officers have little to draw upon except a thorough awareness of the day-to-day problems of battling crime. When explanations of complex legal procedures are cast only against this narrow backdrop, it becomes difficult for the individual officer to develop more than a superficial understanding of the case law. A legal advisor has the background to construct broader gauged training programs, programs that will heighten sensitivity to the competing goals underlying judical decisions and provide a better foundation for assessing them.

POLICY PLANNING

Because total enforcement of the criminal laws is—for reasons given earlier in this report—neither practical nor desirable, discretion in the enforcement of the laws has to be exercised. Generally, the police have been hesitant to articulate or record for either internal use or public information the criteria upon which enforcement decisions are made. The difficulty is that although wide areas of flexibility are now left to police agencies without even general policy guidance from the legislature or the courts, police agencies have not considered it their task to develop and articulate their own policies. As a result, important policy decisions affecting such problem areas as undercover investigations, informants, and alcoholic offenders tend to vary from precinct to precinct and often from officer to officer. Uniformity is lacking and decisions are seldom clear cut within the department itself.

Here, in the development of policies, and particularly those arising from the necessity for selective enforcement, the legal advisor can aid uncertain police executives. According to one former police executive, Herman Goldstein, "the greatest potential and need is in the use of the law-trained man to assist the police administrator in the formulation of policies relating to enforcement and to the processing of the offender." [6]

Another series of tasks concerns the review of cases under investigation, particularly in organized crime. These would include unsolved cases as well as those cleared by arrest, and cases "lost" in court or "dumped" by the prosecutor or grand jury.[7] The goal would be to identify and evaluate current department, squad, and precinct practices in a critical manner, and then to suggest remedies. Some department or squad practices have survived over time only because of insufficient familiarity with the case law. For example, one prosecutor who became familiar with police practices identified several standard procedures that unnecessarily weakened enforcement. One related to enforcement of the laws prohibiting the sale of whisky after hours. In Washington, cases against liquor establishments are made by sending an undercover man inside the premises to make a purchase. The undercover man then swears to a search warrant and a raid is made on the warrant. Under current law, however, it is not necessary to have the undercover man himself sign the warrant, and thereby reveal his identity when a motion to suppress is made in court. The detective in charge of the raid could swear to the warrant on the basis of the information given to him by a reliable informant, the undercover agent.[8] Another example, far more serious in its consequences, "concerns the practice of the homicide squad of rounding up all witnesses to a case and taking them to headquarters to sort out the case. That procedure is potentially defective if one of the witnesses turns out to be the defendant and then confesses or incriminates himself while at headquarters." [9]

LIAISON WITH THE LEGISLATURE AND THE COMMUNITY

Typically, police agencies are remote from the legislative process. When law enforcement officials do recite grievances, they commonly do so without consideration of possible governmental remedies. Consequently, areas which are subject to legislative solutions often remain ignored. A legal advisor could draft needed statutes and evaluate the legislation proposed by others. He could establish communications with the various legislative committees concerned with enforcement and utilize them as a routine forum for the airing of police problems. In addition, the legal advisor could help prepare the testimony of the chief and other officials before legislative committees and, on occasion, could himself represent the department. Unlike the city attorney who presents a package of legislation, some of which may have to be sacrificed, the legal advisor's only task is to make police needs known to the legislature.

Associated with these functions would be various community relations efforts aimed at winning support for law enforcement positions. These could be directed not only to the general public, but also to special governmental agencies, such as the public school and housing authorities, or the local poverty program, with whom information and ideas could usefully be exchanged.

In particular, a need exists for cooperation between the police and the antipoverty programs. There is a common untapped interest in the elimination of crime and poverty. Police agencies could be incorporated into efforts to improve housing, recreation, and mental health facilities, among others. Too often, however, no communication exists between the police and antipoverty workers. A legal unit within the police department could be the means for the identification of common problems.

[6] Letter to the Commission, Feb. 23, 1966.
[7] A legal advisor is suited for this continuing review function, in part because "in many cases the officer will not discuss the problem with the prosecutor because he feels the arrest was good but the prosecutor 'lost' the case in court."

Letter from Walter H. Guibbini, chief trial attorney, San Francisco district attorney's office (Mar. 8, 1966).
[8] Memorandum from Theodore Wieseman, assistant United States attorney, District of Columbia (Mar. 14, 1966).
[9] Ibid.

LIAISON WITH PROSECUTION AND COURTS

Excepting those few departments which employ legal advisors, most police forces receive only sporadic counsel from the prosecutor's office or from individual prosecutors who have developed a special relationship with certain squads or officers.[10] The American Bar Foundation researchers paint a black picture: "While private counsel representing a business client would believe it to be of the utmost importance to consult fully with his client, prosecutors commonly proceed on the assumption that the police need not be consulted. A prosecutor who understood the problems of the police * * * could better decide what issues are in greatest need of clarification." Commonly, "communications between the prosecutor and the police chief are virtually nonexistent."[11]

Perhaps the primary explanation for this lack of coordination is that most prosecutor's offices are understaffed, sometimes severely so, and cannot spare additional manpower for needed consultations with the police. Here the legal advisor could act as liaison officer translating, articulating, and implementing the policies of each agency. He could channel the complaints of the prosecutor and propose remedies for legitimate grievances. He could also maintain communications with sections such as the appellate division, which rarely consult the police, even when issues vital to law enforcement are being litigated. In this way conflict would be minimized and understanding and cooperation increased, not only among local agencies but with Federal investigators and prosecutors as well. In addition, appellate courts would be better informed, since more enforcement data would filter up to them.

Equally important is the need to translate judicial decisions into standard operating procedures. The recent Miranda decision,[12] for example, requires that substantial time and skill be devoted to the preparation of orders detailing interrogation policy. Since most prosecutors' offices do not consider it their responsibility to translate appellate decisions into operating procedures, the task falls to police agencies themselves who typically perform this considerable task without legal assistance, or abandon the effort entirely.

The legal advisor could also serve as an informal liaison with the trial courts, discussing with them police practices that concern or trouble them. In New York City, for example, police executives routinely visit certain courts.

NONCRIMINAL ADVERSARY PROCEEDINGS

Typically, the responsibility for defending civil suits against policemen arising out of official action belongs to the city attorney's office. Sometimes, however, these offices are so overloaded with other cases that they are unable to perform well. And sometimes the lawyers are unfamiliar with the legal issues involved. A legal advisor could assist—or even assume primary responsibility—for defending police officers in false arrest and other suits.

Policemen should not live in fear of civil suit; they should know that they will be supported by able counsel if they are accused of wrongdoing. Otherwise, an officer may become unsure, excessively timid, or lack the incentive to initiate imaginative and vigorous investigations.[13]

PROBLEMS ARISING OUT OF SPECIFIC CASES

Much police work consists of making legal decisions in complicated fact situations with minimal time for deliberation or discussion. An erroneous decision may produce an illegal search or an inadmissible confession that will condemn the investigation to failure and result in the guilty escaping prosecution and remaining free in the community. In these situations where there are few minutes to spare, a phone call to the legal advisor could prove invaluable. If the legal advisor were at headquarters, the precinct, in the cruiser, or otherwise readily available on an around-the-clock basis for visits to the scene, he would be even more effective. Even a telephone conversation, however, would permit key questions to be posed and answered. The routine use of a legal advisor in this capacity would also aid in the identification of practices which are contrary to law or inefficient, or both.

The legal advisor could also, in conjunction with the district attorney, prepare warrants and supporting affidavits, especially those which, due to the danger of destruction or disappearance of the evidence, are needed at once. His routine availability could increase compliance with the judicial preference for arrests and searches on a warrant. In those jurisdictions where the police themselves draw up the information, he could draft the forms and aid in filling them out.

DEPARTMENTAL LEGAL PROBLEMS

The multitude of legal problems affecting the police department as an entity is omitted from discussion here. Many of these legal problems are not unique to the police, but affect governmental agencies generally. Moreover, they are not directly related to crime-combatting activity and are presently handled—on at least a semi-systematic basis—by the corporation counsel or city attorney.

A CIVILIAN LEGAL ADVISOR

As indicated earlier, most police departments, including those in large metropolitan centers, have no legal counsel, and only a few police agencies in the entire country have adequate legal assistance programs. Consequently, opportunities for empirical evaluation of the performance of the legal advisor are minimal, and conclusions about the status of the advisor within the department and the qualifications of the advisor must be drawn cautiously.

Three distinct ways of providing counsel exist, each of which offers special benefits and drawbacks: a civilian employee; a policeman-lawyer; a prosecutor, assigned either on a rotation or permanent basis.

A civilian advisor holds the greatest promise. Unlike the prosecutor, who must to some degree serve two

---

[10] There may be a few model cities, such as San Francisco, where each of the specialized squads has a prosecutor assigned to it, and where the police also have lawyers on the force. Interviews with Attorney General Thomas C. Lynch and Chief of Police Thomas J. Cahill (January 1966).
[11] LaFave, "Arrest: The Decision To Take a Suspect Into Custody," 515–516 (1965).
[12] *Miranda v. Arizona*, 384 U.S. 436 (1966).

[13] In this connection, Superintendent O. W. Wilson, in a departmentwide memorandum, wrote: "I will always support the police officer who, in the performance of his assigned tasks, exercises what he believes to be his legal authority in a reasonable manner. Such an officer need not fear complaints filed against him. He need not fear the threat of a lawsuit. The department and the city will defend the officer against any legal action brought against him and, by statute, will assume liability for any damages which might be assessed," p. 501 (Feb. 5, 1963).

masters—the district attorney and the chief of police—or the policeman-lawyer, who may reflect narrow agency perspectives, the civilian employee is most likely to represent the fullest range of police needs while at the same time reducing police isolation from other municipal agencies and the public. Free from any particular institutional ties, the civilian advisor is likely to be more responsive both to civilians outside of law enforcement and to agencies, such as welfare, education, and housing, which communicate routinely with police agencies. A prosecutor-advisor may be insensitive to policing not geared exclusively to prosecution as, for example, in the handling of the prostitute, the drunk, and the intrafamily assault.

Of course, a legal advisor who is responsible to the police commissioner and not to an outside agency, such as the prosecutor, might lead the department down a legal path different from that charted by the district attorney. Such divergence could produce uncoordinated activity. It could also reflect legitimate police interests, and thus serve to preserve organizational integrity by surfacing important differences in approach. In any event, the relationship between prosecution and police should be no different—and no more difficult—than that existing between trial counsel and house counsel.

If the legal advisor is detailed from the prosecutor's office, there is more likelihood that police and prosecution will travel similar tracks, and that investigations will be prosecution oriented rather than directed to clearance by arrest or to peacekeeping functions. But there is also a greater possibility that the prosecutor-advisor will be overly sensitive to the policies of the district attorney, and comparatively insensitive to possible areas of difference. In some areas, the prosecutor will belong to a different political party than that of the mayor who appoints the police chief. If political rivalry exists, the effectiveness of the prosecutor-advisor will be impaired.

Of course, in a very small department where it is not feasible, financially or otherwise, to employ a civilian, a prosecutor-advisor may be preferable. If the legal advisor is on the staff of the prosecutor, he should have substantial experience in that office, since senior police officers often know more law than junior trial attorneys and so may avoid the errors and omissions which inexperienced prosecutors often make.

Regarding the prior experience of the legal advisor, it is difficult to list specifically any special set of background skills. Presumably there are many career tracks that would adequately prepare one to be an advisor. These include: experience as a prosecutor; private practice, particularly in the criminal field; law enforcement experience, such as with the Federal Bureau of Investigation or the Treasury Department; a police intern program (discussed infra).

MANPOWER NEEDS

It is impossible to calculate with confidence the number of advisors needed now by police agencies across the country. An estimate of the outer limits of manpower needs is dependent upon knowledge of what functions the legal advisor will perform, and these will necessarily vary, often substantially, from department to department. In some places, the advisor will be responsible for training, or legislative relations, or policy planning; in others, he will perform none or all of these duties. A reasonable estimate of minimum needs, however, may be made, even though it is difficult to specify underlying criteria. The following estimates represent the best guess of those most experienced.

There are five police departments servicing cities in excess of 1 million population. At least five legal advisors may be needed to meet minimum needs of these departments and even this figure is probably very conservative. Based on his experience as deputy commissioner for legal matters of the New York Police Department, Franklin Thomas feels that "twice the number recommended would be the absolute minimum to fulfill properly the functions required of such advisors." [14]

Approximately 17 cities range in population between 500,000 and 1 million. At least three advisors should be available. There are about 33 cities within the 250,000 to 500,000 population range. At least two advisors should be budgeted. There are nearly 80 cities under 250,000 and over 100,000 population. At least one advisor would fulfill minimum standards.

In smaller cities, such as those below 100,000 or 50,000 which may not need or be able to afford a full-time legal advisor, pooling arrangements—by which several police agencies in a given area would share a legal advisor—should be made. Fragmentation of police services is notorious and the common use of a legal advisor could be a device not only for acquiring counsel, but of achieving greater coordination among separate police departments.

All of the States, except Hawaii, maintain police or highway patrol organizations. These departments range in sworn membership from 50 men in Nevada to 2,795 men in California. Total personnel as of December 31, 1964, was 26,784 men. At least one advisor should be budgeted for each State, and the largest States, such as New York (2,464 men) and Pennsylvania (2,015 men), should employ several law-trained men. In addition, there are 773 counties which operate road patrols, about 100 of which have uniformed forces of over 100 men. Each of these should employ a full- or part-time advisor.

Totaling these figures, the manpower needed to supply minimum needs ranges from 250 to 400 men skilled in criminal law, administrative law, and police science.

RECRUITING LEGAL ADVISORS

Two innovative programs, one of which is specifically aimed at producing legal advisors, have recently been initiated pursuant to Ford Foundation grants. The program at the Northwestern University Law School is "directed primarily toward the development of police legal advisors." [15] It provides for a 2-year training program for graduate students, the first year being spent in residence at the law school and the second actually working in a police department. The police department receives

---

[14] Letter to the Commission, Nov. 16, 1966.

[15] Revised Proposal to the Ford Foundation (April 1964), p. 2.

the services of the intern free of charge under the terms of the fellowship.[16] At the end of the second year—by which time a thesis must be completed—the trainee receives a master of law degree.

Unlike the Northwestern University program, the "police internship program" at the University of Wisconsin Law School is not "committed to the training of lawyers specifically for assignment in a police agency," but rather to expanding the opportunities for "interested students to become familiar with the major issues confronting the police and other agencies in the criminal justice system."[17] Under the terms of a $260,000 grant, a program for law students to intern with police agencies has been developed. During the summer of 1966, five specially selected students were placed with the Chicago Police Department, and a sixth with a Wisconsin police agency.[18]

Both the Northwestern and Wisconsin programs are imaginative and promising. In particular, the structuring of the Northwestern internship, which gives a lawyer to the police department for a full year, acts as an inducement to the city authorities to retain an advisor on a permanent basis.

Both programs, however, represent only small steps forward in meeting manpower needs. If the necessary pool of talent is to be created within the next 5 years, it is essential now to finance both new training programs, expand existing ones, develop plans for the involvement of more lawyers generally in the police process,[19] and, most important of all, recruit skilled lawyers from the outside.

RESISTANCE TO EMPLOYING LAWYERS IN LAW ENFORCEMENT

Despite the long recognized need for law-trained personnel in police work, there has been over the years only a handful of lawyers working in local law enforcement. While the need has been great, the demand has been low, and the obstacles to employment often overwhelming.

One major source of resistance to the hiring of legal advisors is the city attorney or corporation counsel. Police departments which have retained a legal advisor, as well as those who have unsuccessfully attempted to do so, report strong resistance from the city attorney who commonly claims that servicing the police is his exclusive province. Such a position reflects too narrow a view of what it is the legal advisor does; most of the duties of the legal advisor—outlined earlier in this paper—do not fall within the scope of responsibility of the city attorney's office, nor are they matters that he is especially equipped to handle. In areas where there is overlapping responsibility, as, for example, defending suits for false arrest, a record of vigorous performance by the city attorney could relieve the legal advisor of all responsibility. Too often, however, the city attorney, although unwilling or unable to do the job himself, is also unwilling to permit others to do it.

As a result of opposition from the city attorney, several departments have camouflaged their legal advisor with such titles as "research analyst" or "research director," and generally kept his status unofficial.

Another source of resistance has been paradoxically the police executive himself. The reasons for this resistance are harder to identify since they are rarely made explicit. No doubt they emerge from a general reluctance to hire civilians or change the status quo. To some extent, they derive from ignorance about what it is a legal advisor can do. In addition, in many departments, particularly the more professionalized ones, civil service restrictions combine to prevent the retaining of a lawyer.

A final factor inhibiting recruitment is that attorneys who would be best qualified to serve as legal advisors have access to more attractive career opportunities. Both in terms of prestige and salary the talented prosecutor or private practitioner is unlikely to leave to serve as a police legal advisor. But the gains to the community and the police—measured in more effective and fair law enforcement—are so essential that efforts to establish the position of police legal advisor and to make it an attractive one for skilled attorneys must begin immediately. If salary and career opportunities were at least competitive with other legal positions within the criminal justice system, competent lawyers could be hired. Without question, the position of police legal advisor for a busy department could become one of the most challenging positions in government.

---

[16] Young lawyers, who have 1 or more years' experience, are given annual stipends ranging between $6,500 and $8,500, from which is deducted approximately $2,000 in tuition over the 2-year period. Recent law graduates without experience receive $4,600 for the first year and $7,000 for the second. All stipends are tax exempt. The grant to Northwestern, made in 1964, was for $300,000 extending over 5 years. To date, five fellowships have been granted.

[17] Letter from Prof. Herman Goldstein to the Commission, Feb. 23, 1966.

[18] Prior to the summer internship, the students were given a special seminar to orient them toward police work. Seminar topics included: the police patrol function, aggressive preventive patrol, ferreting out vice activities, policing at the operating level, role of the lawyers in the police agency, and investigating crime.

[19] One set of plans demands greater involvement of the bar associations. Typically, the local bar association has one committee, often several, dealing with the important problems of defendants' rights and the defense of a criminal case. Few have a single committee aiding law enforcement in a comparable manner. Recently, former New York Police Commissioner Michael J. Murphy wrote that "each Bar Association should consider a Legal Advisory Committee to Law Enforcement as part of its community responsibilities." Murphy, supra, note 5. Such committees may accomplish little that demonstrably aids law enforcement, but their mere existence could serve to boost morale, decrease isolation, and set the framework for continuing interchange. The Philadelphia Bar Association recently began a program aimed at training officers to make a pinch that sticks. "Bar To Teach Police New Arrest Wrinkles," Philadelphia Inquirer, April 18, 1966.

Another approach involves the establishment of courses in the law school curriculums that focus on enforcement problems. These could include periods of field observation, and could be elective or required, as is the case at Willamette Law School in Salem, Oreg. There, David Geary, then chief of police, permitted law students to ride in squad cars and observe the complaint desk, radio room, and jails. It may be that municipal governments could subsidize the legal education of students interested in law enforcement, students who would eventually serve as legal advisors.

Chapter 4

Coordination and Consolidation of Police Service

INTRODUCTION

Nearly every critic of local government in recent years has pointed with alarm to the proliferation of local governmental jurisdictions, especially in metropolitan areas. The desire for local self-government no doubt accounts for the zealous development and protection of numerous local units—even when larger, more cohesive units would seem to be a logical solution to metropolitan area problems.

Going hand in hand with the large number of local governments is the apparent need each feels to maintain its own law enforcement program. Commenting on this situation, Prof. Gordon E. Misner says, "Despite gross changes in other facets of our society, the basic organizational structure of law enforcement has remained relatively unchanged since the turn of the century." Continuing, Misner notes that regardless of size, location in relation to other units of general local government, or financial resources, each local governmental unit is deemed "capable" of administering basic law enforcement within its own jurisdiction.[1]

The 1966 "Municipal Yearbook" reported that there were 91,236 governmental units in the United States at the beginning of 1962: 56,507 local governments; 34,678 school districts; 50 State governments; and 1 Federal Government. A further breakdown shows 3,043 counties, 17,977 municipalities, 17,144 township governments, and 18,323 special districts. Of additional interest is that, although the total number of local governments has been reduced in recent years, the reduction has occurred only through the elimination of school districts. Nonschool special districts and municipalities have actually increased in number.

A fundamental problem confronting law enforcement today is that of fragmented crime repression efforts resulting from the large number of uncoordinated local governments and law enforcement agencies. It is not uncommon to find police units working at cross purposes in trying to solve the same or similar crimes. Although law enforcement officials speak of close cooperation among agencies, the reference often simply means a lack of conflict. There is, in fact, little cooperation on other than an informal basis, not a very effective means of meeting current needs.

Formal cooperation or consolidation is an essential ingredient in improving the quality of law enforcement. Crime is not confined within artificially created political boundaries but, rather, extends throughout the larger community. A workable program of formal cooperation or consolidation for law enforcement services within a "common community of interests" is the desired goal for improving the quality of law enforcement at the local level.

DEFINITION OF TERMS

Briefly stated, the concern of this study is an analysis of the problems of local police administration and the potential of coordination or consolidation of services as an aid to the repression of crime. Since the concern of this study is with police functions normally associated with the repression of crime, attention will not focus on police activities related to traffic law enforcement. To be discussed are staff services [2] typical of law enforcement agencies, such as the recruitment, selection, and training of personnel, planning, purchasing, internal investigation, and the like; auxiliary services,[3] such as records and communications systems, detention facilities, laboratory services, and the like; and selected field services,[4] including criminal investigation, delinquency control, special task force operations, vice control, and related activities.

It is important at this point to establish some working definitions of "consolidation," "cooperation or coordination," and "region." In the context of this report, consolidation is the merging, in whole or in part, of one governmental jurisdiction, or function thereof, with another governmental jurisdiction, or function thereof. This definition is made as broad as possible, to include any type of governmental jurisdiction or function and any type of formal agreement which constitutes the assimilation of one unit or function, in whole or part, into another.

Cooperation or coordination presupposes a formal agreement between two or more governmental jurisdic-

---

[1] Gordon E. Misner, "Recent Developments in Metropolitan Law Enforcement," Journal of Criminal Law, Criminology, and Police Science, 50: 497–508, 497, January–February 1960.
[2] Staff services are nonline functions and activities used to develop personnel and departments to effectively meet police responsibilities.
[3] Auxiliary services are nonline functions, separate from staff services, which provide technical, special, or supportive services to other nonline or line elements of a department.
[4] Field services are line functions and activities directly concerned with the fulfillment of primary police responsibilities.

Fragmentation of Urban Police

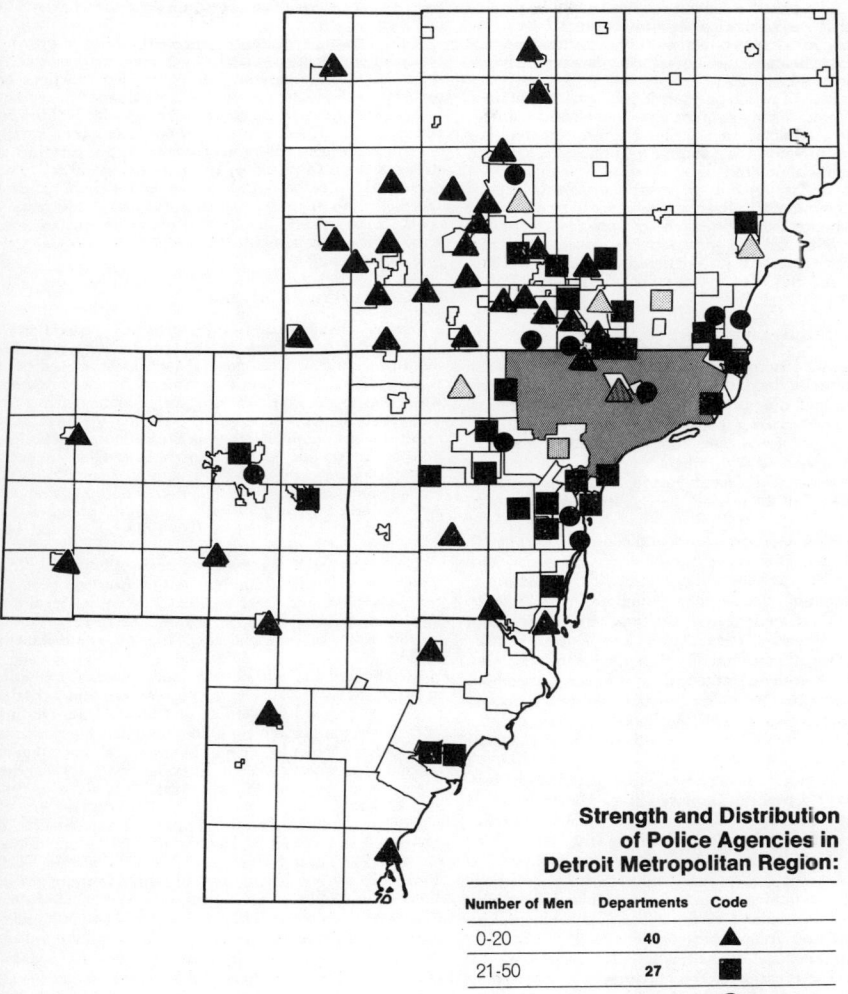

Strength and Distribution of Police Agencies in Detroit Metropolitan Region:

Number of Men	Departments	Code
0-20	40	▲
21-50	27	■
51-100	10	●
101-150	5	△
151-200	2	▨
201-5000	1	▨

tions each with defined responsibilities to jointly provide a common service. This definition is limited to formal agreements and does not extend to informal arrangements.[5] The phrase "defined responsibilities" is used to suggest that each participating unit has a particular responsibility in a cooperative venture, whether in terms of providing financial aid, equipment, personnel, or support by some other means.

A definition of region poses some problems. The word "region" immediately suggests some established boundaries, albeit artificial ones. The English common law concept of a region (or community) as an area having a commonality of interests is accepted as a definition of a region in this study; thus, it is not restricted to defined political boundaries. Rather, one is speaking of two or more governmental jurisdictions with political, economic, social, or other ties and with common problems. And a region may encompass jurisdictions in two or more States such as in the Washington, D.C.-Maryland-Virginia area.

SCOPE OF THE REPORT

Two basic assumptions regarding the status of local government in the United States underlie the ensuing discussion regarding coordination or consolidation of law enforcement services. First, local government will continue as a vital force when some governments are completely consolidated with others. Second, it is desirable to preserve as much local governmental control as is reasonable while increasing the quality and quantity of service.

The sections on coordination and consolidation of staff, auxiliary, and selected field services are concerned with analyzing the problems and potentials of coordination or consolidation of selected police functions. It will be assumed in these sections that proliferation of police jurisdictions is necessary, and that each jurisdiction is capable of providing at least a modicum of service to its citizens. The mission in these sections, then, is to suggest methods of improving selected police functions through coordination or consolidation, with the hope that each jurisdiction will be better able to cope with the problems of law enforcement.

In the section on police service and jurisdictional consolidation, the problem is viewed in a different way. It is assumed that the number of police jurisdictions must be reduced in order to deal effectively with the need for more and better police service. Significant methods used in consolidating police jurisdictions will be described. It is a fair assumption that where these methods have been utilized, it was realized by the affected governmental jurisdictions that fragmented, decentralized policing was either uneconomical or ineffective. It will be assumed, also, that coordination or consolidation of selected police functions was not sufficient and that jurisdictional consolidation was the only answer.

Throughout this chapter it will be evident that quality in police service is the desired goal. If quality can be achieved only through coordinating or consolidating selected police functions, or only through total consolidation of police jurisdictions, these are the routes that should be taken.

Thus, although this study is directed toward improving the quality of police service through coordination or consolidation, the transfer or shift of selected functions or total law enforcement from one unit to another cannot be argued simply in this manner. Present-day realities do not allow it. Interest in local self-rule has been strong enough to develop the present system, and it certainly is strong enough to retard or prevent changes in it. The democratic process implies a desire for local control whether or not there is local control in fact. The section on obstacles to coordination and consolidation describes some of the constraints to the redistribution of law enforcement functions.

RESEARCH METHODS UTILIZED

Several techniques were utilized in the preparation of this report. A detailed review was made of available literature, ranging from general metropolitan studies to studies of specialized police activities. Special attention was given to the literature on existing arrangements for intergovernmental cooperation, even though most such arrangements do not relate to police activities. Publications of the Advisory Commission on Inter-Governmental Relations were carefully reviewed, and some applicable recommendations have been incorporated into this report. Also consulted were other project reports prepared for the President's Commission on Law Enforcement and Administration of Justice.

The project staff also reviewed selected State constitutions, pertinent legislation, opinions of attorneys general, court decisions, and other sources to determine legal authorizations, prohibitions, or restrictions relating to the coordination or consolidation of law enforcement activities.

Members of the project staff made several field visits to a number of governmental jurisdictions and agencies to obtain firsthand impressions and factual data relating to the coordination and consolidation of law enforcement activities. Law enforcement and general government officials were interviewed in Phoenix, Ariz.; Los Angeles County and the cities of Lakewood, Norwalk, Downey, and Oakland, Calif.; the metropolitan government of Nashville, Davidson County, Tenn.; the municipality of Metropolitan Toronto, Canada; Metropolitan Dade County, Fla.; and Nassau and Suffolk Counties, N.Y. Visits also were made to the California Department of Justice; the California Disaster Office; the California Commission on Peace Officer Standards and Training; the Chicago Police Department; the Illinois State Police; the Illinois Division of Criminal Identification and Investigation; and the Sauk-Prairie Police Department, Sauk City, Wis. Discussions were also held with staff members of the League of California Cities and the Association of Bay Area Governments. Other Public Ad-

---

[5] Informal arrangements tend to be those of a mutual-aid nature in which one department agrees to come to the assistance of another as required, usually during emergencies. Such arrangements serve a valid purpose, but they do not materially add to the quality of service provided by a specific department nor do they improve the quality of personnel.

ministration Service personnel provided information regarding law enforcement activities in other cities with which they were familiar, including, among others, Kansas City, Mo.; Baltimore, and Atlanta.

Two conferences were of special value. A 2-day conference, held in mid-June 1966, brought together a number of law enforcement and general government officials of States, counties, and cities; several members of university faculties; and members of the staff of Public Administration Service especially conversant with the problems of law enforcement. The possible areas of coordination or consolidation of law enforcement activities and potential alternative solutions to law enforcement problems were discussed. A second, smaller conference of similar authorities, held in August 1966, reviewed drafts of the project report and evaluated recommendations.

GENERAL FINDINGS AND CONCLUSIONS

The ensuing discussion summarizes the general findings and conclusions of a detailed study of the problems and potentials of coordination and consolidation for the achievement of better police services. The discussion follows the section arrangement of the chapter, presenting first the general findings and then the more important conclusions or recommendations.

COORDINATION AND CONSOLIDATION OF STAFF SERVICES

Findings. On the basis of their potential for coordinated and consolidated action, staff services fall into two major groupings. Recruitment, selection, and training of personnel and planning lend themselves to joint action; whereas public information, internal investigation, and staff inspection are more closely identified with individual jurisdictions.

All police agencies need qualified, trained personnel capable of performing assigned duties. Unfortunately, many lack the necessary resources for recruiting and selecting qualified personnel and for providing the training needed at all levels of service. Many also lack the resources and capabilities for providing the sound, continuous planning that is the basis for evaluating departmental effectiveness and assigning personnel. These endeavors lend themselves to an areawide approach through coordination or consolidation of the efforts of a number of jurisdictions.

Staff activities associated with public information, inspection, and internal investigation are appropriately the tools of the individual police administrator and only rarely, or in limited degree, lend themselves to performance on an areawide basis.

Organized intelligence is a staff service that does not fall precisely into either of the two general groups. In one sense, it is a tool of the individual administrator; however, in order to be fully effective, the organized crime intelligence activities of one department must be coordinated with the activities of other departments engaged in similar and related work.

Primary Conclusions. Police activities related to manpower needs should be organized on the basis of areas large enough to support good programs. Through joint recruitment, selection, and training, police agencies increase their ability to secure the best available personnel. The State should participate in the programs through developing standards and requirements, assisting in making training facilities available to all departments, and establishment of manpower reserves upon which local departments can draw to maintain their strength when their personnel at whatever level are receiving training.

The fulfillment of police responsibilities depends upon the effective use of manpower. To this end, all police agencies need planning assistance on organizational and procedural matters, and access to areawide crime and modus operandi analyses. Such planning tools are beyond the capacity of all but the larger departments.

Other Conclusions. Organized crime intelligence should be shared between local, State, and Federal agencies to the extent possible. Public information services should be coordinated in metropolitan areas. A practical example would be a coordinated public information program between a central city and its suburbs.

Each State should consider the establishment of an independent unit which would have as its sole responsibility provision of internal investigation assistance as required and the initiation of investigations when necessary.

COORDINATION AND CONSOLIDATION OF AUXILIARY SERVICES

Findings. The auxiliary services of records and communications, crime laboratory services, and detention are the police responsibilities best suited to coordination and consolidation on an areawide basis; and with the possible exception of training, these are the services most often performed jointly. Joint action is possible primarily because it involves cooperation only on technical matters; in this, auxiliary services differ significantly from other police functions, particularly field services. Auxiliary services are costly, and resources beyond the competence of most jurisdictions are needed in order to perform them with any degree of effectiveness.

Auxiliary services make it possible for police agencies to fulfill their basic responsibilities by dispatching personnel promptly, bringing to bear the information in records files in the solution of crimes, and studying and analyzing the physical evidence pertinent to a particular investigation. Many police agencies cannot adequately perform these services alone.

Primary Conclusions. The increased pooling of resources among police jurisdictions is essential to the provision of effective records, communications, and laboratory services. Certain records must be maintained, and certain records services provided, on an areawide basis.

Communications systems must be improved through interjurisdictional contractual arrangements, coordination among radio systems, and through an increased role for the State as a coordinating agency.

Crime laboratory services must be available to every police department. With proper training, the routine gathering of evidence can be performed on the local level, but expensive analytical services must be provided by areas capable of supporting them, preferably by the State. Often the resources of poorly operated laboratory facilities in close proximity can be combined to establish one good facility.

One auxiliary service, detention, is not concerned with the fulfillment of basic police responsibilities and should be handled by a correctional agency whenever possible. If it is necessary for the police in some States to continue to provide detention services, consideration should be given to coordination and consolidation among police departments.

COORDINATION AND CONSOLIDATION OF
SELECTED FIELD SERVICES

Findings. Field services are a controversial area for the implementation of coordinated and consolidated police service, primarily because such activities involve the fulfillment of basic police responsibilities that involve direct contact with the public. Opposition to the coordination or consolidation of programs in police service is most apt to be concentrated in this area.

Selected field services, among them criminal investigation, vice and delinquency control, and special task force operations, require specialized training and manpower beyond the capacity of most jurisdictions to supply adequately. Criminal investigation and vice control tend to be concerned primarily with criminals who most frequently operate areawide, rather than within a single jurisdiction. Control of delinquency requires special knowledge, and special task force operations can be characterized as emergency situations requiring large numbers of trained personnel. These selected field services lend themselves to performance through coordinated or consolidated programs covering wide areas.

Primary Conclusions. Since criminal investigation and vice control, particularly, are concerned with a highly mobile criminal element and require significant manpower investments, they are susceptible to areawide performance.

Delinquency control responsibilities are the most local and least susceptible of performance on a coordinated basis. Special training and knowledge are essential, however, to successful programs, and consequently this aspect of delinquency control is applicable to areawide development.

Policing of special events is a proper activity for coordinated action, particularly through the use of mutual aid pacts. In some cases, a statewide task force for this purpose could provide needed manpower which would not be available to individual jurisdictions acting alone.

Other Conclusions. Special tactical units should be organized on an areawide basis in order to be fully effective.

However, the continuing need for manpower, as distinguished from manpower needs for the policing of special events, precludes the use of mutual aid agreements for their establishment. A State or county police organization might provide such units.

POLICE SERVICE AND JURISDICTIONAL CONSOLIDATION

Findings. Not every police department is capable of providing needed staff, auxiliary, and selected field services; nor is every local government capable of providing a desirable quality of police services generally. Many local jurisdictions cannot provide adequate police protection unless they receive assistance from other jurisdictions; and many jurisdictions, for one reason or another, cannot provide even basic patrol services. These situations call for the coordination or consolidation of effort and services.

A number of approaches have been used successfully in consolidating police responsibilities. They include: comprehensive reorganization under metropolitan-type governments; the use of subordinate service taxing districts under a strong county government; intergovernmental agreements; and annexation by municipalities of fringe areas. One additional approach, the use of single-purpose special districts, has been utilized occasionally.

Primary Conclusions. Comprehensive reorganization under a metropolitan-type government offers the best possibilities for fully unifying police services on an area-wide basis, but such reorganization is difficult to accomplish.

The provision of police service through use of subordinate service taxing districts offers a viable means of achieving consolidation within the existing framework of local government, especially through a county policing agency operating under a county charter.

At present, consolidation is perhaps most easily achieved through the use of intergovernmental agreements or contracts. The prime advantages are that permissive legislation is already available, and that consolidation can be accomplished without appreciably disturbing existing governmental structures.

Other Conclusions. Annexation and police special districts are also tools which can be used in achieving consolidation of police responsibilities. Both, however, have serious limitations. Annexation cannot be used effectively when the central city is largely surrounded by other municipal corporations, a situation that frequently prevails. Special districts covering a large territory may be created to provide police protection, thus eliminating jurisdictional problems. However, this method involves the creation of a single-purpose local government over which little popular control can be exercised.

OBSTACLES TO COORDINATION AND CONSOLIDATION

Findings. Obstacles to the coordination or consolidation of the police services of different jurisdictions are similar to the obstacles to restructuring and relocating other functions of local government. The fragmented, decentralized system of police administration parallels the organization of local government generally. However, the obstacles to coordination and consolidation of police services tend to be among the most formidable, primarily because police service is generally one of the most local of governmental services, and also because even the smallest local governmental jurisdictions like to believe that they can provide at least minimal needed police services.

Generally, the political and social pressures inherent in the desire for local self-government, rather than legal restrictions, militate against the coordination and consolidation of police services. Most counties, however, operate under legal restrictions that limit their ability to provide urban-type services, including law enforcement. Moves for the coordination and consolidation of local police services must take into account the strength of the political and social pressures for local self-government.

Primary Conclusions. Broad joint-exercise-of-powers legislation that permits many types of intergovernmental agreements appears to be the most convenient authority under which coordination and consolidation of police services can be accomplished. Action under such legislation involves no changes in existing governmental boundaries or political structures, nor does it negate principles of local self-government. Rather, it represents responsible exercise of the powers of local self-government. All aspects of police service—staff, auxiliary, and field services, and even total police service—can be coordinated and consolidated. Many States already have adopted some form of joint-exercise-of-powers legislation.

COORDINATION AND CONSOLIDATION OF STAFF SERVICES

Staff services of law enforcement agencies are those nonline functions and activities that help to develop departmental personnel, assist the departments to perform their basic police responsibilities effectively, and provide meaningful internal controls. Included in staff services are such activities affecting law enforcement personnel as recruitment, selection, training, staff inspection, and internal investigation. Also included are planning, crime analysis, purchasing, and public information services, among others.

Views on the susceptibility of certain staff services to coordinated or consolidated efforts are mixed. The advantages of coordinated recruitment, selection, and training services seem obvious. However, the value of combined activities in internal investigations and staff inspections and certain other staff services is unclear.

RECRUITMENT AND SELECTION

The need for quality in police officers is one of the major needs in law enforcement today. Except in a few jurisdictions, however, the supply of qualified applicants has not kept pace with demand, and police administrators generally have difficulty in filling vacancies.[6] Recruitment and selection are critical processes in maintaining and building police departments. Recruitment is the process by which potential employees are brought to the initial point in selection, and selection is the process by which qualified individuals are identified.

When two or more jurisdictions conduct joint recruitment and selection programs, several advantages accrue. It is possible to conduct a more widespread and efficacious recruiting program through the pooling of available financial and other resources. More sophisticated advertising of openings usually can be justified, and the potential number of qualified applicants may thereby be increased. Another advantage, especially for smaller jurisdictions, is the opportunity to initiate and conduct recruitment and selection programs under the leadership of professional personnel officers, which should result in more effective recruitment and a higher degree of validity and reliability in screening. The applicant has the opportunity of taking a single test for openings in several jurisdictions.

Joint recruitment and selection may take many forms. For example, a local jurisdiction may request a higher level of government to perform these services. Again, two or more jurisdictions at the same level may join in the recruitment and selection of personnel. Joint recruitment and selection can be partial, stopping at any mutually agreed upon point.

To have a successful program, the participants in a joint venture must agree substantially on how the program is to be conducted and the type of candidates desired. Standards and meaningful prerequisites must be established, and the means for their measurement devised.

Standards. Although the establishment of the basic qualifications of applicants is of major importance, the methods generally used to determine minimum standards or to measure the relative qualifications of applicants have not been especially noteworthy. The establishment of standards for the qualifications of applicants requires specialized knowledge, common sense, and freedom from prejudice or caprice. Attention should be given to standards for intelligence, education, personal and psychological characteristics, background or personal history, and physical characteristics.

The desired level or degree of acceptability may vary from one community to another, and the cooperating agencies need not always agree upon the precise degree of qualification required. If emphasis is placed upon those factors which bear an identifiable relationship to quality in performance, the less significant but more common points of disagreement, such as those concerning residence, physical size, or vision, will become less important to the joint effort. However, the success of a combined recruitment and selection program will depend largely upon the careful working out of a basic core of mutually acceptable standards or qualifications.

---

[6] Raymond L. Bancroft. "Municipal Law Enforcement, 1966," "Nation's Cities," February 1966, pp. 15–17. For a more comprehensive report on personnel problems and requirements, see chapter 5, Police Personnel.

Program Development. Jurisdictions interested in a joint recruitment and selection program must first agree, in principle, upon methods and techniques. Factors of major concern should include:

- ☐ Specific goals.
- ☐ Scope and depth.
- ☐ Reconciliation with existing legal requirements.
- ☐ Organizational and administrative structure and the relationships between and among the participants.
- ☐ Budgetary and staffing requirements.
- ☐ Strategy and tactics.
- ☐ Intent, content, and format of needed brochures, forms, and publications.
- ☐ Protest, appeal, and arbitration procedures.
- ☐ Adherence to recognized professional and scientific practices.
- ☐ Objective, continuing review of processes and programs to determine their relative worth, to measure their validity and reliability, and to insure a consistently high level of performance in keeping with the established goals.

The experience of Bloomington and Burnsville, Minn., two fast-growing Minneapolis suburbs, indicates the practical value of a joint recruitment and selection undertaking.[7]

Bloomington and Burnsville initially agreed that the recruitment program should be scheduled immediately prior to an established annual recruit training program. This timing insured that no men would be without prompt recruit training. The area covered by the joint recruitment effort included the three largest Minnesota cities and their environs, plus some communities in adjacent States. However, the limited number of vacancies did not justify sending a recruiting team to the more distant locations.

Since Burnsville was relatively inexperienced in recruiting, it had no members on the recruitment team, but it participated actively in the selection process. The tests that had been used by Bloomington were determined to be insufficient by Burnsville, so new tests were developed. These were administered by the Bloomington City personnel officer and a police captain. The Bloomington staff also conducted background investigations of the applicants passing the tests. A group interview, a rating interview, and a final interview were used to select candidates. The group interview was conducted by representatives of the two departments, but the rating interview was conducted by police officials of other communities more experienced in this technique. The final interview was conducted by the chiefs of the two departments.

The selection process was completed with a formal offer of employment by the participating jurisdictions. Most of the candidates certified for appointment stated they would be willing to work for either department, and all vacancies were filled. It was agreed by the two jurisdictions that Bloomington would maintain an eligibility list, since it had an established personnel office; and by its merit system rules, Bloomington was required to maintain the list for 1 year.

Other Considerations. Some law enforcement agencies may be reluctant to participate in joint recruitment and selection programs because they do not have salary and fringe benefit schedules competitive with those of other agencies and jurisdictions with which they might join. However, several other factors, including promotional opportunities, community preference, and present residence, may be deciding factors for potential employees.

The Bloomington-Burnsville experience suggests that a joint effort can succeed when interjurisdictional differences have been resolved. It now seems likely that some type of recruitment program involving all of Hennepin County, in which the two towns are located, will soon become a reality.

Despite the advantages of joint recruitment and selection of police officers, such programs are not widespread. Many police administrators, even where favorable conditions exist, are not taking advantage of these efficient and economical procedures, apparently because of an inability or unwillingness to explore possibilities in recruitment and selection beyond their own jurisdictions.

Joint Activities at the State Level. Perhaps more has been done collectively for police service on a statewide basis in California than in any other State. Several groups and agencies have been instrumental in mobilizing police departments to accomplish many things which they could not or would not have done individually. The impetus for a proposed statewide program arose from several factors associated with large-volume demands for personnel and potential large-volume employee retirements. The proposed program will be organized and administered by the California Peace Officer Standards and Training Commission (POST).

In the recruitment phase, POST proposes to utilize the resources of a regional advertising association to conduct a statewide publicity campaign. Promotional materials will be distributed at various locations throughout the State, particularly at colleges, universities, and State employment offices. Trained recruitment teams, which will include educators, interested citizens, and representatives of minority groups, will travel throughout the State, and speak at colleges, universities, junior colleges, and public and parochial schools. A concerted effort also will be made to encourage minority group members who possess requisite qualifications for police service to apply.

In the selection phase, potential candidates will be able to complete an initial screening test at a State employment office. Tests will be graded immediately, and applicants receiving passing scores will be fingerprinted and their records will be checked. It is hoped that the initial written test, given at State employment offices, will suffice for all associated jurisdictions. The list of successful candidates will be distributed to all police agencies in the State, and the individual jurisdictions may then ask an applicant to take an additional examination,

---

[7] Bloomington, Minn., Personnel Office. "Joint Recruitment of Policemen by Bloomington and Burnsville, Minnesota: A Case Study" (Bloomington: Personnel Office, 1965).

and may perform background investigations, and make such other checks as they deem necessary.

Agreement has already been reached on important prerequisites and basic qualifications for police officers. Although the requirements for applicants are not mandated by State law, to qualify for reimbursement of training costs from the State, a police department must hire only men who meet the standards set forth in the California Law Enforcement Standards and Training Act.[8] Since police departments representing 98 percent of the State's population have qualified for this aid, the effect is a State standard for applicants.

The proposed California plan could serve as a guide for other States. While there are many elements in the program, one important feature is implementation on a statewide basis to eliminate a disjointed, uncoordinated search for manpower by hundreds of jurisdictions.

Limited Programs. Should two or more communities be unable to reach agreement on all phases of a recruitment and selection program, this need be no bar to a limited program, such as the use of common forms or of a central employment information center. There is ample precedent for this approach in other employment fields. For example, the League of California Cities administers a test for young men interested in employment as administrative assistants to city managers. After grading by the league, the test results are made available to managers, who may then call in a man for an interview or initiate additional selection processes. The Federal Service Entrance Examination is another example of a single selection device used by a number of individual agencies.

TRAINING

Police training is a recognized need that is receiving increased attention from educational institutions and police and other organizations, and at all levels of government. In its 1966 "National Municipal Policy," the National League of Cities pinpoints its significance.[9]

The enforcement of laws and the regulation of human behavior in our complex urban society requires providing recruits with extensive basic training in all facets of police work and providing veteran officers with regular refresher training as well as specialized training in selected areas of knowledge.

At the national level, the Office of Law Enforcement Assistance provides for grants for professional police training and related education. The Federal Bureau of Investigation and the Federal Bureau of Narcotics have long had an impact on local law enforcement through their training programs.

States have entered into the police training field with laws and assistance programs perhaps more extensively than into any other areas of support for local law enforcement. Twenty-three States now have some form of training legislation; a few provide for mandatory recruit training and some provide financial assistance to local jurisdictions for this purpose.[10]

Universities, colleges, and junior colleges are expanding existing vocational programs and establishing new ones. In fact, hardly a month passes without some new junior or community college law enforcement program being started.[11]

The need for adequate training at reasonable cost seems to indicate that training functions should be coordinated or consolidated. The rate of growth and the variety of approaches in police training programs are of significance when considering training on a multijurisdictional basis.

Despite the current level of activity in police training, much remains to be accomplished and several factors tend to impede progress. Unfortunately, some police administrators insist that their personnel, particularly recruits, be trained only in their own facilities and by their own instructors. This insistence stems largely from a sense of insularity which presumes a nonexistent uniqueness and does not recognize that most departments need officers with the same basic core of knowledge. Although each department must supplement core courses with instruction in local organization, policies, procedures, and regulations, such local orientation is but a small part of total training needs.

A lack of understanding of training as a meaningful support to improved police service is an impediment to training in many departments. This is understandable, in view of the rather general lack of training and education among chiefs of police and their command and administrative staffs. As described in chapters 3 and 5 of this volume, few such personnel have college degrees, even fewer have advanced degrees, and most have had no significant training for their professional responsibilities.

Limited finances and shortages of manpower are complementary problems that may exist in fact or be offered simply as rationalizations for inaction. Financial limitations are real, however, when departments cannot budget for needed complements of personnel and when manpower cannot be provided to allow development of adequate training programs. Manpower shortages are increasingly a problem, even to departments with adequate financial resources. There is growing recognition, however, that manpower shortages can be substantially offset by recruiting top quality personnel and giving them superior training. It is being recognized, more and more, that mere numbers of personnel are not the answer to problems of police efficiency and effectiveness.

Financial limitations and manpower shortages are both factors influencing decisions on training, particularly out-of-city and out-of-State training and educational programs. Many small departments feel they cannot release men even for local or incity training. For example, if one man is released from a five-man department, the others must work overtime and without regular days off, and local police service suffers.

Areawide Training Efforts. Many areawide efforts are being made to satisfy the growing demand for better training. These efforts divide rather naturally into: (1) central city assistance to nearby smaller departments, (2) State and regional training programs, (3) institutes

---

[8] 51 Cal. Penal Code secs. 13500–13523 (1966 Cum. Supp.).
[9] National League of Cities, "National Municipal Policy" (Washington: National League of Cities, 1966), sec. 15-3.
[10] Norman C. Kassoff, "State Laws on Police Training Standards," "The Police Chief," August 1966, p. 13.
[11] Most junior college programs are in California with the remainder concentrated in New York, Florida, and Michigan. In 31 States, no junior college police administration or police science programs exist.

and academies for police training, and (4) university and college programs.

Central City Assistance to Other Departments. Most large departments, historically, have made their training facilities available to surrounding smaller communities. Extension of training programs to smaller communities, under new concepts of reimbursement, may be of increasing value.

In 1965, the Chicago Police Training Academy trained 147 recruits from 35 suburban departments and 4 recruits from a department in a neighboring State. Realizing that the normal 14-week school designed for Chicago needs included studies which did not pertain to all local operations, it ran a special 10-week recruit school for these trainees. In addition, police officers from 77 municipal, county, and State police agencies took correspondence courses offered by the Chicago academy; numerous departments used its reference and film libraries; and the instructional staff of the academy conducted special courses for many outside agencies.[12]

State and Regional Training Programs. There are a number of programs in existence or planned which are based on the concept of areawide service to provide essential training to many departments. For example, the Metropolitan Fund of Detroit, a nonprofit research corporation concerned with intergovernmental relations in the six-county region of southeastern Michigan, has initiated a study of existing facilities and programs for training in the region with the intention of providing information necessary to implement a regional system of police training.[13] The Southeastern Michigan Chiefs of Police organization has established a 6-week recruit program, as has the Metropolitan Police Academy of Michigan, Inc., with headquarters in an armory.[14]

In Oregon, in 1965, an advanced program coordinated by the Oregon Association of City Police Officers trained 852 law enforcement officers at 15 regional schools. In addition, a 3-week basic recruit school was held at a National Guard camp near Portland. Both of these programs had modest beginnings, but in recognition of the need for more intensive training, they have been expanded in recent years.[15]

Through the efforts of the top commanders of six New England State police organizations, and with the aid of an Office of Law Enforcement Assistance grant, the New England State Police Staff College began a training program in 1966 with 36 administrative officers from the six State police organizations in attendance.[16] The objective of the school is to provide executive management training and thus improve the management skills of the police executive, with its goal that of training all men at the rank of sergeant and above. The course lasts 4 weeks and the curriculum is varied according to rank.

Areawide emphasis also appears in some of the recently enacted State training legislation affecting law enforcement agencies. The pertinent sections of the Michigan law provide that the Law Enforcement Officers Training Council shall provide advisory training standards and assist in establishing area training centers in appropriate locations, and shall cooperate with other governmental jurisdictions in establishing and operating these centers.[17]

Following the passage of the New York Municipal Police Training Council Act, the State was divided into 13 areas or training zones, primarily for the purpose of assuring the availability of a training school for every new officer. Zones consist of from two to nine counties, and each zone has a coordinator and a subcoordinator who are responsible for carrying out the purposes of the act within their zones.[18] The council has received a Federal grant to assist it in establishing regional police training centers throughout the State, and it is planned to place them in strategic locations where there are junior and community colleges.[19]

Training facilities now blanket the State of California, and programs are within the reach of practically every department in the State. By January 1967, 46 facilities had been certified to teach the prescribed recruit course and 36 the 80-hour supervisory course. The California POST program also allows credit for preservice college training.

Institutes and Academies. Several institutes and academies, affiliated with a university or a Federal agency, have long provided valuable instruction to the American police. Some date from the mid-1930's. Among those university-affiliated are the Traffic Institute of Northwestern University, the Southern Police Institute of University of Louisville, and the Delinquency Control Institute of the University of Southern California. Other less structured programs also exist—for example, the Annual Institutes on Police and Community Relations at Michigan State University. All such programs need to be maintained and expanded, and additional means need to be found to enroll students. Among the Federal agency programs are the National Academy of the Federal Bureau of Investigation and the training facilities of the Bureau of Narcotics. In October 1966 the 5,000th police official was graduated from the 78th session of the FBI's National Academy.

Universities and Colleges. Institutions of higher learning are sponsoring and supporting two kinds of efforts—recruit and inservice training—and both are increasing in importance. Four-year colleges and universities have long been active in police training, and now the junior and community colleges are undertaking an active role.

The Dade County (Fla.) police training program is a good example of a cooperative effort on the part of a county and a school board.[20] The school board has provided, without charge, State certified instructors and facilities at the Dade County Junior College for both recruit and inservice training. The Dade County Public Safety Department provides an officer to administer the program and maintain liaison with the junior college staff. The whole program is available without charge to all local jurisdictions within the county.

Current Problems. Despite the vast amount of activity in police training, accomplishments still fall short of needs.

---

[12] Chicago Police Department, Training Division, "Annual Report," 1965.
[13] "Metropolitan Fund, Inc., Initiates Training Study," "The Police Chief," August 1965, p. 22.
[14] Claude E. Broom and Marvin G. Lane, "New Academy for Michigan," "The Police Chief," May 1962, p. 20.
[15] Karl A. Van Asselt, "Cooperative Training Program Assists Oregon Local Law Enforcement Officers," "Western City," June 1966, pp. 34-35.
[16] "New England State Police Staff College Holds First Session," "The Police Chief," June 1966, p. 12.
[17] 17 Mich. Stat. Ann. sec. 3.29 (157) (1966 Cum. Supp.).
[18] State of New York, Office for Local Government, Municipal Police Training Council, "Municipal Police Training in New York State" (no date), pp. 12, 52-56.
[19] "State Gets Training Grant," "Public Management," 48: 229, August 1966.
[20] Metropolitan Dade County, Office of County Manager, "Survey of Area-Wide Government Cooperation," mimeograph, Sept. 16, 1963, p. 41.

Failure to recognize the core concept of training is at the root of much of the resistance to areawide, coordinated training. The core concept is widely accepted in Canada. For example, in the Province of Ontario, only two departments, Toronto and Ottawa, have their own recruit training programs. All other departments, including some very large ones, send their recruits to the Ontario Police College; and Toronto, with nearly 3,000 sworn personnel, is considering amalgamating its training facility with the Ontario Police College.[21]

Truly areawide multijurisdictional training programs will probably require State support. This has already been accomplished in many States that have created State police councils which have authority to develop statewide curriculums of sufficient depth in all areas of training, to compel all police officers to take the required courses of study, and to give financial assistance to local departments to allow this to meet mandatory standards.

A State training agency can be in a most favorable position to act. The duties of a State agency, established by law, should include responsibility for determining the need for all phases of training in every department throughout the State, including recruit, inservice, supervisory, specialized, and command and administrative training. The State agency should make an inventory of the training programs of State, county, and local police departments; police associations, Federal agencies; junior and community colleges; and 4-year colleges and universities. Following this inventory, the agency should make recommendations on the location, size, and curriculum of each program and the area it should serve.

Those States that already have agencies are either following this approach or working toward it. The duties of the Michigan council, mentioned above, include this function. The California Commission on Peace Officer Standards and Training has the power "to contract with other such agencies, public and private, or persons as it deems necessary, for the rendition and affording of such services, facilities, studies, and reports to the commission as will best assist it to carry out its duties and responsibilities." The New York Police Training Council has similar duties.

The Manpower Problem. A problem, particularly acute in small departments, is the inability to free men from their regular police assignments to receive training. Many departments are so short of manpower that training can be accomplished only on the job or during very limited periods of time away from it. Indeed, the small number of hours of recruit training specified in some legislation is undoubtedly due in part to the practical limits on the time a small department can spare a man from regular service.

Two solutions to this problem appear possible: (1) A manpower reserve of State police officers available on a statewide basis, and (2) a manpower reserve of officers under the jurisdiction of the county sheriff, county police, or public safety department available on a countywide basis.

A major problem inherent in either a State or county manpower pool is that of stand-in officers performing in accordance with local agency rules, regulations, and procedures. While not categorically rendering the stand-in concept worthless, the issue must be worked out locally. If a force were able to allocate sufficient funds to pay regular officers for overtime work while others were in training, the need for outside personnel to stand in would largely be obviated.

Statewide Manpower Reserve. State police departments may be the agency in which to establish reserves of men for facilitating local training. Legal obstacles to this approach are minimal even where the State agency is one of limited jurisdiction. State officers could be assigned to local jurisdictions and given the necessary authority to enforce local ordinances. The numerical strength of such reserves would have to be determined on the basis of a survey of training needs and the adequacy of replacements at the local level.

In our complex society, the training period for recruits should be a minimum of 10 weeks. With an adequate manpower reserve, this period of training should be within the reach of most departments, and each new recruit should be able to receive this training before he is placed on basic patrol duty. A manpower reserve should also encourage training of shorter duration for command and other inservice personnel.

Countywide Manpower Reserve. A manpower reserve established by the county sheriff or a county police agency may, in many circumstances, be a more likely alternative to a State program. Except for some outstanding exceptions, however, the level of sophistication in county organizations is less than in municipal departments. The alternative of a county reserve can be used only wher there is a county law enforcement agency of sufficient professional competence to be able to assist local departments. Also, many counties do not have enough population to support such a program. In these circumstances the responsibility should go to the State.

PLANNING

There are two vital needs of police departments which can be served by areawide, coordinated planning. One is crime and modus operandi analysis, which calls for areawide planning because of the regional nature of certain crimes and criminal activity. The other is assistance on administrative and operational matters, in which many small departments lack competence and facilities. Both are functions which should be performed on a metropolitan or statewide basis.

Crime analysis is a planning function regardless of the organizational unit in which it is placed. The primary purpose of crime analysis is to study "daily reports of serious crimes in order to determine the location, time, special characteristics, similarities to other criminal attacks, and various significant facts that may help to identify either a criminal or the existence of a pattern of criminal activity." [22]

---

[21] Interview with James Mackey, Chief, Metropolitan Toronto Police Department, June 17, 1966.

[22] O. W. Wilson, "Police Administration" (2d ed., New York: McGraw-Hill, Inc., 1963), p. 103.

Modus operandi, or method of operation, refers to the criminal's individual peculiarities—his methods, techniques, and the tools he uses in the commission of a crime. Modus operandi analysis is concerned primarily with persons, whereas crime analysis relates principally to events although they are interrelated.

Sound police organization and procedures depend upon good planning. Frequently, the emergency nature of police work and the constant attention that must be given to day-to-day operations do not leave enough time for effective planning. Much planning is done daily in all police operations, but, primarily, it is to serve an immediate need. Most police administrators seek to improve their organizations, but many do not know how or do not have enough time to correct deficiencies in organization and faulty procedures. Some large police departments have established planning units to assist the administrator, and, for the most part, these units are staffed by police officers and civilians who know how to analyze the procedures and organizational structures of police departments. It is principally the smaller departments which do not have the time, manpower, or financial ability to plan improvements in their organization and operations.

Crime and Modus Operandi Analysis. The crime analysis unit of the Chicago Police Department, for example, is responsible for the analysis of reports of major crimes for strategic and tactical purposes. When definite and identifiable patterns have been established, reports are sent to the concerned line commanders for appropriate action.

This unit is limited in its operations to the boundaries of Chicago, although it is obvious that crime patterns do not coincide with political boundaries. A trucking theft a year ago in a suburban jurisdiction may be related to a continuing series of such crimes in the central city, yet the central city had no knowledge of this crime, and the suburban jurisdiction was uninformed about the central city crimes. Undoubtedly, many such crimes fail to be cleared because of the lack of areawide crime analysis. The fact that reported crime is increasing in the suburbs faster than in the central cities should give additional support to areawide crime analysis.

Modus operandi analysis which requires the timely submission of case reports and other information and data to a central point is properly a large department or State responsibility. California and Michigan have established rather sophisticated modus operandi files which serve all jurisdictions in the State. The Michigan State Police Department maintains a file on sex offenders and fraudulent checkpassers. Michigan jurisdictions are required by law to submit reports to the sex offender file from which they, in turn, receive the names of suspects best fitting the description of persons wanted. In 1965, 45 percent of the items searched against the fraudulent check file were identified with known fraudulent checkpassers.[23]

The California modus operandi system is fairly complete since California law requires each jurisdiction to submit reports on all felonies daily to the California Bureau of Criminal Identification and Investigation (CII). Crime reports are divided into five major categories: Questioned documents, sex, burglary (including receiving stolen property), fraud, and robbery. Modus operandi analysts are assigned to work on each of these categories. Much of the work performed could be considered crime analysis since it is related primarily to correlating crimes and providing investigative data to local jurisdictions. However, specific subject identification is a primary purpose of the operation.[24]

Staff Assistance on Administrative and Operational Matters. There appear to be few organizations providing staff planning assistance on administrative and operational matters to other agencies and, in fact, there is little recognition of this need. A few consulting organizations, such as the International Association of Chiefs of Police and Public Administration Service, have provided assistance to many jurisdictions on general police matters, and some universities and colleges have occasionally aided local departments on specific problems. There is, however, almost no pooling of governmental resources for planning.

It was precisely for this reason that the Division of Police Administration services was established in the New York State Office for Local Government on January 1, 1966, as a free service to local police departments. The legislature in establishing this division declared:[25]

* * * it is the intent * * * that all units of local government maintaining police forces should be encouraged to promote the highest possible standards of police administration and operations. To that end, this article is enacted to offer such units of local government voluntary advisory services for improving the administration of their police services.

The functions, powers, and duties of the division of police administration services are:[26]

☐ To collect, compile, and disseminate current information regarding general developments in the field of police administration.
☐ To serve as a clearinghouse, for the benefit of police agencies, of information relating to common problems and to assist in the solution of those problems.
☐ To conduct studies and analyses of the administration or operations of any police agency upon request by the head of the agency, and to make the results available to the agency.
☐ To refer police agencies to appropriate departments and agencies of the State and Federal Governments for advice, assistance, and available services in connection with particular administrative problems.
☐ To encourage the further professionalization of police administration.

Interestingly, the division will not answer questions pertaining to the consolidation of departments. This is considered a matter of local concern.

Although in existence only a short time, the division has received many requests for service. One of its recommendations resulted in the consolidation of police communications in one county.[27] In addition to its consulting service, the division is collecting manuals and forms

---

[23] State of Michigan, Department of State Police, "Annual Report, 1965," p. 17.
[24] Interview with O. J. Hawkins, assistant director, California Department of Justice, May 16, 1966.
[25] N.Y. Executive Law, secs. 550–553 (1966 Cum. Supp.).
[26] Id. at sec. 552.
[27] Interview with Charles C. McCloskey, Jr., executive director, Division of Police Administration Services, New York State Office for Local Government, Aug. 5, 1966.

from leading police departments across the Nation, and establishing a reference library in the fields of police science, public administration, and political science.

Conclusions. The New York Division of Police Administration Services represents the first attempt of one government to provide this assistance to other governments on an organized basis. The opportunities for accomplishment in this approach are great. In the future, for example, departments in the same area might be using the same reporting forms to facilitate central records and crime analysis. They may, after study by the division, amalgamate communications or crime laboratories or many other costly facilities if it is shown that economies will result and service levels improved. The division is in a position to bring about standardization and improvement in many areas of New York law enforcement.

ORGANIZED CRIME INTELLIGENCE [28]

Many departments refuse to acknowledge the existence of organized crime and thus rationalize a preoccupation with more local and isolated criminal matters. In many instances, this position has led to virtual operational immunity for the crime syndicates. Further tending to give them freedom of action is the unwillingness of departments freely to exchange intelligence. Often called a trust gap, such reluctance seriously impedes effective local or joint action. The close and unwarranted holding of information by individuals and elements of a department denies it the basis for effective action.

Recent Developments. In recent years, several departments have offered encouraging signs of improved interdepartmental relations which are leading to more effective action. Probably most significant is the belated recognition of syndicated crime as inimical to the country's security and well-being and a problem of great seriousness which cannot be resolved locally.

In 1956, a voluntary organization of law enforcement agencies, the Law Enforcement Intelligence Unit (LEIU), was organized to work for increased sharing of criminal intelligence data. In addition to furthering personal contact between individual members, the LEIU has established a central clearinghouse for criminal intelligence information in the California Bureau of Criminal Identification and Investigation (CII) to which all members contribute and from which they receive information. Membership is divided into three categories: (1) Regular, (2) associate, and (3) affiliate. Regular membership is limited to 70 individuals representing a number of agencies; agencies as such are not members. Regular members are differentiated from the others in that they have voting rights and have access to the complete file maintained by the CII. The membership of LEIU is divided into four zones: (1) Northwestern, (2) Southwestern, (3) Eastern, and (4) Central. Each zone has a chairman, and members in each zone meet annually. The entire membership also meets annually. Discussions of the attributes of LEIU with a number of members indicate that it serves as an excellent means for contact between law enforcement intelligence officials on matters of mutual concern.

The New England State Police Compact developed from discussions of the commissioners of the six New England State police organizations and will come into operation upon ratification by the required three States. The primary provisions of the compact are: (1) A central criminal intelligence file to facilitate the sharing of intelligence information among the member State police forces, and (2) authority to the commissioner of State police of a member State to invite personnel from the State police forces of other member States to work in his State with power of arrest. The second provision is particularly far reaching, permitting the sharing of personnel for investigations, a vital need in long-term surveillance and investigative work.

The Law Enforcement Committee of the New York Metropolitan Council has formed a subcommittee on organized crime. The subcommittee encourages contact between law enforcement intelligence units in the New York City area, but its principal undertaking has been to make the intelligence files of the New York City Police Department available to the other police departments in the area.

The New York State Identification and Intelligence System (NYSIIS) is discussed in a subsequent section in connection with its function as a records exchange center for all types of criminal records. When fully operational, NYSIIS will include criminal intelligence information on the organized criminals of concern to New York and other police departments.

The Oyster Bay conferences, held in New York in 1965 and 1966, assembled representatives of agencies from throughout the United States for the purpose of furthering efforts against organized crime. The conferences have reached some interesting conclusions, among them the need to share information on individuals engaged in organized crime: [29]

> The relationship of the conspiracy and the criminal act must be shared by the investigative agencies if an effective assault is to be mounted against organized crime * * *. The optimum pooling of intelligence information should include both vertical and horizontal dissemination—vertical as between local, State, and Federal levels of government, and horizontal between separate jurisdictions at the same level of government.

The participants did recognize, however, that "a primary consideration for information sharing is security." [30]

Current Needs. A basic need for the uprooting of organized crime is the increased pooling of resources. This includes exchange of information and also making intelligence files available to more people involved in law enforcement. Substantial files of some intelligence units on the activities of organized criminals are unknown to law enforcement officers who could give them major assistance in solving crimes.

Information in the files of large intelligence units should be made available to responsible law enforcement officials on a meaningful basis. It is obviously impractical for an intelligence unit to reveal the contents of working files

---

[28] For a detailed discussion of organized crime intelligence, see chapter 7 of the "General Report" and the separate volume of the Task Force on Organized Crime.

[29] Oyster Bay, New York, 1965 Conference on Combatting Organized Crime, "Combatting Organized Crime." (Albany: Office of the Counsel to the Governor, April 1966), pp. 33–34.
[30] Id. at p. 34.

on developing cases unless it is working in concert with another agency. However, much of the information in intelligence unit files on individuals relates to organized crime's "legitimate" business enterprises, meeting places, personal data, and other information which may be widely disseminated.

Even the largest intelligence unit has difficulty obtaining the manpower necessary to perform continuous surveillance and investigative work to gather information on organized criminals. The members of the New England State Police Compact have recognized this fact and have taken steps to share personnel.

There is a need for agreement on the objectives and definitions of purpose of intelligence units. The effectiveness of many intelligence units is dissipated by activities not even remotely connected with the task of gathering data on organized criminals.

There is continuing need for coordination between the law enforcement agencies of the Federal Government on the one hand, and State and local intelligence units on the other.

Finally, there is a need for better coordination between local and State crime commissions and police intelligence units. Too often the police scoff at the activities of independent crime commissions when, in fact, these agencies can assist the police by making known the actions and objectives of organized crime.

Means must be found to redefine concepts of organized crime intelligence and to strengthen local services. Organized crime intelligence services also should be developed on broader bases. It would be sound to centralize some intelligence services at the State level while leaving intact effective local efforts. Under some circumstances, centralized programs and efforts could cover several States.

It is impossible in this brief analysis to suggest a full program of organized crime intelligence. Such a program is suggested, however, in the "Organized Crime Task Force Volume."

PURCHASING

Purchasing is an activity undertaken by every public jurisdiction, large or small. Traditionally, purchasing was primarily conducted on a departmental basis with little or no centralized purchasing for the jurisdiction. More recently, however, governments, and especially the larger jurisdictions, are abandoning departmental in favor of centralized purchasing. The cities of Chicago, Cincinnati, and Milwaukee are in the forefront in this type of buying. Chicago reports that savings run as high as 15 percent on total expenses of up to 200 million a year![31]

Purchasing is not a static concern—prices change frequently, the uses of products change, new products are developed, and the materials in products may change significantly. Consequently, purchasing requires a special knowledge of products and a firm grasp of specifications development and of negotiating and contracting techniques. It is a function which logically should be performed by a professional purchasing agent with responsibility for all procurement activities within a jurisdiction. Purchasing is a vital tool of management, and the purchasing function is most appropriately carried out under the general direction of the chief administrative office of a jurisdiction rather than at the departmental level.

There are several advantages to programed centralized purchasing: (1) Lower prices may be obtained through volume buying, (2) the quality of goods purchased can be improved through the development of adequate specifications, (3) there is better opportunity to test and inspect products, (4) centralized records and storage facilities are available, (5) items used by many agencies throughout the jurisdiction will be recognized, and (6) a systematic program can be developed and operated for the salvage of obsolete supplies. It would be difficult for most individual departments to operate such programs with their own limited resources.

Some jurisdictions are not of sufficient size to justify the employment of a specialized employee such as a purchasing agent. Frequently, in smaller jurisdictions, the city manager or other local official assumes the centralized purchasing responsibility for all jurisdictional purchases.

There is no need for purchasing to be conducted by individual departments, especially in smaller jurisdictions where volume buying is a significant improvement over departmental buying. The individual department is, of course, the judge of the type of equipment or other supplies best suited to its needs; but this does not mean that the department should conduct its own purchasing program.

Role of Police Department. The police department should identify its needs and assist in the development of specifications to be used in the purchase of items. On occasion, the police department should also perform tests of various types of equipment or supplies to aid in the systematic evaluation of products, a role performed by any department within the jurisdiction.

Intergovernmental Purchasing. Most equipment and supplies utilized by one jurisdiction are the same as those utilized by its neighbors, as responsibilities are commonly the same. Thus, purchasing is very susceptible to a joint or coordinated program. Any intergovernmental purchasing program should not be conducted on a department-to-department basis, but rather should involve entire jurisdictions.

A comprehensive intergovernmental purchasing program was the focus of a detailed study prepared by the Metropolitan Fund, Inc., for the Detroit metropolitan area.[32] The study pointed out the various areas in which cooperative, centralized purchasing could be undertaken between governments, and a program to implement joint purchasing was developed. Certainly, purchases necessary for the operation of a police department could be included in such a joint purchasing program.

Studies of possibilities of joint purchasing have been made in several States, including California,[33] Idaho,[34]

---

[31] "The Christian Science Monitor," Dec. 8, 1966, 1e: 1.
[32] C. T. Hardwick, "Purchasing Study of Local Government in the Southeast Michigan Metropolitan Six-County Region" (Detroit: Metropolitan Fund, Inc., 1965).
[33] James D. Kitchen, "Cooperative Governmental Purchasing" (Los Angeles: University of California, Los Angeles, Bureau of Governmental Research, 1953).
[34] Robert J. Huckshorn, Waino M. Peterson, and A. M. Rich, "Cooperative Centralization of Purchasing for Idaho Municipalities" (University of Idaho, Bureau of Public Affairs Research, 1962).

and Pennsylvania.[35] Los Angeles County now performs a number of purchasing functions for municipalities within the county, and Dade County, Fla., also provides some purchasing services for smaller municipalities within the county.

An example from Pennsylvania illustrates how joint purchasing activities could be beneficial to police departments.[36] It was suggested that a centralized specification agency be established to prepare detailed specifications for products to be purchased. Among the sample specifications are those for two products which every police department utilizes—gasoline and police cars. Pooling the resources of a number of governmental units, complete and detailed specifications were developed which could be of considerable value to all governments—even if actual purchases were not performed jointly. It is doubtful that individual police departments, acting on their own, could have had access to all the information available to the group that developed the specifications.

OTHER STAFF SERVICES

Three staff functions remain to be considered—public information, internal investigation, and intradepartmental staff inspections. Basically, these are responsibilities of the individual chief police administrator, and it is doubtful whether they can be divorced from his immediate control. Many police administrators, however, could profit from what other police departments are doing in these areas, and for this reason there are some limited possibilities for coordination in these functions.

Public Information. In a public information program, primary emphasis should be placed on planning and performing activities which will keep the public aware of what the police are planning and doing. One of the crucial problems, particularly in metropolitan areas, is that many people live and work in different jurisdictions. The life of the suburban resident may be regulated more, and his property protected as much, by the central city police department as by the police department of the community in which he lives. For example, in one Chicago suburban community, 65 percent of the working residents are employed outside the community, primarily in Chicago.[37]

With this in mind, a practical, cooperative public information program could be developed by the central city department and the suburban departments to inform the mobile public and solicit its assistance in observing and reporting suspicious circumstances, and in adopting protective practices designed to forestall burglaries, larcenies, child molestations, and other criminal actions. Such a program could consist of joint appearances at informational programs conducted in the suburban communities, distribution of literature describing the activities of the participating departments, and visits to business and industry to analyze needs, promote sound security practices, and so on. Such joint efforts should do much to improve the image of the central city department, to upgrade the public information programs of the suburban departments, and to stimulate cooperation by the public in many needed ways.

Internal Investigation. In large departments, internal investigation for control purposes is often performed by a unit responsible for providing assistance to line commanders and the chief of police. As discipline is a function of command, it therefore is primarily the responsibility of the individual commanders to oversee this activity. It is usually the line commander's responsibility to control the investigation of complaints against his officers and to ferret out any evidence of corruption in the force. The existence of a separate unit with the sole function of assisting line commanders, however, is of considerable value. At times, this unit will also conduct internal investigations, unknown to line commanders, under the direction of the chief police administrator.

Most large departments have internal investigation units, but small departments usually cannot afford such units and have no place to turn for this assistance. Here outside assistance might sometimes prove valuable. Commenting on this problem, the city manager of a community of 75,000 population mentioned that his department was conducting an internal investigation and needed assistance; but there was no person or agency to which it could turn.[38] This situation describes the condition in a majority of departments.

Pooling resources in internal investigation is fraught with dangers. As has been mentioned, discipline is a function of command, and for this reason, outside assistance might be considered interference. Moreover, many jurisdictions would not be interested in becoming involved in the internal affairs of another jurisdiction. There are also problems implicit in the nature of internal investigation, problems that are not uncommon in an internal investigation operation serving only one department.

Nevertheless, there are enough instances when outside assistance is needed that there should be available an agency totally detached from the normal channels of internal investigation. In California, the attorney general has a constitutional responsibility for coordinating and supervising the activites of the local law enforcement agencies. The department which he heads—the department of justice—is the principal integrating agency for all police functions within the State. Through the efforts of this department, cooperation between all elements of California law enforcement has been achieved. At the same time, however, the attorney general has the responsibility for initiating investigations pertaining to local law enforcement corruption. It is difficult to visualize an agency which has both the responsibility for inducing cooperation and the duty to enforce police morality. It would seem that an agency which has these conflicting objectives must relax one activity to achieve the objectives of the other. Nevertheless, a unit in the office of the State attorney general may be of significant value on matters of internal investigation, provided that this is its only function.

---

[35] Association of Pennsylvania Municipal Managers, 1962 Research Committee, "Inter-Governmental Purchasing Agreements" (University of Pittsburgh, Institute of Local Government, 1962).
[36] Association of Pennsylvania Municipal Managers, 1962 Research Committee, "The Establishment of a Centralized Specification Agency" (University of Pittsburgh, Institute of Local Government, 1962), pp. 9–13.
[37] Northeastern Illinois Metropolitan Area Planning Commission, "Suburban Factbook" (Chicago: NIMAPC, 1962), unpaged. See: Table 17, "Commuting Characteristics, Employed Residents of Suburban Northeastern Illinois Municipalities, 1960."
[38] Interview with Wayne F. Anderson, city manager, Evanston, Ill., June 28, 1966.

In Wisconsin, such conflicting objectives have resulted in the demise of a unit in the attorney general's office.[39] This unit was concerned with two things: (1) Organized crime and (2) problems of internal affairs. Its usefulness in organized crime investigation was hampered as a result of investigations of possible corruption in a large municipal police department. It was reported that Wisconsin law enforcement officials would not cooperate with this unit in crime investigation activities because of its role in the investigation of specific police departments. This is not to say that both activities ought not to be performed; it is only to say that they should be separated.

Perhaps what is needed in every State is a unit which is completely independent, and has no responsibilities other than assisting local law enforcement with problems of internal affairs and, on its own initiative, conducting investigations. To give these units no other responsibilities would enhance their utility. A State unit for internal investigation would be a logical extension of the principle upon would local units are based.

Staff Inspection. In large departments, the chief often assigns staff inspections to a separate unit. The primary interest of a staff inspector is in discovering and examining specific areas where irregularities and weaknesses occur and in keeping supervisory officers informed about them, so that corrective action may be taken. He is not basically concerned with evidences of breaches of integrity but is responsible for identifying and reporting them.

The role of the staff inspector is conditioned by the provisions of a departmental plan. If there is a plan that all units are to follow, it is the duty of the staff inspector to determine that they are all carrying it out. For example, if the department has a plan to be followed in crime reporting, the staff inspector must inspect case reports for compliance with it. Nearly every police department has a manual of rules and regulations; it is the staff inspector, in addition to the line commander, who determines that these rules and regulations are being followed.

Unless two or more departments agree on following similar plans, it is unfeasible to establish coordinated staff inspections. Situations such as in California, requiring submission of crime reports to the State, necessitate some control over local reporting procedures. Staff inspectors from the California Department of Justice are responsible for assuring compliance with this mandatory requirement. All in all, it would seem that intradepartmental staff inspection has little susceptibility for coordination. However, staff inspection on a statewide basis in conjunction with certain State standards is a distinct possibility.

COORDINATION AND CONSOLIDATION OF AUXILIARY SERVICES

Auxiliary services are nonline functions other than staff services which provide technical, special, or supportive services to line or other nonline elements of a law enforcement agency. They include records and communications, detention, laboratory services, and buildings and equipment. After field services, auxiliary services are the most costly part of police management. Generally, auxiliary services as a group are susceptible to joint performance between or among law enforcement agencies.

RECORDS SERVICES

The value of a complete criminal records system to the police effort is well-established. In the words of O. W. Wilson, "The effectiveness of a police department is directly related to the quality of its records."[40] Records are needed:

☐ To provide the information from which intelligent decisions can be made in matching government resources to community needs.
☐ To provide the information to be communicated within and between departments so that police objectives can be accomplished effectively.
☐ To assist in the supervision and control of personnel and the measurement of their accomplishments.
☐ To inform the public.

Advantages of Areawide Central Records. The advantages of an areawide central records operation are an extension of the advantages of a departmental central records system. A departmental central records operation involves the consolidation of all key aspects of criminal, traffic, and service-to-the-public records under a single command. The concept of a central records system is not new. Wilson concluded in 1942 that:[41]

The extent to which the records system facilitates police management * * * depends in large measure upon how it is organized and administered * * *. The records unit is the information center of the police department * * *. All phases of police records work must be fitted together to form an integrated system * * *. A well-administered central records system contributes to the effective operation and management of the police department. A centralized system places the responsibility for the effectiveness of records work in a single division head.

There are many reasons why the concept of a central records system should be expanded to encompass many jurisdictions. Some of the more meaningful advantages are discussed below.

When basic information collected by many jurisdictions is centralized in one place, an inquiring jurisdiction need check only one source for information rather than several. Centralization eliminates duplication of effort and facilitates and reduces the possibility of error, and increases the speed with which an inquiry or search can be handled. For example, when each department in Alameda County, Calif., maintained its own warrant files, the time required for one department to check all of these files was over 39 minutes. When the files were consolidated within the automated police information network (PIN), the total elapsed time from the moment a request was made until the information was received was reduced to less than 2 minutes.[42] The time would have been greater

---

[39] Interview with Prof. Herman Goldstein, University of Wisconsin Law School, June 29, 1966.
[40] Supra, note 22 at p. 384. A more comprehensive description of police records may be found in chapter 11 of the Commission's General Report and in the Task Force volume on Science and Technology.
[41] O. W. Wilson, "Police Records: Their Installation and Use" (Chicago: Public Administration Service, 1942), pp. 8–10.
[42] Bay Area Law Enforcement Information Control Study Committee, "Centralized Electronic Information System" (unpaged, no date).

if a computerized system were not employed, but it still would have been enough less to justify centralization.

If an areawide records operation includes the collection and compilation of statistics, reporting and documentation can be reduced, an accurate overview of crime in the area may be obtained, and detailed analysis of the data will be possible.

A jurisdiction that turns certain records over to an areawide operation may eliminate related files. In the Dade County, Fla., area, for example, one department eliminated its accident report file when the Dade County Public Safety Department instituted centralized collection, processing, and filing of accident reports.[43]

Finally, areawide centralization may result in a reduction of personnel involved in records operations. When the Los Angeles Police Department turned over its stolen property files to the State bureau of criminal identification and investigation (CII), it was able to reduce its work force by 10 people and the CII needed to add only two. The only new cost to Los Angeles was a monthly charge for a telephone line to Sacramento.[44]

Scope of Areawide Central Records. The scope of an areawide records operation will depend upon, among other things, the geographical area covered, the quality of the participating agencies, and the support of the police administration involved. Classes of information that may be made available to all users include:

☐ Operational information services.
☐ Administrative information services.
☐ Reporting and statistical services.

Operational information services are concerned with information of value to field personnel. Included would be data relating to wanted persons, identification of suspects, stolen and wanted vehicles, and other stolen and recovered property.

Administrative information services are concerned with data of value to command and administrative personnel in making decisions. This type of data includes analytical reports based upon data gathered, along with operational information (e.g. time and location of incidents, workload measurement, clearance statistics and analysis, and personnel management data). This is one of the most valuable and least recognized uses of police records.

Reporting and statistical services relate to the collection of crime reporting information for general statistical uses and for compilation of annual or periodic reports to the FBI uniform crime reporting program and to State or local reporting programs. They also encompass central report recording and transcribing services.

The provision of operational information services appears to be most amenable to early implementation on an areawide basis, since there is at present some uniformity of demand, both in content and in volume. Incident reporting and other related data collection and distribution seem the next best suited. There is also sufficient experience with intradepartmental report recording and transcribing systems to warrant consideration of areawide systems.

The provision of administrative information services offers the greatest potential return for individual agencies, but will probably be the most difficult program to secure or to implement, because of a limited knowledge regarding the use of such information by many police administrators. Areawide centralization of vital information such as time and location of police services and manpower deployment is of paramount importance in the effective provision of police service. Until individual agencies, regardless of size, recognize the need for using police records to deploy police forces, the gains made in other uses of police records may be offset by improper or ineffective utilization of manpower.

Other Systems Considerations. A basic impediment to the development and effective use of areawide central records systems is the failure of management to recognize their purposes and values. There are certain records which must be decentralized. This, however, is not a valid argument against areawide central records operations which can provide information promptly to field personnel for use both in emergency and in routine situations, to police administrators to form the basis for sound administrative and operational decisions, and to the public to inform it on police problems and services.

The following factors should be considered in advance of any serious attempt to establish an areawide central records system or a data processing center to provide statistical, analytical, or general operational or administrative informational services.

☐ An effective areawide records system depends upon the utilization of the communications systems of the cooperating jurisdictions. The respective communications operations also must be integrated into a single system working in concert with the areawide records center to the extent that the two systems are interdependent.

☐ Information contained in an areawide central records file must be easily retrievable if the system is to realize its full potential. Data of immediate concern to local agencies (e.g. traffic warrants) should be available locally, while State or Federal systems could house other types of information serving broader needs.

☐ Areawide records services can be effective only with the use of relatively expensive data processing equipment. Therefore, careful study of both the immediate and the long-range costs of an areawide central records operation must precede any decision to establish it. The cost of such equipment may be beyond the ability of the jurisdictions considering the areawide service or may not be justified by volume of work, relative needs, and potential service return.

☐ Lack of agreement on the content of a program would seriously weaken it; therefore, in any areawide records undertaking, all participants must agree upon the type and level of information services to be provided.

---

[43] International Association of Chiefs of Police, "A Survey of Police Services In Metropolitan Dade County, Florida" (Washington: International Association of Chiefs of Police, 1963), p. 10L.

[44] Interview with Dr. John P. Kenney, deputy director, State of California Department of Justice, June 28, 1966.

☐ The information services of police departments vary widely in form and content, and the potential for human or machine error would probably be greater with increased volume. Therefore, control of the quality of information put into an areawide system is especially critical. Control over the timely addition or cancellation of information also becomes increasingly a problem when many jurisdictions are involved.

Organization for Areawide Records Systems. Determination of the size of the area to be served by a central records system presents some problems. Although it is usually less costly and more effective to perform certain functions and maintain certain files for a large than for a small area, the size of the area must be related to the uses to be made of files and the need for immediate service. Time and distance influence the physical location of files and services. For example, police reports must be available to courts or copies provided the public without undue delay. Decentralized demands point up the need to recognize the limits of physical and functional centralization.

The possibilities for areawide records services range from a single National system with various subsystems to State systems, with or without intersystem communications capabilities, to local systems, which can serve as effective areawide records centers. Most current records systems are oriented toward providing operational and/or statistical information, while very few yet provide administrative informational services.

A National System. At the Federal level, the existence of the Federal Bureau of Investigation's (FBI) fingerprint collection attests to the long-time recognition that police records can be centralized on a nationwide basis. Factors of time and distance, however, have mitigated against full use of this system, and many local and State systems also have been developed.

The FBI is also embarking upon an operational information services program which will result in the National Crime Information Center (NCIC). The philosophy behind the establishment of the NCIC is stated as follows: [45]

The logical development of electronic information systems proceeds from local metropolitan systems to statewide systems and then to a national system. In effect, each succeeding system would afford greater geographical coverage. The information stored at each level will depend on actual need, with local metropolitan systems naturally having a data base much broader than that of either the statewide or national system. It is most important to avoid any concept that a national system eliminates the need for systems of lesser geographical scope—metropolitan and statewide systems must develop to serve local needs which could not possibly be met by any national systems. The ultimate nationwide network will not be achieved until such systems develop in each State and the larger metropolitan population centers.

The concept of the NCIC is clear. It is intended to complement, not to replace, local and State systems. The National system should be a coordinating mechanism that will further the exchange of information of mutual concern among smaller, independent but coordinated systems. Provision should be made for use of the system by Federal and regional law enforcement agencies, but parallel or duplicatory systems should be avoided unless for specific backup purposes.

Almost everyone in law enforcement is familiar with the FBI's uniform crime reporting program. From its inception in 1930, this voluntary nationwide program has become progressively valuable to the Nation in documenting the crime problem. Despite its voluntary nature, law enforcement agencies serving over 92 percent of the Nation's population submit data to the program.

State Systems. To date, most of the statewide records systems are manual or mechanized programs dealing with the collection and compilation of simple crime statistics; the provision of clearinghouse service in matters concerning the identification of criminals, victims, and other persons, and wanted or found property and the provision of auto and driver license registration information. Some also provide rudimentary modus operandi and/or crime analysis.

The California Department of Justice, particularly its bureaus of criminal identification and investigation (CII) and of criminal statistics, has long been involved in providing areawide records services to California law enforcement agencies. Services go well beyond the functions normally performed by "State bureaus." The CII alone employs more than 500 persons in activities directly related to operational information services.

The bureau of criminal statistics, concerned primarily with statistical functions, employs more than 40 persons and has an annual budget of approximately $370,000. Its statewide coverage and the fact that the reporting to it of crime is mandatory make the California system perhaps the most complete and accurate in the Nation. Its annual publications, "Crime in California, Delinquency and Probation in California," and "Drug Arrests and Dispositions in California," indicate how far the bureau of criminal statistics has gone in providing local jurisdictions with meaningful statistics. Such a statewide statistical program has several advantages and should be considered when attempting to support and augment the uniform crime reporting program.

The California system may be modified if electronic data processing techniques are introduced. The "total system" approach which is being considered would include not only the CII files for operational information services, but also those of the CII maintained for the

---

[45] "A National Crime Information Center," FBI Law Enforcement Bulletin, May 1966, p. 3.

statistical purposes of the bureau of criminal statistics, files of the bureau of narcotic enforcement, and files of agencies outside the Department of Justice (e.g., Judicial, correctional, motor vehicle registration, and State highway patrol).

There is increasing interest in other States in providing total systems. The New York State identification and intelligence system is being planned to include not only police data, but also data from the files of courts, prosecutors, probation and parole agencies, and correctional institutions.

The proposed Michigan Law Enforcement Information Network (LEIN), to be operated by the Michigan State police, will start with a computer-based file of stolen and wanted vehicles and warrants and then be expanded to include much more data. Plans call for 35 terminals located throughout the State and for complete financing of the system, including terminals and lines, by the State.[46]

There are also some existing or proposed Statewide systems of more limited scope. The California Highway Patrol operates Autostatis (automated statewide auto theft inquiry system), a Statewide file of stolen and suspicious vehicles accessible "on-line" to over 200 police agencies via 150 teletype terminals. The use made of this system is indicated by the fact that approximately 9,000 inquiries per day are logged and, on the average, 1,200 daily file changes are made.[47] A similar system is being readied for implementation by the New York State Police.

Metropolitan Systems. At the local level, the best example of a records system of areawide importance is the Bay Area Police Information Network (PIN). PIN was conceived by the Bay Area Law Enforcement Information Control Study Committee, a group composed of representatives of police agencies in the San Francisco Bay area. The distinguishing features of PIN are its (1) limited scope, (2) areawide nature, (3) "real-time" emphasis, and (4) use of the existing county data processing facility. It was decided early in the planning stage that PIN would be limited to warrants, both criminal and traffic, rather than become involved in a "total systems" approach. In its second progress report, the Bay Area Study Committee states:[48]

While the committee is mindful of the "total systems" approach it is also of the conviction that any "total system" must be based upon local needs and must develop from local experience. Hence * * * our first concern should be to establish * * * an active warrant * * * program and utilize our experience to build toward the "total system". A "total systems" approach would involve a massive conversion of existing * * * files and entry into a new program on such a scale that, while we are certain that the concept is sound, failure * * * could be both economically and politically disastrous.

It was felt that the warrants systems of all area police agencies were sufficiently alike, whereas other records lacked uniformity to a degree which prevented including them in the initial system. Plans call for additional application when possible.

PIN is an areawide service. Each of the 13 police agencies in Alameda County has access to the computerized warrant file without charge; and police agencies outside Alameda County have access upon payment of the following charges:[49]

☐ Terminals, data sets, and lines: 100 percent of actual cost.
☐ Hardware costs: 3½ cents per warrant input per month.
☐ Personnel and other nonhardware costs: $1 per 1,000 population per month.

Charges have been set low to encourage participation by police agencies outside Alameda County. When the 18 cities in San Mateo County became part of PIN, the county assumed all of their costs.

The Chicago Police Department has an automated file of stolen cars and wanted persons. The file contains the following information: Stolen cars, wanted persons, stop orders, criminal and traffic warrants (names), mental institution stop orders, military stop orders, missing persons, revoked and suspended drivers' licenses and licenses of vehicles driven by known criminals. There are some plans to make this file available to other departments through terminals and lines directly to the computer. Several advantages would ensue: (1) An existing data processing facility would be more fully utilized, (2) the system would cover a larger area, and (3) a step would be taken toward a regional records center with data collected from as well as disseminated to additional agencies. The last advantage is perhaps the most important.

Conclusions. In summary, the following conclusions can be drawn from an examination of existing and proposed large area systems:

☐ The scope of a coordinated or consolidated records operation must be based upon such factors as area, population size and concentration, quality and quantity of law enforcement services, and the relative needs of each type or kind of data services.
☐ The appropriations of a particular joint records system should be determined in part by an evaluation of the capabilities of the several agencies to contribute to and use the system.
☐ There are certain readily identifiable classes of data which lend themselves to joint or consolidated recording. They include especially data concerned with operational or field matters and administrative information regarding the analysis of crime and deployment of personnel.
☐ The State should assume major responsibility in the direction and coordination of law enforcement data systems, including the total provisions of certain information services, and support of qualified local or regional systems within the larger system.
☐ An area or statewide system encompassing several major operational information services (e.g., wanted persons, stolen property, stolen autos) should be implemented at the metropolitan level whenever

---

[46] Interview with Capt. John Brown, deputy director, Michigan State Police, Aug. 17, 1966.
[47] Letter from Bradford Crittenden, commissioner, California Highway Patrol, Aug. 15, 1966.

[48] Bay Area Law Enforcement Information Control Study Committee, "Second Regular Progress Report," May 19, 1964, p. 16.
[49] Letter from Gordon F. Milliman, chief, Data Processing Center, Alameda County, Calif., June 9, 1966.

circumstances warrant. However, the State can also perform these services, provided it receives adequate support at the local level.

☐ The receipt and analysis of crime statistics is a proper responsibility of the State. A State program should include the receipt and analysis of crime reports, mandatorily submitted by local departments, and the submission of statistics to the Federal Bureau of Investigation.

☐ Care must be taken in implementing records systems which bring together data from many varied sources of dissimilar responsibilities for the purpose of providing a single, all-encompassing file. Total systems which include information from many other agencies could easily jeopardize the real and meaningful value of a police information exchange.

COMMUNICATIONS [50]

Perhaps the most perplexing situation confronting police communications is the multiplicity of single department radio systems, sometimes sharing the same frequency, in most metropolitan centers. As Professor Misner points out, the availability of communications equipment may tend to aggravate the problems associated with the fragmentation of police resources.[51]

Current Trends. There are enough examples of coordinated and consolidated communications systems to indicate some recognition of this need.

Radio. Perhaps the most usual means of integrating communications systems is through interjurisdictional agreements for the joint use of police radio. The primary motivation for such agreements is cost. When new departments are established, or existing departments decide to become radio equipped, they often join with other departments to provide radio communications or seek service from an established system.

In a 1960 study of interjurisdictional agreements in the Philadelphia area,[52] it was found that agreements covering police radio communications were the most numerous and inclusive. There was a total of 107 agreements encompassing 112 of the 128 departments that had radio-equipped cars, and 13 stations provided this service for the 112 departments. Thus, each station served an average of more than 8 departments, with the range from 2 to 35 departments.

The normal agreement in this area included the provision of full dispatching and maintenance services for an annual charge, with both the base station and the mobile units purchased by the central agency. A second type of agreement provided that individual agencies purchase the mobile equipment, with parts charged at cost, and the central maintenance and dispatching were provided without charge. A third type provided that the individual agencies buy the mobile units and pay for parts and services, with central dispatching available without charge.

In suburban Lake County, Ill., to the north of Chicago, the county communications department operates a radio net for some 20 police departments with base stations and mobile units on a contractual basis. Included in the contract charges are the cost of the equipment and complete maintenance. The county takes out the licenses and thus controls the use of the system, but each department handles its own dispatching.[53]

In the Cleveland suburban area, 26 police departments provide communications services for a total of 64 departments. Thus, communities which cannot afford, or do not wish to operate, their own base station can benefit from the facilities of established departments. The largest of these systems, operated by University Heights, services 13 departments with complete dispatching. The weakness in this system, however, occurs prior to dispatching. Each department answers its own telephones and then relays the information to the dispatcher, a practice that entails delay. Moreover, several departments do not have 24-hour answering service, and contract with private answering services or use other stopgap measures.[54] Ideally, all emergency phone calls should come directly to the dispatching facilities at all times.

Twenty-seven police departments in Dade County, Fla., are serviced by five separate radio systems operated by the Dade County Public Safety Department and the cities of Miami, Miami Beach, Coral Gables, and Hialeah. The Dade County and Miami systems are used by other jurisdictions; the others are used only at the base station city. The Dade County system provides complete radio service free of charge, including telephone answering and dispatching, but each using department must purchase its own mobile radio equipment. The Miami system provides complete service for a monthly charge which covers rental and maintenance of equipment and dispatching. Some departments favor contracting with the Miami system because they do not have to purchase their own equipment.

The successful use of interjurisdictional agreements for the provision of police communication services indicates that when service is economical, facilities are maintained in good order, and cars are dispatched promptly and with precision, radio communications is a police function which can be consolidated.

One of the more common practices in metropolitan areas is the monitoring or cross-monitoring of radio frequencies of adjacent departments. The advantages of cross-monitoring are essentially of an operational nature, but seldom does it result in substantial efficiencies in operation. There is usually no formal agreement between the agencies concerned, and the action taken as the result of an intercepted message is generally voluntary. Further it does not resolve the more fundamental problems of a multiplicity of radio broadcasting stations.

Much the same may be said of the intersystem networks found throughout the Nation. Commonly called point-to-point nets, these systems provide a "party line" that enables a dispatcher in one department to talk with a dispatcher in another. These point-to-point systems carry a considerable amount of administrative traffic,

---

[50] Police communications are discussed in some detail in chapter 11 of the General Report and in the Task Force volume on Science and Technology.
[51] Supra, note 1 at p. 502.
[52] George S. Blair, "Interjurisdictional Agreements in Southeastern Pennsylvania" (Philadelphia: University of Pennsylvania, Fels Institute of Local and State Government, 1961), pp. 38–45.
[53] Interview with Jay McClaskey, supervisor, Lake County Communications Department, June 4, 1966.
[54] Cleveland Metropolitan Services Commission, "Police Protection in Cuyahoga County" (Cleveland: Cleveland Metropolitan Services Commission, 1958), pp. 38–39.

particularly vehicle registration requests and wanted person property checks. However, the basic purpose of these networks is for interjurisdictional communication on emergency matters.

An emerging pattern is a point-to-point system which enables a car on a one-radio system to communicate with a car on another system in emergencies. Such a system, the Illinois State Police Emergency Radio Net (ISPERN), is being implemented in Illinois. In order to establish the communication net, the Illinois State Police relinquished one frequency, and placed it under the control of a governing board to which any police agency desiring access must apply. Once admitted, the agency installs equipment in its mobile units that enables it to broadcast over the ISPERN frequency to all other mobile units on it. Thus far, approximately 30 Illinois police agencies have received permission to install equipment utilizing the ISPERN frequency.

Teletype. Interjurisdictional use of teletype communications has been one of the significant cooperative efforts in law enforcement. Teletype communications networks now span the country through the Law Enforcement Teletype System (LETS). Each State has some form of teletype network linking many or most law enforcement agencies in the State. County systems are on the increase, as are systems linking central cities and their surrounding suburban areas. Direct teletype links with computerized records centers are also utilized by some police agencies.

LETS consists of six circuits, each with a control station and a line running to a switching center in Phoenix, Ariz. When a message is directed to another network or to all networks, the Phoenix center automatically handles the routing and switching according to the coded message instructions received from the sending station. Each of the control stations pays for a share of the equipment common to the entire system. This consists of lines, switching center equipment, and circuit control stations. Because of variations in needs, each station assumes the cost of its own equipment.

At the local level, 11 California counties operate teletype networks, some free of charge to all participating municipalities. The county networks are linked into a statewide system operated by the California Department of Justice. Also, numerous municipal departments and other law enforcement related agencies are linked through the State network. In the Chicago area, several teletype networks link the Chicago Police Department with numerous suburban police departments and with the Illinois State Police. Similar nets are found in most metropolitan areas.

Current Problems. Despite the extensive use of interjurisdictional radio agreements, intersystem radio communications, and nationwide teletype service, much more coordination and consolidation is necessary in order to develop complete areawide communications systems.

One of the primary problems is the existence of many separate police communications systems in close proximity particularly in metropolitan areas. When these systems share the same frequency, the situation becomes acute. Emergency calls in one department are often blotted out by routine calls in other departments which perhaps could have been handled differently.

Other problems relate to the cost of maintaining and operating separate communications systems and to the belief of many police administrators that they lose control over field personnel if radio dispatching is provided by another agency. In its study of police services in Dade County, the International Association of Chiefs of Police commented: [55]

Each system maintains its own service facilities * * * and its own complaint dispatching staff. Each system is looked upon * * * as an important part of the department's operations, and a function which cannot be assigned to another agency without serious loss of supervision and control.

Although his opinion is not universally held, Sheriff Pitchess of Los Angeles County feels that radio communications need not be handled by each individual department if there is available to it a system operated and maintained by a competent central agency.[56]

In the use of teletype communications, cost is still a problem for smaller jurisdictions. Existing systems require the lease of costly telephone lines, and unless State systems pay some or all of the cost of lines, or cost is otherwise reduced, participation by small jurisdictions will not reach its full potential.

Many intersystem teletype systems have fallen into disuse because of continued use of point-to-point radio for routine information needs. A distinction must be made between the two types of systems so that teletype is used for routine information purposes and point-to-point systems reserved for emergency communications.

Possible Solutions. At present, the problems of radio communications are more serious than those of telecommunications. Indeed, coordinated police use of teletype has reached a high point. It is not suggested here that problems in the use of police radio can be solved by consolidating all radio systems in a particular area, for the chances of implementing such a program are not great.

Increased use of interjurisdictional agreements covering radio communications is a possible approach in many areas. Such agreements should include maintenance, dispatching, and telephone answering services. Through contracting for radio services, equipment costs could be reduced, irrelevant communications controlled, and in some instances, positions collapsed or personnel diverted to other tasks.

Short of agreements that would remove the responsibility for radio dispatching from some jurisdictions, much could be done to solve the communications muddle through the use of effective radio-dispatching procedures and dispatcher training.

Improvements will depend, however, upon coordinating agencies, such as the Federal Communications Commission (FCC), giving concentrated attention to police radio communications problems. It is doubtful that the

---

[55] Supra, note 43 at pp. 239–240.
[56] Peter J. Pitchess, sheriff, Los Angeles County, Calif., in "Law Enforcement Regionalization Seminar: Discussion Notes, June 28, 1966" (unpublished, Chicago: Public Administration Service, 1966), pp. 28–29.

present State frequency advisory committees of the FCC, with their limited approach, can meet this need.

The FCC could adopt a policy by which its license granting procedures are handled through the State. Such a policy should assign the States more authority to supervise public safety communications. A State agency could establish standards for and techniques to evaluate the conduct of local police radio, recommend the amalgamation of radio communications systems where feasible, deny licenses to those police agencies which could readily use another agency's communications system, and establish and operate statewide nets for intersystem police radio communications. The merger of radio communications systems should be encouraged through State grants-in-aid.

If the FCC gives the States the power to enforce and coordinate police radio responsibilities, the States would be provided with a valuable management tool and the power of the FCC to regulate civilian communications would be enhanced. Because they are interstate in nature, agencies such as large port authorities should be exempted from conducting business with the FCC through one particular State agency.

Conclusions. On the basis of the above analysis of present problems in police communications, the following conclusions seem warranted:

☐ Areawide communications systems should be developed in concert with areawide records centers to the extent that the two systems are interdependent.

☐ The State should be granted greater power to regulate the use of police radio, including the authority to establish operational standards and to recommend the amalgamation of two or more communications systems. The State's responsibility in this area could be enhanced through the use of grants-in-aid.

☐ Greater use should be made of interjurisdictional agreements whereby one system can provide complete radio communications for two or more jurisdictions.

☐ Police teletype networks should be used increasingly for routine police communications, thus making intersystem radio communications systems available for strictly emergency uses.

DETENTION FACILITIES AND SERVICES [57]

Throughout the country, most detained and sentenced persons are housed in local detention facilities. State and Federal penal institutions normally hold prisoners serving more than a 1-year sentence, whereas local jails or stockades seldom house prisoners for more than 1 year. Local institutions usually hold defendants in felony cases during the judicial process. Upon sentencing, they are sent to State or Federal institutions.

Current Local Practices. Many local police administrators believe that it is necessary to maintain a local detention facility. Nearly every police department has at least a holding facility for temporary detention and many operate full-scale jails, although most are not adequate according to modern penological standards. In many States, sheriffs are required by law to operate such facilities.

Accepted principles of jail management are that prisoners must be segregated by sex, age, and type of crime; be secure; have ample opportunity for work and recreational activity; live under sanitary conditions; and be provided a well-balanced diet. The capital outlay for the personnel, equipment, and facilities needed to meet these standards is prodigious, even in a modest undertaking. For example, to provide continuous round-the-clock supervision of prisoners by one correctional officer requires approximately five full-time men working 40-hour weeks. Such supervision would require an annual outlay of at least $30,000, if the salary and fringe benefits of each officer amount to $6,000 per year.

The most common problems faced by municipal and county jail administrators, according to a State of Washington survey, is a severe shortage of personnel.[58] Many local jails are not supervised round-the-clock by persons on duty in the building, even when prisoners are confined in them. Prisoners are locked in cells, often under unsafe conditions, and helpless in case of disaster. Some jailkeepers, concerned about this problem, have gone so far as to leave cells or even jails unlocked when prisoners are without supervision to obviate potential danger.

In evaluating the local jail program in the State of Washington, the department on institutions noted, "In some instances the best thing that can be said is that the jail is seldom used."[59] It concludes that many local jails are inadequately staffed, poorly maintained, and inefficiently operated. The mere fact that some jails receive only limited use is a sound argument for the elimination of unnecessary facilities and the operation of joint detention programs.

Local jail problems in the State of Washington are in no way unique. For example, Connecticut over the years experienced many similar ills, and dissatisfaction with local jail administration was a factor contributing to the abolishment in 1960 of all county governments.[60]

As an alternative to county jails operated by elected sheriffs, Connecticut established an office of State jail administrator, responsible to the Governor, with control over the detention of all local prisoners throughout the State. This system is separate from the State penal institutions. Jail personnel of the old county system were absorbed into the State merit system at appropriate levels wherever possible. Old facilities were demolished and physical improvements made when necessary. Local police agencies do not operate detention facilities other than units to hold prisoners temporarily until they can be transferred to a nearby State facility.[61]

This type of solution appeals to Sheriff Pitchess of Los Angeles County, who operated the largest county detention facility in the country. In his opinion, the custodial function should be separated from the police, and he

---

[57] The issue of whether police agencies should maintain detention facilities is also discussed in chapter 6 of the General Report.
[58] State of Washington, Department of Institutions, "Jail Information Report" (Olympia: State of Washington, Department of Institutions, Nov. 17, 1964), sec. 1, p. 3.
[59] Id. at sec. 1, p. 2.
[60] Rosaline Levenson, "County Government in Connecticut—Its History and Demise" (Storrs, Conn.: University of Connecticut, Institute of Public Service, 1966), pp. 83–95.
[61] Id. at pp. 165–168, 182–185.

suggests that the proper office to operate it might be the State correctional agency.⁶²

Sheriff Pitchess normally has some 11,000 inmates in custody at any given time, operates one of the most modern jails in the country, and has approximately 1,200 personnel engaged in full-time jail or correctional duties. This operation represents approximately 40 percent of the sheriff's total budget of $50 million, yet he would be willing to turn over complete control of the jail to a qualified agency, and operate his department strictly as a police agency.

The question has been raised whether it is even necessary for the police to be responsible for temporary holding facilities. Many chiefs of police contend that they need to have jail facilities to provide ready access to prisoners for investigative purposes. This argument has increasingly limited validity in light of recent U.S. Supreme Court decisions concerning the interrogation of prisoners. In reference to this question, Prof. Herman Goldstein of the University of Wisconsin Law School says: ⁶³

> The mere fact that [the police] have custody of the individual for a period of time, that he is under their control, has created the widespread image that in this period of time he is subjected to a great deal of coercion and pressure * * * Anyone familiar with this system recognizes that the demands on a prisoner * * * are not that great * * * It seems to me that there is great value in ridding the police of this responsibility, so that * * * once the police arrest an individual they turn him over to an independent agency * * * which has no vested interest in the case, and is not out to prove the man's guilt * * * it places the police in a much more favorable light.

An independent agency responsible for detention seems the logical answer. Sheriff Pitchess feels nothing is accomplished if the detention responsibilities of municipal police departments are merely transferred to the local sheriff, unless the duties of the sheriff are redefined. "You would have the same problem and you would create the same evil in another place." ⁶⁴ If the sheriff operates only detention facilities, improved correctional and detention services are more possible; but if the sheriff remains a law enforcement official, and also has detention responsibilities, the problem has not been solved, merely shifted.

The system used in Connecticut, or in Rhode Island which has a similar detention program, offers the greatest possibility for improvement in jail management. Connecticut through its office of State jail administrator operates all local jails throughout the State in a system separated from the State penal system. This system has improved the management of detention facilities and created a more favorable public attitude regarding jails and law enforcement agencies. Under it, sound correctional training procedures can be developed, greater attention can be given to achieving and maintaining accepted penological standards, and more efficient organization and administration are possible.

In brief, the State should operate jails through an appropriate State agency, and local jails should be discontinued. A logical alternative or interim step would be to have the State agency operate existing facilities, even if they are located in local police buildings.

Police Officer or Correctional Officer. An additional problem at the county and municipal level is the use of sworn police officers in the care and custody of inmates. The work performed by a guard in a jail facility is quite different from the work that should be performed by a police officer, yet most county and municipal jails are operated by such officers. In the Chicago Police Department, for example, nearly 300 sworn police officers are used to operate temporary holding facilities and provide prisoner transportation services. If correctional officers were utilized, 300 additional trained police officers would be available for normal police duties.

The Los Angeles County Sheriff's Department has recently decided to turn, at least in part, to this system. It was found in Los Angeles County that recruitment was hindered because many potential police officers were not interested in working in a detention facility as is usually required at some point while working within the sheriff's department. Consequently, a decision was made to create the new position of corrections officer and use this employee in the minimum security institutions operated by the county.

One difficulty in this approach is evident in the practice of Los Angeles County. In the jail, which is a short-term holding facility where all types of inmates are housed, maximum security is a prime concern. Sentenced prisoners held by the county, however, usually are not convicted felons, and maximum security facilities normally are not necessary. Thus, the county is really operating two facilities—one for presentencing and detained prisoners and another for convicted prisoners sentenced for less than a 1-year period. A sound argument can be made for using sworn personnel in maximum security institutions where incidents are more probable and the risks greater, and correctional officers in minimum security institutions. This argument pertains, however, only to counties or municipalities that continue to provide detention services.

A corollary problem in using sworn police officers in detention work is that it creates a false impression of the number of police personnel available for law enforcement duties, for effective strength is reduced proportionately to the number of personnel utilized for detention.

Sharing Physical Facilities. Several alternatives, other than shifting detention operations to the State or redefining the responsibilities of the office of sheriff, are available. In 1958, the city of Tacoma and Pierce County, Wash., built a new city-county building which includes detention facilities. Each jurisdiction has its own jail, but kitchen and laundry facilities are operated jointly. This limited joint operation has also made it possible to use one facility to house certain catergories of offenders and the other facility to house others. For example, one jail confines all male juvenile prisoners, the other all female prisoners. In this way, neither the city

---

⁶² Supra, note 56 at pp. 8–10.
⁶³ Id. at p. 11.

⁶⁴ Id. at p. 12.

nor the county has to provide the total range of jail facilities.[65]

Basic philosophical or financial problems have arisen in some areas when the merger of two reasonably large jails or correctional systems is considered or contemplated. Efforts to bring the Miami, Fla., city jail system into the Dade County system have been unsuccessful, in spite of the fact that annual savings to the city of Miami would approximate $500,000, because the city of Miami expected compensation from Dade County for the sale of its facilities. The county takes the position that the public has already paid for the facility and to "purchase" it again is unnecessary. A similar difference occurred between the city and county of Los Angeles.

Short of the complete assimilation of one system into another, it is apparent that two jurisdictions can share facilities through a contractual arrangement. Such a program exists between Alameda County and Oakland, Calif., where, under the terms of the contract, Oakland pays the county for each city prisoner detained in the county jail and vice versa.[66]

Los Angeles County provides complete jail service on a contract basis for all cities in the county except Burbank, Glendale, Long Beach, Los Angeles, and Pasadena. The sheriff feels, however, that sufficient centralization has not yet taken place. He says:[67]

> Several custodial agencies should not have charge of the operation of custodial facilities in a metropolitan area. We are constantly in conflict with the larger cities. We take custody of all prisoners charged with felonies. The city which has custodial facilities keeps in custody its own misdemeanants and those charged with violations of the city ordinances.

The Puget Sound Governmental Conference in a recent report, recommended that a regional jail be established in a joint county jail district consisting of King, Kitsap, Pierce, and Snohomish Counties in the Seattle-Tacoma area.[68] The jail would be used for sentenced prisoners while the existing smaller units would be retained for presentence detention. King County is in the process of building a new facility which it is hoped will eventually become a regional jail under a joint jail district.

Conclusions. Municipal jails largely duplicate the services of county jails, especially in the holding of sentenced prisoners. Two sets of conclusions are offered regarding the operation of detention facilities. The first is based on the premise that municipalities will not operate their own facilities.

☐ Municipal police departments should not maintain their own detention facilities. They should turn such operations over to another governmental jurisdiction, preferably an independent State agency. Immediate detention facilities, although perhaps remaining within the walls of a police facility, should be administered by a separate agency.
☐ State governments should establish a jail administration agency with responsibility for the operation and management of all local detention facilities.
☐ If the State does not assume detention responsibilities, the county, through the office of sheriff, should operate all jails within the county. The sheriff, however, should not engage in law enforcement activities.

The second set of conclusions is based upon the premise that local governments will continue to operate jail detention facilities:

☐ Police officers should be used only in maximum security jails, and in supervisory positions, in the care and custody of inmates. Correctional officers should be utilized in minimum security jails.
☐ A number of local jurisdictions should join in the operation of detention facilities, sharing physical facilities under contractual agreements, eliminating duplicate facilities, or establishing jail districts.
☐ The State should establish minimum standards for the operation of jails, training of personnel, security, feeding programs, and related concerns. It should also maintain a full-time inspectional program.

LABORATORY SERVICES [69]

Laboratory services are essential to effective law enforcement. Success in complicated investigation may depend in large part upon the scientific evaluation of pertinent data. The import of recent U.S. Supreme Court decisions suggests that law enforcement agencies must depend increasingly upon scientific analysis of crimes rather than rely upon traditional methods such as interrogation of suspects.

Two distinct activities are involved in laboratory work: (1) The gathering of evidence at the scene of the crimes, and (2) the scientific analysis of evidence. Both activities are essential to the adequate evaluation and use of evidence. Evidence must be gathered and preserved according to established court criteria to guarantee its value in court testimony and for use in laboratory analysis. A laboratory technician can make a detailed and thorough analysis of evidence only if it has been properly gathered, labeled and handled before reaching the laboratory. Evidence that has been mishandled is not admissible in court proceedings.

Competent technicians and good equipment are essential to the success of any laboratory evaluation. This report does not attempt to suggest how many persons or what equipment is needed to perform minimal laboratory services. Suffice it to say that a good laboratory facility is beyond the means of almost all police departments in the United States.

Current Local Practices. The "crime laboratories" of many law enforcement agencies are primarily bureaus of identification which house a number of records but perform no real scientific analysis.[70] Other jurisdictions have fully equipped laboratories filled with the latest scientific tools, but no qualified technicians to operate them. One of the greatest obstacles to the development of regionally

---
[65] Supra, note 58 at sec. 2, p. 36.
[66] See app. A for details of the contract between Oakland and Alameda County.
[67] Supra, note 56 at p. 7.
[68] Puget Sound Governmental Conference, 1962, "Regional Joint County Jail District: A Feasibility Study" (Seattle: Puget Sound Governmental Conference, 1962), p. 15.

[69] For further discussion on crime laboratories, see chapter 11 of the General Report and the Task Force volume on Science and Technology.
[70] Paul L. Kirk and Lowell W. Bradford, "The Crime Laboratory: Organization and Operation" (Springfield, Ill.: Charles C. Thomas, 1965), p. 5.

oriented laboratory operations is the unwillingness of departments to lose their laboratories, even if they are not effectively utilized.

Local practices relating to laboratory services vary greatly. Evanston, Ill., for example, established a police laboratory in 1948, but the facility was never used, primarily because of lack of professional staff, and is now not operational.[71] In Arizona there is only one crime laboratory, that of the city of Phoenix. This facility performs all necessary tests, including some complex work, for the city police department, but services beyond the city are severely limited because it has only two full-time fully trained technicians.[72] The Sauk-Prairie Police Department, serving Sauk City and Prairie du Sac, Wis., sends materials needing scientific analysis to the Wisconsin State Crime Laboratory in Madison.[73] Kansas City, Mo., maintains a laboratory which is equipped to provide such basic services as blood analysis, toolmark identification, firearms identification, and some limited documents examination, but all more sophisticated laboratory work either is not done or is sent to the Federal Bureau of Investigation in Washington, D.C.

In sharp contrast is the laboratory operation of the Chicago Police Department. Operating one of the best equipped and staffed facilities in the country, the Chicago Police Laboratory in 1965 processed materials for 140 jurisdictions, including Federal and State agencies, counties, and other municipalities, in addition to its regular work for the Chicago department. Physical evidence submitted to the laboratory for scientific evaluation involved some 150,000 specimens requiring more than 250,000 individual examinations.[74]

The Chicago Police Department Laboratory serves the needs of the surrounding metropolitan area. With few exceptions, all municipalities in Cook County call upon it for specialized services, and these services are performed free of charge to any requesting agency with a legitimate need. Consequently, much more use is made in the Chicago area of scientific aids in criminal investigation than in many other sections of the country.

In addition to providing laboratory services, the Chicago Police Department will train the personnel of other departments, especially in the collection and preservation of physical evidence but also in some more technical operations. For example, the microanalysis section of the laboratory has the only staff within the Chicago area which can successfully group dry blood stains. The next closest facility with this capability is at the Wisconsin State Crime Laboratory in Madison and the technicians working there were trained by the Chicago Police Department.[75] Because of the capabilities of the Chicago Police Laboratory, and because the department is willing to serve all jurisdictions there is no need for other crime laboratories in the Chicago area.

Finally, since 1934, local agencies have submitted evidence linked to their more sophisticated cases to the FBI Laboratory in Washington, D.C., for analyses. In 1966, the Bureau's facility performed some 304,000 scientific examinations at no cost for local police forces from all 50 States, the District of Columbia, other Federal agencies, and several foreign nations.

Problems in Local Practice. This capsule summary of current local practices in police laboratory services indicates some pervasive problems. Proximity, timeliness, and quality are the most important measures of laboratory service. Some local police forces fail on all three counts because they do not perform scientific evaluations requiring sophisticated analysis, or fail to provide for tests. While it may make good sense for forces in the proximity of Washington, D.C., to use the facilities of the FBI exclusively for scientific analyses, the latter facilities may not be close enough for forces hundreds of miles distant to readily secure timely service. For example, one major police force largely ignores the facilities of the Food and Drug Administration which has a large regional laboratory adjacent to the police headquarters which is capable of performing most necessary examinations. Jurisdictions should attempt to resolve the questions of timeliness and proximity regionally.

Another problem is duplication of facilities. The ability of a department to maintain an adequate laboratory should not be the only criterion in establishing one. Both the city and the county of Los Angeles have such facilities when one would suffice for the area. "The prime concern should be a matter of its availability from a geographic standpoint."[76] Duplication of facilities within the same region should be avoided.

With but one police laboratory in the State of Arizona, many jurisdictions have no opportunity to obtain scientific examination and evaluation of physical data. A number of jurisdictions make frequent use of FBI services, but reservations regarding timeliness and proximity usually apply. Recently, Maricopa County (of which Phoenix is a part) proposed that a central laboratory serving the county and the cities of Phoenix, Scottsdale, Tempe, Mesa, and Glendale be established. Under the proposal, the county would provide the facilities, and all the jurisdictions would share the cost. Such a laboratory would not meet the needs of other jurisdictions in the State, however, which suggests that perhaps the State should provide laboratory facilities. This has been the decision in Wisconsin and in several other States.

When States establish laboratory facilities, they should place them judiciously. The division of criminal investigation and identification in the Illinois Department of Public Safety provides technical service to law enforcement agencies in the State. Recently, the division built a new laboratory facility in Joliet, which is within the area already served by the Chicago Police Department Laboratory. One reason given for the selection of this location was that it is near the population center of the State. Other factors should be considered, however, among them the pattern of requests for assistance from police agencies.

The Role of States in Laboratory Services. The State can provide meaningful laboratory assistance to local police agencies through several possible alternatives.

---

[71] Supra, note 56 at p. 28.
[72] Interview with Lawrence M. Wetzel, assistant chief of police, Phoenix, Ariz., May 10, 1966.
[73] Interview with Robert Rentmeester, Chief, Sauk-Prairie Police Department, Sauk City, Wis., July 18, 1966.
[74] Chicago Police Department, Crime Laboratory Division, "Annual Report," 1965, mimeo, pp. 5-9.
[75] "Microanalysis—The 'Catch-All' Section of the Crime Laboratory," "Chicago Police Star," June 1966, pp. 4-6.
[76] Sheriff Peter J. Pitchess, Los Angeles County, in supra, note 56 at p. 27.

A State Crime Bureau. Several States have established crime bureaus to provide technical services to local law enforcement agencies throughout the State. They are generally not successful in providing complete technical service, tending to emphasize records activities more than laboratory services. Or, if they do provide technical services, these tend to emphasize such routine activities as latent fingerprint and blood alcohol analysis—work, usually accomplished as effectively on the local level.

The first requisite in establishing a State program of laboratory service is to determine what can be done best by the State and what on the local or regional level. Much laboratory work is of a simple, routine nature, if the evidence has been properly collected and preserved. Consequently, local units may well maintain the small laboratory facilities concerned with primary analysis and forward all complex work to a State or regional agency or the FBI Laboratory for detailed or specialized analysis. The State agency could also perform crime scene work in appropriate cases. This arrangement permits all needs to be met; the local facility provides timely service in simple analyses, and the State laboratory provides sophisticated analyses and quality control.

All police laboratory technicians need specialized training in addition to formal training in a specific scientific field, and the State agency could also perform this training function. Gathering and preserving evidence is so crucial to the entire police laboratory program that sound training is mandatory even at the initial level of operation. Qualified instructors should be available to local jurisdictions to assist with inservice training programs, and the State agency also could operate training programs for the instructors of local departments in evidence gathering and preservation. Like the FBI Laboratory services, the entire State program should be available free of cost to any requesting law enforcement agency.

Provision of a State central laboratory would not entirely eliminate the problem of duplication of facilities, but would reduce it to manageable proportions. At the same time, such a program would allow for the training of personnel in the gathering and preservation of evidence.

Other Approaches. In order to obtain a well-integrated operation, it may be desirable to place the smaller local laboratories and the central State laboratory under a single administration. Such an arrangement is in operation in Texas. The same division of work would prevail, but the local jurisdictions would not control their laboratory operations; rather, they would be under the direction of the State laboratory or some other independent agency.

Medical examiners, as well as police, need laboratory services. In many communities a single facility is used for both functions. Prof. Donald E. Clark, formerly sheriff of Multnomah County, Oreg., suggested that police laboratories as such be eliminated and placed under the control of a separate agency, possibly a university or State or local medical examiner.[77] One benefit would be to have expert witnesses not affiliated with the police department—a concern of some courts.

Conclusions. The cost of staffing and operating a laboratory facility capable of handling all needs of a police department is considerable, and a complete program is beyond the financial ability of most departments. At the same time, the need for adequate professional laboratory services is readily apparent. The following conclusions have been reached:

☐ Basic laboratory services must be readily available within each locality or region to handle routine requests for service. Facilities for such services could be operated jointly by two or more jurisdictions with costs shared on an agreed basis. These facilities should perform only those scientific evaluations considered to be routine and those not requiring a heavy investment in limited-use equipment. Duplications in local facilities should be eliminated.

☐ States should provide central laboratory facilities capable of performing almost all complex and sophisticated scientific evaluations needed in police work. Local agencies would forward all complex work to this agency, and perform only routine work themselves. State services should be provided free of cost to all law enforcement agencies. Training of local personnel would be an important aspect of the State laboratory's work. The FBI Laboratory should continue to analyze the sophisticated evidence submitted to it.

☐ Well-developed police laboratories serving metropolitan needs should be continued, freeing State agencies to develop needed laboratory facilities in other parts of the State. Duplication of facilities between local and State agencies, and between local agencies in the same area, should be avoided.

☐ Consideration should be given to coordinating and consolidating laboratory services for medical examiners and law enforcement, and related agencies, in one facility capable of serving all needs. In many areas such services could be provided on a local or regional basis.

☐ Consideration should be given to placing all police laboratories in a State under the direction of a single administration, possibly an independent agency.

A PRIORITY SCALE FOR JOINT PROGRAMS

Equipment and physical facilities are needed for the performance of all staff, auxiliary, and field functions of law enforcement agencies, although needs vary with the type of law enforcement activities undertaken. Usually, the law enforcement agency of a particular government is viewed only as another department when the equipment and space requirements for the entire jurisdiction are being determined. Consequently, the special needs of the police department often are not met.

This fact suggests that the equipment and building needs of law enforcement agencies are susceptible to coordination and consolidation. It should be remembered, however, that while the merger of physical facilities will

---

[77] Supra, note 56 at p. 27.

result in economies, law enforcement will not improve unless there is also joint performance of activities.

Throughout this report, it has been demonstrated that certain law enforcement supportive activities are best performed on a joint basis. Particularly, they include the operation of detention facilities, laboratories, communication centers, records systems, and training facilities— all commonly performed law enforcement supportive activities which require extensive and expensive physical facilities and equipment. If any or all of these functions are performed on a joint basis, it follows that equipment and buildings needs will also be supplied jointly.

It is not necessary for joint operations actually to operate out of the same physical facility in order to have a joint program. If, for example, one police department provides central communications service for several departments, equipment is shared and the other departments can eliminate their duplicate equipment and facilities. In other words, if law enforcement functions are operated on a joint basis, it naturally follows that equipment and buildings will be shared, whether or not only one building is used.

City-County Buildings. One of the current trends in cooperation between municipal and county governments is the construction of city-county buildings. Common housing should be encouraged, although by itself it does not materially assist in law enforcement activities. Location in the same building, however, may be a first step toward the joint performance of law enforcement activities of the two governments.[78]

Mutual Aid Agreements. One of the most common devices providing for the sharing of personnel and equipment is the mutual aid agreement. Some involve formal arrangements, but frequently they are simply informal agreements for mutual use of personnel and equipment when needed. While such arrangements are useful by themselves, they do not materially improve the quality of law enforcement nor are they binding if the participating agencies need to use the same personnel or equipment at the same time. They are apt to be concerned only with personnel and equipment, not physical facilities, a fact that somewhat restricts their usefulness. More attention should be paid to coordinating and consolidating law enforcement efforts on a formal basis, restricting the use of mutual aid agreements to special or emergency circumstances requiring rapid augmentation of the resources of one department or the other.

COORDINATION AND CONSOLIDATION OF SELECTED FIELD SERVICES

Field services constitute a controversial area in coordination or consolidation of law enforcement activities for one simple reason: Field services are line functions and activities concerned with the fulfillment of the primary police responsibilities, and are characterized by direct contact with people. The police in performing such functions as criminal investigation, vice and delinquency control, and special tactical operations are constantly in the public eye and the public becomes possessive about these activities. Communities and law enforcement officials willing to operate joint communications centers often are less willing to consider coordinated or consolidated field operations. Political opposition also is most apt to focus on coordinated or consolidated efforts at the police operational level.

CRIMINAL INVESTIGATION

Criminal investigation is a police function not usually included in recommendations for functional consolidation of selected police services. The nature of investigative work explains a great deal of the reluctance to consolidate, or even to coordinate, efforts in seeking solutions to crimes. It is natural for every department to want to solve the "big case" on its own. This is not a sound argument against coordinating or consolidating criminal investigation functions, but one which is current.

A more valid argument is based upon the responsibility which a chief has for preserving order and protecting property in his community. Misner states:[79]

> Since a chief of police should properly be held responsible for crime conditions within his city, the responsibility for criminal investigation is one of his most valuable assets. If he loses the authority to investigate, or if it is necessary for outside agents to intervene within his jurisdiction, his effectiveness as a police executive is in question. Consequently, the normal police executive protects jealously his authority to investigate crimes.

A third argument against coordinating or consolidating criminal investigation is its initial dependence upon local patrol for effectiveness. A thorough investigation depends largely upon an adequate preliminary field investigation, and often investigations must be initiated a second time because of inadequate preliminary work. It may be argued that separating investigators from the department which is responsible for the preliminary investigation complicates the work.

Many reasons may be advanced, however, for some coordination or consolidation of criminal investigation. Most small departments cannot afford full-time specialists; and if they could, it is doubtful whether they would assign an investigator to conduct extended investigations throughout several jurisdictions. In metropolitan areas, many criminals are the object of investigations by a number of departments, and one department often seeks assistance from others in the area.

Sheriff Pitchess of Los Angeles County, whose department provides assistance to many departments in the county, had this to say about the need of many departments for aid in conducting investigations:[80]

> You do not train a homicide investigator by reading books. * * * When you are confronted with a homicide that is more than just a dead body, you must turn to people who are experts; and the only experts in the field are those who have investigated homicides. Every department in this county, with the exception of Los Angeles and Long Beach, will call us. Pasadena, with over 100,000 population, will also call us, although they are in a better position to train their people because they have homicides. Even Beverly Hills, with perhaps

---

[78] For a discussion of sharing joint physical facilities, see Samuel G. Chapman and Donald E. Rocks, "Planning for Adequate Police Facilities in a Highly Urbanized Setting," "Police," November-December 1966, pp. 11-17.
[79] Gordon E. Misner, "Recent Developments in Metropolitan Law Enforcement, Part II;" Journal of Criminal Law, Criminology and Police Science, 51: 265-272, 268, July-August 1960.
[80] Supra, note 56 at p. 17.

the highest police budget per capita in the United States, used us the other day.

If one department feels that a crime is beyond its capacity to investigate, it should naturally turn to a jurisdiction that has that capacity. However, it sometimes happens that even if a department desires assistance, there is no reliable agency to which it may turn.

The primary advantage of dividing the responsibility for criminal investigations is flexibility. Concentrating all such investigations in single departments unduly restricts the effectiveness of local law enforcement activities and may make the individual departments a series of local watch services. Again, the establishment of a voluntary central criminal investigation operation will have the desired results only if the local departments turn to it when in need.

Consolidated Criminal Investigation. The consolidation of criminal investigation is most apt to occur in areas where the total consolidation of law enforcement has become a virtual reality.

The Suffolk County (N.Y.) Police Department makes investigation services available to all departments in the county. Although these services are provided only upon request, the local departments use them almost exclusively since there are no independent detective operations in the county. The county police department has the sole responsibility for policing the entire western portion of the county with the exception of 2 communities with departments of fewer than 20 men each, and 5 villages with departments of fewer than 5 men each. These seven independent operations provide basic patrol and initial investigative services to their residents, but rely upon the county for followup investigation and case completion. In the eastern part of Suffolk County, basic patrol is provided by the elected sheriff who exercises nominal powers as a peace officer. Basic investigative services are provided by 19 detectives assigned by the county police department to this area; and these men are supported by 61 specialists in auto theft, homicide, arson, and other specialized investigations.

The Metropolitan Police Department of Nashville-Davidson County provides a similar service, but there is an important difference resulting from the way the police services in the two jurisdictions are organized. The Nashville-Davidson department provides complete police service to all Davidson County including the areas served by three small municipal departments, none of which employs criminal investigators. If a citizen in an area served by a separated department needs immediate service, he may call either the metropolitan police or the independent department; but even though it receives the initial call, the independent department usually relays it to the metropolitan department.[81] Thus, the metropolitan department assumes complete control of cases from initial through followup investigation. In Suffolk County, the independent departments are responsible for initial investigation, and the Suffolk County detectives thus must rely upon them for some basic information. In order to improve the capabilities of the independent departments in initial investigations, the Suffolk County Police Department is now giving them extensive inservice training in investigative techniques.[82]

Partial Consolidation of Criminal Investigation. A jurisdiction may choose to employ its own investigators but to call also upon other jurisdictions for assistance. The services of the Dade County Public Safety Department to local jurisdictions are typical of this kind of voluntary arrangement.

In Dade County, 12 independent municipal departments have turned over general criminal investigation functions to the Dade County Public Safety Department, and 10 other departments are given assistance upon request. Only the five largest departments (Miami, Miami Beach, Coral Gables, Hialeah, and Miami Shores) have staffs capable of performing fairly extensive general investigations. The Public Safety Department also investigates all capital crimes in the county except those occurring in the three largest jurisdictions (Miami, Miami Beach, and Hialeah). The various phases of initial investigation are handled by the independent departments. Except when a small department relies completely on the public safety department there is no clear assignment of responsibility between it and the public safety department. The latter, by virtue of its countywide authority, can enter into a local investigation at any time, but only infrequently does it take such independent action.

It is clear that the planners of Metropolitan Dade County intended that criminal investigation be centralized in the Dade County Public Safety Department. The charter provides that Metropolitan Dade County shall have the power to: [83]

> Provide central records, training, and communications for fire and police protection; provide traffic control and central crime investigation; provide fire stations, jails, and related facilities; and subject to section 1.01A(18) provide a uniform system for fire and police protection.

Commenting on the divided situation 6 years after the charter was adopted, John Pennekamp, editor of the Miami Herald, stated: [84]

> Over the years many failures, growing out of the multifaceted police situation, had become apparent. Criminal cases failed of solution in disputes over jurisdiction. In easy criminal cases two or more units wanted to get into the action, to take the credit. When cases became complex there was considerable buck passing with the possible solution evaporating somewhere inside the dispute. Facts were withheld by one unit from the other. Frequently when cases came for trial in court evidence would be missing, lost somewhere in the contest for control of the case.

The International Association of Chiefs of Police (IACP), in its 1963 study of Dade County police services, attempted to bring order out of the apparent chaos relating to the criminal investigation function, by recommending that criminal investigative responsibilities be divided between local police departments and the public safety department as follows: [85]

> Local departments shall conduct all preliminary investigations except those involving fraud, bad checks, and vice operations, and some continuing investigations such as those involving minor thefts, malicious mischief, simple assaults, and domestic problems.

---

[81] Interview with Hubert O. Kemp, chief, Metropolitan Police Department of Nashville-Davidson County, Tenn., June 7, 1966.
[82] Interview with John P. Finnerty, deputy commissioner, Suffolk County (N.Y.) Police Department, Aug. 17, 1966.
[83] "The Charter of Metropolitan Dade County, Fla.", art 1, sec. 101–104.
[84] John Pennekamp, "Behind the Front Page," Miami Herald, Jan. 15, 1963, sec. A, p. 6.
[85] International Association of Chiefs of Police, "A Survey of Police Services in Metropolitan Dade County, Florida," (Washington: International Association of Chiefs of Police, 1963), p. 255.

The public safety department and the detectives of Miami, Miami Beach, and Hialeah Police Departments will conduct all continuing investigations except those assigned to uniformed patrolmen, and some preliminary investigations, including bad checks, fraud, and vice operations.

No action has been taken on these recommendations. Under present arrangements, the local departments benefit greatly from the services of the county department, but the continued existence of numerous detective units causes friction, loss of time, and unsatisfactory areawide investigations.

In Dade County, or elsewhere, it is not feasible to divide the responsibility for investigations according to the type or seriousness of crimes. In each instance it would be necessary to establish a central review unit charged with deciding whether the central unit or the local department would investigate. The local departments with detective forces would be reluctant to approve this approach since it might result in a dilution of their authority. Also, precious time would be lost waiting for decisions of the review unit.

Cooperation and Coordination. Many criminal investigations involve considerable exchange of information among departments. A good investigator pursues all possible leads including those that require consultation with investigators in neighboring departments. These consultations occur because a department, although jealous of its reputation and conscious of the favorable publicity that results from solving a major crime, often must depend upon the help of other departments. While informal cooperation is desirable, it falls short of the organized efforts emphasized in this study. Three examples of more formal cooperation and coordination will be described briefly.

The Kansas City Area Metro Squad is made up of men from 7 sheriffs' departments, 20 municipal police departments, and 2 State Departments (Missouri and Kansas) in the area. Each agency provides a specified number of men for the metro squad, which is governed by a board of directors that has established criteria for participating agencies to use in calling upon it for assistance. Kansas city, Mo., which has approximately 125 men assigned to investigation, calls upon the metro squad as often as Independence, which has approximately 6 detectives. When the metro squad is called, up to 50 detectives may be sent on a major case. Metro squad training classes are conducted, members carry metro squad identification cards, and they work in both Kansas and Missouri. Members of the squad, however, do not have the power to make arrests throughout the metropolitan area. When not on metro squad assignments, members work on regular assignments in their respective departments.

The growing "metropolitan" crime problem was a factor leading to the formation of Atlanta's "Metropol." The idea for the organization developed when the city of Atlanta asked the Atlanta Council of Governments to suggest a program which might improve areawide law enforcement. On June 1, 1965, a meeting was called with representatives of the 38 law enforcement agencies in the 6-county Atlanta region in attendance. Out of this meeting came five projects: (1) Development of areawide teletype services, (2) adoption of uniform radio call signals, (3) establishment of a metropolitan fugitive squad, (4) creation of a metropolitan training school, and (5) publication of a daily bulletin for all departments.

One of the more important projects is the metropolitan fugitive squad made up of officers from the Atlanta Police Department's fugitive squad and from surrounding departments. These men are available to conduct investigative work on a metropolitan basis. Each department provides an automobile which has Atlanta police radios and other common equipment. Consideration is being given to providing all members of the fugitive squad with arrest powers throughout the metropolitan area.

The Major Case Squad of the Greater St. Louis Area, similar to the Kansas City Metro Squad, is comprised of investigators from both Illinois and Missouri police departments. The board of directors of the squad states in its manual: [86]

We feel that larger law enforcement agencies with their greater police facilities should make them available to the smaller municipalities, as a cooperative gesture.

The board goes on to state the specific reasons for the existence of the squad: [87]

☐ A smaller municipality rarely is sufficiently staffed or equipped to investigate a major case.
☐ The perpetrator in many cases resides or takes refuge in the larger city while he preys on the smaller.
☐ Witnesses, leads, and evidence may be found in more than one jurisdiction.
☐ The general pooling of resources seems to be the only answer to the "fight against crime. * * *"

The Major Case Squad has already proved its worth. Only recently activated, the squad failed to clear the crime that led to its establishment, but has already cleared many other crimes.

In contrast to the Kansas City and Altanta operations, each member of the Major Case Squad from St. Louis County has the power to make arrests throughout the county by virtue of deputization by the St. Louis County Police Department.

It should be noted, generally, that though such organizations are multijurisdictional in an operational sense, individual officers' legal authority arises from deputization. Thus, there is no common source of authority or responsibility throughout such organizations.

CONTROL OF DELINQUENCY

The problem of juvenile delinquency, perhaps more so than any other police problem is dealt with by many individuals and agencies. If effort were the criterion for success in reducing or eliminating delinquent behavior, it would have been achieved long ago. Part of the failure to curb juvenile delinquency may lie in the plethora of agencies established to try to cope with it. Many factors

---

[86] Major Case Squad of the Greater St. Louis Area, "Manual of Instructions and Procedures," January 1965, p. 1.

[87] Id. at p. 1.

cloud the issue of delinquency control. First, there is no universal definition of what constitutes delinquent behavior; and indeed, some communities maintain that they have no juvenile delinquency.[88] Second, the police are not sure of their role in curbing delinquent behavior. Third, even if they were, other agencies and individuals have differing views of what this role should be. These unsettled issues have been dealt with at length by others. In this brief section, therefore, suggestions are limited to avenues of approach to the problems of cooperation among the police themselves and between the police, on the one hand, and the total community, on the other.

Cooperation Among Police Departments. Generally, the curbing of delinquent behavior is a primary responsibility of each individual police department regardless of size. It is also the responsibility of each patrol officer. Nevertheless, there are occasions when specialized techniques are useful in dealing with delinquents.

A question may be raised on the desirability of specialization in police juvenile work. The fact that a separate court system for juveniles has been developed is one reason, for it calls for special knowledge on the part of the police to understand the operations of this system as differentiated from the other court proceedings. Also different State and local laws apply to the conduct of juveniles and of adults and it is often necessary to have specialized personnel available to decide what procedures and techniques will conform with these laws.

One alternative is to have specialists from large departments train the personnel of small departments in the techniques of handling juveniles. Because of inadequate training, officers bring many juveniles before the courts unnecessarily when other actions would have served better in particular cases. Universities and college throughout the country have established institutes to train officers in methods of handling juveniles, but not every department is in a position to send such personnel to these schools.

Another approach is to have specialists in large departments handle cases that are beyond the capability of the small jurisdiction. Such action is particularly advantageous when cases must be brought into the juvenile courts.

Areawide associations of police juvenile officers are effective in stimulating the exchange of ideas among police jurisdictions and can serve as a means of increasing the level of competence of small jurisdictions in this field. The Metropolitan St. Louis Police-Juvenile Officers Association is an example. Formed in 1959, the association, although limited to police juvenile officers, has been successful in establishing procedures for the handling of juveniles that are followed by all departments in the area, including those without juvenile officers.[89]

Cooperation Between Police and Other Agencies. A pooling of the resources of police and community agencies is a sound approach to reducing the incidence of delinquent behavior. The Oakland, Calif., associated agencies program, for example, was established primarily because of the difficulties the Oakland Police Department was encountering in trying to deal with juvenile delinquency alone. In a report to the Oakland city manager, the chief pointed out, among other things, that "the 15 police cars we are sending to Technical High School every day are not the answer to this problem."[90] At his urging, the associated agencies program was established. Composed of representatives of some 10 city, county, and State departments, including the police, the group meets regularly to work out ways of dealing with specific kinds of juvenile problems. Similar programs have been developed in other cities.[91] Suffice it to say that all agencies, including the police, are coming rapidly to a realization that juvenile delinquency can be contained only through joining forces.

VICE CONTROL [92]

The Federal Bureau of Investigation does not include violations of vice laws in its documentation of the rising crime rate nationwide. Yet the public is apt to equate vice violations with the increasing problem of crime, and breakdown in the enforcement of vice laws often has been the basis of criticisms of local law enforcement. Many moves for police reorganization have grown out of investigations into local vice conditions.

Vice includes types and classes of personal or group conduct or activity that has been declared through legislation to be inimical to the public welfare and subject to commercial exploitation. Vice is usually considered to embrace prostitution, the illegal use and sale of narcotics, illegal gambling, the use and sale of illegal alcoholic beverages and the illegal sale of legal alcoholic beverages, and the distribution and sale of obscene or pornographic material.

This section defines the relationships that should exist among law enforcement agencies to help in the enforcement of vice laws. In considering this question, a distinction must be made between local and areawide vice activities, although the line between the two is often indistinguishable. Localized vice can be largely controlled by effective local law enforcement, and where the laws prohibiting vice are rigidly enforced, open vice does not exist to any great extent. Real problems occur, however, when vice operations become so deeply imbedded in the community or are so controlled by outsiders that it is practically impossible for local law enforcement agencies to repress them effectively.

Cooperation and coordination in vice control efforts are essential in all vice control activities and are especially important for control areawide. The emphasis in this section is on cooperation and coordination, not on full-scale intervention by outside agencies; although intervention is required when local enforcement fails to curb vice. It is assumed in this discussion that local police departments and officers are diligent in their efforts to enforce the law and have a desire to cope with vice conditions both local and areawide.

Local Vice Problems. Basically, every local vice problem can be handled by the local police department and

---

[88] J. Robert Moskin, "The Suburbs: Made to Order for Crime," "Look," May 31, 1966, pp. 21–27.
[89] Norman Hertel, "Metro Cooperation in Youth Services," "The Police Chief," January 1962, pp. 24–26.
[90] Wayne E. Thompson, "Developing a City's Human Resources," "Public Management," 45 : 74–78, 74, April 1963.

[91] International City Managers' Association, "Inter-Agency Coordination of Juvenile Delinquency Control Programs," Management Information Service Report No. 269 (Chicago: International City Managers Association, June 1966).
[92] See chapter 7 of the General Report and the Task Force volume on Organized Crime.

responsibility should reside at that level. Nevertheless, assistance from an outside agency is occasionally necessary. The training of local officers in the recognition of vice activities and in the enforcement of laws against them is often inadequate, and the needed training may be best supplied by outside assistance as is the case also in other police training. Some departments are so small that lengthy vice investigations would divert manpower from needed patrol activities, as is the case with other criminal investigations. For these departments to pursue many such investigations to their conclusion would be impractical. Manpower can be made available from other jurisdictions. This is also true for surveillance activities where local officers may be not only inadequate in numbers but also well known and easily recognized.

Areawide Vice Problems. It is readily apparent that areawide vice problems are intertwined with the problem of organized crime. Every major investigation of such crime has concluded that there is need for greater cooperation among law enforcement agencies. In only a few areas does a single agency have the responsibility for coordinating the vice control activities of the many agencies involved in them.

Most of the cooperation among police jurisdictions in controlling vice is on an informal basis and conforms to no common pattern. Joint raids are conducted, information is exchanged between chiefs who know one another, and one department may request the services of specialists in another department when it realizes its own inadequacies. Yet all of these efforts, though laudable, are less than adequate. The sum total of agencies involved in vice control call for some coordinating mechanism. Speaking to this problem, one author states: [93]

The * * * local-State-Federal mixture of responsibility, legal structure, and action should be of primary concern. Fragmented, repetitive efforts are commonplace; local detectives find themselves following Federal agents. Amidst the welter of competing interests and separate governmental units, there is much warm talk of cooperation but no mechanism to make coordination work.

Discussing possibilities for control and coordination, he suggests that: (1) the collection of information should be on a broad scale, (2) assimilation or coordination should be on a narrow scale (by one agency), and (3) dissemination should be on a wide scale and action should be taken based upon the patterns emerging from dissimilar and apparently unrelated facts.[94]

At the Federal level a coordinating agency has been established in the Organized Crime and Racketeering Section of the Justice Department's Criminal Division. This unit, with offices in a number of larger cities, coordinates the work of many Federal investigative and prosecutive resources.

At the State level the pattern varies. In some States, the State police provide some coordination areawide in vice control. In Illinois, a State crime commission has been established with duties and responsibilities which appear to provide some coordination in vice control on a statewide basis. This agency has certain investigative responsibilities in vice matters and a wide range of responsibilities associated with organized crime, but it also conducts investigations into the alleged misconduct of local and State legislators and into arson and bomb incidents. In California, coordination of statewide narcotics control efforts is the responsibility of approximately 100 agents of the Bureau of Narcotics Enforcement of the Department of Justice, but this is its sole vice responsibility.

At the local level, any vice conditions existing in a small community with which the local patrol force cannot cope should be made the responsibility of a larger agency with areawide jurisdiction. It will remain the responsibility of the local patrol officers, however, to identify these conditions and bring them to the attention of a larger unit.

SPECIAL TASK FORCE OPERATIONS

The concept of a mobile striking force or task force has been growing in importance in recent years. This may be defined as an element designed to operate as a compact, mobile, effective operational striking force in given locations at times where the record indicates the need for a special concentration of enforcement pressure.

In the words of O. W. Wilson, "A mobile striking force is of value in those situations which call for a saturation of an area either to prevent the outbreak of criminal activity or a racial, religious or nationalist conflict, or when an emergency of major proportions necessitates the assistance of additional personnel.[95] He goes on to say that "in large cities, the continual demand for details to police special events may justify a detail section of the task force for this purpose." [96]

There are two types of situations where there is need for a task force or body of manpower to serve more than one jurisdiction. The first is the special event, whether it be a large public event or a civil disaster or emergency, where the individual jurisdiction cannot provide sufficient police manpower to cope with it and outside assistance becomes necessary. The second is the situation where crimes are beyond the ability of a single jurisdiction to solve because it lacks some special type of tactical operation.

Special Events. The task force concept has been expanded to cover more than one jurisdiction for the policing of special events or emergency situations, although the manpower thus assembled has never officially been described as a task force.

Among the things that must be covered in any agreement for the pooling of resources are the power of arrest and the privileges and immunities of police officers when requested to act outside their own jurisdictions. State police officers have the power of arrest statewide when enforcing State criminal or penal codes, and county law enforcement officers normally have this power throughout their jurisdiction. At the municipal level, the situation is less clear. Extraterritorial arrest powers are limited primarily to situations in which an officer is engaged in fresh pursuit or is executing an arrest warrant. A typical decision has been rendered by the California District Court of Appeals: [97]

We assume without deciding that a * * * police officer lacks the authority of a peace officer to make an arrest under penal

---

[93] Eliot H. Lumbard, "Local and State Action Against Organized Crime," "The Annals of the American Academy of Political and Social Science," May 1963, p. 86.
[94] Id. at p. 88.
[95] O. W. Wilson, "Police Administration" (2d ed., New York: McGraw-Hill, Inc., 1963), p. 250.
[96] Id. at p. 250.
[97] *People v. Alvarado,* 208 C.A. 2d 629 (1962).

code section 836, when he is outside the city limits unless he is engaged in fresh pursuit or is executing a warrant authorizing such arrest.

This type of decision has led California to amend its penal code as follows: [98]

> Upon the request or authority of a chief, sheriff, or chief administrative officer of any county or city, officers from other localities, jurisdictions, or communities shall exercise full police powers as relate to their normal jurisdictions.

Another means of overcoming legal barriers is the local mutual aid agreement, and the number of these in existence attests to its value. (See app. B for a typical mutual aid agreement.) Perhaps the most encompassing provision for mutual aid in the country is contained in the California Disaster Act which establishes the California civil defense and disaster plan. This plan provides the guidelines for full-scale mobilization of police resources in California in the event of civil or military emergency. The plan has been used recently in Vallejo to prevent civil disorder, in the Los Angeles area to help curb disorders following a police-resident incident in the Watts area, and in San Jose to help contain similar problems. Officers can be summoned from all parts of the State to the scene of a disturbance and, while acting under authority of the Disaster Act, they have the same authority they would have if they were acting in their own jurisdictions. The pertinent provision of the act states: [99]

> All of the privileges and immunities from liability, exemptions from law, ordinances and rules, all pension, relief, disability, workmen's compensation, and other benefits which apply to the activity of such officers, agents, or employees of any such agency when performing their respective functions within the territorial limits of their respective public agencies shall apply to them to the same degree and extent while engaged in the performance of any of their functions and duties extraterritorially under the provisions of this chapter.

Tactical Operations. It is difficult to find a single example of a multijurisdictional task force directed to prevent or control specific crime problems. The metropolitan detective units in Kansas City, Atlanta, and St. Louis come closest to this concept although they are strictly investigative units. Multijurisdictional task forces for enforcement purposes, however, have thus far not been developed, although legal and other barriers to such forces could be overcome.

The need for concentrations of police personnel can be determined from an analysis of the crime problems in any given area. Essentially, the deployment of a mobile striking or task force is related directly to crime analysis. If such analysis is performed on an areawide basis, as suggested earlier in this chapter, an areawide task force will be an effective extension of it.

One means of establishing an areawide task force is through some form of mutual aid agreement. Normally, provisions on compensation are not included in such an agreement. However, since a task force will be utilized on a more regular basis than a force mobilized for special events, some consideration needs to be given to its continuing financing.

Cooperative ventures in criminal investigation, however, have not included any provisions for financing; salaries of the men participating in these efforts are paid by their employing departments. The method of financing an interjurisdictional task force must be decided by the participants if mutual aid agreements are utilized. Effective organization calls for a commander and other supervisory personnel, an established set of rules under which the unit will operate, and agreement on the crimes on which the unit will focus its attention. Such a unit may well be organized along the lines of the metro squads of investigators, but it should also have the power to make arrests in any cooperating jurisdiction, and, to be effective, should be continuously employed in its task force capacity.

Implementation of the concept of a multijurisdictional task force by the localities involved will require each participating jurisdiction to donate manpower over an extended period of time, and this may not be possible. Thus, it may be necesary to turn to the county or the State police agency to establish a unit specifically designed to serve local departments in this capacity.

POLICE SERVICE AND JURISDICTIONAL CONSOLIDATION

Thus far, this chapter has considered methods of ameliorating the effects of decentralized local police administration through the coordination or consolidation of staff, auxiliary, and certain field functions. It has not considered coordination or consolidation in relation to basic patrol services; yet, if these services are not considered, it must be on the assumption that every police agency, regardless of size, is capable of providing them effectively if staff, auxiliary, and certain field services are available on a coordinated or consolidated basis. Such an assumption is not valid.

It has been shown that every new police officer needs basic training upon appointment. But even though adequate training programs are available, the fact remains that some police agencies, for one reason or another, will never make use of them. High standards for the recruitment and selection of police officers can be established, but some jurisdictions will escape these provisions. Crime laboratories, records centers, centralized communications, centralized investigative staffs, and other supplementary services can be established with the intent of assisting departments who cannot provide these services for themselves. Once again, some departments, because of a variety of limitations, will not effectively use them.

The number of departments administered and staffed by untrained, part-time personnel is distressing. A recent survey of police manpower in two counties in the Chicago metropolitan area revealed that many of the small departments employ more part-time (not auxiliary) police officers than full-time officers. Indeed, one department was entirely so staffed. (App. C presents the tabulation of this survey.) A similar survey in Onondaga County, Syracuse, N.Y., showed that there are 13 towns and 17 villages employing a total of only 34 full-time police

---

[98] 49 Cal. Penal Code sec. 817 (1966 Cum. Supp.).

[99] 46 Cal. Military and Veterans Code sec. 1587 (1966 Cum. Supp.).

officers and that the bulk of police service is provided by 104 part-time officers.[100]

The cost of providing basic police service is of paramount importance in considering total consolidation. It has been pointed out in previous sections that certain staff, auxiliary, and field services are beyond the resources of many departments to provide. This is also true in many areas with regard to basic patrol services.

Partial or complete consolidation of police services reduces conflicts over jurisdiction; with consolidation there are fewer jurisdictions with which to contend. The compelling reason for consolidation is the elimination of the law enforcement powers of jurisdictions that do not provide quality law enforcement because of administrative deficiencies or financial inadequacies.

This section considers alternative approaches to the consolidation of the police services of two or more jurisdictions. Discussed in turn are consolidation of police services through the establishment of a metropolitan-type government, through formation of a subordinate service district under a county police agency, through annexation, through contract with another jurisdiction for law enforcement, and through the establishment of a separate special district.

POLICE SERVICE UNDER METROPOLITAN GOVERNMENT

There have been many efforts for comprehensive reorganization of local government in metropolitan areas, but with only two noteworthy examples in this country—Nashville, Davidson County, Tenn., and Miami, Dade County, Fla. The major reorganization of local government in Metropolitan Toronto, Canada, has had much impact upon local government in the United States. Each of these reorganizations takes a different form.

Nashville, Davidson County represents a total consolidation of a city and a county into a new government performing areawide services. The Dade County reorganization represents the granting of certain areawide powers to a charter county without affecting the corporate identity of existing municipalities. Toronto is a federated form of government, with the municipality of Metropolitan Toronto providing all services deemed to be metropolitan and the local governments maintaining control of all services deemed to be local. The Toronto structure resembles that of Dade County, but differs significantly from that of Nashville, Davidson County.

Law enforcement services are organized differently in each of these areas. The Metropolitan Toronto Police Department is the largest of the departments and the most consolidated. The Nashville-Davidson County department is similar in form to that of Toronto, but has not met the success of Toronto, in part because it is not the only law enforcement agency in the county. In Dade County, there is no single metropolitan police force, although the county department has countywide jurisdiction.

Metropolitan Dade County. Metropolitan Dade County has a strong county government providing urban-type services in the unincorporated areas and performing certain areawide functions throughout the county. Metropolitan Dade County was the first metropolitan-type government in the United States. Often there is a misconception that there is only one government in Dade County, whereas, in fact, there are 28.

Dade County had a 1963 estimated total population of more than 1 million, 40 percent of whom reside in the unincorporated area of the county and 60 percent in one or the other of the county's 27 municipal corporations. The municipalities range in size from the central city of Miami, with 330,000 persons, to the recently created city of Islandia which is virtually uninhabited.[101]

In May 1957, the voters of Dade County adopted a county charter that brought three basic changes. First, it transformed the former typical county government to the commission-manager form, making numerous elective offices, including that of sheriff, appointive. Second, it gave Dade County home rule and vested in the board of county commissioners the authority to adopt local legislation in a number of areas. Finally, it gave the board of county commissioners the power to carry on a central metropolitan government. Among the enumerated powers of the county are some pertinent to law enforcement, including provision of central police records, crime investigations, communications, jails, and training and setting reasonable minimum standards for all governmental units in the county for the performance of any service or function.

Law Enforcement. Law enforcement services in the county are provided in a variety of ways. Each incorporated municipality except Islandia offers some police protection, and some municipalities provide almost complete law enforcement services. The Dade County Public Safety Department, under the supervision of the director of public safety, who also bears the title of sheriff, provides some law enforcement services for those municipalities that choose to avail themselves of them and also provides complete police service to unincorporated areas. Table 1 shows the services performed by the county for the municipalities.

Law enforcement in Dade County has two principal problems caused primarily by the congeries of jurisdictions. Police strength of the several law enforcement agencies, shown in table 2, is distributed unevenly, some departments consisting of fewer than five men. Also, as is typical in many metropolitan areas, municipal boundaries have little order, and large unincorporated pockets exist in the heart of some municipalities. Law enforcement services in these pockets are the responsibility of the Dade County Public Safety Department, but frequently adjacent municipal departments answer calls for service initially while awaiting the arrival of the county personnel who have primary responsibility. Formal procedures are lacking and residents are confused as to jurisdictional responsibility.

There are solutions to both these problems, under powers granted in the charter, short of the total amalgamation of all police departments in the county. Section 1.01A(18) of the charter, states that the Board of County

---

[100] Onondaga County, N.Y., Division of Research, "Law Enforcement in Onondaga County" (Syracuse: Onondaga County, Division of Research, Mar. 23, 1966), pp. 8–11.

[101] "The First Ten Years: A Proposed Government Information System for Dade County, Florida" (Miami: Metropolitan Dade County Government, Office of County Manager, Data Processing Division, 1966), p. 66.

Table 1.—Services provided by the Dade County Public Safety Department

	Police communications	Fire communications	Police training	Fire training	Drunkometer examinations	Complete fire service	Capital crimes investigation	Natural death investigation	Mobile unit	Crime laboratory	General investigations	Juvenile investigation	Polygraph	Auto inspection administration	Animal control	Arson investigation	Traffic enforcement	Traffic homicide investigation	Transport prisoners	Warrants and copias	Vice investigations	Confinement of felons	Metro court warrants service	Central accident records	Bomb disposal	Wanted information	Identification service	Civil defense	Emergency police ward	Marine patrol	Mutual aid (fire)	Mutual aid dispatcher (fire)	E.D.P. accident records	E.D.P. enforcement records	E.D.P. robbery and burglary reports	Civil service and writs	Criminal intelligence	Underwater recovery	Safety education	Confinement of mentally incompetent	Document examination
Bal Harbour	x	x	x	x	x		x	x	x	x	x	x	x	x	x	x	x	x		x	x	x	x	x	x	x	x	x	x	x	x	x	x	x	x	x	x	x	x	x	x
Bay Harbor Islands	x	x		x		x	x	x	x	x	x	x	x	x	x		x	x	x	x	x	x	x	x	x	x	x	x	x	x	x	x	x	x	x	x	x	x	x	x	x
Biscayne Park					x		x	x	x	x	x	x		x	x		x	x	x	x	x	x	x	x	x	x	x	x	x	x	x	x	x	x	x	x	x	x	x	x	x
Coral Gables			x	x	x	x	x	x	x	x	x	x		x	x	x	x	x		x	x	x	x	x	x	x	x	x	x	x	x	x	x	x	x	x	x	x	x	x	x
Dade County	x	x	x	x	x	x	x	x	x	x	x	x	x	x	x	x	x	x	x	x	x	x	x	x	x	x	x	x	x	x	x	x	x	x	x	x	x	x	x	x	x
El Portal					x		x	x	x	x	x	x		x	x		x	x		x	x	x	x	x	x	x	x	x	x	x	x	x	x	x	x	x	x	x	x	x	x
Florida City	x	x	x				x	x	x	x	x	x		x	x		x	x		x	x	x	x	x	x	x	x	x	x	x	x	x	x	x	x	x	x	x	x	x	x
Golden Beach	x			x	x	x	x	x	x	x	x	x		x	x		x	x		x	x	x	x	x	x	x	x	x	x	x	x	x	x	x	x	x	x	x	x	x	x
Hialeah					x		x	x	x	x	x	x		x	x		x	x		x	x	x	x	x	x	x	x	x	x	x	x	x	x	x	x	x	x	x	x	x	x
Hialeah Gardens			x				x	x	x	x	x	x	x	x	x		x	x		x	x	x	x	x	x	x	x	x	x	x	x	x	x	x	x	x	x	x	x	x	x
Homestead				x	x		x	x	x	x	x	x	x	x	x		x	x		x	x	x	x	x	x	x	x	x	x	x	x	x	x	x	x	x	x	x	x	x	x
Indian Creek			x		x		x	x	x	x	x	x	x	x	x	x	x	x		x	x	x	x	x	x	x	x	x	x	x	x	x	x	x	x	x	x	x	x	x	x
Medley	x		x	x	x		x	x	x	x	x	x		x	x		x	x		x	x	x	x	x	x	x	x	x	x	x	x	x	x	x	x	x	x	x	x	x	x
Miami					x				x		x				x									x	x	x	x	x	x	x	x	x	x	x	x	x	x	x	x	x	x
Miami Beach		x	x	x			x	x	x	x	x				x		x	x		x	x	x	x	x	x	x	x	x	x	x	x	x	x	x	x	x	x	x	x	x	x
Miami Shores			x		x		x	x	x	x	x	x	x	x	x		x	x		x	x	x	x	x	x	x	x	x	x	x	x	x	x	x	x	x	x	x	x	x	x
Miami Springs		x	x		x		x	x	x	x	x	x		x	x		x	x		x	x	x	x	x	x	x	x	x	x	x	x	x	x	x	x	x	x	x	x	x	x
North Bay Village							x	x	x	x	x	x		x	x		x	x		x	x	x	x	x	x	x	x	x	x	x	x	x	x	x	x	x	x	x	x	x	x
North Miami	x	x	x		x		x	x	x	x	x	x		x	x		x	x		x	x	x	x	x	x	x	x	x	x	x	x	x	x	x	x	x	x	x	x	x	x
North Miami Beach	x	x	x	x	x		x	x	x	x	x	x		x	x		x	x		x	x	x	x	x	x	x	x	x	x	x	x	x	x	x	x	x	x	x	x	x	x
Opa Locka	x	x	x				x	x	x	x	x	x	x	x	x		x	x		x	x	x	x	x	x	x	x	x	x	x	x	x	x	x	x	x	x	x	x	x	x
Pennsuco			x				x	x	x	x	x	x		x	x		x	x		x	x	x	x	x	x	x	x	x	x	x	x	x	x	x	x	x	x	x	x	x	x
South Miami			x		x		x	x	x	x	x	x		x	x		x	x		x	x	x	x	x	x	x	x	x	x	x	x	x	x	x	x	x	x	x	x	x	x
Surfside	x	x	x		x		x	x	x	x	x	x		x	x		x	x		x	x	x	x	x	x	x	x	x	x	x	x	x	x	x	x	x	x	x	x	x	x
Sweetwater	x						x	x	x	x	x	x		x	x	x	x	x		x	x	x	x	x	x	x	x	x	x	x	x	x	x	x	x	x	x	x	x	x	x
Virginia Gardens					x		x	x	x	x	x	x		x	x		x	x		x	x	x	x	x	x	x	x	x	x	x	x	x	x	x	x	x	x	x	x	x	x
West Miami				x	x		x	x	x	x	x	x		x	x		x	x		x	x	x	x	x	x	x	x	x	x	x	x	x	x	x	x	x	x	x	x	x	x
Islandia	x				x		x		x		x				x									x				x												x	x

Source: Dade County Public Safety Department.

Table 2.—Police Manpower in Dade County, 1965

Jurisdiction	Population	Police strength (full time)
Dade County	424,720	719
Miami	329,900	627
Miami Beach	73,750	209
Hialeah	76,700	94
Coral Gables	37,600	74
North Miami	31,710	47
North Miami Beach	24,000	38
Miami Springs	12,600	30
South Miami	10,540	29
Miami Shores	9,310	24
Opa Locka	10,440	22
Homestead	9,920	21
Surfside	3,330	18
Bal Harbour	820	14
North Bay Village	2,870	13
Bay Harbor Island	3,660	13
West Miami	5,530	8
Golden Beach	480	6
El Portal	2,150	5
Medley	200	5
Florida City	4,500	4
Biscayne Park	3,070	4
Sweetwater	820	3
Hialeah Gardens	200	2
Virginia Gardens	3,250	2
Pennsuco	260	1
Indian Creek Village	60	(¹)
Islandia	0	0

¹ Private patrol.

Source: "The First Ten Years: A Proposed Government Information System for Dade County, Florida," p. 66.

Commissioners may set reasonable minimum standards for all governmental units in the county for the performance of any service or function. If a governmental unit fails to comply with the established standards, and does not correct deficiencies, the county may take over and perform, regulate, or grant franchises to operate any such service.

In addition, section 1.01A(17) grants the Board of County Commissioners the power to enter into contracts with other governmental units within or outside the boundaries of the county for joint performance, or performance by one unit in behalf of the other, or any authorized function. Neither of these provisions has been invoked thus far in connection with the provision of law enforcement.

The minimum standards provision could be used to remove all law enforcement responsibilities from certain municipalities and have them performed by the Dade County Public Safety Department. This action would require the county to establish certain minimum standards and a system of inspection. Under this provision it is also possible for a municipality to divest itself of law enforcement responsibilities in favor of the county by referendum or ordinance.[102]

The contract provision enables a municipality to contract with the county for police services. One munic-

[102] The powers of Metropolitan Dade County under this provision are not so broad or all inclusive as might appear: In *Miami Shores Village* v. *Cowart*, 108 So. 2d 468, 471 (Fla. 1958) the Florida Supreme Court apparently interpreted this provision to mean that unless a municipality voluntarily abdicates a function, the power of the county to assume such function rests upon judicial determination.

ipality requested the public safety department to estimate the cost of contract policing, but although the county could provide the service for considerably less than the municipality, the city decided that it preferred to have its own police department.[103]

It is the responsibility of the county planning director to study municipal boundaries with a view to recommending their orderly adjustment and improvement. Proposed boundary changes may then be initiated by the Board of County Commissioners, the governing body of a municipality, or by petition of any persons or group concerned. Municipal elections are required in most circumstances to change boundaries.

At present, the chances for a merger of all police departments in Dade County are slight. Since the office of sheriff was returned to appointive status, as a result of a referendum on November 8, 1966, however, coordination and consolidation of certain services may become more attainable. A continuing difficulty arises from the constitutional amendment which gives the county the power to perform a wide range of services but limits its taxing powers to those of other Florida counties which do not have like powers. The present law enforcement budget is supported almost entirely by ad valorem taxes. Expanded services would require an increase in the county tax rate and, unless accompanied by a proportionate decrease in municipal property taxes, the burden on the Dade County taxpayers would be substantial. Another possibility would be to consider new sources of revenue.

A first step toward consolidation could be a merger of the smaller police departments with the county operation by contract or other means. Larger municipalities could continue to be self-sufficient in basic police services, but could gain help from the county agency in staff, auxiliary, and certain field functions.

The powers granted to the county are considerable and could become of greater significance in coordinating and consolidating law enforcement services. Of particular importance is the minimum standards provision which allows the county to exercise important controls over local services.

Metropolitan Nashville-Davidson County. The metropolitan government of Nashville, Davidson County is the most complete metropolitan government in the United States. Separate city and county governments were merged into a new government servicing the entire area. Among the functions performed by the metropolitan government is law enforcement.

Several factors contributing to Nashville's success in forming a metropolitan government are unique. The Nashville-Davidson County area experienced the same suburban population growth as other metropolitan areas, but not the new municipal incorporations that plague so many areas. Only six incorporated municipalities outside Nashville remain in Davidson County.

Mounting population and governmental problems of the area led to the formation of the metropolitan government. In 1953, the State constitution was amended to authorize the legislature to provide for the consolidation of any or all functions of cities and counties in Tennessee.[104] In 1957, the legislature passed a general enabling act which permitted cities and counties having a combined population of more than 200,000 to establish a charter commission that could propose a charter for a consolidated city and county government to the voters.[105] The Nashville area met these requirements, but in 1958 the voters turned down a charter providing for the amalgamation of the governments of the city of Nashville and Davidson County. The issue was decided by the large negative vote in the suburbs and the rural areas.

Meanwhile, Nashville was trying to solve its own problems, particularly those related to a declining tax base. Property taxes were increased and a new vehicle tax was imposed both on residents and on certain nonresidents. The city also annexed by ordinance, and without an advisory vote of the affected residents, an adjacent area that included some 80,000 people. The residents of the newly annexed area were incensed because they were required to pay higher taxes without an appreciable increase in municipal services, and it was in essence the city's annexation policy that provided the necessary stimulus for success when a second election was held on forming a metropolitan government in 1962.[106]

Two provisions of the new charter are particularly relevant to police service in Nashville, Davidson County. First, the county is divided into two districts—an urban services district and a general services district—with residents of the urban services district paying higher taxes for urban-type services.[107] In effect, the urban services district is the old city of Nashville, and the general services district is the entire county. Residents of each area pay for the level of services they receive, including law enforcement. The second provision relates to the expansion of the urban service district.[108] Whenever the metropolitan council finds that areas of the general services district require urban-type services (e.g., more police protection), they are included within the urban services district and are made subject to higher taxes.

Law Enforcement. Prior to reorganization, law enforcement was provided primarily by the Nashville Police Department and the elected county sheriff. The sheriff had a 2-year term, and changes in management and manpower were frequent. In addition, elected constables with constitutional status had some law enforcement responsibilities and were paid on a fee basis. Private police agencies whose personnel had deputy sheriff's commissions provided law enforcement for some areas under a subscription service. Only three municipal police departments were in operation, each of limited proficiency. Police protection in the county was inadequate at best.

Upon establishment of the metropolitan government, approximately 100 sheriff's deputies were absorbed by the new metropolitan police department, which now has an authorized strength of approximately 550 sworn officers and 110 civilians.

The sheriff's sole responsibility, in addition to serving civil processes, is custody and control of the metropolitan

---

[103] Interview with George Leppig, acting sheriff, Dade County, Fla., June 10, 1966.
[104] Tenn. Const . art. XI, sec. 9.
[105] Tenn. Code Ann. sec. 6-3701 (1966 Cum. Supp.).
[106] For a full discussion of events leading to consolidation see David A. Booth, "Metropolitics: The Nashville Consolidation" (East Lansing: Michigan State University, Institute for Community Development and Services, 1963).

[107] "Charter of the Metropolitan Government of Nashville and Davidson County, Tennessee" (Nashville: Metropolitan Government Charter Commission, 1962), sec. 1.03.
[108] Id. at sec. 1.04.

jail.[109] The metropolitan police department has no detention responsibilities. Soon after the charter took effect, the newly elected sheriff initiated court action to restore his criminal law enforcement powers on the basis that he was an independently elected constitutional officer. The Tennessee Supreme Court, however, upheld the charter, stating that the sheriff had no criminal law enforcement powers.[110] No change was made in the constitutional office of constable; but without exception constables no longer perform any law enforcement functions.

Three municipalities continue to have their own departments, but all others rely on the metropolitan police department. Seven private agencies continue serving both incorporated and unincorporated areas by subscription. The metropolitan department patrols the entire county as if the other departments did not exist, and any need for major police services is immediately forwarded by the smaller departments to the metropolitan department.

The division of charges for law enforcement between the urban services district and the general services district presents a problem. The police department budget for the 1966–67 fiscal year is $4.6 million, of which $2.6 million is chargeable to the urban services district for services beyond normal police protection. In other words, the tax rate in the urban services district is based on the entire police department budget, whereas the tax rate for residents of the general services district is based on only that portion of the department's budget considered normal police protection, or 55 percent of the total.

As the population of the suburban areas has increased, the charge for extra police protection to the urban services district has decreased from $4 million in fiscal year 1963–64 to the present $2.6 million. There is some feeling on the part of residents outside the urban services district that they may be paying for more police protection than they receive from the metropolitan police department.[111] The present distribution of charges is not calculated on any precise basis, and calculations are made difficult by the fact that patrol beats of the services districts overlap.

Another problem is the continued existence of private police services and of small municipal police departments. This is unfortunate because of some overlapping jurisdiction and because the residents of areas served by the metropolitan department and the private or small municipal agencies, as a matter of local choice, are paying more for police protection than is necessary. As has been noted, however, jurisdictional problems are minimized by the unquestioned authority of the metropolitan department. As a practical matter, the chief of the metropolitan department feels that the independent departments served a useful purpose in the period following the reorganization before the metropolitan department could adequately cover the suburban and rural areas.[112] This situation has now been remedied through the addition of personnel and an increase in patrol coverage.

The experience of Nashville with metropolitan government is fortunate, but it seems doubtful that its approach can be applied easily to many metropolitan areas, particularly those with numerous established local governments. Its success can be largely credited to the absence of many established local jurisdictions, each with its own set of services and personnel and an established political hierarchy.

Metropolitan Toronto. The Metropolitan Toronto Police Department provides police protection for the entire Toronto metropolitan area, which includes 241 square miles, nearly 2 million people, and 13 incorporated municipalities including the city of Toronto. There are no independent policing agencies in Metropolitan Toronto.

The Metropolitan Toronto Police Department is responsible to a five-man metropolitan board of commissioners of police appointed by the Province of Ontario. It is financed by an assessment on each of the 13 incorporated municipalities, the amount varying with the proportion of the total that each municipality's assessed valuation is of the assessed valuation of all 13 municipalities. Budgetary control is exercised by the Council of the Municipality of Metropolitan Toronto, comprised of areawide representatives and heads of the government of the 13 municipalities. The only ties between the metropolitan police department and the municipality of Metropolitan Toronto are on matters of budget, finance, and taxation. The municipality of Metropolitan Toronto is based upon the concept that certain functions of government in metropolitan areas must be performed on an areawide basis, whereas others can be reserved to local jurisdictions. Police protection is considered a metropolitan function.

In order to understand the development of the metropolitan police department it is necessary to describe briefly the formation of the municipality of Metropolitan Toronto. The primary reason for establishing a metropolitan government was that suburban areas were increasingly unable to supply certain services themselves, and a system of intermunicipal agreements had proved inadequate to the task. A study was conducted in the early 1950's which recommended the establishment of a federated government that would have jurisdiction over matters of common concern to the 13 members of the federation.

Hearings were conducted before the Ontario Municipal Board (the provincial agency concerned with local affairs), with representatives of the 13 municipalities in attendance to present their views. Not every municipality favored the particular solution, but the board recommended it to the Ontario Provincial Legislature, and the legislature thereupon passed the act creating the municipality of Metropolitan Toronto, to take effect January 1, 1954. Law enforcement was not one of the original functions of the metropolitan government.

In 1954, a special committee was appointed by the metropolitan council to study the feasibility of amalgamating the 13 police departments. After hearing arguments from the affected municipalities, and despite the arguments against it by nine of them, the committee rec-

---

[109] Id. at sec. 16.05.
[110] *Metropolitan Government v. Poe*, 383 S.W. 2d 265 (Tenn. 1963).
[111] Interview with Robert Horton, fiscal assistant to the mayor of the metropolitan government of Nashville, Davidson County, Tenn., June 7, 1966.
[112] Interview with Hubert O. Kemp, chief, metropolitan police department of Nashville, Davidson County, Tenn., June 7, 1966.

ommended the merger.¹¹³ The metropolitan council then recommended to the provincial legislature that the 13 forces be merged and following the enactment of legislation, the metropolitan department came into being on January 1, 1957.

Staff and auxiliary services are now provided by the metropolitan police department in a degree that would have been impossible even under partial merger. A 14-week recruit-training program is provided where prior to amalgamation only two departments had recruit-training programs. Centralized communications is a reality. Records are centralized and central investigation is provided for all jurisdictions.

One measure of the effectiveness of the consolidated police department is the rate of crime clearances. In 1957, the clearance rate for major offenses was 39.5 percent; in 1965, it was 46.2 percent. In terms of the cost, the police budget has risen from $11.6 million in 1956 to $27.7 million in 1966, or approximately 140 percent. Total expenditures for fire protection, still a municipal function, have risen, however, by a greater percentage.¹¹⁴

Shortly after the department was formed, criticism was leveled against the consolidation because patrol service has been reduced in certain areas. This criticism was correct in substance, as personnel of the consolidated department were allocated according to need, not prior assignment.

More recently, the concern has been that there is not enough contact between police and community officials. In its brief to the Royal Commission on Metropolitan Toronto, officials of the township of Scarborough stated that: ¹¹⁵

Our concern is that the police force is too centralized and there is too little association directly with the local municipalities. If there were a larger measure of authority at the local level there would be a greater participation by the police in community functions to the end that their association with local residents would be on a more personalized level.

The officials went on to state that the district commander should have more authority, and transfers of personnel should be less frequent so that officers would become more familiar with local problems.¹¹⁶ It is now standard practice for the district commanders to attend meetings of the municipal councils.

The federated form of government in the Toronto area provides some possible approaches to achieving comprehensive reorganization in this country, and the success of the consolidated law enforcement program demonstrates that a total system approach is possible. It should be borne in mind, however, that comprehensive reorganization in the United States depends upon local participation in the decisions to change the structure of government, whereas it is accomplished by the provincial government in Canada.

POLICE SERVICE THROUGH COUNTY SUBORDINATE SERVICE DISTRICTS

It is common practice for county police agencies to provide police services to unincorporated areas of the county. Normally, such services are financed from general county revenues. It is uncommon, however, to find a county department providing police services to residents of incorporated areas with financing through a special tax on these residents—the pattern found in Suffolk and Nassau Counties (Long Island), N.Y.

Suffolk County. Suffolk County is one of the largest and fastest growing counties in the United States. The county police department, through the police district, provides complete police protection services for 560 of the county's 922 square miles, and 765,000 of the county's population of 900,000.

Governmental functions are performed by the county, 10 towns, and 36 villages, each with its own elected officials. The county is made up of two distinct areas, the western and the eastern. Most of the growth has taken place in the western portion, whereas the eastern part remains basically agricultural. In the western half are 5 of the 10 towns and 27 of the 36 villages.

In order to understand law enforcement in Suffolk County, it is necessary to trace the events that led to the formation of the Suffolk County Police Department. Prior to the formation of the department in 1960, law enforcement was provided by some town police departments, some village departments, district attorney investigators, and an elected sheriff. Not only was law enforcement in the county inadequate, but government was not organized to cope with problems inherent in the growth of the area. In order to strengthen both county government and law enforcement, a special act of the State legislature, the Suffolk County Charter, was passed in 1958.¹¹⁷ This charter called for a strong county government and a county police department to be voted on by the electorate of Suffolk County in November 1958. Two votes were taken; one secured the adoption of the charter and the other the formation of the county police department, financed in part through a special police district tax on residents voting to receive complete police service from the department.

Six provisions of the charter pertain to the formation and services of the department. First, each town and village wishing to transfer its law enforcement functions to the county department must vote on the issue and be subject to a special police district tax. Second, in order to form the district, an affirmative vote of three contiguous towns was necessary. Third, any village within a contiguous town joining the police district could, by majority vote, transfer its police functions to the county department, and be subject to the special tax. Fourth, for the future, any town or village contiguous to a town already served by the county department could elect to join it. Fifth, any town or village not choosing to become a part of the police district could contract with the county department for police service for a period of 2 years. And, finally, a decision taken to receive county department service and be subject to the special tax is irrevocable. ¹¹⁸

Initially, the 5 contiguous western towns and 20 of the 27 villages within these towns voted to turn over police

---

¹¹³ Five of the nine municipalities opposed to the merger, however, recommended the centralization of certain staff and auxiliary services. The four in favor of the merger recognized that this was only a partial solution to the problem and that without total amalgamation local municipalities would still be forced to expand police protection to meet the rising population demand. The number of unsolved crimes was also a dramatic argument for amalgamation. See app. D for the arguments for and against consolidation.
¹¹⁴ Interview with Magistrate Charles O. Bick, chairman, Metropolitan Toronto Board of Commissioners of Police, June 17, 1966.

¹¹⁵ H. Carl Goldenberg, commissioner, "Report of the Royal Commission on Metropolitan Toronto," (Toronto: Province of Ontario, 1965), p. 61. This report, commonly called the Goldenberg report, recommended reduction in the number of municipalities from 13 to 4. By act of the provincial legislature, the number was to be reduced to six on Jan. 1, 1967.)
¹¹⁶ Ibid., p. 61.
¹¹⁷ "Laws of New York," 1958, ch. 278.
¹¹⁸ This rather complex method is covered in "Laws of New York," 1958, Suffolk County Charter, ch. 278, secs. 1206, 1207, 1209.

functions to the county police department, and the department came into operation on January 1, 1960. Manpower came primarily from the towns and villages which elected to divest themselves of their police function; 3 of these had more than 100 officers each at the time of merger. The investigators of the district attorney's office were also brought into the new department. Present strength is approximately 1,300 sworn police officers.

Seven villages within the joining towns voted not to join the police district, and so maintain their own departments, the largest of which has fewer than 20 men. An elected sheriff provides a modicum of patrol to the residents of the five eastern towns and the villages within them. In all cases, the county police department supplements the efforts of the independent agencies. The county department also supplies all criminal investigation services and performs most staff, auxiliary, and field functions. Detention, however, is handled by the sheriff.

The police budget is divided into two parts: one is for the services provided solely to the special police districts (in 1966, it amounted to an expenditure of $14 million, or more than 85 percent of the total budget of $16 million), and the other covers the cost of services that are provided countywide. Services to the police district are financed by a tax on the residents of the district; countywide services are financed from county general revenues. Services charged to the respective funds are detailed in table 3.

Table 3.—Distribution of Services Between Those Financed by Police District Tax and Countywide Revenues

FINANCED BY COUNTYWIDE REVENUES

☐ Commissioner of Police and his staff.
☐ Chief Inspector in charge of auxiliary services.
☐ Deputy Chief Inspector in charge of detectives.
☐ Deputy Inspector in charge of Communications and Information Bureau.
☐ Central Records and Statistical Bureau.
☐ Personnel Bureau except Inspection Section.
☐ Property Bureau.
☐ Civil Defense Bureau.
☐ Finance Bureau.
☐ Special Service Bureau of Detectives (e.g. homicide squad, auto theft squad, narcotics squad, etc.).
☐ Squad of detectives assigned specifically to area outside police district.
☐ Crime Laboratory.
☐ Juvenile Aid Bureau.
☐ Part of Planning Bureau.

FINANCED BY DISTRICT TAX

☐ Chief of Police District.
☐ All personnel assigned to Police District including district detectives.
☐ Communications and Information Bureau.
☐ Transportation and Maintenance Bureau.
☐ Traffic and Safety Bureau.
☐ Tactical Platoon.
☐ Marine Bureau.
☐ Inspection Section of Personnel Bureau.
☐ Part of Planning Bureau.
☐ Principal and interest on bonds of police district stations.

Source: County of Suffolk, N.Y. "Budget, 1966," pp. 164-186.

Finally, the wisdom of the charter provision which precludes a town or village electing to join the county police district from subsequently withdrawing might be questioned. But, in order to provide consistent police protection, it has been considered to be necessary.

The county police department was established because existing law enforcement agencies were not able to meet the needs of the increasing population in the western portion of the county. More recently, a request by the county legislators representing the five eastern towns resulted in expansion of the criminal investigation squad serving this area. As population in the eastern section grows the five eastern towns are likely to find that existing law enforcement arrangements will not meet their needs and may turn to the county department.

Nassau County. Nassau and Suffolk Counties resemble one another in their provisions for law enforcement, but with differences that reflect the geographical and political composition of the two counties.

The Nassau County Police Department, with approximately 2,600 sworn officers, provides complete police protection to 45 of the 69 incorporated municipalities in the county. This service is financed by ad valorem tax on their residents. The police district, the area on which the tax is assessed, includes 205 of the county's 300 square miles and 1.1 million of its 1.4 million population. Of the total 1966 budget of $30 million, $21 million is to be expended for services rendered to residents of the police district.

Twenty-four jurisdictions continue to provide law enforcement services through their own police departments, but the county department provides certain supplemental services to them. The cost of these services, financed by countywide revenues, amounts to $9 million for 1966.

The essential differences between the two county departments stem in part from their respective histories. Whereas the Suffolk County Department was established only in 1960, the Nassau County Department dates from 1925. The original force consisted of 55 men transferred from the county sheriff's office (the sheriff no longer has police responsibilities). The police district originally encompassed the unincorporated area of the county and two special districts which have since been dissolved.

To join the police district, the governing body of an incorporated community must adopt a resolution, which must then be acted on favorably by the county board, a more simple method than that employed in Suffolk County. The area policed by the district need not be contiguous, and a municipality may withdraw from the county police district upon petition and a referendum vote. As in Suffolk County, a municipality may contract with the county department for service for a period of 2 years.

The departments also differ in their internal organization and methods. For example, communications are centralized in Suffolk County so that residents need call only one number when desiring service from the county department. In Nassau County there are eight telephone numbers, each terminating in one of eight precinct stations. Cars are dispatched from a central radio room after the message is relayed by direct telephone line from the precinct station. It could be said that the Suffolk County department has used its unique position to better advantage in this respect.

The division of charges between the police district and the county also differs. Whereas more than 85 percent of the Suffolk County department's budget is charged to the police district, in Nassau County the percentage is only 72. The major reason for the difference is that the cost of the total detective force in Nassau County is charged to the countywide budget; whereas in Suffolk County the costs of only specialized units and the detective unit serving the eastern portion of the county are so charged.

Conclusions. In terms of their applicability to other areas, the following conclusions have been drawn on the experience in Suffolk and Nassau Counties:

☐ Provision of police service through a special tax on areas provides this service on an equitable method of financing.
☐ The subordinate service district can provide for a contiguous policing jurisdiction guaranteeing a consistent level of service throughout an area.

ANNEXATION

The practice of adjusting municipal boundaries through annexation is widespread. Annexation is the absorption by a city of territory which is normally contiguous, unincorporated, and smaller than the annexing city. The result is a larger jurisdiction, usually with essentially the same form of local government.

Techniques of Annexation. Annexation practices vary significantly from State to State, but five principal methods are utilized: (1) Legislative determination, in which municipal boundaries are extended by special act of the State legislature; (2) popular determination, in which the voters decide whether an annexation shall take place (this vote may be taken separately or jointly by the voters of the enlarged municipality, the territory to be annexed, and/or the jurisdiction that will lose the annexed land); (3) municipal determination, by unilateral action of the annexing municipality; (4) judicial determination, in which a State court decides whether a proposed annexation shall take place; and (5) quasi-legislative determination, in which a commission or board makes the decisions.[119] Several of the principal methods also may be used in conjunction with one another.

The major strength of annexation as an approach to reorganizing local government is its broadening of the geographical jurisdiction of existing municipalities. It can forestall the creation of special districts or new municipal incorporations and thus help prevent local governmental patterns from becoming more complex. Because annexations are usually of the fringe areas around cities, the cities can then include them in their total program of governmental services and prevent the fringe areas from becoming a source of spillover problems.[120]

Although there is a trend toward making annexation easier to accomplish through the use of quasi-legislative groups like State boundary commissions, in most States the laws do not work to the advantage of an annexing municipality and thus present obstacles to consistent growth through annexation. Also, the prospect of annexation frequently precipitates "defensive" incorporations by fringe areas which work against orderly growth and development. Finally, annexation is of limited use to a city surrounded on all sides by incorporated areas.[121]

Annexation and Police Services. One city which has experienced major growth in recent years through a strong policy of annexation is Phoenix, Ariz. In the 16-year period from 1950 to 1966, the city has grown from 16 square miles to nearly 250, and the population has increased from 100,000 to over 500,000. All of the growth in the area has come through the annexation of unincorporated areas surrounding the city and lying within Maricopa County.

Phoenix actively sought annexations as a means of providing for orderly growth and development of the city through preventing the formation of special districts and new municipal corporations on its outskirts. Most of the area annexed has not added sufficient revenues to meet the cost of the necessary expansion of services, but the city is convinced, under its circumstances, that annexation is the best approach to resolving a number of municipal problems.[122]

Law enforcement service in annexed areas was formerly provided by the county sheriff, who had a huge land area to cover with a small staff. The sheriff provided this service on a request basis, and no significant attempts were made to set up established patrol areas. With annexation, the city police department extended complete law enforcement service to the newly added areas immediately, with a corresponding increase in the size of the department.[123]

---

[119] Advisory Commission on Inter-Governmental Relations, "Alternative Approaches to Governmental Reorganization in Metropolitan Areas" (Washington: Advisory Commission on Inter-Governmental Relations, 1962), p. 58.
[120] Id. at pp. 63–64.
[121] Id. at pp. 64–65.

[122] Interview with Marvin Andrews, assistant to city manager, Phoenix, Ariz., May 10, 1966.
[123] Interview with Lawrence M. Wetzel, assistant chief of police, Phoenix, Ariz., May 10, 1966.

The need for better law enforcement usually is not a prime factor in moves for annexation, but improvement in enforcement services in the added areas is usually a direct result of annexation.

CONTRACT LAW ENFORCEMENT

Intergovernmental agreements are the most widely used means of broadening the geographical base for handling common functions, especially in metropolitan areas. They provide one of the least complicated means of accomplishing coordinated or consolidated governmental services, including law enforcement. Under a contract program, one government agrees to provide certain specified services to another for a fee—in brief, to act as an agent of the other in its jurisdiction.

Contract programs for services are most commonly associated with local government in California, where nearly 3,000 such programs are in operation, including 500 in the law enforcement field.[124] Contract programs in California usually involve an agreement between a county and a city whereby the former provides services to the latter. In Atlanta, Ga., by contrast, the city provides law enforcement services to Fulton County under the terms of a contract. In Connecticut, the State provides law enforcement services to municipalities on a contract basis.

Count to City. Los Angeles County provides complete law enforcement service to 29 of 77 incorporated municipalities within the county. In addition, it provides selected staff, auxiliary, and field services to all jurisdictions. The major advantage of the total program is that the sheriff's department is able economically to provide professional police services directed to the overall needs as well as services adapted to the particular needs of any local community. The major disadvantage is that the municipalities participating in the contract program are not contiguous, and law enforcement, therefore, is somewhat uneven. Total consolidation of the metropolitan area has not been achieved, nor does it seem likely to occur through the contract program.

Beginning in 1954, there have been 29 new municipal incorporations in Los Angeles County, the first since 1939. Each of these new cities was immediately confronted with the basic problem of providing the usual municipal services to its residents. A logical solution was to have the county continue to provide services on a contract basis. The city of Lakewood initiated the program, and it has been accepted in large part by 27 of the other 29 new municipalities. The one exception, the city of Downey, chose to provide its own basic services, including law enforcement.[125]

In evaluating the contract program, one city administrator stated, "A central police authority in the metropolitan area is not the answer in the administration and enforcement of justice. You must have local control because law enforcement is a local government function. The city must participate in all decisions."[126] The city administrator considered contract law enforcement programs to meet this requirement. The station commander of the sheriff's department serving Lakewood functions completely as a chief of police, according to the city administrator, and there are no problems of communication between the administrator's office and the station commander. At no time has the contract program become a political issue in Lakewood, which suggests that the community is satisfied with the quality and level of service it receives.

Cities enter into a contract program with the county on a voluntary basis, and it is this aspect which has contributed to its success. No effort is made to sell a particular kind of service to them. The program has been described by Arthur G. Will, county-city coordinator of all contract programs, as:[127]

* * * a partnership of cities and the county to provide joint services at the least cost while both agencies retain the power of self-determination and home rule. It is further a voluntary partnership under which cities may establish and maintain local identity without heavy initial investment in capital plant, equipment, and personnel. Thus, neither agency loses any of its powers but cooperates for the provision of the services at a mutually satisfactory level.

Objections to Contract Program. Two principal objections have been made to the contract program in Los Angeles County. First, many noncontract cities have felt that the county was subsidizing the contract cities, at least in part, at the expense of noncontract cities. Second, it has been objected that the contract program is an abrogation of local home rule.

It is the express policy of Los Angeles County to recover the entire cost of any services performed for another government; and the State constitution, in fact, prohibits a county from underwriting costs of another government.[128] Table 4 shows a summary of contract charges per unit, per year, from 1958 to 1966. A contract program costs a city less than if it provided the service for itself, largely because of the economies resulting from larger programs, but charges would seem to reflect the actual costs of services accurately.

Table 4.—Rates Charged by Los Angeles County Sheriff's Department for Patrol Car Service to Contract Cities

(July 1, 1958, to June 30, 1966)

Cost elements	July 1, 1958, to Dec. 31, 1962	July 1, 1962, to June 30, 1963	July 1, 1963, to June 30, 1964	July 1, 1964, to June 30, 1965	July 1, 1965, to June 30, 1966
Station:					
Salaries and employee benefits	$68,919	$81,779	$83,414	$88,776	$90,853
Services and supplies	901	1,855	1,893	2,015	2,062
Vehicle expense	4,003	5,337	5,445	5,794	5,930
Administrative overhead:					
Patrol division	525				
Sheriff's department	1,426				
General county	2,626	4,932	5,029	5,352	5,477
Cost for a 24-hour shift using one 1-man car and two 2-man cars	78,400	93,903	95,781	101,937	104,322

Source: Los Angeles County Sheriff's Department.

---

[124] Samuel K. Gove, "The Lakewood Plan," Commission papers of the Institute of Government and Public Affairs (Urbana: University of Illinois, May 1961). table 3, p. 15. (Sometimes the contract plans are referred to as the Lakewood plan, because the program, as it is presently known, originated in the city of Lakewood.)
[125] Ibid. Gove provides a detailed résumé of the development of the contract program in Los Angeles County.
[126] Interview with Marshall W. Julian, city administrator, Lakewood, Calif., May 13, 1966.

[127] Arthur G. Will, "Another Look at Lakewood," address presented to the 27th Annual Conference of the National Association of County Officials, July 11, 1962, mimeo, p. 4.
[128] See Howard H. Earle, "Contract Law Enforcement Services by the Los Angeles County Sheriff's Department," John Donner publication No. 9 (Los Angeles: University of Southern California, 1960), p. 123, for a copy of the General Services Agreement, especially sec. I, which is the basic contract between Los Angeles County and municipalities requesting services.

The cost of a law enforcement program is determined according to an established formula based on the total annual cost of providing one patrol unit. A patrol unit consists of one deputy during the daytime and two deputies during both the evening and the early morning shifts, and the vehicle used in the operation, 24 hours per day throughout the entire year. In addition, the contract includes the prorated costs of other departmental services and operations including investigation, detention facilities, laboratory services, and similar staff, auxiliary, and field services. The cost for one patrol unit in 1966 was slightly more than $104,000.[129] A contracting agency may have as many units as it desires, but must meet the minimum standards established by the sheriff.

The principle of home rule is not violated through the use of a contract program because the program is initiated by the city desiring the service. One city official in testimony to a California legislative committee studying the question of contract programs stated: [130]

The use of the contract plan does not mean an abolition of local home rule. The city council, in electing to use and operate under the contract system, set the level, the type, of services. Each contract has a clause whereby they can be terminated. * * * This is not an abrogation of local home rule. All we did was simply substitute city departments, personnel and payrolls, for county departments, personnel and payrolls, to perform these municipal functions as contractual agents of the city, thereby eliminating a costly duplication.

The legislative committee concluded that home rule was, in fact, not abrogated under the contract program, and this is also the point of view of the League of California Cities, one of the most articulate defenders of home rule prerogatives in the State.[131]

The validity of this position has been questioned, on the basis that the sheriff determines the minimum standard of service, and that the local community may only accept or reject the sheriff's definition of what constitutes minimum service. Richard D. Yerby has concluded that this is a system geared to cost rather than to local flexibility: "as a result, a very limited degree of home rule is preserved." [132]

While this objection might seem to have some merit, it may be countered if home rule is viewed as the right to make basic decisions regarding principle. If the municipality has an opportunity to determine whether it will accept the minimum standard established by the county the principle has not been violated. Also, the municipality can expand the program beyond the minimum level at its own discretion, providing it is willing to pay the additional costs.

City to County. Atlanta and Fulton County, Ga., have together formulated a plan of improvement to strengthen local government in the area while preserving the existing structure. The Atlanta plan of improvement is based upon these premises: (1) All municipal services should be furnished by a city, preferably Atlanta; (2) the county should furnish only traditional county services; (3) areas needing municipal services should be annexed to a city; and (4) until they are annexed, the city should furnish such services by contract.[133]

The plan of improvement originated following the failure of an annexation program in Atlanta in the late 1940's. The legislature thereupon created a local government commission to make a comprehensive study and to report to the legislature a plan for improving government in Atlanta and Fulton County. The suggested plan was completed and submitted to the legislature in 1950 and was approved in an advisory referendum in June 1950. The necessary constitutional amendments were approved in November 1950, and implementing legislation was passed by the legislature in 1951. The plan of improvement went into effect January 1, 1952. A joint performance committee, consisting of equal numbers of city and county officials, handled the details of the transfer of personnel.

The significant features of the Atlanta plan are provisions for continuing annexation by the city of Atlanta of urbanized areas contiguous to it and the reallocation of functions between the city and the county. As a result of the plan, law enforcement has become the sole responsibility of the city which furnishes police service to unincorporated areas under contract with the county.

The city of Atlanta and Fulton County jointly decide the level of police service to be provided in the unincorporated area and prepare the contractual arrangements. Other municipalities in the county continue to maintain their own police departments. The city-county contract is reviewed regularly to reflect changes in police needs. Day-to-day decisions on the allocation of specific personnel and equipment are made by the chief of police of Atlanta, consistent with terms of the contract. Staff, auxiliary, and field services are included in the cost of basic patrol service and are utilized as needed.

All direct expenses incident to and necessary in furnishing police protection and service are reimbursed to the city by the county, with 10 percent added to cover miscellaneous services and administrative expenses. In 1965, the total cost for the contract services was approximately $375,000.

The office of elected sheriff is retained in Fulton County, but he exercises no actual law enforcement powers; the sheriff acts as jailer for the county and serves as an officer of the court for all appropriate civil matters.

State to Local. An unusual contract program for basic law enforcement services, known as the "resident trooper plan," is in operation in Connecticut. The State police, through a contract program, provides a single resident trooper to furnish basic law enforcement service to any requesting municipality that meets certain criteria. Under this plan, 46 towns ranging in population from 1,000 to 17,000 receive law enforcement service.[134] The program is limited by legislation to 46 towns for budgetary reasons.

The State police have full law enforcement jurisdiction in all parts of the State, but they do not exercise this authority in areas that have their own police departments, unless so requested by local officials. Criminal matters not handled by local police are cared for by the State police.[135] The sheriff does not perform any law en-

---

[129] For, a complete description of the method utilized in determining the cost of the contract law enforcement program in Los Angeles County, see app. E.
[130] "Functional Consolidation of Local Government," Final report of the assembly interim committee on municipal and county government (Sacramento: Assembly of the State of California; assembly interim committee reports 1957–59, vol. 6, No. 10), p. 26.
[131] Interview with Jack D. Wickware, assistant counsel, League of California Cities, May 17, 1966.
[132] Richard D. Yerby, "The Police Function," in Beatrice Dinerman, Ross Clayton, and Richard D. Yerby, "Metropolitan Services: Studies of Allocation in a Federated Organization" (Los Angeles: University of California, Bureau of Governmental Research, 1961), p. 99.
[133] Details of the historical development of the Atlanta plan of improvement are summarized in "Governmental Problems in the Chicago Metropolitan Area," a report of the Northeastern Illinois Metropolitan Area Local Governmental Services Commission, ed. Leverett S. Lyon (Chicago: University of Chicago Press, 1957), pp. 276–278.
[134] Letter from Leo J. Mulcahy, commissioner, Connecticut Department of State Police, June 1, 1966.
[135] Ibid.

forcement functions in Connecticut and, in fact, county government has been eliminated. Because of these two factors, the State police have become more involved in local law enforcement than have similar agencies in other States.

Any town, or two or more towns (up to the total of 46), lacking a police department, may contract for a resident trooper. Towns receiving such service jointly must share equitably in the total cost of the program. Appropriate costs of the program are determined by the State police commissioner and approved by the State commissioner of finance and control. Contracts are for a 2-year period and are subject to review by the State attorney general. Under the current arrangement, the State pays 40 percent of the cost of a program and the contracting town 60 percent. The State police commissioner exercises supervisory control over the resident troopers.[136]

Each contract provides for only a single resident trooper, which often does not give adequate police protection, especially when an emergency may remove the trooper from routine duties. In addition, because only one trooper is provided, the community does not receive 24-hour police protection. A State police substation in the immediate area will send occasional patrols through an area when the resident trooper is not on duty, but this is only a partial answer to providing complete protection around the clock.

As the name of the program suggests, the resident trooper resides in the community in which he is providing basic law enforcement. As the system has developed, some troopers use their homes as local State police offices, and frequently their wives will serve as local dispatchers. Assignments to the resident trooper program are made on a volunteer basis, and local officials have a right to approve the appointments to their respective communities. For budgetary purposes, resident troopers are maintained in a category separate from regular State police personnel, although selection and training standards are the same for both groups.

All towns which have resident troopers have locally elected constables, but, although they have police powers, they have not provided effective law enforcement. Normally, they engage in providing school crossing services and related activities. Some communities have arranged to have the local constables under the day-to-day supervision of the resident trooper who directs their activities and training. Such arrangements, however, are not considered part of the contract, and the State does not assist in financing a constable program.

Conclusions. Contract law enforcement is one of the least complicated ways to achieve consolidation of law enforcement services. Under broad joint-exercise-of-powers legislation, governmental jurisdictions can contract for services from other governmental jurisdictions. As later noted in the section on "Obstacles to Coordination and Consolidation," legal authority to contract is found in nearly every State (although some provisions are not so broad as others) or is more easily attained than are other methods of attaining consolidations.

General conclusions are:

☐ Contract law enforcement programs can be effective without altering existing governmental structures.
☐ Any level of government can provide contract law enforcement services to other governments.
☐ A contract program can be effectively utilized to meet law enforcement needs in staff, auxiliary, and certain field services; it also can accomplish complete consolidation of all law enforcement activities.
☐ Costs of a contract program of law enforcement can be distributed equitably among participants and need not work to the disadvantage of nonparticipants.
☐ No contract law enforcement program can be effective if it is based upon arbitrary standards relating to the allocation of personnel and equipment. Each contracting jurisdiction should determine, in conjunction with the contractor, the actual needs of the jurisdiction, and the allocation of personnel and equipment should be based upon this analysis.
☐ Contract programs are limited and voluntary and do not necessarily cover areas that are contiguous.

POLICE SPECIAL DISTRICTS

Special districts for law enforcement are rare—no more than 9 among the more than 18,000 special districts in the United States. Although most States have enacted legislation authorizing many types of special districts, authorizations for police districts also are fairly rare.[137] At the same time, one authority notes that a most persuasive argument for adoption of special police districts is the fact that permissive legislation for such districts requires only a modicum of legal change.[138]

Advantages and Disadvantages. The chief advantage of police special districts may be briefly summarized. First, district boundaries can be drawn to correspond with the most logical areas for providing police service and without regard to existing governmental boundaries. Second, police special districts can be free of immediate local political influence in their day-to-day activities. Third, police districts are legally feasible without need for significant legislative or constitutional change.[139]

In general, special districts do not represent a reorganization of government but, rather, the creation of a new single-purpose unit to furnish a service which, for some reason, existing local units are not providing adequately. Functional specialists and other groups concerned about the performance of existing governments frequently seek to separate the functions in which they are particularly interested and have them performed by special districts. It seems easier to establish a special district than to reform the existing unit.[140]

Special districts normally are financed in two general ways: through user charges and through property tax assessments. The first method does not lend itself to police services as it does, for example, to sewer and water services. The second method places the district in direct competition with units of general local government for

---

[136] Connecticut General Statutes, sec. 29–5 (1958).
[137] John C. Bollens, "Special District Governments in the United States" (Berkeley and Los Angeles: University of California Press, 1967), p. 68.
[138] Max A. Pock, "Are Metropolitan Police Districts Legally Feasible?" "Journal of Public Law," 12: 313–336, 317–318, 1963.
[139] Max A. Pock, "Consolidating Police Functions in Metropolitan Areas" (Ann Arbor: University of Michigan Law School, Legislative Research Center, 1962), p. 40.
[140] Advisory Commission on Inter-Governmental Relations, "The Problem of Special Districts in American Government" (Washington: Advisory Commission on Inter-Governmental Relations, 1964), p. 74.

property taxes. Although in most instances special district tax levies are small in comparison to those of general units of local government, their combined impact can be significant. Overlapping of districts levying property taxes is not unusual as there is no limit on the number of special districts that may tax a given piece of property.[141] Also, special districts may increase the total cost of governmental services unduly because of a duplication of administrative costs.[142]

A principal criticism of special districts is that they may function largely unnoticed and uncontrolled by the public. It is much easier for citizens to focus their attention on units of general government than on special districts. The multiplicity of special districts often prevents the citizen from knowing exactly what is going on in his community. The programs of many districts appear to be completely independent from and uncoordinated with similar programs of general government.[143]

The lack of visibility and public awareness strongly suggests that law enforcement is a function which should not be performed by an independent special district. The nature of law enforcement makes empathy with the public desirable, and such a relationship normally cannot be developed through a special district.

OBSTACLES TO COORDINATION AND CONSOLIDATION

Obstacles to the coordination or consolidation of the police services of different jurisdictions are similar to the barriers faced in restructuring and relocating other functions of local government. They tend to be among the most formidable for the police, principally because police service is generally among the most local of governmental services and because even the smallest local governmental jurisdictions like to believe that they can provide at least minimal needed police service. Often, political and social pressures linked to the desire for local self-government, rather than legal restrictions, offer the most significant barriers to the coordination and consolidation of police services. But it is important for all jurisdictions to be aware of any legal obstacles to coordination or consolidation which may exist.

LEGAL OBSTACLES—CONSTITUTIONAL AND STATUTORY

In some States, existing statute law authorizing local provision of police services, combined with doctrines of "strict construction" of municipal powers, may impede voluntary establishment of formal collaborative arrangements among local units, unless legislation is adopted specifically authorizing such arrangements. But this problem will lessen as an ever increasing number of States enact general "joint exercise of powers" legislation in accordance with recommendations by the Council of State Governments and the U.S. Advisory Commission on Inter-Governmental Relations, as is described later.

Even where statutes clearly authorize voluntary collaboration, or establish metropolitan agencies or otherwise clearly encourage required consolidation or joint administration of traditionally local police service, it is conceivable that constitutional difficulties will materialize in some States. Such statutes may, in a relatively small number of States, be subject to plausible challenge under various constitutional provisions. The basis for such challenges include: (1) "Home rule" provisions purporting to grant the several municipal electorates a range of inviolate control over the structure and/or power of local government; (2) prohibitions against enactment by the legislature of "local" or "special" acts; (3) prohibitions against the establishment of "special commissions" to perform "muncipal" functions; or (4) prohibitions against diversion of municipal assets.

To note that plausible challenges can be raised, however, is neither evidence nor proof that courts will ultimately sustain them. In fact, there is a clear trend on the part of State courts dealing with the four classes of constitutional matters shown above to prevent them from interfering with metropolitan reorganization. Nevertheless, it is suggested that in those States where constitutional prohibitions would not permit the improvement of local law enforcement through coordination and consolidation, that such restrictions be removed through constitutional amendment.

Since the laws relating to home rule vary significantly among the States, it is essential that each jurisdiction examine local constitutional and statutory provisions and court decisions to determine what legal obstacles, if any, may exist to coordination and consolidation of police service. There are several texts notably helpful to the scholar, lawyer, public official, or study group who seeks definitive information pertaining to the legal obstacles and means for surmounting them.[144]

Joint Exercise of Powers. The augmentation of coordination and consolidation of services between or among governmental jurisdictions may be accomplished through intergovernmental agreements. Such agreements open the way to joint efforts and to transfers of responsibilities for the performance of governmental functions.

Objections to Intergovernmental Agreements. It may be argued that intergovernmental agreements tend to impede more comprehensive reorganization by ameliorating current dissatisfaction with a particular condition which in the long run could be dealt with more effectively through governmental reorganization.[145] It is difficult to counter the argument that comprehensive reorganization is the more logical solution to providing better, more efficient local government. It is incumbent upon governments, however, to provide the best possible services within the legal and political frameworks in which they operate. A provision most commonly found, and the one which will offer the fewest political obstacles, is a joint exercise of powers act. Comprehensive reorganization, albeit a desirable goal, is generally not a realistic one for meeting immediate problems.

Counties and municipalities as legal creatures of the State have limited powers, even under home-rule provisions. Express statutory authority is therefore neces-

---

[141] Id. at pp. 34–37.
[142] Id. at p. 75.
[143] Supra, note 137 at pp. 252–256.
[144] These include: Advisory Commission on Inter-Governmental Relations, "State Constitutional and Statutory Restrictions Upon the Structural, Functional, and Personnel Powers of Local Government" (Washington: Advisory Commission on Inter-Governmental Relations, 1962), 80 pages; Charles S. Rhyne, "Municipal Law" (Washington: National Institute of Municipal Law Officers, 1957), 1,125 pages; John M. Winters, "State Constitutional Limitations on Solutions of Metropolitan Area Problems" (Ann Arbor: University of Michigan Law School, Legislative Research Center, 1961), 169 pages; Max A. Pock, "Consolidating Police Functions in Metropolitan Areas" (Ann Arbor: University of Michigan Law School, Legislative Research Center, 1962), 51 pages; and "The Book of the States, 1966–67" (Chicago: Council of State Governments, 1966), 584 pages.
[145] For a more complete discussion of the objections to interlocal agreements, see: Advisory Commission on Inter-Governmental Relations, "Alternative Approaches to Governmental Reorganization in Metropolitan Area" (Washington: Advisory Commission on Inter-Governmental Relations 1962), pp. 29–32.

sary for functional consolidation or joint action through intergovernmental contracts. More than half of the States have now adopted legislation which permits intergovernmental contractual relationships. Unfortunately, however, most of these enabling acts relate only to the particular requirements of a particular area and have been enacted to meet a specific need as it arose. Consequently, a number of States have many uncoordinated statutes pertaining to specific problems and areas. Critics are correct in identifying this type of interjurisdictional authorization as stopgap solutions that do not go to the basic issue of governmental reorganization.

California Joint Powers Act. A notable exception to this pattern is found in California, which has adopted broad joint powers legislation. The Joint Exercise of Powers Act [146] allows any designated public agency [147] to exercise any power common to the contracting parties, even though one or more of the contracting parties may be located outside of the State. This act is as brief as it is broad in scope and serves as one of the most effective vehicles for interlocal cooperation in the United States. Experience in Los Angeles County offers abundant evidence.

Early in this century, Los Angeles County entered into contractual arrangements with a few cities located within the county to assume tax assessment and collection responsibilities for them. Questions were raised about the legal status of the contract program and, in an effort to legitimatize what was already an accomplished fact, the State legislature proposed a constitutional amendment sanctioning the relationship, which was adopted in 1914. The amendment authorized the legislature to provide by general law for the intergovernmental agreements, and the Joint Powers Act of 1921 was the result of this action. The act was redesigned in its current form in 1964 to meet certain criticisms.

Among the features of the California act are provisions that (1) allow the continuance of privileges and immunities, workmen's compensation, and other benefits of employees when engaged in the performance of any of their functions extraterritorially; (2) allow contracting parties to use public funds, supplies, and equipment in carrying out a joint activity; and (3) enable the participating jurisdictions to establish a separate agency to administer or operate a joint program, including such specified powers as the right to enter into contracts, employ personnel, acquire, construct, maintain, manage, or operate buildings, and related powers and activities.

An act of the scope of the California Joint Exercise of Powers Act permits intergovernmental agreements for nearly any type of activity. The Association of Bay Area Governments (ABAG), a council of governments providing an areawide forum for discussion of common problems encompassing a nine-county area around San Francisco, was formed under the aegis of this act, and contract programs for services by a number of California counties to other jurisdictions fall within its scope.[148]

The implications of this act for law enforcement are considerable, and several programs have been worked out under it. A prime example is the police information network (PIN) operated by Alameda County for city and county governments in the San Francisco Bay area. Alameda County provides a police records center for county and municipal governments in the bay area which eventually will house all warrants and other police records on a regional basis. Similar programs for other regions of the State are being studied. Other possibilities under the act would be the joint operation by the State, counties, and municipalities of detention facilities, crime laboratories, training schools, and related programs.

Other Joint Powers Acts. Unfortunately, the joint powers legislation of other States generally is not so broad as that of California. Connecticut, for example, has legislation on interlocal agreements that permits certain types of joint action by public agencies, but the concept of a public agency is not so broad as that of California, and areas for agreements are also limited.[149] In the law enforcement field, only radio communication systems can be operated under interlocal agreements.

Tennessee authorizes an unrestricted range of interlocal agreements, but limits them geographically; only contiguous counties and municipalities within the same county may enter into agreements to provide for the joint operation of functions and services.

Enabling legislation for interlocal agreements that is restrictive in nature is not an effective means of fostering interlocal cooperation. Broad and all-encompassing legislation is needed.

The Council of State Governments proposed a model interlocal or joint exercise of powers act in its "Suggested State Legislation Program for 1957." (A complete copy of the model act can be found in appendix F.) This model suggests provisions for States that wish to initiate legislation or revise existing acts. Under the model, a State will authorize joint or cooperative activities on a general basis, which allows the local governmental units to decide what functions they wish to contract for or perform in concert. The act does not suggest that new powers be granted to localities but encompasses only existing powers. The model act would also permit agreements between jurisdictions located in more than one State. Most existing legislation does not provide for agreements across State lines, but patterns of population frequently would make such agreements advantageous.

An act similar in scope and content to the model act should be adopted by all States to further intergovernmental activities. At present, at least six States (Indiana, Kentucky, Maine, Nebraska, Utah, and Virginia) have adopted the model act in substance. The California Joint Exercise of Powers Act is even more permissive than the model act.

Interlocal Agreements Across State Lines. A question has been raised whether States can authorize agreements for interlocal cooperation across State lines because they are assumed by some to be interstate agreements or compacts requiring consent of the U.S. Congress under the Federal Constitution. While this question has not

---

[146] 32A Cal. Govt. Code, secs. 6500–6514.
[147] The broad concept of a public agency in this act includes the Federal Government or any Federal department or agency, the State of California, an adjoining State or any State department or agency, a county, city, public corporation, or public district of California or any adjoining State.
[148] Interestingly, the legal authority upon which the so-called Lakewood plan was formed in Los Angeles County is the State constitution (art. XI, sec. 7.5), which authorizes charter counties to provide contract services, if so stated in the charter. No one questions the fact, however, that the Joint Exercise of Powers Act encompasses the contract services program. See: Jack M. Merelman, "Legal Machinery for Providing Services," in "County Government 1963, Proceedings, sixth Biennial County Government Institute" (Sacramento: County Supervisors Association of California, 1963), p. 7.
[149] Conn. Gin. Stat. secs. 7-339e—7-3391 (1966 Rev.).

been settled through court decisions, it may be argued that because the powers exercised by local governments are under jurisdiction of the States, not the Federal Government, it is within their power to authorize interstate cooperation at the local level.[150] Because some legal doubt still exists, however, it seems appropriate that the Advisory Commission on Inter-Governmental Relations review the problem and make appropriate suggestions to clarify these questions.

OTHER OBSTACLES

Relinquishment of Responsibility. Another argument made against coordinating or consolidating law enforcement services is that no government should allow another to assume responsibilities it will not undertake itself. Criminal activities, however, are not confined within political boundaries, but spill over into other governmental jurisdictions, and single jurisdictions, therefore, cannot adequately repress them. The objection that no government should allow another government to provide a service that it cannot itself provide fails to acknowledge the fact that not every governmental jurisdiction is financially or otherwise capable of providing comprehensive services.

Governments have a basic responsibility to provide needed services for their constituents. If it is beyond the ability of an individual jurisdiction to provide adequate basic services, there are three alternatives: (1) Abolish the jurisdiction and make some other jurisdiction responsible for the services; (2) continue inadequate services; and (3) seek, through joint action, to meet its local responsibilities more adequately. The first choice usually is not feasible politically. The second choice invites an increase in criminal activity and direct action by a higher level of government to protect the public security. The best alternative is the third, the initiation of joint programs with other governmental jurisdictions. Such action is not a rejection or relinquishment of responsibilities but, rather the recognition that certain problems require resources beyond the capacity of a particular jurisdiction.

Difficulties in Achieving Local Government Reorganization. Comprehensive reorganization has been a usual goal of reformers in trying to restructure local governments for the provision of more adequate services. Political and other obstacles to comprehensive reorganization of local government, especially in metropolitan areas, are, however, formidable. The failure of most such attempts is well documented;[151] the principal successes in the United States, in Nashville-Davidson County and Dade County have also been treated in depth elsewhere.[152] It is sufficient here merely to note what types of obstacles will be met.

The Advisory Commission on Inter-Governmental Relations suggests some of the difficulties in its report on attempts at government reorganization in 18 of the Nation's standard metropolitan statistical areas:[153]

☐ Proposals for governmental reorganization in metropolitan areas have faced a largely apathetic public.
☐ Reorganization efforts should not be undertaken lightly, but with full recognition of obstacles to their success.
☐ Any consequential local government reorganization in a metropolitan area will inevitably involve "political" issues.
☐ One condition for success in metropolitan reorganization is an intensive and deliberate effort to develop a broad consensus on the best attainable alternative to the status quo.
☐ Enlistment of popular support for governmental change in a metropolitan area calls for the use of a variety of promotional methods, suited to the diverse composition of the electorate.

In brief, a comprehensive reorganization of local government in metropolitan areas faces many hazards. The success of such an endeavor is related directly to the degree of local consensus that has been achieved and, most particularly, to the degree of consensus reached by the political leadership.

Robert C. Wood, now Undersecretary of the U.S. Department of Housing and Urban Developments, has noted that the political leadership of a metropolitan area must be involved in the decisions regarding the functional coordination or consolidation of services. In the past, most such proposals have been advanced largely by the technicians involved in the immediate administration of a functional specialty, "Little real attention was paid to the construction of meaningful political communities, or to the question of obtaining political responsibility, although these objectives were honored in passing."[154] Such proposals have raised almost insuperable problems of representation and shifts in political influence and have called for a surrender of local political privileges and prerogatives in return for only increased administrative benefits.

It is imperative that questions regarding representation and political influence be met before programs of coordination and consolidation of local government activities can be adopted. Especially in the area of law enforcement, where so much local control is being exercised, such programs must enlist the agreement of the political leadership of the governments involved.

Councils of Governments. A device that holds some promise of lessening the impact of political obstacles to consolidation and coordination is the council of governments. A council of governments is a voluntary association of governments, usually county and municipal, which attempts to solve areawide problems on a common basis. Currently, eight such councils exist, and the ninth is in the planning stages.[155]

The best known council is the Association of Bay Area Governments (ABAG), which includes in its membership 8 counties and 78 municipalities in the San Francisco Bay

---

[150] John M. Winters, "Interstate Metropolitan Areas" (Ann Arbor: University of Michigan Law School, Legislative Research Center, 1962), pp. 85–95.
[151] See: Government Affairs Foundation, Inc., "Metropolitan Surveys: A Digest" (Chicago: Public Administration Service, 1958); James A. Norton, "The Metro Experience" (Cleveland: The Press of Western Reserve University, 1963); and Henry J. Schmandt, Paul G. Steinbicker, and George D. Wendel, "Metropolitan Reform in St. Louis" (New York: Holt, Rinehart, and Winston, 1961).
[152] See Edward Sofen, "The Miami Metropolitan Experiment" (Bloomington: Indiana University Press, 1963); and David A. Booth, "Metropolitics: The Nashville Consolidation" (East Lansing: Michigan State University, Institute for Community Development and Services, 1963).
[153] Advisory Commission on Inter-Governmental Relations, "Factors Affecting Voter Reactions to Governmental Reorganization in Metropolitan Areas" (Washington: Advisory Commission on Inter-Governmental Relations, 1962), pp. 24–33.
[154] Robert C. Wood, "A Division of Powers in Metropolitan Areas," in "Area and Power: A Theory of Local Government," ed. Arthur Maass (Glencoe, Ill.: The Free Press, 1959), p. 60.
[155] The eight existing councils of government are: ABAG, San Francisco area; New York Metropolitan Regional Council, New York City area; Metropolitan Atlanta Council of Local Governments, Atlanta area; Metropolitan Washington Council of Governments, District of Columbia area; Mid-Willamette Council of Governments, Salem, Oreg., area; Puget Sound Governmental Conference, Seattle area; Regional Conference of Elected Officials, Philadelphia area; Southern California Association of Governments, Los Angeles area; and East-West Gateway Coordinating Council, St. Louis area. A ninth council is now being formed in the Detroit metropolitan area.

area. It has been described as a "comprehensive, multiple, but limited purpose, regionally based institution for developing cooperative, coordinated approaches to areawide problems."[156] A significant factor is that ABAG is an association of the political leaders of its member jurisdictions. Organized under the California Joint Exercise of Powers Act, ABAG is capable of bringing authority to bear upon areawide problems because it is politically viable, representative of the local government in the area, and also because it is concerned with maintaining effective local government institutions.[157]

While ABAG has not been directly concerned with the coordination or consolidation of law enforcement service, other councils of government have been.[158] The Metropolitan Washington Council of Governments has prepared a detailed study for a computer-based regional law enforcement records system which will encompass the District of Columbia, several Virginia and Maryland counties, and the city of Alexandria.[159] The Metropolitan Atlanta Council of Local Governments took the lead in establishing Metropol (the Metropolitan Police), the areawide police unit which provides communications, training, and investigative services to a six-county area.[160] In all, five of the eight existing councils of government have some concern with law enforcement activities.[161]

A council of governments, with a committee on law enforcement, can be an effective vehicle in metropolitan areas for promoting consolidation or cooperation in law enforcement activities. Four of the councils are now engaged in negotiating cooperative agreements among member units, and three also mediate disputes. All of the councils have been active on an informal basis in promoting interjurisdictional agreements.[162] It is a simple step to include law enforcement as part of a council's total program.

Because these councils of government are comprised primarily of the political leaders of the member jurisdictions, the political obstacles to coordinated or consolidated programs are not so great as when the development of such programs originates with the day-to-day administrators. It would appear that the problem of political representation and influence suggested by Undersecretary Wood can be met through such an association. As noted, one of the strengths of ABAG is its interest in preserving local government. Thus, a council of governments may also allay some of the fears of home rule advocates.

Economic Obstacles. Any program of coordinated or consolidated services in law enforcement (or any other governmental activity) must be concerned with financing. As noted, one impediment to the participation of low social-ranking communities in joint ventures is the fear of increased costs. Higher-ranking communities may want to provide even more law enforcement service than is really needed—because it is considered a public amenity. Also, no central city wants to be in the position of financing a joint program for the benefit of suburban communities. Each of these situations, then, poses problems of costs.

For example, suburban areas in the Chicago metropolitan area have approximately 49 percent of all assessed property valuation and the city of Chicago and Cook County have the remaining 51 percent. The suburban areas, however, are not paying anything approaching 49 percent of the total law enforcement expenses in the metropolitan region under the current fragmented system. A metropolitan police force, financed by property taxation, would call for increased taxes in the suburbs unless Cook County and the city of Chicago absorbed the increased costs. Suburbs would not view a redistribution of the tax burden favorably,[163] even if more effective law enforcement resulted. This points to a basic difficulty in coordinating or consolidating law enforcement services—cost of any such program must be distributed on an equitable basis.

Several techniques have been devised to redistribute costs for services, including special service districts, subordinate service districts, contractual agreements calling for specified payments for services rendered, and related approaches. Each of these techniques has its individual problems with regard to equitable distribution of costs, but each provides partial answers to the dilemma. Suffice it to say at this point that it is as important to provide for the proper distribution of costs as it is to include the political leadership in any joint program of coordinated or consolidated law enforcement services.

---

[156] Randy H. Hamilton, "ABAG Appraised: A Quinquennial Review of Voluntary Regional Cooperative Action Through the Association of Bay Area Governments." (Berkeley, Calif.: Institute for Local Self Government, 1965), pp. 5–6.
[157] Id. at pp. 55–56.
[158] Interview with Warren Schmid, executive director, ABAG, May 18, 1966.
[159] Systems Science Corporation, "A Regional Law Enforcement Systems Design," a study prepared for the Metropolitan Washington Council of Governments (Bloomington, Ind.: Systems Science Corporation, 1966).
[160] "Metropol: Working Together for Better Law Enforcement," "Georgia Municipal Journal," September 1965, pp. 8–11.
[161] Citizens Research Council of Michigan, "Research Brief on Staff Services and Programs of Councils of Government" (Detroit: Citizens Research Council of Michigan, 1966), p. 11.
[162] Id. at p. 9.
[163] Gilbert Y. Steiner, "Metropolitan Government and the Real World: The Case of Chicago" (Chicago: Loyola University, Center for Research in Urban Government, 1966), pp. 12–14.

APPENDIXES

A. JAIL CONTRACT AGREEMENT, CITY OF OAKLAND AND ALAMEDA COUNTY, CALIF.

B. POLICE COOPERATION AGREEMENT, CITIES OF ALLENTOWN, BETHLEHEM, AND EASTON, PA.

C. NUMBER OF FULL-TIME AND PART-TIME POLICE OFFICERS IN COOK COUNTY, ILL. (EXCLUDING CHICAGO)

D. ARGUMENTS FOR AND AGAINST UNIFICATION OF THE 13 POLICE DEPARTMENTS IN THE METROPOLITAN TORONTO AREA INTO A METROPOLITAN POLICE DEPARTMENT

E. METHOD OF DETERMINING COST FOR CONTRACT LAW ENFORCEMENT SERVICES IN LOS ANGELES COUNTY

F. INTERLOCAL COOPERATION ACT

Appendix A

JAIL CONTRACT AGREEMENT—
CITY OF OAKLAND AND ALAMEDA COUNTY

This agreement, made and entered into this ___ day of _____, 1960, by and between the City of Oakland, a municipal corporation organized and existing under and by virtue of the laws of the State of California, hereinafter called "City," and the County of Alameda, a political subdivision of the State of California, acting by and through its board of supervisors, hereinafter called "County:"

WITNESSETH:

Whereas, each of the parties hereto now owns and maintains jail facilities; and

Whereas, pursuant to section 4004.5 of the Penal Code of the State of California, City and County may enter into an agreement, through their respective legislative bodies, whereby City shall furnish jail facilities for County prisoners upon such terms as may be mutually agreed upon; and

Whereas, it is considered necessary and desirable and in the public interest that the County and the City exercise the rights and privileges afforded by said section.

Now, therefore, it is mutually agreed by and between the City and the County as follows:

1. The jail facilities owned and maintained by the City are hereby made available and furnished for holding prisoners held for examination, held for trial, or held subsequent to sentencing until transported to other facilities.

2. The reimbursement for costs of maintaining prisoners in the parties respective jail facilities shall be computed and paid as herein provided, to wit:

   (a) For each person sentenced and transported to the County owned and maintained jail facilities a rate of $3.11 per day; however, said rate may be modified as provided in (c) of this paragraph, provided that any such payment shall be made solely for such persons as have only been charged with, and found guilty of, violations of city ordinances or city charter provisions.

   (b) For each person sentenced and transported to the City owned and maintained jail facility a rate of $3.11 per day; however, said rate may be modified as provided in (c) of this paragraph, provided that no such payment shall be made for prisoners charged only with the violation of city ordinances or city charter provisions.

   (c) The parties further agree that the rate established in (a) above may be adjusted annually based on costs of operation of said County jail facility and set by resolution of the Board of Supervisors adopted before the first of May and effective on the first of July of each year, and that the rate for prisoners maintained by City, as provided in (b) above, shall increase or decrease automatically to equal the rate when set by County's Board of Supervisors by resolution.

3. It is mutually agreed by and between the parties hereto that the term "per day," as used in paragraph 2 of this agreement, shall mean the 24-hour period from midnight to midnight, or any fraction thereof, that a prisoner is held in the jail facilities: except that such term shall not include, nor shall charge be made for, any fractional period of time the prisoner is held upon the date of his discharge from the jail facilities.

4. In the event that prisoners charged with or found guilty only of violations of city ordinances or charter provisions are removed to the County Hospital for examination, medical services, or hospital care, City shall reimburse County at the rate per day fixed by

the Board of Supervisors of County together with the additional cost of necessary guards and for the safekeeping of such prisoners.

5. The amounts due under this agreement by the County to the City, and by the City to the County, shall be due and payable 30 days from and after the receipt of itemized invoices by each party to this agreement for services rendered to it by the other.

6. This agreement shall be in force from and after the first day of July 1960, and may be modified or terminated at any time by mutual consent of the parties. Either party may terminate by giving notice to the other party in writing of its intention so to do at least 2 months prior to the end of the fiscal year in which it is so terminated.

CITY OF _____

BY _____

COUNTY OF ALAMEDA, a body politic and corporate and a political subdivision of the State of California.

BY _____
(Chairman of the Board of Supervisors)

Appendix B
POLICE COOPERATION AGREEMENT—CITIES OF ALLENTOWN, BETHLEHEM, AND EASTON, PA.

Whereas, increasing population and an increasing number of common problems have tended to obliterate municipal boundaries in the enforcement of laws of the Commonwealth of Pennsylvania in the Lehigh Valley; and

Whereas, there is an urgent need for uniformity and continuity in the enforcement of such laws in the Lehigh Valley; and

Whereas, cooperation among adjoining cities in the exercise and performance of their governmental powers, duties, and functions is authorized by the Act of Pennsylvania Assembly of 1959, September 29, Public Law 990, as amended (53 P.S. 472 et seq.).

This Agreement executed by the cities of Allentown, Bethlehem, and Easton.

WITNESSETH:

1. Each of the parties intends to be legally bound by the terms of this Agreement and has executed the Agreement in accordance with authority conferred by Ordinance or Resolution duly enacted by its city council.

2. The mayor of each municipality shall swear in the police officers below the rank of sergeant of the other two municipalities as auxiliary policemen of his municipality.

3. In the event of emergency, the mayor of the municipality affected may call on the mayors of the other two municipalities for the services as auxiliary policemen of such number of personnel and such equipment as he deems essential. On the receipt of such a call, the mayor called upon shall assign to service in the requesting community such number of personnel as auxiliary policemen and such equipment as in his judgment may be released for such purpose.

4. Personnel and equipment from any municipality assigned on such an emergency call shall be subject to recall by the mayor of that municipality.

5. At periodic intervals, compensation on the basis of payroll cost of personnel supplied and fair rental for equipment supplied shall be mutually determined.

In Witness Whereof, this Agreement has been executed in sextuple as of the ___ day of _____.

ATTEST: CITY OF ALLENTOWN:

_____ BY _____
(City Clerk)   (Mayor)

ATTEST: CITY OF BETHLEHEM:

_____ BY _____
(City Controller)   (Mayor)

ATTEST: CITY OF EASTON:

_____ BY _____
(City Clerk)   (Mayor)

Appendix C
Number of Full-time and Part-time Police Officers in Cook County, Ill. (Excluding Chicago) 1966

Municipality	Estimated population (in thousands)	Cook County Full-time officers	Cook County Part-time officers	Grand total	Municipality	Estimated population (in thousands)	Cook County Full-time officers	Cook County Part-time officers	Grand total
Alsip	8.5	7	4	11	Markham	17	13	3	16
Arlington Heights	42.5	40	0	40	Matteson	4	5	1	6
Barrington	6.5	15	14	29	Maywood	29	40	10	50
Barrington Hills	2.5	7	6	13	McCook	0.5	12	3	15
Bartlett	2.5	3	3	6	Melrose Park	25	36	20	56
Bedford Park	.75	15	0	15	Midlothian	14	10	8	18
Bellwood	22.8	24	15	39	Mount Prospect	31	28	0	28
Berkeley	7	7	8	15	Niles	29.5	43	0	43
Blue Island	25	17	4	21	Norridge	17	10	0	10
Bridgeview	9.5	8	11	19	Northbrook	19	23	0	23
Broadview	9.6	18	6	24	Northfield	5	14	0	14
Brookfield	23	23	0	23	Northlake	16	20	5	25
Burnham	3	3	3	6	North Riverside	8.5	16	8	24
Calumet City	30	23	8	31	Oak Forest	11	6	15	21
Carpentersville	22	20	0	20	Oak Lawn	49	49	0	49
Chicago Heights	40	55	0	55	Oak Park	63	76	0	76
Chicago Ridge	8.2	8	10	18	Olympia Fields	2.5	3	7	10
Cicero	70	98	0	98	Orland Park	4.5	4	8	12
Cook County Sheriff		176	0	176	Palos Heights	5.3	3	12	15
County Club Hills	5	2	11	13	Palos Park	3	1	10	11
Countryside	3	8	0	8	Park Forest	32	21	0	21
Des Plaines	50.7	55	0	55	Park Ridge	40	40	0	40
Dixmoor	3.2	0	12	12	Phoenix	4.2	7	13	20
Dolton	2.5	14	8	22	Posen	4.5	3	8	11
East Chicago Heights	4.7	5	4	9	Richton Park	1	0	7	7
Elk Grove Village	13.5	21	5	26	Riverdale	13.6	12	0	12
Elmwood Park	24	21	0	21	River Forest	12.6	25	0	25
Evanston	80	127	0	127	River Grove	10	11	0	11
Evergreen Park	25	26	23	49	Riverside	10	15	0	15
Forest Park	15	23	0	23	Robbins	7.5	10	10	20
Franklin Park	22	27	12	39	Rolling Meadows	15	14	5	19
Glencoe	11	18	0	18	Sauk Village	6	3	7	10
Glenview	24	29	0	29	Schaumburg	7	7	15	22
Glenwood	3.5	2	5	7	Schiller Park	10	11	20	31
Hanover Park	6.6	3	10	13	Skokie	69	117	0	117
Harvey	33	26	15	41	South Chicago Heights	5.5	4	7	11
Harwood Heights	9.5	9	12	21	South Holland	18.5	11	10	21
Hazel Crest	9	7	12	19	Stickney	7	9	10	19
Hickory Hills	8	3	14	17	Stone Park	4.5	12	2	14
Hillside	12	24	10	34	Summit	10.3	12	13	25
Hoffman Estates	17.5	14	0	14	Thornton	3.9	1	14	15
Hometown	7.6	1	26	27	Tinley Park	8.7	8	5	13
Homewood	17.8	16	0	16	Villa Park	25.4	26	0	26
Justice	5.5	2	10	12	Westchester	22	20	6	26
Kenilworth	3	11	0	11	Wheeling	12.5	15	0	15
La Grange	17.5	29	0	29	Wilmette	32	32	0	32
La Grange Park	17	24	0	24	Winnetka	13.4	27	0	27
Lansing	22	15	26	41	Worth	10.3	8	8	16
Lincolnwood	14	24	0	24					
Lyons	11	14	14	28	Total		2,060	591	2,651

Appendix D

ARGUMENTS FOR AND AGAINST UNIFICATION OF THE 13 POLICE DEPARTMENTS IN THE METROPOLITAN TORONTO AREA INTO A METROPOLITAN POLICE DEPARTMENT [a]

ARGUMENTS AGAINST:

1. Police administration would be removed from the close contact with the residents of local municipality.
2. The local police force has a much better appreciation of local problems, and the means whereby they may be solved.
3. The present arrangements are satisfactory and adequate.
4. Police protection in the suburban municipalities is not less sufficient than in the city of Toronto.
5. The concentration of all calls through one communication center would result in the "jamming" of such center with consequent delays.
6. The formation of a metropolitan Toronto police force was not recommended by the Ontario Municipal Board in the recent amalgamation proceedings, and this decision should not now be interfered with in any summary or less exhaustive review.
7. All area municipalities do not have the same police problems, and therefore, local police forces can best deal with local situations and enjoy the pride of local residents.
8. Transfers of personnel to distant divisions would result in hardship for such personnel due to excessive traveling.
9. It would be too difficult to unify police services of the entire area in one operation and if the proposal is considered at all it should be done by degree.

ARGUMENTS FOR:

1. Duplication of police services would be eliminated.
2. A central communications department would remove costly delays which now exist in emergency and critical situations where speed is an important factor in apprehending an offender.
3. A properly equipped crime laboratory could be established which would provide expert witnesses for court actions.
4. A proper system of centralized records of offenders would be available to the entire area and eliminate delays involved in searches of several police files.
5. Uniform control of traffic would result from direction received from a central traffic bureau.
6. Specialized bureaus could be established which would operate over the entire metropolitan area and release personnel for the very important and too often neglected duties of foot patrol.
7. The entire metropolitan area would have the benefit of central (a) morality branch, (b) traffic branch, (c) criminal investigation branch, (d) criminal identification branch, (e) training school, and (f) transportation of prisoners.
8. Substantial savings to the taxpayer through central control of purchasing would result.
9. Policing the metropolitan area would be more efficient, and the costs of such policing would be equalized over the various municipalities.
10. A unified police force would provide better control over those criminals who operate as receivers and disposers of stolen goods by making it possible to provide adequate surveillance of such persons.
11. The number of unsolved crimes in the metropolitan area indicates that a change in police organization is necessary.
12. Differences that presently exist in wage schedules for police officers doing similar work in different municipalities would be eliminated.
13. Local councils should no longer attempt to direct and administer the activities of a local police force.
14. Adequate finances would be available to properly equip a unified force.
15. There would be one police commissioner who would administer the entire metropolitan area in an impartial manner resulting in a uniform enforcement of police regulations and the criminal code, free from the possibility of local political interference.
16. Unification and modernization of police departments by the formation of a metropolitan police force would result in greater benefits to every municipality.

[a] Source: "Report No. 1 of the Special Committee Re(garding) Unification of the Police and Fire Departments in the Metropolitan Area: For Consideration by the Council of the Municipality of Metropolitan Toronto" (Toronto: Municipality of Metropolitan Toronto, Sept. 29, 1955), pp. 2-4.

Appendix E

METHOD OF DETERMINING COST FOR CONTRACT LAW ENFORCEMENT SERVICES IN LOS ANGELES COUNTY [a]

The basic unit of contract law enforcement service is one car on continuous around-the-clock duty in three 8-hour shifts—one 1-man shift and two 2-man shifts.

The chargeable rate is based on the combined direct operating costs of four selected stations whose workloads consist mainly of providing law enforcement service to contract cities.

The operating costs of these stations were determined from the budget allocation records maintained by the sheriff's department. From these costs, the following items were deducted:

1. Cost of services applicable to other contracts such as prisoner maintenance, school safety officers, crossing guards, etc.
2. Costs indicated by the sheriff as representing the normal staffing of each of the four stations. (Staffing required if patrol car services were not rendered to contract cities.)

The remaining costs, plus applicable county retirement and social security contributions and workmen's compensation insurance, were allocated between one- and two-man cars fielded by each of the stations as follows: station supervision was allocated on the basis of the salaries of patrol deputies assigned to cars. Station support such as detectives, clerical, desk sergeants, etc., were allocated on the basis of number of one- and two-man car shifts fielded in the ratio of 1 to 1.5, respectively. Services and supplies costs were allocated on the basis of the aggregate salary costs including supervision and support previously distributed to the one- and two-man cars.

The station costs allocated to one-man cars and the cost allocated to two-man cars were then divided by the number of one- and two-man car shifts, respectively. This computation provides the basic cost per one-man and two-man car shifts. In addition, auto expense and applicable county indirect expense were added to the station cost per car shift.

County indirect expense recovers the cost of activities of service departments (auditor-controller, county counsel, purchasing agent, etc.) and expenditures from centralized service appropriations (utilities, telephone, insurance, etc.) which are not charged to operating departments.

The cost per shift of one 1-man and two 2-man cars were combined to arrive at the cost for around-the-clock services. Each fiscal year, this rate is updated to reflect salary adjustments provided for deputy sheriffs.

The sheriff's departmental and divisional administrative overhead and central support services were not considered a chargeable cost in the computations made subsequent to 1962. The exclusion of these costs recognizes that the sheriff retains his countywide responsibility for law enforcement, and that the only proper charge to contract cities are for the additional costs incurred in order to provide the contracted services. Accordingly, all sheriff overhead and central support activities (special units, crime laboratory, training, etc.) were considered applicable to the sheriff's statutory responsibility and, therefore, not chargeable to a contracting city.

[a] Los Angeles County sheriff's department.

Appendix F
INTERLOCAL COOPERATION ACT [a]

[Title should conform to State requirements.]
(Be it enacted, etc.)

SECTION 1. PURPOSE. It is the purpose of this act to permit local governmental units to make the most efficient use of their powers by enabling them to cooperate with other localities on a basis of mutual advantage and thereby to provide services and facilities in a manner and pursuant to forms of governmental organization that will accord best with geographic, economic, population and other factors influencing the needs and development of local communities.

SEC. 2. SHORT TITLE. This act may be cited as the Interlocal Cooperation Act.

SEC. 3. PUBLIC AGENCY DEFINED. (a) For the purposes of this act, the term "public agency" shall mean any political subdivision [insert enumeration, if desired] of this State; any agency of the State government or of the United States; and any political subdivision of another State.

(b) The term "State" shall mean a State of the United States and the District of Columbia.

SEC. 4. INTERLOCAL AGREEMENTS. (a) Any power or powers, privileges or authority exercised or capable of exercise by a public agency of this State may be exercised and enjoyed jointly with any other public agency of this State, and jointly with any public agency of any other State or of the United States to the extent that the laws of such other States or of the United States permit such joint exercise or enjoyment. Any agency of the State government when acting jointly with any public agency may exercise and enjoy all of the powers, privileges, and authority conferred by this act upon a public agency.

(b) Any two or more public agencies may enter into agreements with one another for joint or cooperative action pursuant to the provisions of this act. Appropriate action by ordinance, resolution, or otherwise pursuant to law of the governing bodies of the participating public agencies shall be necessary before any such agreement may enter into force.

(c) Any such agreement shall specify the following:

1. Its duration.
2. The precise organization, composition, and nature of any separate legal or administrative entity created thereby together with the power delegated thereto, provided such entity may be legally created.
3. Its purpose or purposes.
4. The manner of financing the joint or cooperative undertaking and of establishing and maintaining a budget therefor.
5. The permissable method or methods to be employed in accomplishing the partial or complete termination of the agreement and for disposing of property upon such partial or complete termination.
6. Any other necessary and proper matters.

(d) In the event that the agreement does not establish a separate legal entity to conduct the joint or cooperative undertaking, the agreement shall, in addition to items 1, 3, 4, 5, and 6 enumerated in subdivision (c) hereof, contain the following:

1. Provision for an administrator or a joint board responsible for administering the joint or cooperative undertaking. In the case of a joint board, public agencies party to the agreement shall be represented.
2. The matter of acquiring, holding, and disposing of real and personal property used in the joint or cooperative undertaking.

(e) No agreement made pursuant to this act shall relieve any public agency of any obligation or responsibility imposed upon it by law except that to the extent of actual and timely performance thereof by a joint board or other legal or administrative entity created by an agreement made hereunder; said performance may be offered in satisfaction of the obligation or responsibility.

(f) Every agreement made hereunder shall, prior to and as a condition precedent to its entry into force, be submitted to the attorney general who shall determine whether the agreement is in proper form and compatible with the laws of this State. The attorney general shall approve any agreement submitted to him hereunder unless he shall find that it does not meet the conditions set forth herein and shall detail in writing addressed to the governing bodies of the public agencies concerned the specific respects in which the proposed agreement fails to meet the requirements of law. Failure to disapprove an agreement submitted hereunder within [* * *] days of its submission shall constitute approval thereof.

[(g) Financing of joint projects by agreement shall be as provided by law.]

SEC. 5. FILING, STATUS, AND ACTIONS. Prior to its entry into force, an agreement made pursuant to this act shall be filed with [the keeper of local public records] and with the [secretary of state]. In the event that an agreement entered into pursuant to this act is between or among one or more public agencies of this State and one or more public agencies of another State or of the United States, said agreement shall have the status of an interstate compact, but in any case or controversy involving performance or interpretation thereof or liability thereunder, the public agencies party thereto shall be real parties in interest, and the State may maintain an action to recoup or otherwise make itself whole for any damages or liability which it may incur by reason of being joined as a party therein. Such action shall be maintainable against any public agency or agencies whose default, failure of performance, or other conduct caused or contributed to the incurring of damage or liability by the State.

SEC. 6. ADDITIONAL APPROVAL IN CERTAIN CASES. In the event that an agreement made pursuant to this act shall deal in whole or in part with the provision of services or facilities with regard to which an officer or agency of the State government has constitutional or stat-

---

[a] Source: Council of State Governments, "Suggested State Legislation Program for 1957" (Chicago: Council of State Governments, October 1956), pp. 93–97.

utory powers of control, the agreement shall, as a condition precedent to its entry into force, be submitted to the State officer or agency having such power of control and shall be approved or disapproved by him or it as to all matters within his or its jurisdiction in the same manner and subject to the same requirements governing the action of the attorney general pursuant to section 4(f) of this act. This requirement of submission and approval shall be in addition to and not in substitution for the requirement of submission to and approval by the attorney general.

SEC. 7. APPROPRIATIONS, FURNISHING OF PROPERTY, PERSONNEL, AND SERVICE. Any public agency entering into an agreement pursuant to this act may appropriate funds and may sell, lease, give, or otherwise supply the administrative joint board or other legal or administrative entity created to operate the joint or cooperative undertaking by providing such personnel or services therefor as may be within its legal power to furnish.

SEC. 8. [Insert severability clause, if desired.]

SEC. 9. [Insert effective date.]

Chapter 5

Police Personnel

As with any enterprise, the effectiveness of our Nation's law enforcement agencies depends upon the competence of personnel: [1]

> It is impossible to separate the performance of local governments from the abilities of their personnel. Ordinances are not self-executing and no other service of local government has meaning except as it is planned, directed, and delivered by people. If these things are done well, communities may thrive; if poorly, the future demand may outstrip all services, all facilities, all planning.

Commission surveys show that there is substantial variance in the quality of police personnel in the United States. They indicate that, in general, law enforcement personnel meet their difficult responsibilities with zeal, determination, and devotion to duty. They also indicate that many actions of individual police officers and administrators are ill-conceived. This is cause for concern; for rising crime rates, social unrest, and expanding police functions demand personnel of ever-increasing competence.

This chapter will explore the nature of the challenge confronting the police. It will describe the persons needed to meet this challenge, and some methods for attracting them into the police service. Finally, it will discuss programs for improving the overall quality of police personnel.

THE POLICE TASK: ITS CHALLENGE AND DIVERSITY

THE COMPLEXITIES OF CRIMINAL LAW ENFORCEMENT

It is generally assumed by the public that the police enforce the criminal laws and preserve peace mechanically, by simply arresting anyone who has deviated from legislative norms of acceptable behavior.

Unfortunately, some police spokesmen publicly enunciate this same view. As chapter 2 has explained, this concept of mechanical enforcement of all criminal laws dramatically underplays the difficulties of the police role. First, the police do not have the resources to enforce all criminal provisions equally. Second, the other parts of the criminal justice system simply cannot cope with all law violators.[2] Further, the police are faced with enforcing numerous laws regulating social conduct—drunkenness, prostitution, and gambling to name a few—which are often unpopular, ambiguous, unenforceable, or which can apply to the common activities of law-abiding citizens even though they were intended to apply only to the activities of certain kinds of criminals.

In light of these inherent limitations, individual police officers must, of necessity, be given considerable latitude in exercising their arrest power. As a result, no task committed to individual judgment is more complex or delicate. A mistake in judgment can precipitate a riot or culminate in subsequent criminal activity by a person who was erroneously released by an officer. An unjustified arrest can seriously, and perhaps permanently, affect the future course of a man's life. The importance of the arrest power and the need for rational exercise of this power cannot be overstated.

A further complication is that the framework of procedural rules within which the police must function is often unclear and difficult to apply. Only years of litigation may resolve ambiguities in procedural rules, but a police officer must make his own resolution instantly, under stress, and often without advice.

Since the police are also expected to prevent crime, they must constantly be alert to potential violations and must attempt to reduce the opportunity for criminal behavior. This requires vigilance on the part of police officers, an intuitive sense for suspicious conduct, and an understanding of human behavior.

The police are also regularly called upon to resolve volatile situations for which legislative or judicial direction is either vague or nonexistent. Calls for assistance besiege police departments, and officers must respond to such problems as domestic disputes, unruly juveniles, or suspicious persons. Many of these problems will not result in arrest or do not even involve criminal conduct. But only the police are available to render assistance, and as a result, every officer must resolve delicate social situations, even in the absence of a clear direction to do so.

THE COMPLEXITIES OF POLICE ADMINISTRATION, SUPERVISION, AND TECHNICAL SERVICES

Police work is not only complicated for police officers on the street. Administrative and supervisory personnel must operate a complex business, which entails assessing

---

[1] "Government Manpower for Tomorrow's Cities: A Report of the Municipal Manpower Commission." (New York: McGraw-Hill, 1962), p. 20.
[2] Frank Remington, "The Law Relating to 'On the Street' Detention, Questioning and Frisking of Suspected Persons and Police Arrest Privileges in General," in Claude R. Sowle, ed., "Police Power and Individual Freedom: The Quest for Balance" (Chicago: Aldine Publishing Company, 1962), p. 20.

community needs; determining policy; selecting, training, deploying, and supervising personnel; and utilizing a budget in the best possible manner. Further, a department must have a technical staff that responds to the need for optimum recordkeeping and information retrieval; communications; community relations; and analysis of evidence. In large municipalities, the administration of a police department is a massive undertaking. In 1965, the New York Police Department employed 28,363 personnel and had a budget of over $364 million; the Chicago Police Department had a budget of over $90 million and had 11,726 employees.[3]

In summary, and as was observed in 1931 by the Wickersham Commission,[4] policing a community is one of the most complex responsibilities confronting any governmental agency: [5]

Reviewing the tasks we expect of our law enforcement officers, it is my impression that their complexity is perhaps greater than that of any other profession. On the one hand we expect our law enforcement officer to possess the nurturing, caretaking, sympathetic, empathizing, gentle characteristics of physician, nurse, teacher, and social worker as he deals with school traffic, acute illness and injury, juvenile delinquency, suicidal threats and gestures, and missing persons. On the other hand we expect him to command respect, demonstrate courage, control hostile impulses, and meet great physical hazards. . . . He is to control crowds, prevent riots, apprehend criminals, and chase after speeding vehicles. I can think of no other profession which constantly demands such seemingly opposite characteristics.

THE NEED TO IMPROVE PERSONNEL ASSIGNMENTS

CURRENT USE OF THE PATROLMAN AND DETECTIVE

Under traditional police organization, the initial responsibility for confronting the entire range of police problems rests with the patrolman. Along with responding to criminal behavior, the patrolman is responsible for such matters as enforcing traffic regulations and for performing a myriad of services for the public. On any tour of duty a patrolman may confront a burglary in progress, an incapacitated drunk, an injured or ill person, a violation of a littering ordinance, an unlicensed peddler, a suspicious person, a traffic violation, a person locked out of his residence, or a domestic dispute.[6]

As a result of these divergent demands, patrolmen often are overextended to the point of being unable to give adequate attention to criminal matters. In spite of rising crime rates and a continuing low rate of crimes cleared by arrest, a patrolman must normally devote a considerable portion of his time to the performance of noncrime related tasks. A survey of the Kansas City Police Department in 1966, for example, revealed that patrol officers devoted only 32 percent of their time to criminal matters.[7] This problem is not easy to solve. The nonenforcement tasks the police perform are extremely important, and in most places the police are the only people available to perform them.

In nearly all departments, a patrolman does not conduct follow up investigations on criminal offenses; this task is performed by a detective. However, since there are relatively few detectives in a police department— normally about 10 percent of all sworn personnel [8]—they also are overwhelmed by their caseloads. As a result, extensive investigations can be undertaken only on major crimes, and little, if any, time can be devoted to a systematic search for witnesses, or for leads on the perpetrators of most offenses.

The existing wide range of patrol responsibility hampers efforts to attract more highly qualified personnel into police service. Present police departments are monolithic in structure. All sworn police personnel, regardless of individual qualifications or experience, normally begin their careers as patrolmen, assigned to patrol or traffic duties. Normally, personnel must remain in this category from 1 to 5 years before being eligible for promotion or transfer. Since a police officer serving in this capacity must respond to all demands upon police, whether they involve removing a cat from a roof or arresting a robbery suspect, his status is adversely affected both within and outside of the police agency. Police work, therefore, tends to attract persons who are willing to perform its mechanical aspects and to accept its status and compensation. For example, in a survey conducted of the Metropolitan Police Department of Washington, D.C., in 1966, it was revealed that over 60 percent of the applicants for positions in that department were holding clerical, sales, manufacturing, or transportation jobs at the time of application and that the majority of the remaining applicants were in the military service.[9]

Few persons whose ability or academic achievement gives them other professional career opportunities are willing to spend as many years performing mechanical, undemanding duties which consume a large part of a recruit's time in most police departments. Insofar as personnel assignments diminish the attractiveness of police work they reduce police effectiveness: [10]

If progress is to be realized in achieving professional stature, there must be a separating out of functions so that those of a purely ministerial nature are performed by persons of lesser talents receiving compensation commensurate with the job. Admittedly, there are major problems involved in accomplishing such a classification of employees in smaller agencies where flexibility of personnel is important. But the need is greatest within the large departments and it is in these departments that the concept that all police tasks are equally important so seriously impairs the possibility of achieving professional status for those who are engaged in what might be termed the "guts" of police work.

It seems evident that a more rational division of assignments, particularly in the larger departments, would greatly alleviate some of these deficiencies. This was noted by the British Royal Commission in their 1960 Interim Report on Police: [11]

The reason for this failure [to recruit a proper share of able and well-educated young men] is not in our view, that the police service is inherently unattractive as a career. . . . It lies in the

---

[3] International City Managers Association, "Municipal Yearbook, 1966." (Ann Arbor: Cushing-Malloy, 1966), p. 444.
[4] National Commission on Law Observance and Enforcement, "Report on the Police." (Washington: U.S. Government Printing Office, 1931), p. 19.
[5] Statement of Dr. Ruth Levy, Director, Peace Officers Research Project, Health Department, City of San Jose, Calif. Presented at Conference for Police Professors, Michigan State University, April 6-8, 1966.
[6] In 1933, a job analysis of the police service in California determined that police work required over 3,000 types of skills and applications of knowledge. "Analysis of Police Service." (Sacramento: California State Department of Education, 1933).
[7] Survey conducted by Public Administration Service for the President's Commission on Law Enforcement and Administration of Justice.

[8] O. W. Wilson, "Police Administration." (2d ed., New York: McGraw-Hill, 1963), p. 293.
[9] Century Research Corp., "Recruitment and Retention Factors in the Metropolitan Police Department," prepared for the President's Commission on Crime in the District of Columbia and the Office of Law Enforcement Assistance. (Arlington: Va., 1966), table 11, p. 23.
[10] Herman Goldstein, address delivered at the University of Wisconsin on May 13, 1965, as quoted in "The Police Function in the United States, American Bar Association Project on Minimum Standards for Criminal Justice, Committee on the Police Function." (Sept. 8, 1966), p. 3.
[11] Royal Commission on Police, "Interim Report, 1960." (London: Her Majesty's Stationery Office, 1960), p. 19.

neglect of those responsible to adjust the opening stages of a police career, in the way that other professions have found it necessary to do, so as to attract able candidates. It cannot be doubted that it is the early prospects that influence young people to choose one career rather than another. Nor does it call for any great insight or a deep knowledge of psychology to understand how the police service must appear at a disadvantage in this respect compared with almost any other profession today.

THE REVAMPING OF EXISTING PATROL AND
INVESTIGATIVE ASSIGNMENTS

A promising way to attract better personnel, to utilize them more effectively in controlling crime, and to provide better service for the community is for departments to divide police functions more rationally among their personnel. At present a patrolman is equally responsible for the most complex and the most menial of police tasks. The wide range of skills required in performing all these tasks seems possible of attainment for only limited numbers of personnel.[12] This being so, these tasks should be divided according to the skills required to perform them. For example, instead of having all patrol officers respond to all demands placed upon a department, the most competent officers should devote their time to the police work that requires the greatest degree of ability, education, and judgment.

To implement this recommendation, police departments in large and medium-sized cities should establish three classes of officers, which for purposes of this report will be referred to as the police agent, the police officer, and the community service officer (CSO). Tasks would be assigned to these officers on the basis of the skills, intelligence, and education necessary to perform those tasks well. An individual would then devote his time to working on matters suited to his level of competence. This proposal has been evaluated and influenced by police practitioners at all departmental levels and by other experts from across the country.

It is recognized that some departments are simply too small to revamp current patrol responsibilities, and that many rural departments devote nearly all of their time to the enforcement of traffic regulations and the performance of services for their communities. These departments, therefore, are compelled to use their personnel for all tasks.

The Police Agent. A critical need exists in law enforcement (1) to identify the tasks that require the highest degree of judgment, intelligence, education, initiative, and understanding of a community and of human behavior; (2) to assign these tasks to the most competent personnel, and (3) to accord proper status to the officers who perform these tasks. Although these are obvious principles, they are not widely followed in the police service.

To accomplish this end, police departments should establish a distinct classification of officers, designated herein as police agents, who would be assigned to the most complicated, sensitive, and demanding police tasks. For example, police agents could be assigned to patrol high-crime neighborhoods or areas of social unrest, to investigate major crimes, or to respond to the more serious domestic disputes or a gathering of troublesome juveniles.

As described later in this chapter, a police agent should have considerable educational attainment: At least 2 years of college and preferably a baccalaureate degree in the liberal arts or social sciences. For the present, however, the position of agent should also be open to officers who cannot make such an academic showing but who demonstrate a capacity for imaginative and responsible work.

Agents would replace, but have a much wider responsibility than, the existing detective. In most departments, the detective is limited to an investigative function. Many tasks currently performed by detectives, such as routine followup investigations on certain classes of crime, could be assigned to police officers, and in some cases, to community service officers.

An obvious advantage of the police agent position is that it could make police work an attractive career for highly qualified young men. This involves more than merely creating a new title, of course. A police agent must be accorded the status and compensation of a skilled professional who requires a minimum of close supervision. He should be permitted great latitude in his performance and should be judged by his ability to solve problems and to reduce crime as well as apprehend offenders.

While it is not possible to describe, in detail, the scope of police agent responsibility for all departments, the following is illustrative of some functions that could appropriately be performed by the most competent personnel:

(a) Serve as a uniformed patrol officer in high crime and high tension areas;
(b) Investigate major crimes in a plainclothes capacity;
(c) Acquire an understanding of and develop solutions for police-community problems;
(d) Make difficult arrests;
(e) Investigate crimes in which juveniles are involved;
(f) Enforce gambling, vice, and narcotic statutes;
(g) Maintain contact with citizens in the community to ascertain potential signs of strife.

The character of problems requiring the attention of police agents will necessarily change from time to time. An agent may be needed to patrol a sensitive neighborhood in uniform for a period of time, but could next be assigned to a series of major investigations. The crux of the agent concept is that the best officers in a department should be used flexibly to confront problems placing the greatest demand for talent upon police personnel.

The Police Officer. The police officer would perform the police duties of enforcing laws and investigating those crimes that can be solved by immediate followup investi-

---

[12] August Vollmer, "The Police and Modern Society." (Berkeley: University of California Press, 1936), pp. 221–223.

gations or are most likely to have suspects close to the crime scene. He would respond to selected called for services, perform routine patrol, render emergency services, and enforce traffic regulations and investigate traffic accidents. In addition to these responsibilities, the police officer would be an integral part of the police teams discussed in the General Report, working in concert with police agents and CSO's in solving crimes and meeting other police problems.

Since a substantial portion of police time is currently devoted to these tasks, police departments would undoubtedly need a greater number of police officers than agents. The ratio of officers to agents would depend to a large extent on the magnitude and character of a community's crime and social problems. Police officers would be encouraged and assisted to qualify for the position of police agent.

The Community Service Officer. The purposes of creating the position of community service officer are many: (1) To improve police service in high crime rate areas; (2) to enable police to hire persons who can provide a greater understanding of minority group problems; (3) to relieve police agents and officers of lesser police duties; (4) to increase the opportunity for minority group members to serve in law enforcement, and (5) to tap a new reservoir of manpower by helping talented young men who have not been able as yet to complete their education to qualify for police work.

Problems of major proportions confront the police in deprived communities. Aside from the existence of substantial crime in many of these communities, the police face widespread hostility and resentment. One of the primary reasons for this hostility and resentment is the failure of the police and citizens living in impoverished conditions to understand each other's problems. There is a critical need to improve this understanding. For example, although a primary function of the police is to perform many services for the community, there is little recognition of this fact by citizens in slum sections of a city. And it is they that often have the greatest need for such services. Further, since relatively few persons from slum communities become police officers, police personnel have limited knowledge of conditions that encourage criminal behavior in these communities.

The need to improve police operations and efficiency, as described in chapter 3, has further isolated the police from the slum community. To reduce the time it takes for police personnel to respond to called for services, they have become motorized. Thus, in most cities, a police officer no longer walks his beat. Another movement in police departments is to centralize police operations and reduce the number of neighborhood precincts. For example, in 1961 the Chicago Police Department reduced the number of precincts from 38 to 21, and in a 1966 survey of the Metropolitan Police Department of Washington, D C., the International Association of Chiefs of Police recommended that the existing 14 precincts be consolidated into 6 districts: [13]

In the 19th and early 20th centuries police precinct stations were a necessary convenience to the public and served as work centers to reduce the time and distance involved in an officer's travels from his place of duty to his station. Today, however, the widespread use of the telephone and modern police radio and transportation systems have drastically reduced the need for neighborhood police stations. The consolidation of unnecessary facilities can result in considerable economies to the taxpayer because of the savings involved in operational and maintenance costs and in the reduction of utility expenses.

Although the move toward more efficient and economical police operations is a necessary one, it must be accompanied with efforts to gain a greater understanding of slum problems and to provide adequate police services for the poor. It is doubtful that these goals can be accomplished without a greater participation of minority group persons in police service. For these reasons—and because of the need to broaden recruiting efforts—the position of community service officer should be established in urban police departments. This officer would be recruited primarily from neighborhoods of the type he would serve.

It is visualized that the CSO would be a young man, typically between the ages of 17 and 21, with the aptitude, integrity, and stability to perform police work. A CSO would be, in effect, an apprentice policeman—an entirely new type of police cadet working on the street under close supervision, and in close cooperation with the police officer and police agent. He would not have full law-enforcement powers or carry arms, neither would he perform clerical duties as many police cadets do today.

The duties of the CSO would be to assist police officers and agents in their work and to improve communication between police departments and the neighborhood as a uniformed member of the working police. He would render certain carefully selected police services to these neighborhoods. For example, the CSO might play an important role in police work with juveniles; refer citizen complaints and problems to appropriate agencies; and perform services such as emergency aid for the sick, the mentally ill or the alcoholic. The CSO would, moreover, investigate certain minor thefts and loss of property; provide continuing assistance to families encountering domestic problems; and work with specialized police units such as a community relations unit.

To counteract the isolation of the police from the community created by the present centralization of police operations and the motorization of personnel, small neighborhood offices could be established in deprived communities which could serve as locations where the community service officer, the police agent, and police officer could be contacted or could be available for consultation with citizens during certain hours of the day.

Applicants for the position of community service officer would not have to meet the conventional educational requirements of a department. For example, a high school diploma should not be a rigid prerequisite for serving as a CSO. Rather selection should be made on an individ-

---

[13] International Association of Chiefs of Police, "A Survey of the Metropolitan Police Department, Washington, D.C." (Washington: I.A.C.P., 1966), p. 448.

ual basis with priority being given to applicants with promising aspirations, honesty, intelligence, a desire and a tested capacity to advance his education, and an understanding of the neighborhood and its problems. And an applicant might well be selected despite a minor offense record. Otherwise, it might be difficult to recruit members of minority groups as CSOs since Commission studies reveal that there is a 60 percent probability that a Negro youth who grows up in the slums will have such a record. Programs to assist CSOs to continue their education and to become eligible to serve police departments in other capacities are discussed in subsequent sections of this chapter.

This new division of functions should increase the attractiveness of police work by making it possible for a college graduate to assume the responsible position of agent after a brief internship but without long prior service as a patrol officer, and for officers and CSOs to become agents as soon as they qualify and vacancies exist. The opportunity to continue with education at the expense of and with the help of a police department would surely increase the attractiveness of police work to members of minority groups—or to any young men who are unable to further themselves because of insufficient schooling. Creating the positions of CSO and agent might do much to solve the manpower problems of those departments that have them, and might be the fastest way of recruiting large numbers of well-qualified and experienced minority group officers. However, it is important to add in the latter connection that every department should strengthen its efforts to recruit minority group police officers and agents who do not need to go through the CSO phase. A department that admits minority group personnel only at the CSO level will merit the charge that it is practising a subtle kind of discrimination.

THE ROLE OF CIVILIANS IN POLICE WORK

Many tasks now performed by sworn officers do not require police skills. Police officers are now used in many departments as record clerks, school crossing guards, lab technicians, court bailiffs, receptionists, and mechanics. For example, in 1965, over 100 sworn police officers were used for the purpose of regulating taxicabs in New York City.[14] Many tasks now performed by sworn officers should be assumed by civilian personnel within a department.

Several departments have already recognized the value in utilizing civilian personnel for the performance of collateral police tasks. In 1965, 10.7 percent of the total personnel in police departments were civilians.[15] This represents an increase of nearly 3 percent over the total used in 1960.[16] For example, nearly all large departments are now using "meter maids" to enforce parking regulations. This is an encouraging trend and law enforcement agencies should increasingly utilize civilians to perform clerical and mechanical functions.

Civilians are needed for the performance of more than mechanical tasks, however. There are critical needs in police departments for skilled specialists in such fields as fiscal planning, personnel management, law, research and planning, and science and technology. Many departments now utilize sworn personnel for all staff and technical positions, even when such personnel do not possess the requisite skill for these positions. Police administration and operations will suffer as long as this continues

Career Development and Educational Standards

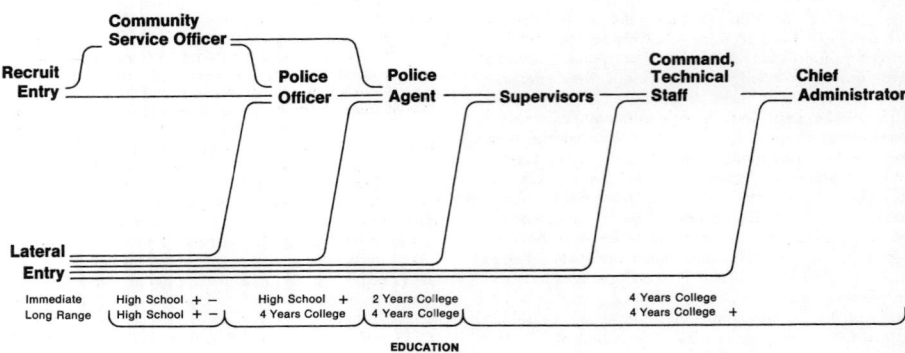

[14] Law enforcement task force, appointed for the period of governmental transition, "Report to Mayor-Elect John V. Lindsay." (New York: 1965), p. 8.
[15] U.S. Department of Justice, Federal Bureau of Investigation, "Uniform Crime Reports—1965." (Washington: U.S. Government Printing Office, 1966), p. 152.
[16] Bruce Smith, revised by Bruce Smith, Jr., "Police Systems in the United States." (2d rev. ed., New York: Harper and Brothers, 1960), p. 114.

to be the case. Hence, because skills needed for fiscal planning or for research are unrelated to the skills required of police officers, police departments should not restrict such positions to sworn personnel. Instead, whether they be civilians or sworn officers, persons should be selected who possess the ability and academic background necessary to meet the demands of specialized positions.

Several departments have already recognized the value of using civilians with specialized skills in certain administrative and staff capacities. For one, Superintendent O. W. Wilson, of the Chicago Police Department, has utilized civilians in research and training, and recently hired a civilian as the department legal advisor; and the Ventura, Calif., County Sheriff's Department has a civilian business manager.

The President's Commission on Crime in the District of Columbia, in its "Report on the Metropolitan Police Department," suggested that several divisions within that department could be administered by civilians: [17]

In the future more responsibilities should be assigned to highly trained civilians. Civilians can bring needed technical disciplines to the Department as it begins the reorganization and modernization outlined by the IACP and recommended by this Commission. In the new organization plan there are important Divisions which could properly be commanded by civilian directors. In the areas of planning, training, communications, public information, recordkeeping, computerization and many others, there are important jobs requiring professional skills not now available within the Department. The reorganization presents a unique opportunity to add to the Department's complement of skills and thereby equip it to provide better service to the community.

The recommendation that certain administrative and staff positions should be assigned to specialists does not mean that sworn personnel should be precluded from serving in these positions. It does mean, however, that sworn personnel should be selected for administrative, supervisory, and staff assignments only if they possess the requisite skills.

THE ROLE OF WOMEN IN POLICE WORK

Women were first appointed to the American police service 56 years ago by the Los Angeles department. This was 4 years before they were appointed to the Metropolitan Police of London and 7 years after the first female was commissioned on the European Continent in Stuttgart, Germany.[18] The first American woman police were charged with: [19]

The protection of young girls and the prevention or minimization of social evils . . . the return of runaway girls to their homes, the warning of young girls, the suppression of dance hall evils, . . . petty gambling in stores frequented by children . . . [and] the sale of liquor to minors, service at railroad depots, the conducting of investigations and the securing of evidence.

In 1960, there were 5,617 female police officers and detectives in the United States. Of these, all but 400 served in urban areas.[20]

The role of the policewoman today is essentially what it always has been. Female officers serve in juvenile divisions, where they perform investigative and social service oriented activities for women, teenaged females, preteen youngsters (both male and female), and infants. In addition, some larger forces, including those of New York, Detroit, and Los Angeles, routinely assign female officers to other operational commands, where they participate in narcotics and gambling law enforcement and routine patroling.

Policewomen can be an invaluable asset to modern law enforcement, and their present role should be broadened.[21] Qualified women should be utilized in such important staff service units as planning and research, training, intelligence, inspection, public information, community relations, and as legal advisors. Women could also serve in such units as computer programming and laboratory analyses and communications. Their value should not be considered as limited to staff functions or police work with juveniles; women should also serve regularly in patrol, vice, and investigative divisions. Finally, as more and more well-qualified women enter the service, they could assume administrative responsibilities.

NEEDED QUALITIES AND THE SELECTION PROCESS

It has often been stated that policing a community is personal service of the highest order, requiring sterling qualities in the individual who performs it.[22] The Commission's evaluation of police work confirms this observation. Few professions are so peculiarly charged with individual responsibility.[23] Officers are compelled to make instantaneous decisions—often without clearcut guidance from a legislature, the judiciary, or from departmental policy—and mistakes on judgment could cause irreparable harm to citizens, or even to the community.

Complexities inherent in the policing function dictate that officers possess a high degree of intelligence, education, tact, sound judgment, physical courage, emotional stability, impartiality, and honesty.[24] While innumerable commissions and expert observers of the police have long recognized and reported this need, communities have not yet demanded that officers possess these qualities, and personnel standards for the police service remain low.

The failure to establish high professional standards for the police service has been a costly one, both for the police and for society. Existing selection requirements and procedures in the majority of departments, aside from physical requirements, do not screen out the unfit. Hence, it is not surprising that far too many of those charged with protecting life and property and rationally enforcing our laws are not respected by their fellow officers and are incompetent, corrupt, or abusive. One incompetent officer can trigger a riot, permanently damage the reputation of a citizen, or alienate a community against a police department. It is essential, therefore, that the requirements to

---

[17] The President's Commission on Crime in the District of Columbia, "A Report of the President's Commission on Crime in the District of Columbia on the Metropolitan Police." (Washington: U.S. Government Printing Office, 1960), p. 31.
[18] Elmer D. Graper, "American Police Administration." (New York: The MacMillan Co., 1921), p. 226.
[19] Id. at pp. 228–229.
[20] U.S. Bureau of Census, "U.S. Census of Population 1960. Subject Reports: Occupational Characteristics—Final Report PC (2)–(7A)." Washington: U.S. Government Printing Office, 1963), table 1, p. 9.

[21] This was also recognized by the President's Commission on Crime in the District of Columbia, supra, note 17 at p. 30.
[22] Supra, note 11 at p. 19; and Leonard V. Harrison, "Police Administration in Boston," vol. II. (Cambridge: Harvard University Press, 1934), p. 28.
[23] Leonard V. Harrison, "Police Administration in Boston: Harvard Law School Survey of the Boston Police Department," vol. III. (Cambridge: Harvard University Press, 1934), p. 30.
[24] Supra, note 12 at p. 223.

serve in law enforcement reflect the awesome responsibility facing the personnel that is selected.[25]

Higher standards . . . must be established. Whatever may be achieved in remedying police defects must be done through enlisting the services of intelligent men of excellent character, who are sufficiently educated to perform the duties of a policeman. . . . The police organization suffers in reputation and society pays the bill when policemen are dishonest, brutal, stupid, or physically or tempermentally unsuited.

The purpose of this section is to determine what attributes must be possessed by police personnel, what characteristics should preclude an applicant from serving the community as a law enforcement officer, and what deficiencies exist in the current selection process.

EDUCATION

The Need for Advanced Education. The quality of police service will not significantly improve until higher educational requirements are established for its personnel. As was indicated earlier in this chapter, the complexity of the police task is as great as that of any other profession. The performance of this task requires more than physical prowess and common sense:[26]

It is nonsense to state or to assume that the enforcement of the law is so simple that it can be done best by those unencumbered by a study of the liberal arts. The man who goes into our streets in hopes of regulating, directing or controlling human behavior must be armed with more than a gun and the ability to perform mechanical movements in response to a situation. Such men as these engage in the difficult, complex and important business of human behavior. Their intellectual armament—so long restricted to the minimum—must be no less than their physical prowess and protection.

The need for highly educated personnel was recognized as early as 1931 in the report of the Wickersham Commission.[27] But despite the admonition of that commission to improve low entrance standards, educational requirements remain minimal in most departments.

In 1961, a survey conducted of over 300 police departments showed that 24 percent of those departments had no minimum educational prerequisite, while less than 1 percent required any level of college preparation.[28] In one region of the country, the New England States, over 72 percent of the departments surveyed did not even require their applicants to have high school diplomas.[29]

Although minimal educational requirements have not prevented some persons with higher academic achievement from pursuing careers in law enforcement, these exceptions are few in number. In a survey conducted of 6,200 officers in 1964, only 30.3 percent had taken one or more college courses and only 7.3 percent possessed a college degree.[30] A more recent survey of over 5,700 police officers employed by police agencies in the metropolitan area of Detroit revealed that over 75 percent of these officers had not attended college.[31] In the Metropolitan Detroit survey, it was further shown that nearly 13 percent of the officers had not received high school diplomas. In many departments, particularly in New England and Southern States, a majority of the officers are not high school graduates. For example, a 1962 survey of one Connecticut department revealed that 53 of the 85 sworn officers had not completed high school.[32]

Sworn personnel, who, in various unpredictable situations, are required to make difficult judgments, should possess a sound knowledge of society and human behavior. This can best be attained through advanced education:[33]

A superior officer of any police department should certainly be conversant with the structure of our government and its philosophies. He must be well grounded in sociology, criminology, and human relations in order to understand the ramifications of the problems which confront him daily. He must understand what makes people act as they do and what impact his actions in the performance of duty will have on them.

Minimum Educational Requirements. Due to the nature of the police task and its effect on our society, there is need to elevate educational requirements to the level of a college degree from an accredited institution for all future personnel selected to perform the functions of a police agent. The demands on the police should preclude a lower requirement for persons responsible for confronting major crime and social problems. Functions to be performed by the police officer, although not as demanding, are also complex. Hence, all future personnel serving in that capacity should be required to have completed at least 2 years of college preparation at an accredited institution.

While such educational requirements could be implemented in only a limited number of departments today, it is imperative that all law enforcement agencies strive to achieve these goals as quickly as possible. As an appropriate first step, all departments should immediately establish a requirement that no person be employed in a sworn capacity until he has received a high school diploma and has demonstrated by appropriate achievement tests the ability to perform successfully college level studies.[34] Cities and counties which fail to recognize the vital necessity of upgrading the educational levels of their departments are guilty of perpetuating ineffective police service and are not providing their citizens with adequate police service and protection. To assist departments in ultimately reaching desirable requirements, educational standards should be increased progressively as conditions permit. The ultimate goal is that all personnel with general enforcement powers have baccalaureate degrees.

At least twenty-two departments, twenty-one of which are in California, have already established minimum college requirements, varying from one semester of college education to a 4-year degree. For example, the San Jose Police Department has had a minimum entrance requirement of 2 years of college since 1957 and the Berkeley Police Department has had the same requirement since 1960.[35] The only non-Federal law enforcement agency now requiring that all entering officers have a 4-year college degree is the Multnomah County Sheriff's Department in Oregon.[36]

Although it is recognized that most departments are encountering difficulty in filling current positions under

---

[25] August Vollmer, "The Police in Chicago," in "Illinois Crime Survey," John H. Wigmore, ed. (Chicago: Association of Criminal Justice, 1929), p. 360.
[26] Quinn Tamm, "A Change for the Better" in "The Police Chief." (Washington: I.A.C.P., 1962), p. 5.
[27] Supra, note 4 at p. 56.
[28] George W. O'Connor, "Survey of Selection Methods." (Washington: I.A.C.P., 1962.)
[29] Ibid.
[30] George W. O'Connor and Nelson A. Watson, "Juvenile Delinquency and Youth Crime: The Police Role." (Washington: I.A.C.P., 1964), p. 79.
[31] Michigan State University, Institute for Community Development, "Police Training in the Detroit Metropolitan Region: Recommendations for a Regional Approach." (Detroit: The Metropolitan Fund, 1966), p. 69.
[32] "Police and Fire Services of the City of Meriden, Conn." (Chicago: Public Administration Service, 1962), p. 121.
[33] Statement of Stephen Kennedy, former Commissioner of Police, cited in Franklin M. Kreml, "The Role of Colleges and Universities in Police Management," "The Police Yearbook." (Washington: I.A.C.P., 1966), p. 40.
[34] National League of Cities, "National Municipal Policy." (Washington: National League of Cities, 1966), p. 67.
[35] Donald E. Clark and Samuel G. Chapman, "A Forward Step: Educational Backgrounds for Policemen." (Springfield: Charles C. Thomas, 1966), p. 21.
[36] Id. at p. 3.

existing entrance requirements, little attempt has been made thus far to attract college students and graduates into the police service. In 1966, 55 percent of all high school graduates enrolled in college and this percentage will continue to increase.³⁷ The police service can be one of the most rewarding and challenging callings in government, and police departments should be in a position to compete for college graduates. Positive programs for attracting highly qualified students into law enforcement careers will be discussed in a later section of this chapter.

The need to elevate educational standards is not limited to sworn officers of lower rank. The 1964 national survey conducted by the International Association of Chiefs of Police disclosed that only 33.6 percent of the police administrators had attended college, and of this figure, only 9.2 percent possessed one or more college degrees.³⁸ These percentages approximate the educational level of subordinate officers, and with reason. In nearly all agencies, police administrators are selected from among men of lower rank within the department. Although a great majority of the chief administrators in our nation's police departments have achieved enviable records as outstanding police officers, only a few have achieved the appropriate level of training and education in management and administration to administer a law enforcement agency.³⁹

> The police officer who has walked his beat as a patrolman, investigated crime as a detective, and managed the technical routine of stationhouse activity as lieutenant or captain, is not fitted by this experience to administer the complex affairs of a large police department.

In the early part of the 20th century, a police chief would typically be appointed by a mayor. On many occasions this appointment was used as a method of rewarding friends or repaying political favors. The misuse of this appointing authority was illustrated in the Wickersham Commission "Report on Police" in 1931: ⁴⁰

> As an illustration, a few years ago the mayor of Indianapolis was called upon to introduce the police chief of that city to an assemblage of police chiefs during one of their conferences. In the course of his introductory remarks the mayor said, "I know that my man is going to be a good chief because he has been my tailor for 20 years. He knows how to make good clothes; he ought to be a good chief."

Stringent civil service regulations were enacted in many communities to counter this evil, and the requirement that a chief of police had to be selected from among men presently in the department ensued. Stamping out one evil, however, simply created another, since the men selected were often not qualified to assume the administration of the department. The operation and management of a large police department is as complex as administering a business of comparable resources and requires similar skills.⁴¹

In that respect, there are problems of police management that are quite similar to problems of big business, and soluble in familiar managerial techniques; efficiency, planning, communication, and technological innovation.

It can no longer be assumed that the affairs of a police department can be administered effectively by a person whose single qualification is extensive police experience. With few exceptions, the completion of 4 years at a college or university is a minimum requirement for top administrative and staff positions in other branches of government.⁴² No less should be demanded of administrative and supervisory personnel in our police departments.

Therefore police departments, and particularly larger departments, should take immediate steps to establish the minimum educational requirement of a baccalaureate degree at an accredited institution for all major administrative and supervisory positions. The need for an influx of trained or experienced persons possessing college credentials into top management positions is a current and critical one. Although the educational requirements for many supervisory and middle management positions may have to be increased progressively—in the same manner as for the police officer and the police agent—a baccaluareate degree requirement should immediately be established for all future chief administrators. Further, and as will be more fully discussed in the later section on career development, all present supervisors, middle managers, and administrators should be exposed to advanced training in supervisory and management principles. If no candidate within a department is fully qualified to fill a vacancy for chief of police, this position should be opened to applicants from outside of the department who do possess the requisite qualifications. In some jurisdictions, this will require a revision of civil service regulations. The position of chief administrator has already been opened to outside applicants in such large cities as Chicago, Boston, Philadelphia, New York, Syracuse, Detroit and Baltimore, as well as numerous medium-sized and small departments.

Educational Programs for Law Enforcement. There is a current and rapidly growing movement among colleges and especially junior colleges to develop degree programs for potential and existing law enforcement personnel. In 1966, there were 134 degree programs which could be identified as oriented toward police service, 100 of which were 2-year degree programs in police science offered at junior colleges.⁴³ To encourage the development of such programs, the U.S. Department of Justice, through its Office of Law Enforcement Assistance, has been providing grants to institutions interested in establishing such programs or improving existing ones.

The Commission's examination of these programs disclose that many of them are highly vocational in nature and are primarily intended to provide technical skills necessary in performing police work. College credit is given, for example, for such courses as traffic control, defensive tactics and patrol procedures. Although there is a need for vocational training, it is not and cannot be a substitute for a liberal arts education: ⁴⁴

> The trained man has developed skills and attitudes needed to perform a complex task. The educated man has developed his capacity to judge the worth, the performance, and the excellence of human action.

---

³⁷ Figures obtained from the National Center for Educational Statistics, Office of Health, Education, and Welfare, Aug. 1966.
³⁸ Supra, note 30 at p. 79.
³⁹ Raymond B. Fosdick, "American Police System." (New York: The Century Co., 1921), p. 220.
⁴⁰ Supra, note 4 at p. 20.

⁴¹ Franklin M. Kreml, "The Role of Colleges and Universities in Police Management," "The Police Yearbook." (Washington: I.A.C.P., 1966), p. 36.
⁴² Supra, note 1 at p. 168.
⁴³ "Police Science Programs of Universities, Colleges, Junior Colleges in the United States," "The Police Chief." (Washington: I.A.C.P., 1966), p. 50.
⁴⁴ Supra, note 41 at p. 39.

The wisdom of giving degree credit for technical courses, therefore, must be questioned. Training may be properly offered at college or junior college facilities but not as part of the school's basic program. The facilities of these institutions, since they are designed for teaching, may serve as the location for basic or specialized police training programs. Twenty-six out of forty-four California certified police academies are, for example, coordinated and financed through the junior college system in that State.[45] When courses are offered for vocational training, however, they should be considered as such and not as degree credit offerings of the institution.

While there has been some progress made in determining the training needs of police personnel, there has been far too little analysis either by the police or by colleges and universities of their educational needs. First of all, the diverse demands on the police dictate that departments recruit persons with specialized educational backgrounds in various disciplines. For example, lawyers are needed as legal and administrative advisors; business and public administration experts are needed for fiscal and management positions; engineers and scientists are needed for communications and other technological programs; and personnel with a variety of backgrounds are needed for planning and research.

That being the case, the educational requirements cannot be identical for all police positions. A police agency must select personnel on the basis of their qualifications to fulfill a particularized need. Although it is obvious that certain subjects such as sociology, psychology, history, and political science should be taken by police agents and officers in order to give them greater insight into human behavior and the governmental process, much more research is needed to determine which specific courses of study are most beneficial. Colleges and universities have long ignored the problems and educational needs of law enforcement.[46] As FBI Director J. Edgar Hoover has observed, these institutions "should be initiating and increasing courses of study oriented toward the development of a career police profession."[47]

Until the educational needs of field officers are more fully evaluated, however, undergraduate programs should emphasize the social sciences and liberal arts. The complex responsibilities and duties of police work require that field personnel understand their community and conditions which breed criminal and delinquent conduct. This understanding can best be gained through a liberal education.

Independent Examination of Educational Qualifications. There are pitfalls in relying upon a college or junior college degree as the sole means of measuring whether an education is suitable to meet minimum requirements. Experience in other disciplines and in law enforcement has revealed that there are "diploma mill" institutions that award the requisite degree but that fail to provide a meaningful education.[48] For this reason, police departments should either require that a college degree be obtained from an institution accredited by a recognized accrediting body or should independently test candidates to measure their educational achievement.

Also, until such time as educational requirements are elevated to acceptable levels, police departments should administer tests to all applicants to determine capacity and potential and should accept only those applicants who demonstrate an ability to perform successfully university level studies. Nearly all departments today administer written examinations to their applicants. In a survey conducted in 1961, 98 percent of the departments surveyed conducted entrance examinations to test mental ability.[49] However, many of these examinations either test for knowledge of police work alone or do not appropriately measure intelligence. For example, one written examination given to applicants of a metropolitan police department in Tennessee measured memory and general knowledge of police practices, local government, and general information only.[50] The written examination given to applicants of the Metropolitan Police Department of Washington, D.C., consists of an 80-question multiple choice aptitude test. When the examination was given to 206 applicants in three cities in June of 1965, 188 passed.[51]

If a department accepts applicants with an educational achievement of a high school diploma or less, it should administer and have interpreted by trained experts an intelligence test of trustworthy reliability and validity, such as the Wechsler Bellevue, the California Mental Maturity Test, or the Otis Quick Scoring Mental Ability Tests.[52] Too, it should accept only those applicants whose intellectual capacity is above average.

INDIVIDUAL CHARACTERISTICS

Just as advanced education and above average intelligence are fundamental requisites for law enforcement personnel, so are emotional stability, commonsense, and integrity. In addition, the law enforcement officer must be free of prejudices which might interfere with the proper carrying out of his responsibilities:[53]

> The police are frequently confronted with emotion-charged situations that tempt strong responses from them. Important to success in dealing with such situations is a stability impervious to work-related and other emotional stresses and unhampered by prejudices and undesirable attitudes in getting along with people under trying circumstances.... Police service affords unusual opportunities and temptations to accept graft, to indulge in other forms of dishonesty, immorality, and excesses and to wreak vengeance on persons who have offended. Successful police service is predicated on the integrity, morality, and fairness of the members of the force.

It is doubtful whether current selection procedures in most police departments effectively screen out persons unsuited for police work. In the early years of this century, personal qualifications were deemed sufficient if laudatory letters were received from friends or "ward heelers" in support of a candidate.[54] Although there have been improvements in procedures for evaluating personal characteristics in the past 35 years, they are not widely used. Further, there are as yet no reliable screening

---

[45] State of California, Department of Justice, Commission on Peace Officer Standards and Training, "California Peace Officers Standards Program." (Sacramento: California Department of Justice, 1966).
[46] L. Dana Gatlin, "Police Chiefs Win Diplomas," Christian Science Monitor. (Boston), August 20, 1966, p. 3, col. 1.
[47] J. Edgar Hoover, "Message from the Director, FBI Law Enforcement Bulletin," editorial. (Washington: U.S. Department of Justice, Federal Bureau of Investigation, May, 1964.)
[48] Supra, note 41 at p. 39.

[49] Supra, note 28.
[50] I.A.C.P., "A Survey of the Department of Metropolitan Police, Nashville-Davidson County, Tennessee." (Washington: I.A.C.P., 1964), p. 86.
[51] Supra, note 13 at p. 100.
[52] Robert L. Thorndike and Elizabeth Hagen, "Measurement and Evaluation in Psychology and Education." (New York: John Wiley & Sons, 1956), p. 254.
[53] Public Administration Service, "Police Services in Portland, Maine." (Chicago: Public Administration Service, 1955), pp. 109–110.
[54] Supra, note 4 at p. 66.

devices to identify applicants who are emotionally unfit for police employment.[55] Although reliable methods may have been devised for measuring suitability for a limited number of other occupations and professions, these methods are not as effective in measuring fitness for police work.[56]

Selection techniques in law enforcement cannot merely emulate those devised for business, industry, or teaching. Law enforcement, which vests authority and power in its representatives, also imposes on them stresses unlike those encountered in any other profession.

Even though it is not yet possible with existing knowledge to ascertain all factors which contribute to the development of a good or an unfit policeman, procedures for discovering undesirable traits in applicants do exist and are being used by some departments.[57] These methods, their value, and their limitations, are the subject of this section.

Character Investigation. If properly conducted a background investigation can provide invaluable information on the character of applicants.[58]

In a recent survey by the National League of Cities, 278 of the 284 cities surveyed reported that a background investigation was employed to investigate the character of police applicants.[59] This survey indicated that a majority of the cities checked identification records at the local, State, and Federal levels, and also checked character references supplied by the applicants.[60] In many cities, however, character investigations are extremely limited in scope and investigators seldom probe deeply enough to uncover the information needed for professional evaluation.[61]

Few municipal forces have yet devoted enough attention to the character investigation of applicants. Civil Service routines often merely require that the applicant provide character vouchers or "references" which are accepted without further question.[62]

This is not true, however, of all departments. For example, during the period between August 1957 and October 1964 over one-fourth of the applicants of the Los Angeles Police Department were rejected on the basis of intensive background investigations after they had successfully passed written, oral, and medical examinations.[63]

No department should admit any person into the police service until his background has been comprehensively investigated. Trained investigators should examine school, credit, and criminal records; interview persons used as references and other persons in the applicant's neighborhood; and interview past and present employers. The investigative process should extend to other communities as well, if the applicant has lived elsewhere. To assist in the check of criminal records, the fingerprints of each applicant should be obtained. Prior convictions, work habits, prejudices, emotional stability, among other characteristics, should be determined to ascertain whether the applicant is fit to perform police work.[64] Since background investigations are expensive, if properly conducted, they should be restricted to those who otherwise have qualified.[65]

Emotional Stability. Within the past 30 years, many police administrators and educators have contended that prospective policemen should be examined for personality defects prior to their appointment.[66] The emotional stability to withstand the stresses of police work must, of necessity, be a primary requisite of police personnel. Officers must rationally cope with violence, verbal abuse, resentment, and emergencies. The emotionally unfit cannot meet these stresses. Although a comprehensive character investigation will eliminate many socially maladjusted applicants, personality defects in some of the applicants will be latent and not easily discernible.[67]

For this reason, several police departments conduct psychological and psychiatric examinations. A survey of over 300 police departments by the International Association of Chiefs of Police in 1961 revealed that 50 departments administered such examinations.[68] In 1955, Thomas W. Oglesby, then a personnel technician for the city of Pasadena, Calif., conducted a survey that disclosed that 14 cities with population of over 100,000 had formalized programs for psychiatric or psychological testing of police applicants.[69] These examinations vary considerably. For example, in Philadelphia, applicants are interviewed by a psychiatrist; in Kansas City, a clinical psychologist interviews applicants. In Los Angeles, the psychiatrists who interviews applicants also administers two tests—The Minnesota Multiphasic Personal Inventory (MMPI) and the Group Rorschach, primarily to determine neurotic and psychotic tendencies.[70]

Between 1953 and 1957, of the 760 persons tested by the Los Angeles Police Department for personality disorders, 86, or 11.3 percent, were rejected as not meeting acceptable psychiatric standards.[71] Fifty-one percent of these applicants were found to be latently or borderline psychotic and 22 percent were diagnosed as schizoid personalities.[72] Although there is considerable conflict over the reliability of such tests as they relate to vocational success or failure in police work,[73] properly administered tests and interviews can eliminate many of the emotionally unfit.

Psychological tests, such as the MMPI, and interviews to determine emotional stability should be conducted by all departments. These examinations should be administered only by trained professionals and their limitations should be fully understood. Federal and State funds should be made available in the form of research grants for the purpose of devising reliable tests or other means of evaluating the characteristics of applicants which may be detrimental to successful police work.

A majority of police departments use another procedure, the oral interview, to assess the character of applicants.[74] Under this procedure, a selected group of offi-

---

[55] Dr. Ruth Levy, "Summary of Report on Retrospective Study of 5,000 Peace Officer Personnel Records," "The Police Yearbook." (Washington: I.A.C.P. 1966), p. 61.
[56] Id. at p. 61.
[57] Dr. James H. Rankin, "Preventive Psychiatry in the Los Angeles Police Department," "Police." (Springfield: Charles C. Thomas, July–August 1957), p. 28.
[58] Richard H. Blum, "Police Selection." (Springfield: Charles C. Thomas, 1964), pp. 157–177.
[59] Raymond L. Bancroft, "Municipal Law Enforcement, 1966," "Nation's Cities." (Washington, D.C.: National League of Cities, February 1966), p. 20.
[60] Id. at p. 20.
[61] Supra, note 50 at p. 86.
[62] Supra, note 16 at p. 130.
[63] Samuel Haig Jameson, "Controversial Areas in 20th Century Policing: Quest for Quality Training in Police Work" in Walter C. Reckless and Charles L. New-man, "Interdisciplinary Problems in Criminology: Papers of the American Society of Criminology, 1964." (Columbus: Ohio State University, 1965), p. 130.
[64] Supra, note 58 at pp. 157–177.
[65] Supra, note 8 at p. 148.
[66] Thomas W. Oglesby, "The Use of Emotional Screening in the Selection of Police Applicants," "Police." (Springfield: Charles C. Thomas, Jan.–Feb. 1958), p. 49.
[67] Supra, note 57 at p. 24.
[68] Supra, note 28.
[69] Supra, note 66 at p. 49.
[70] Supra, note 28.
[71] Supra, note 57 at p. 27.
[72] Id. at p. 27.
[73] Supra, note 5.
[74] Supra, note 28 at Table 22.

cers or a combination of officers and civilian personnel specialists interview individual applicants, then subsequently determine the applicant's suitability. This procedure has numerous advantages. Representatives of the department have the opportunity to evaluate the demeanor and attitude of the applicants, and through probing questions can determine their ability to handle stress situations and to respond appropriately to judgmental questions.[75] However, since this technique of screening is primarily a subjective one, it has received criticism which arises out of three considerations: [76] (1) the difficulty of developing valid and reliable oral tests; (2) the difficulty of securing a reviewable record on an oral test; (3) public suspicion of the oral as a channel for the execution of political influence through the destruction of anonymity.

Although each department, utilizing skilled representatives, should have the opportunity to evaluate its applicants for police positions, the opinions derived from an oral interview, which is necessarily subjective, should not be the sole method used for disqualification. If this procedure is appropriately utilized along with background investigations and psychological testing, the selection process could become a reliable method for screening out the unqualified.[77]

Even if more reliable devices for screening applicants were used in all departments, candidates with personality disorders or other defects cannot always be discovered before they are accepted into police service. It is essential, therefore, that procedures exist to remove such officers before permanent tenure makes removal extremely difficult. Such procedures are discussed in a later section on probationary period.

Physical Requirements. Any police officer working in the field must possess physical courage, stamina and agility. These qualities may help to save his own life or the lives of others. But existing requirements on physical stature and condition in many departments are unduly restrictive, with the result that many applicants, who may otherwise have exceptional qualifications, are summarily rejected because of height, weight, or vision. For example, in 1956, a survey conducted by the International Association of Chiefs of Police revealed that nearly 85 percent of the police departments surveyed had a mandatory height requirement of 5'8" or higher.[78]

All departments should eliminate inflexible mandatory physical requirements. While physical characteristics and conditions such as freedom from disabling diseases or physical handicaps should be carefully considered in the selection process, factors such as height should be considered along with other attributes of the candidate, rather than be automatically disqualifying.[79]

Height, like age, is a factor which must be evaluated in terms of the full abilities of the candidate. It should not be used as a hurdle with a fixed standard except to eliminate persons below normal standards lacking other compensation qualities. Physical stature is a single factor which should not deprive the police service of individuals who are capable of physically defending themselves. The police image is not likely to suffer any severe damage if fully capable men are employed despite their lack of height.

Likewise, there is little justification for requiring near perfect uncorrected vision of all applicants. Sight requirements are often set at 20/20 uncorrected for both eyes, or slightly less for one eye, correctable to 20/20.[80] Other occupations, in which excellent vision is of equal necessity, have less stringent standards. For example, the Federal Aviation Agency will license commercial pilots whose vision is 20/100 as long as the vision is correctable to 20/20.[81] Professional athletes, who participate in body contact sports such as basketball or football, often wear corrective contact lenses, and this does not adversely affect their ability to perform. Also, police departments continue officers in employment after selection even though they subsequently require corrective lenses.

Many departments are beginning to recognize the arbitrariness of traditional standards. In 1965, the Philadelphia Police Department lowered the height minimum from 5'8" to 5'7" and began accepting recruits with vision defects correctable by spectacles.[82]

In place of mandatory rigid requirements for all entering personnel, physical requirements should be assessed on an individual basis. The opinion of an examining physician on whether an applicant is fit to serve would prove far more reliable than mandatory civil service requirements.[83]

For this reason, a police administrator should be given the discretion to establish flexible standards. These standards may vary in relationship to the position being filled. For example, if a person is hired from outside of the department to fill a staff position, physical stature and vision would not have to meet minimum standards required of sworn personnel.

Residency Requirements. A major deterrent to recruiting is local restrictions on the residency of applicants. A 1961 survey by the International Association of Chiefs of Police revealed that nearly 75 percent of the responding departments had preservice residency requirements varying from 6 months to 5 years.[84]

These requirements can be traced back to the depression era when employment was scarce and municipalities attempted to give job preferences to local residents.[85] Since nearly all police departments are encountering great difficulty in filling current positions, these restrictions now serve only to inhibit attempts to improve the quality of police personnel. Many departments, such as the Metropolitan Police Department of Washington, D.C., and the Public Safety Department of Dade County, Fla., have deleted residence requirements and nearly all police experts are calling for their removal: [86]

Preemployment residence in the community should not be required of candidates, for it reduces the number of qualified applicants from whom the most promising may be selected. Qualified young men who are residents of other cities or of small communities and rural areas often lack attractive opportunities in their local police service and are frequently interested in service in the departments of a larger community. Local-residence candidates deny the community the opportunity to recruit prom-

---

[75] Supra, note 28.
[76] Statement from Stahl, as quoted in Blum, supra, note 58 at p. 182.
[77] A. C. German, "Police Personnel Management." (Springfield: Charles C. Thomas, 1963), pp. 51–55.
[78] Supra, note 28.
[79] Supra, note 28.
[80] Supra, note 50 af p. 82.
[81] Federal Aviation Agency, "Regulations: Part 57, Medical Standards and Certification" (Washington: U.S. Government Printing Office, Nov. 23, 1965).
[82] The Sunday Oregonian (Oct. 30, 1966), sec. 4m, p. 24, col. 5.
[83] Supra, note 77 at p. 17.
[84] Supra, note 28.
[85] Federal Bureau of Investigation, "Police Management—Recruitment and Selection of Personnel," "FBI Law Enforcement Bulletin," (Washington: U.S. Dept. of Justice, FBI, Oct. 1966), p. 16.
[86] Supra, note 8 at p. 137.

ising candidates who may, in some instances, provide a quality of leadership lacking among local applicants.

Each department should attempt to obtain the best policemen that can be recruited anywhere in the country.[87] Police and city administrators should immediately take steps, therefore, to remove local residency requirements and should also encourage the removal of State residency requirements, if they exist. This is consistent with the recent recommendation of the American Bar Association in their minimum standards for police recruit qualifications and selection.[88]

Age Requirements. In most cities, the minimum permissible age for becoming a policeman is 21, although some cities require that recruits be 25.[89] Thus, police departments that accept applicants who have completed high school or less cannot actively recruit persons until they have been out of school for at least 3 years. The effect of this delay is that many of the talented high school graduates will begin other careers, and therefore, will be otherwise committed before they are eligible for the police service.[90]

The 21 years of age standard restricts recruitment. Potential police applicants who graduate from high school find it necessary to obtain other employment and are likely to fall in career channels which take them away permanently from their original police interests and aptitudes.

As a result, police departments often attract applicants who have already experienced one or more job failures.

If police departments required all applicants to possess a college degree, a minimum age requirement of 21 would not create a significant problem. But as long as the police continue to recruit high school graduates or even junior college graduates—and this is likely for some time—it is essential that the police be permitted to compete more effectively for younger men.

There are at least two potential methods of overcoming this problem. First, the minimum age requirement for police service could be reduced to 18, 19, or 20. This would allow the police to recruit persons before they become committed to other careers. At least five cities, Chicago, Oak Park (Michigan), Minneapolis, Houston, and Dallas, already hire persons under the age of 21 to serve as police officers.[91] The Houston Police Department in 1964 hired 26 men under the age of 21. It was the unanimous view of that department's supervisors that these officers performed successfully and that the department would continue to select mature men of 19 and 20 to become police officers.[92]

Police departments should carefully evaluate their existing minimum age requirements. In the light of the great responsibility of policemen, however, there is is some question whether age requirements should be automatically lowered for all applicants. It may be more appropriate to establish a special procedure whereby the minimum age requirement could be waived when a person under the age of 21 demonstrates the necessary maturity and intelligence to merit special consideration.

The second, and possibly the most promising, method of bridging the period between graduation from high school and the age of 21 is the development of an entirely new type of cadet program—the CSO concept.

Under the traditional cadet or trainee program, a police department hires persons between the ages of 17 and 21 and assigns them the responsibility of performing nonsworn police tasks or assisting sworn officers until they qualify to take the entrance examination. Such a program has been in existence in England since the 1930's and now constitutes the primary source of recruiting men to police service.[93] In a 1966 survey by the National League of Cities it was reported that 52 police departments in the United States now have cadet programs.[94] In the New York City Police Department, those in its trainee program perform certain clerical and other tasks not directly related to crime control, receive police training and earn salaries competitive with other salaries paid to high school graduates. The trainee can take his qualifying examination before reaching 21 and when he reaches the minimum age required for sworn status, can immediately enter the service as an officer.

Many of the departments that initiated cadet programs found them wanting.[95] The primary reasons are that the work done by cadets often did not justify the expenditures for the program, that a limited number of persons were attracted to the program, and that many cadets left the program and did not become sworn officers.[96]

Most cadets now perform clerical functions only and, therefore, learn little about police work or the rewards of a police career. If cadets were given financial aid to continue their education and received extensive police training as CSOs, assisting police officers and police agents, as well as performing noncrime related functions, CSO programs could serve as a valuable recruiting device and a method of upgrading the quality of personnel. Education and incentive programs for CSOs will be more fully described in the next section of this chapter.

In summary, the current minimum age in most police departments may unnecessarily restrict the recruiting base and discourage persons, otherwise qualified, from pursuing careers in law enforcement. Communities should adjust current requirements and should experiment with CSO-type programs for the purpose of interesting qualified persons in law enforcement careers.

Concomitant with minimum age restrictions, most communities impose maximum age restrictions on police department applicants. A 1961 survey by the International Association of Chiefs of Police revealed that 30 percent of the departments surveyed barred persons over 30 years of age and 80 percent barred men over 35 years.[97] Many police experts favor lowering the maximum age requirement to 29. For example, the International Association of Chiefs of Police has recommended that the maximum age be reduced to 29 : [98]

The upper age limit of 35 is considered to be too high. There are many advantages in lowering the upper limit. It assists in reducing turnover because young men, not having established themselves in a trade or occupation, are less likely than others to leave the force during periods of economic prosperity . . .

---

[87] Supra, note 53 at p. 110.
[88] "Minimum Standards for Police Recruit Qualifications and Selection: American Bar Association Project on Minimum Standards for Criminal Justice," Committee on the Police Function (Sept. 8, 1966), sec. II, p. 6.
[89] Supra, note 28.
[90] Supra, note 58 at p. 52.
[91] Glenford S. Leonard, "Police Career Development", "The Police Yearbook" (Washington: I.A.C.P., 1966). pp. 87–89. Supra, note 82 at cols. 1–8.
[92] Id. at p. 87.
[93] Supra, note 11 at p. 30.
[94] Supra, note 59 at p. 17.
[95] Indiana University, Department of Police Administration, "Recommendations Based Upon a Study of Police Cadet Programs in the United States," submitted to Office of Law Enforcement Assistance, Department of Justice (April 1966).
[96] Ibid.
[97] Supra, note 28.
[98] I.A.C.P., "A Survey of Police Services in Metropolitan Dade County, Fla." (Washington: I.A.C.P. 1963), p. 39.

Younger men can also be expected to fulfill their maximum working years with greater endurance for the tremendous physical exertions required of the working officer. In addition, younger men present easier training subjects and are probably more readily amenable to the discipline necessary in a police operation. For these reasons a maximum age should be established that is no higher than 29.

While every effort should be made to recruit younger men for police service, it is doubtful that mandatory maximum age requirements of 29 would always serve the best interests of a department. In some cases, a highly qualified person, who had pursued a successful career in another law enforcement agency or in another profession, such as the military service, may possess skills needed by a police department. To prevent the automatic rejection of such persons, maximum age requirements should be maintained at higher levels—the Federal Bureau of Investigation has a maximum age requirement of 41 [99]—or police administrators should be given wide latitude in waiving a lower maximum age requirement when they consider such waiver to be justified.

PROBATIONARY PERIOD

Regardless of how carefully a department may select and screen its personnel in accordance with the best techniques known today, these procedures alone do not accurately measure fitness to perform police work.[100] The police service and other government agencies have long recognized that a period of probation is necessary to judge the qualities of new employees. Full evaluation must be made of a police recruit's ability to determine whether he can cope with the unusual demands of the police service and to detect weaknesses which may develop under actual working conditions. Since civil service commissions, central personnel agencies, or police boards often select police personnel, a probationary period is the only method, aside from a brief oral interview, by which a chief administrator can evaluate officers and eliminate those who do not meet the needs of the department.[101] In a 1956 survey of 368 departments by the International Association of Chiefs of Police, it was reported that 93 percent of these departments required new appointees to serve a period of time on probationary status.[102] However, in over 74 percent of these departments, the probationary period was limited to 6 months or less.[103] Only 2 percent of the departments had a probationary period longer than 1 year.[104] In contrast, the probationary period for the police in England and Wales is 2 years.[105]

Few departments today make appropriate use of the probationary process. An earlier national commission indicated that this was common of all government agencies: [106]

In spite of the frequently heard complaint that the examinations are even now unsatisfactory, and that the departments are now filled with incompetents, this commission was able to find scarcely a single jurisdiction which is giving systematic attention to the probationary period.

Probation should involve a systematic evaluation of performance and a correction of deficiencies in the selection process by "dismissing the inept recruit in the early stages of his service . . . before he has acquired the extraordinary protection thrown about him by tenure-of-office acts." [107] Since current selection methods cannot screen out all persons who are unsuited for police work, a comprehensive evaluation of recruits during probation is extremely important. For example, in the Berkeley, Calif. Police Department an average of 20 percent of the recruits initially accepted into the department are removed prior to the end of their 2-year probationary period.[108] Between October of 1961 and September 1962, 10 percent of the recruits hired by the Department of Public Safety of Dade County, Fla., were dismissed during their probationary period.[109]

In most departments, however, the length of the probationary period and methods of evaluation are insufficient to measure the effectiveness or the personal characteristics of recruits. The first 3 to 6 months of a recruit's employment should be devoted to a training program. Thus, little opportunity will exist to observe performance in a variety of working situations until after training is completed. A reliable evaluation cannot be made in a few months. For this reason, a probationary period should be 18 months in length, and certainly no less than 1 year.

Even an extended period of probation will not be meaningful, however, unless a careful evaluation of each recruit is undertaken. In many departments, probationary officers are not closely supervised and no formal reports are made of their performance. As a result, it is typical for officers to be elevated to regular status automatically upon the completion of their probationary period. The performance of all officers, both during and after recruit training, should be systematically observed and formally rated by all training instructors, immediate supervisors, and carefully selected officers who have worked with the probationary officer.[110] And if, for example, a probationary officer demonstrates biases which prevent him from impartially performing police work, he should be rated as unqualified. Along with ratings, citizen complaints rendered against probationary officers should be evaluated both to protect the officer and to determine possible derogatory qualities and conduct. All noted deficiencies in performance and aptitude should then be assessed to determine whether they are rectifiable. If they are not, the officer should be dismissed from the service.

Dismissal of probationary officers is complicated by the civil service law in many jurisdictions.[111] A 1961 survey showed that civil service regulations in 82 of the 345 cities surveyed required police departments to show the same documented cause for dismissing probationary officers as for dismissing regular personnel. Far greater latitude for dismissal should be granted to the hiring authority during a probationary period.

In many cities, however, incompetent personnel is not removed during probationary periods solely because of the unwillingness of chief administrators to exercise their power of dismissal.[112]

While much remains to be done to improve civil service law and regulations with respect to police probation, the whole prob-

---

[99] U.S. Department of Justice, "Facts About a Career in the FBI." (Washington: U.S. Government Printing Office, 1966).
[100] Supra, note 28.
[101] Supra, note 77 at p. 67.
[102] Supra, note 28.
[103] Ibid.
[104] Ibid.
[105] Supra, note 16 at p. 132.
[106] Commission of Inquiry on Public Service Personnel, "Better Government Personnel." (Washington: 1946, U.S. Government Printing Office), pp. 48–49.
[107] Supra, note 16 at p. 132.
[108] Supra, note 58 at p. 152.
[109] Supra, note 98 at p. 50.
[110] Supra, note 13 at p. 104.
[111] Supra, note 28.
[112] Supra, note 16 at pp. 132–333.

lem will remain unchanged until municipal police administrators more frequently exercise the powers of dismissal lodged with them. Until this is done, little sympathy need be accorded to the police chief who complains that he does not possess sufficient power to discipline the rank and file; for even when the chief's powers in this respect are complete and unrestricted during the probationary period, almost never are they exercised, with the result that the errors arising out of inadequate selection processes quickly come under the full protection of civil service laws and regulations.

Thus, it is incumbent upon all chief administrators to take action quickly and remove any officer who does not possess the requisites to meet effectively and impartially the demands placed upon police personnel.

AUTHORITY FOR REMOVAL

Even the careful screening of officers during probation will not insure that a department will be free of personnel who are corrupt, incompetent, or emotionally unqualified to perform police work. While the need to protect career officers from arbitrary dismissal by chief administrators is recognized, civil service regulations in a majority of our cities unduly restrict the authority of an administrator to weed out undesirable officers. In many cities, he has no authority to dismiss, but only the authority to recommend that a civil service board determine whether there is cause for dismissal.

The experience of removal procedures under civil service has revealed that officers are normally dismissed only under flagrant circumstances. Even if an administrator is desirous of upgrading the quality of his personnel and removing all officers who do not meet the standards of his department, it is doubtful whether, under current procedures in many cities, he would be able to do so. Commission surveys report that these conditions contribute to a situation where too many officers remain in police departments even though they are unsuitable for public service and tarnish the image of all police personnel.

The primary authority for removal should be vested in the chief administrator of a police department. To curb abuses of authority, an independent agency, such as a civil service commission, should review dismissals.

THE EFFECT OF RAISING STANDARDS

This report has strongly urged that selection standards be significantly raised. This has been done with the full realization that the nation's police departments are seriously understaffed.

The raising of standards, however, should actually have the overall effect of attracting more and better candidates by bolstering the prestige of police service. There are many able young men who will be willing and even eager to enter police work if police departments offered professional opportunities. As a former Chief of Police of Kansas City, Mo., recognized almost 10 years ago: [113]

Some have reasoned that current police working conditions, longer hours, and lower salaries than private industry, are large enough obstacles in the way of obtaining new police personnel. They say that if we add another barrier, such as preservice State examinations, the employment problem will become more acute. I have reminded them that there is no permanency to *status quo;* there must either be progression or regression in our push to better standards. If we make the acquisition of a police position too easy, we discourage incentive and invite inefficiency. Any move on our part that tends to make the attainment of the policeman role a more honorable and proud accomplishment will tend to attract more and better recruits, men of the kind and type we now seek with eagerness.

Departments which have college requirements, such as the Multnomah County Sheriff's Department, have reported that the elevation of standards has enhanced, not hindered, recruiting efforts.[114]

This of course will require more than a mere appeal to college men or better public relations. First, as was emphasized above, police departments should relax unduly restrictive standards relating to height, weight, eyesight and residency. Police departments will often have to decide which is more important—an officer who is intelligent and has insight into community enforcement problems or an officer with lesser intelligence and education who meets all the present rigid physical and residency requirements. The decision should be that modern professional policing must place a priority on education, intelligence, and emotional stability, and provide greater flexibility in physical requirements.

Second and most important, higher educational standards can be successfully implemented only if police organizations are drastically reorganized and improved to attract able recruits. The two can only be accomplished together. Consequently, the police departments of this nation must simultaneously work to recruit better educated personnel and to examine and change their own operations to make police service a challenging and rewarding career.

ATTRACTING PERSONNEL

The Nation's police departments are encountering serious difficulty in maintaining their forces at authorized strength. A survey conducted by the National League of Cities in 1966 disclosed that over 65 percent of the departments surveyed were understaffed; that these departments were 5,840 officers, or 5 percent below authorized strength; and were 11,864 officers, or 10 percent below preferred strength.[115] In 1965, for example, Baltimore was 229 officers below strength; Cleveland, 512; Pittsburgh, 80; Kansas City, 215; and Memphis, 78.[116]

Since, on the average, police departments are currently 5 percent below authorized strength, since the authorized strength of police departments has increased at the rate of approximately 3 percent each year,[117] and since an average of 5.4 percent of existing personnel leave their departments each year (due to resignation, dismissal, retirement, or death)[118] 50,000 new police officers will be needed in 1967 alone.

Commission recommendations for the addition of community service officers and staff specialists will require

---

[113] Bernard C. Brannon, "The Set of the Sail," "Police." (Sept.–Oct. 1957), p. 17.
[114] Letter from Donald Clark, former Sheriff, Multnomah County, Portland, Oreg. (September, 1966).
[115] Supra, note 59 at p. 16.
[116] Police Department, Kansas City, Mo. "1965 Survey of Municipal Police Departments" (Cities of 300,000 population, 1960 Census), Oct. 25, 1965.
[117] Memorandum from Michael S. March, Assistant Chief, Education, Manpower, and Science, U.S. Bureau of the Budget, May 1, 1966, table 4.
[118] Supra, note 59 at p. 16.

even greater numbers of police personnel. But mere addition of manpower without accompanying efforts to make the best use of existing personnel strength might serve only to aggravate the problem of inefficiency. In many departments police personnel are being wasted on trivial duties. In others, increased investment in staff work or more sophisticated equipment would do more to improve police work than investment in more men. Switching from 2-man to 1-man patrol cars would in some instances free large numbers of policemen for added patrol or investigative duties. Each department should assess its manpower needs with considerations such as these in mind and ask for additional men only when the organization, policies, and practices of the department are such that the increased personnel can be effectively utilized in the reduction of crime. When the case for this need has been made, it is the responsibility of each jurisdiction to see that this need is met.

Although police departments are encountering difficulty in hiring new officers, this is not due to a dearth of applicants, but to a lack of qualified applicants. In 1961, only 22.3 percent of the applicants for positions in 368 police departments were accepted.[119] The applicant success rate in many departments is far lower. For example, in 1965, only 2.8 percent of the candidates for the Los Angeles Police Department were eventually accepted into the force.[120] In 1966, only 29 of 1,033 applicants were hired by the Dallas Police Department.[121]

There is a critical need, therefore, for police departments to attract more acceptable applicants to careers in law enforcement. This is particularly true in light of the recommendation that educational standards be elevated and that candidates be more carefully screened to insure acceptable emotional stability. As was noted by the British Royal Commission on Police in 1962, police work is not inherently unattractive as a career.[122] The investigation or prevention of crime, the protection or assistance of citizens, and the administration of a complex governmental agency all provide stimulating career opportunities for the talented and the educated.

This chapter has already discussed the inhibiting effect on police recruitment of the single level of entry into police work for recruits, and of restrictive physical and residency requirements. These are by no means the only deterrents to attracting able police recruits. There are other "policies and practices that are obsolete and inadequate in today's competitive labor market." [123]

THE POLICE IMAGE

There is limited understanding by the public of the nature of the police task. The public as a whole may see the police as a whole as the front line of defense against crime, but more often than not individual citizens encounter individual policemen when the policemen are directing traffic, rendering emergency treatment, issuing citations for parking or traffic violations, providing information, or performing other routine duties. On the other hand, to some persons who are poor or who are in minority groups, the police are viewed as oppressive enforcers of the status quo. Although support and respect for the police is increasing, the status accorded to the police is still far lower than that of other professions that compete for college graduates. In a 1961 survey of status given to occupations, the police ranked 54th out of 90 occupations, which tied them with playground directors and railroad conductors.[124]

In short, the primary challenges confronting law enforcement are often not apparent to the public, and the police, to date, have done little to highlight the demands on their personnel that do call for professional skills. Little effort is devoted to describing the complexity of investigating or preventing crime, of reducing delinquent behavior, of administering police operations, or of solving community problems. Instead of promoting the advantages of a career in the police service, police departments, all too often, tarnish the attractiveness of police service. Police administrators frequently bemoan the plight of the policeman, the low compensation, the long hours, and the hostility and resentment of the public. Although the police should publicly discuss their problems, this can be accomplished, as it is in other professions, without undermining the attractiveness of police service itself. The hardships confronting the police, if positively presented, are precisely the challenges that could make the police service attractive to the highly skilled. As Glenford S. Leonard, the Director of Public Safety of Oak Park, Mich., recently stated: [125]

If we continually complain that our image is being adversely affected by our problems . . . (then) it is being affected. I believe that we should start insisting and advertising that it is a career service of action, of prestige, and of the greatest importance in our democracy. We may even convince ourselves of this, and if we do, we have taken a big step toward attracting people. . . .

CONDITIONS OF EMPLOYMENT

Compensation. If the police service is to be an attractive career opportunity, it must offer compensation that is competitive with other occupations or professions that seek men of education or ability. In most communities, the police service presently does not offer competitive salaries to the college graduate or to other talented persons.

In 1966, the median starting salaries for patrolmen ranged from $4,920 in smaller communities to $5,834 in cities of over 500,000 population.[126] Starting salaries varied from $2,820 in Durant, Okla., to $8,790 in Anchorage, Alaska.[127] In most cities, the maximum salaries paid to patrolmen were not significantly higher than the entrance salary. The maximum median salary in 1966 was $5,650 in smaller communities and $7,008 in larger cities or an average increase of only $730 and $1,174 respectively over starting salaries.[128]

Of the 228,798 sworn personnel reported in the 1960 census of occupational characteristics, only 464 earned salaries of more than $15,000 and only 4,500 earned over $10,000.[129] These figures clearly reflect the limited financial oportunities in the police service today.

---

[119] Supra, note 28.
[120] American Trial Lawyers Association, "Crime and Its Causes in Los Angeles." (Lancaster, Calif.: Golden West Publishing Co., 1966), p. 7–8.
[121] "Police Academy Accepts Only 3%," *The Times-Herald* (Dallas, Tex., Aug. 28, 1966), p. 1, col. 1.
[122] Royal Commission on Police, "Royal Commission on the Police, 1962, Final Report" (London: Her Majesty's Stationary Office), p. 94.
[123] Detroit Free Press, Aug. 4, 1965, sec. B, p. 6, col. 1.

[124] Albert Reiss, "Occupations and Social Status." (New York: McMillan Co., 1961).
[125] Supra, note 91 at p. 84.
[126] Supra, note 3 at p. 435.
[127] Id. at p. 436.
[128] Id. at p. 435.
[129] Supra, note 20 at p. 304.

Although it is difficult to determine what occupations or professions compete with the police for personnel, it can be seen that police salaries are below those of most skilled occupations. In 1960, the median salary for professional and technical workers was $7,124; for craftsmen and foremen, $5,699; and for police, $5,321.[130]

In Seattle policemen are paid $375 a month less than cable splicers;[131] in Nashville, electricians earn an hourly rate of $3.22 in contrast to the police rate of $2.55;[132] and retail buyers in Los Angeles earn a median salary of $9,492 as compared with maximum salary of $8,820 paid to patrolmen.[133]

As earlier indicated, starting and maximum salaries for the police service should be competitive with salaries offered by other employers who seek men of the same age, ability, education, and experience. This will require that police salaries for all positions be increased in nearly all cities. For example, police departments must attract competent college graduates to perform as police agents. In many cities, this will require that starting salaries range from $7,000 to $10,000—based upon 1967 wage levels—with maximum salaries for police agents exceeding $15,000. Special agents for the Federal Bureau of Investigation now earn starting salaries of $8,421 and can ultimately earn $16,905 in that same position.

Not all police salaries, at least in the foreseeable future, will have to be competitive with salaries offered college graduates. Many police officers will continue to be high school graduates or will have only completed 2 years of college. Salaries for this position, however, should at least be competitive with salaries paid to craftsmen and other skilled laborers.[134] In many communities this will require a starting salary—again based upon 1967 wage levels—between $6,000 and $9,000 with a maximum salary of at least $12,000. Many large departments are already paying beginning salaries to patrolmen which fall within this range. For example, the San Francisco Police Department has a starting salary of $8,220; Los Angeles, $7,692, and New York, $7,032.[135] But in these departments, as well as nearly all others, the maximum salary opportunity is limited. Although the starting salary in San Francisco is comparatively high, the maximum salary for patrolmen is only $600 higher.[136] Since the number of supervisory and administrative positions in any police department are limited, relatively few sworn officers advance to these levels. Also, since it is essential that highly skilled personnel remain as police officers and police agents, all departments should create greater career opportunities within these positions.

The median salary for the top police executive, the police chief, ranges from $7,504 in smaller communities, to $17,600 in cities of over 500,000 population.[137] In only 8 of 38 cities of between 300,000 and 1 million population, do captains receive more than $11,000. Sergeants receive $9,600 or more in only nine cities.[138] Supervisors and administrators in police departments must receive salaries comparable with the magnitude of their responsibility. Administering a police department requires skills similar to those required of management in private industry. Before a police department can attract persons who could ultimately assume management responsibility and who aspire to do so, the salary paid to supervisors and administrators must be closely competitive with analogous responsibility in that community.

In many cities, police salaries are tied to the salaries of other government employees. For example, it has been a tradition for police and fire department salaries to be identical. Police compensation should be based solely on the nature of work being performed by various classes of personnel within the department as well as within the entire structure of local government. Since policemen and firemen perform entirely different jobs, neither service should base its salaries upon those of the other. If, considering all factors, firemen require higher salaries, they should be so compensated. The opposite should also be true.

In addition to competitive salaries, all police departments should insure that fringe benefits such as retirement plans, group health and life insurance, and vacation and sick leave are comparable to those offered in private industry. At one time, many police departments had fringe benefits which were superior to those offered by private industry, and they assumed that benefits such as early retirement or lengthy vacation periods were a substitute for competitive salaries. However, since most occupations and professions now have comparable or superior fringe benefit programs, police departments can no longer rely upon these benefits as the sole means of attracting personnel.

In summary, the police cannot be expected to recruit competent personnel until communities are willing to pay the price for improved police performance. Many communities have already recognized this need, but starting and maximum salaries are still insufficient in nearly every department. Until salaries are increased to competitive levels, the police service will fight a losing battle in its efforts to upgrade the quality of its personnel.

Working Conditions. Another deterrent to the attractiveness of careers in law enforcement is the working conditions of many police departments. All too often, police precinct stations are old, cramped and badly maintained; equipment is deficient; and clerical help is limited. These conditions adversely affect police morale and detract from the professional nature of police work:[139]

> Police morale is adversely affected as long as police activities are housed in outmoded buildings and personnel are forced to work with inferior equipment. Without proper facilities and equipment even the most conscientious officer finds it difficult to perform his tasks properly. Good police buildings and equipment also create a favorable public impression enhancing the prestige of the department.

Recent surveys of several departments indicate that deplorable working conditions are widespread. For example, in Baltimore, the walls of the police headquarters building "were dirty, inadequate lighting made the lobby appear dingy, and the disinfectant used to clean the floors permeated the air with a pungent smell."[140] In Woodbridge, N.J., "police headquarters was inadequate in area,

---

[130] Id. at p. 232–233.
[131] Seattle Police Officers Guild, "A Study of Wages and Working Conditions in the Seattle Police Department." (Seattle: Police Officers Guild, 1966).
[132] Supra, note 50 at p. 111.
[133] Los Angeles City Government, "Wage and Salary Survey in Los Angeles County." (Los Angeles: Printing Division, 1966), p. 6. The patrolmen's salary was obtained from the 1966 "Municipal Yearbook," supra, note 3 at p. 444.
[134] Supra, note 50 at p. 111.
[135] Supra, note 3 at pp. 444–445, 450.
[136] Id. at p. 445.
[137] Id. at p. 436.
[138] Supra, note 116.
[139] I.A.C.P., "A Survey of the Police Department, Baltimore, Maryland." (Washington: I.A.C.P., December 1965) p. 475.
[140] Id. at p. 478.

poorly laid out, inadequately lighted, unsanitary, and unattractive." [141] There are 900 persons in the headquarters building of the Washington, D.C., police occupying less space than had been allocated for 385.[142] Further, in many departments uniforms are drab; the numbers of automobiles and other equipment are totally inadequate; and sworn officers are often required to write or type their own reports and maintain their own records.[143]

Competent officers cannot easily be attracted or retained under conditions such as those described above. All police buildings should be attractive, provide adequate space and be well maintained. Modern equipment such as dictating machines should be used for reports, and officers should only be required to perform work suited to their ability.

Professional Climate. As was earlier indicated, the police service will not stimulate the interest of the college graduate unless tasks are more rationally separated among different classes of officers and immediate opportunities are provided for the qualified to confront the most difficult law enforcement problems. It will also be essential that police departments encourage the use of professional skills. At the present time, personnel are closely regimented in most departments and initiative is not encouraged. For example, there is far more emphasis on making arrests and following orders than on questioning traditional procedures or solving community problems. This is not an appealing environment for a person of professional stature. Thus, the overregimentation of personnel, which was noted in a 1934 survey of the Boston Police Department, continues to exist today: [144]

> Too often the military aspect of organization pushes the essentially individual character of police work into the background. A policeman is regimented with his fellows. He is given a uniform, badge, and number; he is assigned to a squad and platoon; he carries a book of rules in his pocket and a schedule of duty calls in his mind. He is a cog in a machine. Everything seems to be numbered, labeled, covered by rules, and arranged far in advance. Yet, when he goes out on post he is alone and on his own responsibility.

Unquestionably, police organizations must have certain military characteristics; officers must be responsive to departmental policies and must act in a disciplined fashion during emergency situations. However, police work also requires considerable independent judgment and an ability to adjust police practices to complex and changing conditions. Extreme regimentation prevents these needs from being fulfilled.

Therefore, if the police sincerely want professional recognition, they must afford professional status to their sworn officers. Unnecessary regimentation should be removed, independent judgment should be encouraged, and criticism of existing practices should be solicited. Police departments traditionally have resisted change and have been wary of the intellectual. As long as this attitude prevails, the police will never successfully compete for the type of person they so desperately need. Although other factors, such as compensation, bear heavily on the ability to attract qualified applicants, none bears as heavily as the professional opportunity available to the officer.

RECRUITMENT PROGRAMS

The Commission has suggested many reforms calculated to enhance the attractiveness of careers in law enforcement for the college graduate or other qualified persons. But improvements in career opportunities alone will not alter the current crisis. Concomitant with reforms, the police must adopt vigorous recruiting programs. At the present time there is little coordinated effort among law enforcement agencies to stimulate interest in careers in law enforcement. As a result, each of the 40,000 separate agencies must undertake its own recruiting program, and these programs rarely extend to the college campus.

If law enforcement is ever to upgrade the existing levels of personnel, it must do so by concentrating recruiting efforts among college students or among persons who have the capacity to perform college work. In light of the current unfortunate image of police work, successes in such recruiting programs may initially be limited. It will be necessary, therefore, to develop programs to stimulate interest in law enforcement. The following proposals suggest some methods for attracting the college graduate or other persons with needed skills. There is an additional need to attract persons with less education, but with a knowledge of the community, to serve as community service officers. Methods to accomplish this end are explored in chapter 6.

The Coordination of Recruiting Efforts. While many police departments currently have extensive recruiting programs, recruiting efforts by a majority of the law enforcement agencies are haphazard, poorly financed and limited to the community where the individual department is situated. Several of the smaller police departments do not have sufficient funds to undertake extensive recruiting efforts, and because of strict residency requirements, the search for candidates must be restricted within city boundaries.

It is imperative that all departments be permitted to recruit on a nationwide basis. Residency requirements currently imposed on police departments should, therefore, be removed, as has already been done in such cities as Washington, D.C., and Miami, Fla. Also, aside from recruiting programs conducted by individual departments, all law enforcement agencies within a State should jointly engage in statewide campaigns—and even campaign nationally—for the purpose of describing the challenge of law enforcement careers and the available opportunities for qualified candidates. Innumerable advantages exist in jointly administered recruitment programs: (1) potential candidates would be informed of all vacancies in police departments throughout a State; (2) comprehensive efforts to promote careers in law enforcement could be undertaken; (3) more extensive budgets could be appropriated for recruiting at substantially less cost than would necessarily have to be incurred by individual departments; and (4) common procedures for applying for

---

[141] The New York Institute of Criminology, "Report of Survey: Police Department Township of Woodbridge, Middlesex County, New Jersey." (New York: The New York Institute of Criminology, May 19, 1962), p. 52.
[142] Supra, note 17 at p. 41.
[143] Id. at p. 43; See also Bureau of Police, St. Paul, Minn., "A Study and Report." (East Lansing: The Eastmans 1962) pp. 79, 142.
[144] Supra, note 23 at p. 30.

positions for all departments could be devised. Joint programs could easily be administered by State commissions on police standards, which are described in a later section of this chapter. Recommended joint recruiting programs were extensively described in chapter 4, and will not therefore be repeated here.

Incentive Programs. Because of the immediacy of the recruitment problem and of the urgent need for college graduates in law enforcement, special financial incentives should be offered to persons who desire to complete their education and pursue careers in the police service. For example, under the National Defense Education Act of 1965, the Federal Government is currently providing loans to college students.[145] Under this act, 50 percent of a loan is forgiven if a student becomes a full-time teacher in an elementary or secondary school or in an institution of higher education.[146] This act should be amended to apply also to students entering the police service. As a supplement to this act, State or local governments could also provide student loans which would be partially or totally forgiven over a period of years if students enter police departments within that jurisdiction.

Another method of stimulating interest in law enforcement would be for police departments to provide part-time employment to college students as civilians, thereby enabling them to finance their college educations. If, upon graduation, the student enters the department in either a civilian or sworn capacity, he could receive retirement and pay credit for the time employed while attending college. Retirement and pay credits are given to graduates of the military academies who pursue careers in the military service. Such a program is also now being used by the Arlington County Police Department.[147]

It was earlier recommended that police departments establish programs for the purpose of attracting qualified high school graduates into police service before they select other career opportunities. At the present time, cadets are primarily used to perform clerical tasks, and are admitted into police departments as sworn officers upon reaching the age of 21. To derive greater benefits from a cadet or police intern program, participants should be required to attend an accredited college or university on a full-time basis. While attending a college or university an intern could perform clerical tasks, field work, or staff functions for the police department on a part-time basis during the school year, and full-time during summer vacations. For example, the intern could assist police officers and police agents, or could serve as community service officers. The police department, with Federal, State or local financial assistance, could defray the college expenses of the intern as well as pay him a salary and these expenses would have to be repaid only if he did not enter the police department and serve a specific length of time upon his graduation from college.

At least 19 police departments now require their cadets to take college courses.[148] However, in many of these programs, the cadet is required to pay for his own education and his academic courses are frequently restricted to technical police science courses. For example, cadets in the Chicago Police Department are required to enroll in at least two units of college study each year "along police career lines." [149] A majority of the other departments which do pay the college tuition for cadets also restrict college study to police science subjects.[150] As was earlier observed, police science programs, as presently constituted, do not fulfill the educational need of police personnel.

For this reason, cadets and interns should be required to enroll in the broader college offerings at accredited institutions. If cadet programs are utilized in this way, their attractiveness will be enhanced and they could serve as a valuable method of recruiting qualified persons into the police service.

CAREER DEVELOPMENT

TRAINING

Recruit Training. No person, regardless of his individual qualifications, is prepared to perform police work on native ability alone. Aside from individual intelligence, prior education, judgment, and emotional fitness, an officer must receive extensive vocational training before he can understand the police task and learn how to fulfill it: [151]

When recruits are properly selected they bring to the job considerable native ability but little knowledge or experience in police work. In a short time, they must be prepared to operate alone on the streets under a variety of conditions that call for knowledge of laws and ordinances, legal procedures, police practices, and human relations. As they progress, they must not only acquire more of the same kind of knowledge but also should develop some specialized understanding of investigative techniques and scientific crime detection. This will enable them to conduct initial or preliminary investigations and to preserve vital evidence for the specialists who will assist them on difficult cases.

Training "is one of the most important means of upgrading the services of a police department." [152] The need for such training, however, was not fully recognized until the decade prior to World War II.[153]

In years gone by, it was an opinion among both police and public that any man of general ability could learn to "police" by doing it. Consequently, the then prevailing "training" philosophy was one of providing the recruit with a uniform and badge; arming him with a baton, revolver, and handcuffs; assuring his geographical orientation by issuing him a local street map; and instructing him to "hit the street" and enforce the Ten Commandments. This philosophy conforms conveniently with that which proclaims "there is more justice and law in the end of a night stick than is to be found in all law books."

Although the Wickersham Commission reported in 1931 that formalized recruit training was no longer controversial, its survey of 383 cities in that year showed that only 20 percent of these cities conducted such training.[154] In the majority of the cities surveyed, particularly the smaller cities, there was not even a pretext of training.[155]

---

[145] United States Senate. Subcommittee on Education of the Committee on Labor and Public Welfare, "National Defense Education Act of 1958, as amended by the 88th Congress." (Washington: U.S. Government Printing Office, November 1964), p. 22.
[146] Id. at p. 22.
[147] FBI National Academy, "Police Cadet System: Research Paper". (Washington: Department of Justice, June 3, 1964), p. 34.
[148] Supra, note 95.
[149] Chicago Police Department, "Personnel Division—Cadet Program." (Chicago: Police Department, 1966.)

[150] See e.g., Report of President's Commission on Crime in D.C. Supra, note 17 at p. 28.
[151] Winters, "Recruit and In-Service Training: A Must" Speech delivered to the First Annual Southern Institute for Law Enforcement, the Florida Institute for Continuing University Studies, Tallahassee, Fla., Nov. 7–8, 1963.
[152] Supra, note 17 at p. 32.
[153] Supra, note 32 at p. 110.
[154] Supra, note 4 at p. 71.
[155] Id. at pp. 70–71.

Briefly, then, in the counties, towns, and hamlets of this class, it must be stated that assumption of badge, revolver, and the authority of law, has as a prerequisite no training or police experience, in fact, nothing.

Spurred by the Federal Bureau of Investigation, which dramatized the need, set standards, and provided curricula and instructors for police training, the police have made great strides in the past 30 years in widespread institution of formal recruit training programs. In 1965, a survey of 1,352 cities conducted by the International City Managers Association found that 1,135 of these cities conducted some type of recruit training for their police officers.[156] A recent survey of 269 law enforcement agencies by the National League of Cities, conducted in 1966, reported that 97 percent of the agencies surveyed had formal training.[157] But another survey of 4,000 police agencies conducted in 1965 by the International Association of Chiefs of Police revealed that 85 percent of the officers appointed were placed in the field prior to their recruit training.[158]

Even though a substantial number of today's police departments require their recruits to undergo some initial training, an examination of many of these programs reveals that the vocational training needs of recruits are inadequately met in most departments.

Content of Training Programs. In 1934 a survey of one police department indicated that the primary courses offered in its recruit training program were:[159]

Criminal law of the State and common law.
Ordinances and bylaws of the city.
Rules and regulations of the police department.
Traffic signals with hand and arm.
First aid to sick and injured, and Schaeffer prone pressure method of resuscitation for cases of suffocation by drowning, gas, hanging, electric shock, smoke, and ammonia fumes.
Military drill (U.S. Army Drill Regulations) in the school of the soldier—squad, platoon, and company.
U.S. Army calisthenics.
Use and care of the revolver; dry practice and practice with fixed ammunition.
Use of gas masks, gas bombs, bulletproof vests, and Winchester (riot) shotgun.
Jiu jitsu holds and breaks.

While it is obvious that such a training program is totally inadequate to prepare recruits for police work, few of our smaller police departments today provide even this amount of training. For example, the city of Meridan, Conn., had almost no regular training aside from firing range instruction until 1961.[160] This is not true of our Nation's larger departments, however. Metropolitan police departments, particularly those in cities of over 500,000 population, have greatly expanded the scope of their training programs. These now include instruction in such subjects as investigation, field procedures, crowd control, basic sociology and race relations, administration of justice, criminal evidence, and juvenile procedures.

While a few of these programs are highly commendable, it remains doubtful whether even a majority of them provide recruits with an ample understanding of the police task. For example, very few of the training programs reviewed by the Commission provide course material on the history of law enforcement, the role of the police in modern society, or the need for discretion in law enforcement. The fact that appropriate consideration is not given to police discretion was also noted by the President's Commission on Crime in the District of Columbia:[161]

Throughout the training program there must be a frank recognition of the fact that policemen exercise broad discretionary powers in enforcing the law. The maxim that policemen exercise no discretion but only enforce the law must give way before the blunt realities of the law enforcement process. One important test of a good recruit training program, therefore, is the extent to which it equips the recruit to exercise his discretion wisely when confronted with actual enforcement problems. In the past the department has neglected this important ingredient of recruit training; we urge that the curriculum be extensively reshaped to reflect more fully the actual dimensions and difficulties of police work in the District of Columbia.

Current training programs, for the most part, prepare an officer to perform police work mechanically, but do not prepare him to understand his community, the police role, or the imperfections of the criminal justice system.

Some police departments are just beginning to recognize the significance of improving the relationship of the police with the community, and particularly with the minority community. Although several departments have incorporated courses on police-community relations, these units are limited, both in time and substance. For example, two of the largest police departments devote under 10 hours of their over 400 hours of training exclusively to police-minority group relations. Thus, an earlier observation on police training in the United States is still applicable today:[162]

It can be said of police training schools that the recruit is taught everything except the essential requirements of his calling, which is how to secure and maintain the approval and respect of the public whom he encounters daily in the course of his duties.

Length of Training Programs. In those departments that provide recruit training, programs vary in length from less than 1 week in many of the smaller departments to as many as 20 weeks.[163] The recruit training program of the Los Angeles County Sheriff's Department in 1966 consisted of 820 hours. While a majority of the departments in cities above 250,000 population provide 8 weeks or more of training, the average department in the remaining communities provides not more, and typically less, than 3 weeks of training.[164] Cost factors are undoubtedly the primary reason for this disparity. Very few small departments can afford to establish extensive programs.[165]

It is economically feasible to provide recruit training to a class of 20 men whereas it is not feasible to do so with a group of 2 or 3 men. Thus, the smaller cities are confronted with the problem of either going so far under strength, awaiting a recruit group of adequate size, or of hiring men in small numbers without providing training.

---

[156] Supra, note 3 at p. 435.
[157] Supra, note 59 at p. 20.
[158] I.A.C.P., "Police Training," report submitted to the President's Commission on Law Enforcement and Administration of Justice. (Washington: I.A.C.P., 1966).
[159] Supra, note 23 at p. 70.
[160] Supra, note 32 at p. 110.

[161] Supra, note 17 at p. 35.
[162] Charles Reith, "The Blind Eye of History: A Study of the Origins of the Present Police Era." (London: Faber and Faber limited, 1952), p. 115–116.
[163] Supra, note 158.
[164] Ibid.
[165] Supra, note 28.

The latter course has been taken far too often. Some of the small departments, however, do send their recruits to training academies in nearby departments, community colleges, or state academies.[166] But most of the smaller agencies cannot spare an officer for any prolonged period of time and local governments are often unwilling to pay the salary and expenses necessarily incurred in sending a recruit to another part of the State for extensive training.

The choice then is typically between sending a recruit for a limited time or not sending him at all. When the demands on the police are considered, it is doubtful that any department can fulfill training needs in less than the 400 hours utilized by the majority of the departments in the cities over 500,000 population.

Relatively few departments provide supervised field training as an adjunct of classroom instruction. A 1966 Survey by the National Council on Crime and Delinquency reported that only 23 of 109 departments, for example, provided field observation of street problems. Classroom instruction will not suffice in and of itself. Ideally, a recruit should initially receive classroom orientation on the nature of the police task and law enforcement responsibility. The remainder of the training program should be balanced between closely supervised field training experience and classroom sessions devoted to problem solving situations which closely parallel actual street problems. Under such a training program, classroom instruction and field experience could be interspersed over a period not exceeding 6 months.

At least two police departments now combine recruit training with supervised field experience. In the Tucson, Ariz., Police Department, recruits devote 1 week of field work to each of the three principal departmental divisions as part of their formal training. The San Diego Police Department has 2 weeks of classroom and range instruction and devotes the remaining 12 weeks to a blending of classroom instruction and field experience. After the first 2 weeks, the recruit normally spends 4 hours of each day in the classroom and 5 hours obtaining field experience under the supervision of carefully selected police officers. The sixth hour of the daily field training portion is spent in a critique session reviewing experiences and problems. The benefit of these programs is that a recruit can better assimilate classroom instruction that is related to actual incidents in the field. Through exposure to actual field problems, investigations and crime incidents the need and value of classroom training becomes vividly apparent to the trainee. In summary, formal training programs for recruits in all departments, large and small, should consist of an absolute minimum of 400 hours of classroom work spread over a 4- to 6-month period so that it can be combined with carefully selected and supervised field training.

Methods of Instructions. Consideration must also be given to present methods of instruction. In nearly all training programs, the administrative and teaching staff are comprised totally of sworn officers who have been assigned to the academy on a full- or part-time basis.[167] The need for use of experienced officers to train recruits in performance of police work is an obvious one. Certain courses, however, could more appropriately be taught by or with the assistance of civilian specialists. For example, talented instructors from other disciplines should be used for instruction of such specialized subjects as law, psychology, race relations, and teaching techniques. The FBI National Academy has long had civilian instructors as part of its visiting faculty. For example, in 1966, the following civilian instructors taught at the National Academy: a professor of psychology, a sociologist, a chief clinical psychiatrist, four judges from various levels of the court system, a professor of history, a physicist and a chemist to cover the field of criminalistics, a superintendent of schools, and a representative from the news media. This is done on only a limited basis in most police departments today, although FBI instructors do teach subjects in many training programs. In 1965 alone, FBI personnel provided 42,224 hours of instruction to over 149,000 persons.

Most training courses are taught almost exclusively by lecture method, even though the limitations of such instruction have long been recognized by professional training directors and educators. The extent to which training academies utilize methods of instruction other than the lecture method was reported in a 1966 survey of the National Council on Crime and Delinquency:[168]

TEACHING TECHNIQUES
(Survey of 109 police departments—1965)

Technique	Number and percent using
1. Lecture and discussion	105 (96.33)
2. TV-films and recordings	68 (62.38)
3. Simulation of practice	45 (41.28)
4. Actual practice	37 (33.94)
5. Practice in use of work devices	30 (27.52)
6. Field observation of communication facilities and conditions	23 (21.10)
7. Discussion of assigned readings	19 (17.43)

This survey indicates that many police departments are either unaware of newer educative techniques or do not recognize the need for them. In order to insure that department instructors are qualified to teach in a training academy, all regular instructors should be required to complete a teacher training course of no less than 80 classroom hours taught by professional educators. This is the number of hours that the Federal Bureau of Investigation requires its special agents to complete before they are assigned to teach police subjects.

Continuing Training Programs. Deficiencies in current police training are not limited to recruit programs. New laws are enacted and old ones amended; the enforcement needs of a community change, and new concepts of police technology and department policy emerge. These facts dictate that training be a continuing process.

In a recent survey of the 54 police agencies within the metropolitan area of Detroit, only one-third of these departments provide refresher training for its personnel.[169]

The Nation's departments that do provide continuing training are typically large departments that also conduct

---

[166] Ibid.
[167] Department of Health, Education, and Welfare, National Council on Crime and Delinquency and Office of Juvenile Delinquency and Youth Development, "Pilot Study of Correctional Training and Manpower," 1966.
[168] Ibid.
[169] Survey of the International Association of Chief of Police, Washington, D.C., (1966).

extensive recruit training programs. But even in these departments, intensive inservice training is normally limited. There are some notable exceptions, however. For example, after police officers in the Los Angeles Police Department complete their basic training, they return to school after 1 year on the job for an intermediate course that ranges from 40–80 hours. This course marks the end of their 1-year probationary period. Between the 3rd and 5th year each officer in the department returns for another training course of the same length. Between their 7th and 14th year all officers must again return for a formal training period of 40–80 hours. The Federal Bureau of Investigation sends each of its special agents back to its training academy for a comprehensive 2-week refresher course after approximately 2 years of service, and thereafter such training is given every 5 years.

Much of the existing inservice training is given in brief, daily form. For example, many departments conduct rollcall training for from 5 to 20 minutes at the beginning of each tour of duty, and utilize excellent training aids such as "Training Key" or Sight/Sound films provided by the International Association of Chiefs of Police. While the short, daily training sessions for police officers have great value, these programs should be supplemented by an annual period of intensive inservice training. The necessary length of such training will vary among departments. It is doubtful, however, that yearly training needs can be fulfilled in less than 1 week.[170]

THE DEVELOPMENT OF CAREER OPPORTUNITIES

Of equal concern is the fact that little consideration is given to preparing personnel for supervisory and administrative positions. As was indicated earlier in this report, an officer is not qualified to administer the complex affairs of a large department or to supervise the performance of others simply on the strength of police experience acquired in subordinate positions.

Supervisory and middle-management personnel perform functions and have responsibilities largely unrelated to their early experiences within the agency. Additional skills needed by prospective administrators and supervisors must be acquired through advanced education and specialized training.

Inservice Education. The future elevation of educational requirements will not alter the fact that a majority of today's police officers have not advanced beyond high school. In line with the critical need to upgrade the educative achievement of police personnel, it is essential that departments undertake massive programs to provide the opportunity for interested personnel to continue their educations.

One State, Virginia, has enacted legislation to enhance this opportunity. By a statute adopted in 1966, the Virginia Department of Education was authorized to pay 50 percent of all tuition costs to any officer who attends college. The department of education was further authorized to pay the remaining tuition costs when it received evidence that the officer continued to serve with the same department for 1 year following the completion of such courses.[171] Several cities, such as Tucson, provide financial assistance to their officers to enable them to take college courses. Such programs are commendable, and local, State, and Federal funds should be provided to assist police personnel to continue their educations.

Since it is extremely difficult for any person to acquire a meaningful education on a part-time basis, it would be preferable if a department could allow personnel to devote a complete year, for example, to college work. Military programs permit personnel to return to college for 1 academic year to complete requirements toward an advanced degree. They also permit those who have not completed baccalaureate degree requirements to return for up to 1 academic year while on a leave status. As recommended in chapter 13 of the General Report, Federal and State Governments should provide assistance to local governments so that similar programs can be initiated for the police service.

Most personnel, however, will undoubtedly have to acquire college education on a gradual basis by enrolling in one or two courses each semester. This gradual route to education unfortunately poses many hardships for police personnel. Duty rotation and court appearances often present conflicts with off-duty education, and many officers are not within commuting distance of a college or university. It is essential, therefore, that meaningful correspondence courses be available for interested officers. State and Federal Governments should finance the development of university extension level courses for police personnel.

Few departments today provide sufficient encouragement for personnel to return to school. For example, the fact that an officer has an advanced degree does not, in most cases, qualify the officer for a pay increment and is not normally one of the factors considered in promotions. A department should provide these additional incentives to encourage officers to advance their educations.

As was recommended earlier in this chapter, no officer should be eligible to qualify for promotion to police agent, supervisor, or administrator until he has acquired a baccalaureate degree. Based upon the current level of educational achievement, however, it is obvious that such a requirement would be unattainable at the present time. Until such a goal is attainable, however, departments should progressively increase educational standards for these positions at the earliest opportunity. Such a concept is not new to the police field. For example, in 1962 a consultant to the St. Paul, Minn., department made the following recommendation:[172]

> Patrolmen should not be appointed to the rank of sergeant until they have had 1 year of college work; 2 years should be required for promotion to lieutenant; 3 to captain; and 4 years to positions above this rank. . . .

In addition to requiring higher educational standards for such advanced positions, all departments should provide pay incentives for college education. For example, a pay increase could be provided for each year of college

---

[170] Supra, note 31 at p. 113–114.
[171] Va. Code Ann., tit. 23, sec. 23–9 (1966 Cum. Supp.).
[172] "Survey of the Bureau of Police: St. Paul, Minnesota." (East Lansing: The Eastmans, 1962), p. 128.

education completed, with a substantial increase for personnel completing the work required for a degree. The California Commission on Peace Officers Standards and Training has suggested an education incentive program which certifies officers who attain specified levels of education and experience, and thereby qualifies such officers for pay increase:

SUGGESTED EDUCATION INCENTIVE PROGRAM, CALIFORNIA COMMISSION ON PEACE OFFICERS STANDARDS AND TRAINING

1. Must possess the P.O.S.T. Basic Certificate to qualify for the final step in the pay scale for police officer, deputy sheriff or higher ranks.
2. Possession of P.O.S.T. Intermediate Certificates shall qualify the officer for a 5 percent pay increase.
3. Possession of P.O.S.T. Advanced Certificates shall qualify for a 10 percent increase.
4. To remain eligible to receive the incentive program pay increase, the applicant must requalify each year by completing no less than 50 hours of education or training which would be recognized by P.O.S.T. as courses credited toward intermediate or advanced certificate or by completing a project approved by the department head. All education, training or projects approved under this section (annual qualification) shall be completed on the officer's own time unless otherwise approved by the department head.

For the purpose of annual qualification, the department head may specify and approve credit courses other than those recognized by P.O.S.T. when in his judgment the course has added to the professional development of the training or education specified.

Career Development Training. While a liberal education provides the foundation for enlightened leadership, it cannot totally provide the required specialized knowledge for police administration.

The demands on administrators, supervisors, or specialists also require advanced skills not developed by basic police training.[173] And yet, only a few large metropolitan departments provide even a limited amount of executive training.[174] To require vocational training for entry level officers, but not for specialists, supervisors, or administrators within a department, is incongruous. In the Los Angeles Police Department, each newly appointed sergeant, lieutenant, and captain must complete an advanced training course in preparation for his newly assigned duties. The sergeant's course is 160 hours, the lieutenant's and captain's courses vary from 40-80 hours. A command officer's school is also held periodically for ranks above captain whenever the need for training at this level is apparent. Such advanced training for supervisory and administrative positions is essential. Each State, therefore, should establish mandatory statewide standards which require that all personnel, prior to assuming supervisory or administrative responsibilities, complete advanced training offered either by the department or by college or university institutes. Such training could include subjects in leadership, fiscal management, supervisory decisionmaking, and psychological aspects of supervision. Further, specialized training should be provided to personnel assuming responsibility for staff functions such as planning and research and police-community relations.

Colleges and universities should cooperate with individual departments in order to provide model career development programs. Several universities and colleges already provide specialized training for law enforcement in traffic, police-community relations, criminal investigation, criminalistics, and police administration. Such offerings are currently provided by the Northwestern University Traffic Institute, the Southern Police Institute, Indiana University, Michigan State University, and numerous colleges and universities in California.

During the past 32 years, the Federal Bureau of Investigation has also conducted inservice training at its National Academy for over 5,000 officers. In 1966, the Department of Justice provided a grant to the Harvard Business School to conduct an institute for improving management skills of the chiefs of police of 40 large cities.

The concept of management institutes should be encouraged, and State and Federal funds should be allocated for the purpose of greatly expanding the role of college and universities in providing middle and upper management training.

PROMOTION

In most cities today, police departments provide promotions on the basis of a merit system. In the early years of this century, police promotions were the subject of political abuse.[175] To preclude such abuses, civil service procedures were adopted which required that promotions be based upon written examination, length of service, and existing rank.[176] While these criteria lessened the opportunity for political influence and favoritism, they did not insure the selection of the most highly qualified personnel for positions of greater responsibility. The current promotion system is based largely upon the premise that experience and knowledge of police fieldwork are the prime requisites for serving as administrator or supervisor.

The qualities needed for serving in such capacities, however, cannot be measured by seniority and experience alone:[177]

Seniority may be taken into account but should not govern promotion, and promotion by competitive examination would be quite unsuited to the police system because of the importance of initiative, tact, judgment, and other personal qualifications which cannot be gauged by means of an examination paper.

There is an assumption in the police service that fairness dictates that personnel with the longest term of service receive a preference for promotions. The effect of such preference, however, is to delay the advancement of more qualified personnel:[178]

An omnipresent management problem is how to overcome a feeling deeply ingrained in most cultures that the most competent and accomplished younger person should wait out his time in deference to a mediocre individual with longer service.

---

[173] Samuel G. Chapman, "Developing Personnel Leadership," "The Police Chief." (Washington: I.A.C.P., March 1966), p. 24.
[174] Supra, note 21 at pp. 28, 29.
[175] Supra, note 8 at p. 132.
[176] Supra, note 16 at p. 133.

[177] The British Home Office Committee on the Police Service in England, Scotland, and Wales quoted in Harrison, supra, note 23 at p. 92.
[178] John Pfiffner, "The Supervision of Personnel." (New York, Prentice-Hall, 1951), p. 408.

Under existing procedures, an officer, regardless of his qualifications, must normally wait several years before he can be considered for promotion to the rank immediately above his own. For example, in Baltimore, a patrolman must serve in that capacity for 5 years before being eligible for sergeant, and all other officers must wait 2 years before being eligible to apply for the next higher rank.[179] If a person has the necessary leadership qualities, no reason exists to restrict his opportunity for advancement as long as he meets other qualitative standards. The seniority factor should be reduced to a bare minimum. In reviewing the police system throughout the Nation today, it is believed this admonition would apply to all but a few departments.

It is equally inappropriate to rely heavily upon high achievement in written examinations:[180]

> Written promotional examinations, on the other hand, do not test those qualities of leadership or administrative capacity which are presumably a major consideration in promotion to higher ranks. Such qualities are, therefore, largely ignored before the more familiar techniques of personnel management which do not attempt any such evaluation of human personality.

Current promotion procedures should be altered in most departments. As stated previously, the period of seniority should be reexamined and in most departments greatly reduced. While there may be merit in requiring all candidates to take a competitive written examination, the results of such an examination should be only one of the many factors to be considered. Other factors should include: (1) An officer's prior performance and reputation in previous jobs as well as within the department and in the community; (2) an officer's educational achievement; and (3) an officer's demonstrated leadership potential and ability to assume greater responsibility. In order to ascertain prior performance and personal qualities, each department should adopt a system of rating personnel. For example, prior performance could be rated by having immediate supervisors, other officers and special units submit reports on the proficiency and conduct of the candidate. Personal qualities could be evaluated by background investigation and oral interviews.

LATERAL ENTRY

Under existing police structures, nearly all local enforcement agencies restrict advanced appointments to personnel within the department. The only exception to this restriction is that some departments exempt the position of chief administrator from Civil Service, and it is possible for persons who are not in the department to compete for this position. A consequence is that America's police personnel are virtually frozen into the departments in which they started. An officer whose special skills are in oversupply in his own department cannot move to a department where those skills are in demand. An officer who seeks to improve his situation by moving from a small department where opportunities for advancement are few to a large department where they are numerous cannot do it, nor can a city officer who would like to work in a small community follow his inclinations. A department that cannot fill important jobs adequately from its own ranks is precluded from seeking experienced officers elsewhere.

To improve police service, competition for all advanced positions should be opened to qualified persons from both within and outside of the department. This would enable a department to obtain the best available talent for positions of leadership.[181]

To limit promotional appointment to those within any agency is to repress initiative, creativity, and critical judgment. . . . All promotional processes must be geared to the objective of getting the finest leadership possible.

If candidates from within an agency are unable to meet the competition from other applicants, it should be recognized that the influx of more highly qualified personnel would greatly improve the quality of the service.

Before it will be feasible to encourage interchange of personnel among police departments, however, current civil service rules, retirement systems, department hiring restrictions and statutes will require revisions in several sections of this country:[182]

> The rules and statutes, indeed, usually attach penalties to or prohibitions against circulation—such as local residence requirements, promotion barriers, cumbersome transfer procedures, the loss of pension and retirement benefits. The rules are set heavily against circulation, a fact which is emphasized not only by the presence of these barriers but also by the absence of personnel procedures to overcome them. To these conditions, adverse to mobility among bureaucracies, must be added a stronger version of the seemingly universal habit of organized groups to prefer promotion from within rather than the recruitment of "new blood" at the intermediate and higher levels.

Many of these longstanding tight personnel restrictions are stifling the professional development of the police service, and should, therefore, be removed. In addition, to encourage lateral movement of police personnel, a nationwide retirement system should be devised which permits the transferring of retirement credits.

Without question, the police service desperately needs an influx of highly qualified college graduates. It is doubtful whether suitable graduates will be attracted to police service if they are required in all cases to initiate their career at the lowest level of a department, and it is further doubted that this would be an appropriate method of utilizing such personnel. For this reason, college graduates should, after an adequate internship, be eligible to serve as police agents. Persons who have adequate education and experience should be allowed to enter directly into staff and administrative positions.

MINIMUM STATEWIDE STANDARDS FOR SELECTION, SCREENING AND TRAINING

A study of police personnel problems indicates that, while all departments are in need of extensive upgrading of recruiting efforts, minimum standards, selection procedures and training, the needs are more pronounced for the smaller police departments. Many of these departments provide little or no training, use ineffectual selec-

---

[179] Supra, note 139 at p. 197.
[180] Supra, note 16 at p. 134.
[181] A. C. Germann, "Recruitment, Selection, Promotion, and Civil Service," report submitted to the President's Commission on Law Enforcement and the Administration of Justice (Washington: 1966), p. 110.

[182] Wallace S. Sayre, "The Recruitment and Training of Bureaucrats in the United States." "The Annals of the American Academy of Political and Social Science." (Philadelphia: Academy of Political and Social Science, March 1954), p. 39.

tion and screening techniques, and have no organized recruiting programs. This results in substantial variation in the quality of police service, not only in different areas of the country, but within the same State.

The apparent reason for this disparity is that many of our Nation's police departments and local governments either do not have sufficient funds to correct current deficiencies or do not have the expertise to recognize them. The general level of police service will not significantly improve unless each State assumes greater responsibility for upgrading all local law enforcement agencies.

Each State, therefore, should establish a commission on police standards or expand an existing commission on police training and empower such commission to:

- ☐ establish minimum statewide selection standards;
- ☐ establish minimum standards for training; determine and approve curricula; identify required preparation for instructors; and approve facilities acceptable for police training;
- ☐ certify sworn police personnel;
- ☐ conduct and stimulate research by private and public agencies designed to improve police service;
- ☐ make inspections to determine whether Commission standards are being adhered to; and
- ☐ provide such financial aid as may be authorized by the legislature to participating governmental units.

The proposed role of a State commission is fully described in chapter 8.

Chapter 6

The Police and the Community

THE SCOPE OF THE PROBLEM

THE IMPORTANCE OF POLICE-COMMUNITY RELATIONS

The need for strengthening police relationships with the communities they serve is critical today in the Nation's large cities and in many small cities and towns as well. The Negro, Puerto Rican, Mexican-American, and other minority groups are taking action to acquire rights and services which have been historically denied them. As the most visible representative of the society from which these groups are demanding fair treatment and equal opportunity, law enforcement agencies are faced with unprecedented situations on the street which require that they develop policies and practices governing their actions when dealing with minority groups and other citizens.

Even if fairer treatment of minority groups were the sole consideration, police departments would have an obligation to attempt to achieve and maintain good police-community relations. In fact, however, much more is at stake. Police-community relationships have a direct bearing on the character of life in our cities, and on the community's ability to maintain stability and to solve its problems. At the same time, the police department's capacity to deal with crime depends to a large extent upon its relationship with the citizenry. Indeed, no lasting improvement in law enforcement is likely in this country unless police-community relations are substantially improved.

Effect on the Police Department as an Organization

Hostility, or even lack of confidence of a significant portion of the public, has extremely serious implications for the police. These attitudes interfere with recruiting, since able young men generally seek occupations which are not inordinately dangerous and which have the respect and support of their relatives and friends.

Public hostility affects morale and makes police officers less enthusiastic about doing their job well. It may lead some officers to leave the force, to accept more prestigious or less demanding employment.

Many police officers now view their relations with the public as poor. This attitude is reflected in surveys of patrolmen as well as in frequent statements by police officials.

Recently a survey of policemen in a western municipal department disclosed that 70 percent thought that the prestige of police work was fair or poor while only 29 percent said good and 2 percent excellent. Twenty-six percent of the officers believed that "relations with public" was the principal problem faced by police.[1] Another survey of officers in a big-city department found that over 70 percent had an acute sense of citizen hostility or contempt.[2] A Commission survey of police officers conducted in eight precincts in three large cities found that the officers considered "prestige and respect one gets from a job" next to last among the factors they liked about police work; when asked what was least liked about police work when they entered the force, 22 percent cited public lack of respect; only the hours worked were rated lower.[3]

A dissatisfied public will not support the police enthusiastically when such issues as police salaries, sufficient numbers of officers, and adequate equipment and buildings are pending before State legislatures, city councils, or civilian executives. Perhaps most significant of all, when the police and the public are at odds, the police tend to become isolated from the public and become less capable of understanding and adapting to the community and its changing needs.

Direct Effect on Police Operations

Poor police-community relations adversely affect the ability of the police to prevent crime and apprehend criminals. People hostile to the police are not so likely to report violations of law, even when they are the victims. They are even less likely to report suspicious persons or incidents, to testify as witnesses voluntarily, or to come forward and provide information. For example, a study in St. Louis found that 43 percent of Negroes and 36 percent of whites believed that "most of the city residents seem to be afraid to contact their police." [4] Yet citizen assistance is crucial to law enforcement agencies if the police are to solve an appreciable portion of the crimes that are committed: [5]

To most Negroes, policemen constitute an outgroup whose members are antagonistic toward them. Consequently, they will do nothing to help the police * * * They are afraid they will be treated as roughly as the criminal.

---

[1] Jerome H. Skolnick, "Justice Without Trial: Law Enforcement in Democratic Society" (New York: John Wiley & Sons, Inc., 1966), p. 50.
[2] James Q. Wilson, "Police Attitudes and Citizen Hostility," quoted in supra, note 1 at p. 62.
[3] Albert J. Reiss, Jr., "Police Officer Attitudes Toward Their Work and Job" (Ann Arbor: University of Michigan, 1966), table 7, report prepared for President's Commission on Law Enforcement and Administration of Justice. This report is a preliminary draft which is being included with the Commission's records in the National Archives. It is presently being revised and supplemented by the University of Michigan and will be embodied in research studies to be published by the Commission.
[4] Edmund Joseph Casey, "Citizen Attitudes Toward the Police and Law Enforcement" (unpublished Ph. D. thesis, St. Louis University, 1966), p. 100.
[5] Mayor's Law Enforcement Committee, "Report" (Houston: Office of the Mayor), pp. 82, 84. As cited in address by Arthur B. Caldwell, "The Police Image—Civil Rights and Law Enforcement" (Berkeley, University of California, Sept. 27, 1962).

Public hostility can and does influence police field operations. For example, it may make officers reluctant to act; it may also induce the use of unnecessary force, verbal abuse, or other improper practices. The danger under which the policeman must work may make him "less judicious, indeed less discreet, in the exercise of his authority." [6] When unfriendly crowds begin to gather, officers will necessarily have to call for reinforcements and use greater force to secure the offender and control the onlookers. Even if not excessive, such force will often lead to increased police-public tensions. On the other hand, "the cooperation of the public * * * diminishes, proportionately, the necessity of the use of physical force and compulsion for achieving police objectives." [7] Hostility by racial minorities or others may also provoke police officers and therefore increase the likelihood that they will discriminate in exercising their discretion. Consequently, poor police-community relations tend to perpetuate themselves.

Effect on Individual Police Officers

Statistics compiled by the FBI reveal that 20,523 officers were assaulted, 6,836 injured, and 53 killed during 1965.[8] Many of the serious injuries and deaths were inflicted by felons or other persons attempting to escape and therefore had little, if anything, to do with problems of police-community relations. However, many of the minor assaults (and some of the more serious ones as well) resulted, at least partially, from general hostility toward the police. Consequently, poor community relations can increase the danger of police work.

Perhaps even more important, poor police-community relations place a serious personal burden upon a police officer. Though the number of incidents which result in police injury is a small proportion of total police contacts with the public, the prospect of facing danger in hostile neighborhoods is constantly present. Like any other person, the officer resents having to work day in and day out, frequently for low pay and in danger, for people who often verbally abuse him or silently dislike him.

Effect on Community Stability

Any interference with proper police operations reduces the ability of the police to handle crime and maintain law and order. In addition, poor police-community relations has contributed to the disturbances and riots which have increasingly afflicted our cities for the last 3 years. Between January 1964 and June 1966, 32 disturbances or riots occurred in which 2 or more persons were injured or there had been substantial property damage.[9] Poor police-community relations, together with poor housing, unemployment, and oppressive commercial practices, were basic underlying factors in these riots. In addition, more often than not, riots were set off by some quite ordinary and proper action by a policeman. Some riots, however, started after improper or at least unwise police conduct.

It is the purpose of this chapter to determine the reasons for, and the extent of, the difficulties of police-community relations and to examine ways to improve these relations. Although the extent of the problem varies from jurisdiction to jurisdiction, the programs which will be suggested in the following pages should be particularly applicable to all communities that have a substantial minority population.

PUBLIC ATTITUDES TOWARD THE POLICE

The General Public

Contrary to the belief of many policemen, the overwhelming majority of the public has a high opinion of the work of the police. A national survey conducted by the National Opinion Research Center (NORC) for the Commission produced these answers to the following questions: [10]

Do you think that the police here do an excellent, good, fair, or a poor job of enforcing the laws?

	Percent
Excellent	22
Good	45
Fair	24
Poor	8

How good a job do the police do on giving protection to people in the neighborhood?

	Percent
Very good	42
Pretty good	35
Not so good	9
No opinion	14

The results of other surveys are substantially consistent with this one. A Louis Harris poll in 1966 found that 76 percent of the public rated Federal agents as good or excellent in law enforcement and the comparable figures for State and local agencies were 70 and 65 percent respectively.[11]

Similarly, a Gallup poll in 1965 showed that 70 percent of the public had a "great deal" of respect for the police, 22 had "some" respect, and only 4 percent had "hardly any." [12] Surveys by NORC in 1947 and 1963 showed that 41 and 54 percent, respectively, thought that the police had an "excellent" or "good" standing in the community. This improvement was one of the most noteworthy for any occupation during the 16-year period. Moreover, a NORC study in 1964 concluded that about 40 percent of the population believed that the social standing of policemen was too low and only 10 percent thought it was too high.[13] The survey of three precincts in Washington, D.C., made by the Bureau of Social Science Research (BSSR) for the Commission found that 60 percent thought that the police had a high reputation in their neighborhood; 85 percent thought that the police deserve more thanks than they get; 68 percent thought that the police should get more pay; and 78 percent thought that "just a few policemen * * * are responsible

---

[6] Supra, note 1 at p. 68.
[7] Charles Reith, "A Short History of the British Police" (London: Oxford University Press, 1948), p. 64.
[8] U.S. Department of Justice, Federal Bureau of Investigation, "Uniform Crime Reports—1965" (Washington: U.S. Government Printing Office, 1966), pp. 33, 152–153.
[9] Technical Information Center, "Locations of Riots Involving Minority Group Members Chronologically from January 1, 1964, through June 1966 as Reported by the New York Times" (Washington: U.S. Commission on Civil Rights, 1966), pp. 1–4.
[10] National Opinion Research Center, "A National Sample Survey Approach to the Study of the Victims of Crimes and Attitudes Toward Law Enforcement and Justice" (Chicago: unpublished, 1966) ch. 8, p. 1.
[11] Louis Harris, "Eye-for-an-Eye Rule Rejected," The Washington Post, July 3, 1966, sec. E, p. E-3, col. 4.
[12] Gallup poll, "Tabulation Request Survey AIPO No. 709" (prepared for the President's Commission on Law Enforcement and Administration of Justice, 1966), p. 1.
[13] Robert W. Hodge, "The Public, The Police, and The Administration of Justice" (Chicago: National Opinion Research Center of The University of Chicago, 1965), pp. 4, 7.

for the bad publicity."[14] It is interesting that a recent survey in England showed that 83 percent of the public expressed great respect for the police, 16 percent mixed feelings, and only 1 percent little or no respect.[15]

The public generally believes that the police do not engage in serious misconduct. A Gallup poll in 1965 showed that only 9 percent of the public believed that "there is any police brutality in this area."[16] The 1966 NORC survey found, in answer to the question, "How good a job do the police do on being respectful to people like yourself?", that the public answered:[17]

	Percent
Very good	59
Pretty good	26
Not so good	4
No opinion	10

The BSSR survey of Washington, D.C., disclosed that 78 percent of those who reported having contact with the police considered that the officer acted properly during the last contact.[18] Almost none believed that the officer used unnecessary force; 4 percent thought that he acted unethically, unfairly, or illegally; 4 percent thought that he was rude, and 11 percent that he was indifferent, ineffective or otherwise did poor work.[19] The Harris poll in 1966, found that only 4 percent of the public believed that many law enforcement officers in their community take bribes.[20]

The University of California surveys for the Commission in San Diego and Philadelphia found that the large majority of white community leaders thought that police-community relations were good, although there was some dissent.[21] The general findings of the Michigan State University survey of 16 jurisdictions were similar.[22]

These studies might seem to suggest that there is no widespread police-community relations problem. And, if the persons showing greatest skepticism toward the police were evenly distributed through all kinds of communities and neighborhoods, this would be true. In fact, however, this is not so.

The Negro Community

Police Effectiveness. The NORC survey shows that nonwhites, particularly Negroes, are significantly more negative than whites in evaluating police effectiveness in law enforcement. In describing whether police give protection to citizens, nonwhites give a rating of "very good" only half as often as whites and give a "not so good" rating twice as often. These differences are not merely a function of greater poverty among nonwhites; they exist at all income levels and for both men and women.[23]

Other surveys indicate a similar disparity in views. The Louis Harris poll, for example, shows that 16 percent fewer Negroes than whites—a bare majority of 51 percent—believe that local law enforcement agencies do a good or excellent job on law enforcement.[24] A survey in Watts found that 47 percent of the Negroes believed that the police did an "excellent or pretty good" job while 41 percent thought they were "not so good" or "poor."[25]

In Washington, D.C., the BSSR survey found that Washington Negroes have decidedly different attitudes than whites as to how the police carry out their duties, as the responses to the following statement indicate:

You would have to replace at least half the police force to get a really good police.

	Nonwhite males	Nonwhite females	White males	White females
	Percent	Percent	Percent	Percent
Agree	40	28	18	11
Disagree	40	52	60	62
Don't know, etc.	20	20	22	27

About half the Negroes, in contrast to two-thirds of the whites, believed that the police deserve more respect than people in the neighborhood give them. However, almost as many Negroes as whites believed that the police had a high reputation in the neighborhood (almost 60 percent), deserved more thanks than they got (over 85 percent), and thought that the police should get more pay (68 percent).[26] A poll in Detroit in 1965 found that 58 percent of Negroes did not believe that law enforcement was fair, and an earlier poll in 1951 found that 42 percent of Negroes believed that it was "not good" or "definitely bad."[27]

Police Discourtesy and Misconduct. Negroes show even greater attitude differences from whites with regard to police discourtesy. The NORC national survey found, as to respectfulness to "people like yourselves," the following differences between the attitudes of Negroes and whites:[28]

	White annual income		Nonwhite annual income	
	$0 to $2,999	$6,000 to $9,000	$0 to $2,999	$6,000 to $9,000
	Percent	Percent	Percent	Percent
Males:				
Police very good	56	67	34	31
Police not so good	4	4	22	6
Females:				
Police very good	62	66	28	41
Police not so good	3	1	12	45

---

[14] Bureau of Social Science Research, "Salient Findings On Crime and Attitudes Toward Law Enforcement in the District of Columbia" (a preliminary technical report submitted to the U.S. Department of Justice, Office of Law Enforcement Assistance, 1966), pp. 13A, 13B.
[15] Royal Commission on Police, "Royal Commission on the Police; 1962 Final Report" (London: Her Majesty's Stationary Office, 1962), p. 103.
[16] Supra, note 12 at p. 2.
[17] Supra, note 10 at ch. 8, p. 1.
[18] Supra, note 14 at p. 16.
[19] Ibid.
[20] Supra, note 11 at col. 5.
[21] Joseph D. Lohman and Gordon E. Misner, "The Police and the Community" (Berkeley: University of California School of Criminology, 1966), vol. I, p. 50; vol. II, p. 78. Report prepared for the President's Commission on Law Enforcement and Administration of Justice by the School of Criminology at the University of California. The study consisted of intensive analysis of police-community relations problems and programs in San Diego and Philadelphia, with six-man teams visiting the two cities for 6 weeks each. During this time, they accompanied the police in their daily work and interviewed hundreds of police officials and officers, judges, lawyers, minority group leaders, civic leaders, juveniles, and average citizens.
[22] Raymond Galvin and Louis Radelet, "A National Survey of Police and Community Relations" (East Lansing: Michigan State University, 1967), p. 12. Report prepared for the President's Commission on Law Enforcement and Administration of Justice by the National Center on Police and Community Relations at the School of Police Administration and Public Safety of Michigan State University. Questionnaires were sent to the police departments in all cities with populations of over 100,000; a 10-percent sample of cities between 25,000 and 100,000 population; the 30 most populous counties; and all State police agencies. Separate questionnaires were sent to approximately a half-dozen civic and minority group leaders knowledgeable in police-community relations in the same cities; visitations of 1 or 2 weeks at a time were made by teams with 1 to 3 men to 12 medium and large cities, 2 rural counties, and 2 State agencies. In addition, there was a review of the police-community relations literature and a reliance on the Institute's extensive experience concerning other localities throughout the country.
[23] Supra, note 10 at table 8-2.
[24] Supra, note 11 at col. 5.
[25] John F. Kraft, Inc., "Attitudes of Negroes in Various Cities" (New York: John F. Kraft, Inc., 1966), p. 25. Report prepared for the Senate Subcommittee on Executive Reorganization.
[26] Supra, note 14 at 13A.
[27] Richard W. Ouderlugs, "How Citizens Rate Police Department on Racial Fairness" Detroit News, Feb. 3, 1965, sec. A, p. 1, col. 3.
[28] Supra, note 10 at table 8-3.

A 1965 Gallup poll showed that only 7 percent of white males but 35 percent of Negro males believed that there was police brutality in their area; 53 percent of Negro males thought that there was none.[29]

A survey of the Watts area of Los Angeles concerning opinions on the existence of "brutality" found: [30]

Existence of police brutality	Total	Age		
		15 to 29	30 to 34	45 and over
	Percent	Percent	Percent	Percent
A lot	22.2	24.4	25.0	17.1
A little	24.6	35.6	22.7	14.3
None at all	15.1	17.8	11.4	14.3

Thus, nearly 47 percent of all respondents and 60 percent of all those from 15 to 29 years of age believed that there was at least some police brutality. Of those who had answered "a lot" and "a little," approximately half claimed that they had witnessed it.[31]

Another survey of Negroes in the general area of Watts by the University of California at Los Angeles found that a high percentage of those surveyed believed the police engaged in misconduct, said they had observed acts of misconduct, or indicated that such an act had happened to someone they knew or to themselves: [32]

Police	Happened in area	Saw it happen	Happened to someone you know	Happened to you
	Percent	Percent	Percent	Percent
Lack respect or use insulting language	85	49	52	28
Roust, frisk, or search people without good reason	85	52	48	25
Stop or search cars for no good reason	83	51	49	25
Search homes for no good reason	63	22	30	7
Use unnecessary force in making arrests	86	47	43	9
Beat up people in custody	85	27	46	5

This study also shows that males below the age of 35 were most critical of the police. For example, 53 percent of young males reported they had been subjected to insulting language; 44 percent to a roust, frisk, or search without good reason; 22 percent to unnecessary force in being arrested; and 10 percent to being beaten up while in custody. Well over 90 percent of young males believed that each of these kinds of incidents occurred in the area and 45 to 63 percent claimed to have seen at least one of them. There were no substantial differences based on economic levels. Negroes with higher education reported more insults, searches without cause, and stopping of cars without cause.[33]

The BSSR survey of Washington, D.C., found that over half of the Negroes and only a quarter of whites thought that "many police enjoy giving people a hard time." Ten percent of Negro men and 6 percent of Negro women claimed to have seen unjustified police use of violence in contrast to no white men and 3 percent of white women. The BSSR study also showed a clear difference between Negroes and whites in their beliefs concerning police discrimination between whites and Negroes. Sixty percent of Negro males, as compared to 29 percent of white males, said the police did discriminate. Of those who believed that Negroes were treated worse, the following differences existed as to the kind of discrimination

	Rudeness	Picked on more	Brutality
	Percent	Percent	Percent
Negro males	53	60	48
White males	25	38	

Yet, as many Negroes as whites (almost 80 percent) said that "there are just a few policemen who are responsible for the bad publicity." [34]

A survey in Harlem in 1964 concerning police brutality showed that of the 63 percent of the respondents with an opinion, 12 percent thought that there was a lot of brutality, 31 percent a little, and only 20 percent none at all.[35]

A survey of junior high school students in Cincinnati found that only 41 percent of the Negro boys and 58 percent of the Negro girls disagreed with the statement that "the police are mean." The following figures show the difference between white and Negro teenagers: [36]

	Police accuse you of things you didn't do	Police try to act big shot	Police try to get smart with you if you ask a question
	Percent	Percent	Percent
White girls	40	33	34
White boys	56	46	45
Negro girls	60	51	55
Negro boys	65	69	70

A study of teenagers in Kalamazoo, Mich., in 1957 similarly found that "only 41 percent of the Negroes (teenagers) gave favorable answers when questioned on the fairness of the police, while 79 percent of the whites responded favorably." [37]

Surveys may not accurately reflect the full extent of minority group dissatisfaction with the police. In-depth interviews with members of minority groups frequently lead to strong statements of hostility, replacing the neutral or even favorable statements which began the interview. For example, a study of 50 boys from the slums of Washington concluded that, as a result of real or perceived excessive force, humiliation, and other police practices, they regarded the police as "the enemy." [38] Attacks on police officers, interference with arrests, disturbances and riots starting with police incidents, and verbal abuse by citizens offer abundant testimony to the strong hostility. The way in which such hostility can become an important factor in a riot is illustrated by the following statement of a resident of Watts to an interviewer: [39]

> Two white policemen was beating a pregnant colored lady like a damn dog. They need their heads knocked off. I agree 100 percent for the Negroes going crazy—they should have killed those freaks. Yes, treating niggers like dirty dogs.

This incident, which was thought by many people in Watts to have been the cause of the 1965 Los Angeles riot,

---

[29] Supra, note 12 at p. 21.
[30] Supra, note 25 at p. 13.
[31] Ibid.
[32] Walter J. Raine, "Los Angeles Riot Study; The Perception of Police Brutality in South Central Los Angeles Following the Revolt of August 1965" (Los Angeles: University of California, 1966), at fig. 1.
[33] Id. at figs. 6, 7, 8.
[34] Supra, note 16 at 13B.
[35] Supra, note 25. New York Times Survey, July 27, 1964, quoted in tables from Watts survey.
[36] Robert G. Portune, "Attitudes of Junior High School Pupils Toward Police Officers" (University of Cincinnati, 1966), p .2.
[37] Peter Feddema, "Negro and White Student Attitudes Toward the Police" (unpublished paper quoted in Burton Levy, "Law Enforcement and Civil Rights" (Lansing: Michigan Civil Rights Commission, 1966)), p. 3.
[38] Paul A. Fine, "Neighbors of the President" (New Brunswick: Paul A. Fine Associates, 1963), p. 126. Report prepared for the President's Committee on Juvenile Delinquency and Youth Crime.
[39] Supra, note 25 at p. 2.

never occurred.⁴⁰ But many Negroes apparently were prepared to believe that police officers act in such an improper manner.

A survey of Watts' residents by the University of California at Los Angeles showed that 21 percent thought that police mistreatment was the cause of the riot.⁴¹ In contrast, only 2 percent of whites considered police brutality as the cause. The study further found that those Negroes who believed that the police abused people (used excessive force, beat up persons in custody, were insulting, and engaged in other misconduct) or who claimed to have seen such abuse or to have been subjected to it, were more likely to have been active participants in the riots.⁴²

The Commission's studies of police-community relations in 11 localities throughout the country showed serious problems of Negro hostility to the police in virtually all medium and large cities. In short, as the Philadelphia Urban League's 1965 report states, "many Negroes see the police as their enemies; and they see them as protectors of white people, not as protectors of Negroes, as well." ⁴³

Police Honesty. The NORC survey disclosed that sharp differences exist as to how citizens view police honesty. About two-thirds of whites, but only one-third of Negroes thought the police to be "almost all honest;" less than 2 percent of whites thought that they were "almost all corrupt" in comparison to 10 percent of nonwhites.⁴⁴ A Louis Harris poll in 1966 found that approximately 15 percent of Negroes (almost four times as many as whites) believed that most police officers in their communities took bribes.⁴⁵ A survey in St. Louis found that 46 percent of Negroes in contrast to 24 percent of whites believed that "dishonesty is one of the characteristics of many of our police." ⁴⁶

Need for Police Protection. Although surveys disclose that Negroes are substantially more hostile to the police than whites, Negroes also feel strongly about the need for police protection. This is not surprising since a much greater proportion of Negroes than whites are the victims, as well as perpetrators, of crime. For example, in Watts, of the 41 percent of Negroes who believed that the police are doing a "not so good" or "poor" job (47 percent thought the police were doing an "excellent or pretty good job"), many cited lack of adequate protection as the basis of their opinion rather than brutality, discourtesy, or discrimination.⁴⁷ The Cincinnati survey of junior high school students showed that 83 percent of the Negro boys agreed that "without police there would be crime everywhere." ⁴⁸

A survey of Harlem in 1964 showed that 39 percent of the respondents considered "crime and criminals" as the biggest problem for Negroes in the area. This was the third highest category, following economic complaints and housing. Complaints about police misconduct were not one of the nine most frequently mentioned categories.⁴⁹ A subsequent survey in Harlem found that 21 percent of those interviewed believed that dope addiction was the area's biggest problem and 11 percent thought crime and juvenile delinquency were the biggest problems; these were the first and third most frequently mentioned problems. As to problems in their block, those interviewed ranked them in the following order: ⁵⁰

	Percent
1. Crime in the streets	28
2. Dope addiction	20
3. Need for better police protection	15
4. Murders	3
5. Drunks in the hallways of buildings	3

A 1966 Louis Harris poll in Washington found that Negroes as well as whites considered crime and law enforcement the greatest community problem.⁵¹ The staff report of the U.S. Civil Rights Commission on "Police-Community Relations, Cleveland, Ohio" concluded that the "most frequent complaint [of Negroes] is that of permissive law enforcement and that policemen fail to provide adequate protection and services in areas occupied by Negroes." ⁵² Neighborhood groups in the Bedford-Stuyvesant area of New York came to the same conclusion. And the Michigan State survey found that this was one of the two most frequent criticisms of the police by minority groups throughout the country.⁵³

Most Negroes, regardless of their feelings, do not physically or verbally react with hostility in routine situations. A Commission study which viewed thousands of police-citizen interactions in several cities found that 11 percent of the citizens reacted deferentially, 76 percent civilly, and only 6 percent antagonistically. The differences between Negroes and whites were negligible.⁵⁴ Negroes talk frequently about the "good cop" who, while fully enforcing the law, treats them as fellow human beings. And, as has been shown, Negroes greatly desire better police protection. Consequently, there is every reason to believe that relations between the police and Negroes can be substantially improved.

However, the problem may be aggravated unless immediate steps are being taken to improve police-community relations while America's cities are becoming more heavily populated by minority groups. For example, in Washington, D.C., Negroes now constitute a majority of the population; in 9 other cities, they constitute over 40 percent of the population and in 17 more, over 30 percent. By 1970, it is projected that Negroes will constitute half the population in 4 cities of over 100,000 population; 40 percent or more in 10 additional cities including Baltimore, Detroit, Newark, St. Louis, New Orleans, and Nashville; and 30 percent or more in 23 more cities including Atlanta, Memphis, Chicago, Cleveland, Philadelphia, and Cincinnati.⁵⁵ The problems inherent in policing such cities by police forces comprised largely of white officers may become even worse if effective action is not taken.

---

⁴⁰ Governor's Commission on the Los Angeles Riots, "Violence in the City—An End or a Beginning?" (Los Angeles: Office of the Governor, 1965), p. 12.
⁴¹ T. M. Tomlinson, "Los Angeles Riot Study Methods Negro Reaction Survey" (Los Angeles: University of California, 1966), table 25.
⁴² Supra, note 32 at fig. 22–25.
⁴³ Philadelphia Urban League, "Year End Report; 1965." Cited in supra, note 22 at p. 16.
⁴⁴ Supra, note 10 at table 8–4.
⁴⁵ Supra, note 11 at col. 5.
⁴⁶ Supra, note 4 at p. 101.
⁴⁷ Supra, note 25 at pp. 25–26.
⁴⁸ Supra, note 36 at p. 2.
⁴⁹ Supra, note 25. New York Times survey, July 27, 1964, quoted in tables from Watts survey.
⁵⁰ Robert B. Semple, Jr., "Negroes in Poll Ask More Police," New York Times, Sept. 4, 1966, sec. 1, p. 1, col. 4.
⁵¹ Louis Harris, "Crime Is Top Problem in District, Area's Negroes and Whites Agree," the Washington Post, Oct. 2, 1966, sec. A, p. 1, col. 1.
⁵² Supra, note 22 at p. 14.
⁵³ Supra, note 22 at pp. 14–15.
⁵⁴ Donald J. Black and Albert L. Reiss, Jr., "Police and Citizen Behavior in Routine Field Encounters: Some Comparisons According to the Race and Social Class Status of Citizens" (Ann Arbor: University of Michigan, 1966), table 3, report prepared for the President's Commission on Law Enforcement and Administration of Justice. This report is a preliminary draft which is being included with the Commission's records in the National Archives. It is presently being revised and supplemented by the University of Michigan and will be embodied in research studies to be published by the Commission.
⁵⁵ "Negroes Nearing Majority in Major Northern Cities," *Congressional Quarterly*, XXIV: 1860–1863, Aug. 26, 1966.

Other Minority Groups

The American Negro is not the only minority group which expresses hostility toward the police. The Michigan State University survey found that Latin Americans also tend to "look upon the police as enemies who protect only the white power structure." [56] The University of California survey in Philadelphia found that some Puerto Rican leaders felt even more alienated from the police department than did Negroes.[57] Such findings are consistent with the evidence provided by the 1966 riots among Puerto Ricans in Chicago and Perth Amboy, N.J., disturbances which were started by conflicts with the police and were followed by expression of community problems relating to the police.

Both the University of California and Michigan State University surveys revealed that relations between Mexican-Americans and the police in San Diego and other western cities could be improved.[58] A survey in Los Angeles found that Mexican-Americans were generally less negative toward the police than Negroes but considerably more so than whites, as the following figures show: [59]

	One of the very best police departments in the country	Definitely below standard in comparison with other police departments
	Percent	Percent
Whites	30	8.5
Mexican-Americans	22.8	14.5
Negroes	14.4	20.3

	Police always respect constitutional rights of suspected criminals	Police often conscienceless and brutal in performing duties
	Percent	Percent
Whites	34.8	11.1
Mexican-Americans	21.2	44.4
Negroes	12.1	38.2

Youth

Tension also exists between the police and youth generally. For example, responses to the following question in a 1965 Gallup poll showed significant differences based on age: [60]

How much respect do you have for the police in your area—a great deal, some, or hardly any?

Age	A great deal	Some	Hardly any	Don't know
	Percent	Percent	Percent	Percent
20–29	57	31	8	4
60–69	76	19	2	3

A recent survey among junior high school students in Cincinnati showed that only 44 percent of white boys disagreed with the statement that the "police accuse you of things you didn't do;" only 54 percent disagreed that the "police try to act big shot" and that the "police try to get smart with you when you ask a question." The favorable answers by white girls were approximately 12 to 16 percent greater.[61]

The Poor

Two recent polls show that the poor have generally less favorable attitudes toward the police than more affluent citizens. The NORC survey showed, as to the effectiveness of the police in enforcing the laws, the following attitudes of white males broken down by income levels: [62]

Annual income	$0 to $2,999	$3,000 to $5,999	$6,000 to $9,999	Above $10,000
	Percent	Percent	Percent	Percent
Excellent	17	25	24	32
Good	49	43	47	41
Fair	24	25	22	23
Poor	10	7	7	4

A 1965 Gallup poll obtained the following responses to this question: [63]

How much respect do you have for the police in your area—a great deal, some, or hardly any?

	A great deal	Hardly any
	Percent	Percent
Under $3,000 a year	65	6
Above $10,000 a year	75	2

Sixteen percent of those earning under $3,000 thought that there was police brutality in their area while only 8 percent of those earning more than $10,000 believed so.[64]

POLICE PROGRAMS DIRECTLY RELATED TO COMMUNITY RELATIONS

The purpose of this section is to analyze particular police policies and procedures as they bear on community relations. Of course, all of the observations made do not apply to any one force. Particular police departments are doing many different kinds of things relating to police-community relations, some good and some bad. Moreover, the inability of the police to remedy their problems with minority groups and the poor is little different from the similar failure of welfare, education, housing, and other government agencies.

Unless, however, the legitimate grievances relating to the police are confronted frankly and effectively, improvement of police-community relations will be impossible. Modification of police procedures on the street, stronger internal discipline over officers, greatly enlarged and strengthened police-community relations units, improved procedures for handling citizen complaints, better screening to eliminate candidates for the police force who are biased, and many other measures deeply affecting police agencies and police work will be necessary.

---

[56] Supra, note 22 at p. 30.
[57] Supra, note 2 at vol. II, p. 106.
[58] Supra, note 21 at vol. I, p. 92; and supra, note 22 at pp. 12, 30.
[59] G. Douglas Gourley, "Public Relations and the Police" (Springfield: Charles C. Thomas, 1953), pp. 75–76.
[60] Supra, note 12 at p. 13.
[61] Supra, note 36 at p. 2.
[62] Supra, note 10 at table 8–1.
[63] Supra, note 12 at p. 15.
[64] Id. at p. 22.

Of course, the entire burden cannot and should not be placed on the police. Local governments must be willing to pay for the higher salaries which will attract better police officers and for the training which is urgently necessary. The community must be willing also to have a genuinely integrated police force and to have its laws enforced without discrimination. The public, moreover, must recognize that it cannot demand that the police stamp out crime regardless of how the methods used may affect community relations. Minority leaders must be willing to distinguish their grievances against other groups from those against the police, to criticize the police responsibly, to withhold allegations until the facts are known, and to attempt to prevent criticism from descending into violence. Community organizations must be willing to criticize the police when criticism is needed, yet to rally support for the police so that they can carry out their essential functions.

To a considerable extent, the police are the victims of community problems which are not of their making. For generations, minority groups and the poor have not received a fair opportunity to share the benefits of American life. They suffer from bad housing, inferior education, unemployment, underemployment, or low wages. They have been discriminated against and abused by welfare and public housing officials, private landlords, and businessmen. Their frustrations and bitterness are taken out, at least in part, on the policeman as the most visible symbol of a society and its law which have often treated them so unjustly.

The police are sometimes blamed for the evils of the rest of the criminal justice system. When a suspect is held for long periods in jail prior to trial because he cannot make bail, when he is given inadequate counsel or none at all, when he is assigned counsel that attempts to extract money from him or his family even though he is indigent, when he is paraded through the courtroom in a group or is tried in a few minutes, when he is sent to jail because he has no money to pay a fine, when the jail or prison is physically dilapidated or its personnel brutal or incompetent, or when the probation or parole officer has little time to give him, the offender will probably blame, at least in part, the police officers who arrested him and started the process.

Still, the primary responsibility for improving police-community relations must rest with the police. As a responsible and organized public service agency, they must take the initiative in making good police-community relations a reality.

Police-community relations have two essentially different aspects. First, the substantial majority of Americans respects its police force, supports its actions, and looks to it for protection. Second, a significant number of people, largely the poor or members of minority groups, fears and distrusts the police. Ironically, this latter group often has the greatest need for police protection because it usually inhabits the most crime-ridden sections of our cities.

The task of building strong police-community relations is different with each population group. In one case, it may be a matter of translating a general endorsement into concrete assistance to the police in preventing crime, obtaining adequate salaries, and the like. In minority communities, the effort must begin at a more basic level with a frank exploration of the attitudes and practices which cause hostility on both sides.

In this section three main techniques presently employed by police departments to work with the community are analyzed: (1) police-community relations units; (2) citizen advisory committees; and (3) special programs which bring the police into continuing contact with the community.

POLICE-COMMUNITY RELATIONS UNITS

Although the Commission's surveys clearly indicate that most police departments are keenly aware of serious community relations problems, they have been slow to institute programs to confront them. A 1964 survey conducted by the International Association of Chiefs of Police and the United States Conference of Mayors found that only 46 of 165 cities either with populations over 100,000, or with more than 30,000 population and 5 percent non-white population, had extensive community relations programs; of these only 37 had a community-relations unit within the department.[65] Only 6 out of 145 cities with between 30,000 and 100,000 population and less than 5 percent nonwhite residents, had a formal community relations program of any kind.[66]

In the last few years there has been some progress. In several major departments community relations units recently have been established.[67] The need for such a unit or its expansion has often been recognized after a major disorder, as in Watts, or after an inflammatory racial incident, as in Seattle.[68] Nevertheless, the 1966 Michigan State University survey showed that only 38 percent of the cities over 100,000 population had a community relations unit.[69] In short, most of the smaller departments still have no unit or program; and in many large cities, community relations are handled without any central organization because of lack of sufficient funds, personnel, initiative, or other reasons.[70]

The belief is prevalent in many departments that it is enough if "every policeman is a community relations officer" and if the chief's "door is always open" to citizen complaints, suggestions, and problems. Yet the Michigan State study found that departments without units tended to concentrate their community activities on improvement of their public image.[71] This conclusion is consistent with that of the International Association of Chiefs of Police and United States Conference of Mayors which found that only a handful of departments without community relations units had any formal community relations program.[72]

Although, ideally, every man on the force should indeed be a community relations officer, he also has a full-time job of patrol or investigation. What is in effect every officer's business can end up being no one's business. Even if, as in some departments, community relations officers are appointed in each precinct, this is not a total

---

[65] International Association of Chiefs of Police and United States Conference of Mayors, "Police-Community Relations Policies and Practices" (Washington: IACP, 1965), p. 9.
[66] Id. at p. 11.
[67] Supra, note 22 at p. 6.
[68] Los Angeles Police Department, Memorandum No. 27, Sept. 28, 1965; the New York Times, July 24, 1966, p. 45, col. 6.
[69] Supra, note 22 at p. 60.
[70] Id. at p. 66.
[71] Id. at p. 126.
[72] Supra, note 65 at p. 11.

solution. Without a central unit to plan overall programs, conduct training, represent the force with citywide citizen groups, and supervise precinct-community relations efforts, the job will either not get done or will lack the expertise, coordination, and leadership which are needed.

While a police-community relations unit is essential, the mere existence of a unit does not, of course, guarantee its effectiveness. Too often such units have been regarded by the rest of the department as the sole repository of the responsibility for good community relations. The activities of the units are not well known in other parts of the department and have rarely affected the activities of individual officers or substantially influenced departmental policy in such police activities as field interrogation, recruitment, assignment of personnel, and integrated patrols.[73]

Conversely, both the Michigan State University and University of California studies found that community relations units have not generally won the confidence of minority groups. Individual community relations officers have often been liked and respected by minority leaders. But the units have usually been known only to a small proportion of the minority community and then generally only to the middle class. Those who respect the officers of the unit have generally seen them as distinct from the department and as having little support from it. This belief is often confirmed by the unit's lack of influence and prestige within the department itself.[74]

Several factors, discussed below, vitally affect the success of a community relations unit.

Responsibility

Community relations programs cannot be effective if responsibility is split between various police units. In one large city, for instance, a public information division handles press relations, speeches, tours, and citizen crime prevention programs; a human relations section working out of the field services division investigates incidents with religious, racial, or ethnic overtones and gives advice concerning high-tension situations; and, a community relations coordinator, in the office of the chief of patrol, coordinates neighborhood police-community workshops. On the other hand, in St. Louis one division handles all community relations.[75] Similarly, San Francisco's community relations unit has been given full responsibility for formulating and executing a community relations program.[76]

Relationship to Headquarters

In the administrative hierarchy, community relations units too often appear as an afterthought. In 1966 the community relations unit in Washington, D.C., functioned as part of a special services division which also has responsibilities relating to civil defense, court liaison, communications and records, and the police reserve corps.[77] The head of the five-unit division reported to the executive officer to the chief. In Philadelphia the community relations unit was one of five units responsible to the special investigations chief, who reported to the deputy commissioner for investigations, who in turn reported to the chief. The rank of the commander of the unit depended upon the man assigned to the job, which carried no particular rank of its own.[78] The Michigan State survey showed that of 18 departments whose community relations units it studied, 1 was commanded by the chief himself, 1 by a civilian director, 2 by deputy chiefs, 1 by a deputy inspector, 1 by an inspector, 2 by captains, 5 by lieutenants, and 5 by sergeants.[79]

If community relations units are to be successful, they must clearly have prestige and authority. Consequently, responsibility for community relations must be placed at the highest possible level. In large departments, the units should be commanded by officers who are one, or at most two, ranks below the chief, and who report directly to him. In smaller departments this may mean that the chief himself, or a close assistant, should assume charge of community relations. In any event, community relations should not be treated on an organizational par with maintenance or records as is now so often the case.

The unit's status within a department may also be affected by its physical location. In Washington, D.C., the community relations unit was formerly located in an obscure office on the second floor of the fourth precinct nine blocks from central headquarters.[80] In another city, the unit was located three blocks from headquarters because of lack of room in the central building.[81] Although space is usually at a premium in expanding police departments, a vital community relations program demands both the symbol of status and the physical proximity to the center of authority which comes from being located in headquarters.

Relationship to Precincts

Community relations officers should be assigned to each precinct and to special squads. Most police-community relations units now have inadequate personnel for such assignments. In Philadelphia, Chicago, and Nassau County, however, officers have been assigned to each precinct. In St. Louis, community relations officers have been assigned to three high-crime districts (they are responsible both to the unit and the precinct commanders), and the Los Angeles department has assigned a lieutenant as a community relations officer in each precinct with serious police-community relations problems. New York City is in the process of establishing precinct-community relations councils at which a lieutenant, appointed by the precinct commander, will be present and run community relations programs within the precinct. In San Francisco, two men in each district station are assigned to work on community relations in coordination with the central police-community relations unit.[82]

The prime value of a full-time precinct-community relations officer is that he can ensure that community relations does not become merely a job for the headquarters unit and can see that community relations permeates every aspect of police activity. The actions that most critically

---

[73] Supra, note 22 at pp. 67–68, 72; supra, note 21 at vol. I, p. 46, and vol. II, p. 65.
[74] Supra, note 22 at pp. 62–63, 67–68; supra, note 21 at vol. I, pp. 56–59, and vol. II, pp. 65, 286.
[75] Supra, note 22 at pp. 33–35.
[76] Id. at pp. 44–48.
[77] President's Commission on Crime in the District of Columbia, "Report on the Metropolitan Police Department" (Washington: U.S. Government Printing Office, 1966), pp. 6–7. The report of this Commission resulted in a reorganization of the department.
[78] Supra, note 22 at pp. 74–77.
[79] Id. at exhibit I.
[80] Inter-Religious Commitee on Race Relations, "Police-Community Relations Unit" (Washington: Inter-Religious Committee on Race Relations, 1966), p. 2.
[81] Supra, note 22 at p. 62.
[82] Supra, note 22 at p. 69; supra, note 21 at vol. II, p. 273; "3 Policemen Get Community Relations Jobs," St. Louis Post Dispatch, Mar. 19, 1966, sec. A, p. 3, col. 8; New York Times, July 24, 1966, p. 45, col. 6; Los Angeles Department Memorandum No. 1, Jan. 6, 1966.

affect police-citizen relations emanate from the officer on the beat. The community relations officer can assist by advising the commander on policy needs and on specific incidents which affect community relations. He can also help individual officers, conduct rollcall training, maintain close communication with neighborhood groups whether formally organized or not, ascertain community tensions and develop programs to deal with them, and provide information for the central unit concerning conditions and programs of the precinct. These duties may require more than one officer in particularly large precincts or ones with especially difficult community relations problems.

Assignment of a community relations officer in a precinct or special unit, however, requires a delicate balance. It is no coincidence that in most of the successful programs a strong effort has been made to make community relations activities the responsibility of the district commanders.[83] The precinct community relations officer must insure that the precinct commander, the commanders of the canine, traffic, and other special squads, the supervising sergeants and lieutenants, and the patrolmen assume more, not less, responsibility because he is there. His is an educative and advisory function; they should retain the responsibility for community relations within their areas. Otherwise, the officers may ignore him, as they now often ignore community relations officers, and afford little or no consideration to the long-run improvement of community relations in the neighborhood in carrying out their activities.

Preferably, precinct-community relations officers should have staff responsibility to the central community relations unit and line responsibility to the precinct commander. The central unit must maintain close contact with the precinct officers and have staff supervision over them so that it can provide expert and coordinated leadership to the entire community relations program.

Support of the Department

In every police department visited, the Michigan State survey found problems relating to the support of community relations units by police chiefs, supervisors, or ordinary police officers, and often by all three. On close examination, this was found to be true even of departments where community relations programs have earned national respect.[84]

In one city, where the unit suffered from a lack of strong unambiguous support from the chief, a law enforcement survey found that the chief's directives: [85]

... are insufficient to properly direct, guide, and encourage community relations activities. The language of the order, for example, merely states that "the Police-Community Relations Unit shall cooperate with all precincts and units in their problems pertaining to police-community relations" but it does not establish any real relationships between the operating units and the Police-Community Relations Unit. The role of the operational units is not defined at all. Line operations are without direction in community relation activities because formal policy has not been established in directives.

The Inter-Religious Committee on Race Relations has stated that the Washington unit "enjoys very little prestige within the Department" and "is practically a stepchild." [86]

In one city, where the unit had been formed as a result of outside community pressures, the chief of police refused to make an announcement concerning the formation of the unit and did not invite its commander to a key departmental meeting concerning community relations. In another city, one district commander expressed resentment at being drafted into community discussion groups at the precinct level.[87] The result was that these programs were ineffective.[88]

A former Negro commander of a community relations unit said that few police top administrators "personally and honestly believe in [police-community relations]. It has been forced on them so they have to go along with it— just giving a lot of lip service and speeches and no meaningful action that will develop trust of the police in the Negro community." [89]

There is a natural tendency for line officers to compare their jobs of keeping order and catching criminals with those of community relation officers, who are sometimes seen as dabbling in social work and negotiating with persons hostile to the police.[90] Unless this attitude is met forcefully by the top leadership in the department, the unit cannot attract capable personnel, cannot feel free to question police policies and practices affecting community relations, cannot have sufficient influence on ordinary officers, and cannot gain the real confidence of minority groups. Line officers should be shown how necessary, difficult, and challenging the role of a community relations officer is and how capable and skillful an officer fulfilling that role must be.

The community relations unit must have the full support of the entire department, and such a commitment must be reflected in specific directives from the chief concerning the unit's function and responsibilities. The directives in turn must be effectively communicated through recruit and inservice training. It is even more effective if the chief or his deputies exhibit personal interest in the unit through attendance at community meetings or programs designed by the unit.

Authority and Jurisdiction

The problems of police-community relations differ markedly in quality and degree among cities, and the functions of community relations units and programs will reflect those differences. At the outset, it is well to distinguish community relations from related matters with which this subject is often confused.

The primary function of many community relations units is seen as explaining and justifying police policies and practices to the general public. Hence, the Michigan State survey found that over 70 percent of the units reporting handled the department's public relations; indeed, in many cities, the very title of the office indicates that it has largely a public relations or information responsibility.[91] In two large cities, police administrators

---

[83] Supra, note 22 at p. 68.
[84] Id. at pp. 60–68.
[85] International Association of Chiefs of Police, "A Survey of Metropolitan Police Department of Washington, D.C." (Washington: IACP, 1966), p. 418; supra, note 77 at p. 72.
[86] Supra, note 80.

[87] Supra, note 22 at p. 85.
[88] Id. at pp. 60–68.
[89] Supra, note 21 at vol. II. p. 66.
[90] Supra, note 22, at table II.
[91] Springfield, Mass., Daily News, Apr. 19, 1966, p. 4, cols. 1–2.

felt that their community relations problems would be resolved if they could hire professional public relations firms.[92] Both the University of California and Michigan State studies found that most departments believed the primary purpose of community relations was to sell the police image to the public.[93]

Public relations and community relations have different objectives. The latter requires that the police and public candidly and openly face the issues concerning their problems. Public relations programs, in contrast, are designed to create a better image and this often requires attempting to have the department accepted as it is. Consequently, emphasis on public relations will often lead departments to mistake the nature of the problem as merely a failure to communicate the correct police image to the public. Needed community relations personnel are then used for purposes of preparing press releases and giving speeches to community groups. As a result, minority groups and others will become convinced that the department is not willing to face up to the serious community relations problem. As the University of California study found, the entire community relations program will be seen as a "public relations puff," a "snow job," or "con game."[94]

This of course does not mean that police departments should have no public relations unit or program. Police departments are obligated like other organizations to give the public a fair picture of police activities and policies, including those affecting community relations. In doing so, it is important that police departments be less secretive and work with the mass media to disclose as much information as possible to the public. But the different functions and methods of public and community relations suggest that they be handled by different personnel and units. Otherwise, the credibility of the community relations program in openly facing police-community problems is likely to be seriously impaired.

In addition, it is important that police-community relations units not design their activities to gain intelligence information. If police-community relations are improved, citizens will as a matter of course be more willing to volunteer information to the police. However, if a community relations unit deliberately engages in intelligence activities, many citizens—and particularly those already suspicious of the police—will refuse to participate in its activities.

Citizen Contacts. A commonly accepted function of community relations units is working with citizen groups—sending speakers to such groups, participating in their programs, and listening to their grievances. Over 95 percent of the units responding to the Michigan State survey were involved in such efforts. In addition, in more than 62 percent of the units, the community relations staff ran school programs in order to develop friendly relationships and a positive police image with the children in the community.[95] Units also run or conduct a variety of other programs including neighborhood advisory committees, police-community relations institutes, and tours of police stations.

These programs are discussed below. There can be no doubt that a primary purpose of community relations units is to plan and run programs for the purpose of maintaining communication and dialogue with as many civic organizations and individuals as possible. And particular emphasis should be placed on those groups and individuals likely to be most hostile to the police.

Policy Formulation. In most police departments the problems of community relations are rarely translated into policies except under public pressure. It is essential that police-community relations units have a formal role in formulating policies affecting community relations, such as by membership on the high-level policymaking board, which the Commission recommended in chapter 4 of the General Report. The community relations unit should be heard on such decisions as deployment of saturation patrols, assignment of minority members of the force, integration of patrol teams, use of the canine corps, and enforcement of policies relating to minor crimes like disorderly conduct.

The community relations unit must also observe how such policies are actually carried out from the standpoint of community relations and how the community reacts to them. This is consistent with the way other units or divisions in police departments are ordinarily run:[96]

> The division that develops an operational plan is responsible for its objective, is interested in its purpose, and is qualified to direct it; consequently, it is the logical division to inspect the operation of the plan. For example, to ensure the successful operation of a traffic-control plan, the traffic division should inspect the work done by other divisions insofar as that work is a part of the plan. * * *
> The indirect control thus provided is vital to the success of special operations.

Personnel Decisions. The most promising way to avert future police-community tensions is to recruit, train, and promote only those men with a sound respect for people. Community relations specialists should participate in the planning of the series of psychological interviews, written tests, and background investigation given to applicants for police employment. They should attempt to ensure that greater numbers of minority group members seek careers in police work by improving recruitment programs and by preventing discrimination, whether conscious or not, against such applicants. This will require participation in the selection process itself.

The same considerations apply to promotion. The precinct community relations officers should regularly evaluate officers from the standpoint of community relations, on the basis of knowledge concerning the officer's work and the opinion of the community. Such an evaluation should constitute an important factor in rating or promotion decisions. Promotion criteria should be

---

[92] Supra, note 22 at p. 85.
[93] Supra, note 22 at pp. 49–50. Some departments do, however, assign to the unit the job of handling civilian complaints against the police. Over 24 percent of the units in the Michigan State survey did so, including Philadelphia, which actually investigates the complaints. See supra, note 22 at pp. 60, 90b.
[94] Supra, note 21 at vol. I, p. 58, quotations from citizen interviews. See also id. at vol. II, pp. 82–83.
[95] Supra, note 22 at p. 90b.
[96] O. W. Wilson, "Police Administration" (2d ed., New York: McGraw-Hill Book Co., 1963), p. 115.

scrutinized to insure that minority officers are treated fairly.

Training. The Michigan State survey found that 67 percent of community relations units now participate in training. Personnel from the community relations unit should have considerable responsibility for providing that portion of a force's recruit and inservice training directly affecting community relations, including such topics as civil rights and the purpose of good community relations. In addition, they should be consulted routinely on training concerning other subjects which affect community relations, such as procedures for making arrests and field investigations, the use of weapons, and riot control.

Handling of High-Tension Situations. One of the fundamental purposes of a community relations unit is to prevent, if possible, situations of high tension between the police and community residents, and to help deal with such situations when they occur. Accordingly, the preventive aspects of the unit's work directly relate to its awareness of when and why tensions exist. This kind of knowledge can only come from having staff regularly in the field, contacting both residents and precinct personnel, analyzing citizen complaints, and making occasional special attitude surveys. When tensions are diagnosed, the unit has the responsibility of bringing them to the prompt attention of line command officers and participating in staff decisions as to how they can be alleviated, for example by changing personnel policy, issuing public statements, initiating a series of community meetings, planning joint programs with citizen groups, or making specific suggestions to other municipal agencies whose actions may be contributing to the problem.

One example reported in the Michigan State survey in San Francisco illustrates imaginative work in easing tension: [97]

After a series of rock throwing incidents in a neighborhood heavily populated by minority groups, tension in the community was running high. [A]s a result of efforts on the part of the community relations unit and minority group leaders, a rock cleanup campaign sponsored by a local newspaper resulted in a sharp reduction of community tensions. Labor organizations, trucking companies, and other firms offered their time and equipment to work with the youths, many of whom had criminal records. This action resulted in praise from previously hostile community residents.

When antipolice feeling is generated by an isolated incident of police misconduct, the community relations unit can help ease the feelings of community residents. While it probably should not be directly responsible for the investigation of incidents likely to lead to official action against the policeman involved, it can work in other ways to reduce resentments. It can, when appropriate, suggest an official investigation,[98] keep the investigative unit informed of the nature and level of community tensions, and, if requested, assist in gathering information. Of course, the unit should ensure that the investigation and hearing procedures are fair and adequate, and should be prepared to explain to citizens the actions being taken by the department. Such a role may include holding one or more community meetings, open to the whole neighborhood.

The community relations unit should participate in the planning that precedes demonstrations and in making preparations for handling any incidents that may arise in their course. Close and continuing relationships with the civil rights and other groups involved often means that advance steps can be taken jointly to prevent incidents, and to deal with them promptly and firmly when they do arise. Such preplanning has worked successfully in San Francisco.[99]

The unit's preventive work also extends to the area of planning and participating in police responses to disturbances or riots. The unit must be involved in every aspect of preparing the department's riot or civil disturbance plan and the training of carefully selected line personnel for facing such an eventuality. The unit should know, through its contacts with residents throughout the community, of high-tension situations, and should be able to mobilize citizen support to prevent disturbances or flare-ups from spreading. It should know who the likely leaders of such disturbances are, what voices in the community they respond to, and who has the best chance of interceding successfully.[100]

Evaluation and Research. A community relations unit must constantly evaluate its own programs. New ideas are frequently tried, but the programs have rarely received sufficient professional evaluation. Too often, the level of attendance at community meetings or the number of resolutions passed by civic organizations is the criteria for success or failure.

One means of evaluation is through attitude surveys conducted among residents. Such surveys can indicate how residents view the police, where community relations programs have succeeded and where they have failed, and what areas need concentrated effort. Similar evaluation should be conducted of the attitudes of recruits and line officers before and after departmental training sessions. Such evaluations may require outside organizations, staffed with persons having competence in statistics, sociology, and psychology. The importance of such periodic research to confirm or repudiate the basis and direction of any police-community relations program, and to suggest when police policies should be changed or new programs initiated, cannot be overemphasized.

In summary, the job of a community relations unit transcends public relations and friendly contacts with community residents. It includes continuing involvement in aspects of policymaking, personnel decisions, and training which have a community relations impact. This means playing a key role in police planning for demonstrations and civil disturbances and in preventing minor incidents that can trigger a major outburst. In a few cities, as will be discussed later, the units have gone even further and begun to take a part in actively helping residents with nonpolice problems such as job placement and referrals for help.

---

[97] Supra, note 22 at pp. 49–50.
[98] This is authorized in San Diego, according to the San Diego Police Department Manual of Rules and Regulations, as cited in supra, note 21 at vol. I, p. 41.
[99] Thomas J. Cahill, "Seminar: Police Training for Inter-Racial Problems," The Police Chief, December 1963, pp. 34–37; 35–37.

[100] This was done successfully by a New York police-community relations officer in Brooklyn during the summer of 1966. Paul L. Montgomery, "East New York Peaceful, But Police Stay on Alert," New York Times, July 25, 1966, p. 1, col. 2.

Personnel

Numerical Strength. The strength of existing community relations units often varies substantially between cities without any logical relationship to the population of the city or the size of the police department. In a survey of 165 cities over 100,000 population, or with a population of between 30,000 and 100,000 population and more than 5 percent nonwhite population, units ranged from 1 to 10 men, with an average of 3.[101] Washington, D.C.'s unit has a deputy chief, an inspector, and 3 lieutenants; San Francisco has 12 officers including a lieutenant, assistant inspector, and sergeant; Denver has a deputy chief, lieutenant, and 2 patrolmen. Philadelphia's unit is the largest, with 46 officers headed by a captain, 3 lieutenants, and 5 sergeants. In contrast, Buffalo assigns line officers part time to a "community relations committee" to deal with community crises as they arise.[102]

Police departments have generally assigned an insufficient number of personnel to community relations work. The appropriate number is properly related to a city's population, its economic, social, racial, and ethnic characteristics, the amount and kind of tension or hostility which is directed against the police, and the gross number of men on the force. However, in view of serious police-community relations problems in most cities and the broad responsibilities which should be assumed by community relations officers, considerably more personnel must be assigned to perform this work. It is doubtful that departments can adequately fulfill their responsibilities unless they assign at least one percent of their sworn membership to community relations work.

Caliber. The Michigan State survey found that community relations officers are generally not picked on the basis of the best man for community relations; instead, they often are chosen on the same criteria as line officers, or they are next on the appropriate list, or they are physically limited to light duty.[103] Applicants for such positions are few and transfer requests out of the units have been frequent, probably due in large part to the fact that the units are not accepted as an integral and important part of the department. One unit reported a 50 percent turnover in personnel during its first 10 months of operation.[104] When this happens, the unit loses the benefit of an officer with on-the-job experience.

Only a few cities have employed civilians. The Chicago police-community coordinator in 1965 was "borrowed" from the National Conference of Christians and Jews; the directors of the St. Louis program have been nonpolicemen, and a university sociologist has been used as a consultant.[105]

Minority groups are typically represented in such units. For example, in one western city, with large groups who speak only a foreign language, the police department assigned an officer who was fluent in it.[106] Negroes are also often assigned, occasionally as commanders of the units.

The Michigan State survey found frequent examples of skilled officers in police-community units who are doing an exemplary job in view of the serious handicaps imposed on them. As a general policy, however, the following changes in personnel policies appear to be necessary if the community relations units are to perform their delicate mission effectively:

1. The head of the unit should be a person who will command the respect of the rest of the force and bring prestige to the objectives of the unit. At the same time, he must be genuinely dedicated to the importance of his task and generally accepted by those whose attitudes toward police are negative, particularly the poor and minority groups. If a capable sworn officer is available, he is generally preferable to a civilian. Police officers are often suspicious of civilians and particularly those connected with community relations. Until the unit is firmly established within the department and has the respect of all levels of personnel, a ranking officer is most likely to be able to give the unit the status it deserves.

2. Subordinates should be selected especially for ability in the field of community relations. Visible integration of minority members in the unit is highly desirable. Precinct-community relations officers should be of the rank of sergeant or lieutenant in order to provide the necessary authority. In areas which are predominantly Negro or Spanish-speaking, a Negro or Spanish-speaking officer may have a significant advantage in dealing with the residents.

3. Work in community relations should be made attractive to police officers so that they will compete to obtain such positions, just as they do for plainclothes work. This requires that the units be given real authority and that ranking officers make clear the importance of the unit's work. In addition, community relations work should be afforded at least parity with other assignments when promotions are being made. This would induce superior personnel to seek community relations positions, make clear to all officers the importance of community relations, and in the long run result in more ranking officers with prior experience in community relations activities.

4. Civilian experts in such fields as psychology, sociology, and urban problems should be recruited as full-time employees of units in large departments. Both large and small departments can also utilize experts from universities and other sources as consultants for planning and carrying out training programs and for other important tasks.

5. As discussed in chapter 5, community service officers, recruited from neighborhoods, should perform a variety of police functions. One important role for such an officer would be to assist the community relations officer in the precinct or the central community relations unit by circulating through the community to identify local problems and grass-roots leaders by personal contacts and neighborhood meetings.

Staff Training. Before assignment to the unit, community relations officers today rarely receive any special training. They may attend, for a week or less, a

---

[101] Supra, note 65 at p. 9.
[102] Supra, note 22 at p. 68; supra, note 21 at vol. II, p. 61; Inter-Religious Committee on Race Relations, "Police-Community Relations Unit" (Washington, 1966), p. 2.
[103] Supra, note 22 at pp. 74–75.
[104] Id. at p. 76.
[105] Id. at pp. 34, 54.
[106] Id. at p. 62.

community relations institute. Although such institutes are valuable, they alone do not provide sufficient training. The officers need special training in such fields as the psychology, culture, and problems of minority groups and the poor, the dynamics of crowd behavior, the history of the civil rights movement, and the attitudes of various segments of the public toward the police. Large departments can appoint several community relations officers at once and then train them for several weeks or months. Smaller departments can send one or two officers to statewide or regional training sessions. Universities, junior colleges, and groups with sufficient expertise should be encouraged to run these programs.

Periodic inservice training is essential since problems and techniques change so rapidly, and community relations officers should be encouraged to attend classes at local universities or take correspondence courses in sociology, psychology, and related subjects.

CITIZEN ADVISORY COMMITTEES

Police departments must become increasingly aware that isolation from the neighborhoods they protect can interfere with good policing, as well as with good police-community relations. For the most part, police readily acknowledge the need to keep attuned to developments and attitudes in the surrounding neighborhoods. Perhaps the most promising mechanism that has evolved for this purpose is the police advisory committee. Yet a 1964 survey by the International Association of Chiefs of Police and United States Conference of Mayors found that of the 165 reporting cities with over 100,000 population, or between 30,000 and 100,000 population and more than 5 percent nonwhite population, only 8 had organized precinct committees and only 19 a citywide committee.[107] Since that time, however, a number of other cities have initiated such committees.

The advisory committees take different forms in different places. Basically they consist of groups of citizens, usually formed, under police auspices, to discuss policing problems. They have no formal authority, but act as advisers to the department leaders. A brief summary of the organization and activities of these committees follows:

(1) St. Louis.—What was probably the first police advisory committee in the Nation was formed in St. Louis in 1955. Its stated objectives were "to promote increased cooperation between the police department and other community agencies" and to "educate private citizens to their responsibilities in the preservation of law and order."[108] Three district committees were formed by the citywide committee in high-crime Negro and poor white areas.

The committees, composed largely of clergymen, social workers, and other responsible leaders, met monthly with the district commanders. During its first few years, police support was erratic, and citizen interest waned. In 1957 a full-time professional, paid from private funds, was hired to infuse the group with new vitality. He was later named the department director of community relations and worked out of the office of the Board of Police Commissioners. The committees floundered again in 1959 when the director resigned. Many of the district committees became dormant. In 1960, an expanded office of community relations served as liaison for the district committees and advisor to the district commanders. In 1963 and 1964, however, many district committees again became inactive.

The citywide committee now meets regularly with the chief and acts as a screening body for programs and actions of the district committees. The nine district committees consist of the district commander and several officers and representatives from churches, PTA's, social agencies, and civil rights organizations in the community. Each group elects its own officers and has an executive committee to plan activities. Subcommittees work in such areas as juvenile crime, auto theft, public relations, and traffic. District committee and subcommittee chairmen from all over the city meet periodically, and a newsletter is circulated to all members. Among the activities sponsored are: Citizens Against Crime, a membership card program to encourage citizens to report suspicious occurrences; Boy Scout Explorer troops for poor and minority youth; rides for high school students as observers in patrol cars; and precinct open houses.[109] Representatives of the department have met with civil rights leaders both at their own meetings and at police headquarters in an attempt to give both police personnel and civil rights leaders a chance to discuss police and community problems.[110]

(2) San Francisco.—After a visit to St. Louis in 1962, Chief Thomas Cahill initiated, under the auspices of a community relations unit, neighborhood committees in three of nine police districts. Section chairmen, appointed for each geographical area of a district, enlisted several citizens to work with them. The various section chairmen constituted an executive committee for the district to plan public meetings at a different location each month. Citizens aired their concerns at these public forums.[111]

Other variations exist. Cincinnati has an informal advisory committee of minority group representatives which meets with the chief on an ad hoc basis as problems arise.[112] New York City is developing precinct community relations councils in each of 76 precincts patterned after existing precinct youth councils which bring public and private youth agency personnel together regularly with police to discuss treatment of youthful offenders. The councils will be formed by the precinct commanders, and a lieutenant will be assigned to represent the commander at meetings.[113]

Effective communication between the police and the neighborhood is essential, and an advisory committee offers an excellent means to achieve it. However, as the following discussion illustrates, existing committees have been seriously deficient.

---

[107] Supra, note 101 at p. 9.
[108] Curtis Bronston, "Police Planning Operations and Techniques," The Police Chief, June 1963, p. 38.
[109] Supra, note 22 at pp. 33–43.
[110] Community Relations Service, United States Conference of Mayors, "Police-Community Relations in St. Louis" (undated, p. 4).
[111] Supra, note 99 at pp. 34–87; supra, note 22 at pp. 44–47.
[112] Supra, note 22 at p. 102.
[113] Philip H. Dougherty, "Broderick Orders Police to Form Precinct Community Councils," New York Times, Dec. 10, 1965, p. 55, col. 4.

Neighborhood Advisory Committees

Composition of the Committees. According to the Michigan State survey, most neighborhood advisory committees consist mainly of businessmen, civic organization leaders, clergymen, and other people whose "stake in the community" is readily apparent.[114] Generally, membership includes only those persons who agree with the police or otherwise do not cause trouble.[115] It is doubtful that such persons are representative of those who are hostile to the police or that they are even cognizant or sympathetic to citizen grievances. The study found that "all current programs (surveyed) have failed to reach the very segments which are in conflict" with the police or other "grassroots" people.[116] Although it is difficult to reach low-income persons, few attempts have even been made.[117]

Such a limited focus is essentially self-defeating. The police need to keep avenues of communication open with the kinds of people who harbor the greatest hostility toward them, who most need an escape valve for their antagonisms, real or imagined, and who have the most to say about police practices on the street. This is important not only to influence these people, but also to give the department an accurate picture of the attitudes of persons on the street. All too often, community relations units do not have this knowledge and therefore cannot realistically plan or program for meeting community problems.

Persons who are hostile may be argumentative, disruptive, or otherwise difficult to deal with. Allegations may be made which are, or which appear to be, radical or irresponsible. However, this free discussion allows the committees to become vehicles for meeting conflict head-on in a controlled forum. The possibility of unpleasantness at a meeting is obviously preferable to leaving these confrontations to the streets.

Police advisory committees should attempt to attract as many participants as possible. There should be at least one committee in each precinct and more where precincts cover large areas or community relations problems are particularly serious. Many of the residents will not, or cannot afford to, venture far from their immediate neighborhoods. St. Louis, for example, established special committees, which are branches of the regular district committees, inside public housing projects.[118] As it is difficult to persuade corner gang members, tavern habitues, frontdoor stoop dwellers, and exconvicts to participate in general meetings, special committees aimed at these groups seem necessary.

The neighborhood committees should involve not only a broad spectrum of the community but many police officers as well. They should not be limited to the precinct commander, his immediate assistants or the community relations officers. They should include, at least on a rotating basis, officers at the sergeant and patrolman rank who bear the daily brunt of putting community relations into practice.

Purpose of the Meetings. At present the meetings of most citizens committees include little frank and open discussion of controversial police policies; more typically they feature explanatory talks concerning crime conditions in the area and other noncontroversial subjects. The introduction of controversial topics by citizens was generally discouraged in meetings which were attended during the Michigan State survey. In one city, when such issues as stop-and-frisk were raised, the questions were met with the adamant refusal of the police to discuss them.[119] In another meeting, the commander became defensive whenever police practices were questioned and changed the subject. The citizens did not express their true feelings because, as one later said, it "is useless for the police become hostile and [they are] not really interested in listening."[120] The study concluded that while the program looked good on paper and was widely so regarded, it did not really open communication with persons hostile to the police.[121]

Such meetings do have the potential for dispelling myths and pointing up problems about police practices. But those attending need to have confidence that they will get honest answers to such urgent questions as: Under what circumstances are Negroes stopped in white neighborhoods? Why are late strollers stopped so often for questioning? Why are juveniles told to move on? How are areas selected for saturation patrols? Complaints, whether or not they have basis, should be solicited and seriously considered; for as long as they are expressed in rumors, they will create friction. Relatively high-ranking officers should be present to give authoritative answers and to take steps to alleviate abuses when this is necessary.

Neighborhood committees also allow the police and public to consider the enforcement of minor crimes statutes in the area. There is a measure of discretion in the way these ordinances are enforced that allows the police to take account of community mores, cultural patterns, poverty, and housing conditions. Open discussion with neighborhood residents as to what their tolerance is for noise, for drunks on the streets, or for youths congregating on hot summer nights will help to produce law enforcement which protects rather than harasses the residents and induces citizens to aid and respect, rather than harass, the police. Where police discretion is involved, an accurate reading of community sentiment is an invaluable guide to the law enforcement officer.

This lesson is brought home by an incident in 1966 in Perth Amboy, N.J. A newly enacted antiloitering ordinance was applied to Puerto Rican slum dwellers whose leisure time was often spent in street socializing. After disturbances occurred and large numbers of police had to be assigned to that area every night, city officials finally agreed to redraft the ordinance and submit it to Puerto Rican representatives for their comments.[122]

The police should also use such community gatherings to discuss and elicit citizen views of police enforcement practices in the precinct. The use of dogs, saturation patrols, stop-and-frisk, and other practices all affect community relations. Consequently, the opinions of residents should be considered as one relevant factor as to how these measures are used. Moreover, such discussion will

---

[114] Supra, note 22 at p. 70.
[115] Id. at p. 72.
[116] Supra, note 22 at p. 91.
[117] Supra, note 22 at pp 80–81.
[118] Id. at pp. 42–43.
[119] Id. at p. 72.

[120] Id. at p 71.
[121] Id. at p. 72.
[122] James R. Sikes, "Jersey Disorders Laid to New Law," New York Times, Aug. 2, 1966, p. 13, col. 5; "Perth Amboy Gives Puerto Ricans Plan," the Washington Post, Aug. 5, 1966, sec. A, p. 6, col. 3.

sometimes result in community acceptance of legitimate crime-prevention activities which, without explanation, may appear threatening to area residents. For example, the use of dogs has aroused resentment among Negro residents in several cities; yet, in St. Louis, where the neighborhood residents were thoroughly educated by the police beforehand as to why and in what circumstances dogs were to be used and with what restrictions, no opposition emerged.[123]

In short, the ideal precinct committee would act as a real participant in police policy formulation within the bounds of law and the requirements of effective crime control. Successful counterparts are now performing in some poverty programs and school systems.[124] Moreover, the modern urban police department needs closer citizen contacts to maximize its integration into neighborhood life. With a real role to play in police-community relations, such committees will become more attractive to area residents and accordingly more valuable to the police as barometers of community reaction to their performance and as a means of confronting the basic police-community problems of the neighborhood.

Organization of Committees. Where active, representative neighborhood organizations already exist, the police may profitably utilize them as the focus for their dialogue with the community. It takes great effort to organize a new group which will be independent and representative; seasoned groups may already command more prestige and membership than a new one could acquire in several years. Confederations of block clubs, for instance, would be more likely to convey community sentiment accurately than a new group solicited by the police.

If a new group must be formed, the police may wish to encourage neighborhood residents to form it on their own, or to enlist the aid of antipoverty agencies or settlement houses which have expertise and resources for community organization. They also often have good contacts with low-income residents; and, they sponsor block clubs, credit unions, and youth organizations whose members could be encouraged to join in genuine exchange with the police. And if only a few representatives attended the police meetings, they could in turn transmit the message to their groups and thereby influence large numbers of their own membership.

Even where an existing group is used, however, the committees should be a major part of the work of the precinct community relations officer. To ensure success, the precinct commanders must give full support to the program and subordinate personnel must also participate. The Michigan State survey found that committees often floundered because of lack of sympathy or leadership by district or precinct commanders, lack of participation by low-ranking officers, and inadequate police staff assistance.[125] It should be the responsibility of the community relations officer to ensure that the necessary police support is provided.

The police should be careful, however, to avoid an appearance of dominating the meetings, choosing the agenda, or vetoing topics. The Michigan State survey found that where police took an interest in neighborhood committees, the district commander often took them over and denied the citizen any feeling of real participation.[126] The committee should determine its own membership, plan the subject matter of the meetings, and make independent policy judgments.

Citywide Advisory Committees

Citywide committees serve a different function. They bring together the police leadership and the city's civic leaders so that the department can discuss with the community's leaders citywide issues involving departmental practices or policies and allied problems. They can also coordinate the activities of the local precinct councils.

To accomplish this, however, the committees must have the wholehearted support of the chief and his top-ranking subordinates, frequent contacts with them through a regular schedule of meetings, and an opportunity to offer views on important issues before pertinent police policies are formulated or put into effect. The committees must also maintain their independence if they are to remain representative of the community rather than a department satellite. Free discussion and democratic self-government must characterize such groups, if their views are to be persuasive in the community at large.

Such committees, like the neighborhood committees, must be representative of all citizens in the city. The Michigan State survey found that in most cities they were not. In one large midwestern city, for example, the 15-man committee has had 1 Negro member, although the city's population is 35 percent Negro and racial antagonism has figured prominently in police-community tensions.[127] Race alone is not, of course, always the determinant factor in representation; the upper middle class Negro often has less in common with the ghetto slum dweller so far as police problems are concerned than do other slum dwellers regardless of color. Citywide committees should therefore strive to include several articulate representatives of the poor who have the respect of their peers. Probably the best way to obtain such representatives, as well as to coordinate the activities of the neighborhood committees, is to have each of the local precinct committees represented on the citywide council.

Committees of Minority Group Leaders

Many police chiefs have little continuing contact with the leadership of minority groups. As Cincinnati and St. Louis have found, ad hoc committees composed entirely of minority group leaders are useful in dealing with police issues. Since citywide councils must be broadly representative, some important minority leaders will not be members. The ad hoc committee can be an additional channel to minority neighborhoods where police hostility is heavily concentrated. Planned demonstrations, community tensions, and other problems may be discussed privately with the chief of police before positions are polarized by public exchanges or a crisis has already occurred.

Minority committees must also be representative of

---

[123] Supra, note 22 at p. 38.
[124] See "Break Up Is Urged of School Boards," New York Times, July 15, 1966, p. 15, col. 4; "S.W. Residents Elect School Advisers," the Washington Post, Sept. 1, 1966, sec. B, p. 7, col. 1–2.
[125] Supra, note 22 at p. 70.
[126] Id. at pp. 70–74.
[127] Id. at pp. 80–82.

the broad spectrum of opinion within minority groups. Membership cannot be confined to the less militant Negro organizations if more extreme groups reflect the views of a significant number of Negroes. The chief must be readily accessible, strongly support such a committee, and zealously guard its independence if it is to be of any real assistance to him. And, whether or not such a committee exists, he must be accessible to all kinds of minority leaders.

SPECIAL POLICE-COMMUNITY RELATIONS PROGRAMS

Besides citizen advisory committees, existing community relations activities normally are of three types: programs to educate the public concerning some aspects of police work, programs to prevent crimes, and programs to provide services other than law enforcement to the community. These programs may be run by community relations units, advisory committees, public information officers, juvenile squads, or line officers. Each activity must be analyzed on the basis of the target population, the expectations as to what will be accomplished with that group, and a judgment whether the return is worth the expenditure of effort.

Public Education Programs

Citizens who distrust the police will not easily be converted by information programs they consider to come from a tainted source. However, even for these groups, long-term education based upon honest and free dialogue between the police and the public can have an effect. Indeed, this is one of the basic goals of the citizen advisory committees.

On the other hand, citizens who are neutral or supportive can benefit from increased understanding of the complicated problems and tasks of the police. Informational programs can also generate support for more personnel, salary increases, sufficient equipment, and other resources to improve the efficiency of police work. It can help the cooperative citizen to avoid becoming a victim of crime and show him how to work more effectively with the police. And, to the extent that the police department is genuinely working at improved community relations, dissemination of this information to the press and other media does have a positive effect on community relations.

Contacts with Civic Organizations and Individuals. Most police departments (95 percent in the Michigan State survey) readily accept speaking invitations to appear before civic organizations.[128] Many run a speaker's bureau with a list of officers who can speak on specialized subjects such as narcotics, the canine corps, or traffic control. The San Diego bureau, for example, offers a choice of 35 speakers and is supervised by the community relations unit.[129] the St. Louis speakers bureau makes an average of 50 speeches monthly; and St. Louis, Chicago, Philadelphia, and Oakland have pamphlets available on police topics.[130]

The Michigan State survey found, however, that the speakers are not always chosen to fit the level of sophistication of the group;[131] different organizations may require a precinct commander, a patrolman, a community relations expert, or a college-trained administrator. Too often the topics offered are noncontroversial, and, if important, constitute merely a recitation of a department's outstanding programs. The survey found that many of the speakers were hesitant to engage in debate on police policies or to acknowledge possible departmental error.[132] The groups with which the police had most contact were business or civic organizations. As a Philadelphia police inspector told the University of California survey:[133]

[A]ny time I've ever attended a community meeting, I don't care what you try to get across, * * * they're not the people you want to get it across to, because they're not the problem.

Police departments, through community relations units and precinct community relations personnel, should attempt to maintain close liaison with, not merely make occasional speeches to, organizations of most importance to community relations. Active efforts should be made to reach out to low-income groups. The topics which interest these people may be the ones closest to their everyday experience, i.e., police protection in the area, arrest policies, and others. For the same reason, close contact should be maintained with militant civil rights organizations, civil liberties unions, and the like. The mere presence of a police officer in front of such a group, willing to listen and to explain, can have a positive effect by dispelling stereotypes of the police probably accepted by many in the audience.

For example, in San Diego, the lieutenant in charge of the community relations unit is personally involved in the Citizens Interracial Committees, the National Conference of Christians and Jews, and the citywide and neighborhood committees of the local antipoverty agency. His assistant works with the Student Non-Violent Coordinating Committee, other Negro civil rights groups, and the American Civil Liberties Union.

In addition to maintaining contact with community organizations, personnel should be in contact on the street with persons who do not belong to civic organizations. As a police captain in a Washington, D.C., slum neighborhood has said:[134]

I feel their attitude could be changed—especially the younger ones. We've got to reach the people who don't go to meetings, or to church. * * * At one time, the man on the beat was the best source. But now we just don't have enough men for regular beats.

The people who do not belong to organizations—including, no doubt, the young men who cause the police the most difficulty—are probably in the majority in high-crime neighborhoods.

Tours, Cruises, and Demonstrations. In many cities, the public is offered tours of headquarters, demonstrations of police equipment, and rides in police cars on patrol. In St. Louis, there is an annual invitation for

---

[128] Id. at p. 88.
[129] Supra, note 21 at vol. I, p. 41.
[130] Supra, note 22 at p. 89.
[131] Id. at p. 89.
[132] Id. at p. 89; supra, note 21 at vol. I, pp. 41–45.
[133] Supra, note 21 at vol. II, p. 75.
[134] Ken Schlossberg, "The Drunk Arrest: A Trouble Spot," Washington Daily News, Dec. 21, 1965, p. 5, col. 3.

school children and citizen groups to come to police headquarters; and police cadets conduct tours for 1,000 persons a month. An annual open house with special demonstrations of police equipment, canine corps, and defense tactics is staged in each district. High school and college students ride in police cars on patrol.[135] New York City has experimented with a police-citizen art show at the precinct to show the people that "they are welcome and * * * can have friendships [there]."[136]

It is difficult to evaluate the effect of such attempts to broaden civilian understanding of the police. Although such programs can help the public understand the problems encountered daily by a policeman, it must be acknowledged that the public who responds to such programs is probably not the public involved in police-community tensions. In short, such efforts can be of some assistance but should never be allowed to become the core of a community relations program.

Police-Community Relations Institutes. Police departments, often under the sponsorship of private organizations, participate in institutes with the public on the subject of community relations.[137] The St. Louis department participated in an institute sponsored by the NAACP in 1966 with police representation from every district. The Dayton department in 1965 participated in such an institute organized by the Human Relations Commission for 40 of its command personnel and 83 community leaders; and Texas A. & M. University holds such an institute for police and community leaders from 4 neighboring States.[138] These institutes give the police and community representatives a concentrated block of time together to explore their problems in depth.

On the other hand, institutes lack the continuity and followup of an advisory committee that meets regularly. A combination of the two techniques involving many of the same participants holds promise. The institutes can help make the participation of community leaders and police officers in neighborhood or citywide advisory committees more effective. For maximum value, the institutes, like the committees, should include representatives of the poor from high-crime areas, as well as high and lesser ranking police personnel, and the discussion must be candid and nondefensive.

Institutes held on a neighborhood basis are valuable in reaching persons not affiliated with organizations. For example, with the cooperation of local ministers, the Philadelphia community relations unit has initiated a series of neighborhood meetings in high-tension areas. The audience is broken into small discussion groups led by a district police officer to discuss neighborhood police problems.[139]

With the assistance of a financial grant from the Office of Law Enforcement Assistance of the Department of Justice, the Newark Police Department is bringing together 150 of its men of the rank of sergeant and below with 150 residents of the poverty districts, mainly young men between 20 and 30, to discuss problems between the police and community. The participants consider high-tension situations by playing out the roles natural to them in such encounters and accompany each other on police patrol and community activities. Expert lecturers address the group on the effects of poverty, the causes of criminal behavior, and intergroup reactions. The program, to cover 25 hours over a 10-week period, will be evaluated through analyses of the participants' attitudes before and after the sessions.[140]

With financing from the Office of Juvenile Delinquency in the Department of Health, Education, and Welfare, Boston has already completed a program of 12 weekly informal discussions in the Roxbury area between 18 residents (representing a cross-section of the neighborhood, including 2 juveniles and a mother on welfare) and 10 policemen (including a captain and 4 sergeants). Detailed interviews showed that while only a few participants changed their points of view, all seemed able to discuss police-community problems on a basis of friendship and honesty by the end of the program and most learned about the problems of the other group.[141]

School Programs. Over 80 percent of the departments in the Michigan State survey ran special school programs to tell pupils about police work or to explain special laws or problems which affect young citizens.[142] The aim of such efforts is to portray the policeman as a community helper, rather than as an antagonist.

The St. Louis school program is one of the most complete. It begins in Headstart preschool classes when a patrolman comes to talk to the children about crossing streets safely; continues in grades one through four with more advanced talks and films on pedestrian conduct; and in grades five through eight provides further instruction on the role and duties of a police officer, and a special tour of police headquarters. A "Say Hi" program gives membership cards to school children who wave or yell "hi" to policemen they see. In high school, a Negro professional football player from the St. Louis Cardinals acts as a community relations consultant and, accompanied by an officer who is usually the district commander, narrates a film on police work. Social science classes are assisted by the district citizens committees to organize small-group field projects which may involve working with the police in such tasks as assisting juvenile officers in delinquency prevention programs. District and citywide prizes are offered for the best reports on these projects. A youth council composed of five representatives from each high school meets with police officials five times a year to plan the school programs. Selected high school and college students also ride in unmarked police cars with officers chosen at random and instructed to answer all questions.[143]

The New York City police have experimented with comic books on police work, training courses for elementary school teachers, and composition and drawing assignments for the children on the role of the policeman as their friend.[144] Programs in other departments include: intensive 4-day courses, with field trips, on police work in all six grades of high-crime area schools in one precinct (Washington, D.C.); provision of officers to answer the questions of teenage panels at open meetings (Washing-

---

[135] Supra, note 22 at pp. 40-41.
[136] Mayor John Lindsay, quoted in Alfred Friendly, Jr., "Police Station Art Is Given a Lift in Harlem," New York Times, May 10, 1966, p. 47, col. 1.
[137] Institutes attended largely by police officers have training rather than police-community dialogue as the primary purpose. Such institutions are discussed below.
[138] Supra, note 22 at pp. 290-296.
[139] Id. at pp. 57-58.
[140] Newark Human Rights Commission. "Application for Police-Community Relations Training Programs." (June 1, 1966-June 30, 1967), pp. 4-11.
[141] Boston University Law-Medicine Institute, "Police-Community Relations Pilot Project" (Washington: Department of Health, Education, and Welfare, 1966), pp. 6-7, 9, 21-25, 50-51, and 57.
[142] Supra, note 22 at tables I and II.
[143] Clement S. Mihanovich, "Programming for Citizen Participation in Police Action Programs," The Police Chief, March 1965, pp. 27-31; supra, note 22 at pp. 38-39; supra, note 110 at p. 4.
[144] Lauder C. Hamilton and Bernard R. Kaplan, "The Police and the Schools," The Police Chief, November 1965, pp. 32-40; Bernard R. Kaplan and Sidney Lodge, "The Police and the Schools," The Police Chief, June 1965, pp. 24-28.

ton, D.C.),[145] integrated two-man teams visit schools on an informal basis to discuss students' conceptions of the police (Kansas City, Mo.); [146] participation in a month-long law enforcement unit for grades five through eight featuring posters, student interviews with policemen, essay contests, panel discussions, and precinct tours (Gilroy, Calif.); [147] and junior and senior high school programs taught by qualified police instructors on specific police topics such as curfew regulations, arrest laws, and use of force (San Diego, Calif.)[148]

How much and for how long the appearance of a friendly policeman in the classroom affects pupil attitudes will vary. Those who already see the police as friends will receive confirmation in the schools. Those who have had hostile or threatening encounters on the street, or whose family or friends have had direct conflicts with the police, will often be skeptical.

In the upper grades, the police lecturer may perform an educational function if he informs juveniles of the laws which affect their conduct, the police criteria for stopping or taking juveniles into custody, and the kind of processing a juvenile goes through as well as its effects in later life. His account must, however, square with the facts of street life as the ghetto or slum teenager knows them, and the policeman must be willing to discuss frankly the complaints of the students. If the police officers try to convince students of ideas inconsistent with their experience, the result may be to make them more distrustful and cynical than before. For example, in Philadelphia, a settlement house had to discontinue a program that taught juveniles about due process of law because what they were taught did not conform to their own experiences.[149]

The participation of nonpolice experts in designing courses is indispensable if they are to justify either the school's or the police department's time. For example, the University of Cincinnati under a Law Enforcement Assistance Act grant is developing a model curriculum on law enforcement for permanent use in Cincinnati schools. Scheduled for trial in 1967, the unit's success in molding constructive attitudes toward the police will be evaluated by student and teacher interviews. While more modest in scope, the same kind of intensive curriculum development is needed as has been occurring in the science field under the leadership of the National Science Foundation.

Crime Prevention Programs

Police-citizen programs to combat crime are dealt with in another section of this report. It suffices here to recognize that such programs can be useful to build support with citizens already favorably disposed toward the police. For either as individuals or in organizations like civic groups and neighborhood advisory committees, citizens can be involved in aiding the police.

In addition, the University of California study found a police reserve program in San Diego useful for community relations. Two hundred reserves, of whom 25 are Negroes, aid the regular force by working at special events and by accompanying 1-man patrols. The result is that members of minority groups and police officers have developed greater respect for each other.[150]

Community Service Programs

Routine police duty involves many kinds of assistance to the public which has nothing to do with crime. Help in getting emergency aid for injured or sick persons, animal and human rescue missions, suicide prevention, redirecting confused or lost travelers, finding missing persons—all these are community relations activities in the truest sense of the word and are rendered on an ad hoc basis. For example, a New York City policeman who had been recently accused of brutality was cheered by a Negro crowd after he successfully saved a newborn infant's life.[151]

It is sometimes suggested that at least some of the service functions can be more efficiently handled by one or more specialized government agencies which would allow the police to concentrate more fully on activities more directly related to combatting crime. However, "[p]olice time spent in furthering good relations may be justified even if it does not contribute directly to law enforcement." [152] As an English author has written in answer to the argument that the rendering of services is not part of the duties and functions of the police: [153]

The answer is that the friendliness, confidence, respect, trust and affection that they receive from the people are almost the sole basis of the power and efficiency of the police of Britain.

Recreation Programs. Several police departments or citizen advisory committees sponsor Boy Scout Explorer troops, specializing in police-related subjects. In Washington, D.C., and New York City, officers escort boys and girls from minority neighborhoods on tours to local showplaces and ballgames, and give Christmas parties and dinners for them.[154]

Police athletic leagues and boys clubs are common. In many cases, the funds for these activities must be solicited on a volunteer basis by the policemen themselves. The Police Boys Club in Washington, D.C., for example, has 8,300 members and includes baseball, football, basketball, and track teams; it operates on a $400,000 budget, has a full-time officer from each precinct assigned to it, and has both police and civilian volunteers.[155] These kinds of programs have broad support from the police; a recent survey found that 75 percent of police officers believed that police agencies should operate such recreational programs.[156]

Police-sponsored recreational programs have been criticized on the grounds that they overlap recreation department efforts; police solicitation of funds is said to raise question of propriety; and the boys who participate are not the kind who would get into trouble any-

---

[145] "Youngsters to Question Police Panel," the Washington Post, June 25, 1966, sec. E, p. 1., col. 3; "Police Panel Attracts 250 to Church," Washington Post, Apr. 9, 1966, sec. B, p. 7, col. 4.
[146] Catholic Reporter, Kansas City, Mo., July 1, 1966, p. 4, cols. 5–6.
[147] C. J. Laizue, "Crime Prevention Program," (Gilroy, Calif.: Gilroy Police Department, undated).
[148] W. S. Sharp, "San Diego Police Department Student Contact Program" (San Diego: San Diego Police Department, undated) pp. 1–2.
[149] Supra, note 21 at vol. II, p. 153.
[150] Id. at vol. I, p. 156.
[151] "Patrolman Accused of Brutality Saves Life of Negro Baby," New York Times, July 19, 1966, p. 29, col. 8.
[152] New York Law Enforcement Task Force, "Report to Mayor-Elect John V. Lindsay" (New York: Office of the Mayor, 1965), p. 7.
[153] Charles Reith, "A Short History of the British Police" (Fair Lawn, New Jersey: Oxford University Press, 1948), p. 112.
[154] M. A. Farber, "Policemen Show They Wear Hearts Under Nightsticks," New York Times, Feb. 25, 1966, p. 33, col. 8; "2nd Precinct Starts Fund to Help Needy Children," the Washington Post, Apr. 26, 1966, sec. A, p. 2, col. 6; supra, note 22 at pp. 41–42.
[155] For example, see William Raspberry, "City Funds Needed for Boys Club," Washington Post, Apr. 21, 1966, sec. B, p. 1, col. 1.
[156] George W. O'Connor and Nelson A. Watson, "Juvenile Delinquency and Youth Crime: The Police Role" (Washington: International Association of Chiefs of Police, 1964), p. 125.

way.[157] Such problems, however, if they exist can be overcome.

Police recreational programs offer opportunities to improve relations with children and their parents. They can change the negative image of the police in slum neighborhoods. As one Negro teenager in Washington said after a visit to the Police Boys Club:[158]

> [S]ometimes, when you go down there you see polices there boxing. * * * I didn't even know it was a police til somebody told me. He looked just like a teenager to me. * * * I didn't even know police take up activity like that. I didn't think they care for nothing like that. I just think they care for getting drunks and beating them in the head and all that kind of stuff.

The effort should be concentrated with the poorest children, minority groups, and when possible, youngsters with past records of delinquency or misconduct. For example, in Washington, D.C., a baseball league in each precinct consisted of half precinct officers and half hardcore delinquents.[159] The programs should be financed by means other than police fund solicitation. And they should be manned, whenever possible, with police officers, not paid staff or civilian volunteers, even if extra time or pay allowances are necessary.

Social Services to the Poor, Exoffenders, and Other Citizens. Many people think of the police first when they are in any kind of trouble; as a result, police departments frequently must relay complaints and refer persons to other government agencies. Information and complaint bureaus are set up in some police departments to guide the confused citizen through the bureaucratic maze of municipal government. This kind of public service should be expanded so that police who observe conditions on patrol that require attention from other agencies—uncollected garbage, locked playgrounds, housing code violations, consumer frauds—would take the initiative in reporting them to the appropriate agency. Although police personnel are already overextended in most communities, this valuable service could be performed for the most part by the community service officers discussed in chapter 5.

A few departments have become deeply involved in remedial work with the social and economic problems of residents. In San Francisco, the community relations unit has assigned six full-time community relations officers to the Economic Opportunity Council and to the Youth Opportunities Center of the U.S. Employment Service to help boys with police records to secure jobs.[160] It has also taken on cases like the following:

1. A mother came to the office of the police-community relations unit with her daughter who had recently failed a civil service examination for clerk-typist. The mother informed the officers that she had attended several public meetings of the unit and wondered if they could help her. The officers conducted an investigation into the educational deficiencies of the young woman and made the necessary arrangements for enrolling her in an adult training center to correct these deficiencies.[161]

2. Several complaints were received by the police-community relations unit that recreation facilities were inadequate for many youths, especially in minority group neighborhoods. It was felt that this lack of recreation caused many youths to commit crimes, particularly on weekends. The unit contacted recreation officials in the city and arranged to have the recreation centers remain open for part of the weekend and provided police volunteers to staff and supervise the activities.[162]

The Atlanta Police Department also has assigned policemen to antipoverty centers as youth counselors to help juveniles obtain available services.[163] "Operation Help" in Honolulu has a social worker on police call to help with the problems of juveniles brought to the station.[164]

Active police involvement in what may be labeled "social work" programs raises profound questions about the role of the police. The traditional view espoused by most departments surveyed by Michigan State was that the police should stick to the role of preventing crime and enforcing the law; few regarded the "causes" of crime as their concern. Many police officials feel that they do not have resources to spare for any new functions and other persons criticize the lack of expertise of police officers to do social work.[165]

On the other hand, new roles might well be welcomed by police officers. A survey of police officers found that over 65 percent believed that juvenile officers should try to find jobs for older juveniles who come to their attention.[166] A Commission survey of police officers in eight precincts in three large cities found that the thing most liked about police work was the "feeling that comes from helping people." Forty-three percent of the officers considered this the thing that they liked best and 70 percent made it one of their first three choices.

In fact, police officers now spend much of their time in "social work" roles. They attempt to settle disputes between spouses and between neighbors, counsel children about attending school and obeying their parents, and decide when to make arrests for nonserious offenses, partially on the basis of whether the criminal process will be likely to help the individual or society.

Plainly, police service programs cannot be of sufficient size to solve the "causes" underlying criminality. But an expanded police role must be judged not only by whether it alleviates social conditions, but also whether it assists the police in improving community relations. Significantly, the Michigan State survey has found that the San Francisco program has probably been more successful in reaching the hard-core poor and members of minority groups, and changing their image of the police from an adversary to a friendly one, than any other community relations program.[167]

These programs point the way toward a reevaluation of the basic police role which may have a more significant long-term effect than merely improvement of the police image. The possibility has been suggested that eventually the police may become part of a broader social service team which will include social workers, psychiatrists, and

---

[157] Supra, note 77 at p. 59.
[158] Supra, note 38 at p. 127.
[159] Jesse W. Lewis, Jr., "Young Toughs, Police to Assault Ball as Teammates to Improve Relations," the Washington Post, Sept. 3, 1966, sec. B, p. 3, col. 6–8.
[160] Supra, note 22 at p. 47.
[161] Id. at pp. 47–48.
[162] Supra, note 22 at pp. 50–51.

[163] "Police-Counselors," Atlanta Journal, May 30, 1966, p. 16, col. 1.
[164] John M. Pfittner, "Some Role Alternatives for the Police Juvenile Activity" (Los Angeles: University of Southern California, 1964), pp. 23–24.
[165] Supra, note 22 at pp. 92–94.
[166] Supra, note 156 at p. 124.
[167] Supra, note 22 at p. 90.

doctors acting as an intake screening unit for all kinds of antisocial or disturbing conduct. Individual decisions would then be made on what should be done with each case—whether the man should be processed through court, treated at a hospital or mental health clinic, or given social counseling and help in finding a job or in going back to school. Besides its other merits, the effect would be to improve police-community relations by reducing the adversary role of the police and by making them part of a broader process than merely arrest and conviction. Consequently, increased experimentation with new helping roles for the policeman, especially with youths and ex-offenders, is promising.

At the same time, precinct stations might well be a part of community service centers. Meeting halls and athletic facilities could be opened to the public; other services, such as employment assistance or family counseling, could be in adjoining offices. While the consolidation of precincts is reducing the number of police buildings, small police centers—manned by sworn police officers and community service officers [168]—might be part of other public and private service facilities. The result of such programs would be to reduce the separation of the police from the community.

Because of their insight into crime-breeding conditions, police officers and their organizations should be in the forefront of groups seeking legislation and other means to provide housing, employment, and recreational facilities, improve the schools, and otherwise overcome poverty and discrimination. Occasionally, police officials have taken such leadership. For example, the executive committee of the Michigan Association of Chiefs of Police recommended: [169]

That the people of Michigan must oppose segregation in housing and education, because it creates distress for all who are entitled to the responsible exercise of their freedom, and creates tension which reduces the ability of the police to serve all people;
That the people of Michigan must protect their liberty by providing equal opportunities for employment, limited only by fitness and ability, so that every race and persuasion may enjoy the fruits of our prosperity, and so that one of the causes of poverty and crime may be reduced * * *.

Such police support, besides serving other beneficial purposes, is in the self-interest of police officers themselves since poverty and discrimination are basic causes of much of the hostility toward the police. As Vice President Humphrey told the 1966 annual convention of the International Association of Chiefs of Police: "[Y]ou're the ones that have to deal with the results of the social problems on the streets. You men are the ones who must stand there and be pelted with rocks." [170] The Vice President's suggestion that the police support proposals to overcome these problems offers the opportunity for the police and civil rights and poverty groups, which have often been in tragic conflict, to join in a program of common interest.

PERSONNEL

The characteristics of personnel within a police department have a direct bearing upon police-community relations. If, for example, police departments hire officers who are prejudiced against minority groups or who do not understand minority group problems, serious conflicts will develop. And if police departments, through their hiring or promotion policies, indicate that they have little interest in hiring minority group officers, the minority community is not likely to be sympathetic toward the police.

In chapter 5 of this volume, a variety of matters pertaining to personnel—recruitment, selection, promotion, and training—were examined. Several of these matters raise issues which have particular relevance to police-community relations and they are, therefore, discussed here.

POLICE PERSONNEL GENERALLY

Selection Standards

The standards for selection of law enforcement officers have a major impact upon the capacity of a department to maintain good police-community relations. Appropriate standards will determine whether a department will restrict its hiring to persons who are qualified to understand and serve the community as a whole. Few departments have appropriate standards today.

Education. If educational standards are raised as recommended in chapter 4 of the Commission General Report and chapter 5 of this volume, it should have a significant, positive long-term effect on community relations. Police personnel with two or four years of college education should have a better appreciation of people with different racial, economic, and cultural backgrounds or, at the least, should have the innate ability to acquire such understanding. Studies support the proposition that well-educated persons are less prejudiced toward minority groups than the poorly educated.[171]

Higher educational standards, however, may also create collateral problems which must be overcome. A study of police handling of juveniles in two cities, one in the East and one in the West, found that officers in the eastern city, whose education was more limited, generally came from poor neighborhoods and appeared to understand better such neighborhoods and their inhabitants. At the same time, these officers tended to be antagonistic toward new ethnic groups which entered their neighborhoods. On the other hand, while many of the officers in the western city's force had at least some college education, these officers had limited personal experience with the poor.[172] This study suggests that when higher educational standards are adopted in a department, special efforts must be made to train officers, regardless of their background, concerning the problems of the poor.

Raising educational standards may also interfere with the concrete and immediate benefit of being able to add an adequate number of officers with minority group backgrounds. Such a result need not and cannot be permitted to occur; otherwise, the higher standards are likely to be seen by members of minority groups as a new and subtle form of discrimination just when they are beginning to satisfy the existing standards. Therefore, in

---

[168] See ch. 5, Police Personnel.
[169] Michigan Association of Chiefs of Police, Press Release, May 19, 1966, p. 2.
[170] As cited in Leonard Downie, Jr., "Police Chiefs Urged to Fight Slums," the Washington Post, Oct. 6, 1966, sec. A, p. 1, col. 4.

[171] See Robin M. Williams, Jr., "Strangers Next Door: Ethnic Relations in American Communities" (Englewood Cliffs: Prentice-Hall, Inc., 1964), p. 54.
[172] James Q. Wilson, "The Police and the Delinquent in Two Cities" (unpublished report), pp. 26-27.

localities with large numbers of persons from minority groups, severe problems of police-community relations, and shortages of officers from these groups—which unfortunately today means almost all cities—a program for raising minimum educational standards must be accompanied by financial aid and other methods of providing the educational opportunity which will enable members of minority groups to meet the new standards in adequate numbers.

Psychological Stability and Racial Attitudes. Screening out candidates whose emotional instability makes them clearly unfit for police work—through psychological tests and psychiatric interviews—should also improve the capacity of police forces to improve community relations. Unthinking anger at abuse from a citizen or panic at facing a hostile crowd causes obvious community-relations problems.

A more difficult issue is whether officers should be screened also for racial and other bias. Some police officials believe that officers must be not only emotionally stable but "free of bias or prejudice." [173] Other police experts contend that police officers can be trained and disciplined to overcome personal prejudices by strong department leadership.[174] It is doubtful, however, that the complete exclusion of all persons who are biased is realistic in view of the high proportion of the population generally who have prejudices against certain types of people. Moreover, persons with relatively slight prejudices will probably control them if properly trained and supervised. On the other hand, there is a serious problem as to officers who have strong prejudices.

The precise extent to which prejudice affects the conduct of the officer on the street is not known. Social scientists, however, believe that discriminatory action is influenced not only by individual attitudes, by the social structure, and by the views of the rest of the group, but also by the policies of the organization.[175] This would indicate that policy directives of a department, if enforced, can affect the actions of individual officers. On the other hand, the seriousness of strongly held prejudices by numerous officers should not be minimized.

Few police departments have yet devised systematic methods for screening out biased officers. In one Commission study of police practices in several large northern cities, it was found that a large proportion of officers expressed strong racial prejudice to neutral observers; and the Michigan State survey similarly found that officers often show prejudice in private references to minority groups.[176] Further, a study of juvenile officers in a western police force of particularly high standards found that 18 of 27 officers openly admitted a dislike of Negroes, attributing their attitude to experiences as police officers, and another study of officers generally in that city found that "hostile feelings toward the Negro are characteristic of policemen in general * * *" [177] And a survey of Philadelphia policemen, made in the 1950's, found that over 59 percent of white patrolmen said that they would object to riding with Negro officers in a patrol car, and over one-third said that they would object to taking orders from a Negro sergeant or captain.[178] The same survey found that some Negro officers were extremely hostile to Negro offenders and have emotions of shame, indignation, and disgrace concerning Negro crime.[179]

Whatever bias an officer has when he joins the force, without adequate training it will often get worse. Officers see the worst side of life and, in view of the higher crime rate, especially the worst side of the ghetto. As a result, their stereotypes of Negroes, as well as of other minority groups, may be strengthened. And such prejudices are likely to become increased by virtue of the large number of other officers who express prejudice.[180]

The study of Philadelphia policemen during the 1950's found that those white officers who were prejudiced—i.e., believed there were too many Negroes on the force, and objected to riding with Negro patrolmen, taking orders from a Negro sergeant, or having Negro patrols in white neighborhoods—believed more often that it was necessary to be stricter with Negro offenders. For example, of officers who objected to riding with Negro patrolmen, 65 percent found it necessary to be stricter with Negro offenders and 32 percent did not. Of those who did not object to riding with a Negro patrolman, 29 percent found it necessary to be stricter with Negro offenders and 66 percent did not.[181] The study of a western police department found that racial prejudice did not have any apparent effect as to some assignments. In other assignments, however, including patrol, it had an effect such as in treatment of Negroes as suspects on the basis of a vague description.[182] A study of patrolmen in one city also found that these patrolmen stopped and interrogated Negroes more frequently than other youths, often e en in the absence of evidence that an offense had been committed, and Negroes usually received more severe dispositions by the officer for the same violations. One reason for this difference in treatment was long-held prejudice on the part of the individual officer.[183] The Commission's studies in several northern cities, however, found no discriminatory treatment against Negroes in comparison to whites of the same economic level; indeed, if anything, low-income whites received slightly more severe treatment.[184]

With adequate training, supervision, and discipline, officers can often be trained and induced to overcome personal prejudices which exist generally in our society. But this is not enough. It is extremely difficult for the best police leaders to prevent all verbal abuse or, in times of crisis, unnecessary physical force. It is even more difficult to curtail subtle forms of discrimination in the exercise of discretion such as arresting a Negro in situations in which a white man would not be arrested, apply-

---

[173] Supra, note 96 at p. 136.
[174] E. Wilson Purdy, "Meeting Current Problems," in Nelson A. Watson, ed., "Police and the Changing Community" (Washington: International Association of Chiefs of Police, 1965), p. 156.
[175] Supra, note 171 at p. 348.
[176] Supra, note 22 at p. 341; Donald J. Black and Albert J. Riess, Jr., "Patterns of Behavior in Police and Citizen Transactions," (Ann Arbor: University of Michigan, 1967), table 25, report prepared for the President's Commission on Law Enforcement and the Administration of Justice.
[177] Irving Piliavin and Scott Briar, "Police Encounters With Juveniles," American Journal of Sociology, 70:206–214, 212; supra, note 1 at p. 82.
[178] William M. Kephart, "Racial Factors and Urban Law Enforcement" (Philadelphia: University of Pennsylvania Press, 1957), pp. 185, 187. The University of California, while making no detailed survey, surmised that prejudice among Philadelphia's police officers had somewhat declined in recent years. Supra, note 21 at vol. II, pp. 192–193.
[179] Ibid. at p. 118.
[180] Supra, note 171 at pp. 96, 345–348.
[181] Supra, note 178 at pp. 106–107, 196–200.
[182] Supra, note 1 at pp. 83–87.
[183] Supra, note 177 at p. 212.
[184] Donald J. Black and Albert J. Reiss, Jr., "Police and Citizen Behavior in Field Encounters: Some Comparisons According to the Race and Social Class Status of Citizens," (Ann Arbor: University of Michigan, 1966), p. 10, report prepared for the President's Commission on Law Enforcement and Administration of Justice. This report is a preliminary draft which is being included with the Commission's records in the National Archives. It is presently being revised by the University of Michigan and will be embodied in research studies to be published by the Commission.

ing handcuffs tighter to a Puerto Rican, or talking more harshly to a Mexican-American. In other words, just as the justification for having far better educated officers is that they must operate alone and make difficult decisions in situations of high tension and great importance, so the same reasons underline the need to have officers who do not harbor substantial prejudice against minority groups. Otherwise, the community, and particularly minority groups, cannot be expected to have confidence in police judgment.

While there is no one psychological test which can reliably identify all candidates who are emotionally unfit for police service, a combination of tests and oral psychiatric interviews can pinpoint many serious character defects. For example, character investigations can include interviews with friends, teachers, fellow employees, and others who are acquainted with the candidate. After the applicant has been appointed, the probationary period, if properly used, offers unique opportunity to evaluate the extent to which a recruit is fit or unfit. Precinct community relations officers, by using their contacts in the neighborhood and by talking to the recruit's police associates, should be able to evaluate the recruit's attitude and performance.

Disqualifying candidates and recruits who would be likely to allow prejudice to affect their action is crucial. It is also important that ability in police-community relations receive special positive weight in the selection process. Strength in this area should outweigh slight deficiencies in less important matters such as height and weight.[185] The police-community relations unit should determine that the selection process adequately evaluates the potential ability of applicants to work with citizens.

Preemployment Residence. The Commission has recommended that preselection residence requirements be eliminated to allow recruitment of the best possible officers wherever they may live. Nevertheless, efforts should be devoted to recruiting qualified candidates who live in the general area by such methods as recruiting at local universities and high schools. As the President's Commission on Crime in the District of Columbia states, "such a policy will make the police force more representative of the citizens it serves" [186] and will result in having officers with greater appreciation for the problems of the locality.

Promotions

Police-community relations ability should be an important factor in attaining promotion. This may be the most effective way to make service to the community an important part of the police role along with prevention of crime and the apprehension of criminals. Officers will begin to understand that the department values an officer who is good at keeping the peace by persuasion and building support for the department as much as one who shows superior ability in criminal investigations. And the positive incentive of promotion is often more effective than the negative one of discipline in preventing physical or verbal abuse.

Moreover, as has been emphasized above, the attitude of supervisory, and especially command, personnel is crucial if police-community problems are to receive the attention from the department which they require. If such officers understand the community and are willing to modify police practices whenever necessary, rank-and-file police officers are likely to conform. On the other hand, if supervisory officers have no special police-community relations sensitivity, improvement is likely to be slow.

If police-community relations ability and achievement are to be considered in promotion, they must be built into the formal process. The written examination should include, as in San Francisco, questions concerning urban life, the people who live in the city, and other community relations subjects,[187] as well as technical police subjects. The police-community relations officer in a precinct should know, based upon his contacts in the neighborhood and with the officers, which officers are prejudiced,[188] which treat people with discourtesy, and which make illegal arrests. He should also know which officers have earned the respect of the people in the area he patrols. Regular reports by the precinct police-community relations officer, based in part on interviews with neighborhood residents, should be considered as part of the efficiency evaluation which is periodically made and considered for promotion.

Assignments

The Commission's study of police procedures in several large cities found that often men who were acknowledged as among a department's worst were assigned to police minority group neighborhoods. In fact, such assignments have sometimes been given as punishment, a kind of exile.[189] This practice is harmful to minority groups since they will receive inadequate police protection and possibly more unfair treatment so long as police departments deliberately choose inferior personnel to serve them.

The problems of high-crime rates and difficult police-community relations make poor, minority group neighborhoods the most challenging for the police. There is little routine patrol. Officers are frequently involved in crime and community relations situations of great difficulty. The best officers should, therefore, be chosen for these areas—officers with intelligence, emotional stability, lack of prejudice, and sensitivity to the special problems of minority groups. As an incentive to take these positions, departments might give officers who have performed well in high-crime neighborhoods special credit toward promotion because doing good work is more difficult there.

Officers serving in high-crime neighborhoods should be assigned in the same area for extended periods, perhaps a year or longer, to enable them to understand the culture and attitudes of the people. They should, if possible, be assigned to particular beats to permit them to know the citizens and develop friendly relations with them. Moreover, patrol officers should keep the same beats, and supervising officers should retain the same geographic areas in

---

[185] The President's Commission on Crime in the District of Columbia recommended this kind of flexibility. Supra, note 77 at p. 21. See also O. W. Wilson, "Police Administration," supra, note 96 at pp. 139–140.
[186] Supra, note 77 at p. 25.

[187] San Francisco Police Department, "Police-Community Relations" (San Francisco: Police Department, 1967), pp. 4–10.
[188] O. W. Wilson suggests that lack of prejudice should be considered in promotion. Supra, note 96 at p. 153.
[189] Supra, note 21 at vol. II, pp. 162, 191.

order that they can be held responsible for community relations in a specific neighborhood.

In some cities short-term assignments are typical. Whereas San Diego officers usually keep the same assignment for 3 months,[190] in Philadelphia, juveniles congregating on the same corner at the same time each night will see five different officers during a single month, because shift changes occur every 6 days.[191]

As a result, the same persons may well be stopped repeatedly by different officers or the officers may use methods which are unnecessary or harmful merely because officers and citizens are not known to each other. The problem is well expressed by police officers in Philadelphia:[192]

> Every situation is different, and every corner is different, and I think that each policeman, as he is out there awhile, gets to know the individual corner and the individual crowd.
> * * * You can have a group of fellows on one corner, which will be there every night of the week, and you don't bother them—they don't bother anybody. * * * You may have the same amount in the next block or on the other side of the street, that you know, they are the troublemakers.
>
> *   *   *   *   *
>
> I still think the old adage of the old beat man on the corner knew everybody is very, very helpful in many, many areas; because you take a new man and put him on the street on a beat, he doesn't know the area, he doesn't know the people, and they don't know him. * * * He'll get challenged every time. As soon as he opens his mouth to move somebody or gets into any situation whatsoever, somebody is going to be there to challenge him, because they don't know him.

Post-Employment Residence

Many police authorities believe that police officers should not live in areas in which they work. In Philadelphia and other cities, a strict policy forbids this, and if an officer moves within the precinct where he is stationed, he is promptly transferred. The rationale is that an officer will have difficulty in impartially enforcing the law among his friends and this will diminish the officer's ability to perform his duties.[193] In contrast, in many cities in England, the government provides housing for policemen in the area where they work.[194]

Aside from convenience, local residence avoids the impression that the police come from the outside world to impose law on the poor and minority groups, and also avoids the risk of police isolation from the needs, moods, and customs of the community. As a Negro woman in Washington, D.C., has said:[195]

> The biggest gripe people have is they don't know the police. Most of the policemen live outside the community. They never see us unless we have trouble or make trouble.

Perhaps more effectively than any amount of training, off-duty contact between police and the people they serve prevents the stereotyping of police by citizens, and of citizens by police.

Either encouraging or preventing police residence near their duty stations involves risks and advantages. However, the acute alienation of minority group communities from the police should weigh heavy in the scale. Except where special problems of corruption exist, police departments should review their residence policies of prohibiting officers to live in or near the precincts where they work.

Wherever possible, police officers should be encouraged to live within the city limits, for it is important that officers have a feeling of commitment to the city, above and beyond their obligation to police it. As O. W. Wilson has written: "[L]ocal residence after appointment is desirable except in communities where compliance with such a requirement would work an undue hardship on policemen because of limited suitable housing facilities."[196]

It is also important to develop new techniques to provide both recruits and officers direct contact with the problems of the poor and minority groups. For example, it might be beneficial if recruits or selected officers visit over an extended period with a carefully selected family in a low-income minority group neighborhood or act as aides in a social work or antipoverty agency. Discussions with neighborhood residents and with outside experts might be held to focus particular aspects of the experience. The recruit might enter such a program immediately after his police field training experience.

The result would be to present graphically the hardship and complexity of life in a minority slum, to demonstrate that the citizen of the slum is not always the staggering drunk or the abusive husband. And it might help the officer to build a creative understanding of the role of a policeman.

Community Service Officers

In chapter 5, a new category of police personnel—the community service officer—is discussed. This officer could make a major contribution to police-community relations. Many would later be able, through assistance in improving their education, to serve as police officers or police agents. Since many community service officers would be drawn from minority groups, this would make a substantial contribution to increasing the percentage of minority employees on the force. Of course, the existence of a group of CSO's drawn from minority groups in no way obviates the necessity of seeking minority group personnel for other police jobs.

The very presence of the CSO in the neighborhood would symbolize a closer relationship between the police and the community. Some community service officers would be assigned to assist precinct community relations officers. Many more, however, would be assigned to other duties, and particularly to assist precinct line officers in their regular patrol and investigative work. They would help to inform the officers with whom they work of the culture and attitudes of the community and, conversely, would help to inform the community of the officers' concerns. They could, together with sworn police agents and officers, staff neighborhood offices so that the residents had a place near their homes to come for assistance, a need which becomes increasingly important as precincts are consolidated in the interests of efficiency and economy. They could enable a department to refer citizen

---

[190] Ibid., at vol. I, p. 161.
[191] Id. at vol. II, p. 157.
[192] Id. at vol. II, pp. 143–145.
[193] Id. at vol. II, pp. 51–52.
[194] Supra, note 15 at p. 106.
[195] Supra, note 134 at p. 5, col. 3.
[196] Supra, note 96 at pp. 137–138.

complaints, like violations of the housing code or the closing of a school playground to other governmental agencies and to handle more service calls, such as getting a homeowner into his locked house or getting a drunk off the street. They could seek to refer delinquent children to a social service agency. They could—as in the Richmond, Calif., project where five neighborhood aides have been assigned to a juvenile unit—work with juveniles who were in trouble and explain to parents why their children had been arrested. And, as that same project has shown, they could be extremely effective in organizing community meetings to deal with problems relating to the police.[197]

It is essential, however, that the community service officer not be used for all "helping" functions of the police department while police officers are thereby left to concentrate on law enforcement alone. Such a division of functions would make the police officer seem even more isolated than at present.

MINORITY GROUP PERSONNEL

Attraction and Selection

The Need. Police departments in all communities with a substantial minority population must vigorously recruit minority group officers. The very presence of a predominantly white police force in a Negro community can serve as a dangerous irritant as exemplified by the following comment:[198]

> Why in the hell—now this is more or less a colored neighborhood—why do we have so many white cops? As if we got to have somebody white standing over us. * * * Now if I go to a white neighborhood, I'm not going to see a lot of colored cops in no white neighborhood, standing guard over the white people. I'm not going to see that; and I know it, and I get sick and tired of seeing so many white cops, standing around.

To some extent such a statement is likely to be the result of accumulated resentment by Negroes of white persons generally, and such prejudice appears to be most prevalent among those who are more poorly educated, have the lowest incomes, and live in high-crime neighborhoods.[199] To an even more important degree, however, the problem is symbolic. In neighborhoods filled with people suffering from a sense of social injustice and exclusion, many residents will reach the conclusion that the neighborhood is being policed not for the purpose of maintaining law and order but for the purpose of maintaining the status quo.

In order to gain the general confidence and acceptance of a community, personnel within a police department should be representative of the community as a whole. But the need for competent minority group officers is more than a symbolic one. The frequent contact of white officers with officers from minority groups on an equal basis can help to reduce stereotyping and prejudice of white officers. Minority officers can provide to a department an understanding of minority groups, their languages, and subcultures, that it often does not have today. This obviously has great practical benefits to successful policing. In some cities, for example, the lack of knowledge of Spanish has led to conflicts between the police and Spanish-speaking people.[200] Personal knowledge of minority groups and slum neighborhoods can lead to information not otherwise available, to earlier anticipation of trouble, and to increased solution of crime.

Police officers have testified to the special competence of Negro officers in Negro neighborhoods. For example, while a study in Philadelphia found that commanding officers were divided as to whether Negro policemen are more effective in Negro neighborhoods than white policemen, more than three-fourths of the patrolmen thought that Negro policemen did better jobs. The reasons given include: they get along better with, and receive more respect from, the Negro residents; they receive less trouble from Negro residents; they can get more information; and they understand Negro citizens better.[201]

Police officials in other cities agree. The chief of police of Greenville, Miss., has said that "[o]ne of the things that police all over the Nation know is that Negro policemen can spot trouble in the Negro district faster and do what is needed [better] than whites."[202] Similarly, the chief of police of Evansville, Ind., has remarked that Negro officers "are in a better position to control their districts due to the knowledge of their own people, personal acquaintance, hangouts, permanent residents and transients."[203]

But the same standards for selection which must be demanded of white officers must also be required of minority officers for equivalent positions. While the mere addition of policemen from minority groups will undoubtedly improve police-community relations, it will not end hostility to the police if such officers are prejudiced or abusive. The University of California survey found substantial hostility to Negro officers among Negroes in San Diego and Philadelphia on the ground that they were harsher than white officers.[204] An earlier study of the Philadelphia Police Department found that many white and Negro officers said that the latter were harsher with Negroes. This study also found that many Negro officers were indignant and ashamed because of the high number of Negro offenders.[205] There is even some evidence that in some places, low-income Negroes prefer white policemen because of the severe conduct of Negro officers.[206] Observations of consultants in several cities revealed proportionally at least as much physical abuse by Negro officers as by white officers.[207]

The need for greater numbers of qualified minority group officers in nearly all police departments in communities with substantial minority group populations is easily documented. A 1962 survey by the U.S. Civil

---

[197] Gordon E. Misner, "The Development of 'New Careerist' Positions in the Richmond Police Department" (Walnut Creek, Calif.: Contra Costa Council of Community Services, 1966) pp. 44–45.
[198] Harlem resident, as quoted in Kenneth B. Clark, "Dark Ghetto" (New York: Harper & Row, 1965), p. 4.
[199] Supra, note 171 at pp. 216–248.
[200] Supra, note 21 at vol. II p. 190.
[201] Supra, note 178 at pp. 48–45, 59–61, 83–85.
[202] U.S. Civil Rights Commission, "Administration of Justice Staff Report" (Washington: U.S. Government Printing Office, 1963), ch. 11, p. 23.

[203] Id. at p. 24.
[204] Supra, note 21 at vol. I, pp. 93, 101; vol. II, pp. 116, 132–133.
[205] Supra, note 178 at p. 118.
[206] Elliott M. Rudwick, "The Unequal Badge: Negro Policemen in the South" (Atlanta: Southern Regional Council, 1962), p. 11.
[207] Albert J. Reiss, Jr., "The Use of Physical Force in Police Work" (Ann Arbor: University of Michigan, 1966), p. 10, report prepared for President's Commission on Law Enforcement and Administration of Justice.

Rights Commission of all cities with Negro populations of over 5,000 showed that 124 cities in the South and the border States had 1,128 Negro officers. There was 1 Negro officer for every 3,125 Negroes, in contrast to 1 white officer for every 490 whites, a disproportion of over 6 to 1.[208] The number of Negro officers has risen in many southern cities since 1954, but the disproportionate representation of white officers r e m a i n s extreme: [209]

Negro Personnel in Representative Southern Cities

City	1954	1959	1961	1962	1966	Percent of Negroes on force 1966	Percent of Negroes in city 1960
Atlanta	16	31	40	45	73	9.3	38
New Orleans	12	43	36	37	44	4	37
Tampa	10	13		13	13	2.6	17
Richmond	21	21	30	34			42
Nashville	16	19	23	32			38
Winston-Salem	14	12	13	10	10	4.9	37
Birmingham, Ala.	0	0	0	0	1	0.2	40
Washington, D.C.				417	531	18.5	54

One hundred and six northern and western cities had a total of 2,937 Negro officers in 1962. This was 1 Negro officer for every 1,351 Negroes, in contrast to 1 white officer for every 442 whites. The following table shows the contrast in representative cities outside the South: [210]

Police Personnel in Representative Cities Outside the South According to Race

City	Percent of Negroes in city, 1960	Number of Negro officers, 1962	White officers per 1,000 whites in population, 1962	Negro officers per 1,000 Negroes in population, 1962	Number of Negro officers, 1966	Percent of Negroes on force, 1966
Indianapolis	21	79	2.01	0.81	93	10
Tucson	3	1	1.26	0.14	3	1.1
Oakland	23	15	2.24	0.18	16	2.3
Boston	9	37	4.09	1.59	44	1.8
Detroit	29	154	3.54	0.32	170	3.9
Jersey City, N.J.	13	27	3.33	0.74	33	4
San Francisco	10	28	2.57	0.38		
Cleveland	29	108	2.83	0.43		
Cincinnati	22	62	2.00	0.57		
Elizabeth, N.J.	11	15	2.32	1.28	12	4.4

Of 170 sheriff's offices in the South and border States in counties with over 5,000 Negro population in 1962, 120 had no Negro deputies; the other 50 had an aggregate of 137. There was an average of 1 Negro deputy for every 25,000 Negroes and 1 white deputy for every 4,000 whites.[211] In the North and West, of 102 sheriff's offices, 33 had no Negroes and the remainder had 546. The disparity between Negro and white deputies was less than for any other category of law enforcement agencies—there was 1 Negro deputy for every 8,333 Negroes and 1 white deputy for every 5,000 whites.[212] The following table shows the number and proportion of Negro officers in responding counties in several States: [213]

Personnel in Representative Sheriffs' Offices According to Race

State	Number of sheriffs' offices responding	Number of white deputies	White deputies per 1,000 whites	Number of Negro deputies	Negro deputies per 1,000 Negroes
Alabama	13	57	0.13	0	0.00
Virginia	10	74	0.15	3	0.03
Florida	16	703	0.37	25	0.06
North Carolina	26	260	0.22	9	0.02
California	12	4,392	0.44	215	0.29
Michigan	13	757	0.15	105	0.15
New York	9	953	0.15	25	0.04

Of 12 State police and highway patrols in southern and border States, only 1, Maryland, had a Negro officer in 1962. In 19 northern and western States, 1 State, Illinois, had 24 Negro officers, and the other 18 States together had only 9, plus 3 in training. Of these, California and Pennsylvania had only three each and Michigan and Ohio had none.[214]

In short, in every city, county, and State where statistics are available, Negroes are under represented, usually substantially, on police forces. Although the number of Negroes in police departments has been increasing, in some places rapidly, there is indication that the percentage of Negroes on police forces may level off well below their percentage of the population unless police departments are much more effective in recruiting in the future. Thus, while Washington, D.C., has one of the highest proportions of Negro officers in the country—18.5 percent—and this figure has been rising, the proportion of Negro recruits remained static from 1962 through 1965 at between 22 and 26 percent,[215] although in the 1960 census, Washington had a Negro population of 54 percent. And of 165 cities with populations over 100,000, or over 30,000 with more than 5 percent nonwhite population, 71 percent reported difficulty in recruiting nonwhites.[216]

The Reasons for Under-Representation. In most large cities, police officials are genuinely interested in attracting more officers from minority groups—Puerto Ricans and Mexican-Americans as well as Negroes.[217] But, there can be little doubt that in many communities, both in the North and South, discrimination in the selection of officers has occurred in the past and exists today. There are very striking and puzzling differences in the percentage of Negroes employed by police departments. For example, in New York City, the standards are approximately the same for employment in the New York City Police Department and a policeman for the City Housing Authority. Yet, the former has approximately 6 percent Negroes, the latter 55 percent.[218] The Illinois State Police had, in 1962, eight times the number of Negro officers as the next highest State police agency.

Furthermore, some police departments have dramatically increased their proportion of officers of minority groups within relatively short periods of time. For example, Philadelphia increased the percentage of Negroes on the force from 3.6 percent in 1952 to 13.6 percent in 1956. In Pittsburgh, the percentage of Negro police

---

[208] Supra, note 202 at p. 3.
[209] Supra, note 206 at p. 5; supra, note 202 at pp. 5–7, app. II, table 15; supra, note 22 at pp. 286–7.
[210] Supra, note 202 at app. II, table 16; supra, note 22 at pp. 286–287.
[211] Supra, note 202 at ch. 12, pp. 2–3.
[212] Id. at p. 6.
[213] Id. at pp. 5, 8.
[214] Id. at ch. 12 at tables 5 and 6, pp. 13 and 15.

[215] Commissioners' Council on Human Relations, "Human Relations in the Metropolitan Police Department—A Progress Report" (Washington: Government of the District of Columbia, 1966), p. 6.
[216] Supra, note 65 at p. 8.
[217] Supra, note 22 at pp. 261, 264.
[218] Peter Kihss, "State Senator Says City Police Lag in Putting Negroes in Ranks," New York Times, Feb. 22, 1966, p. 20, col. 2.

doubled between 1952 and 1962. And in Chicago the percentage quadrupled between 1952 and 1961.[219]

Past discrimination or even the belief that discrimination does or has existed has much the same effect as actual, present discrimination. Thus, the President's Commission on Crime in the District of Columbia found that although the Metropolitan Police Department's policy was opposed to discrimination, "we doubt that many Negro citizens believe that the policy is being vigorously implemented." [220] Plainly, such a prevalent view hinders recruitment.

Even in the absence of discrimination, a substantial discrepancy would remain. Of 117 departments with acknowledged difficulty in recruiting nonwhites, 48 said that the problem was too few applicants and 83 noted failure to pass the examination and meet other standards.[221] The same factors underlying the disproportionate failure of members of minority groups in the selective service examination and other written tests operate in police recruitment. In Miami, the number of Negro officers dropped from 85 in 1959 to 74 in 1962, apparently because the recruiting standards for Negroes, which had been lower, were raised to match those for whites. Negro leaders in Miami have reported that one reason for the reduced number of Negroes was that most Negroes cannot meet the present entrance requirements because of inferior economic and educational background.[222]

In Philadelphia, a study completed in 1957 found that about 50 percent of applicants for the police department were Negro. While a somewhat higher percentage of Negroes than whites failed the physical examination or had a criminal record, most of the discrepancy in the relative proportion of Negroes selected was a result of written examination. Some of the key personnel on the Civil Service Commission, which gave the tests, were Negro, and the tests were apparently given fairly. The study concluded that educational deficiencies were the main reason for the failure of Negroes to qualify.[223]

The manner in which discrimination and educational deficiencies can operate together to interfere with increased recruitment of Negroes is shown by a study of selection procedures in Detroit. Of the 1,566 applicants for the Detroit police force in 1959, there were 434 Negroes. This approximated the proportion of Negroes in the city. Of this group, 71 whites and 2 Negroes were eventually selected.

An investigation by the Commission on Community Relations found that 178 whites but only 36 Negroes were allowed to pass the preliminary screening even though they failed to meet one or more qualifying criteria. More than a score of the whites and none of the Negroes from this group were eventually employed. The Commission found that white applicants were favored in this process.

Despite the fact that the anonymity of the individual was maintained in processing the written examination, 49 percent of the whites and 80 percent of the Negroes failed.

Of the remaining 115 whites and 11 Negroes, 4 whites and 4 Negroes were eliminated by preliminary oral interviews. The Commission found that the decision to drop two of the Negroes was questionable. Ten whites and one Negro were then dropped on the basis of a background investigation. Of the 101 whites and 6 Negroes who appeared before the Oral Examination Board, 71 whites and 2 Negroes passed. The Commission again questioned the subjective reasons used to drop two of the Negroes.[224]

Remedies

Any program to increase the proportion of members of minority group police officers must begin by persuading qualified candidates to apply. However, the hostility of Negroes to police forces is so strong that Negro officers are frequently disliked by their fellow Negroes. And Spanish-speaking persons have traditionally regarded policing as not an appropriate occupation.[225] Consequently, the problem of attracting candidates requires police departments to improve all aspects of police relations with minority groups.

On the other hand, the unattractiveness of police work to minority groups should not be overemphasized. Negroes frequently apply in substantial numbers. A recent survey of three precincts in Washington by the Bureau of Social Science Research found that 54 percent of the Negro men responding, in contrast to 50 percent of the white males, disagreed with the statement that "a man would make a mistake if he became a policeman." [226]

Improvement of Recruitment Techniques. Police forces generally rely heavily upon referrals from their own members as a source for qualified recruits. A study in St. Louis showed that 42 percent of applicants and 57 percent of those appointed were referred by precinct police officers.[227] Since relatively few police officers are from minority groups, referrals are an inadequate source of minority group candidates. Consequently, new recruiting techniques must be developed. Particular effort must be made to recruit minority members from low-income areas because differences in attitudes and opinions frequently separate middle- and low-income persons within the same minority groups almost as much as persons of different races.

The police recruiting unit should include officers from minority groups. These units must go to high schools and colleges which have largely Negro students, as departments in New York and elsewhere have begun to do.[228] Civil rights and church organizations should be asked to participate in drives to get recruits. Recruitment subcommittees of neighborhood advisory committees can run continuing programs. Advertising campaigns have sometimes produced large numbers of minority candidates.[229] Advertisements can picture minority group as well as white officers. Athletes, movie stars, and other prominent personalities can be enlisted. Employment agencies can be notified of the special interest of the department in minority candidates.

It is important, however, in recruiting programs that standards and the selection process be carefully explained.

---

[219] Supra, note 202 at ch. 11, p. 16.
[220] Supra, note 77 at p. 165.
[221] Supra, note 55 at p. 8.
[222] Supra, note 202 at ch. 11, pp. 4 and 5.
[223] Supra, note 178, pp. 132, 141–145.
[224] Supra, note 202 at ch. 11, pp. 8, 10–16.
[225] Supra, note 22 at pp. 271–272.

[226] Supra, note 14 at p. 13b.
[227] Supra, note 22 at p. 266.
[228] Bernard Weintraub, "Police to Recruit at Negro Schools," New York Times, June 30, 1966, p. 42, col. 6.
[229] Ernest Reuter, "Report on Investigation of Discrimination in the Gary Police Department" (Gary, Ind.: Gary Human Relations Commission, unpublished report, 1966), p. 5.

Police departments reject as many as 97 percent of their applicants with the national average for rejection being 77.8 percent. Consequently, if minority group applicants attracted by broadly based recruiting drives do no better than applicants generally, these programs will produce an extremely large group of rejected men, many of whom are likely to suspect racial discrimination. It is therefore essential that screening for such basic standards as age, height, physical fitness, and intelligence be done early in the process and that the reason for rejection be carefully explained.

Not all recruiting programs need be aimed so generally. The existing cadet programs and the community service officer proposal in chapter 5 can be used to attract and train members of minority groups. One of the problems in existing cadet programs, however, is that their success in attracting minority group persons has often been as limited as programs for recruiting police officers directly. For example, in the District of Columbia, of the first 25 cadets appointed in 1965 only 6 were Negro despite the fact that Washington is 54 percent Negro.[230] The proportion of 24 percent is almost exactly the percentage of Negro recruits to the police force in recent years.

Programs should be devised which are especially aimed at members of minority groups. During the past year, such programs have been developed to train young men to become police officers using funds of the Manpower Development and Training Act administered by the Department of Labor. The New York City program is illustrative. Since recruiting was concentrated in Negro and Puerto Rican neighborhoods, 70 percent of the 1,100 trainees were from these groups. The recruiting itself and the initial screening was administered by the city's Youth Board, the State Unemployment Service, and four poverty program agencies rather than by the police force. Three hundred of the trainees were high school graduates who were trained for 6 months in law enforcement, human relations, automobile driving, clerical skills, and patrolmen's duties. Eight hundred of the trainees are high school dropouts who receive 6 months of general educational courses to enable them to pass the high school equivalency examination, after which they go on to the 6 months of special training. The trainees are given counseling and have a police officer as a "Dutch Uncle." Assistance is provided in overcoming medical problems and students are given $20 to $70 per week during training.[231]

The regular standards of the police departments apply to entrance into the programs and final determination is made by the police department. Students who are below the minimum age of 21 at the completion of the training program may enter the regular cadet program or take civilian positions within the police department until they can qualify to become officers. Trainees are given instruction in office skills so that if they are rejected as police officers, they can be helped to obtain clerical positions within the police force or other jobs in the city government or private industry.[232]

Similar programs are starting in other cities—Los Angeles, St. Louis, Oakland, Miami, Baltimore, and for Spanish-speaking candidates, Chicago. Some of them concentrate on persons who, on their first attempt barely failed to meet the medical and educational standards of the police force,[233] others on persons who only failed to pass the written test. While as yet these programs are too new to be evaluated, they seem to offer great promise. They may provide a realistic means for police departments to attract recruits from low-income minority groups without lowering police standards.

Removal of Discriminatory Policies. The recruitment of minority groups requires that all forms of discrimination in the selection of officers be ended. Indeed, even the appearance of discrimination must be eliminated if members of minority groups are not to be discouraged from applying. This can be accomplished by screening personnel officers with particular care for prejudice. Written examinations should be analyzed to ensure no cultural or other bias against minority group exists.

Officers from minority groups should participate in the selection process. For example, in Washington, D.C., a Negro physician is on the four-man board which screens for medical and psychological problems; and in New York, two of the three highest ranking Negroes examine all rejections of minority applicants subject to the final determination of the Commissioner.[234] Minority officers should, whenever feasible, serve on personnel interviewing boards both to prevent discrimination and to observe strong points of minority applicants which other officers might miss.

In addition, no recruiting drive can succeed as long as police departments discriminate against their own minority officers. In some police departments the legal powers vested in an officer depend on whether he is white or Negro. For example, a 1961 survey found that 28 police departments (31 percent of those surveyed) restricted the right of Negroes to make felony arrests. In 18 of the departments, the officer could hold a white suspect until a white policeman appeared; if none was available, the Negro officer could make the felony arrest. In 10 others, the Negro officer could not arrest a white suspect at all, although 3 required the Negro policeman to keep the suspect under surveillance. The power of Negro officers to arrest for misdemeanors was even more limited.[235]

In only 11 of 41 sheriffs' departments surveyed in the southern and border States could Negro officers arrest a white felon. In three northern counties, Negro deputies were allowed to arrest white felon suspects only if a white deputy was not immediately available.[236] An earlier survey of the South in 1959, which covered a greater number of small communities, found that over half required Negro officers to call white officers to arrest a white suspect.[237]

As described later, many police forces appear to have denied equal opportunity for promotion to members of minority groups. Officers from minority groups have often been segregated by being denied entrance to specialized units, by being usually assigned to Negro areas, by being required to patrol with members of their own race,

---

[230] Supra, note 215 at p. 14.
[231] Kenneth Gross, "City Woos Dropouts as Police Trainees," New York Post, Mar. 24, 1966, p. 57, cols. 2, 3.
[232] New York State Department of Labor, "Information Sheet—Police Cadet" (New York: State Printing Office, 1966), p. 1.
[233] Supra, note 215 at p. 7.

[234] Emmanuel Permutter, "Police to Review Minority Hiring," New York Times, Mar. 17, 1966, p. 1, col. 2.
[235] Supra, note 202 at ch. 11, p. 26.
[236] Id. at ch. 12, pp. 9–11.
[237] Supra, note 206 at p. 10.

by being assigned to a separate shift or even by having lockers in a different room.[238] They have often been made to feel unwelcome or have been harassed by other officers.[239] In many communities, Negro officers have been discouraged from participating in policemen's associations or have been completely excluded.[240] All these actions have significantly affected the morale and attitudes of minority officers and have surely served as a negative influence on attracting minority group persons to seek careers in police service.

Precinct policemen from minority groups are the best possible advertisement for a police career. At present, many Negro policemen cannot honestly sell police work because they feel that discrimination exists within their departments. If police departments really wish to attract recruits from minority groups, all aspects of segregation and discrimination must end. Minority officers must have full opportunity for promotion and assignment to prestigious units, must not be segregated in patrols or in particular areas of the city, and must have the same powers of arrest as any other officers.

Minority group police officers must be genuinely welcomed. No one wants to work in an organization where his colleagues are merely tolerant. One ancillary benefit of programs such as police athletic leagues is the opportunity they provide for members of a police force to accept one another fully. All other police organizations must likewise be fully open to minority officers.

Selection Standards. Certain selection standards may have the unintended effect of arbitrarily barring large numbers of minority group applicants who could adequately perform police work. For example, minimum height restrictions prevent many Puerto Ricans, Mexican-Americans, and Orientals from joining police forces. The minimum height requirement was recently changed in Chicago from 5 feet 8 inches to 5 feet 7 inches, in part because of the need to recruit Puerto Ricans. Similarly, restrictions on flat feet and other physical defects have barred many Negroes; eyesight problems, many Oriental-Americans.[241] In the review of traditional physical requirements which the Commission has recommended, an important factor should be the extent to which inflexible standards tend to interfere with the recruitment of members of minority groups.

Careful consideration should also be given to the evaluation of applicants' criminal records. Young men who have grown up in poor, and particularly minority group, neighborhoods run a very great risk of acquiring a police record.[242] In such circumstances, arrest records or conviction of a minor offense does not necessarily mean that the applicant is irresponsible or of poor character. While police departments cannot lower their requirements as to good moral character for the sake of recruiting members of minority groups—the loss in community respect alone would be too great a price—criminal records should be realistically evaluated. A minor record should be considered as part of an analysis of the moral character of the applicant based on all available information, rather than an automatic disqualification.

Promotions

Increasing the number of ranking officers from minority groups is as important as, and closely related to, recruiting new officers of minority group background. Successful recruitment and promotion opportunities are obviously interdependent. For example, in one western city, three Negro officers left a city department after failing to get promotions and joined the county sheriff's department where all were promoted, one reaching the rank of captain. This story is still being told by Negroes as one reason for Negroes not seeking employment in the city department.[243]

There is an even more marked disproportion of minority group supervisory personnel than of minority group officers generally throughout the police service. A survey in 1952–53 of 19 of the 25 largest departments in the country showed that there were only 40 Negro sergeants, 14 lieutenants, and 1 captain. Negroes constituted 3.8 percent of the patrolmen, 1.1 percent of the sergeants, 0.9 percent of the lieutenants, 0.2 percent of the captains, and 0 percent of higher ranks.[244]

The 1962 survey of the Civil Rights Commission of localities with a Negro population of over 5,000 showed that Negroes were still seriously underrepresented at command and supervisory levels. In the southern and border States, 30 departments had a total of 70 Negro sergeants; 8 communities had a total of 9 Negro lieutenants; only St. Louis and Kansas City, Mo., had Negro captains.[245]

The following table compares the ratio of white supervisory officers to white officers generally and Negro supervisory officers to Negro officers in southern and border State cities:[246]

	Sergeants	Lieutenants	Captains
White	1:8	1:20	1:37
Negro	1:16	1:125	1:246

In the 106 northern cities responding, 6 had a total of 9 Negro captains, 17 had a total of 26 Negro lieutenants, and 48 had a total of 141 Negro sergeants. The following table compares the number of white and Negro supervisory officers to white and Negro officers generally in these cities.[247]

	Sergeants	Lieutenants	Captains
White	1:9	1:25	1:45
Negro	1:20	1:108	1:311

Thus, Negro officers have been unsuccessful in gaining higher rank outside of the South.

The following table compares white and Negro ranking officers in several cities over a period of years:[248]

---

[238] Michael Banton, "The Policeman in the Community" (New York: Basic Books, Inc., 1964), p. 54.
[239] William Raspberry, "Police Rift Widens Here Among White and Negro Officers," Washington Post, September 23, 1966, sec. B, p. 1, cols. 1, 2.
[240] Supra, note 21 at vol. II, pp. 49–50; and supra, note 202 at ch. 11, pp. 30–31.
[241] Supra, note 22 at pp. 277–279.
[242] For example, a study of Baltimore in 1939 to 1942 found that in almost all Negro areas, more than 20 percent of the boys between 10 and 15 had been before a juvenile court and in many areas the percentage was over 70 percent. Forty percent of Negro boys aged 14 and 15 came before the court. Bernard Lander, "Towards an Understanding of Juvenile Delinquency" (New York: Columbia University Press, 1954), pp. 20, 32.
[243] Supra, note 22 at pp. 270–271.
[244] Supra, note 178 at p. 138.
[245] Supra, note 202 at ch. 11, p. 17.
[246] Id. at ch. 11, p. 18.
[247] Id. at ch. 11, p. 21.
[248] Supra, note 202 at app. II, tables 15, 16; supra, note 178, at p. 138; supra, note 22, pp. 286–287.

Ranking Officers in Representative Cities According to Race

City	1950, percent Negroes in population	1952-53								1960, percent Negroes in population	1962							
		Patrolmen		Sergeants		Lieutenants		Captains and above			Patrolmen (including corporals)		Sergeants		Lieutenants		Captains and above	
		W	N	W	N	W	N	W	N		W	N	W	N	W	N	W	N
Washington, D.C.	35	1,378	205	68	0	75	1	37	0	54	2,086	406	157	8	79	3	70	0
Detroit	16	3,565	96	344	3	167	1	42	0	29	3,640	148	340	5	152	1	56	0
St. Louis	18	1,240	75	196	5	36	1	23	0	29	1,393	125	192	12	35	2	31	2
Chicago	14	5,927	260	474	7	148	1	60	0	23	7,708	1,188	962	50	231	4	65	2
San Francisco	6	1,178	5	194	0	42	0	120	0	10	1,273	28	210	0	50	0	23	0
Newark	17	1,030	19	71	1	57	0	21	0	34	970	88	96	3	88	2	22	0
Dallas	13	289	4	46	0	14	0	24	0	19	717	8	249	5	45	0	30	0
Cincinnati	16	607	51	43	2	35	1	18	0	22	664	57	69	2	34	3	19	0

In the 30 State police or highway patrols responding in 1962, other than Illinois, there were no Negro supervisory or command personnel. Of the 24 Negro officers in Illinois, however, there were 2 corporals, 1 sergeant, and 1 lieutenant.[249]

The notable disproportion of Negro officers promoted to that of Negro officers recruited and selected is partly explainable by the recency of recruitment of many of the minority officers. It may take several years before recently appointed Negro officers are eligible for promotion into supervisory and command positions. In addition, the frequently more limited educational background of minority group officers takes its toll in promotion examinations.

But there is also evidence that discrimination is practiced against minority group officers, perhaps more in promotion than in recruitment. The promotion in some police departments of one or two Negroes to relatively high rank is often only a token show of nondiscrimination.[250] The Michigan State survey found, in a number of police departments, that Negro officers are discouraged from taking promotion examinations.[251] There have been examples of separate tracks and hidden job ceilings for minority group officers.[252] The very upsurge in promotions of minority group officers in cities such as Washington, D.C., Philadelphia, and Chicago—the number of Negro ranking officers in Chicago rose from 10 sergeants and 1 captain in 1960 to 50 sergeants, 4 lieutenants, and 2 captains in 1962 after Superintendent O. W. Wilson announced a policy of nondiscrimination[253]—suggests that these departments had not promoted qualified Negroes before.

A police department should have several qualified higher ranking minority group officers if it is to be responsive to the needs of minority neighborhoods. If minority groups are to feel that they are not policed entirely by a white police force, they must see that Negro or other minority officers participate in policymaking and other crucial decisions. The interaction of white officers with ranking minority officers can do much to reduce the stereotyping of minority groups by the white officers and therefore lessen racial or ethnic prejudice.

Finally, minority supervisory and command officers can be of unique value to the police in improving community relations. For example, a Negro captain was able to quiet police-community tension after a riot in Harlem when he was appointed as the first Negro to head a precinct there.[254] Similarly, in Washington, D.C., after a disturbance, the only two Negro captains on the force were assigned to the area.

The elimination of discrimination in promotions is a more complicated problem than that involved in the original selection of personnel. The relatively few officers involved in the selection process can be screened for prejudice and minority officers can be included in the review to help guarantee its honesty and dispel possible appearances of discrimination. Insofar as promotions are based on written examinations, similar methods can be used. However, in many police departments, efficiency reports play a major role in evaluating candidates for promotion. This means that crucial determinations are made throughout the department concerning the practices and ability of minority officers by every supervisor who has such an officer under his command.

It is essential that efficiency reports on minority officers receive special attention. Chiefs should issue strong statements on the necessity of avoiding even subtle forms of discrimination. The police-community relations units should scrutinize efficiency reports on minority officers, and it should be made clear that discrimination will result in strong disciplinary action.

In some jurisdictions an outside agency in the local government is given responsibility to determine whether promotions in all government agencies have been based in part on discrimination. For example, in the District of Columbia, any District employee, including any police officer, can file a complaint of discrimination with the Commissioners' Council on Human Relations. If conciliation by the council fails, a three-man panel is selected; one person is chosen by the complainant, one by the executive director of the council, and one by the first two panel members. The person selected by the executive director is a District government employee, from a department other than the one involved, who has been

---

[249] Supra, note 202, at ch. 12, at p. 14.
[250] Supra, note 22 at p. 283.
[251] Id. at p. 270.
[252] Supra, note 202 at ch. 11, pp. 18–19.
[253] Supra, note 202 at ch. 11, p. 22.
[254] Michael T. Kaufman, "Police Shake-Up Begun by Leary: Top Aide Chosen," New York Times, Feb. 26, 1966, p. 1, col. 1.

recommended by his department and approved by the executive director. The panel's recommendation, together with a recommendation by the executive director, is submitted to the Commissioners who make the final decision.[255]

Assignment to a prestigious unit or special training may also be important to advancement. If these opportunities are denied because of race, nondiscrimination in promotion may be of little importance. Such assignments should therefore receive the same kind of special attention.

But promotion of officers from minority groups will often require more than nondiscrimination. Minority officers now often leave the forces or do not take promotion examinations because they are convinced that past discrimination continues.[256] The study of Philadelphia police officers in the 1950's found numerous Negro officers who had given up hope of promotion:[257]

> Well, I wanted to go higher, but I felt beat before I started—felt like I never had a chance, so I never took the exam.
>
> * * * * *
>
> When I was younger naturally I wanted to get ahead. I kept taking the exams but never made it. I finally realized it was prejudice. I haven't taken any recently. I'm too old now—satisfied where I am.

Since police departments urgently need more high-ranking minority officers, it is essential that each department make every reasonable effort to overcome the legacy of the past. Nondiscriminatory policies should be forceful and publicly stated. Officers from minority groups should be encouraged to take promotion examinations. One method would be to urge ranking officers from minority groups to assist other minority officers in preparing for the examinations, as has been done with success in the District of Columbia.[258] While it may cause other problems, consideration might be given to reducing the time requirements which minority officers must spend in grade before being eligible for promotion where it is determined that promotion has been denied in the past because of discrimination.[259]

In some departments, promoting officials choose among the top several candidates. The highest ranking positions are generally not filled on the basis of competitive examinations at all. For example, in New York all appointments above the level of captain are made at the discretion of the Police Commissioner, and in Washington, D.C., appointments to captain and above do not involve examinations.[260] A major factor in the exercise of this discretion should be the urgent need for high-ranking minority officers.

One important application of the lateral entry concept discussed in chapter 5 would be the recruitment of talented members of minority groups who previously had not thought of a police career. As the President's Commission on Crime in the District of Columbia emphasized, lateral entry allows a police department to overcome this problem without waiting for officers from minority groups to be promoted slowly through the ranks.[261]

Assignments

The problem of assignments for minority group officers is largely the problem of integration—integration of patrols where two-man patrols are used, integration of the personnel assigned to white as well as minority neighborhoods and integration of specialized units. In many ways, the stresses to be expected are the same as those experienced in the integration of any large organization.

Particular Units and Duties. While it is not clear how much of this discrimination still exists, Negro officers have been discriminated against in the South by being assigned to separate precincts and divisions[262] and throughout the country in assignments to foot patrols rather than to cars and to desk jobs. The study of the Philadelphia police, for example, showed that at least until 1956, the latter kind of discrimination was common in most precincts.[263] Similarly, until 1960, Negroes were not usually assigned to patrol cars in Chicago; and in at least one precinct, if no white officers were available, some cars did not go out.[264] While by 1962, the situation had improved as to both motor assignments and desk positions, the Civil Rights Commission survey in 1962 showed that of the 68 nonsouthern counties with Negro deputies, in 18 all field patrols were white, and Negro deputies were given other jobs to do.[265]

Discrimination against Negroes in entering detective units has been general in the South. A study of Negro police in that region showed that there were only 56 Negro detectives in 1954 and 87 in 1959, among the 146 agencies responding (which included most of the larger ones), and 101 among 98 agencies in 1961.[266]

Outside the South, discrimination against Negroes in assignments to detective units is also widespread. Until a new administration appointed 10 in 1962, Newark had only 1 Negro detective.[267] Whether or not it is the result of present or past discrimination, in many cities during 1966 the proportion of detectives was significantly smaller than that of patrolmen:[268]

City	Detectives			Patrolmen		
	White	Negro	Percent	White	Negro	Percent
Washington, D.C.	118	20	14.5	1,770	455	20.4
Boston	166	1	.6	1,904	42	2.1
Detroit	350	12	3.3	3,287	149	4.3

On the other hand, in some cities like Indianapolis, Buffalo, and Atlanta, the proportion of Negro officers doing detective work is above the proportion of Negro patrolmen on the force.[269]

Many of the same methods for ending discrimination in promotions apply equally to the assignment of Negroes to plainclothes duty. It is important that all openings to special police assignments be filled on the basis of ability. The program, recently introduced in the District of Columbia, to post notices of openings and to solicit

---

[255] See "City Adopts Tough Code on Hiring," Washington Post, Aug. 26, 1966, sec. E, p. 10, col. 1.
[256] Supra, note 22 at pp. 269–271; supra, note 21 at vol. I, pp. 154–155; William Raspberry, "Promotions in the Police Department—Is There Discrimination?" the Washington Post, Oct. 16, 1966, sec. B, p. 1, cols. 1–7.
[257] Supra, note 178 at pp. 129–130.
[258] Alfred E. Lewis, "Police Name 2nd Negro as Captain," the Washington Post, Mar. 2, 1966, p. 1, col. 3.
[259] Waiting periods were partially suspended in Chicago and Philadelphia a few years ago. Supra, note 22 at p. 288.

[260] Supra, note 218; supra, note 77 at p. 166.
[261] Supra, note 77 at pp. 31–32.
[262] See, e.g., supra, note 202 at ch. 11, pp. 29–30.
[263] Supra, note 178 at pp. 36–37, 46–55, 161.
[264] Supra, note 202 at ch. 11, p. 32.
[265] Supra, note 202 at ch. 12, p. 11.
[266] Supra, note 206 at pp. 5–7.
[267] Supra, note 202 at ch. 11, p. 31.
[268] Supra, note 22 at table IV, p. 286.
[269] Id. at table IV, p. 286.

written applications, provides an excellent basis for non-discriminatory determinations.[270]

Patrols. Segregation presently exists in patrol assignments in many departments. A recent survey showed that of 165 cities either with populations over 100,000, or with populations of between 30,000 and 100,000 but with 5 percent nonwhites, 4 never assigned Negro and white officers together, 40 did so only for special details, 54 did so occasionally, and 74 did so "generally."[271] The Michigan State survey found that of the eight departments in the South responding, three used integrated patrols. In contrast, outside the South, 19 of 26 departments used at least some integrated patrols.[272]

These figures, however, overstate the amount of real integration. Where, for instance, the composition of patrols or teams has been left to the voluntary choices of the individuals involved, the result has usually been mostly all-white and all-Negro teams.[273] For example, in the District of Columbia in 1966, almost half of Negro officers doing patrol work were still riding in all-Negro cars and in several precincts there were no integrated patrols at all.[274] Progress has been slow because precinct commanders "defer to the prejudices of individual officers."[275] In many other cities with integrated patrols, the proportion of Negro officers in all-Negro teams is even greater and consequently there is only token integration. Official color blindness is not a sufficient remedy. The department policy must make clear both to police officers and to the community that the department will not tolerate segregation within its own ranks. As long as segregation exists, even by voluntary choice, departmental exhortations about improving police-community relations will not be taken at face value by minority citizens. Minority officers will believe that racial prejudice governs decisions throughout the department, and that belief will have a serious effect on their morale and on the recruitment of other minority officers.

The mere lack of contact between white and minority group officers on the force will make other measures to end prejudice and discrimination less effective. Studies of prejudice show that stereotypes tend to be modified and prejudices reduced when whites have contacts with Negroes on an equal footing.[276] As a white police officer told the Philadelphia study, "When somebody's shooting at you, it doesn't matter what color you are."[277] The same study found that the more white officers worked with Negro policemen, the less they were prejudiced against them.[278]

Integration of police forces is also necessary because of the special competence of minority group officers in minority group neighborhoods. The description of an incident in Washington by a Negro officer indicates the value of integrated patrol:[279]

My partner and I were chasing a Negro suspect into an all-Negro neighborhood * * * when the man shut himself up in an upstairs room and began shouting that the police were trying to get to him to beat him up.

It would have been inviting trouble to send a white officer into the crowded building to get him * * *. So I went up and got him and told the people on the way out why we were arresting him. There was no trouble.

Neighborhoods. Police-community relations in minority group neighborhoods will benefit materially from the assignment of more minority group officers than would be the case if the officers were distributed evenly throughout the force, i.e., were assigned on a completely nonracial basis. With an even distribution, Negro officers would represent less than one-fifth of total officer strength in Negro precincts in Washington, D.C., whose police force has one of the highest proportions of Negroes of any in the country. And the percentage of Puerto Ricans and Mexican-American officers in neighborhoods where these groups live would be even less.

On the other hand, the significantly disproportionate assignment of most minority officers to minority neighborhoods raises the appearance of segregation which would be as harmful as segregated patrols, teams, or units. In the past, minority group officers have been restricted entirely or primarily to minority group neighborhoods. A study in 1959 showed that in 129 southern cities, Negro officers were allowed to patrol only Negro neighborhoods in 107 cities and were assigned primarily to Negro neighborhoods in another 6.[280] The Civil Rights Commission survey in 1962 found that in the southern and border States, 92 percent of city police departments and 90 percent of county sheriffs assigned Negro officers solely or primarily to Negro neighborhoods. Only seven cities and four counties made assignments without regard to race.[281] A much smaller survey in 1966 showed that Negro officers patrolled in white areas in 7 of 11 southern localities responding.[282]

Outside the South, the Civil Rights Commission survey in 1962 found that 85 percent of city and 93 percent of county law enforcement agencies claimed that they assigned Negro officers without regard to race.[283] In 14 cities and 3 counties, however, law enforcement agencies admitted that Negro officers were primarily assigned to Negro areas. These cities included Los Angeles, Indianapolis, Kansas City (Kansas), Detroit, and Syracuse.[284]

Such assignment of minority group officers exclusively or almost exclusively to minority neighborhoods is strongly opposed by most Negroes. For example, 87 percent of Negroes interviewed in a survey in St. Louis opposed exclusive assignment of Negro officers to Negro areas; in contrast, a significant majority of whites supported it.[285] Segregation—whether based on the preferences of officers or citizens—is indefensible and cannot be tolerated.

This problem should be met by assigning minority group officers where they will be most useful, while at the same time avoiding segregation. The best resolution of the dilemma presented by these conflicting goals seems to be along three lines. First, although a somewhat disproportionate number of minority group officers should be in

---

[270] "New Police Assignment Procedure for City Issued by Chief Layton," the Washington Post, July 21, 1966, sec. K, p. 1, col. 6.
[271] Supra, note 65 at p. 9.
[272] Supra, note 22 at p. 284.
[273] Id. at p. 261.
[274] Commissioners' Council on Human Relations, supra, note 215 at p. 19.
[275] Supra, note 77 at p. 58
[276] Supra, note 171 at pp. 156–159, 167–168, 185, 191, 217, 220.
[277] Supra, note 178 at pp. 71–72.
[278] Ibid. at pp 98–99, 188–189.
[279] Leonard Downie, Jr., "Two Against Crime," the Washington Post, Potomac, Magazine, Dec. 19, 1966, pp. 6–7.

[283] Supra, note 206 at pp. 13–14.
[281] Supra, note 202 at ch. 11, p. 23; ch. 12, p. 9.
[282] Supra, note 22 at pp. 284–285.
[283] Supra, note 202 at ch. 11, p. 23; ch. 12, p. 10.
[284] Id. at ch. 11, p. 24; ch. 12, pp. 10–11. Similarly, in Boston, Negro officers were predominantly assigned to Negro districts or to cases involving Negroes. See report of the Massachusetts Advisory Committee to the U.S. Commission on Civil Rights, "50 States Report" (Washington: U.S. Government Printing Office), pp. 253–254.
[285] Supra, note 4 at table 13, p. 97.

minority neighborhoods, many officers also should be stationed in other areas. Second, the minority group officers stationed in minority group neighborhoods should be rotated to other neighborhoods. Third, the disproportionate assignment of minority group officers should, of course, cease when the police-community relations problems of minority group neighborhoods are not so acute as to justify such extraordinary measures.

TRAINING

Chapter 5 presented the problems of existing police training in this country. Recruit training was found generally to be inadequate. Inservice training, if it existed at all, usually was likewise insufficient.

Police-community relations training also suffers from lack of attention and is unlikely to improve substantially until overall police training is upgraded in quality and extent. It has long been treated as a stepchild which, until recently, has been barely accepted into the curriculum. Improvement in police training generally will not automatically result in better community relations training. This, together with the special complexity of police-community relations curricula and techniques, warrants separate discussion of this training area.

Purpose of Police-Community Relations Training

A recent survey found that most cities with community relations training concentrated on public relations.[286] Such a program attempts to teach the police officer how to improve the image of the police and conduct himself in a way which will not alienate the public. It concentrates on such matters as why community relations is important to the police department, how to talk courteously to citizens, and how and why to avoid physical or verbal abuse and discrimination. These ideas are often included in training sessions concerning arrest, field interrogation, traffic citations, and the other points of contact between the police and public. The theory is that officers who are taught about police policies will follow them in a professional, well-organized department.

Another type of community relations training equips the police officer to understand the various kinds of individuals with whom they will come in contact and the various neighborhoods and the city. This is directed not so much at the basic arms-length ability to avoid offense, as at the intelligent exercise of discretion. Subjects such as basic psychology and sociology, the history and culture of the city and its various parts, and the history and purpose of the civil rights movement, help officers to distinguish between offenses which should result in arrest and those which should not, to deal with groups of youths who have congregated, and similar issues.

Finally, community relations training is sometimes intended to change attitudes and prejudices of recruits or police officers. There is evidence that intensive experiences, particularly in small groups, can have an effect with persons who are only mildly prejudiced.[287] Some of the subjects taught for this purpose would be those also included in the curriculum for the purpose of improving the officer's ability to exercise discretion. Role-playing or small discussion groups may be used to help the officer to think through his own emotions and beliefs.

Each of these three types of training is important, and each reinforces the others. It is essential that the officer know the community relations policies of the department, understand individual and community characteristics which should affect his discretion, and have proper attitudes.

Recruit Training

There are two different aspects of training in police-community relations. First, community relations training should be made part of a more general instruction on arrest procedures, field interrogations, use of firearms. Second, some community relations subjects can only be taught separately. The amount of recruit training devoted specifically to community relations problems is woefully inadequate in most jurisdictions. A survey found that 22 of 165 police departments in cities either with over 100,000 population, or with between 30,000 and 100,000 population but over 5 percent nonwhites, gave no human relations training of any kind and that the average training in the others was only 11 hours in length. Of 145 cities with between 30,000 and 100,000 population and less than 5 percent nonwhites, only 43 gave any such training.[288] Of the 53 police departments responding to the Michigan State survey, only 20 gave more than 20 hours of community relations training and only 4 more than 40.[289] The chart on the following page shows the number of hours of separate community relations training given in certain agencies.[290]

Clearly, in the majority of police departments, the amount of time given specifically to human and community relations must be dramatically increased. Few police officers today have a proper background in psychology, sociology, or the culture of the poor, minority groups, or juveniles. In any jurisdiction with a serious community relations problem or a substantial number of residents from minority groups, 60 hours of such training seems a bare minimum and 120 hours highly desirable. The training could be given as a combination of basic and inservice training over a period of time. Such training could also, as in California, be offered by community colleges. Even in other localities, the complex problem which police have in dealing with human beings in difficult circumstances indicates adequate instruction must be provided. Before an officer can become expert in deriving the truth from conflicting statements, in knowing how to handle quarreling spouses and delinquent youths, in determining when an arrest for drunkenness or loitering is useful or necessary and when it will merely harm an individual or inflame a minority community, and in calming tense and hostile crowds, he must acquire information and understanding concerning human relations. It is doubtful that this can be acquired in less than 60 hours.

---

[286] Supra, note 65 at pp. 7, 11; supra, note 22 at pp. 303, 310.
[287] See, e.g., George E. Simpson and J. Milton Yinger, "Racial and Cultural Minorities" (rev. ed., New York: Harper & Rowe, 1958), pp. 772–773, 776–777.
[288] Supra, note 65 at pp. 7, 11.
[289] Supra, note 22 at pp. 304–309.

[290] Ibid. This data cannot be taken as exactly accurate. Police departments themselves made the classification as to what constituted community relations training and what kind it was. There is probably considerable inconsistency in placing training in particular categories and some exaggeration of the amount of community relations training given.

Hours of Separate Community Relations Training in Representative Police Departments—1966

City	Human relations	Public relations	Sociology	Psychology	Civil rights	Total	Community relations training — Total percent training hours
500,000 plus population:							
Washington, D.C.	40	(¹)	0	0	2	42	42/165 = 25.5 percent.
Kansas City, Mo.	4	4	0	0	2	10	10/504 = 2 percent.
Detroit, Mich.	22	0	4	0	6	32	32/480 = 6.7 percent.
Boston, Mass.	30	8	6	4	10	58	58/520 = 11.2 percent.
Atlanta, Ga.	4	2	1	2	4	13	13/288 = 4.5 percent.
250,000 plus population:							
Dayton, Ohio	6	4	10	8	4	32	32/680 = 4.7 percent.
New Orleans, La.	4	7	0	0	(¹)	11	11/560 = 2 percent.
Minneapolis, Minn.	40	12	22	(²)	6	84	84/400 = 21 percent.
Oakland, Calif.	0	8	0	0	0	8	8/320 = 2.5 percent.
Birmingham, Ala.	10	2	0	0	1	13	13/300 = 4.3 percent.
100,000 plus population:							
Savannah, Ga.	2	1	0	0	0	3	3/192 = 1.6 percent.
Yonkers, N.Y.	8	2	0	0	0	10	10/500 = 2 percent.
Independence, Mo.	8	8	8	8	8	40	40/480 = 8.3 percent.
Below 100,000 population:							
West Allis, Wis.	8	32	0	0	2	42	42/240 = 17.5 percent.
Portsmouth, Ohio	0	0	0	0	0	0	0/80 = 0 percent.
County agencies:							
Dade County, Fla.	2	14	0	16	6	38	38/616 = 6.2 percent
Nassau County, N.Y.	7	12	6	6	6	37	37/436 = 8.5 percent
State agencies:							
Texas Department of Public Safety	3	3	5	5	2	18	18/820 = 2.2 percent.
Minnesota Highway Patrol	0	0	0	0	1	1	1/576 = .2 percent.

¹ Included in human relations.   ² Included in psychology.

Of course, much more than additional time in the curriculum is required for effective community relations training. The following curriculum which was used in St. Louis in 1966, although limited in time, suggests the kind of comprehensive, carefully planned curriculum devoted to community relations which is necessary: [291]

SAINT LOUIS METROPOLITAN POLICE DEPARTMENT

Community Relations and Human Behavior Curriculum for Recruit Officers

Hours

I. Psychiatric Growth and Development of the Individual 5
    Father Trafford Maher, S.J.
    Saint Louis University

II. The American Culture 3
    Dr. George Hyram
    Saint Louis University

III. Human Behavior 2
    Dr. Lawrence Nicholson
    Harris Teachers' College
    and Saint Louis University

IV. Social Disorganization 12
    Alcoholism, narcotic addiction and drug abuse 4
    Dr. Joseph Kendis and Staff
    Department of Psychiatry
    Washington University
    Suicide 2
    Dr. Eli Robbins and Staff
    Department of Psychiatry
    Washington University
    Social maladjustment and sex deviation 2
    Dr. Lee Rainwater
    Washington University
    Mental illness 3
    Dr. Robert Felix
    Department of Psychiatry
    Saint Louis University
    Delinquent and criminal behavior 1
    Mr. William Handy
    Community Relations Manager

V. The Saint Louis Community 5
    Dr. William Moore
    Carver School

VI. Mechanics of the Police-Community Relations Program 1
    Mr. William Handy
    Community Relations Manager

VII. Psychology of Prejudice 5
    Father Trafford Maher, S.J.
    Saint Louis University

VIII. Mass Media Relations 1

Total 34

Other appropriate subjects could include how to handle violations of civil rights laws (such as fair housing or public accommodation statutes), the history and culture of poverty and of minority groups, and the extent and effects of racial discrimination.

The person teaching the course is at least as important as the subject matter. Where police forces have sworn officers who are good teachers with expertise in psychology or sociology, they should be used as instructors. This is not the case in many departments today, so the use of civilian instructors from universities or elsewhere becomes essential.[292] Ideally, police departments should use both police officers and civilian experts as instruc-

[291] Id. at p. 313.

[292] Id. at pp. 313, 322.

tors.[293] The police instructors can impress upon recruits that community relations is important to the department—that it is a vital part of law enforcement. The civilians can often teach the more complex subject matter.

The effectiveness of civilian instructors is increased if they understand the nature of police work. Where possible, police departments should add civilian experts on a full-time, or regular part-time basis to their community relations units, where they can also be of assistance in areas other than training. In any event, they should be encouraged to become interested in the law enforcement field on a continuing basis.

Civilians who are not experts should also participate in police training. For example, civil rights leaders and even ordinary, although articulate, citizens from the poor community could make notable contributions by giving recruits their point of view, telling about how the poor and deprived view various issues. However, community relations training should not be confined to isolated lectures by guest speakers, each speaking an hour or two in the classroom. The training program must be unified.

Along with classroom work, field training must be given. It is frequently said that when recruits leave the training course, they soon forget all they have learned and instead adopt the practices of the officers with whom they work. If the results of the community relations training sessions are to be strengthened rather than undermined, the officers accompanying the recruits in their field work must be carefully screened for their abilities and attitudes relating to community relations and should receive clear instructions concerning how to help the recruits improve their abilities in this area.

Inservice Training

Inservice training is of particular importance in community relations. Many officers received little or no community relations training at the time they were recruits. Even if they had, the practice of community relations in police work is extremely difficult and the lessons of recruit training may be forgotten if not reinforced. And minority group problems and other issues of importance to community relations are constantly changing.

Most police departments have no inservice community relations training although the number that do is increasing.[294] In those that do, it is usually too brief. Even in one of the Nation's outstanding inservice training programs, only 2 of the 36 class hours in 1963 could be considered to be devoted specifically to community relations training. A balanced program of community relations training for officers now on the force would have the following components:

Rollcall Training. Other aspects of department policy need constant repetition at rollcall and the same holds true of policies affecting police-community relations. In addition, rollcall offers the opportunity for precinct community relations officers to talk on a regular basis to all officers in the precincts about problems which they have found to be bothering the neighborhood and the precinct's program for dealing with them.

Community Relations Retraining for Patrolmen. Regular inservice training should exist in all departments and be expanded. If it is to have any significant effect, a minimum of 10 hours of formal community relations training a year would seem essential as part of any inservice program, and it is probably most effective if given in one or two blocks of time.

A number of police departments in the last 2 years have initiated special, concentrated community relations training programs for all or large portions of the force, often under grants from the Federal Government. The Office of Economic Opportunity recently funded a program in Detroit for all 1,800 officers in "inner-city precincts," which was run by the department in conjunction with the city's Commission on Community Relations and the local antipoverty program. Each of the 8 sessions began with a lecture for about 60 officers and discussions of the lecture. The officers then broke into 6 groups to discuss police handling of a specific police incident such as a house search, street loitering, or a crowd, which was either role-played or described aloud—why it occurred, how the officers in the incident handled it, and how it should have been handled. The incidents were the kind which raise the most serious police-community problems. Each discussion group reported back to the entire meeting.[295]

The Office of Law Enforcement Assistance in the Department of Justice has made a grant to the New Orleans Police Department to give the entire 1,100-man force and 100 key personnel from surrounding parishes an 18-hour course featuring lectures and small discussion groups. That office has also given a grant to have a private corporation, which has conducted training previously in other fields, train 1,000 of the 2,900 officers in the Washington, D.C., department for 24 hours in groups of 25.[296] And analysis of eight sessions of lectures and discussion concerning community relations for all officers in Lake County, Ind., which was funded by the Office of Economic Opportunity, showed that the attitudes toward minority groups of police officers with a low degree of prejudice had been affected.[297]

Training for Supervisory and Command Officers. Separate training for command and supervisory personnel has been rare.[298] But unless supervisory officers are trained, the community relations training of recruits and patrolmen is likely to mean little. Lower ranking officers naturally respond to the expectations of their supervisors. The latter make policy, enforce discipline, devise community relations programs, talk to the press and citizens' groups, and otherwise set the tone of the entire department.

Training should therefore start at the top, and the course of study should be longer than can be afforded for all personnel. Supervisory and command personnel

---

[293] Id. at pp. 304–309.
[294] Id. at p. 314; supra, note 21 at vol. I, p. 150.
[295] United States Conference of Mayors, "Police-Community Relations Training in Detroit" (1966) 4 pp.; the Detroit program is based on Arthur I. Siegel, Phillip J. Federman, and Douglas G. Schultz, "Professional Police Human Relations Training" (Springfield: Charles C. Thomas, 1963).
[296] Alfred E. Lewis, "Police Face Course in Diplomacy," the Washington Post, July 3, 1966, sec. B, p. 4, col. 4.
[297] Gary, Ind., Application for grant to Office of Law Enforcement Assistance, 1966, pp. 3–7.
[298] Supra, note 22 at pp. 323–324.

probably should receive at least 50 hours of community relations training at or near the time of promotion and then regular training after that.

In addition to the subjects in the recruit's and patrolman's curricula, higher officers should receive training in subjects of particular relevance to them. These might include how to deal with citizen organizations, particularly those of minority groups; the structure of citizens' organizations in the city; and the use of discipline and incentives to ensure that community relations policies are carried out.

Special Training. Some kinds of specialized training are of great significance for police-community relations. Programs in basic Spanish, such as those which have been given in New York, Philadelphia, San Diego, and Chicago,[299] should be provided for officers working in communities with a substantial Spanish-speaking population. In addition, policemen should receive special instruction on the culture of the residents of various neighborhoods and the community resources available to them. A special 8-hour course has been given several times in Philadelphia on "crime and race" because of misconceptions relating to crime causation and statistics.[300]

Police-Community Relations Institutes. Police-community relations institutes are of two types. Some are intended to provide a forum where the community and the police may discuss current issues and build mutual understanding. Such discussions, like all community meetings focusing on police problems, have training implications, and officers should be sent to them for this purpose.

Other institutes, which are attended largely by police officers, are held principally for training purposes. If community representatives are present, they are intended to give citizen opinion as part of the training. An example of this type is the National Institute at Michigan State University, which has been held annually since 1955 under the auspices of the National Conference of Christians and Jews. The 1966 meeting attracted 442 participants from 155 cities and 30 States, of whom 80 percent were police officers generally of supervisory rank.[301] Such meetings allow officers to compare their problems and the programs which they have employed to remedy them.

TECHNIQUES OF COMMUNITY RELATIONS TRAINING

The importance of imaginative educational techniques, such as discussion groups, problem solving, and roleplaying was described in chapter 5. Such techniques are of particular importance for instruction relating to community relations.

Frequently, recruits or officers are completely indifferent or even hostile to such training because they do not regard it as "real police work."

The President's Commission on Crime in the District of Columbia found that community relations training by the Metropolitan Police Department "seems to have created antagonism to the principles taught rather than adherence." [302] Thus, unless carefully planned, community relations training may reinforce antagonism to minority groups and community relations generally. On the other hand, if properly carried out, such training can help to persuade the recruit or officer to adopt a different attitude toward the role of a police officer and different groups in the community.

Universities and other groups having experts from various disciplines should be encouraged to develop new techniques and curricula, to run training programs, and to evaluate them. For example, in Philadelphia, community relations training was initiated by a psychological consulting firm, and the present program was developed and taught by a sociologist from the University of Pennsylvania.[303] Most of the other innovative programs discussed in this section were run by outside groups in conjunction with police departments.

POLICE FIELD PRACTICES

A community's attitude toward the police is influenced most by the action of individual officers on the street. While community relations units, neighborhood advisory committees, and fair procedures for processing citizen complaints are essential for reducing existing friction between the police and the community, these programs will have little enduring effect if persons are not treated justly in their contacts with police officers. This is particularly true of persons in slums or minority group neighborhoods who, because of more frequent contact with the police, are more aware of police practices.

Although many allegations of police misconduct or discriminatory treatment are unwarranted, Commission surveys reveal that police practices exist which cannot be justified. For example, the Commission found that abusive treatment of minority groups and the poor continues to occur. Many established police policies—such as the use of arrests for investigative purposes—alienate the community and have no legal basis. Departments may utilize procedures, such as the use of dogs to control crowds, without balancing the potental harm to police-community relations. And some valuable law enforcement techniques, like field interrogation, are frequently abused to the detriment of community relations. Too few departments give necessary guidance to assist their personnel in resolving potentially explosive social and criminal problems.

It is not possible for the police to enforce the law and preserve the peace without incurring some hostility and resentment. This is inherent in the very nature of police work. The major criticisms of the police, however, result from the particular methods used in accomplishing these functions. The purpose of this section is to examine police practices which appear to antagonize certain portions of the community, to determine the propriety of such practices, to show the need for all departments to establish reasoned policies governing police practices, and to analyze the sometimes competing considerations which must be weighed before establishing such policies.

---

[299] Supra, note 22 at pp. 322–323; supra, note 21 at vol. II, p. 43.
[300] Supra, note 21 at vol. II, p. 76.
[301] Annual Report (Michigan State University, National Center in Police and Community Relations, July 1, 1965–June 30, 1966), p. 9.

[302] President's Commission on Crime in the District of Columbia, Report of the President's Commission on Crime in the District of Columbia" (Washington: U.S. Government Printing Office, 1966), p. 210.
[303] Supra, note 21 at vol. II, p. 76.

This section does not constitute an effort to determine whether particular police practices are unconstitutional. Plainly, some practices described in this section, such as physical abuse, are illegal; others raise constitutional questions; and still others may be constitutional but unwise. Here the sole focus is on police practices which do or may affect community relations regardless of constitutional issues.

POLICE CONTACTS WITH CITIZENS ON THE STREET

It is extremely difficult for a policeman to maintain his composure in all street situations even though this is expected and demanded of him in nearly all police departments. For example, the Law Enforcement Code of Ethics, which has been adopted by nearly all departments and police associations, requires the following: [304]

I will * * * maintain courageous calm in the face of danger, scorn, or ridicule; develop self-restraint; and be constantly mindful of the welfare of others.
I will never act officiously or permit personal feelings, prejudices, animosities or friendships to influence my decisions * * *.
I will enforce the law courteously and appropriately without fear or favor, malice or ill will, never employing unnecessary force or violence * * *

But the capability of a policeman, and particularly one who works in a high-crime rate or slum neighborhood, to act in a restrained manner is constantly tested. There are countless pressures which increase the difficulty of performing police work calmly and with restraint. Typically, an officer is expected to maintain order on the street, to keep "a clean beat," to disperse mobs, to remove "undesirables," whether or not legal tools for accomplishing these results are available. A policeman's authority is daily challenged by unruly juveniles anxious to detect any weakness or fear. In dangerous neighborhoods, he may be mocked, threatened, or even spat upon. Police work requires that policemen continually see the tragedy of victimized citizens and the sordid lives of the reprehensible and unfortunate elements of the community. And, a policeman must always live with the prospect that he may be subject to attack without warning.

Even if an officer is of the highest quality, his work and the people with whom he must deal may cause him to become disillusioned or angry. If he is not of the highest quality or if he has not been properly trained, if he is prejudiced or hotheaded, he may succumb to his anger or resentment and physically or verbally abuse someone who offends him.

The problems of police-citizen contacts are multiplied and exacerbated when the citizens involved are youths. Youths commit a large and increasing proportion of crimes. They are out and around, noticeable to the patrolling officer. They travel in groups, which may make them appear more suspicious and at least potentially harder to control. They spend time in such local gathering places as pool halls, recreation centers, record shops, and street corners, and they often acquire information useful to the police. The antipathy toward the police that they might have at any age by virtue of race, neighborhood, or experience is heightened by youth's natural dislike for authority.

It is hardly surprising that youths and policemen are not always on the best of terms. Various factors influence their reactions to and relations with each other. Informal street contacts are rarely recorded, and little factual information is available about their real extent and nature. Several recent studies and field research projects, however, have begun to explore the causes of friction between police and juveniles.

In one study, a series of interviews was conducted with San Francisco gang boys—white, Mexican, and Negro—over a 2-year period.[305] While the survey was limited to gang members, it has broader significance both because its observations and analyses deal with activities of the boys independent of their gangs and because gangs and their members probably have greater contact than other youths with the police.

As the San Francisco observers point out, besides needing to obtain information from youths and to apprehend them when they have violated the law, the police also feel an obligation to receive respectful behavior from them, both to symbolize their law-abiding attitude and to attest their acceptance of the particular police officer's authority. The youths in question, however, feel an equal need to establish and maintain their autonomy—a need that, in the case of many lower class gang boys, has been a way of life since they were children and successfully asserted their independence of overworked, ineffectual, or absent parents. One of the most tangible ways in which gang boys assert autonomy is their claim to control of a street corner, city block, or other geographical area as the inviolable site of their activities. But the gang's private hangout is also the policeman's beat and: [306]

Although the boys attempt either subtly or violently to convince outsiders that their behavior at the hangout is a strictly private affair, the police tend to insist with equal conviction that all behavior on public property is their legitimate concern.

According to one sociologist, the Chicago police illustrate the conflict by saying, when displaced by a gang's hangout behavior, "Give me that corner!" [307]

The struggle for street corner control may be the backdrop for encounters between police and juveniles, but it is the more pointed, circumscribed encounters—stops, searches, trips to the stationhouse—that shape their views of each other. As the San Francisco sociologists point out, when policemen are suspicious of youths in a strange neighborhood, or their furtive actions, or their gathering together in groups, they are often supported in their suspicions by common sense and experience, as well as by want of alternative means to solve crimes and preserve public order. But feeling themselves both demeaned and challenged, the youths may react with more or less open defiance and hostility, slouching or smirking or answering the officers in an offhand or uncooperative manner, thereby challenging the policeman, in turn, to "put-up-or-shut-up." In that situation the officers, fearful of losing face

---

[304] Law Enforcement Code of Ethics. See ch. 7, Police Integrity.
[305] Carl Werthman and Irving Piliavin, "Gang Members and the Police," in David Bordua, ed., "The Police" (New York: John Wiley & Sons, 1967), pp. 56–98. The study of the police reported in this chapter was conducted by the Survey Research Center at the University of California under a grant from the National Institute of Mental Health. The study of gangs was carried out by the Survey Research Center and the Center for the Study of Law and Society at the University of California under grants from the Ford Foundation and the Department of Health, Education, and Welfare. Aaron V. Cicourel, whose recent study of police handling of juveniles in two California cities will appear in a forthcoming book, states that the "actual encounters [he] witnessed over a 4-year period support the Werthman analysis of the problem of police authority." ("The Social Organization of Juvenile Justice" ch. 7, p. 73, of unpublished manuscrip.)
[306] Id. at p. 62.
[307] Ibid.

and sacrificing authority on future occasions, may feel virtually forced either to arrest the juveniles for a vague or minor offense (suspicion of robbery, loitering, disturbing the peace, violating curfew regulations) or to make it appear that they are being let go out of the goodness of the officer's heart. The San Francisco study concludes that "this is why criminal records of many gang boys are often heavily laced with such charges as 'suspicion of robbery' and 'suspicion of rape.' " [308] Similarly, a study of disorderly conduct arrests of both adults and juveniles in the District of Columbia found that in almost a quarter of them the arrest had been made only for loud and boisterous talking or obscene remarks to the police. [309]

The San Francisco gang study, in taped interviews of youths, found that the appearances of authority thereby gained is more than offset by the resentment and disrespect created: [310]

> One day we were standing on the corner about three blocks from school and this juvenile officer comes up. He say, "Hey you boys! Come here!" So everybody else walked over there. But this one stud made like he didn't hear him. So the cop say, "Hey punk! Come here!" So the stud sorta look up like he hear him and start walking over. But he walking over real slow. So the cop walk over there and grab him by the collar and throw him down and put the handcuffs on him, saying, "When I call you next time come see what I want!" So everybody was standing by the car, and he say, "All right you black * * *! Get your * * * home!" Just like that. And he handcuffed the stud and took him to juvenile hall for nothing. Just for standing there looking at him.

Demeanor appears to affect police disposition after arrest as well as arrest in the first instance. Juvenile officers and patrolmen interviewed in the San Francisco study estimated that demeanor is the major factor in 50 to 60 percent of juvenile dispositions.[311] Another study of juvenile offenders reports police officials in agreement that "defiance on the part of a boy will lead to juvenile court quicker than anything else." [312] The more general significance of demeanor is illustrated by a study of a western police department, in which it was found that charges against speeders, prostitutes, and other offenders depended in large part on the suspect's demeanor.[313]

Not all policemen equate unusual attire or surroundings with actual or potential lawlessness, and not all interpret defiance as need or justification for custody. This distinction is not lost on youths: [314]

> Those two studs out in Lakeview wouldn't always be on our back for playing neither. We'd be standing on the corner pulling some kinda phoney (!) * * *, and they'd pull up to find out if we was up to something. But they talked to us nice. They wouldn't let us get away with nothing, and I, mean, them cats would bust you if they had to. But they talked to us nice.

Such officers—as the gang boy himself points out—are not necessarily softer, more lenient, or less effective. But by avoiding ethnic slurs, by recognizing and making allowance for the exuberance and the naturally combative and nonconforming attitudes of adolescents, these policemen allow adolescents to escape the uncomfortable spotlight of constant suspicion. Such a spotlight is not only frequently undeserved but it may encourage the youths to act as their audience, the police officers, appear to expect.

Verbal Abuse and Discourtesy

Commission studies reveal that there are abuses in some cities which range from simple discourtesy to clearly unwarranted excessive use of force against persons of all ages. In focusing on such abuses, it is important to bear in mind that in the large majority of instances officers were observed to handle themselves with courage and often with restraint. Therefore, it is important that the following material not be read as a general description of the conduct of all police officers, but rather as a description of certain conduct which cannot be tolerated regardless how frequent or infrequent it may be.

No matter is more important to police-community relations than the manner in which police officers talk to people on the street. The Michigan State survey found that while allegations of excessive physical force receive the most attention, verbal abuse and discourtesy were probably greater irritants to community relations.[315] If officers are abusive, insulting, or condescending, the most insignificant contact can become an occasion which arouses hostility against the police. On the other hand, if police officers are polite, forthright, respectful, and, where appropriate, friendly, a field interrogation, a traffic ticket, or even an arrest can actually increase the respect of the citizen, as well as others who see the incident, for the police.

Commission surveys revealed that a number of officers treat citizens in a demeaning manner. In one Commission study, observations were made in several cities of several hundred routine contacts between police and citizens, usually in a home or on the street. Most of the persons interviewed were witnesses, bystanders, and victims, rather than suspects. The study showed 9 percent of the persons received a polite request from the officers; 5 percent received an impersonal summons which was neither polite nor nasty; 66 percent were interrogated without introduction; and 15 percent of the interrogations began with a brusque or nasty command like "Come 'ere, punk" or "Get your * * * over here, pork chop." [316]

Discriminatory statements, in particular, produce both anger and strong counterprejudice among minority groups.[317] The use of racial epithets, such as "nigger," "coon," "boy," and "Pancho" appears to be widespread, even though their use is condemned by responsible police administrators. The President's Commission on Crime in the District of Columbia found that "offensive terms such as 'boy' or 'nigger' are too often used by officers of the Department" and that "in most cases, the language is chosen deliberately to demean the citizen and demonstrate the superiority of the officer." [318] And a study of police handling of juveniles in two police departments stated that, while the observer never heard derogatory remarks made to Negroes by officers on the professionalized force, he heard dozens of insults and derogatory remarks by officers in the less professionalized depart-

---

[308] Id. at p. 91.
[309] Patricia M. Wald and Joel E. Hoffman, "Report on the Disorderly Conduct Statute of the District of Columbia" (unpublished manuscript: July 16, 1966), p. 25.
[310] Supra, note 305 at p. 90–91.
[311] Id. at p. 74.
[312] Nathan Goldman, "The Differential Selection of Juvenile Offenders for Court Appearances" (Washington: National Council on Crime and Delinquency, 1963), p. 106.
[313] Supra, note 1 at pp. 90, 94, 95, 108, 111. See also the similar accounts of Philadelphia police officers in supra, note 21, vol. I, p. 112; vol. II, pp. 145, 146, 156, 168, and 169.
[314] Supra, note 305 at p. 68.
[315] Supra, note 22 at p. 17.
[316] Supra, note 184 at table 14.
[317] Supra, note 171 at pp. 46–48, 253, 257–258, 283, 301.
[318] Supra, note 77 at pp. 66–67.

ment.[319] It is precisely this type of language which solidifies the conflict between minority groups and the police. Many police departments have regulations which require that citizens be treated with courtesy and respect and train their officers accordingly. One of the most far-reaching is that of the San Diego Police Department: [320]

> We should treat all juveniles as we would want our own children treated, even the "hard core young hoodlum," for our job is to help juveniles toward good citizenship and build respect for the police and not to create "cop-haters" and criminals. *Always be fair, impartial, honest, and constructive.* [Emphasis in original.]

A similar rule might properly be applied to adults as well.[321]

But the general instructions of most departments are neither sufficiently forceful nor specific as to the manner in which police officers should conduct themselves with regard to citizens. General police statements concerning the need for courtesy are not enough. All departments, for example, should formulate clear policies which prohibit the use of racial epithets. A similar recommendation was made by the President's Commission on Crime in the District of Columbia: [322]

> The chief of police should issue a directive concerning verbal abuse of citizens by police officers, which identifies and prohibits the use of trigger words such as "boy" or "nigger." The Metropolitan Police Department should make it clear that violation of its order will be cause for disciplinary procedures. Current department statements on the subject, which urge that "undue familiarity with the use of such terms as 'bud,' 'Junior,' 'Mac,' be avoided," are neither sufficiently forceful nor directly related to the problems of the community.

Shortly after that report, the chief of police issued a more specific directive than had previously existed.

Other police departments also prohibit certain forms of address. For example, the Chicago Police Department has the following policy: [323]

> At all times Departmental personnel will:
> 1. Never show any bias or prejudice against race, religion, or any other group or individual.
> 2. Act, speak, and conduct themselves in such a manner as to treat all persons with complete courtesy and with that respect due to every person as a human being.
> 3. Never "talk down" to any group or individual or engage in the use of derogatory terms such as "nigger," "boy," "wop," "kike," "chink," "shine," "burrhead," "dago," "polack," "bohunk," and the like * * *

Some departments, such as Baltimore, require that their officers address persons as Mr. _____, Mrs. _____, Sir, or Madam.[324] Such forms of address should be used as a matter of common courtesy.

Of course, it is often difficult for officers to be respectful when dealing with citizens who are abusive or disrespectful. But, as was expressed by the President's Commission on Crime in the District of Columbia after it deplored the use of abusive language both by police and citizens: "Officers must be held to a higher standard of conduct in performing their official duties." [325] This view was also expressed by O. W. Wilson, the superintendent of police in Chicago: [326]

> The officer * * * must remember that there is no law against making a policeman angry and that he cannot charge a man with offending him. Until the citizen acts overtly in violation of the law, he should take no action against him, least of all lower himself to the level of the citizen by berating and demeaning him in a loud and angry voice. The officer who withstands angry verbal assaults builds his own character and raises the standard of the department.

Consequently, if citizens show disrespect for an officer, such conduct, alone, while reprehensible, does not justify making an arrest or taking other action.

Finally, police officers should be encouraged to talk to citizens about nonpolice matters while on duty, as they are in New York, rather than prohibited from conducting such conversations with citizens.[327] The BSSR survey of three Washington, D.C., precincts shows that hostility in Negro males declines as informal contacts with the police increase.[328] These contacts allow the police to establish friendships rather than having solely the role of making arrests and interrogations.

Physical Misconduct

Unjustified use of force, like verbal abuse, cannot be tolerated in law enforcement. Many persons, and particularly those from minority groups, believe that police officers sometimes or even frequently engage in excessive or unnecessary physical force. The Commission was not able to determine the extent of physical abuse by policemen in this country since recent studies have generally not been systematic. Earlier studies, however, found that police brutality was a significant problem. For example, the National Commission on Law Observance and Enforcement (the Wickersham Commission), which reported to President Hoover in 1931, found considerable evidence of police brutality.[329] The President's Commission on Civil Rights, appointed by President Truman, made a similar finding in 1947.[330] And in 1961, the U.S. Civil Rights Commission concluded that "police brutality is still a serious problem throughout the United States." [331]

The Commission believes that physical abuse is not as serious a problem as it was in the past. The few statistics which do exist suggest small numbers of cases involving excessive use of force.[332] Although the relatively small number of reported complaints cannot be considered an accurate measure of the total problem, most persons, including civil rights leaders, believe that verbal abuse and harassment, not excessive use of force, is the major police-community relations problem today.[333] It is clear, how-

---

[319] Supra, note 172 at p. 30.
[320] J. R. Laffoon, "Field Interrogation" (San Diego, Calif.: San Diego Police Department, July 1965), p. 38.
[321] Id. at pp. 41–44.
[322] Supra, note 77 at p. 74.
[323] Supra, note 22 at p. 187.
[324] Richard Severo, "Strong Police Command Vital to Avert More City Violence," the Washington Post, June 30, 1966, sec. A, p. 6, cols. 1, 2, 3.
[325] Supra, note 77 at p. 74.
[326] Supra, note 96 at p. 188.
[327] Thomas A. Johnson, "New Police Plan Used on Crowds," New York Times, July 25, 1966, p. 16, col. 6.
[328] For a similar result, see Donald Lowell Johns, "A Study of Some Factors Related to the Formation of Attitudes Toward the Police" (unpublished masters thesis, University of California at Berkeley, School of Criminology, 1966), pp. 122, 144.
[329] National Commission on Law Observance and Enforcement "Report on Lawlessness in Law Enforcement" (Washington: U.S. Government Printing Office, 1931).
[330] President's Commission on Civil Rights, "To Secure These Rights" (New York: Simon & Schuster, 1947), pp. 25–27.
[331] "The 50 States Report," submitted to the Commission on Civil Rights by the State Advisory Committees, 1961 (Washington: U.S. Government Printing Office, 1961), 687 p.
[332] In fiscal year 1965, FBI statistics show that there were only 9 convictions out of 1,787 cases of excessive force investigated and in fiscal 1966 there were 1,671 excessive force complaints investigated and only 3 resulted in convictions. These data were provided by Jerome Daunt, Chief, Uniform Crime Reporting Section, FBI, Mar. 7, 1967.
[333] Supra, note 22 at p. 66; Walter Gellhorn, "When Americans Complain" (Cambridge, Mass.: Harvard Press, 1966), pp. 176–177; William Raspberry, "Physical Violence May Be Gone, But Police Brutality Still Exists," the Washington Post, May 27, 1966, sec. B, p. 1, cols. 1, 2, 3.

ever, that excessive force remains a serious problem in parts of the South. There are too many well-documented instances of brutality against Negroes and civil rights workers in the recent past to doubt that it still occurs today. For example, during the Mississippi march in the summer of 1966, State, county and local law enforcement officers on several occasions struck demonstrators.[334] On numerous other occasions, law enforcement officers have watched white citizens attack civil rights demonstrators or have otherwise failed to prevent or halt private violence.[335]

Moreover, one study undertaken by the Commission also determined that excessive use of force still remains as a significant problem outside the South as well. During this study, Commission observers systematically accompanied police officers on regular patrol in a number of major cities—primarily in high crime and slum precincts—for periods ranging from 5 to 8 weeks. During the survey, observers witnessed, during 850 8-hour patrols, 5,339 police-citizen encounters—encounters which included police contacts with suspects, witnesses, victims, and bystanders. While watching these encounters, Commission observers reported that there were 20 instances where officers used force where none was clearly required or where its use was plainly excessive. Of the incidents observed, most did not appear to be based upon racial prejudice. More than half of those subjected to excessive force were white. Almost all of the victims appeared to be poor. They included drunks, sexual deviates, or juveniles who were regarded by the police as hoodlums, and most appeared to contest verbally the police officer's authority.[336] Three of the 20 examples of the incidents observed are as follows: [337]

White officers responded to a man with a gun * * * and heard three shots fired. Then the white man with the gun got a drop on the officer—somehow they got the gun away and handcuffed him (gun was a 12 gauge 1905 musket). When they got him to the station garage, they kicked him all over, but the principal one was the officer who had been in danger when the man had the drop on him. He beat him as the others held him up. I got to the scene and the lockup man whistled for them to stop but they didn't. The Lieutenant arrived with everyone else and said there's going to be a beef on this one so cover it up and go find the empty shells. Someone call an ambulance (he needed it badly). Then the Lieutenant took complete control. They got the shells, got a complainant who said the three shots were an attempt to kill the officer, and he would sign a complaint, say he called an ambulance, etc. They wrote a cover for the incident. The officer who beat the man most was shaken by then but the others gave him support, telling him how brave he was and how wise he had been not to kill the guy at the scene, etc. They then set about to put all the stories in order and I was carefully notified of it in detail so I would have it straight. I had enough rapport with these officers that they talked about it even after. The man was in pretty bad shape when he got to the hospital.

* * * * *

The officers were flagged down by a white man and woman. "The man who flagged us down said a Negro was inside the (public transportation station) causing trouble. The woman said he had sworn at her as did the man. One said: 'What's a nigger doing here; he should be down on * * *' The two white officers went in and grabbed him. They shoved him into a phone booth. Both officers beat him with fists and a flashlight and also hit him in the groin, then they dragged him out and kept him on his knees. He said he had just been released from a mental hospital that day. He begged them not to hit him again and let him go back to the hospital. One officer said: 'Don't you like us Nigger; we're here to help you! You're a crazy nigger.' They took him to the car and he kept begging them not to hurt him. Then they put him on the wrong bus—he wanted to go to the hospital and they sent him the wrong way. The last thing the Negro man said was: 'You police just like to shoot and beat people.' Officer No. 1 said: 'Get moving nigger or I'll shoot you.' The offender was crying and bleeding as he was put on the bus. Officer No. 2 said: 'He won't be back.'"

* * * * *

The dispatch was drunks in a cemetery. "We found the drunks sleeping in the cemetery. They were white men between 25 and 45 years of age. Officer No. 1 (white) ripped the shirt off one drunk in searching him. He also hit him in the groin with his nightstick. Officer No. 2 ripped back of pants of another drunk. The officers laughed as they forced them to climb over the fence and they laughed because the buttocks of the one was completely exposed. One officer said: 'I ought to run you * * * in.' As they left over the fence, another said: 'Those * * * * * won't be back—a bunch of * * * winos.'"

While this limited study gave the Commission no basis for stating the extent to which police officers use force, it did confirm that such conduct still exists in the cities where observations were made.

One other study conducted in a large city revealed that when juveniles show disrespect to officers, many of the officers prefer to settle the challenge to their authority by physical means. This study indicated that certain officers would justify their use of force by deliberately provoking the juvenile until he could be considered to be resisting arrest. This technique is described in the statements of one police officer and one juvenile taken during interviews in this city: [338]

For example, when you stop a fellow for a routine questioning, say a wise guy, and he starts talking back to you and telling you that you are no good and that sort of thing. You know you can take a man in on a disorderly conduct charge, but you can practically never make it stick. So what you do in a case like this is to egg the guy on until he makes a remark where you can justifiably slap him, and then if he fights back, you can call it resisting arrest.

* * * * *

Another reason why they beat up on you is because they always have the advantage over you. The cop might say, "You done this." And you might say, "I didn't!" And he'll say, "Don't talk back to me or I'll go upside your head!" You know, and then they say they had a right to hit you or arrest you because you were talking back to an officer or resisting arrest, and you were merely trying to explain or tell him that you hadn't done what he said you'd done. One of those kinds of things. Well, that means you in the wrong when you get downtown anyway. You're always in the wrong.[339]

A survey of policemen in one midwestern city in 1951 also indicated that many officers had misconceptions about when they are justified in using force. Officers were asked to respond to this question: "When do you

---

[334] Gene Roberts, "Police Seize 11 in Rights March," New York Times, June 24, 1966, sec. 21, col. 4; "175 Negroes Are Pursued and Clubbed," the Washington Post, July 11, 1966, p. 1, col. 3. See supra, note 331 at p. 1.
[335] U.S. Commission on Civil Rights, "Law Enforcement: A Report on Equal Protection in the South" (Washington): U.S. Government Printing Office, 1965), pp. 174–175; "Court Told How Police Ignored Negro Beatings," the Washington Post, Sept. 16, 1966, sec. A, p. 6, cols. 1, 2. See also supra, note 331 at pp. 29–44, 105–109.
[336] Supra, note 207 at pp. 16–17.
[337] Id. at pp. 1, 2, and 8 of appendix.
[338] William A. Westley, "Violence and the Police," American Journal of Sociology, 59; 34–41, 38, as quoted in Werthman and Piliavin, supra, note 305 at pp. 92–93.
[339] Supra, note 305 at p. 93.

think a policeman is justified in roughing a man up?" They gave the following responses: [340]

Reason	Percentage
Disrespect for police	37
To obtain information	19
For the hardened criminal	7
When you know the man is guilty	3
For sex criminals	3
When impossible to avoid	23
To make an arrest	8

The interviews provided considerable detail concerning the officers' rationale. They believed that the use of force to obtain evidence which would justify an arrest in a felony case was acceptable—"to rough him up a little, up to a point * * * You feel that the end justifies the means." [341] Force was seen to be permissible with sex criminals when the officer knew that a person was guilty, did not have enough evidence, and considered it necessary to ensure that the criminal was punished. The officers said that force was justified in cases involving disrespect such as: [342]

I was on the beat, and I was taking [a man] down to the station. There were people following us. He kept saying that I wasn't in the army. Well, he kept going on like that, and I finally had to bust him one. I had to do it. The people would have thought I was afraid otherwise.

The officers believed that the only way to treat certain groups of people, including Negroes and the poor, is to treat them roughly. [343] On the other hand, this study did conclude that illegal force was not used as frequently and with as little provocation as the officers' statements would suggest.

To prevent physical abuse by police officers requires that all police departments take great care in selecting personnel, formulate strong policies on permissible conduct, dismiss officers who engage in physical misconduct, regularly review personnel practices, comprehensively investigate all complaints made against individual officers, and strongly discipline those officers who misbehave. Methods for accomplishing this are described in chapters 2 and 3 of this volume. Policies should be formulated to bar not only unnecessary force but describe, to the extent possible, the amount of force which is permissible for making arrests and carrying out other police activities. Such policies can best be enforced if all officers who use physical force for any reason are required to report in writing the circumstances under which the force was used. [344]

Discrimination

The University of California study found that members of minority groups in Philadelphia and San Diego generally believed that discrimination is practiced against both middle class and poor persons from minority groups. [345] Polls of minority groups show similar results. [346] It is extremely difficult to establish the extent to which such allegations are accurate since discrimination is likely to be only one of several factors which affect an officer's decision in any particular situation. Negroes, other minority groups, and the poor are arrested and probably stopped in disproportion to their numbers. However, these groups frequently live in high-crime areas. Consequently, normal, completely fair police work would doubtless produce the arrest or stopping of larger numbers of these groups.

Two studies of referrals to juvenile courts in several cities found that the police referred significantly more Negro than white juveniles for the same types of offenses, particularly for minor offenses. [347] Another study of police handling of juveniles in two large cities found that the eastern, nonprofessional police force referred three times as many Negro juveniles to court as whites. On the other hand, the western, more professional police force tended to treat similar types of offenders alike. [348] And, the Commission's study, based on observation of routine police work in several northern cities, found that the police did not discriminate between whites and Negroes of the same economic class; instead, police conduct seemed to depend on economic status and on whether the person was a drunk, a homosexual, or otherwise an outcast. [349]

As was described earlier, a high percentage of Negroes believe that the police provide inadequate protection in minority communities. [350] Lack of protection can take the form of police being slow to respond to calls, having inadequate personnel, or tending to ignore offenses by one minority person against another in contrast to those by members of minority groups against whites or whites against whites. While the lack of attention paid to investigating violations against others of the same race is probably decreasing, it still exists in many localities. [351] For example, the American Bar Foundation study undertaken in mid-1950's found that it exists especially in large cities and particularly as to serious offenses such as aggravated assault. [352]

Police officers should not base decisions to arrest, stop, use force, or the like, in whole or in part, on race, poverty, or civil rights activity. All decisions must be based on objective evidence which creates suspicion, proof of guilt, or threat of danger to the officer or public, as the law requires.

Field Interrogation

In many communities, field interrogations are a major source of friction between the police and minority groups. Many minority group leaders strongly contend that field interrogations are predominantly conducted in slum communities, that they are used indiscriminately, and that they are conducted in an abusive and unfriendly manner.

The police consider field interrogations to be an important method of preventing and investigating crime, since they rarely encounter a crime in progress. Normally, by the time a police officer has arrived at a crime scene, the perpetrator has fled, people have gathered, and confusion has ensued. Further, the police believe that they

---

[340] Supra, note 338 at p. 38. Only one reason was counted—either that first mentioned or that given most heatedly or at greatest length—for each officer. Dr. Westley believed that the officers were cautious with him because of recent criticism by the chief of police and the community about the use of violence.
[341] Id. at p. 36.
[342] Id. at p. 39.
[343] Id. at p. 40.
[344] This was also recommended by Chief Stanley R. Schrotel in "Supervising the Use of Police Authority," Journal of Criminal Law, Criminology and Police Science, 47; 590–599.
[345] Supra, note 21 at vol. I, p. 78, 107; vol. II, pp. 105, 153.
[346] Supra, note 14 at 13B.

[347] Supra, note 312 at pp. 42–44, 57–58, 65–67, 73–75, 88–89; supra, note 177 at p. 212.
[348] Supra, note 172 at pp. 9–10, 29–30.
[349] Supra, note 305; supra, note 184 at pp. 9–10, 14–17.
[350] Supra, note 21 at vol. I, p. 139.
[351] Supra, note 1 at p. 172; report to the U.S. Commission on Civil Rights, Delaware Advisory Committee, "50 States Report" (Washington: U.S. Government Printing Office, 1961), p. 92; George E. Simpson and J. Milton Yinger, "Racial and Cultural Minorities" (rev. ed.; New York: Harper & Brothers, 1958), pp. 511–512.
[352] Wayne R. LaFave, "Arrest: The Decision to Take a Suspect into Custody" (Boston: Little, Brown and Co., 1965), pp. 110–114.

can prevent much crime if they are permitted to stop and question persons whose behavior strongly suggests that a criminal act is being contemplated:[353]

A law enforcement officer in the performance of his duties will be confronted with innumerable situations in which it seems necessary to make some inquiry of a person whose name he does not know, and whom, if further action is not taken, he is most unlikely ever to find again. An inquiry may appear appropriate because such a person is behaving in a suspicious or unusual manner which suggests a possible involvement in crime. Thus, he may be a person running with a heavy package at 2:00 a.m. in a business neighborhood. Or he may correspond to a description of the perpetrator of a recent crime, but because he is traveling in an automobile it is impossible to be sure. Or he may be walking slowly down a street at night, looking into the windows of parked cars.

The person to whom the officer would like to direct an inquiry may clearly not be involved in criminality. He may be a person who was near the scene of a crime, and thus a potential source of information. Or it may be impossible to tell in advance whether the person to be stopped is a suspect or a source of information.

The limits of police authority to stop persons briefly for purposes of criminal investigation are unclear in most jurisdictions. In some States, there is specific statutory authority for officers to stop suspicious persons. For example, a recently enacted statute in New York gives an officer authority to stop for questioning a person whom "he reasonably suspects is committing, has committed, or is about to commit" a felony or other specified crimes and authorizes the officer to use whatever force is necessary to effectuate such stops.[354]

In most States, however, there is no specific statute which defines this authority. As a result, police departments are given little guidance as to when a person may be stopped, whether or how long he may be detained, whether force may be used to detain him, what degree of force may be used, whether a person may be searched, whether he may be compelled to answer certain questions, and under what circumstances he must be advised of his legal rights.

A few police departments have policies governing the conduct of field interrogations. Training materials of the Oakland, Calif. Police Dept., for example, carefully describe the types of persons who should be stopped;[355] the San Diego, Calif. Police Dept. specifically forbids officers to restrain persons being questioned against their will;[356] and the Tampa, Fla. Police Dept. defines conditions under which a person may be searched.[357]

The Commission believes that there is a definite need to authorize the police to stop suspects and possible witnesses of major crimes, to detain them for brief questioning if they will not voluntarily cooperate, and to search such suspects for dangerous weapons when such a precaution is necessary. This need was also recognized by the reporters for the American Law Institute Model Pre-Arraignment Code Project:[358]

If, as some have argued, the only power to restrain a person, even briefly, is by arresting him on reasonable grounds to believe him guilty of a crime, the police will be foreclosed from responding to confused, emergency situations in the way that seems most natural and rational. For in such circumstances, where a crime may have been committed and a suspect or important witness is about to disappear, it seems irrational to deprive the officer of the opportunity to "freeze" the situation for a short time, so that he may make inquiry and arrive at a considered judgment about further action to be taken. To deny the police such a power would be too high a price in effective policing and in the police's respect for the good sense of the rules that govern them, in order to avoid brief inconveniences that most innocent persons would be prepared to undergo.

Misuse of field interrogations, however, is causing serious friction with minority groups in many localities. This is becoming particularly true as more police departments adopt "aggressive patrol" in which officers are encouraged routinely to stop and question persons on the street who are unknown to them, who are suspicious, or whose purpose for being abroad is not readily evident. The Michigan State survey found that both minority group leaders and persons sympathetic to minority groups throughout the country were almost unanimous in labelling field interrogation as a principal problem in police-community relations:[359]

* * * race has an undue influence on who is stopped.

* * * practice is o.k., but the way it was carried out was unfriendly, abusive, etc. Not against method, but how it is used.

Personally, I found it offensive and was affronted on occasions of its use in New York.

Spanish-Americans are picked up sooner.

Many Negroes stopped in other neighborhoods and questioned. Happens more to Negroes than to others.

The Commission has found that field interrogations, used sometimes in conjunction with aggressive, preventive patrol, are often conducted on a broad-scale basis by many police departments. First, field interrogations are often conducted with little or no basis for suspicion. In San Diego, written reports were made of over 200,000 stops in 1965 and there were probably about as many stops which were not recorded.[360] The effect on attitudes which can result is revealed by the following comment of a lower income Negro:[361]

When they stop everybody, they say, well, they haven't seen you around, you know, they want to get to know your name, and all this. I can see them stopping you one time, but the same police stopping you every other day, and asking you the same old question.

A study of juvenile offenses in a western city with high police standards found that Negroes were stopped more frequently than other juveniles "often even in the absence of evidence that an offense had been committed."[362]

Second, field interrogations are sometimes used in a way which discriminates against minority groups, the poor, and the juvenile. For example, the Michigan State survey found, on the basis of riding with patrol units in two cities, that members of minority groups were often stopped, particularly if found in groups, in the company of white people, or at night in white neighborhoods, and that this caused serious problems.[363] Similarly, in a midwestern city, using aggressive patrol and field interrogations seems to cause, as in San Diego, the major problem

---

[353] American Law Institute, "A Model Code of Pre-Arraignment Procedure; Tentative Draft No. 1," 1965, p. 95.
[354] New York Code Criminal Procedure § 180–a(1); see Uniform Arrest Act, § 2; supra, note 353 at pp. 6–10.
[355] Oakland Police Department, "Departmental Training Bulletin," Mar. 7, 1966.
[356] Supra, note 320 at pp. 41, 44.
[357] Tampa Police Department, "Training Bulletin," vol. XII, No. 6, Dec. 10, 1962, p. 3.
[358] Supra, note 353 at pp. 96–97.
[359] Supra, note 22 at pp. 333–334.
[360] San Diego Police Department, "Field Interrogation—Burglary Graph," (San Diego: San Diego Police Department, 1966); supra, note 21 at vol. I, p. 127.
[361] Supra, note 21 at vol. I, p. 86.
[362] Supra, note 177 at p. 212.
[363] Supra, note 22 at pp. 327–336.

in police-community relations.³⁶⁴ In contrast, in Philadelphia the field interrogation is used less and is not a major item of criticism by minority groups or others.³⁶⁵

Finally, field interrogations are frequently conducted in a discourteous or otherwise offensive manner which is particularly irritating to the citizen. For example, even in San Diego, where officers are instructed specifically and at length to give the citizen an explanation and to act courteously,³⁶⁶ the University of California study found that an explanation is frequently not given. In some cities, searches are made in a high proportion of instances not for the purpose of protecting the officer but to obtain drugs or other incriminating evidence. In New York, for example, where searches are permitted only when the officer reasonably believes he is in bodily danger, searches were made in 31.6 percent of stops reported.³⁶⁷ However, a Commission survey of police practices in several large cities, found that one out of every five persons frisked was carrying a dangerous weapon—10 percent were carrying guns and another 10 percent knives.³⁶⁸

While the same problems exist as to field interrogations of juveniles as with adults, there are also additional difficulties. As was described earlier, juveniles are subjected to particularly close scrutiny by police officers. The study in San Francisco, for example, found that juveniles are frequently stopped when they travel outside their own neighborhoods: ³⁶⁹

If we go someplace, they tell us to go on home. Because every time we go somewhere we mostly go in big groups and they don't want us. One time we was talking in Steiner Street. So a cop drove up and he say, "Hey! Hanky and panky! Come here!" And he say, "You all out of bounds, get back on the other side of Steiner Street."

* * * *

If boys from Hunter's Point or Fillmore [Negro neighborhoods in San Francisco] go in all white districts, the police will stop you and ask you where you from. If you say Fillmore or Hunter's Point, they'll take you down to the station and run checks on you. Any burglaries, any purse snatchings, anything.

The same study also found that the police are suspicious and make field interrogations of certain individuals because of clothing, hair, and walking mannerisms: ³⁷⁰

Why do they pick us up? They don't pick everybody up. They just pick up on the ones with the hats on and trench coats and conks [a Negro hair style]. If you got long hair and hats on, something like this one, you gonna get picked up. Especially a conk. And the way you dress. Sometimes, like if you've got on black pants, better not have on no black pants or bends [a kind of trouser] or levis. They think you going to rob somebody. And don't have a head scarf on your head. They'll bust you for having a head scarf.

* * * *

The way you walk sometimes. * * * Don't try to be cool. You know. They'll bust you for that. * * * Last night a cop picked me up for that. He told me I had a bad walk. He say, "You think you're bad."

White youths who wear the clothes and have the look of possible delinquents are likewise stopped sometimes without evidence of criminality.³⁷¹

The study concluded that the juveniles understood being sought and interrogated for their illegal activity: ³⁷²

If you done something and you be lying and yelling when the boys from juvy come around and they catch you lying, well, what you gonna do? You gonna complain 'cause you was caught? Hell man, you can't do that. You did something and you was caught and that's the way it goes.

But they were indignant about field interrogation for offenses they did not commit—when "we were just minding our own business when the cops came along." And they particularly resented being singled out because of their clothes or hair: "Hell man, them cops is supposed to be out catching criminals! They ain't paid to be lookin' after my *hair!*" ³⁷³ The juveniles consider this harassment by the police as a policy of confinement by a "foreign army of occupation." ³⁷⁴

In order to balance the need for field interrogations and the harmful effect on police-community relations which may result from their indiscriminate use, State legislatures should define the extent of police authority to stop and question persons, and police departments should adopt detailed policies governing this authority whether or not legislation exists. Such legislation and policies should have the following principles:

☐ Field interrogations should be conducted only when an officer has reason to believe that a person is about to commit or has committed a crime, or that a crime has been committed and he has knowledge of material value to the investigation.
☐ Field interrogations should not be used at all for minor crimes like vagrancy and loitering.
☐ Adequate reason should be based on the actions of the person, his presence near the scene of a crime, and similar factors raising substantial suspicion, and not on race, poverty, or youth.
☐ The stop should be limited in time.³⁷⁵ The sole purposes should be: (a) to obtain the citizen's identification; (b) to verify it by readily available information; (c) to request cooperation in the investigation of a crime; and (d) to verify by readily available information any account of his presence or any other information given by the person.
☐ The citizen should be addressed politely and should receive a suitable explanation of the reason for the stop.
☐ An officer should be allowed to conduct a search of the person only if he has reason to believe that his safety or the safety of others so requires.
☐ Officers should be required to file a report each time a stop is made in order to record the circumstances and persons involved.³⁷⁶ Even greater care should be taken with these records, than with arrest records so that the police do not use them to establish the delinquency or bad character of the person stopped. Moreover, the records should not be available to persons outside of public law enforcement agencies.

---

³⁶⁴ Supra, note 21 at vol. I, pp. 85, 127–128, 142.
³⁶⁵ Supra, note 21 at vol. II, pp. 170, 173.
³⁶⁶ Supra, note 1 at pp. 87–88; supra, note 360 at pp. 29–30, 43–44. The San Diego Department explicitly requires an explanation because of the sensitive community relations problems involved in field interrogations. The same is true of Oakland. See supra, note 355 at p. 8.
³⁶⁷ New York City Police Department, Quota Circular, Misc. 15, Oct. 13, 1965.
³⁶⁸ Albert J. Reiss, Jr., "Personal and Property Searches in Radio Dispatched Police Work: An Overview of the Data from Three Cities," (Ann Arbor: University of Michigan, 1966) pp. 4–6. A report prepared for the President's Commission on Law Enforcement and Administration of Justice. This report is a preliminary draft which is being included with the Commission's records in the National Archives. It is presently being revised and supplemented by the University of Michigan and will be embodied in research studies to be published by the Commission.
³⁶⁹ Supra, note 305 at pp. 77, 79.
³⁷⁰ Id. at p. 80.
³⁷¹ Supra, note 177 at pp. 212, 213.
³⁷² Supra, note 305 at p. 71.
³⁷³ Supra, note 305 at p. 82.
³⁷⁴ Supra, note 305 at p. 96.
³⁷⁵ Supra, note 353 at p. 6. The American Law Institute draft model statute specifies 20 minutes.
³⁷⁶ Some police forces now have such a requirement. See, e.g., St. Louis Police Department, "Special Order 60–S–122," Aug. 9, 1965, p. 1; New York Police Department Circular Order No. 25.

One of the most difficult questions in connection with a stop and attendant search is whether the results or fruits of a search other than weapons, should be used by police. While there are serious objections to barring evidence of crime discovered in a lawful search, the admissibility of evidence such as betting slips or narcotics found during a stop may encourage the misuse of the search power.[377]

EXERCISE OF THE ARREST POWER

Arrests for Investigation

Although there is no legal basis for arresting persons simply as a means of detaining them while an investigation of their possible involvement in crime is conducted, this has been a common practice in a number of departments.

The American Bar Foundation study of police practices in three midwestern States found that in cities with substantial crime problems, arrests are often made on suspicion—such as refusing to answer questions or giving an equivocal answer during a field interrogation.[378] In 1960, the Washington, D.C. Police Department made 4,684 arrests for investigation, but only 257 (5.5 percent) of the arrested persons were ever charged with the commission of a specific offense. Of those arrested, 1,349 were held for 8 hours or more. This practice was abolished in 1963 as a result of a study in 1962 condemning it.[379]

In Detroit, from 1947 to 1956, 219,053 arrests of a total of 658,808 nontraffic arrests were listed by the police department as arrests for investigations.[380] In 1956, of 73,827 arrests, only 40,641 persons were formally charged with commission of an offense; 33,186, or 45 percent, were arrested for investigation. Of the latter, only 6,490 were subsequently charged with a crime and the others were released without charge. The suspect would be detained for an average of at least 3 days before release or before being brought before a magistrate. Authority for the practice was provided in the police manual.[381] The 1964 police department statistics still showed that 8,140 arrests out of 63,125 nontraffic arrests were classified merely as "detention." [382]

Sixteen of fifty-five departments responding to a Commission survey in 1966 admitted the use of investigative arrests.[383] In Baltimore, for example, 3,719 (6.6 percent) of the 56,160 nontraffic arrests during 1964 were recorded as arrests for investigation. Of those arrested on this basis, 98 percent were dismissed without going before a magistrate.[384]

Occasionally, police departments engage in dragnet arrests on suspicion after serious crimes have been committed. In Detroit, in December 1960 and January 1961, after a series of rapes and murders of women, persons were stopped on the street, searched, and in about 1,000 cases arrested.[385] In 1964, after two brothers killed one policeman and seriously wounded another, Baltimore police officers searched more than 300 homes, most belonging to Negroes, looking for the gunman. The searches were often made in the middle of the night and were based almost entirely on anonymous tips. The U.S. Court of Appeals for the Fourth Circuit stated: [386]

Lack of respect for the police is conceded to be one of the factors generating violent outbursts in Negro communities. The invasions so graphically depicted in this case "could" happen in prosperous suburban neighborhoods, but the innocent victims know only that wholesale raids do not happen elsewhere and did happen to them. Understandably they feel that such illegal treatment is reserved for those elements who the police believe cannot or will not challenge them.

As reported in the Uniform Crime Reports prepared by the Federal Bureau of Investigation, 76,346 arrests for suspicion were listed for the year 1965, in jurisdictions with approximately 70 percent of the Nation's population.[387] These statistics almost certainly understate the number of investigative arrests in the country. In jurisdictions where the practice is not permitted, such arrests are frequently made by using the drunkenness, vagrancy, and other petty offense laws. [388] Similarly, the American Bar Foundation found that in the three States it studied, a common practice was to arrest a suspicious person and then book him for an offense which occurs frequently in the area or for an offense for which he resembled generally the person wanted.[389] A captain in a Kansas sheriff's department said that it was no problem to arrest a person without a specific offense in mind since "it is no difficult matter to find some sort of a 'want' on the State teletype that will fit the man's description." [390] An instructor in a training session said that "[It] is a poor policeman who cannot find a description to fit the suspect, as you officers have at least 30 days of daily bulletins in your notebooks." [391]

One nationally recognized governmental consulting firm, which has done considerable consulting with police agencies, recently reported that the widespread use of investigative arrests demonstrates inadequate policy, supervision, and investigative personnel: [392]

The practice of allowing or perhaps even condoning such arrests reflects an unawareness of the impropriety and, in fact, the illegality of most such arrests. It has developed as a result of failure to formulate policy and adequate procedures on the part of the chief and the command staff.

Aside from the legal and constitutional implications of arrests for "suspicion" or "for investigation," the frequency of occurrence of such arrests tends to reflect upon the competency and attitude of the investigator, and quality of investigations surrounding the cases for which these arrests are made * * *

Thus, it may be seen that departments and individual investigators who tend to rely heavily upon indiscriminate and casual arrests of known criminals, suspects, and others will generally perform rather inadequate and unprofessional investigations.

Arrests for investigation or on suspicion, whatever label is attached, should be abolished by all departments that now utilize them. This practice has long been a source

---

[377] Supra, note 353 at p. 10. Reporters of the American Law Institute Pre-Arraignment Code have this issue under further study.
[378] Supra, note 352 at pp. 249–250, 295.
[379] "The Report and Recommendations of the Commissioner's Committee on Police Arrests for Investigation, Washington, D.C., July, 1962.
[380] Harold Norris, "Arrests Without Warrant," "Crisis," October 1958, 65: 486.
[381] Supra, note 352 at pp. 302, 306; Detroit Bar Association Committee on Civil Rights, "Report on Detroit Police Department Policy of 'Arrests For Investigation'" as published in "United States Commission on Civil Rights, hearings held in Detroit, Michigan," (Washington: U.S. Government Printing Office, 1961), p. 505.
[382] See also Michigan Civil Rights Commission, "Report on Investigations of Law Enforcement Claims Against the Detroit Police Department," June 24, 1966, p. 4.
[383] Supra, note 22 at p. 338.
[384] Baltimore Police Department, "Annual Report" (1964), pp. 33–43.

[385] Arnold S. Trebach, "The Rationing of Justice" (New Brunswick: Rutgers University Press, 1964), p. 6.
[386] Lankford v. Gelston, Fourth Cir., No. 10, 384, decided June 23, 1966, pp. 2, 3, 16, 17.
[387] Federal Bureau of Investigation, "Uniform Crime Reports, 1965" (Washington: Department of Justice, 1966), p. 109.
[388] The use of these statutes for investigative purposes is described more fully later in this chapter.
[389] Supra, note 352 at p. 296.
[390] Ibid.
[391] Id. at p. 297.
[392] Public Administration Service, "The Savannah Police Department, Part V: Guidelines to Measurement and Evaluation" (Chicago: Public Administration Service, 1964), p. 21, 22.

of justified community hostility. They not only seriously inconvenience the citizen or even result in his incarceration, but they result in an arrest record which may greatly affect his present or future employment.

Arrests for Harassment

The police in some cities use their arrest power to harass persons whom they do not intend to prosecute because of insufficient evidence or because of the practice of the courts in giving light sentences. The harassment arrest is primarily used as a mechanism for annoying persons who are allegedly involved in vice practices such as prostitution, gambling, or illegal liquor sales. The American Bar Foundation study found in Detroit, during 1956-57, for example, over 1,000 arrests were made for gambling and liquor violations during a 6-month period in one precinct. Ultimately, however, only 60 cases were presented for prosecution.[393] These arrests were made because, as an assistant prosecutor commented: "the prosecutor's office and the police department are forced to find other means of punishing, harassing, and generally making life uneasy for the gamblers." [394]

The same study found that as many as 40 or 50 prostitutes a night were arrested and released the next day because they were found on the street in an area where prostitution was practiced and they had a prior record of arrests for prostitution. Negro women with white men were almost always charged. A police official asserted that the arrests were part of "a harassment program'. The police department has no other means of dealing with prostitution." [395]

Similarly, in Cleveland, of 1,202 women arrested and taken to a particular precinct in a Negro area of Cleveland for investigation in connection with prostitution, 1,075 were Negro. Only 96 were charged. The 224 white men arrested were all released on the stated ground that they were needed to testify against the women. The uniform release of these men has been a cause of great resentment in the Negro community.[396]

While the police are under considerable pressure to contain vice within a community and to keep undesirable persons off the streets, the current practice of using the arrest power in situations in which there is no intent to submit the case for prosecution is deplorable. Police departments, therefore, should establish policies which specifically prevent illegal harassment arrests, and which direct that arrests be made only if probable cause exists that a crime has been committed.

Arrests for Minor Crimes

Arrests for minor crimes, such as vagrancy, disorderly conduct, use of obscene language, loitering, failure to move on, blocking the street or sidewalk, drunkenness, drinking in public, and curfew violations, constitute almost one-half of all arrests made each year in the United States.[397] There is evidence that such arrests create great antagonism against police officers in slum communities. For example, many complaints filed with the review board in Philadelphia involve such ordinances and not a single complaint has involved an incident during commission of a felony.[398] The reason for hostility resulting from minor crimes is probably that while most offenders know when they have committed major crimes and expect that they will be arrested for them, the issue as to most alleged minor crimes is not as clear and the offender does not usually believe, whether or not he has acted illegally, that he has done anything sufficiently wrong to justify arrest. The comments of two men in Harlem suggest the antagonism that can result: [399]

A bunch of us could be playing some music, or dancing, which we have as an outlet for ourselves. We can't dance in the house, we don't have clubs or things like that, so we're out on the sidewalk, right on the sidewalk; we might feel like doing dancing, or one might want to play something on his horn. Right away here comes a cop. "You're disturbing the peace!" No one has said anything, you understand; no one has made a complaint. Everyone is enjoying themselves. But here comes one cop, and he'll want to chase everyone. And gets mad. I mean, he gets mad! We aren't mad. He comes into the neighborhood, aggravated and mad.

* * * * *

Last night, for instance, the officer stopped some fellas on 125th Street * * *. [T]he officer said, "All right, everybody get off the street or inside!" Now, it's very hot. We don't have air-conditioned apartments in most of these houses up here, so where are we going if we get off the streets? We can't go back in the house because we almost suffocate. So we sit down on the curb, or stand on the sidewalk, or on the steps, things like that, till the wee hours of the morning, especially in the summer when it's too hot to go up. Now where were we going? But he came out with his nightstick and wants to beat people on the head, and wanted to—he arrested one fellow. The other fellow said, "Well, I'll move, but you don't have to talk to me like a dog."

Minor crime statutes are frequently misused. They are employed as a means of clearing undesirables or unsightly persons from the street or driving them out of town, aiding the police in detaining a suspected person during an investigation of a more serious crime, and regulating street activity in slum neighborhoods. Often, under pressure from the community, the police will "declare a war on bums, prostitutes, homosexuals, and narcotic traffickers" by making wholesale arrests for vagrancy, disorderly conduct, drunkenness, or loitering.[400] Justice William O. Douglas found that in Tucson, between 1958 and 1960, the poor were discouraged to come to the city for employment by the policy of picking "up any vags spotted within the city limits." [401] In 1966, a District of Columbia judge found that "the typical accused under [the vagrancy] law is a miserable derelict whose principal offense is poverty and affinity for cheap wine, or an individual, male or female, suspected of engaging in prostitution or homosexuality." [402] The court concluded that the "basic design" of the vagrancy law is "preventive conviction imposed upon those who because of their background and behavior are more likely than the general public to commit crimes and * * * the statute contemplates such convictions even though no overt criminal act has been committed or can be proved." [403] Recent studies of the use of public drunkenness statutes in two cities found that they were often employed to arrest skid row types who were not drunk

---

[393] Supra, note 352 at p. 473.
[394] Id. at p. 478.
[395] Id. at p. 456.
[396] U.S. Civil Rights Commission, staff memorandum, "Police-Community Relations, Cleveland, Ohio" (Feb. 21, 1966), pp. 3-4.
[397] Supra, note 387 at pp. 108-109.
[398] Supra, note 21, vol. II, at p. 232.

[399] Kenneth B. Clark, "Dark Ghetto" (New York: Harper & Row, 1965), pp. 4-5.
[400] Caleb Foote, "Vagrancy Type Law and Its Administration," University of Pennsylvania Law Review, 104: 603-650, 613.
[401] Tucson Daily Citizen, Jan. 4, 1960, quoted in William O. Douglas, "Vagrancy and Arrest on Suspicion," Yale Law Journal, 70: 1-14.
[402] *District of Columbia* v. *Ricks*, No. D.C. 3050-66, decided June 16, 1966, p. 10.
[403] Id. at p. 2, 3.

but were aesthetically displeasing.[404] Until 1965, one department was arresting women under an ordinance which made it a crime for a "woman of notorious character" to walk or ride up "the streets of this city."[405]

This practice is even more harmful to a person than an unwarranted field interrogation, since the suspect is not merely stopped, but he is arrested and confined, at least until he can make bail. While such arrests may serve some investigative value to the police, there is grave question as to their propriety.

The American Bar Foundation, in its study of 1956–57, found that the "Police assume that these [vagrancy] statutes are intended primarily as aids to investigation."[406] For example, if the police desire to undertake an in-custody investigation of a person, and investigative arrests are not used, they often arrest a person for violating a vagrancy-type statute. In one observation made during the American Bar Foundation study, a man was seen near a pawn shop with a jacket on his arm. When questioned, he said that he was unemployed because he had just come to the city to find work and that he had no identification because his wallet had been stolen; he also gave other evasive answers. The officers arrested him for vagrancy because they suspected him of burglary but lacked evidence. Similarly, a man suspected of homicide was arrested for vagrancy so that a prolonged investigation could be made while he served his sentence.[407] Other statutes were found to be used for the same purpose. A man suspected of carrying narcotics, whom the officers did not have evidence to arrest, was arrested for a minor traffic violation which would ordinarily result in a warning and his car was searched.[408]

Arrests for failure to move on, loitering, blocking the sidewalk, or public drinking are predominantly made in slum neighborhoods. One reason is that more officers are stationed in these neighborhoods because of the greater amount of serious crime. As a result, residents sometimes charge "over policing" at the same time they seek more protection from crimes such as robbery and burglary. Minor crime statutes, however, are also more used in poor areas because it is harder to keep order there. As a precinct captain in Washington, D.C. stated:[409]

> We do tend to enforce the drunk laws more rigidly on 14th Street than in, say, Crestwood, a better part of the precinct. If we overlooked things on 14th Street, we would have a more serious problem.

The source of these difficulties in enforcement of minor crime statutes reaches beyond the police. The community often demands that the police rid the city of undesirable persons, harass persons engaged in vice activities, and keep the unsightly off the streets, even though the police do not have legal means of doing so.[410] Thus, until the public recognizes the dilemma facing the police in regulating such behavior, the police will continue to be placed in an untenable position.

As recommended in chapter 5 of the General Report, the content and use of minor crime statutes should be carefully reexamined in all communities. Obviously, certain minor crime statutes are necessary in order to regulate reasonable conduct on the street. If persons are disorderly and disturb others, if they block the streets and sidewalk, if they use obscene language in public, police action is warranted. Many existing statutes, however, which base criminality on suspicious conduct, a prior record, or poverty, are of questionable legal validity and usually of considerable harm to community relations.

At least some minor crime statutes should be eliminated. In chapter 9 of the General Report, the Commission recommended the abolition of criminal drunkenness statutes. Besides its other virtues, this would reduce the tension which frequently results, particularly in minority communities, from the arrest of drunks. The neighborhood reaction would doubtless be different if citizens knew, as the Commission recommends, that drunks were merely taken to a sobering up facility and then released or treated.

Most statutes which are used to regulate street conduct are so broad that almost unlimited discretion is given to the police officer to arrest persons on the street or, as with a failure-to-move-on statute, to regulate conduct by the threat of arrest. Such statutes should be amended to cover only conduct which reasonably disturbs the public or is an immediate threat to the peace. Even if this is done, however, there would still be a need for police departments to formulate guidelines concerning their permissible use.[411] The guidelines should clearly bar discriminatory enforcement of minor crime statutes either against individuals or in particular neighborhoods. The District of Columbia Crime Commission Report noted that "until recently, there were no criteria issued by the police to assist the officer in exercising * * * discretion wisely."[412]

Arrest Quotas

It is often alleged that police officers and perhaps even precincts have arrest quotas. As a result, it is contended, officers who have not made a sufficient number of arrests begin to make frivolous or marginally warranted arrests relating to minor crimes and that supervising officers order patrolmen to clear the streets of drunks and the like. The police, on the other hand, generally deny that such quotas exist.[413]

The difficulty in determining whether arrest quotas exist is that they need not be absolute requirements. The effect is virtually the same if precincts and individual officers are expected to make an approximate number of arrests as evidence that they are carrying out their responsibilities in a diligent and effective manner. Such expectations can be as effective as a regulation.

The Commission has little evidence that police forces use quotas for evaluating officers. Two Commission surveys did find, however, that, in both a midwestern and a western city, one means by which superior officers evaluated officers was by the number of field

---

[404] Emory University, Department of Psychiatry, "Alcohol Project," Sept. 23, 1963, p. 18.
[405] "Atlanta Prostitutes Win Fight to Curb Arrests on Streets," New York Times, Dec. 10, 1965, p. 38, col. 5.
[406] Supra, note 352 at p. 88.
[407] Id. at p. 151.
[408] Ibid.
[409] Supra, note 134 at p. 35, col. 5.
[410] See, ch 2, Law Enforcement Policy: The Police Role.
[411] For example, the Corporation Council in the District of Columbia has recently issued a ruling, construing the move-on statute to mean that the person does not commit an offense when he fails to move after being ordered by an officer unless there are circumstances which "(a) amount to an actual obstruction of vehicular or pedestrian traffic, or (b) constitute an immediate threat to public safety, public peace, or public order." Milton D. Korman, Letter to the Commissioners, "Authority of Police Officers to Order Persons Congregating on Public Streets to Move On," June 7, 1966, p. 13.
[412] Supra, note 77 at p. 67.
[413] Supra, note 21 at vol. I, pp. 126–127, 162.

interrogations each had made.[414] In one of those cities a ranking officer stated: [415]

> Our first line supervisors [Sergeants] have a responsibility to keep statistics on each officer's production—not an average, but his production—to find out whether a particular officer's performance is consistent with what his [s]quad's average might be. As a result, if a particular man is low, we expect an explanation.

Police work is far too complicated and delicate a job to judge an officer's work or qualifications for promotion on the number of arrests he has made. Furthermore, arrest quotas, if they exist as either explicit requirements or implied expectations, can lead to improper activity by policemen. Patrolling officers have the complex and difficult responsibility of exercising their discretion based on the circumstances of the particular case. No part of this calculation should consist of the number of arrests the officer has made in comparison to a preestablished quota or expectation set by the department.

USE OF FIREARMS TO APPREHEND OR ARREST SUSPECTS

Police use of firearms to apprehend suspects often strains community relations or even results in serious disturbances. For example, the San Francisco riot of 1966 started after a juvenile was shot and killed while fleeing from a stolen car.[416] Severe tensions were aroused in Los Angeles during May 1966, after an officer's firearm accidentally discharged and killed a man who had refused to stop his automobile until it was forced to the curb.[417] In St. Louis, disturbances began in September 1966 after police officers shot and killed a person who had his hands handcuffed behind him in a police car located in the courtyard of police headquarters. The police assert that the suspect threatened officers in the car with a tear gas pistol he had in his belt behind him which the officers had failed to find in a search earlier.[418]

When studied objectively and unemotionally, particular uses of firearms by police officers are often unwarranted. For example, an American Bar Foundation study revealed one instance where a foot patrolman signaled a speeding driver to stop. When the driver did not, the officer fired five times at the speeding car.[419]

A study by an American Civil Liberties Union affiliate in a medium-sized city found that officers fired guns more than 300 times in a 2-year period and over one-third were during automobile chases involving juveniles.[420] An average of 240 persons per year were fatally injured by police between 1950 and 1960.[421] The Michigan State study concluded that police officers often use guns indiscriminately and that this was due, in large part, to overemphasis of danger in police work.[422] While the murder of a single police officer is a tragedy, as of 1955, the rate of total police fatalities while on duty (including accidents) was 33 fatalities per 100,000 officers which was less than the rate of deaths on duty in mining (94), agriculture (55), construction (76), and transportation (44).[423]

It is surprising and alarming that few police departments provide their officers with careful instruction on the circumstances under which the use of a firearm is permissible. For example, a 1961 survey of Michigan police forces found that 27 out of 49 had no firearms policies.[424] A survey in 1964, of 45 of the 51 American cities of over 250,000 population, found that 3 had no written firearms policy,[425] and, while others had comprehensive policy statements, many were quite limited. For example, one simply prohibited warning shots, one instructed its officers to "exercise the greatest possible caution," and 10 urged officers to use "good judgment." [426] While it is true that many departments have oral firearms policies, these policies have normally developed through customary practices that rarely are the product of careful analysis and are usually not well understood by patrolmen.[427]

It is essential that all departments formulate written firearms policies which clearly limit their use to situations of strong and compelling need. A department should even place greater restrictions on their use than is legally required. Careful review of the comprehensive firearms use policies of several departments and discussions with police administrators indicate that these guidelines should control firearms use:

1. Deadly force should be restricted to the apprehension of perpetrators who, in the course of their crime threatened the use of deadly force, or if the officer believes there is a substantial risk that the person whose arrest is sought will cause death or serious bodily harm if his apprehension is delayed. The use of firearms should be flatly prohibited in the apprehension of misdemeanants, since the value of human life far outweighs the gravity of a misdemeanor.[428]

2. Deadly force should never be used on mere suspicion that a crime, no matter how serious, was committed or that the person being pursued committed the crime. An officer should either have witnessed the crime or should have sufficient information to know, as a virtual certainty, that the suspect committed an offense for which the use of deadly force is permissible.

3. Officers should not be permitted to fire at felony suspects when lesser force could be used; when the officer believes that the suspect can be apprehended reasonably soon thereafter without the use of deadly force; or when there is any substantial danger to innocent bystanders. Although the requirement of using lesser force, when possible, is a legal rule, the other limitations are based on sound public policy. To risk the life of innocent persons for the purpose of apprehending a felon cannot be justified.

4. Officers should never use warning shots for any purpose. Warning shots endanger the lives of bystanders, and in addition, may prompt a suspect to return the fire. Further, officers should never fire from a moving vehicle.

5. Officers should be allowed to use any necessary force, including deadly force, to protect themselves or other

---

[414] Supra, note 22 at pp. 335–336; supra, note 21 at vol. I, p. 142.
[415] Supra, note 21 at vol. I, p. 126.
[416] Lawrence E. Davies, "Calm is Restored in San Francisco," New York Times, Sept. 30, 1966, p. 1, col. 5.
[417] Peter Bart, "Inquest Tightens Tension in Watts," New York Times, May 21, 1966, p. 13, col. 1.
[418] Donald Janson, "St. Louis Orders Riot Crackdown," New York Times, Sept. 29, 1966, p. 39, col. 3.
[419] Supra, note 352 at p. 213.
[420] American Civil Liberties Union, "Police Power vs. Citizens' Rights" (New York: The American Civil Liberties Union, 1966), pp. 4–5.
[421] Gerald D. Robin, "Justifiable Homicide by Police Officers," Journal of Criminal Law, Criminology and Police Science, 54: 228–229. Robin also notes that an average of 240 persons per year were fatally injured by police intervention between 1950 and 1960—approximately six times the number of officers killed by criminals.
[422] Supra, note 22 at pp. 344–346.
[423] Supra, note 421 at pp. 228–231.
[424] Samuel G. Chapman and Thompson S. Crockett, "Gunsight Dilemma: Police Firearms Policy," Police, May–June 1963, p. 54.
[425] Cincinnati Police Department, "Police Regulations Governing Use of Firearms Survey," Apr. 22, 1964, p. 1.
[426] Id. pp. 9–54.
[427] Supra, note 424 at p. 22.
[428] This is already prohibited in many States by statute.

persons from death or serious injury. In such cases, it is immaterial whether the attacker has committed a serious felony, a misdemeanor, or any crime at all.

6. In order to enforce firearms use policies, department regulations should require a detailed written report on all discharges of firearms. All cases should be thoroughly investigated to determine whether the use of firearms was justified under the circumstances.

If all departments formulated firearms use policies which include the above principles and these policies were consistently enforced, many of the tragic incidents which had a direct bearing upon community relations could have been avoided.

POLICE TACTICAL PROCEDURES

Police-community relations are not affected by the actions or conduct of individual officers alone. Often, departmental procedures which are intended to reduce crime, quell riots, or promote efficiency have a major effect on police-community relations. For example, in order to reduce crime in a high-crime area, a police department may saturate it with substantially increased numbers of police officers or decide to use trained dogs and handlers. In order to make more efficient use of its personnel, a police department may use motor rather than foot patrol or one-man rather than two-man motor patrols. Such practices, although often far more efficient and economical, can sometimes antagonize the public or at least reduce the opportunity for friendly contacts which are the basis of good community relations.

Motorized Patrols

The Nation's police forces are increasingly patrolling in cars rather than on foot because motor patrol is plainly more efficient—officers can cover many times more area in the same period of time—and police officers have more to do.[429] The change to motor patrol can, however, significantly affect police-community relations. The University of California study found that since officers on motor patrol in San Diego had such a heavy workload and were without portable police radios, they rarely left their automobiles to meet citizens in a nonenforcement situation.[430] Similarly, a study of another western city which almost exclusively used motor patrol found that the officers had "little opportunity to build up an intimate familiarity, much less an identification, with any neighborhood." [431]

On the other hand, an officer on foot has the opportunity to have informal and friendly exchanges with the people whom he quickly comes to know personally. The public can develop a greater understanding of the officer and his job. The officer similarly can learn the culture and opinions of the people in the area and can learn to appreciate them as individual human beings and not as a nameless part of a racial, religious, or ethnic group.[432] As Professor Oscar Handlin has noted:

I think it is fair to say if one thinks of the large municipalities as a whole, the links between the police and the communal organizations have not been strengthened in the last quarter of a century and in some ways have been weakened. In an earlier period the policeman walking his beat at least had a certain familiarity with the institutions of his own immediate district. I'm not putting too much emphasis on that nor do I wish to romanticize that gallant figure; but nevertheless he knew something about the actual people and the actual organizations in the district of the beat which he walked.

Similarly, the Commissioner of the London Metropolitan Police said:[433]

The policeman in a car, on a motorcycle, or absent from his beat becomes a cipher. * * * [T]he greatest safeguard of public relations, as well as the greatest preventive measure against crime, lies in making good deficiencies on the beat.

The recent Royal Commission Report concluded that: [434]

In spite of heavy and conflicting demands on their limited resources we regard it as most important that chief police officers should bear in mind the need to allocate an adequate number of men to beat duties, where they will be in touch with the public.

The question then is: Can the need for greater efficiency be coupled with sufficient informal contact to improve police-community relations?

There are several possible patrol techniques and new personnel assignments which can accomplish both the objective of greater efficiency and substantial informal contact. First, foot patrolmen or community service officers should probably remain in high-crime, high-tension areas where the streets are usually crowded. Second, patrolmen in other areas could ride motor scooters which permit easier contact with residents.[435] Third, patrolmen either on scooters or in automobiles could park their vehicles at one end of a block (or two) and then walk around it. If they have portable police radios, they could still be summoned immediately to proceed to the scene of an emergency.[436] Alternatively, as in Philadelphia, a two-man car can be used with one partner walking a beat with a portable radio to communicate with the man in the car.[437] Thus, motor patrolmen are in effect considered as foot patrolmen using cars to increase their mobility. Fourth, informal citizen contacts by patrol officers using traditional motor patrol methods can be increased by having them work, along with precinct community relations officers, with community organizations.

One-Man Patrols

Police departments are increasingly changing from two-man to one-man motor patrols.[438] Again, this allows scarce personnel to cover more area at less cost.

The one-man patrol in itself has no major effect on police-community relations unless it leads to changes in other police procedures. It has been suggested that an

---

[429] Governmental Research Institute, "One-Man Police Patrol Car Operation," and O. W. Wilson, "Put the Cop Back on the Beat," both appearing in Samuel G. Chapman, ed., "Police Patrol Readings" (Springfield: Charles C. Thomas, 1964), pp. 129 and 97.
[430] Supra, note 21 at vol. I, pp. 114, 161–162.
[431] Supra, note 172 at p. 27.
[432] Oscar Handlin, "Community Organization as a Solution to Police-Community Problems," The Police Chief, March 1965, p. 22.
[433] Supra, note 15 at p. 106.
[434] Ibid.
[435] The police of New York City, New Rochelle, Washington, D.C., North Bergen, N.J., and Newport, R.I., reported to the Commission that they were experimenting with the use of motor scooters in conjunction with programs to provide transportation for men formerly assigned to foot patrol.
[436] O. W. Wilson, "Put the Cop Back on the Beat," and Thomas J. Rogers, "Review of Foot Patrol in Chicago," both appearing in Samuel G. Chapman, ed., "Police Patrol Readings" (Springfield: Charles C. Thomas, 1964), pp. 97–101; 105–110. Also, police in New York City, Oakland, Berkeley, Kalamazoo, and Meriden, Conn., have been equipped with portable police radios. This concept is discussed in detail in ch. 3.
[437] Supra, note 21 at vol. II, p. 190; and Norman L. Clowers, "One and One-Half Man Cars." Police, March–April 1960, appearing in Samuel G. Chapman, ed., "Police Patrol Readings" (Springfield: Charles C. Thomas, 1964), pp. 102–105.
[438] Supra, note 429 at pp. 129–130.

officer, making an arrest when alone is more likely to try persuasion than force.[439] On the other hand, in San Diego, police policy is to handcuff all persons arrested regardless how minor the crime or inoffensive the person. The reason given is that an officer driving an arrested person alone to the station is so vulnerable to attack that handcuffs are required.[440] Similarly, if officers, particularly in areas of great hostility to the police, are nervous or afraid of being alone, this may well lead them to use a gun or nightstick where it is not needed.

Such problems can be met in ways other than the general use of two-man patrols. When difficult arrests are to be made, at least a second car can be dispatched to the scene. Two-man patrols can be used in high-tension areas even if not needed in other parts of the city. In any event, it is important that the change to one-man patrols not inadvertently lead to police practices harming relations with the public.

Tactical Forces

Increasingly, large urban police forces are creating special units to more effectively control crime. In Washington, it is the tactical force; in New York, the tactical patrol force; in Chicago, the task force; and in Detroit, the tactical mobile unit.[441] In Washington, the force has consisted of 200 regular officers working an extra 8 hours a week.[442] In New York, the force is a carefully selected group of 450 men, which is soon to be increased to 690. All are 6 footers, under 30 years of age, unmarried, picked on the basis of physical ability and intelligence, and are specially trained.[443] Tactical units usually perform special functions such as patrolling in high crime areas, controlling disturbances and riots, and handling demonstrations and other large crowds.

The use of tactical units with relation to disturbances, riots, and crowds in itself need not present any community relations problem. On the contrary, since such units generally receive special training over an extended period of time and have greater experience in handling crowds, it is likely that they will be both more effective from the standpoint of the police and more disciplined and fair in protecting the public. On the other hand, the aggressiveness of one tactical force consisting of highway patrol officers—a ranking officer has called it "a skull-cracking division"—has produced strong public hostility.[444] As a result, one ranking officer has said that

"[W]henever there are sensitive situations developing in my district, or if disturbances actually have broken out, I will be better off if the highway patrol does not come into any district and stimulate violent reaction."[445]

It is important both for effective law enforcement and police-community relations that patrolling officers become intimately acquainted with their assigned neighborhood. Consequently, if crime is high in an area and additional officers are needed in an area on a long-term basis, they should be permanently assigned and special task forces should not be used on routine patrol.[446] Temporary saturation of an area by officers unfamiliar with it should be used only when it is essential in special circumstances such as the likelihood of a disturbance or riot, or an outbreak of robberies, burglaries, or other serious crime problems.

When extra forces are assigned to an area, it is important that they avoid straining police-community relations. Even though most people who live in high-crime areas strongly desire additional police protection,[447] resentment is likely to be increased further if the additional police spend much of their time making many more arrests for minor crimes such as loitering, vagrancy, and drunk-and-disorderly.[448]

The possible community relations problems can be met in several ways. For example, tactical unit officers should not be used to enforce minor crime statutes except in unusual circumstances. When the objective is apprehension rather than deterrence, officers in plain clothes should be used.[449] It is always important that the reason for the use of tactical forces be carefully explained by community relations officers in neighborhoods where they are likely to be used.

Use of Dogs

Although used from time to time since the turn of the century, dogs have been extensively employed in American law enforcement agencies only since 1960. They have been used for searching for intruders in warehouses, stores, and parks; for handling crowds; for tracking suspects; and for finding runaway children. Only in the past 10 years have they been generally used for deterring crime, protecting the officer, and making arrests during routine patrol in high-crime areas. Various police forces report their dog-handler teams have had considerable success in performing all these functions.[450]

Unfortunately, considerable hostility has arisen from using dogs to control crowds, for civil rights demonstrations, and on routine patrol in minority areas.[451] In Washington, D.C., which has the largest canine corps in the country with 92 doghandler teams, the corps formerly patrolled routinely on foot, mostly at night, in high-crime areas.[452] Negro citizen groups in Washington, D.C. have made the use of dogs one of their principal complaints against the police. As one resident asked at a neighborhood meeting, "What do the police use them for anyway except to scare us?"[453] The occasional times when a dog has attacked the wrong person[454] increased Negro fears. As a result, the District of Columbia government agreed in 1965 not to use dogs for crowd control or in any place that is "congested" with people.[455]

The President's Commission on Crime in the District of Columbia in its 1966 report concluded that there existed no adequate measure of the effectiveness of the canine corps; dogs are often hard to handle during the

---

[439] Supra, note 38 at pp. 69, 151–152.
[440] Supra, note 21 at vol. I, p. 143.
[441] Newsweek, June 27, 1966, p. 24.
[442] Supra, note 77 at p. 56.
[443] "Police Increase Tactical Force," New York Times, June 14, 1966, p. 18, col. 6.
[444] Supra, note 21 at Vol. II, p. 46.
[445] Ibid.
[446] Supra, note 9 at p. 250; supra, note 77 at p. 52.
[447] Supra, note 25 at pp. 25–26; supra, note 36 at p. 2.
[448] Supra, note 77 at p. 57. About this issue, the District of Columbia Crime Commission noted that "It has been suggested to the Commission that a number of the many drunk-and-disorderly arrests being made by police officers assigned to the Tactical Force emanate in part from the boredom inherent in its current operations."
[449] Id. at p. 57.
[450] Samuel G. Chapman, "The Dog in Law Enforcement," Police, June 1960, pp. 52–56; Samuel G. Chapman, "Whether to Use Police Dogs," Police, September-October 1961, pp. 62–67; Samuel G. Chapman, "Dogs in Police Work" (Chicago: Chicago Public Administration Service, 1960), pp. 14, 26–27, 39, 40, 43, 46–48; supra, note 96 at pp. 250–251.
[451] Supra, note 22 at pp. 18, 26; California Advisory Committee to the U.S. Commission on Civil Rights, "Report on California: Police-Minority Relations," August 1963, p. 22.
[452] Supra, note 77 at pp. 53–54; "Use of City Canine Corps Stirs Comments," the Washington Post, Nov. 4, 1965, sec. E, p. 4, cols. 1–6
[453] "Use of City Canine Corps Stirs Comments," the Washington Post, Nov. 4, 1965, sec. E, p. 4, cols. 1–6.
[454] "K-9 Corps Dog Bites Wrong Man in Chase," the Washington Post, May 6, 1966, sec. C, p. 3, cols. 1, 2.
[455] "Use of City Canine Corps Stirs Comments," the Washington Post, Nov. 4, 1965, sec. E, p. 4, cols. 1–6.

hot summer months; animosity has developed between observers and the police where dogs have sniffed drunks during arrests. The most serious disadvantage is that "there is a risk that people may see themselves as controlled, rather than protected, by the dogs."[456] Consequently, the Commission recommended that the corps not be expanded without proof of its effectiveness; that "great caution" be exercised in deploying dogs in populated areas; that all requests for use of dogs in particular areas be clearly justified; and that clear directives be issued.[457]

It is likely that in many areas the large majority of residents will accept the prudent use of dogs for routine patrol if this is carefully explained. Even in Washington, D.C., where criticism of their use has been great, the survey by the Bureau of Social Science Research found that 46 percent of Negro men and 60 percent of Negro women who responded favored more use of police dogs.[458] And in St. Louis, after talks in the schools to civic groups, public demonstrations of the use of dogs, and other dissemination of information to the public, the use of such dogs has produced little, if any, consternation in the Negro community.[459]

There is considerable doubt, however, whether dogs should ever be used to control crowds. While the policies of most departments were to use dogs as a last resort in crowd control, if at all, the Michigan State University survey found that they were frequently present at disturbances as "backup" units or for "shows of force."[460] Their use might well increase violence and produce further harm to community relations.

Handling Crowds, Demonstrations, and Riots

Crowds. The police handling of a crowd which could possibly become a riot raises substantial community relations problems. Although the police naturally seek to assemble sufficient personnel to prevent a riot, police in unnecessarily massive numbers may be regarded by minority and perhaps other groups as a provocation.[461] The possibility of provocation through oversaturation can be minimized without interfering with adequate protection, by holding some units on a standby basis a few blocks away and assigning them out of the area as tensions lessened.

It is crucial that careful procedures be developed in advance on proper handling of crowds and that such planning take into account different kinds of crowds. For example, careful preparation was made for dealing with a possibly dangerous crowd prior to a Labor Day motorcycle race at Marlboro, Md., in 1965. Part of the police planning included discussion about how to avoid harsh, indiscriminate treatment of the motorcyclists which could result in unifying them against the police. The police officers were instructed to treat motorcyclists like any visiting motorists in the county. During the weekend, motorcyclists were not harassed, but law violators were dealt with fairly and firmly. The result was not only immediately effective in preventing a riot but the lack of police harassment created good relations for the future.[462]

Demonstrations. One of the primary responsibilities of the police is to protect the constitutional rights of citizens. Part of this responsibility involves cooperating with all legal demonstrations no matter how repugnant the participants or cause may be to policemen personally. They must protect demonstrators against the illegal action of bystanders, and they must take official action against demonstrators if laws are violated.[463] The police must treat competing pickets (who are acting lawfully) equally but must be mindful of the prospects for friction between opposing groups. Such demands are among the hardest facing the police today.

Unfortunately, police action has not always met these necessary standards. As shown earlier, the police, particularly in the South, have sometimes themselves attacked peaceful and clearly legal demonstrators with excessive force and have failed even to try to protect demonstrators from violent attack. These actions, which have received national press and television coverage, have reduced respect for the police not only in the South but throughout the country.

On the other hand, many police forces have received strong, public praise from leaders of demonstrations for their cooperation and fairness regarding demonstrations, such as during the huge and peaceful march on Washington, D.C., in 1963. Such success is not the result of chance. Chief Thomas Cahill has described the elaborate preparations used in San Francisco. The police seek out the leaders of the demonstrators, and then plan with them together. At one demonstration, the police told its leaders of the advisability of monitors with armbands for every 100 demonstrators so that the demonstrators could police themselves. Few uniformed officers were in sight although others were in the vicinity. The demonstration, as Chief Cahill described it, "was one of the most orderly demonstrations that I have ever seen. The leaders paid tribute from the platform, not only to the participants, but also to the police department for their cooperation and assistance."[464]

Before another sit-in demonstration, the leaders came to Chief Cahill's office and told him of the action they proposed to take. They said that they expected to be arrested and together with the Chief they discussed the charge which would be brought. The sit-in occurred, the demonstrators were arrested, and no other problem developed.[465]

Similarly, in New York, peace groups have informed the police department about demonstrations. Ground rules have been established such as placing placards on light, blunt sticks rather than sharp sticks or heavy poles. The number of demonstrators had been limited to prevent unreasonable interference with other citizens.[466]

These examples show that the police can work closely with the leaders of demonstrations and that the latter will frequently work with the police. This requires, however, that the police be completely fair—that they not use the cooperation of the demonstrators against them. It

---

[456] Supra, note 77 at p. 54.
[457] Id. at p. 55.
[458] Supra, note 14 at p. 13B; the same study discloses that 53 percent of the white men and 68 percent of the white women responding favored the use of dogs.
[459] Supra, note 22 at p. 38.
[460] Supra, note 22 at pp. 347–349.
[461] Supra, note 21 at vol. I, p. 158.
[462] Robert Shellow and Derek V. Roemer, "The Riot That Didn't Happen," (unpublished report, 1965).

[463] "New York City Police Commissioner States Policy on Demonstrations," The Police Chief, July 1963, p. 14; Quinn Tamm, editorial, "Police Brutality—Or 'Smokescreen'?" The Police Chief, December 1963, p. 7.
[464] Supra, note 99 at p. 37.
[465] Ibid.
[466] Michael J. Murphy, "Civil Disobedience," The Police Chief, June 1963, pp. 58–59.

also requires that the police be willing to deal with all kinds of groups including those which are generally hostile to them.[467]

It is also important that personnel at demonstrations have special training and experience. For example, Philadelphia has a special squad of 22 police officers, 11 of whom are Negro. The squad has been unusually successful in dealing effectively with demonstrations while maintaining good relations with the demonstrators.[468] Similar results have been achieved by giving special training to a civil disobedience unit in a populous suburban Maryland county near Washington, D.C.[469] The officer should be trained to avoid an unnecessary show of force which would suggest police antagonism to the demonstration, although the police should be ready to handle any situation which might arise. Before reporting to their stations, all officers should be specifically informed about the demonstration, and police strategy, and be briefed on contingency plans.[470]

Finally, if arrest is required, demonstrators should be treated courteously and humanely. As former Commissioner Murphy of New York has stated: [471]

We may well be headed toward a situation where we will feel obliged to say "pardon me" as we escort the violator to the waiting patrol wagon. But, gentlemen, if our work is to be done properly that "pardon me" will in no way interfere with the speed and efficiency of the arrest process.

Riots. The police have little control over the social, economic, or other factors which create riots; however, a good and comprehensive community relations program is the best method of riot control available to the police, for most riots are at least triggered by police action.[472] If the police had genuinely good relations with all segments of the public, some riots could doubtless be prevented.

Police activities to prevent riots can cause serious police-community relations problems. For example, on some occasions, a show of force can be unwarranted and provocative.[473]

The unanswered question is: Could other police measures have met the objections of the neighborhood residents and still have prevented a riot? Some alternatives might have included using fewer cars, patrolling in unmarked cars, and patrolling without the show of weapons. For example, in Philadelphia, the police have had unusual success in employing as little force as possible although much greater additional force is nearby.[474] Similarly, in Washington, D.C., when a disturbance began in August 1966, the police sealed off the crowd and called in civilian leaders who could calm it.[475]

Once a disturbance or riot is in progress, of course, the dominant consideration must be to end it. However, even then, it is extremely important that the means used be weighed for their effect on police-community relations. This is essential since actions which stir up antagonism in turn may prolong the riot and increase the likelihood of future ones. Alternative methods of equal, or virtually equal, effectiveness may be available for controlling the riot which will cause less serious damage to police-community relations. For example, the common police technique in controlling riots is to use a massive amount of force to break up the rioters into small groups as soon as possible. Snipers are generally answered in kind; batons, dogs, and tear gas may be used.

In contrast, New York City, during the summer of 1966, employed a different method. When a mob formed, the police did not try to break it up directly. They blocked off streets but left open an avenue of "escape" for the mob. The mob ther generally dissipated. No shots were fired by the police in answer to sporadic sniping and the emphasis was on restraint. Despite a week of disturbances, no major riot resulted, police casualties were light, and the department earned considerable praise from the community.[476]

It is debatable which methods are most effective for preventing and controlling a riot. Certainly, it is unfair to second guess police action long after the event. Yet it is important to note that the techniques used in New York and Washington improved, rather than hurt, community attitudes toward the police. At least, these examples show that considerations of police-community relations should be a major factor in developing plans relating to disturbances and riots.

To help local departments plan, the Commission assisted the FBI in preparing a manual, "Prevention and Control of Mobs and Riots," which was published by the FBI in April, 1967.

ENSURING FAIRNESS

INTERNAL PROCEDURES

The best way to deal with police misconduct is to prevent it by effective methods of personnel screening, sufficient training, constant retraining, and supervision. A department that clearly articulates its community-relations policies and holds its members to abide by them should receive a minimum of complaints from citizens. However, there will always be citizen complaints, warranted and unwarranted, about treatment by the police. And there will always be misconduct by individual officers about which no complaint will be made. How complaints should be handled and how misconduct should be dealt with has been the subject of perhaps the fiercest of the many controversies about the police that has raged in recent years.

Without question, the best means for ensuring that personnel are complying with departmental policies and general notions of fairness is through effective internal police procedures. Internal discipline can be swifter and, because imposed by the officers' own superiors, more effective. If properly carried out, internal discipline can assure the public that the department's policies concerning community relations are fully meant and enforced. This is particularly true when the department's own investigation discovers misconduct without any citizen complaint.

Strong discipline shows the public that misconduct is

---

[467] Supra, note 174 at pp. 156–158.
[468] Supra, note 21 at p. 84.
[469] Robert Shellow, "Reenforcing Police Neutrality in Civil Rights Confrontations," Journal of Applied Behavior Science, 1:243–254.
[470] Supra, note 174 at p. 163.
[471] Supra, note 466 at p. 59.
[472] See Assessment Task Force Volume of the report of the President's Commission on Law Enforcement and the Administration of Justice.
[473] Supra, note 21 at vol. I, pp. 80–81.
[474] Id. at vol. II, pp. 39–41, 190–191.
[475] Claude Koprowski and Jesse W. Lewis, Jr., "Police Curb Outbreak in Northeast," the Washington Post, Aug. 24, 1966, sec. A, p. 1, col. 1.
[476] "More Stress Put on Role of Police 'Peace Officer'," Jamaica, N.Y., Long Island Press, July 28, 1966, sec. 1, p. 14, cols. 1, 2 Thomas A. Johnson, "New Police Plan Used on Crowds," New York Times, July 25, 1966, p. 16, col. 6.

merely the action of individual officers—the few who violate the rules in any organization—and not action which is customarily tolerated in the department. Consequently, high priority should be given to improving internal police procedures so that they can satisfy as much of the public as possible concerning their fairness and effectiveness.

Internal Investigations

Formal machinery within every police department for the investigation of complaints against police activity or employees and for the determination of whether departmental policy is being carried out is an absolute necessity. Most large police departments now have procedures of some kind for dealing with charges of misconduct by their members, whether those charges originate inside or outside of the department. When such machinery is fully and fairly used, in concert with internal investigation and inspection programs, it succeeds both in disciplining misbehaving officers and deterring others from misbehaving.

The job of ensuring fairness and good community relations requires continuous monitoring and creates a need at all times for information as to how well departmental directives are being carried out and what new problems are developing. There are numerous means through which an aggressive leadership can fill this need. For example, if the department has an active program of working with community groups, much information can be gained through direct communication. An alert inspection unit will provide valuable information, particularly regarding problem areas and the relative effectiveness of different personnel units and techniques. Internal investigations also provide important information about the conduct of individual officers. Once the department has obtained information concerning possible misconduct or violations of policies relating to community relations, it must give the same dedication and attention to further investigation and, when appropriate, punishment as it gives to other vital areas of police work.

Many police agencies have recognized this need and are seeking to meet it. But in many, the programs are seriously inadequate and in all those examined during the Commission's studies there is room for improvement. The purpose of this section is to suggest machinery for handling complaints and enforcing policy.

American police departments have long faced problems in fighting corruption and the best departments have responded by developing specialized investigative machinery to deal with them. These internal investigative units, described in chapters 3 and 7, operating independently under a senior officer, have proved valuable in attempts to control corruption. The internal investigation units should be just as diligent in sampling the conduct of its officers and ferreting out misconduct against citizens as in ferreting out corruption. For example, they should be willing to observe police conduct on the street, to have men in stationhouses to determine whether physical abuse occurs, and to utilize other promising investigative techniques. In 1966, Chicago established an Undue Force Unit within the Internal Investigation Division. The Unit is commanded by a Lieutenant and consists of 8 Negro and 7 white investigators.

Policemen all too often, because of misplaced loyalty, overlook serious misconduct by other officers. This has relevance to community relations as well as corruption. The Michigan State survey indicates that there is seldom any established procedures to accommodate the complaint of one officer against another and that "nearly every organization contacted made it extremely difficult both formally and informally for a patrolman to inform higher officials of improper conduct on the part of his fellow officers or his supervisors. The departments nearly always require an exhaustion of the chain of command before pressing a complaint elsewhere." [477]

An officer should in no way be discouraged from reporting misconduct of other personnel. This will only serve to perpetuate misconduct. Rather, a department should provide a suitable procedure whereby misconduct of other officers and of superiors can be reported outside of normal channels, if necessary. In 1966 such procedures were in effect in the Boise, Idaho, force: [478]

Reporting Violations of Laws, Ordinances, Rules or Orders

If you know of other members or employees violating laws, ordinances, or rules of the department, or disobeying orders, you shall report same in writing to the chief of police via official channels. If you believe the information is of such sensitivity or such gravity that it must be brought to immediate personal attention of the chief of police you may bypass official channels.

Citizen Complaints

No department can be expected to operate without some misconduct at times by some of its personnel. Every department can, however, be expected to attempt to discover its faults, correct them where possible, and learn from them. Since law enforcement is primarily a business which deals with the public and must have its trust, complaints by citizens offer a unique opportunity—a channel for communication that may otherwise not exist, a means for discovering failures to follow department policies, a method for the redress of grievances, and an early warning of larger troubles. How a department treats such complaints is a general index of its concern or lack of concern for community relations.

Although some departments have recognized the vital role that a good complaint procedure can play in police administration, too few forces today have adequate procedures for dealing with complaints. The Michigan State survey found, that "there exists a widespread distrust of the internal police trial procedures by the major minority groups around the country." [479] The University of California study made a similar finding as to Philadelphia and San Diego.[480] Although some of the reasons for distrust are unjustified, there is a basis for the feeling that many departments have adopted procedures which discourage rather than encourage the filing of complaints and which are unfair either to the complainant or to the officer complained against.

---

[477] Supra, note 22 at pp. 137–138.
[478] Police Department of Boise, Idaho, "Police Manual," p. 6, quoted in supra, note 22 at p. 141.
[479] Supra, note 22 at p. 223.
[480] Supra, note 21 at vol. I, pp. 57–58, 89, 172–173; vol. II at p. 100.

Reception of Complaints. Since citizen complaints are extremely important to police departments, efforts should be made to encourage citizens with grievances to file them. Unfortunately, police officers and departments often regard a citizen complaint as an attack on the police as a whole rather than a complaint against an individual officer,[481] and therefore, attempt to discourage citizens from filing them. The discouraging of citizen complaints not only deprives a department of valuable information but also convinces the public that the kinds of practices complained about are condoned or even expected.

Several methods of discouraging complaints have been practiced in the past. In one large eastern city, for example, the police department used to charge many of those who filed complaints of police misconduct with filing false reports with the police. In 1962, 16 of 41 persons (almost 40 percent) who filed complaints were arrested for filing false charges, in comparison with the arrest of only 104 of 33,593 persons (0.3 percent) who filed similar charges against private citizens.[482] Officers sometimes told prospective complainants that all statements must be made under oath and that they could be charged with false reporting. Such a statement is apt to discourage complaints whether or not such charges are actually filed. In 1965, the Commissioners of the District of Columbia issued an order forbidding the police to file a charge of "false report" without their specific approval.[483] However, the practice, as of 1966, was to drop criminal charges against a person if he would agree to withdraw his complaint or agree not to file one. Similar procedures have discouraged complaints in New York and other localities.[484]

In Philadelphia, the police review board found in 1959 "that it seemed to be standard police procedure to charge a person with resisting arrest or disorderly conduct whenever the person charges the police with brutality."[485] It also found some evidence that two complainants had been intimidated—one by arrest at the completion of the hearing and one by harassment before it. Following the board's recommendation, the Commissioner ordered that such practices be "immediately discontinued."[486] However, the University of California study found that there is still "fear of police retaliation if a complaint is lodged against a police officer."[487] An observer from Michigan State University reported the following incident: [488]

A Negro stopped the police supervisor with whom our staff member was riding. The Negro indicated that two officers had mistreated him earlier in the night and he wanted to make a formal complaint. * * * The supervisor suggested to the complainant that the complaint was going to cause everybody a lot of trouble. He recommended that the whole thing be dropped because if it was not the complainant would have to miss a lot of work, etc., to pursue it. After listening to the supervisor, the complainant went on his way, and as far as the staff member knows, the complaint never received further attention.

The survey concluded that, through a variety of techniques "there was a tendency to discourage complaints against police officers." [489]

The mechanics of receiving complaints often tends to discourage potential complainants from taking any action. Some procedures are so little known, so complex, or so hard to pursue that the ordinary citizen either gives up or never tries in the first place. Indeed, 75 percent of police departments have no formal complaint requirements at all.[490]

Police departments should ensure that officers in no way discourage the filing of complaints. Once complaints are filed, they should be transmitted immediately to the proper bureau. When made a complaint should be accepted: (1) whether reported in person, in writing, or by telephone; (2) whether made anonymously, sworn to, or in any other form; and (3) whether from the victim, an eyewitness, a person who has merely heard of the incident, or an organization such as a civil rights group.

Prosecution for other charges should never depend in any way on whether the defendant has made or dropped a complaint. Even if the complaining citizen wishes to drop the complaint, the department should continue its investigations, if only to prevent any possibility that complaining witnesses will be discouraged or intimidated. As in Chicago, records of all complaints should be kept and, as in Detroit, settlements should be reviewed by the Chief of Police or another high-ranking official.[491]

Departments should advertise widely, as Oakland and New York have done, that they seek out all complaints of police misbehavior of any type.[492] Complaint forms should be available for civic organizations, civil rights groups, antipoverty agencies, and neighborhood advisory committees.[493] Advisory committees should be constantly reminded to encourage residents with complaints to bring them forward.[494]

Complaint Investigations. Although 90 percent of police departments surveyed by Michigan State and the National League of Cities now require an investigation of all citizen complaints, many forces do not have a designated special unit for dealing with complaints. Those forces lacking such units in the survey group tended to be State police organizations, departments in cities below 75,000 population, and southern departments. But there were some larger cities as well. The following tabulation shows the means available in departments for processing citizen complaints: [495]

	Michigan State Survey N=57		National League of Cities Survey N=395	
	Number	Percent	Number	Percent
No special unit	27	47.3	114	28.8
Special unit	29	50.8	191	48.3
No answer or other	1	1.7	90	22.8

---

[481] Supra, note 21, vol. I, pp. 153–154; vol. II at pp. 100, 187.
[482] National Capital Area Civil Liberties Union, "A Proposed Revision of the System for Processing Complaints Against Police Misconduct in the District of Columbia," June 1964, p. 17.
[483] Ibid.; supra, note 77 at pp. 76–78.
[484] Ibid.
[485] Philadelphia Police Review Board, "First Annual Report," Sept. 15, 1959, p. 5.
[486] Id. at p. 6.
[487] Supra, note 21, at vol. II, p. 164; vol. I at p. 174.
[488] Supra, note 22 at p. 192.
[489] Id. at p. 217.
[490] Note, "The Administration of Complaints by Civilians Against the Police," Harvard Law Review, 77:502.

[491] Supra, note 490 at p. 502.
[492] "Police Complaint Procedures," Oakland Police Department, Bulletin from the Office of the Chief, June 10, 1966, p. 1; Police Commissioner Vincent D. Broderick, "Improvements in the Procedures of the Police Department's Civilian Complaint Review Board," statement before the Committee on City Affairs of the City Council of New York City, June 29, 1965, Community Relations Press Release No. 62.
[493] Ibid. In Oakland, copies of the complaint form have been provided in bulk to churches, business associations, civil rights and poverty groups. See Id. at p. 2.
[494] Supra, note 22.
[495] Supra, note 22 at p. 194. The National League of Cities data are from its Department of Urban Studies.

Although the best police practice has long recognized the utility of internal investigative units for controlling corruption, the Michigan State survey found that of those forces which had some kind of special unit, only half were internal investigation units: [496]

Units	Departments responding	
	Number	Percent
Internal investigation	15	50.0
Bureau of Staff Services	5	16.6
Community relations	2	6.6
Personnel	2	6.6
Other	6	20.0

The Michigan State study confirmed that discipline is still regarded as a function of line supervisors. It noted that, even in a department with an internal investigation unit, in 70 percent of complaints investigated, the investigation was performed by the district personnel where the accused officer was assigned.[497] In total, fewer than 5 percent of the 191 departments responding to a 1963 survey relied exclusively on a special unit to investigate citizens' complaints.[498]

An internal investigations unit—or a designated individual in smaller departments—is necessary both to organizational control and to good community relations. The Michigan State and University of California surveys found that in departments without units, where investigations were conducted by the line unit involved, they were often haphazard and dependent on the attitude of the particular line commander; an independent, objective investigation was more difficult to obtain and, even if this was accomplished, suspicion of the result was more likely; records were generally inadequate; and department regulations were often not followed or were unclear.[499] Consequently, as the International Association of Chiefs of Police and the President's Commission on Crime in the District of Columbia recommended for the Washington, D.C., Police Department, all citizen complaints should be handled, not merely supervised, by the specialized unit.[500] The unit should be commanded by a high ranking officer who reports directly to the chief.

According to the Michigan State study, the caliber of investigations varied from completely inadequate to excellent. The difference tended to depend on the attitudes of the supervisors and investigators—that is, on the commitment of the department to ferret out misconduct directed at citizens. Investigators sometimes discourage complaints by calling on complainants repeatedly at work or coming to their homes in marked police cars.[501] The study concluded that most departments needed closer supervision of investigators to ensure adherence to regulations and adequate investigation.[502]

Resolution of Complaints. The Michigan State survey found numerous weaknesses in procedures to resolve complaints. For example, in one department, the commander of the internal affairs bureau indicated that there had been some civil judgments holding policemen liable but that the department did not believe any of the cases merited disciplinary action. The department had no records concerning any of these cases. Between 1960 and 1965, this department had investigated 121 excessive force complaints and had sustained none.[503]

During the survey, approximately 300 departments were polled regarding their internal disciplinary proceedings. Of the 63 departments reporting, 5 percent found that 40 to 50 percent of the complaints they received had some merit and were sustained. In contrast, 50 percent of the departments found that less than 10 percent of the complaints they received were valid. Ten percent of the departments could not decide 70 to 100 percent of the complaints as true or not while 40 percent could decide in at least 90 percent of the complaint situations.[504] A more detailed examination of excessive force complaints in five cities, based in part on confidential departmental records, also indicates a wide variation in the number of complaints sustained.[505]

These figures reveal, as was found by Michigan State, that "there is such a wide variation in the disposition of complaints that the public at times has cause to suspect that the police may not always be handling their complaints properly." [506] As Deputy Chief Klug of Cincinnati has said: [507]

> The thing that bothers me is that police continue to receive huge numbers of complaints but there are only a few instances where the complainant is upheld. They can't be wrong that much—and we can't be right that much.

Police complaint investigative procedures in most departments must be substantially improved to obtain results which are just to all the parties and give the appearance of fairness. At present, the procedures in most departments have many deficiencies. For example, a study by the Harvard Law Review in 1963 found that 70 percent of police departments surveyed had no formal hearings even for serious complaints; almost half with hearings held them in secret; the complainant could not examine witnesses in 20 percent; he was entitled to the department's investigative report in only 5 percent; and in 20 percent, the complainant and officer were not entitled to the assistance of counsel.[508] The Michigan State survey found that the trial board in one city is ineffective because of the lack of the subpoena power; that in many cities the secrecy of trial boards leads to public distrust; that the denial to complainants of a right to a hearing or, if one is held, to present witnesses or to testify themselves, produces charges of unfairness; and that organizational and procedural complexity, the lack of information given to the public, and lack of supervision of police personnel discourages many complaints.[509]

All departments must reassess their existing hearing procedures to determine whether they meet appropriate standards of fairness for all parties. Certainly, such reassessment should determine whether departmental hearing officers are properly screened to ensure against decisions which are based upon prejudice or preference. A reassessment of hearing procedures should also confront issues such as whether both parties should be entitled to

---

[496] Id. at pp. 196, 198.
[497] Id. at p. 211.
[498] Supra, note 490 at p. 504.
[499] Supra, note 22 at pp. 202–204, 218–221; supra, note 21 at vol. I, pp. 170–172, 174; and vol. II at p. 239.
[500] Supra, note 77 at pp. 80–81.
[501] Supra, note 22 at p. 220.
[502] Id. at pp. 218–223.
[503] Id. at p. 172.
[504] Id. at pp. 201a, 201b.
[505] Supra, note 22 at pp. 169, 171.
[506] Id. at p. 203.
[507] Richard Severo, "Today's Police Cast in Role of an Enemy of Society," the Washington Post, June 26, 1966, sec. A, p. 6, cols. 1, 2, 3.
[508] Supra, note 490 at pp. 505–508.
[509] Supra, note 22 at pp. 223–227.

counsel, whether both should have subpoena power, whether both should be entitled to be present during the entire hearing, whether both should have the right to cross-examination, whether transcripts should be provided, whether hearings should be formal or informal and whether all hearings should be opened to the public.

The following procedures seem consistent with the best practices:

1. Minor complaints should be resolved through informal procedures or summary punishment wherever possible. Often a formal apology from the department or the expunging of an arrest record will be sufficient where such a complaint has merit.

2. Serious complaints, such as physical or verbal abuse, discrimination, or harassment, should always go through normal departmental procedures for serious punishment unless the investigation shows no evidence at all of misconduct.

3. Such procedures should include, as is now the practice in most departments, a hearing before a trial board unless the department is so small that the chief of police can himself conduct the hearing. If a board is convened, its members should be carefully screened for impartiality and lack of prejudice. The hearing should be open to the public; the complainant and any witnesses he desires should be present; both the officer and the complainant should have subpoena powers, be represented by counsel, and be able to see the investigative report if they so desire; there should be opportunity for cross-examination by both the officer and the complainant; if desired by any party, a transcript should be made; and the decision should be prompt—probably no more than a month, except in unusual cases, after a complaint is filed. The trial board should render an opinion containing findings of all important facts and explaining its reasoning.

In some cities, disciplinary hearings are conducted by civil service commissions or by other agencies which are independent of the police department. In these cities, the agencies responsible for discipline must undertake the same type of reassessment of procedures that must be undertaken by police departments. Where necessary, laws or ordinances should be revised.

Discipline. The need for reassessment is not limited to hearing procedures. It is also essential that existing disciplinary policies be reexamined. Many persons have charged that where officers are found guilty of misconduct relating to abuse of authority or community relations, they are either punished too lightly or not at all. On the other hand, in some cities, associations of police officers or police unions complain that disciplinary actions assessed by the chief or statutory authority are often too severe for minor misconduct. The Michigan Civil Rights Commission concluded with regard to one large department:[510]

The record of disciplinary actions taken by the Department in civil rights violations shows a practice of differential treatment. Disciplinary action went beyond written reprimand in only two instances where civil rights violations were charged. In too many cases the disciplinary measures invoked are not consistent with the seriousness of the offense. * * *

The Commission has emphasized to the Department the principle that disciplinary measures taken in civil rights cases must receive the same consideration as discipline applied in other violations.

The Michigan State survey concluded that "probably the strongest criticism that can be offered is that seldom is meaningful disciplinary action taken against officers guilty of one or more of the forms of brutality."[511]

In contrast, many police departments impose severe and automatic punishments for comparatively minor violations of regulations. For example, in Philadelphia, department regulations impose the same penalty—reprimand to 5 days' suspension for a first offense—for "[u]sing rude or insulting language or conduct offensive to the public" as for "unexcused tardiness" or "occupying a seat in a public conveyance while in uniform to the exclusion of paying passengers."[512]

Clearly, police departments must take steps to insure that punishments more suitable to the offense committed are given. This will require that all departments examine penalties to determine whether they are effective in deterring future misconduct and whether they are justified when the nature of the offense is considered.

Publicizing the Decision. Once the decision on a complaint has been made, the complainant should be notified of the decision and of the basis for it And the public should have access to the facts of the case and the nature of the decision. Unless the public has access to reliable information, it is likely to assume the worst.[513] On the other hand, if complainants are told of the disposition, "[t]hey would know that the Department is concerned and that their complaint was not thrown in the wastebasket."[514]

Michigan State found that in 50 of 57 police departments notification of disposition of the complainant was given automatically, but that in 4, it was given only on request and in 3, not at all. Only 25 of the 57 departments surveyed by Michigan State, however, made investigative reports public to any extent while 32 did not at all.[515]

In addition, when an incident or series of incidents has raised tension in an area, it will often be desirable for the determination to be announced and explained directly to the residents of the area either through the community relations unit, a neighborhood advisory meeting, or some other similar procedure.[516] An annual report by the police department providing such facts as the number and kinds of complaints, the kinds of people who made them, the disposition of the complaint, and the punishments imposed can also make a useful contribution to better public understanding.

EXTERNAL REVIEW

In view of the increasing involvement of government officials in the lives of citizens, adequate procedures for the consideration of such individual grievances as citizens may have against such officials are essential. So far as possible, it is desirable that procedures for the considera-

---

[510] Supra, note 382 at p. 5.
[511] Supra, note 22 at p. 186.
[512] Supra, note 21 at vol. II, pp. 201–202.
[513] Id. at vol. I pp. 172, 175.
[514] Interview with a Mexican-American leader in San Diego, supra, note 21 at vol. I, p. 92.
[515] Supra, note 22 at p. 200.

[516] The San Mateo County Sheriff's Department notifies the NAACP, American Civil Liberties Union, or other appropriate "social action groups that might reasonably be expected to have an interest" in citizen complaints, and these groups are kept informed as the investigation proceeds. If the group decides to conduct an investigation, the Sheriff's Office cooperates with it. San Mateo County, California Sheriff's Office Information Bulletin No. 25, "Procedure for Handling Personnel Complaints Involving Persons from Minority Groups," pp. 1–2.

tion of individual grievances against policemen—as well as grievances against other governmental officials or employees—be established within the governmental agency involved.

In all jurisdictions, if a complainant remains dissatisfied with the internal disposition of a case, there are other avenues of appeal outside the police agency: The local prosecutor; the courts; elected officials such as councilmen or the mayor; the State's attorney general; and the U.S. Department of Justice. In some jurisdictions, other forums exist such as civil rights or human relations commissions, civilian review boards, and ombudsmen. While these institutions have procedures for processing citizen grievances about the conduct of public officers or employees, they are frequently too formal, awesome, expensive, or geographically far removed from the often bewildered citizen. Some of them lack the machinery or resources to process grievances properly. Some can take action only if a criminal law has been violated and many acts of misconduct complained of do not qualify as a basis for criminal action.

In going beyond the established legal procedures, the Commission found it unreasonable to single out the police as the only agency which should be subject to special scrutiny from the outside. The Commission, therefore, did not recommend the establishment of civilian review boards in jurisdictions where they do not exist, solely to review police conduct. The police department is only one of a number of official agencies with whom the public has contact, and in some cases, because the police are the most visible and conspicuous representatives of local government, they may be the focus of more attention than they deserve. Incompetence and mistreatment by housing, sanitation, health, and welfare officials can be as injurious to citizens as mistreatment by the police and should be equally subject to public scrutiny. These officials, like policemen, are public servants.

If an agency's internal procedures for review of citizen grievances are ineffective or fail to inspire public confidence, including the confidence of those who may have legitimate grievances, further recourse is essential. The form that such further recourse should take is dependent on local needs and governmental structure.

The following section examines the various methods now utilized in different jurisdictions for external review of citizen complaints. Essentially, they present the several alternatives from which each jurisdiction can choose the most appropriate method of civilian recourse. It deserves emphasis that the following description of various techniques that some jurisdictions are using or have used for external review of citizen complaints is included here to make available the results of research by the Commission staff and consultants. It is not intended in any way to indicate endorsement by the Commission or its Police Panel. The position of the Commission and the Panel on the subject of external review is set forth in the preceding paragraphs of this section and at page 103 of the Commission's General Report.

Review by Civilian Officials

Unless limited by a statute assigning final authority to discipline police officers to the police chief, civil service commission, or some other body, the mayor or city council normally has the power to review any such determination. However, this authority is rarely exercised effectively because the elected officials neither have the time nor the staff to consider carefully individual cases. As a result, the relatively few complaints made to elected officials are generally referred to the police department for investigation and determination with little, if any, review by the elected officials.

In 50 of 55 cities responding to the Michigan State University survey, no such review existed. In two cities, there was further review before a civilian board appointed by the chief executive; in two, before the public safety director; and in one, the chief executive.[517]

In the District of Columbia, the Board of Commissioners reviews all summary hearings and trial board cases. The Board almost invariably approves the disciplinary actions. From 1962 through 1965, the Board affirmed 86 of 92 trial board determinations, modified 3, and reversed 3.[518]

In Cincinnati, either the officer or the complainant can appeal to the civilian director of public safety who is superior to the chief of police. The chief of police can decide to hold a new hearing.[519]

In Chicago, a five-man police board, appointed by the mayor, supervises the police department. In disciplinary matters, the case is presented to the board by the city council and the five members sit as a reviewing body. The accused officer may appear with counsel if he chooses. While it does not now do so, the police board has authority to hear appeals by citizens from the police superintendent's decision.[520]

Court Review

Some kinds of police conduct have traditionally been subject to review by the courts. It is very difficult to determine what impact this kind of review has had on police-community relations. It seems likely, however, that, except where the exclusionary rule has been applied, judicial influence has not been substantial. There are several reasons why this is so.

Criminal Law. The relevance of the criminal law to police-community relations is limited by the fact that many forms of police misconduct affecting police-community relations, such as verbal abuse, coercion of respect and the like, are not violations of the criminal law. It is further limited by the problem of proof and credibility of testimony. In many cases, the only witnesses to the misconduct are the policeman and the alleged victim, and often the alleged victim and nonpolice witnesses are from minority groups, are poor or unemployed, or have criminal records.[521] Finally, many prosecutors are reluctant to bring charges except in serious cases because they work so closely with the police.[522]

---

[517] Supra, note 22 at p. 200.
[518] Supra, note 77 at p. 77.
[519] Supra, note 22 at p. 206.
[520] Id. at pp. 213–214.
[521] Supra, note 331 at p. 63.
[522] Id. at p. 80.

In some jurisdictions, special procedures have been established to insure that complaints against the police which may amount to criminal offenses are brought to the attention of the prosecutor. In Los Angeles County, the district attorney has gone a step further and established a special section within the division of investigation to deal with alleged official misconduct. This section investigates complaints of illegal conduct against all local officials including the police, monitors investigations of particular officers by the police departments themselves, and investigates all homicides by police officers.[523]

Such procedures are helpful. However, the basic problem is to assure that prosecutors enforce the criminal law as vigorously against public officers as against private citizens. Since it is sometimes difficult for local prosecutors to prosecute local public officials, authority should be given to State's attorneys general to bring such cases when necessary.

The principal Federal criminal statute with relevance to police misconduct is section 242 of title 18 which prohibits the deprivation "under the color of any law * * * of any rights, privileges or immunities secured or protected by the Constitution or laws of the United States * * * on account of such inhabitant being an alien or by reason of his color or race." In *Screws* v. *United States*, however, the Supreme Court interpreted the statute to require that the prosecution prove not merely that the defendant sheriff had beaten a helpless prisoner to death but that he "had the purpose to deprive the prisoner of a constitutional right." [524]

In 1961, the Civil Rights Commission found this statute largely ineffective and criticized the forcefulness with which it had been enforced.[525] In 1965, it found that enforcement had improved somewhat due to the addition of personnel to the Civil Rights Division of the Department of Justice. Seventy-three cases had been brought in 2 years, an increase of 75 percent.[526] In April 1966, the President asked Congress to authorize an additional 100 FBI agents and supporting personnel to deal with this kind of crime and Congress did so.

In 1961 and again in 1965, the Civil Rights Commission recommended that section 242 be clarified by specifically making it a crime to perform, maliciously under color of law, certain prescribed acts including the following: [527]

1. Subjecting any person to physical injury for an unlawful purpose;
2. Subjecting any person to unnecessary force during the course of an arrest or while the person is being held in custody;
3. Subjecting any person to violence or unlawful restraint in the course of eliciting a confession to a crime or any other information.

Civil Remedies. If an officer is guilty of misconduct, civil damages are legally available. Damages may include losses for physical injuries, medical costs, loss of earnings, harm to reputation, injury to property, and, in some instances, pain and suffering. Abuse which is purely verbal, however, is not usually recompensable. If a judgment is awarded, it can influence the future action of officers or policies of a department, regardless of whether the judgment is paid by the officer himself, an insurance company, or the city.

In a few jurisdictions, civil actions are frequently brought in cases involving excessive force. During 1965, citizens filed 237 suits against New York City alleging police brutality; in 35, claims totalling $169,482 were settled or were sustained at trial. From July 1, 1963, to July 1, 1964, 326 actions were brought and the city paid out $232,425 in 72 cases.[528]

While civil cases are more frequent than criminal cases, particularly in large cities, civil litigation also has serious difficulties. The chief witnesses are still likely to be the alleged victim and the officer. Even if a victim is successful, the officer may not be able to pay the judgment. Unless the prospect of payment is substantial, there is little incentive for the victim to incur the costs of investigation and counsel necessary to the suit or for counsel to take the case on a contingent fee basis.[529]

In many States, the alternative of suit against the city or State which employs the officer is blocked by the doctrine of sovereign immunity. In an increasing number of others, however, this has been changed by statute or court decision.[530] Most of the judicial decisions have involved negligent actions by government officials and therefore it is often not clear whether the governmental entity is liable for nonnegligent misconduct, the kind which most often affects community relations. In Illinois and Connecticut, police officers are entitled to indemnification for recoveries against them.[531] And in some States, policemen and sheriffs must post bond for the conduct of their officers.[532]

Procedures should be adopted in all jurisdictions to permit citizens to recover civil damages if they can prove damages due to officer misconduct. This may require waiver of sovereign immunity, requirements of bonding, provision for payment of counsel, or other changes in the law. In some instances, however, bonding and indemnification may lessen the deterrent effect.

The Federal civil statute, 42 U.S.C. 1983, is almost identical to the Federal criminal statute except that it does not require proof that the officer intended to deny the citizen a constitutional right. It covers not only excessive force but arrest without probable cause, illegal searches,[533] and other violations of constitutional rights by police officers, and provides for injunctions as well as money damages.

In the 2-year period beginning in 1959, only 42 such suits were brought "for police brutality"—with few judgments awarded—and in 1961, the Civil Rights Commission concluded that this section was ineffective.[534] The Civil Rights Commission therefore recommended that the statute should be amended (1) to allow suits against the local government as well as the police officer and (2) to allow the district courts to award costs and reasonable attorney's fees both in cases for damages and in cases for injunctive relief.[535] No action has yet been taken on this recommendation.

---

[523] Frank Riley, "The D.A.'s Answer to Police Brutality," Los Angeles Magazine, March 1966; District Attorney Evelle J. Younger, "Report to the Governor's Commission on the Los Angeles Riots," Oct. 28, 1955, pp. 42, 46–47.
[524] 325 U.S. 91, 107.
[525] Supra, note 331 at p. 67.
[526] Supra, note 335 at pp. 112–118.
[527] Supra, note 331 at pp. 112–113; and supra, note 335 at p. 178, note 2.
[528] Walter Gellhorn, "When Americans Complain: Government Grievance Procedure" (Cambridge: Harvard Press, 1966), p. 184.

[529] Supra, note 331 at p. 71.
[530] Id. at pp. 81–82; Marshall S. Shapo, "Municipal Liability for Police Torts: An Analysis of the Strand of American Legal History," University of Miami Law Review 17: 475–518.
[531] Id. at pp. 505–506.
[532] See, e.g. Ken. Rev. Stat. 95: 750 (1959).
[533] *Monroe* v. *Pape*, 365 U.S. 167.
[534] Supra, note 331 at p. 69.
[535] Id. at p. 113.

Court Exclusion of Evidence. In addition to those cases in which the courts are asked to review police conduct directly by way of a prosecution or civil action for damages, police conduct may come before the courts in the course of a normal prosecution. For example, a court may be asked to admit evidence which a police officer seized illegally or to accept a confession which the police obtained in some way not in accordance with law. In this kind of case, the Supreme Court has over a period of time developed a set of rules which prohibits the use of this kind of evidence. The impact of these rules, however, is limited to police conduct which is designed to obtain evidence for use in a criminal case.[536] This is only one type of abuse which must be protected against, and only a small proportion of police abuses have this purpose.

Civilian Review Boards

Many citizens, particularly those from minority groups and civil rights organizations, have been dissatisfied with police internal review procedures. They have urged the creation of civilian review boards to investigate and determine the validity of citizen complaints. Civilian review boards of one sort or another were established in Washington, D.C. (in 1948), Philadelphia (in 1958), Minneapolis and York, Pennsylvania (in 1960), Rochester (in 1963), and New York City (in 1966). Boards have been proposed in many other cities, including Chicago, Cincinnati, Detroit, Los Angeles, Oakland, Newark, Pittsburgh, and Seattle. Bills have been introduced in the California, Massachusetts, and New York legislatures to require large cities or the State to form such boards.[537]

But civilian review boards have had a stormy history. The boards in Philadelphia and Rochester have been the subject of court suits with injunctions against their operation during part of their lives. The board in Washington, D.C., was severely criticized for inaction and was thoroughly reorganized in 1965. The boards in Minneapolis and York never actually operated, and the board in New York City after a very heated campaign, was rejected by the electorate and has been replaced by a board composed of civilian police employees.

While those boards which have gone into operation differed somewhat in organization and detail, their basic concept has been the same. They have been advisory only, having no power to decide cases. The New York City and Washington, D.C., boards have even lacked the power to indicate their views on the merits of the case, being limited to recommending whether a police trial was necessary or not. The details of operation of four such boards are described in the following chart: [538]

Civilian Review Board, Organization and Procedures

	New York	Philadelphia	Rochester	Washington
1. Number of members	7 (3 police)	8 (including 2 former police officers)	9	7 (2 attorneys)
2. Staff	Civilian executive director, deputy director and assistant director, 2 civilian hearing officers and staff of police officers	Full-time executive secretary	Part-time executive secretary	None
3. Jurisdiction	Any misconduct concerning community relations	Any misconduct concerning community relations	Excessive or unnecessary force	Any misconduct
4. Who may complain	Any person or group including anonymously	Victim or interested person or organization	Victim or his representative	Victim only
5. Who investigates	Board staff	Police board can also investigate	Police, but board can supplement	Police (internal investigations unit)
6. Informal settlement	Unknown	Adjustment encouraged if no "substantial physical injury"		
7. Hearing held	At discretion of board	If complainant requests unless "no cause whatsoever for citizen's complaint"	If complainant requests	At discretion of board
8. Hearings open to public	No	Yes	No	No
9. Representation by counsel allowed.	Yes	Yes	Yes	Yes
10. Counsel provided	Both sides if indigent	Indigent complainant	Indigent complainant	No
11. Evidence rules apply	No	Ye	No	Unknown
12. Cross-examination	Yes	Yes	Yes	Unknown
13. Subpoena power	Yes	No	Yes	Yes
14. Power to decide	No	No	No	No
15. Can recommend punishment	No, can recommend only police trial board	Yes	Yes	No, can recommend only police trial board or summary punishment
16. Recommendation made public	No, parties notified	Unknown	Board's discretion	Not until Commissioners act
17. Miscellaneous	Unknown	Can recommend expunging of record	Unknown	

Prior to its reorganization in 1964, the Washington, D.C., board handled only 54 cases. Twenty-three complaints were disposed of without formal action, 8 referred for police action, no disposition was made of 14, and 9 dispositions are unknown. The board did not explain the basis for its findings even to the police.[539]

After its reorganization, the board assumed jurisdiction in 39 cases prior to June 1966. Of the cases returned to the board in which the police found no misconduct, the board took no further action in five because of the difficulty of resolving the facts, dismissed six, recommended trial boards in four, and asked the police for more information in three.[540]

The Philadelphia board has received and disposed of by far the largest number of cases. Its case load has steadily increased from 32 the first year to 75 the second and 131 in 1965. The character of the complaints re-

---

[536] Supra, note 352 at p. 488; supra, note 1 at pp. 224–225.
[537] Supra, note 490 at pp. 511–512.
[538] Philadelphia Police Advisory Board, Rules of Practice, published in Philadelphia Police Advisory Board, "Seventh Annual Report," Dec. 31, 1965, exhibit A; Philadelphia Police Advisory Board first through sixth annual reports; District of Columbia Executive Office, Order No. 65–798, June 11, 1965, quoted in supra, note 77 at pp. 77–80; Rochester Municipal Code, ch. 10; Rochester Police Advisory Board, first and second annual reports; New York Police Department, "Civilian Complaints—Revised Procedures," General Order No. 14, May 2, 1966.
[539] Supra, note 77 at p. 77.
[540] District of Columbia Complaint Review Board, Statement to the Board of Commissioners, May 19, 1966; Harrison Young, "Review Board Asks Trial in 2 Charges of 'Police Brutality,'" the Washington Post, Aug. 5, 1966, sec. C, p. 1, cols. 6–8.

ceived from 1958 until the middle of 1966 were as follows: [541]

Brutality (presumably including verbal abuse)	239
Illegal entry and search, etc.	108
Harassment	125
Other	99
Total	571

Almost two-thirds of the complaints were filed by Negroes, although the city is almost three-fourths white. Over 50 percent of the complainants had no prior arrest record.[542]

In Philadelphia, the disposition of complaints for the period October 1958 through December 1965 was as follows: [543]

	October 1958 to December 1965
Number of complaints	704
Number withdrawn, closed, settled without hearing or complainant failed to appear	320
Suspensions recommended	15
Reprimands recommended	23
Improper police action (no discipline taken and record of complainant expunged)	49
Cases undecided	174

In many cases, citizens sought an explanation of police powers or other information. Some cases were settled by an apology by the officer or by modification of some police activity. Most cases, through the middle of 1966, have been settled without a hearing. Board actions have included commendation of the police officer, recommendations for psychiatric examination, disciplinary action or dismissal (2 cases), suspension of 1 to 30 days (23 cases), and reprimand (19 cases). In a number of cases, the board recommended discipline stronger than that recommended by the original police investigation.[544]

During its first 28 months, the Rochester advisory board received 50 complaints: [545]

Unnecessary or excessive use of force	21
False arrest	12
Harassment	9
Refusal to allow accused to telephone his lawyer or family	4
Indignities	3
Loss or destruction of personal property	2
Denial of medical attention	2
Discourtesy	2
Illegal search	1
Others	6

Of these, only 16 were within the narrow jurisdiction of the board—physical abuse. Forty percent of the complaints were filed by Negroes. Of the 16 complaints within the board's jurisdiction, 6 were dismissed on procedural grounds or withdrawn, 1 decided in favor of the police and 1 against, and 8 had not been decided at the time an injunction was issued against the board.[546] In the case decided in favor of the police, the board questioned "the propriety of the police procedures employed on this occasion" and the chief of police said that "the conduct of the police at the scene is being reviewed in its entirety." [547]

In New York, approximately 100 complaints were filed per week during the board's operation. In contrast, an average of 200 complaints were filed per year under the earlier procedure from 1960 to 1964.[548] Of the first 300 complaints to the review board, 158 alleged unnecessary force, 61 abuse of authority, 67 discourtesy, and 14 ethnic abuse. More complainants lived in middle-class white neighborhoods than poor ghetto areas. Of the first 407 complaints, 140 came from whites, 113 from Negroes, 38 from Hispanic persons, and the race of 116 was unknown. Of the 146 cases disposed of by the board during its existence, the charges in 109 were found to be unsubstantiated after investigation, 21 were conciliated, 11 were outside the board's jurisdiction and referred elsewhere, disciplinary action was recommended to the Commission in 4, and in 1 the officer received a reprimand. In none of the cases did the board split between the police and civilian members.[549]

In addition to handling individual cases, civilian review boards have been concerned about police policies affecting police-community relations. The Philadelphia board, for example, has recommended special training on the use of handcuffs, formulation of policies on the use of force, and prohibition of the arrest of persons at interracial gatherings or interracial couples merely for being interracial. The police department, as a result, did forbid arrests based on the interracial composition of a group.[550]

In Washington, D.C., after a case where a woman alleged that an off-duty officer shouted obscenities at her, the board suggested that the Commissioners consider specific rules of conduct for off-duty policemen. On the basis of three cases, it asked for study of the "move on" statute, including the development of policies as to how policemen should handle inquiries from third persons concerning why arrests are made and how to address persons they are urging to move on.[551]

Civilian review boards have many of the same weaknesses which exist in internal police machinery in many departments. Citizens have had difficulty in obtaining complaint forms, the procedures of the board have not been widely known, and the boards have been slow in their determination of cases. For example, in Philadelphia, only 8 percent of the cases were concluded within a month and 31 percent in less than 4 months; 12 percent took over a year.[552]

A considerable portion of the boards' problems have also been due to lack of staff and delays in receiving reports from police departments. For example, in Philadelphia, less than half the police investigations are finished in under three months even though the University of California study concluded that the investigations could have been completed much more quickly. The

---

[541] Supra, note 21 at vol. II, p. 236.
[542] Id. at vol. II, pp. 231, 248, 266, 267. In addition, the existence of prior arrests was not ascertained for 19 percent of the complainants. Id. at p. 267.
[543] Philadelphia Police Advisory Board, "Seventh Annual Report," Dec. 31, 1965, exhibit B.
[544] Supra, note 21 at vol. II, pp. 230-231.
[545] Rochester Police Advisory Board, second annual report, Oct. 1, 1965, pp. 3, 5. The total includes more than 50 allegations because some complaints involve multiple allegations.
[546] Id. at pp. 3-4.
[547] Cited in Prentiss L. Pemberton, "Rochester's Police Advisory Board—After Eighteen Months," November 1964, p. 3.
[548] New York City Council, "Report to the Committee on City Affairs from its Subcommittee on Proposed Civilian Complaint Review Board," May 18, 1965, p. 963.
[549] Bernard Weinraub, "Few Poor People Accusing Police," New York Times, Oct. 21, 1966, p. 1, col. 7; Bernard Weinraub, "Leary Reports Anti-Police Verdict in 3 of 113 Review Board Cases," New York Times, Oct. 17, 1966, p. 1, col. 4; "Few Complaints Against Police Result in Charges, Board Finds," New York Times, Mar. 4, 1967, p. 24, col. 1.
[550] Philadelphia Police Advisory Board, fourth annual report, Sept. 30, 1962, p. 4; Philadelphia Police Advisory Board, third annual report, Sept. 30, 1961, pp. 4-5; Philadelphia Police Advisory Board, first annual report, Sept. 15, 1961, p. 5.
[551] District of Columbia Complaint Review Board, "Statement to the Board of Commissioners," May 19, 1966, p. 1. Subsequently, the Corporation Counsel issued an opinion limiting the scope of the "move on" statute.
[552] Supra, note 21 at vol. II, pp. 246, 247.

investigations in Philadelphia have also been of uneven quality.

Despite these difficulties, the boards have had some success. The Philadelphia Police Commissioner has shown a willingness to voluntarily follow the civilian review board's recommendations in most cases.[553] In 1959, Police Commissioner Gibbons testified in court, in answer to a question whether the board had harmed morale, that "the board has not only aided me, but has aided the police department."[554] The board works in close cooperation and constant contact with the top echelons of the police department so that complaints can be frequently settled quickly and informally without a hearing. And while the rank-and-file officers generally oppose the board, the University of California study concluded that morale had not been perceptibly impaired.[555] The Rochester director of public safety has also said that the board had not impaired the efficiency or morale of the police in that city.[556] The President's Commission on Crime in the District of Columbia concluded that the Washington board "has impressed the Commission with its desire to be fair and thorough."[557] The members of the boards generally have been distinguished citizens and the procedures adopted appear to be fair.

The attitudes of minority and civil liberties leaders have been generally favorable but not enthusiastic. For example, in Rochester, three Negro leaders are reported to have said that the board does not "solve tensions over law enforcement" but it is "a constructive step;" it has "done some good" and "given the police a more positive name;" it has "helped both the police department and citizens by preventing emotional reactions from beclouding issues."[558] In Washington, D.C., the procedure has been criticized by Negroes because it has attracted so few complaints and shown its investigative work done by the police.[559] In Philadelphia, the Michigan State study found that the public is more confident of obtaining a fair hearing and that some believe that the police board of inquiry has been led into conducting its proceedings more fairly.[560] The University of California study found that some minority leaders believe that the board is ineffective and a few even believe that it has no value. However, most find that the board does alleviate tensions at least to some extent and show confidence in it by referring complaints. But perhaps most important, the University of California study found that the complainants themselves were favorably impressed with the treatment they received.[561] The study concluded that the board *"has worked* as an avenue of redress for civilian grievances against members of the police force."[562]

Ombudsman

The first ombudsman was appointed in Sweden in 1809. The idea has since been adopted in Finland in 1919, Denmark in 1955, Norway and New Zealand in 1962, and Great Britain and Nassau County, N.Y., in 1966.[563]

In Sweden, the ombudsman is chosen by Parliament and is usually a jurist. He has eight lawyer assistants. He does not have the power to order administrative officials to take action except that he can order prosecutions. However, this power is now seldom used; he usually makes a public reprimand or criticism. He also helps complainants to obtain compensation for damages either from the official or the government and recommends appropriate interpretations of law or changes in it. Jurisdiction over municipal officials was added in 1957 to that over all national officials, including judges, except for Ministers of the Government.[564]

The ombudsman receives complaints in writing. The complainant need not have first complained or appealed to the administrative agency. The ombudsman asks the appropriate administrative agency for all relevant documents and for an explanation. If he needs further information, he can ask the police to investigate or hold a hearing of his own. He also initiates investigations without a complaint being filed, often on the basis of regular inspection tours.[565]

During the 19th century, most cases involved the courts, prosecutors, police, and prisoners.[566] Matters stemming from acts of these same agencies are still being considered. But a review of the yearly reports reveals "the insignificant number of really flagrant violations of the law which have caused intervention."[567] The ombudsman in Sweden has "kept up a constant defense of the rules guaranteeing personal security from abuse of police power" for almost 150 years.[568] In recent years the growth of other administrative agencies has produced a shift of emphasis:[569]

The Swedish Ombudsman: Administrative Scope of Cases, 1960–63

	1960	1961	1962	1963
Courts	210	171	178	241
Public prosecutors	123	171	81	108
Police	190	101	168	213
Execution of verdicts	40	35	44	55
Prison administration	111	123	106	146
Care of mental cases	91	110	123	102
Other health and welfare	80	76	93	99
Public utilities	8	13	14	17
Ecclesiastical authorities	20	32	14	19
King in Council and Parliament	10	8	6	6
Private associations and persons	56	38	22	59
Inquires, unclear complaints, etc.	52	71	58	65
Others	314	322	373	395

During these same years, the ombudsman disposed of cases as follows:[570]

	1960	1961	1962	1963
Dismissed	263	190	217	287
Transferred or canceled	20	29	19	22
Investigated, no direct action	669	592	620	746
Criticisms, etc.	273	208	194	276
Prosecutions	8	7	4	6
Proposals to government	5	16	2	14
Pending	240	278	385	430
Total Cases	1,478	1,320	1,441	1,781

---

[553] Philadelphia Police Advisory Board, Second Annual Report, Sept. 30, 1960, p. 5.
[554] Transcript, Court of Common Pleas No. 2, December term 1959, No. 207, pp. 75–76.
[555] Supra, note 21 at vol. II, pp. 258–260.
[556] Supra, note 548 at p. 559.
[557] Supra, note 77 at p. 79.
[558] Quoted in supra, note 547 at p. 6.
[559] Leonard Downie, Jr., "Complaint Board Criticized," the Washington Post, Oct. 31, 1965, sec. K, p. 1, cols. 5–8.
[560] Supra, note 22 at p. 215–216.
[561] Supra, note 21, vol. II, pp. 100, 111, 217, 249, 253–254.
[562] Id. at p. 271.
[563] Alfred Bexelius, "The Ombudsman for Civil Affairs," in Donald C. Rowat, ed., "The Ombudsman, Citizen's Defender," (London: George Allen and Unwin Ltd., 1965), p. 24; Paavo Kastari, "The Chancellor of Justice and the Ombudsman," in Donald Rowat, ed., op. cit., p. 61; I. M. Pedersen, "Denmark's Ombudsman," in Donald Rowat, ed., op. cit., p. 97; J. F. Northey, "New Zealand's Parliamentary Commissioner," in Donald C. Rowat, ed., op. cit., p. 127. James H. Sikes, "L. I. Ombudsman Is a Busy Adviser," New York Times, Nov. 20, 1966, p. 53, col. 1.
[564] Alfred Bexelius, supra, note 563 at pp. 21–22, 25–28.
[565] Alfred Bexelius, op. cit., pp. 28–29.
[566] Id. at p. 36.
[567] Ibid.
[568] Stig Jagerskiold, "The Swedish Ombudsman," University of Pennsylvania Law Review 109: 1076–1099, 1098.
[569] Donald C. Rowat, ed., supra, note 563 at p. 330.
[570] Id. at p. 329.

The Swedish ombudsman's primary function is securing sounder government for the future, as well as reviewing current complaints. In resolving pending cases, the ombudsman often recommends that the government or the individual official right the wrong which was done, such as by returning private property, granting a license, or paying damages.[571]

The Finnish ombudsman has essentially the same functions. The ombudsman's investigations are often conducted by police officers even if the conduct of other officers is at issue. In 1963, the complaints made to him consisted of:[572]

Courts:
Sentences too severe or wrong	215
Other procedural faults	51
Public prosecutors and police	82
Execution of punishments	102
Prison administration	105
Ordering into institutional care	18
Other health and welfare	11
Other administration	96
Conduct of military officials	5
Private associations and persons	72
Other	30
Total	787

In Denmark the ombudsman, who has a staff of ten, has jurisdiction over the ministers of the government but not the courts. Although he has the power to order prosecution or administrative disciplinary proceedings, these powers have never been used. Instead, he reports to the complainant and, if the matter is important, to the appropriate Minister or Parliament. His major power is the ability to provoke public criticism, although he sometimes recommends particular administrative or legislative changes.

The ombudsman may consider substance, procedure, delay, inconvenience, or impoliteness. The action under review need not have been illegal; he can criticize "mistakes" or "unreasonable" exercise of discretion.[573]

In Denmark, far fewer cases are initiated sua sponte than in Sweden. Complaint investigation ends (or is not commenced at all) the moment it appears to be baseless. The Danish ombudsman is concerned more with future general consequences of governmental activity than with the effect on the complainant. Formal hearings are not usually held; instead, the parties are generally interviewed separately.[574]

Danish cases were disposed of in the following manner from 1960 to 1963:[575]

	1960	1961	1962	1963
Dismissed without investigation	603	584	689	725
Dismissed after summary investigation	288	307	239	254
Formally investigated (including direct action)	209	174	152	151
Total	1,100	1,065	1,080	1,130
Criticisms, etc.	49	48	36	53
Recommendations, etc.	12	16	14	10

Very few cases involve the police. From 1960 to 1963, 35, 32, 9, and 15 cases out of a total of 209, 174, 152, and 151 respectively, which were formally investigated, involved either the police or prosecution.[576] The police cases investigated by the ombudsman have included: a citizen who claimed that he was held unduly long without trial, which was not upheld since he was being examined for mental illness; several cases involving allegedly illegal searches, in one of which a technical violation of the requirement of written consent to a search was found; and two cases involving alleged abusive language where the ombudsman found lack of evidence.[577] The scope of the ombudsman's province even included action in a 1957 case involving the handcuffing of a woman while being taken to the police station. In this case the ombudsman, who had no objection to the use of cuffs in this specific case, found that the Danish police were generally uncertain about when they might be used, so he recommended some guidelines. In another case, the ombudsman told the police that they had no right to keep the fingerprints of an arrested person who was subsequently absolved.[578]

In matters concerning the police, the citizen may complain directly to the ombudsman without first going to the local chief constable or Ministry of Justice. If he deems the matter worthy of inquiry, the ombudsman asks for a report from the Ministry which may ask in turn for a report from the local constable. The ombudsman may then decide the matter or may himself make a further investigation. The subsequent determination is sent to the complainant, Ministry of Justice, and others principally concerned.[579]

In New Zealand, local authorities are not within the ombudsman's jurisdiction. Sixteen of 535 cases decided in an 18-month period ending in 1964 involved the police; in contrast, 106 involved the social security, 52 the inland revenue, and 36 the education departments.[580] During 1965, the ombudsman received 34 complaints concerning the police, found 13 worthy of full investigation, and concluded that 4 complaints were justified. For example, the ombudsman criticized police procedures in committing a man for mental observation; criticized an officer for remarks made during an interrogation; and explained to a woman the propriety of the police questioning suspects in making investigations.

The ombudsman of Nassau County, N.Y. (formally called the Commissioner of Accounts), received 172 complaints from July 1, to December 31, 1966. Only 16 of these concerned the police. None involved brutality and only two police discourtesy. The others related to police protection, the issuance of permits, traffic control signals, and the like.[581]

In other countries, the ombudsmen's recommendations have not always been followed. Often the ombudsmen have to temper their recommendations to take into account the likelihood of support from the government or Parliament. They have not always vigorously defended citizens against invasion of basic rights.[582] Nonetheless, they have had a substantial impact on public administration in most of the countries where they have existed. For example, a police chief in Finland was proud of the fact

---

[571] Walter Gelhorn, "Ombudsman and Others" (Cambridge, Mass.: Harvard University Press, 1966), pp. 213–214.
[572] Id. at p. 70.
[573] Id. at pp. 433–434.
[574] J. M. Pedersen, "Denmark's Ombudsman," in Donald C. Rowat, ed., op. cit., pp. 78–81; Kenneth Culp Davis, "Ombudsman in America: Officers to Criticize Administrative Action," University of Pennsylvania Law Review 109: 1057–1076, 1059–1060; Bert Christensen, "The Danish Ombudsman," University of Pennsylvania Law Review 1100–1126, 1110–1116.
[575] Donald C. Rowat, supra, note 563 at p. 333.
[576] Id. at p. 334.
[577] Thomas A. Aaron, "The Control of Police Discretion: The Danish Experience" (Springfield, Ill.: Charles C. Thomas, 1966), pp. 51–95.
[578] Supra, note 571 at pp. 37–38.
[579] Supra note 577 at pp. 51–95.
[580] Donald C. Rowat, supra, note 563 at pp. 336–337.
[581] Samuel Greason, report from the Office of Commissioner of Accounts to County Executive Eugene H. Nickerson, July 1, 1966, to Dec. 31, 1966 (Jan. 3, 1967), pp. 1–2.
[582] Supra, note 571 at pp. 37–41, 87–90.

that the ombudsman had not criticized his force in 11 years. However, he went on to say: [583]

> [W]e have had inquiries about matters that had been sent to the * * * Ombudsman, and so we are well aware that complaints can be made. Of course, too, we have all heard about the prosecution of K. [a police chief in another city] for unnecessarily keeping a sick man in jail. That is very much on our minds because we have not in the past had any system for dealing with sick prisoners. After what happened to K. we can't continue to be easy going. We are working on that problem right this minute.

And another senior official said "Don't let anyone tell you that police officers don't care about those fellows in Helsinki. * * * [W]e know they can and do concern themselves with us, and that makes us careful." [584]

In addition, as the Swedish ombudsman has noted, the ombudsman has helped protect administrative officials as well as the public: [585]

> One important aspect of the ombudsman's activity that is frequently overlooked is the rejection of unwarranted complaints. Obviously it is of great interest to the official attacked that accusations of abuse are not left open, and that it is made evident by an impartial agency that the complaints were not justified. Also, it is of great importance that accusations made in the press, or otherwise, regarding abuse by the authorities are taken up for investigation by an agency free of bureaucratic influence, and that these investigations are available and the true facts made known to the general public. Since the ombudsman gives the grounds for decisions rejecting complaints, the petitioner will receive an explanation of what to him appeared to be wrong. By the rejection of unwarranted complaints after proper investigation and on grounds clearly stated, the ombudsman contributes to strengthening public confidence in the authorities and thus to the feeling of well-being in the society.

Similarly, an official in New Zealand said that "when [the ombudsman] goes over something we have done and says he finds nothing wrong, he takes the wind out of the sails of the Doubting Thomases." [586] In addition, the same official noted that "people will complain to him when for one reason or another they won't complain to me, and this gives me an added opportunity to police my own department." [587] At the same time, most complainants are apparently satisfied even when their position has been rejected.[588]

In summary, both citizens and government officials are generally enthusiastic about the ombudsmen in the countries where they now exist.[589]

Local Human Relations Commissions and Other Local Agencies

Local human relations commissions and other local agencies exist in many cities around the country to assist the community with problems involving racial or religious discrimination. In some communities these agencies handle citizen complaints against the police.

In Pittsburgh, a human relations commission conducts investigations of any case which might affect intergroup relations, including those involving brutality or other police misconduct. The board makes findings and recommendations as to discipline in each case. These are transmitted, with the investigative report, to the director of public safety.[590] During 1965, the Pittsburgh Commission processed 18 such cases: [591]

Disposition	Number of cases	Number of officers
Misconduct and physical abuse found, suspension recommended	2	5
Misconduct and physical abuse found, reprimand recommended	4	8
Complaint dismissed:		
Failure of complainant to proceed	2	
Lack of jurisdiction	1	
Lack of evidence to support complaint	6	
Pending	3	
	18	

Some human relations Commissions which do not regularly process civilian complaints are asked to investigate particularly serious incidents. For example, in New Haven, the local commission was asked by the mayor and the police to investigate two disturbances involving arrests. Finding some of the actions justified and some not, the Commission recommended disciplinary action against six officers and made extensive recommendations concerning the establishment of a community relations program and training.[592]

In New York City, the department of investigation can conduct an inquiry into any aspect of any department of the city government, including the police, and, in doing so, may subpoena witnesses and hold hearings. Unlike an ombudsman, the department does not purport to be independent; rather it investigates on behalf of the mayor. It maintains a complaint bureau and, in addition, investigates complaints sent to Box 100, the address of the widely publicized complaint bureau of the mayor. Writing to that address guarantees the writer that he will be free from harassment. While the 150 letters sent weekly to Box 100 generally concern pleas for assistance such as for housing and complaints about other agencies of government, some—about 100 a month—have been allegations that police officers were corrupt, discourteous or unresponsive to pleas for assistance. The department of investigation frequently acts privately, but a study of its files in 1965 showed positive consequences in many cases.[593]

In Baltimore, the Complaint Evaluation Board—composed of the State attorney general, the Baltimore prosecutor and city solicitor, a representative of the police commissioner, and the executive secretaries of the State and city interracial commissions—considers all citizen complaints against the police. It can either accept the police department's recommendation or recommend other action such as independent investigation by the State police. The board does not hold hearings or make investigations itself.[594]

In Denver, a six-member Mayor's Committee on City-Citizen Relationships was established in 1965 to receive citizen complaints involving any city department, and investigate and make specific recommendations to the mayor concerning the merits of the complaint and possible punishment. It has no staff and does not hold hear-

---

[583] Id. at p. 74.
[584] Ibid.
[585] Alfred Bexelius, supra, note 563 at p. 42.
[586] Quoted in supra, note 571 at p. 153.
[587] Ibid.
[588] Id. at pp. 436–438.
[589] Id. at pp. 45, 87, 91, 152–153, 192.
[590] Pittsburgh Commission on Human Relations, "Procedure for Processing Complaints of Civilians Against City of Pittsburgh Police Officers Charging Misconduct or Brutality," June 16, 1965, pp. 1–3; Pittsburgh Commission on Human Relations, "Working Together," 1965 annual report, pp. 4–6.
[591] Id. at p. 6.
[592] New Haven Commission on Equal Opportunities, "Report Based On Its Investigation of Police Activity on December 10, 1965, and December 25, 1965," Apr. 20, 1966, pp. 19–21.
[593] Supra, note 528 at pp. 166–170; editorial, "Another Reason for a 'No' Vote," New York Times, Oct. 29, 1966, p. 28, col. 1.
[594] Ralph G. Murdy, "Civilian Review Boards in Review," FBI Law Enforcement Bulletin, July 1966, pp. 14–18.

ings. In the first year, it received 25 complaints, including 22 involving the police, 1 the welfare department, and 2 the city hospital.[595]

Michigan Civil Rights Commission

The Michigan Civil Rights Commission was established by the new 1963 State constitution. Unlike most State civil rights commissions, which have no authority over local government affairs, it has jurisdiction over all cases of social or religious discrimination involving local and State government agencies as well as fair housing, employment, and public accommodation statutes. The eight-member Commission investigates the cases and holds hearings. It does not simply render advisory opinions; it can seek court enforcement of its orders.[596] Although its jurisdiction includes review of complaints against law enforcement agencies, the Commission, in order to avoid interference with legitimate police activities, has attempted to resolve problems through "cooperation rather than by coercion." [597]

The Michigan Commission received 478 cases during 1964 in the following categories: [598]

	Number	Percent
Employment	286	59.8
Housing	60	12.6
Law enforcement	77	16.1
Public accommodation	47	9.8
Education	8	1.7

Over 88 percent of the complainants were Negroes.

During its first 2 years, 1964 and 1965, the Michigan Commission handled 161 cases involving law enforcement agencies. The complaints were resolved in the following fashion: [599]

Probable cause—adjusted [settlement with police department]	33
Probable cause—order [to comply]	1
No probable cause—dismissal	45
Lack of jurisdiction	5
Withdrawn by claimant	4
Under investigation	73

Only one of these cases required issuing a formal order to comply and in none were the courts involved. Of the first 77 law enforcement cases filed, 74 involved the police, 2 the prosecutor, and 1 the courts; 76 alleged discrimination on the basis of race and 1 on the basis of religion.[600]

One hundred and fourteen of the first 168 complaints against law enforcement agencies through March 30, 1966 involved the Detroit Police Department: [601]

Physical abuse	62
Harassment	48
Verbal abuse	29
False charges	16
Failure to take complaints	9
Property damage	4

Examples of the kinds of cases where the Commission found probable cause and followed through until the cases were settled include the following: [602]

In one case a citizen complained to officers and was himself struck and charged with an offense. The responsible officers were reprimanded and transferred, and the department apologized to the claimant. In another instance, a citizen was stopped on suspicion and was injured in the scuffle that followed. The citizen was released on bond a few hours later, and the same officers again stopped the citizen for investigation. One officer was warned, one was reprimanded, and the charges against the citizen were dropped.

The Michigan Commission has not limited its concern to a case-by-case aproach. It has developed with city officials and police chiefs programs for the recruitment of minority group officers and community relations instructors for senior police personnel. It has reviewed a series of disciplinary actions by the Detroit Police Department and encouraged the imposition of punishments more consistent with the severity of the offense. Following recommendations made after specific cases, the Detroit police force issued an order discontinuing arrests for investigation in liquor and gambling cases and distributed a memorandum and amended manual concerning proper procedures for handling complaints about violations of equal accommodations laws. After members of a civil rights group were arrested and abused, meetings with civil rights organizations were started in the precincts.[603]

CONCLUSION

The purpose of this chapter has been to review the problem of police-community relations in the United States and to recommend numerous possible ways to meet it. It is well, in conclusion, to reemphasize the basic principles which must underlie any meaningful community relations program.

1. No police-community relations program can be effective without the full and complete support of the chief of police and other ranking police officers. Unfortunately, many lower ranking policemen have sensed that the strong statements of their superiors on police-community relations were not really meant—that they were intended to placate minority groups and civilian officials. They often see that action is taken only in times of crisis. If police officers know that other objectives are given far higher priority, they will continue to operate as in the past. Consequently, police-community relations programs have generally received inadequate support from middle level commanders and from officers on the street.

2. Improved community relations is not merely the job of police-community relations units or of citizens organizations. Instead, as a distinguished group of citizens advised Mayor Lindsay: [604]

Community relations is not a part-time task of the Police Department, or a mere postscript to its traditional work. We believe that community relations is essential to all law enforcement and therefore an integral part of all police work. Im-

---

[595] American Civil Liberties Union, "Police Power and Citizens' Rights" (New York: American Civil Liberties Union, 1966), p. 45.
[596] Michigan State Constitution, art. I, sec. 2, art. V, sec. 29; Michigan Civil Rights Commission, rules, Aug. 11, 1964.
[597] Office of Attorney General Frank J. Kelly, statement of Dec. 22, 1964, p. 2; memorandum of agreement between the Michigan Civil Rights Commission and the Detroit Police Department on "Procedural Steps in Investigations of Civil Rights Complaints," Apr. 22, 1966.
[598] Michigan Civil Rights Commission, "1964 Annual Report," p. 14.
[599] Michigan Civil Rights Commission, "Law Enforcement Cases Handled by the Michigan Civil Rights Commission," Jan. 1, 1964 through Dec. 31, 1965, p. 1.
[600] Supra, note 598 at pp. 14, 16.
[601] Supra, note 382 at pp. 1, 2.
[602] Ibid.
[603] Id. at pp. 4–5; supra, note 598 at pp. 11–12.
[604] Law Enforcement Task Force of New York City, "Report to Mayor-Elect John V. Lindsay," Dec. 31, 1965 at p. 15.

proving community relations is a full-time assignment of each man on the force. * * * [Healthy community relations] * * * can only be achieved by inculcating an attitude—a tone—throughout the force that will help facilitate a creative rapport with the public.

3. The commitment of the chiefs of police must result in more than honest, hard work to improve community relations. Many of the things which may need to be done will seem to interfere with other objectives and needs of the department. For example, harsher penalties for officers who engage in serious misconduct, increased promotion of qualified Negro officers to higher ranks, and even discussion with the more aggressive civil rights leaders may alienate some police officers and perhaps, at least temporarily, lower morale. Restricting use of certain minor crime statutes, of dogs, and of field interrogations may mean that police officers will have somewhat less control over occurrences on the street or even lead, in the short run, to apprehending fewer criminals. However, if these measures help to improve community relations, the result will probably be to improve considerably the ability of the police to control crime.

The solution is not, of course, to choose any policy merely because it results in more support by the public, or a portion of the public. A chief of police has to consider other objectives. Nevertheless, since police-community relations create serious problems in cities throughout the country, such relations must be one of the principal criteria in evaluating any policy or activity of the department. Indeed, in view of the extremely serious problems and the possibility that police relations with certain segments of the community may worsen, it may often be the most important factor.

4. An effective police-community relations program requires simultaneous efforts in many areas. Otherwise, any individual effort, no matter how well conceived, is likely to be ineffective. For example, neighborhood advisory committees will work well only if, in response to committee discussion, the police department is genuinely willing to reevaluate its policies concerning the activities of officers on the street and its methods of handling civilian complaints. Similarly, more Negro police officers, particularly as superior officers, are needed to gain the confidence of the Negro community. Yet, qualified Negroes are unlikely to join the force as long as the police are strongly disliked by much of the Negro community and as long as present Negro officers believe that they are discriminated against in promotion and assignments or that other officers are hostile to them. Consequently, the recruitment of more Negroes requires a concentrated effort to improve the practices of patrolmen on the street, to open communications between the police and the Negro, and to end all forms and appearances of discrimination within the department.

5. Police-community relations will probably not improve substantially unless policing as a whole improves. More educated policemen are essential, which means, in turn, higher salaries and better working conditions. Police morale must be raised. Yet, morale is affected by almost everything occurring within the department, from salaries to the caliber of supervision. Consequently, while police-community relations is treated separately in this chapter, this subject cannot in fact be separated from the rest of the problems in policing today.

6. Police-community relations is not merely a problem of a particular police force. The public tends to see the police as one group just as they view lawyers, doctors, or the members of any other profession. Consequently, when the police in one area are abusive, for example, to peaceful demonstrators, respect and support for police officers everywhere is weakened. It is even more true that when one of numerous police agencies within an area engages in acts which offend the public, other police departments in the area are significantly harmed.

7. The problem between the police and the community, particularly the minority community, is not merely a product of lack of communication or information. It will not be solved merely by having the police and the community talk together or by having the police educate the community concerning their role and activities. Instead, the conflict concerns real points of disagreement, such as how the police treat citizens on the street, whether they discriminate in applying the law, and how citizen complaints are handled. Discussion and education can only help if the police (as well as citizens) address the serious problems and attempt, where necessary and possible, to change their policies and activities to meet citizen objections.

8. Police officials and officers often adopt a defensive attitude toward those who criticize and are hostile to them. Many of the people most hostile to the police are ordinary citizens acting honestly out of firm belief. It is therefore essential that the police explore problems openly—that, indeed, the police seek out their critics so that problems can be met together.

9. The movement toward the professionalization of the police must include a professional approach towards community relations problems. As the Michigan State study concluded: [605]

> In their rapid movement toward professionalism, the police have sometimes overemphasized crime suppression to the detriment of the police and community relationship. Many aspects of the police's traditional public service goal are now shunted aside as being nonprofessional or unprofessional.

Professionalization within the police world has, in considerable part, meant greater attention to efficiency. One-man patrol cars are becoming more common; field interrogations are made more systematically; officers are expected to spend more time in patrol and less time talking to citizens; and the number of precinct stations is being reduced. These and other changes may improve police effectiveness against crime. Yet, they may also interfere with the development of friendly and informal contacts between police officers and the public which are so necessary to community relations. Consequently, many of these new trends may have to be adapted or compensated for, if police-community relations are not to be harmed.

---

[605] Supra, note 22 at pp. 30–31.

Professionalism must mean more than mere efficiency.

The problem of police in a democratic society is not merely a matter of obtaining newer police cars, a higher order of technical equipment or of recruiting men who have to their credit more years of education. What must occur is a significant alteration in the ideology of police, so that police "professionalization" rests on the values of a democratic legal order, rather than on technological proficiency.[600]

10. The police must be willing to adapt to change. One area of change, which is the concern of a large part of the Commission's report, concerns new technology. Perhaps, even more important, however, there have been extremely significant social changes in this country since World War II. The proportion of juveniles has risen and they have increasing freedom; citizens of all ages are rejecting conformity and challenging accepted ideas and institutions; the poor are seeking to be treated with dignity and to receive their fair share of America's wealth; and minority groups, particularly Negroes, are demanding both the end of all forms of discrimination and equal opportunity in all aspects of American life.

These groups are becoming increasingly sensitive to being frequently stopped and questioned or arrested for minor crimes. They are increasingly sensitive to police disrespect whether real or imagined. They are increasingly willing to challenge slum landlords, unscrupulous merchants, other agencies of government, and particularly the police as the symbol of the law.

The police cannot ignore these changes. Nor can or should they stop them. If the police—from the chief to the patrolman—learn to understand the way of life and aspirations of the Mexican-American juvenile, the poor white, or the middle-class Negro, they will be able both to enforce the law and to improve relationships with the entire community.

11. For too long, the public has either ignored or even increased tensions between the police and portions of the community. While it is the responsibility of police departments to improve community relations, the public too must bear its share of the responsibility. Besides paying the financial cost, the public must forego the temptation, to which it has too often succumbed, to use the police *against* minority groups, to encourage the use of methods which are illegal or offensive. The public must be willing to have the police serve equally and fully all segments of the community. It must demand that elected civilian officials exercise responsibility and control over the police as well as over all other government agencies. It must be willing to participate in community relations activities such as neighborhood and citywide advisory committees. It should, through a variety of civic organizations, investigate the reasons for police-community tensions in their localities, support constructive police activities to improve community relations, and work for the reforms which are necessary. Unless interest is shown in these and many other ways, progress in police-community relations is likely to be slow and inadequate to meet this serious problem.

12. While many suggestions have been made in this chapter, there is no pat answer to improving police-community relations. The problem, particularly between the police and minority groups, is a deep and complex one involving many other issues and institutions of our society. The problems and therefore the remedies are different in different localities. Experimentation with new ideas is therefore essential.

Yet, as the surveys and other information described in this chapter show, the problem exists—particularly in our cities—throughout the country. At least some of the causes and some of the remedies are clear. There can be no excuse if the police and the community do not begin to meet the problem before them in frank fashion.

13. Finally, much has been said about the ineffectiveness of existing community relations programs. It must be remembered, however, that 10 years ago, there were almost no such programs. Today police departments are generally aware of the problem and are beginning to take serious action. Programs exist in many places and new or expanded programs are constantly being announced. Therefore, the weakness of the programs must be considered in the light of the substantial progress.

Unfortunately, however, progress is not nearly fast enough. Impatience, frustration, and now violence are growing quickly in minority communities and these trends are likely to accelerate. Consequently, if the problem is not to get worse, to the serious detriment of both the police and the community, drastic and creative action is urgently needed.

---

[600] Supra, note 1 at p. 239.

Chapter 7

Police Integrity

THE NEED FOR ETHICAL CONDUCT

Exacting ethical standards and a high degree of honesty are perhaps more essential for the police than for any other group in society. Because the police are entrusted with the enforcement of the fundamental rules that guide society's conduct, a policeman's violation of the law or his corrupt failure to enforce it dishonors the law and the authority he represents. Dishonesty within a police agency can, almost overnight, destroy respect and trust that has been built up over a period of years by honest local government and police officials. Nothing undermines public confidence in the police and the process of criminal justice more than the illegal acts of officers. Support for the police in their work, and the bringing about of crucial changes such as those recommended by the Commission to strengthen the police, can easily be impaired by a belief that the police themselves are not taking every possible measure to eradicate corruption and unethical conduct.

As this chapter will point out, the dishonest policeman is, in many cases, strongly influenced by the corruption of others—politicians, businessmen, and private citizens. Although he is inherently no more resistant to temptation than anyone else, his position exposes him to extraordinary pressures. In many cases practices that are accepted in other fields and occupations—such as tipping and doing favors—are particularly difficult to avoid in police work. Conflicting pressures are often placed upon the police. For example, police are required to enforce parking and gambling laws, though most of the community might prefer them not to. Public resistance to the enforcement of such laws greatly increases the temptation to accept favors, gratuities or bribes, or simply to ignore violations. Police dishonesty is, of course, a series of private tragedies for the officers who become involved. It also affects the morale of thousands of honest policemen who suffer from popular identification with those involved in corruption or misconduct. When the "dishonest cop" headline appears, honest police officers throughout the country are adversely affected, "the feeling of pride slips and * * * a hint of shame takes hold." [1]

Field studies undertaken by the Commission and the work of its consultants have revealed that at least in some cities a significant number of officers engage in varying forms of criminal and unethical conduct. The Commission's limited studies afford no basis for general conclusions as to the exact extent of police dishonesty or the degree to which political corruption affects police service today. But these studies have shown that even in some of the departments where the integrity of top administrators is unquestioned, instances of illegal and unethical conduct are a continuing problem—particularly in slum areas, where the most incompetent officers tend to be assigned in some cities. Administrators with whom the Commission has consulted acknowledge that dishonesty is a problem that must be frankly confronted if their objective of eradicating such misconduct is to be achieved.

PATTERNS OF DISHONESTY

The violations in which police are involved vary widely in character. The most common are improper political influence; acceptance of gratuities or bribes in exchange for nonenforcement of laws, particularly those relating to gambling, prostitution, and liquor offenses, which are often extensively interconnected with organized crime; the "fixing" of traffic tickets; minor thefts; and occasional burglaries. The Commission's work also revealed some instances of police officers in high-crime neighborhoods engaging in such practices as rolling drunks and shakedowns of money and merchandise in the very places where respect for law is so badly needed.

POLITICAL CORRUPTION

Government corruption in the United States has troubled historians, political reformers, and the general public since the middle of the 19th century.[2] Metropolitan police forces—most of which developed during the late 1800's when government corruption was most prevalent—have often been deeply involved in corruption.[3] The police are particularly susceptible to the forms of corruption that have attracted widest attention—those that involve tolerance or support of organized crime activities. But the police, as one of the largest and most strategic groups in metropolitan government, are also likely targets for political patronage, favoritism, and other kinds of influence that have pervaded local governments dominated by political machines. Against both forms of corruption,

---

[1] Mort Stern, "What Makes a Policeman Go Wrong," Denver Post, Oct. 8, 1961, sec. A, p. 1, col. 1.

[2] See e.g., Lincoln Steffens, "The Shame of the Cities" (New York: McClure, Phillips, 1904), 306 p.

[3] Charles Reith, "The Blind Eye of History" (London: Faber & Faber Ltd., 1952), p. 83.

responsible police leaders have fought a continuing battle—one that appears to be steadily gaining.[4]

The remnants of corrupt political control allied with organized crime and vice operations have, however, continued to plague some cities—as evidenced by widely publicized incidents during the past 10 years, particularly concerning organized crime activities. In Newport, Ky., for example, city officials and police were indicted in 1963 for permitting organized vice and gambling activities to flourish.[5] In 1961, corruption in Boston was exposed through a nationwide television documentary which showed 10 policemen entering and leaving a bookmaking establishment in a locksmith's shop. Prior to release of the film, the Internal Revenue Service, acting upon complaints originating from the New England Citizens Crime Commission, raided the shop; but when State police raided the shop 4 weeks later it was again operating openly. As a result of this scandal, a survey of the department was ordered, and the police commissioner was replaced.[6]

In May 1961, a raid by agents of the Internal Revenue Service on a gambling establishment in New Kensington, Pa., uncovered corruption there. The subsequent election of a reform mayor and the appointment of an honest chief of police ended a regime that "was so closely controlled by organized crime that the community seemed helpless in its grip." [7]

Perhaps the most notorious such incident was the gangland-type murder of State Attorney General-elect Albert L. Patterson, resulting in a cleanup of Phenix City, Ala., in 1955. Both the sheriff and the mayor resigned their offices, were charged, and paid fines for wilfully neglecting their duties. Scores of gamblers went to prison.[8]

Another form of political corruption—where police appointments are considered a reward for political favors and police officials are consequently responsive primarily to the local political machine—is still a fairly open and tacitly accepted practice in many small cities and counties. It recurs too, from time to time, in larger cities, though generally in less conspicuous form.

Even in some cities where reforms have ended open political control of the police, policemen who make trouble for businessmen with strong political influence may still be transferred to punishment beats, and traffic tickets may still be fixed in some places through political connections. Honest and conscientious police chiefs often have an extremely difficult time eliminating these practices.

Such assignment practices may be present in the lower ranks of individual precincts or bureaus, and, if detected, are often difficult to prove with the certainty needed to take action under cumbersome civil service regulations. Appeal to a mayor, city council, or prosecutor may of course be fruitless, since they themselves may be involved in or condone such practices. The general public often accepts this style of city government as simply "the way things are," and the policeman who tries to buck such a system is likely to be ostracized by his companions and lose any chance he may have had to advance in his career. Political corruption in police personnel practices, although rarely dramatic enough to make headlines, can in itself destroy the morale of the honest and conscientious officer, and deter able men from careers in law enforcement.

NONENFORCEMENT OF THE LAW

Chapter 2 has discussed the problems that confront the police when they are faced with enforcement of laws in such areas as gambling, prostitution, liquor, and traffic. In many cases there are strong community pressures against enforcement of such laws. In others neither the police nor the rest of the criminal justice system have the resources or ability to attempt full enforcement and in these cases a pattern of selective nonenforcement prevails. Some prosecutors and judges react to selective enforcement problems by dropping cases or imposing fines low enough to be accepted as part of the overhead of illegal business. This can create an environment in which dishonesty thrives.

Sometimes enforcement policies are decided openly and rationally by such means as chapter 2 suggests; in such instances selective enforcement is properly regulated. But in others, nonenforcement may become the occasion for bribery or other corruption. Thus, in the prohibition era, millions of people sought and found ways to disregard the ban on liquor, and police attempts at enforcement were met with citizen condemnation and offers of payment for tolerance of community norms.

While the wholesale corruption of prohibition days has passed, illegitimate nonenforcement remains a problem. One west coast police official described in this fashion how a bookie once attempted to influence him:

These people really work on you. They make it seem so logical—like you are the one that is out of step. This bookie gave me this kind of a line: "It's legal at the tracks, isn't it? So why isn't it legal here? It's because of these crooks at the Capitol. They're gettin' plenty—all drivin' Cads. Look at my customers, some of the biggest guys in town—they don't want you to close me down. If you do they'll just transfer you. Like that last jerk. And were the Judge, what did he do?: Fined me a hundred and suspended fifty. Hell, he knows Joe citizen wants me here, so get smart, be one of the boys, be part of the system. It's a way of life in this town and you're not gonna change it. Tell you what I'll do. I won't give you a nickel; just call in a free bet in the first race every day and you can win or lose, how about it?" [9]

The corrupt offer may come from the law-violator, as in the previous example. But initiation of such offers is not confined to people so clearly involved in illicit enterprises. A patrol division commander in one city described another common situation:

This fellow was president of his local service club and he was always shoving something into the officer's hand saying, "here's a little trinket for the wife!" He did the same thing with delivery men and others in return for small favors. In our case it was in appreciation for the officer not tagging overparked or doubleparked customers' vehicles in front of the shop. He really didn't see any harm in what he was doing.[10]

In another city it was common practice for a detective to provide a list of names of selected police officers to

---

[4] Ralph Lee Smith, "The Tarnished Badge" (New York: Thomas Y. Crowell Co., 1965), p. 230.
[5] "Challenge to Morality," Christian Science Monitor (Boston), Jan. 9, 1963, p. 9, col. 3.
[6] Ibid. Also, see Dwight S. Strong, "New England: The Refined Yankee in Organized Crime." The Annals, 347: 40-50, 48 (May 1963).
[7] Supra, note 5 at col. 2.
[8] Supra, note 5 at col. 1.
[9] This example was one of many provided to the staff of the Commission by police officials from various cities in the United States.
[10] Ibid.

leading law firms and large hotels for distribution of liquor at Christmas time. In the same city it was customary for detectives assigned to the pawn shop detail to receive special Christmas gifts from each of the downtown pawnbrokers.[11]

These practices may be little different in kind from exchanges that commonly occur in the business world, but they have a far more ominous implication when they involve public officials. And they may lead to far more serious misconduct.

Certain traffic accidents provide the setting for another form of mutual consent bribery:

> In an accident situation where the officer can cite either party, he may stall, maybe give a slight hint—or the citizen may take the initiative. The citizen generally tells the officer a sad story, walks over to the officer's car and leans over the front door. This is the cue. What actually happens is that money is dropped onto the floor of the car. The officer then decides not to issue any citation and leaves in his car—after he has also secretly collected a reward from the tow-car operator. . When he "discovers" the money on the floor of his car he now has money from two sources. These cases are very difficult for internal investigations units to make, but it can be done if enough manpower is made available.[12]

In some cities corruption has been so highly organized within a precinct or department that there are regular fees for permitting various activities, collected at set intervals by a "lieutenant's man." In one large eastern city, for example, contractors who wished to unload materials at curbside had to pay a given per diem to the precinct captain—ostensibly to cover the cost of a patrolman to supervise traffic, though in fact there was no basis for such a charge for police services, and no special assistance was given. In another city, workmen at construction sites have been known to line up during their morning coffee break each day to pay a dollar to the beat patrolman for not ticketing their illegally parked cars.

THEFT

The problem of theft by police officers sometimes takes a form less blatant than the occasional, well-publicized burglary such as the Summerdale incident, which resulted in the reorganization of the entire Chicago police department in 1960, and the 1961 apprehension in Denver of a ring of police burglars, which resulted in dismissal of 52 men. In some cities, the Commission determined that some officers kept stolen property recovered by investigation, stole small items from stores when a patrol inspection disclosed an unlocked door, or emptied the pockets of drunks before they were taken to the stationhouse.

A ranking police official from a southwestern city illustrated the problem with this example:

> One night one of our men discovered an unlocked jewelry store. He flushed out the building for a possible burglar, and when he discovered all was secure he checked the safe. It was also unlocked and contained several trays of diamond and ruby rings. He yielded to temptation and took a ring for his wife. He rationalized by thinking the owner would collect insurance when he discovered the loss and that way nobody would really lose.[13]

[11] Ibid.
[12] Ibid.

A pattern that was described by more than one police official was that of storekeepers who also take the attitude that insurance will cover losses and, as a mark of appreciation when policemen discover an unlocked door or investigate a burglary, invite them to help themselves to merchandise that can be reported as having been stolen.

Some officers have also been known to take building material and actually transport it in police vehicles. In one city officers picked up nails, tools, bundles of shingles, roofing paper and other items from the "midnight supply company" while working their shift. They were remodeling their houses and rationalized their act on the basis of numerous reports of stolen property from building contractors presumably much of it taken by workmen on the job. One of the officers was a former building trade worker and looked upon this form of "toting" as an accepted practice.

KICKBACKS

Particularly in the case of traffic offenses there is also an opportunity, which has sometimes resulted in publicized incidents, for policemen to receive payments for referring business to others such as towing companies, ambulance companies, garages, and lawyers who specialize in traffic accident damage suits. In one large city, for example, lawyers' "runners" with radio-equipped cars sometimes showed up at accidents. The result was an automatic $25 for the police officer handling it if the victim could be influenced to accept the attorney.[14] Licensing, inspection, and truck weighing duties also have afforded opportunities for this sort of unethical conduct.

THE BACKGROUND OF THE PROBLEM

Since such conduct continues to be a problem of concern for police officials, inquiry is required into the underlying factors that contribute to dishonesty and violation of ethics. A number of these are apparent from the incidents used in previous examples.

POLITICAL DOMINATION

The problem of old-style domination of the police by political machines has attracted the most intensive reform efforts from the police themselves. As a result, the effort to establish independent, professional law enforcement has made considerable headway over the past 30 years. This movement has not been without its own problems, however; the tradition of improper political interference is deep-rooted.

Further, civil service regulations in many jurisdictions have sometimes restricted the reform attempts of honest police executives. In many cities, for example, it is extremely difficult to remove officers who have engaged in serious acts of misconduct.

It is obvious that improper political interference contributes to corruption. Patronage appointments lower the quality of personnel and encourage all officers to

[13] Ibid.
[14] Ibid.

cooperate with politicians, even in improper circumstances. Although a man might withstand this temptation for himself, it may be impossible or even pointless for him to separate himself from the practices of his superiors or partners.

DISHONEST SUPERIORS AND FELLOW OFFICERS

Not long ago, the police commissioner of a large city expressed publicly his pessimism about the ability of training to protect new recruits from the pressures of improper conduct. He preferred to assign his best young officers to a tactical force that operated as a unit entirely separate and apart from the traditional organization. In that way, he said, it kept them out of "the system," where a new man was sometimes subjected to heavy pressures to conform to unethical practices, such as splitting tow-truck rebates and accepting gifts from merchants.

In many cases, of course, an honest recruit if properly trained and motivated will decide to report a matter to his superiors and assist in prosecuting disciplinary action. For example, proper action was taken by the officer in the following case:

Nothing is more despised by honest policemen than the corrupt officer who leads younger men into a pattern of graft. If this kind of an officer is part of a two-man motor patrol, he must convince his partner to go along with the shakedown or he can't operate. This happened to me when I was a young officer. But I avoided involvement. Instead we made a case against him and he was fired. My sergeant backed me all the way.[15]

But this is often not easy. In some cases superiors, too, may be involved in dishonesty. When this is known to the officer he should report the incident to a superior he trusts, even if he must go as high as the chief himself or to an outside agency. To protect the officer supervisors can, in most instances, develop a case without revealing the identity of the reporting officer.

All police officers have taken an oath to uphold the law and to support the regulations of their department. While in some cases proper action may be difficult and require considerable fortitude, the general problem cannot be overcome until there is a strong determination within all law enforcement agencies to rid the profession of the "rotten apples." Failure to do so by withholding information should be cause for severe disciplinary action. This rule is firmly enforced within the Federal Bureau of Investigation and may be one of the strong influencing factors responsible for its outstanding record of integrity.

Whenever a number of dishonest officers are tolerated by other officers within a police organization, an atmosphere of mutual support and protection may develop, and eventually it may taint the entire police system. This was illustrated in the 1961 Denver scandal when it became apparent that there were varying degrees of involvement. The illegal practice centered about a small group of corrupt officers. The majority of the officers involved were passive participants; their grave error was only the failure to recognize a sworn obligation to report the activity to officials who could have taken proper action.

The personal ethical standards of police supervisors and executives exert great influence in establishing an agency's attitude toward dishonest police behavior. If an officer suspects that others support or simply condone dishonesty, his own definition of what comprises proper conduct may shift to accord with his concept of departmental norms.

Supervisors may create an atmosphere that supports corruption if they place popularity among patrolmen above their supervisory responsibilities. Such an official may be willing to excuse infractions of departmental rules. He may keep from the police chief information that an officer accepted a number of small items from a local merchant. He may realize that a patrolman is engaging in misconduct, but to avoid controversy and to maintain what he considers a good working relationship, he may remain silent.

Chiefs of police who are suspected of improper action can exert an even more serious influence. Such men may symbolize to young officers the standard for reaching the top. When the chief is known to be responsive to improper political pressure or even to take orders from criminal elements, corruption can be considered a necessary route to promotion. At the least, the existence of dishonesty at the top levels of command may influence an officer to accept favors.

PUBLIC PARTICIPATION

One major reason why police dishonesty continues is that large sections of the public contribute to it or condone it.

It is not merely the professional gambler offering a patrolman a free bet who promotes corruption, but the motorist, who thinks little of offering a traffic officer $5 to avoid a ticket, or the businessman who presses gifts and gratuities on police in return for indulgences or other favors.

Even where such practices seem relatively harmless in and of themselves, they may easily establish an atmosphere wherein it becomes impossible to resist more serious bribery. More generally, it is unrealistic to expect a police force to maintain absolute integrity in a city where petty corruption and political favoritism is accepted by the public.

The widespread practice among other segments of the community of using positions of authority to elicit small gifts or favors may similarly influence the police. Police executives have often compared a businessman's accepting gifts from manufacturers and salesmen with an officer's accepting gratuities from merchants in his patrol area. While such conduct by the police is clearly unethical, the fact that the practice is accepted in the business world understandably leads some officers to question the harm of accepting small gratuities.

LACK OF ENFORCEMENT POLICY

A considerable number of the most serious and persistent kinds of unethical conduct are connected with failure

---

[15] Ibid.

to enforce laws that are not in accord with community norms. Among these are laws concerning gambling, prostitution, liquor, and traffic. The failure of police administrators and other law enforcement officials—and ultimately of legislators and the general public—to acknowledge frankly the paradoxes confronting enforcement officials, has meant that only rarely have explicit policies and guides to enforcement in these areas been developed and enforced.

RECRUITMENT, TRAINING, AND COMPENSATION

The inability to attract and retain men of higher character and the failure to screen applicants carefully enough contribute to the problem of dishonesty. A failure to confront in training the various ethical dilemmas that may be faced by a policeman can compound this situation. Recruits may get the idea that a department's command really does not care about ethics in borderline situations. Or they may simply never realize that some practices constitute ethical violations, especially if they have not been so informed, and if they see other officers engaging in such practices.

Low salaries may also contribute to police dishonesty, both by making it more difficult to recruit able men and by providing a convenient rationale for illegal enrichment.

ISOLATION

The climate of isolation between police and community that exists in some places, particularly in slum neighborhoods, has a pervasive influence in supporting misconduct. In such neighborhoods a policeman tends to see only the bad and to have contact with residents only when they have committed an offense. He may come to feel that the problems he is to deal with are insoluble and that he has no support or cooperation from the community. It is easy for the man who feels himself to be an outcast to react by disregarding standards of ethics and law.

A dishonest officer in such precincts may also, in fact, be less liable to exposure. In too many such cases there is little formal contact between responsible police officials and residents. The latter may feel with justification that to protest dishonest police behavior is futile.

These neighborhoods are characterized as undesirable assignment districts, and, in fact, many officers have been transferred there because of past misconduct. Often too, these neighborhoods may have a history of being ignored not only by the police but by the many agencies of government. Consequently, when a department contains a few dishonest officers, and when the story heard is of police tolerance of misconduct, the slumdweller who wants to rely upon the police for protection and counsel may eventually become seriously disillusioned not only with the police but also with all branches of government. This is one important reason why it is recommended in chapter 5 that the most highly qualified officers be assigned to high crime areas and to areas of social unrest.

This same isolation tends also to close off discussion of progressive ideas of law enforcement. Outside surveys and research that would analyze organizational structure, personnel, and other important police matters might also uncover dishonest practice. Therefore, corrupt officers, especially those who might hold supervisory positions, will seek to discourage such research. As a result, lax departments may continue with practices that have been discredited and replaced years before in other cities by responsible police officials.

MAINTAINING POLICE INTEGRITY

It is the police themselves, in the vast majority of cases, who are ridding their profession of the unethical and the corrupt. An ever-increasing number of law enforcement leaders are realizing that vigilance against such practices is a continuing part of their responsibilities. For over 40 years Director J. Edgar Hoover and his associates throughout the FBI organization have set an outstanding example of integrity within a law enforcement agency. Through the influence of its special agents throughout the country, working in close contact with local police officers, and through its training programs at the FBI National Academy and local training schools, the FBI has encouraged thousands of police officers to emulate its standards.

National, State, and local police associations have also done a great deal to encourage police integrity. The Law Enforcement Code of Ethics has been adopted by all major police associations and agencies throughout the Nation. In California, for example, State law requires that police ethics be taught and that the code be administered as an oath to all police recruits training in the 45 police academies certified by the State Commission on Peace Officers Standards.[16] In 1955, the International Conference of Police Associations[17] developed a lesson plan for the teaching of ethics within police organizations. The California Peace Officers Association and the Peace Officers Research Association maintain highly active committees on police standards and ethics and are responsible for most of the high ethical standards established throughout the State. And the International Association of Chiefs of Police constantly strives to establish and maintain honest police leadership. Other police consulting firms have made similar recommendations. Through numerous surveys of police departments, it has pointed up the need for maintaining police integrity through the establishment of internal investigation units. The Fraternal Order of Police has stressed the need for attracting high caliber police recruits through adequate salaries, sound retirement systems and other benefits.

Such groups should increase their activity in this field. Local police associations especially must be alert to the problem, recognizing the relationship between maintaining integrity and good conduct and improving the public image of the police. This can lead to more adequate pay and equipment, along with improved working conditions. Associations that come to the aid of dishonest

---

[16] Admin. Code of Cal., tit. 2, ch. 2, sec. 1003.

[17] Until 1955, known as the National Conference of Police Associations.

officers render an obvious disservice, not only to themselves, but to the entire police profession.

There are a number of specific directions in which action to ensure integrity should be taken.

POLITICAL ACCOUNTABILITY

Political accountability of the police should be resolved solely at the executive level. The police chief should be responsible to only one executive, and not to minor officials. These officials should bring their suggestions and questions about law enforcement problems to the attention of the political executive. If he considers the matter appropriate for police action, it should be his responsibility to communicate it to the chief of police. General enforcement policies should be discussed among police, prosecutors, and community groups. These should be approved by the political executive and given full publicity in the community, especially with those directly affected.

LAW ENFORCEMENT CODE OF ETHICS

As a Law Enforcement Officer, my fundamental duty is to serve mankind; to safeguard lives and property; to protect the innocent against deception, the weak against oppression or intimidation, and the peaceful against violence or disorder; and to respect the Constitutional rights of all men to liberty, equality and justice.

I will keep my private life unsullied as an example to all; maintain courageous calm in the face of danger, scorn, or ridicule; develop self-restraint; and be constantly mindful of the welfare of others. Honest in thought and deed in both my personal and official life, I will be exemplary in obeying the laws of the land and the regulations of my department. Whatever I see or hear of a confidential nature or that is confided to me in my official capacity will be kept ever secret unless revelation is necessary in the performance of my duty.

I will never act officiously or permit personal feelings, prejudices, animosities or friendships to influence my decisions. With no compromise for crime and with relentless prosecution of criminals, I will enforce the law courteously and appropriately without fear or favor, malice or ill will, never employing unnecessary force or violence and never accepting gratuities.

I recognize the badge of my office as a symbol of public faith, and I accept it as a public trust to be held so long as I am true to the ethics of the police service. I will constantly strive to achieve these objectives and ideals, dedicating myself before God to my chosen profession . . . law enforcement.

[18] Oakland Police Department "Manual of Rules and Regulations," (Oakland, Calif.: Oakland Police Department, 1960).

ARTICULATION OF POLICY

Police departments should establish policies that outline in detail proper and improper police practice. As discussed in chapter 2 such policies should be stressed in training, reviewed fully with all officers, and publicized in the community at large. The public should be expressly informed of its duties in helping prevent corruption. It should be stressed that prompt action will be taken against persons who participate in violations. Departments should define as unethical the acceptance of gifts, gratuities and favors by police officers, and should outline the common situations in which temptations to engage in dishonest conduct may arise. And such a rule must be enforced. The Oakland Police Department rules and regulations provide the following:

Section 310.70 Gifts, Gratuities, Fees, Rewards, Loans, etc., and Soliciting

Members and employees shall not under any circumstances solicit any gift, gratuity, loan, or fee where there is any direct or indirect connection between the solicitation and their departmental membership and employment.

Section 310.71 Acceptance of Gifts, Gratuities, Fees, Loans, etc.

Members and employees shall not accept either directly or indirectly any gift, gratuity, loan, fee, or any other thing of value arising from or offered because of police employment or any activity connected with said employment. Members and employees shall not accept any gift, gratuity, loan, fee, or other thing of value the acceptance of which might tend to influence directly or indirectly the actions of said member or employee or any other member or employee in any matter of police business; or which might tend to cast any adverse reflection on the department or any member or employee thereof. No member or employee of the department shall receive any gift or gratuity from other members or employees junior in rank without the express permission of the chief of police.

Section 310.74 Rewards

Members and employees shall not accept any gift, gratuity, or reward in money or other consideration for services in the line of duty to the community or to any person, business, or agency except lawful salary and that authorized by Section 96.4 of the Charter of the City of Oakland which reads as follows: "The Board of Trustees may on notice from the chief of police reward any member of the department for conduct which is heroic or meritorious. The sum or amount of such reward shall be discretionary with the Board of Trustees but it shall not exceed in any one instance one month's salary and may be paid only out of funds provided by the Council and the Council may on application of the Board of Trustees provide money for such purposes." (Commission note: No reward has been granted since 1950.)

Section 310.80 Free Admissions and Passes

Members and employees shall not solicit or accept free admissions or passes to theatres and other places of amusement for themselves or others except in the line of duty.[18]

Assignments which represent particular opportunity for extortion or bribery should receive special attention in both written policy and spot checking by an internal investigation unit. Particular attention should be given to department assignments that offer unusual opportunities for dishonesty. Vice or gambling squads are obvious examples. Some of the most routine assignments, such as traffic enforcement and inspection duty, may also contain leverage for extortion.

Reasonably precise procedures should be established to govern individual decisions where the exercise of discretion may be bargained for, such as the policing of bars, the assignment of wrecked or illegally-parked automobiles to towing companies and the removal of sick and injured persons by ambulance. Departments should also establish policies and regulations governing situations in which officers may take advantage of their position of authority in nonduty situations such as offduty employment which conflicts with police interests and the acceptance of price concessions from businessmen. And procedures should be formulated which adequately control the care, custody, and release of property and evidence held by the police, especially money, liquor, jewelry; and firearms.

INTERNAL INVESTIGATION UNITS

Internal investigation units should be established in all medium-sized and large police departments. These should serve in the dual role of general intelligence and investigation of specific reported cases of police misconduct.

In small departments, the chief, or at least a ranking officer, should be responsible for a planned program to ensure integrity. These units should also give attention to causes and manifestations of misconduct, and they should suggest to the police executive appropriate ways to prevent corruption. Such an internal investigation unit should operate separately from the law enforcement intelligence units, which have been established in many larger departments to provide information for attacks on organized crime. Otherwise, it might be impossible for the intelligence unit to gain the confidence and trust of officers and informants.

By broadening their responsibilities beyond investigating reported cases for prosecution, internal investigation units can keep the police administrator aware of various activities within the department that are most vulnerable or have the potential of becoming vehicles of dishonesty. They may also detect unreported instances of unethical conduct.

The problem of misconduct should not be treated as a series of isolated incidents. As an example, one department may discover officers who accept money or goods from local merchants in exchange for nonenforcement of traffic violations of customers or supply companies. The investigation unit may be able to discover the identity of most of the officers responsible, prove the charge, and have them dismissed from the department and prosecuted. At that point, the case is closed.

To stop here, however, leaves unsolved the question of why these officers become involved and others did not, and why some districts were especially prone to have dishonest officers and others were not. Analysis of the information gathered by the investigation unit may provide a variety of answers. One may be that officers who have turned dishonest have pressing debts, or supervision is lax. Or again, such officers may have remained in one assignment for periods greater than others.

Such information is of obvious value in preventing further dishonesty. Unless the study is carried this far, there is at least some reason to suspect that these contributory factors eventually may bring about a reappearance of dishonest practices.

Where cities do not have the resources to maintain adequate internal investigation units, the chief of police should seek assistance from the State attorney general or the State police in attacking internal integrity problems. State governments should provide the necessary trained investigators to assist local authorities. Chapter 4 suggests that police manpower should be pooled in a metropolitan area or among a cluster of cities, to provide the internal investigation support necessary to maintain police integrity. In some areas where professional police organizations exist at the county level it may be possible to provide an internal investigation unit to serve the entire county. In those States where the attorney general has responsibility to move against police dishonesty at the city and the county level this responsibility should be vigorously carried out by him.

PROSECUTION OF CASES OF DISHONESTY

Police officials have sometimes argued that instances of police misconduct should be quietly resolved within a department itself. Evidence seems to indicate, however, that a department achieves greater respect from the community when dishonest officers are openly and vigorously prosecuted.

Similarly, private citizens and businessmen who offer bribes should also be prosecuted to discourage people who presently feel that only the most serious corruption is considered important enough to investigate or prosecute.

PERSONNEL SELECTION

Perhaps the most fundamental method of maintaining integrity in law enforcement is through careful selection of personnel. All of the selection techniques available today must be used, including comprehensive background investigations and reliable tests to determine aptitude and emotional stability. As pointed out in chapter 5, personnel testing experts recognize that it is much more difficult to predict latent dishonesty than to predict some other forms of deviant human behavior. Research in depth is needed to devise adequate testing procedures which will provide the police with more reliable screening techniques than now exist.

TRAINING

Officers should be taught the importance of ethics in law enforcement. Training should fully delineate the pitfalls that an officer will face and explain how he can avoid them.

It should clearly indicate the types of action to be taken by the officer under different circumstances, including, for instance, how he should proceed when he witnesses or learns of dishonest acts on the part of another officer. Training should also cover departmental policies for proper decisionmaking and should emphasize proper conduct as a factor in maintaining good community relations.

Training should especially emphasize the obligation of all officers to rid the profession of the unethical, and it should instill in the trainee a feeling of pride in his important work. In this regard FBI Director J. Edgar Hoover has stated: [19]

If every officer and law enforcement agency must suffer in some degree from charges made against other officers, we cannot afford to take a passive view, shrugging the matter off as none of our business.

I believe it is the duty of every officer in every law enforcement agency to take a personal interest in maintaining a high standard of conduct with his organization. To do otherwise invites public disgrace. The traitor to ethical standards of law enforcement will be discovered, but often not until he has brought a great deal of harm to both the public interest and the reputation of his organization and fellow officers. We should separate such elements from the profession at the earliest opportunity.

No matter what laws are passed or rules made, public service still demands the highest in personal integrity. We must demonstrate that the men of law enforcement have it in abundance.

PRIVATE POLICE

Traditional police tasks are not always performed by governmental police agencies alone. In order to reduce the threat of vandalism and theft, for example, industrial plants and department stores, among others, often hire private security agencies to provide protective services above and beyond that provided by a local police department. Although the right of these agencies to arrest, to search, or to question is no different from that given to any private citizen, their presence can serve as an added deterrent to persons who are seeking an opportunity to commit crimes. When someone is caught in the act of violating the law, security personnel typically either release the offender after a warning—if the misconduct is minor—or turn him over to the local police.

Recently the Governor of Florida hired a private security agency for quite a different purpose—to uncover facts about crime conditions and corruption within his State. The agency, which is responsible to the Governor alone, has been soliciting information about organized crime and reviewing books and records of selected public officials. As a result, it has accumulated files on individuals and has made at least one arrest.

Any agency that assumes responsibility for law enforcement must be held to high standards of integrity and respect for individual rights. Since it is not possible to subject private agencies to the necessary controls and safeguards that are imposed upon public police agencies, private police agencies should not be used to perform essential public law enforcement tasks, such as the gathering of criminal intelligence, for any branch or agency of government or for any elected or appointed official.

---

[19] J. Edgar Hoover, "Message from the Director." FBI Law Enforcement Bulletin (Washington: U.S. Department of Justice, December 1951).

Chapter 8

Implementation Through State Commissions on Police Standards

ROLE OF POLICE STANDARDS COMMISSIONS

A State Commission on Police Standards can do much to improve local law enforcement. Without removing control of law enforcement from local agencies, a Commission can help to establish adequate personnel selection standards, to strengthen training procedures, to coordinate recruitment, and to improve the organization and operations of local departments.

Commissions on Police Standards and Training now exist in several States. Some of them are more effective than others; all could be significantly improved. In most States, the Commissions do not have the power either to establish mandatory standards or to give financial assistance to local departments. This lack of authority limits their impact. If properly constituted and empowered, however, State Commissions on Police Standards could play a significant role in the process of upgrading police effectiveness.

STATE STANDARDS

A Commission should begin its work by selecting a strong and active full-time staff with access to a wide network of experts in law enforcement agencies, the rest of the criminal justice system, and colleges and universities. The Commission should then evaluate the current situation in its State through studies and hearings. The Crime Commission's work disclosed that the qualifications of police officers were generally lower in small departments than in large ones. It also found that small communities suffered because their resources to train, equip, and compensate personnel could not compare with those of larger cities. The Commission's research revealed that recruitment and promotion in many departments is governed by inflexible standards that are often unrelated to the real needs of law enforcement. A State Commission could help resolve many of these problems.

MINIMUM SELECTION AND PROMOTION STANDARDS

An important early step for State Commissions is to set basic minimum selection standards applicable to all departments. The recommendation in chapter 5 of this volume that all future police officers be required to have a high school diploma and proven ability to do college work could be one such standard. A requirement that an extensive background investigation and an oral interview be conducted of all potential officers is another. It would be a mistake, however, for a state-level body to establish minimum standards of residence, height, weight and age; the Commission recommends flexibility in such standards, so that individual departments can meet their own recruitment needs. The role of the State Commission here should be to encourage civil service reforms to achieve such flexibility and to promote programs and services that can help departments adjust to more flexible standards. Frequent physical fitness and medical examinations, for example, might replace rigid physical requirements. An example of existing minimum standards for recruitment is contained in the regulations of the California Commission on Peace Officer Standards and Training:

Minimum Standards for Recruitment

(a) The minimum standards shall be the following:
 (1) Citizen of the United States.
 (2) Minimum age of 21 years.
 (3) Fingerprinting of applicants with a search of local, State and national fingerprint files to disclose any criminal record.
 (4) Shall not have been convicted by any State or by the Federal Government of a crime, the punishment for which could have been imprisonment in a Federal penitentiary or a State prison.
 (5) Good moral character as determined by a thorough background investigation according to specifications entitled, "The Personal History Investigation" published by the Commission.
 (6) Graduation from high school or a passing of the General Education Development test indicating high school graduation level, or a score on a written test of mental ability approved by the Commission and equivalent to that attained by the average high school student.
 (7) Examination by a licensed physician and surgeon. Only those applicants who are found to be free from any physical, emotional or mental condition which might adversely affect performance of his duty as a peace officer shall be eligible for appointment. The applicant's declaration of medical history and the physician's findings upon the examination shall be recorded on forms which shall include but are not limited to all of the items set forth in the specification entitled, "Physical Examination" published by the Commission.
 (8) An oral interview shall be held by the hiring authority or his representative, or representatives, to determine such things as the recruit's appearance, background, and ability to communicate.
 (b) It is emphasized that these are minimum entrance standards. Higher standards are recommended whenever the availability of qualified applicants meets the demand.

It might be desirable in some situations to set different basic standards for departments in communities of different sizes, to ensure that incentive for improvement is given to large cities as well as to smaller towns. Organizational criteria or recommended educational standards for supervisors, for example, will often vary according to department size; clearly the chief of a force of 20 men does not need qualifications as broad as the chief of a 2,500-man force.

An important and difficult problem that State Commissions should also consider is the screening and evaluating procedures for recruitment, retention, and promotion of police personnel. Some departments may need advice about how to conduct adequate background investigations, how to structure personnel interviews, or how to evaluate officers during a probation period. In addition to determining methods for assessing applicants' character, aptitude, and career potential, State Commissions could suggest ways of assessing applicants' attitudes in order to keep prejudiced persons out of police service and to aid in assigning men to duties for which they are best fitted by temperament and background.

There is also a definite need to set standards for promotion and retention, on the basis of educational achievement and on-the-job performance. Here again, a State Commission could suggest appropriate means for such evaluation. And when departments encounter difficulties in implementing reforms, the experience and resources of a State Commission would be invaluable.

Chapter 5 discusses the advantages of permitting lateral entry of qualified persons into all positions within a police department. Few departments permit this today because of rigid civil service regulations, retirement requirements and other restrictions. State Commissions could be especially effective in suggesting ways of removing impediments to lateral entry.

Not the least of the responsibilities of a standards commission would be convincing local governing bodies and law enforcement officials of the desirability of undertaking innovations of all sorts, and helping to put these innovations into effect.

TRAINING STANDARDS AND PROGRAMS

Strengthening recruit, inservice, and career development training is the area in which a State Commission can be of most immediate help. With some exceptions, only the largest departments have been able to conduct independent training programs adequate to meet the needs of today's police service. And even large departments in many cases need help in developing specialized programs on subjects such as riot control, community relations, legal developments, ethics, discretionary decisionmaking, and implementation of policy. Regardless of size, all departments should be afforded the opportunity to use programs prepared and presented by qualified instructors. Commissions could encourage the use of talented civilian instructors from other disciplines to teach specialized subjects such as law, psychology, or race relations.

The first step in establishing training programs is to develop a curriculum and to determine the minimum number of classroom hours required for each subject. Standards should be set for facilities, course materials, classroom and field techniques, training aids, and qualifications of instructors. State Commissions could help recruit and orient instructors, and provide grants for developing better teaching materials and methods.

The two States which have the most extensive programs in training for policemen are California and New York.[1] Although these programs have the same objective of establishing statewide minimum standards for training, the procedures for accomplishing this end differ. In New York, all recruits must satisfactorily complete a prescribed training program of 240 hours before they are qualified to serve as policemen in the State. Under the law, the Municipal Police Training Council must approve police training schools, certify instructors, and certify police officers who have satisfactorily completed a basic training program. The State of New York, however, does not provide financial assistance to local departments to help them comply with the mandatory standards.

California, on the other hand, has enacted a statewide program of police training which is voluntary in nature. The Commission on Peace Officer Standards and Training is empowered to establish minimum standards for training and is authorized to reimburse all qualifying jurisdictions in an amount not to exceed one-half of the necessary living expenses incurred by the policeman if he is required to take his training away from his home. The State Commission now requires recruits to receive a minimum of 200 hours of prescribed basic training and first line supervisors a minimum of 80 hours of supervisory training before a department can qualify for State aid. During 1966, 98 percent of the population was served by police agencies which adhered to minimum standards for police training. The 2,700 recruits for California departments received an average of 370 hours of basic training. The New York and California programs each have their advantages, but it would seem that higher training standards could be accomplished more quickly if a State provided financial assistance to local departments.

A State Commission might also initiate continuing education programs for potential officers who meet all department qualifications except the educational requirement. Courses could be provided through the Department of Education or through government grants. Commissions could also be instrumental in developing training programs along new lines, such as a program designed to fulfill the needs of the community service officer.

State Commissions should draw heavily on the resources of police science programs in colleges and universities for their work in the training area, as California has done. Since basic college preparation for the police should gradually be directed away from strictly technical or vocational courses, these latter resources could best be used to improve the level of training programs. Police science program coordinators could, for example, be used by a State Commission in setting up a model training school to serve a cluster of smaller departments; in coordinating the annual intensive refresher courses that should serve as a core for continuing training; and in planning curriculum development and instructor training programs.

The challenges in the training area are, in short, enormous, and the need for aggressive, imaginative efforts by State Commissions is urgent. In the training field par-

---

[1] See Cal. Penal Code secs. 13500–13523; N.Y.S. Exec. Law Art. 19–F, secs. 480–487.

ticularly, such commissions can have a direct impact on the caliber of law enforcement throughout an entire State.

POLICE ORGANIZATION AND MANAGEMENT

Commissions can also help greatly to improve police organization, management, and operations. This is a more difficult task than improving training or raising personnel standards. And while it is not always possible to prescribe exact minimum standards for police organizations, State Commissions can encourage improvements in the organization and operation of departments by sponsoring surveys and by making recommendations for upgrading the operations of individual departments. They can also conduct studies to recommend ways of coordinating or pooling the resources and services of groups of departments. Commissions could provide the kind of foresight and planning that is needed on a statewide basis to permit the establishment of computer systems and the standardization of records and forms to accommodate such systems.

Surveys of police agencies have been undertaken with success for many years by the International Association of Chiefs of Police, the Public Administration Service of Chicago and others, but they have reached only a few of the Nation's 40,000 police departments. In many cases, departments that had been surveyed did not have sufficient expertise to implement the recommendations that were made. If, however, a survey were to be conducted under the auspices of a State Commission, its field representatives could assist a department in adopting recommended changes.

In 1965, the State of New York established a Division of Police Administration Services with the following functions: [2]

1. To collect, compile and disseminate current information regarding general developments in the field of police administration and operations.
2. To serve as a clearinghouse, for the benefit of police agencies, of information relating to their common administrative problems.
3. To conduct studies and analyses of the administration or operations of any police agency, when requested by the head of such agency, and to make the result thereof available for the benefit of such agency.
4. To refer police agencies to appropriate departments and agencies of the State and Federal Governments for advice, assistance, and available services in connection with particular administrative problems.
5. To encourage the further professionalization of police administration.
6. To do all things necessary or convenient to carry out the functions, powers and duties expressly set forth in this article.

During its first year of operation, the agency received requests for assistance from 36 separate local law enforcement departments in New York on such matters as records surveys; revised rules and regulations; manpower allocations; and organizational charts. The staff for the new agency is not yet large enough, however, to engage in extensive research or survey work.

The objectives of the New York program are worthy ones. Other States are encouraged to create an agency similar to New York's and appoint sufficient qualified staff. But, as is suggested in the following section, one State agency should assume responsibility for supervising both peace officer training and improving police organization, management, and field operations statewide.

RECOMMENDATIONS FOR ORGANIZATION AND OPERATION OF STATE COMMISSIONS

As early as 1952, the American Bar Association, in conjunction with the National Conference of Commissioners on Uniform State Laws, recognized the need to develop a State Council to serve as a catalyst in improving law enforcement. Together they published a Model Police Council Act. This act, with significant revisions, served as a model for the States of New York and California, which established State Police Standards Commissions in 1959. Since then, many variations of this legislation have been enacted in other States.

It is crucial that legislation creating a Commission on Police Standards be broad enough to authorize the commission to take the following actions:

☐ To adopt regulations establishing mandatory minimum standards relating to educational, mental, moral, and physical fitness, which shall govern the selection of police officers.
☐ To establish mandatory minimum training standards with the authority to determine and approve curricula; to identify required preparation for instructors; and to approve facilities acceptable for police training.
☐ To certify police officers who have acquired various levels of education, training, and experience necessary to perform adequately the duties of the police service.
☐ To conduct surveys of the administration and operation of police departments or aid governmental units in providing for surveys to be conducted by other agencies or consulting firms, and to assist governmental units in the implementation of recommendations.
☐ To conduct studies and make recommendations concerning means by which participating police agencies can pool individual resources.
☐ To conduct and stimulate research by public and private agencies designed to improve police administration and law enforcement.
☐ To make such inquiries and inspections as may be necessary to determine whether or not the standards established in the regulations are in fact being adhered to.
☐ To provide such financial aid as may be authorized by the legislature to participating governmental units.

THE IACP MODEL POLICE STANDARDS COUNCIL ACT

In 1966, after considerable research, a Model Police Standards Council Act was drafted by the Advisory Council on Police Training and Education and the Professional Standards Division of the International Association of Chiefs of Police, under a grant from the Ford Foundation. While the language in some of its sections differs slightly from that suggested above, the adoption of this Act, including the broad powers suggested above, and

---

[2] See N.Y.S. Exec. Law Art. 20, secs. 550–553.

the provision of adequate financing would permit any State to implement the essential programs described in this chapter. The Model Police Standards Council Act is attached as appendix A.

THE CONTINUING ROLE OF STATE COMMISSIONS

A State Commission can provide the focus that is needed by law enforcement agencies to give greater impetus to their progress. In addition to the areas outlined above, it can, for example, be an effective voice in promoting greater coordination among law enforcement agencies, among agencies within the administration of justice, with community groups, and with other units of government.

Moreover, it can be one of several action agencies in helping the State and local planning units, proposed in chapter 13 of the "General Report," to develop and carry out its programs. Some States may prefer to make the State Commission on Police Standards an arm of the State planning agency; others may want them to be independent of one another. In either case, a State Commission on Police Standards should provide invaluable information and expertise on police problems and needs to a State planning agency and in return should receive assistance in the development of new programs and standards for local law enforcement.

But the State Commission on Police Standards and Training can also initiate the research that must continually test, challenge, and evaluate professional techniques, procedures and indeed its own minimum standards in order to keep abreast of social and technical change. And though the task is difficult, it can help develop within the ranks of law enforcement the vision, inventiveness, and leadership that is necessary to meet the complex challenges facing the police of our cities.

APPENDIX A
MODEL POLICE STANDARDS COUNCIL ACT OF――

(Title should conform to State requirements. The following is a suggestion: "An act establishing a Police Standards Council; providing certain educational and training requirements for members of police forces; and for related purposes.")

(Be it enacted, etc.)

SECTION 1. FINDINGS AND POLICY

The legislature finds that the administration of criminal justice is of statewide concern, and that police work is important to the health, safety, and welfare of the people of this State and is of such a nature as to require education and training of a professional character. It is in the public interest that such education and training be made available to persons who seek to become police officers, persons who are serving as such officers in a temporary or probationary capacity, and persons already in regular service.

SECTION 2. POLICE OFFICER DEFINED

As used in this Act:
"Police officer" means any full-time employee of a police department which is a part of or administered by the State or any political subdivision thereof and who is responsible for the prevention and detection of crime and the enforcement of the penal, traffic, or highway laws of this State.

SECTION 3. POLICE STANDARDS COUNCIL

(a) There is hereby established a Police Standards Council, hereinafter called "the Council," in the Executive Office of the Governor. The Council shall be composed of 15 members, as follows: Five chief administrative officers of local government police forces, at least 3 of whom shall be from forces maintained by incorporated municipalities; 5 officials or employees of local government who have general executive or legislative responsibilities with respect thereto so chosen as to represent county government and municipal government; [the head of the State police], 1 representative of higher education, 2 public members and the Attorney General.

(b) Except for the Attorney General and the [head of the State police] who shall serve during their continuance in those offices, members of the Council shall be appointed by the Governor for terms of 4 years: provided that no member shall serve beyond the time when he holds the office or employment by reason of which he was initially eligible for appointment. Notwithstanding anything in this section to the contrary, the terms of members initially appointed to the Council by the Governor upon its establishment shall be: three for 1 year, three for 2 years, three for 3 years, and four for 4 years. The Governor, at the time of appointment, shall designate which of the terms are respectively for 1, 2, 3 and 4 years. Any vacancy on the Council shall be filled in the same manner as the original appointment, but for the unexpired term.

(c) The Governor annually shall designate the chairman of the Council, and the Council annually shall select its vice chairman. The chairman and vice chairman shall be designated and selected from among the members of the Council.

(d) Notwithstanding any provision of any statute, ordinance, local law, or charter provision to the contrary, membership on the Council shall not disqualify any member from holding any other public office or employment, or cause the forfeiture thereof.

(e) Members of the Council shall serve without compensation, but shall be entitled to receive reimbursement for any actual expenses incurred as a necessary incident to such service.

(f) The Council shall hold no less than four regular meetings a year. Subject to the requirements of this subsection, the chairman shall fix the times and places of meetings, either on his own motion or upon written request of any [five] members of the Council.

(g) The Council shall report annually to the Governor and legislature on its activities, and may make such other reports as it deems desirable.

SECTION 4. POWERS

In addition to powers conferred upon the Council elsewhere in this act, the Council shall have power to:
1. Promulgate rules and regulations for the administration of this act including the authority to require the submission of reports and information by police departments within this State.

2. Establish minimum educational and training standards for admission to employment as a police officer: (a) in permanent positions, and (b) in temporary or probationary status.

3. Certify persons as being qualified under the provisions of this act to be police officers.

4. Establish minimum curriculum requirements for preparatory, inservice and advanced courses and programs for schools operated by or for the State or any political subdivisions thereof for the specific purpose of training police recruits or police officers.

5. Consult and cooperate with counties, municipalities, agencies of this State, other governmental agencies, and with universities, colleges, junior colleges, and other institutions concerning the development of police training schools and programs or courses of instruction.

6. Approve institutions and facilities for school operation by or for the State or any political subdivision thereof for the specific purpose of training police officers and police recruits.

7. Make or encourage studies of any aspect of police administration.

8. Conduct and stimulate research by public and private agencies which shall be designed to improve police administration and law enforcement.

9. Make recommendations concerning any matter within its purview pursuant to this act.

10. Employ a Director and such other personnel as may be necessary in the performance of its functions.

11. Make such evaluations as may be necessary to determine if governmental units are complying with the provisions of this act.

12. Adopt and amend bylaws, consistent with law, for its internal management and control.

13. Enter into contracts or do such things as may be necessary and incidental to the administration of its authority pursuant to this act.

SECTION 5. EDUCATION AND TRAINING REQUIRED

(a) Police officers already serving under permanent appointment on the effective date of this act shall not be required to meet any requirement of subsections (b) and (c) of this section as a condition of tenure or continued employment; nor shall failure of any such police officer to fulfill such requirements make him ineligible for any promotional examination for which he is otherwise eligible. The legislature finds, and it is hereby declared to be the policy of this act, that such police officers have satisfied such requirements by their experience.

(b) At the earliest practicable time, the Council shall provide, by regulation, that no person shall be appointed as a police officer, except on a temporary or probationary basis, unless such person has satisfactorily completed a preparatory program of police training at a school approved by the Council, and is the holder of a bachelor's degree from an accredited institution. No police officer who lacks the education and training qualifications required by the Council may have his temporary or probationary employment extended beyond 1 year by renewal of appointment or otherwise.

(c) In addition to the requirements of subsections (b), (e), and (f) of this section, the Council, by rules and regulations, shall fix other qualifications for the employment and promotion of police officers, including minimum age, education, physical and mental standards, citizenship, good moral character, experience, and such other matters as relate to the competence and reliability of persons to assume and discharge the responsibilities of police officers, and the Council shall prescribe the means for presenting evidence of fulfillment of these requirements.

(d) The Council shall issue a certificate evidencing satisfaction of the requirements of subsections (b) and (c) of this Section to any applicant who presents such evidence as may be required by its rules and regulations of satisfactory completion of a program or course of instruction in another jurisdiction equivalent in content and quality to that required by the Council for approved police education and training programs in this State.

(e) After the effective date of this act, each candidate for employment as a police officer who receives passing scores on his employment entrance examinations shall have credits, as established by the Council, added to his total examination scores for studies which he has satisfactorily completed at an accredited institution of higher learning in a program leading to a degree.

(f) Each police officer who is a candidate for promotion also shall receive educational credits as determined in section 5 on promotional examinations.

SECTION 6. POLICE TRAINING SCHOOLS AND PROGRAMS: GRANTS UNDER THE SUPERVISION OF COUNCIL AND THE STATE

(a) The Council shall establish and maintain police training programs through such agencies and institutions as the Council may deem appropriate.

(b) The Council shall authorize the reimbursement to each political subdivision and to the State 50 percent of the salary and of the allowable tuition, living, and travel expenses incurred by the officers in attendance at approved training programs, providing said political subdivisions or State agencies do in fact adhere to the selection and training standards established by the Council.

SECTION 7. APPROPRIATIONS

(a) Except as otherwise specifically provided in this Section, the Council shall be supported only by appropriations made by the legislature.

(b) The Council may accept for any of its purposes and functions under this act any and all donations, both real and personal, and grants of money from any governmental unit or public agency, or from any institution, person, firm, or corporation, and may receive, utilize, and dispose of the same. Any arrangements pursuant to this subsection shall be detailed in the annual report of the Council. Such report shall include the identity of the donor, the nature of the transaction, and the conditions, if any. Any monies received by the Council pursuant to this subsection shall be deposited in the [State treasury] to the account of the Council.

(c) The Council, by rules and regulations, shall provide for the administration of the grant program authorized by this Section. In promulgating such rules, the Council shall promote the most efficient and economical program for police training, including the maximum utilization of existing facilities and programs for the purpose of avoiding duplication.

(d) The Council may provide grants as a reimbursement for actual expenses incurred by the State or political subdivisions thereof for the provisions of training programs to officers from other jurisdictions within the State.

SECTION 8. SEVERABILITY

The provisions of this act shall be severable and if any phrase, clause, sentence, or provision of this act is declared to be contrary to the Constitution or laws of this State or of the United States or the applicability thereof to any government, agency, person, or circumstance is held invalid, the validity of the remainder of this act and the applicability thereof to any government, agency, person, or circumstance shall not be affected thereby.

SECTION 9. REPEALING CLAUSE

All acts or parts of acts not consistent with this act are hereby repealed.

Chapter 9

The Community's Role in Law Enforcement

The previous chapters of this volume have detailed the steps, both long and short range, the police should take to increase their effectiveness. However, crime is not the business of the police alone.[1] On an average night in a city of half a million population, 65 police officers will be on patrol duty. No matter how well trained, well organized, and well equipped they are, they cannot be at the scene of every crime when it is committed, and this would be true if they numbered 65 or 650. The police need help from citizens, from private organizations, from other municipal agencies, and from crime prevention legislation. This chapter will give examples of how citizens can aid the police by protecting themselves and by creating new resources for crime prevention and the rehabilitation of criminals.

The role of other municipal agencies working in concert with the police in anticrime planning is examined, along with ways in which private citizens can create a continuing partnership with the police dedicated to preventing crime and solving those crimes already committed. Prevention-oriented ordinances and regulatory action are proposed.

In short, the police need help, all the help the community can give them. Methods proposed in this chapter utilize only a portion of the total community resources which could feasibly be marshalled to aid law enforcement.

The Commission had neither time nor resources to survey and evaluate specific programs for community assistance to law enforcement throughout the Nation. However, in the course of its work it did receive information about such programs, and it was assured by citizens and police officials in a number of communities that such programs were of great value. The intention of this chapter is to report this information, and to urge police departments and citizen groups throughout the country to consider its practical application in their own communities.[2]

CITIZEN PRECAUTIONS AGAINST CRIME

It is evident that, without significant inconvenience to themselves, citizens can take several commonsense measures that will reduce the threat of crime to their persons or property. For example, the number of crimes that involve negligence on the part of their victims is needlessly high. Departing homeowners act sensibly when they lock their doors and windows securely; leave automatically activated night lights burning during lengthy absences; lock the garage doors and cancel milk and newspaper deliveries; and alert the neighbors or police to their absence. A survey of housebreakings in the District of Columbia in 1965 revealed that almost three-quarters of all intrusions were made while the owner was gone, 20 percent of them through unlocked windows or doors.[3] The kind of property most commonly stolen from homeowners is radios, TV's, tape recorders, cameras, and other salable items. Many homeowners wisely choose to record the serial numbers of goods for later tracing by the police in case of theft or burglary.

Individuals can also maintain a reasonable awareness of danger in other facets of their daily lives. This includes maintaining a healthy alertness in encounters with strangers at the door or on the streets and avoidance of situations which leave the potential victim defenseless to personal attack or powerless to summon aid. These are normal, not hysterical, responses to modern urban life. Similarly, children can be matter-of-factly warned of the dangers of advances from strangers in a way that does not frighten or confuse them.

Simple precautions are particularly important in preventing auto thefts. Car owners should remove the keys from the ignition and lock their cars when they park. The District of Columbia crime survey showed 50 percent of stolen cars in 1 month were unlocked; 19 percent of the owners had left the keys in the ignition.[4] And a national survey in 1965 showed an even greater degree of owner negligence; 42 percent of the stolen cars had the ignition unlocked or the keys visible![5]

Storeowners and businesses have an even greater responsibility to make the task of the potential theft, robbery or burglary a more difficult one. They can do so by keeping a minimum amount of cash on hand, varying routines for taking money to the bank, balancing cash registers away from checkout counters, locating safes in well-lighted spots highly visible from the outside of the building, and using two-man teams to open and close the stores.

Pyramid telephone warning systems are in operation in some cities among liquor stores, grocery chains, gas sta-

---

[1] As one commentator has picturesquely put it: "Law enforcement is not a game of cops and robbers in which the citizens play the trees."
[2] For a provocative article about citizen cooperation with the police, see Howard James, "Wake Up! The Police Need Help!" "The Christian Science Monitor," Apr. 11, 1966, p. 9, cols. 1–4.

[3] "Report of the President's Commission on Crime in the District of Columbia" (Washington: U.S. Government Printing Office, 1966), pp. 80–88.
[4] Id. at pp. 97–104.
[5] FBI, "Uniform Crime Report, 1965" (Washington: U.S. Government Printing Office, 1965), p. 18.

221

tions, and clothing merchants. For example, upon receiving a report of a check fraud, shop-lifting incident, confidence game, or robbery in one store, the police telephone appropriate merchants and warn them. Those merchants in turn telephone others, giving the details of the crime and if possible, a description of the suspects. Such crimes often are committed in series, and on many occasions pyramid warnings have brought about the apprehension of suspects when they attempted subsequent crimes. And in some places, merchants have rigged a system which sends an alarm to other stores within a four-block radius, and once warned, shopkeepers watch for fleeing suspects from their vantage points. In some instances, this system has resulted in information vital to the later identification of suspects.

Adequate illumination of premises both inside and out, and secure locks are among the most useful anticrime precautions the businessman can take. The Oakland, Calif., police have found that most commercial burglaries occur in establishments with inadequate night lighting. Also, 60 percent of Washington, D.C., commercial burglaries are known to have taken place at night, over half through unlocked or breakable windows, one-third by forcing locks. Also, 64 percent of burglarized businesses are located on the ground floor.[6]

Alarm warning systems seem advisable in many cases, especially if the owner has supplied the police ahead of time with a floor plan of the store so that officers can plan a strategic entry, perhaps in time to surprise the burglar in the act. Also high walls, dead-end driveways, and heavy shrubs or foliage provide protective cover for night intruders. Such barriers should be lighted, shrubs trimmed, and areas generally opened to maximum visibility consistent with usefulness and aesthetics.

EDUCATION IN CRIME PREVENTION

Public education to alert citizens and businessmen on how to avoid becoming victims of crime can be a valuable adjunct to a crime control program. In many cases such campaigns are undertaken by the police, in other cases by interested citizens or by businessmen's groups. The best ones are often a cooperative effort. The American Association of Federated Women's Clubs and the National Auto Theft Bureau have conducted auto theft prevention campaigns in several cities, accompanying the police on their rounds, and leaving pamphlets in unlocked cars and attaching warnings to parking meters on the dangers of leaving keys in the ignition.

Another women's organization, the General Federation of Women's Clubs, has campaigned for better street lighting throughout the country. Businesses ranging from grocery chains to banks to diaper institutes have paid for pamphlets distributed to their customers on precautionary measures citizens may take to avoid crime. The Insurance Institute has made special appeals to clients on safeguarding furs and jewelry. Also the service clubs in one city bought etching tools so that the police could imprint serial numbers on valuable possessions of willing citizens. In another community, similar groups have provided a film library so that the local police department could supplement their appearances before citizens and school groups with moving pictures on such subjects as vandalism, narcotics, personal defense, and burglary protection. A midwestern sheriff has a "junior posse" of over 25,000 youngsters who distribute crime prevention literature to homeowners and apartment residents.

The police of several European countries, including Finland, Germany, and Sweden, are engaged in special programs which could be utilized by American forces. They have police advisory storefront offices set up in cities for crime prevention exhibits and staffed by police officers ready to offer advice to citizens. An English Home Office report has considered cataloging in central registries the crime prevention efforts of local police forces to permit interchange of successful techniques.[7] The report also describes the experience of English police with the crime prevention officer who is especially detailed to call on victims, offer advice and followup services, distribute crime prevention literature, undertake security needs studies, and train police force members in prevention techniques.

In 1967, under a grant by the Office of Law Enforcement Assistance of the Department of Justice, high schools in Des Moines, Iowa, are conducting a special course for 125 seniors on "The Science of Law Enforcement and Citizen Responsibility." In New York, Chicago, and Cincinnati, the police are participating in the development of materials to be used by elementary school teachers in explaining to their pupils how to avoid dangerous situations and when and how to contact the police. And the Des Moines police are running a 2½-month crime prevention course to educate the business community in how to cope most effectively with robberies, larcenies, bad checks, and vehicle thefts. Police in other cities sponsor robbery clinics for banks, savings and loan organizations, and other firms that handle large amounts of money in the routine course of business. In Oakland, the police have distributed weekly bulletins to storeowners, including details about and pictures of bad check artists or shoplifting rings operating around the city.

Crime prevention campaigns, if they involve a substantial segment of the community's residents and business people, in all probability can affect crime rates. To be effective they must, however, be built around up-to-date, accurate, and specific crime prevention advice. Moreover, the specific needs of different groups in the community must be taken into account; for example, old people, young children, nighttime workers, and neighborhood grocers all have different problems vis-a-vis crime. Appeals to each group should be individualized whenever possible; direct personal contact is superior to mere literature handouts. Social and professional groups can be an invaluable asset to the police in making the crime prevention message relevant to the interests of their members, and in turn such groups can help in getting the message over to the community as a whole.

Many members of the community, however, do not

---

[6] Supra, note 3 at pp. 80-88.
[7] "Report of Working Group on Crime Prevention Methods" (London: Her Majesty's Stationery Office, 1956), p. 3.

belong to such groups. The fact is that the most crime-ridden areas in the city are usually both the poorest and the most socially disorganized. For example, in the District of Columbia over one-half of all serious crime areas are in 5 of the 14 precincts. Any campaign that does not make a special effort to include or reach these residents through poverty centers, block organizations, churches, and schools should expect little success.

CITIZEN AID TO LAW ENFORCEMENT

In addition to taking normal precautions against crime, citizens can mobilize to help the police and other branches of the criminal justice system. The ancient frank pledge of medieval villagers can have its counterpart among modern urban dwellers who complement police action in deterring, reporting, and rehabilitating law violators.

CRIME REPORTING PROGRAMS

Several communities have experimented successfully with concerted campaigns to impress upon citizens the urgency of reporting promptly to the police all relevant information about crimes or suspicious incidents. In Chicago a million citizens and 300 citizen-organizations are involved in "Operation Crime Stop." Members are asked to call the police about any suspicious happening and to report the nature of the incident, number, and description of the persons involved, and the license numbers of any cars used. Those citizens whose information leads to the solution or prevention of a crime are publicly honored each month. "Operation Crime Stop," inaugurated on April 13, 1964, is credited by the Chicago Police Department with assisting in 7,000 arrests.

The District of Columbia Police Department launched a "Signal Ten" program in December 1966 to stimulate citizen aid to the police. The first step in this program was specifically directed against robberies. Thirty thousand leaflets were distributed to business firms; they provided the emergency police number, instructions on how to react to an armed robbery, and space on the leaflet in which witnesses could write information on crimes they witnessed and sketch the offender's appearance. Five hundred thousand small cards also were handed out to patrolmen for dispersal to robbery witnesses on the scene. They solicited the witnesses names and requested that relevant information about the crime be noted on the card. Similar programs are now in operation in Chicago and New Orleans. A Florida sheriff's department has had good results with a junior deputy program that encourages youngsters to watch for and report suspicious incidents.

The police of San Diego city and county report that the "Stamp Out Crime Crusade," founded and financed by the Independent Insurance Agents Association of California in 1965, is making a notable contribution to local crime prevention efforts. Pointed toward increasing public awareness of crime problems and encouraging citizens to assist the police, the crusade was introduced statewide in California in 1966. After 1 year of operation in San Diego, Police Chief W. S. Sharp noted the program's success: [8]

> The type of support and public awareness that the crusade has created is most welcome. Law enforcement in this city has felt its effects. In addition to a number of positive actions by citizens, we detect a swell of public support and cooperation that we have never known before.

In addition, Sheriff J. C. O'Connor of San Diego County noted: [9]

> Where once the public all too often turned the other way, there is now a willingness to "stand up and be counted," and frequently in the face of great physical danger.

Some groups have suggested that the common law doctrine of misprision of felony [i.e., concealment of felony] be revitalized to penalize witnesses who fail to report offenses they witness or learn about.[10] At the present time, where this doctrine is in effect, prosecutions usually require that the defendant be charged with active concealment of the crime or criminal rather than with mere apathy or inaction.[11] Updating the doctrine to encompass a more affirmative duty to report offenses or aid in police investigations seems worthy of further study. A comparable requirement now exists in some states to report all serious traffic accidents.

CITIZEN PREVENTIVE PATROLS

Groups of citizens in a few communities or neighborhoods complement police preventive patrols. For example, in Washington, D.C., several private citizens with "ham radios" in their cars have formed a "React" program to patrol three high crime precincts on weekends. On Friday and Saturday nights between 8 and 12 midnight, peak hours in the city's criminal activity, they cruise their beats in teams of two, alert to any potentially unruly teenage gatherings or other suspicious activity. Their function is merely to transmit information to a base station, which relays it to the police dispatcher for appropriate police coverage or surveillance. In other cities, radio band operators' clubs perform similarly, watching for stolen cars, suspicious circumstances, runaways, and escapees.

Many cities and counties have civilian police reserve units which, with sworn police officers or in groups of two or more, patrol beaches, parks, and playgrounds. In some instances they are trained to handle crowds during parades and special events, to assist in search and rescue operations, and to direct traffic. In appropriate instances they work alone. One community has stationed civil defense personnel with mobile radio equipment at posts in high hazard areas to report on disturbances or incipient difficulties.

In addition to this kind of citywide help, the residents of many neighborhoods carry on their own watchdog activities, keeping an eye on absent homeowners' property, reporting suspicious incidents and, in some cases, making neighborhood rounds.

---

[8] Letter from W. S. Sharp, Chief of Police, San Diego, to Andrew H. Ekern, chairman, Stamp Out Crime Crusade, May 3, 1966.
[9] Letter from J. C. O'Connor, Sheriff of San Diego County, to Andrew H. Ekern, Chairman, Stamp Out Crime Crusade, Nov. 14, 1966.
[10] Goldberg, "Misprision of Felony: An Old Concept in a New Context," 52 A.B.A.J. 148 (1966). Also see Sykes v. Director of Public Prosecutions (1961), 3 Weekly L.R. 371 (H.L.) Lord Denning.
[11] See Neal v. U.S., 102 F. 2d 643 (8 Cir. 1939), Interpreting 18 U.S.C. 251.

In some cities, taxicab fleets and utility company cars with their own communications systems have stepped forward and offered to serve as extra "eyes and ears" for the police. Kansas City, Mo., has "Operation Barrier," an emergency alert program involving 14 taxi, trucking, and public utility firms with over 700 radio-equipped vehicles. A direct telephone network links police dispatchers with the agency dispatchers. Police emergency broadcasts can be relayed to private vehicles, and their drivers can assist the police in identifying and tracking down offenders, all at no cost to the city. The private vehicles check in periodically with the agency dispatcher for police information. Birmingham, Chicago, Denver, Detroit, Green Bay, Wis., and New Orleans also have routine arrangements for furnishing descriptions of missing or wanted persons by radio to taxicab drivers for lookout purposes. The District of Columbia police furnish descriptions of wanted persons or cars to the mobile equipment of the city's electric and gas companies and to the bureau of traffic engineering and operations. The effectiveness of these local liaison programs inspired a recent congressional resolution to encourage direct radio communication between the police and taxicab drivers on a national scale.[12]

ENCOURAGING THE GOOD SAMARITAN

Every day in our cities the police or the victims of crime must depend on the willingness of strangers and onlookers to summon aid, render emergency services, and even help subdue assailants. In other periods, sheriffs and law enforcement officers could compel citizens in attendance at such emergencies to pitch in and help. Those on the scene were deputized as a "posse commitatus" under pain of criminal penalty for refusal.[13] There was also a common law duty on the part of citizens to prevent the commission of a felony when possible.

Such doctrines may appear highly unrealistic in today's urban setting of frequently hostile crowds, which often refuse aid or even obstruct the police in making arrests, and sometimes coldbloodedly turn their backs on victims. Improved police-community relations is probably the only long-range solution to this problem, but communities might also give consideration to removing any legal impediments that could inhibit well-motivated citizens from offering aid. For example, good samaritan laws might absolve them from legal liability for any likely consequences of their intervention; crime compensation laws might provide reimbursement for injuries or losses suffered in the incident.

Public education campaigns might well include instructions to witnesses on how best to assist police in need and what kind of aid would most benefit crime victims. Sometimes a citizen is afraid of becoming involved in a prolonged prosecution which can cause him loss of time on the job. Some departments consequently protect the anonymity of emergency callers on behalf of others. Witness fees commensurate with the inconveniences suffered by citizens while doing their legal duties might also aid in crime emergencies.

CITIZEN RESOURCES FOR CRIME PREVENTION

Through group efforts and on an individual basis citizens can provide auxiliary resources for all parts of the criminal process. Many civic groups and businesses have sponsored nationwide and local showings of documentary films like "The Thin Blue Line" or "Every Hour, Every Day."[14] In New Orleans one organization raises money for educational grants to police officers. In Spanish-speaking Harlem, a group of residents is teaching patrolmen their language. Oakland merchants have worked out an arrangement with the police department for handling first offender shoplifters without formal arrest, or in the case of juveniles, by referral to youth officers. In St. Louis unarmed adults guard school entrances at off-hours against unwelcome intruders. El Monte, Calif., has a "block mother" program sponsored by the local PTA in which one specially selected mother in each block has an open house with a sign in the window that she will help children who are lost, troubled by strangers, or hurt. The block mother also identifies children in need of supervision, trouble spots, and suspicious activities going on in the block. Many other cities have introduced similar programs.

Private groups can be especially effective in developing needed services for delinquency prone youths. PTA's can provide volunteer parents, foster homes, remedial tutoring and daytime supervised activities in high delinquency areas. They can see that inner city schools are equipped with adequate numbers of social workers and guidance counselors, and that housing developments have sufficient play space. The YMCA and the American Friends Service Committee pioneered in the detached youth worker field, sending their young men into public housing projects and onto street corners to divert gangs into constructive activities. Organizations like "Big Brothers" work with boys to steer them into constructive growth patterns. Many inner city churches have devoted considerable time and resources in reaching out to the disadvantaged youth in their areas and giving them comfort, counsel, organized recreation, and teenage centers. Washington, D.C., ministers in one precinct have developed a referral service to which youngsters apprehended by the police for minor crimes that do not require court referral can be sent for help in solving their problems. This kind of neighborhood mobilization is an immense asset to the police in underserviced or especially troubled areas of the city. Other church groups have opened store-front clinics for narcotics addicts and halfway houses for released prisoners.

Many police forces have formed school safety patrols. These organizations, comprised largely of fifth and sixth graders, provide youths an opportunity to be of service to others and to identify with a worthy cause—safety and order. Some programs offer every participant the chance to attend a summer camp. The internationally known Berkeley Junior Traffic Police, founded by the late Chief August Vollmer, has been functioning since 1923 and has served as the model for hundreds of similar programs

---

[12] H. Cong. Res. 633, May 4, 1966.
[13] See *Monterey County* v. *Rader*, 248 Pac. 912 (1926); 80 C.J.S. Sheriffs and Constables, sec. 34. Cf. Va. Code Ann. secs. 18.1–301; 15.1–79.

[14] The International Association of Chiefs of Police, Inc, 1319 18th Street NW., Washington, D.C., welcomes inquiries about the availability of films of this kind.

throughout the Nation. Automobile associations have been laudably active in backing such programs too.

Another aspect of crime prevention involves citizen help in reintegrating previously institutionalized offenders into the community. Citizen interest is particularly needed in the rehabilitative field as tangible evidence that the community is ready to welcome back an offender into its midst and help him to avoid a return to crime. Private industries and unions make an invaluable contribution to controlling recidivism when they go into the prisons and run training programs that prepare inmates for decent jobs on release, and when they hire releasees. Universities like Harvard or Chicago, which conduct special educational programs in the prisons, also contribute.

For accused or convicted offenders living in the community, private groups, settlement houses, churches and unions can become private sponsors and supervisors helping with jobs, housing, and counsel. Often they can make the difference between successful probation or parole and return to prison, or between a defendant who is allowed release until trial and one who must stay in jail for want of bail. Professionals throughout the institutions of criminal administration carry such heavy caseloads that personal contact with their charges is the exception rather than the rule. Private citizens can provide the kind of individual backup in the community that is critical to the success of the rehabilitative effort.

COMMUNITY PLANNING AGAINST CRIME

Crime prevention can be built into almost every aspect of community planning. Unfortunately it is too often ignored because of the compartmentalization of municipal and county agencies. Crime is looked upon as the exclusive province of the police department and not the concern of those in charge of education, housing, urban renewal, health, welfare, or streets and highways. Both the police themselves and the other municipal agencies are guilty of this type of myopia. One police official described it thus:[15]

Community service agencies and law enforcement agencies have become polarized and isolated, each acting as though they are operating at opposite ends of the services continuum.

A Commission-sponsored survey of 95 high ranking public officials in 4 large cities revealed that the police were not significantly involved in community planning. The planning agencies on the one hand were "insular" in their relations with the police department and cautious about information exchange. The police seemed indecisive about what role they should play in any nonlaw enforcement planning.[16]

Increasingly, however, the police must become active participants in all aspects of community planning related to combatting crime. This can encompass almost the entire spectrum of local government. For instance, the police should be aware of public transportation developments insofar as they may relate to crime at terminals or on public transit conveyances. Divisions within public works department should adopt building designs and lighting provisions that minimize crime hazards. Parks and recreation departments need advice on the location, lighting, and supervision of playgrounds and recreation areas. City planning and development commissions include zone controls, which influence population movements and demands for police service. Building and safety departments should take action to abate attractive nuisances, hazards, abandoned buildings and wells, and lots. Streets and highway departments oversee street lighting, driveway requirements, traffic flow, adequacy of off street parking, and parking lot regulation. The fire department may be needed for emergency use in crowd control, fire prevention at accident scenes and disasters, and arson investigations. Public and parochial schools have problems with vandalism, youth gangs, perverts and narcotics pushers. The health department can be a valuable source of information about changing patterns of drug use, venereal disease, alcoholism, and prostitution.

There are some notable examples of successful collaboration between the police and other agencies in crime prevention. For instance, one police department conducted intensive door-to-door surveys in especially crime-prone areas to determine what the residents thought their chief crime problems were and what the residents thought should be done about them. They received responses along the following lines which confirm that public order is indeed a multidepartmental task:

☐ The fire department should eliminate fire hazards and burn off lots being used for juvenile misbehavior.
☐ Schools should provide better perimeter lighting for the schoolyards and structures after hours.
☐ The recreation department should offer more attractive programs designed to use up idle youth energy.
☐ Juvenile probation officers should intensify their contact with probationers in the area.
☐ Public utilities should provide additional street lighting.
☐ The alcoholic beverage commission should crack down on liquor dealers who sell to minors.

Police officers who compiled the survey's results submitted the citizen complaints to the appropriate agencies for remedial action.

In another city, the police became an integral part of a master plan review team to screen all redevelopment plans for safety and crime hazards. Together with other agency representatives, they drew up a model set of criteria for evaluation of such projects. These criteria included accessibility of buildings to patrol units, proper traffic flow and off street parking provisions, lighting requirements, location and regulation of cul de sacs, playgrounds, common greens, fences, and security entrances. During the course of their combined effort, the team talked to juvenile delinquents in custody to ascertain their

---

[15] Bruce C. Weller, "The Police Role in Prevention," "The Police Chief," July 1966, 33: 54.
[16] Richard Laskin and Margaret G. Oslund, "An Exploratory Study of Inter- Organizational Contacts, Communication and Coordination" (report to the Office of Law Enforcement Assistance, Department of Justice, August 1966).

patterns of housebreaking and theft so that proper preventive measures could be taken.

In the San Francisco Bay area, subway designs are submitted to the police for personal safety factors and the South San Francisco Police Department also screens building permits for compliance with sound crime prevention principles of lighting, building design, location, and alarm provisions. Regional teams of youth officers, teachers, school nurses, and guidance counselors regularly review youth delinquency problems in another community.

There are other types of collaboration programs. Personnel of Chicago's youth division meet weekly with representatives from the family and juvenile courts, schools, and the welfare department to keep each other abreast of new developments in areas of mutual interest. The Oakland associated agencies program operates out of the city manager's office and brings together representatives of the police, schools, probation and parole departments, health, education and welfare specialists and California Youth Authority personnel to discuss and resolve juvenile problems. A similar coordinating council in Alameda County, Calif., operates to inform participating youth agencies of action and policy changes which may affect each others operations.

Chapter 13 of the "General Report" recommends that the mayor of every city have a special staff, adviser, or committee to coordinate all agencies directly concerned with or potentially useful in crime control. In Los Angeles, the county runs an "Operation Take Hold," which coordinates all crime control activities through the office of the district attorney with the assistance of an advisory council and a crime control coordinator.

Internally, police departments might facilitate broad range liaison with other governmental units through creation of community planning units, headed by officers or civilians skilled in interdisciplinary planning. The community service officers described in chapter 5 could receive citizen complaints or requests for service of all sorts, contact the relevant agencies, and follow up the contacts by attempting to resolve community problems or refer them to other agencies.

Another route to closer integration seeks to end the physical isolation of the police at the precinct level from other agencies that deal with neighborhood problems. Experimental projects have been suggested to house the police, along with welfare, health, probation, parole, housing, and employment officials, in community centers located in the neighborhoods, on the theory that physical proximity alone might have pronounced effects upon exchange of information and coordination. Preliminary efforts have been made in this direction by departments like Atlanta's, which places officers in poverty centers. Those officers participate in weekly meetings to which the neighborhood residents can bring their complaints about police and other government actions. In some European departments, such as in Oslo, police officers give advice and help to unemployed or homeless persons. The Copenhagen police have also devoted considerable effort to helping unemployed miners.

Police participation in municipal policymaking would be especially valuable in regard to adequate illumination on streets, alleys, in the rear of commercial buildings, in parks, playgrounds, and other spots where darkness can make the criminal's task easier.[17] Although no accurate data has been collected on the precise crime deterrence of improved lighting, the presumption that light will impede criminality seems a reasonable one. Better lighting means a victim may become aware of his attacker in time to defend himself or summon help; it also increases the chances of witnesses being able to identify the offender. Or it may deter the criminal from acting at all. Police experience should be available in determining the right kind of lighting, its location and spacing, for different uses and in different parts of the city. The police can keep track of where certain kinds of crimes are committed, how frequently and at what times of the day or night. Any experiments must take into account the myriad of variables which affect the incidence of crime; this information, in great part, is in the exclusive possession of the police.

Cities should also make it easier for citizens in distress to summon police aid. Several cities have opened traditionally locked police callboxes to the public. Others have publicized a direct public telephone contact number for emergency use. Many have installed telephonic police-fire-ambulance emergency reporting callbox systems and placed them at strategic outdoor locations throughout the city. New York City has set callboxes at closer proximity to one another. Surely joint research and planning between the police and other city authorities must continue in order to arrive at the most expeditious communication medium for citizens to use in crime emergencies.

LEGISLATION AND FEDERAL ACTION TO COMPEL CRIME PREVENTION

The alternative to persuasion and public education in the crime prevention field is legislation compelling manufacturers and owners of personal property and real estate to maintain certain basic security standards. The most frequent suggestions are in the area of property security codes and automobile thefts. In addition, suitable firearms control legislation can make an important contribution to reducing the danger of crime in the United States. While the problem of firearms control is highly complex, owing to the American stratification of government, the need for Federal, State and local legislation is urgent, as described in chapter 10 of the Commission's "General Report."

AUTO THEFTS

Many communities already have key ordinances which lead to fines for car owners who leave their autos unlocked or with keys in the ignition. Ordinarily, however, these ordinances are not enforced with sustained vigor. Also, the relevance of automobile title laws to theft has been

---

[17] Many claims are made that better lighting reduces crime. Claims of a 90 percent reduction in robberies in Fort Wayne; 96 percent reduction in aggravated assaults in Salt Lake City; 85 percent decline in stolen cars in Pittsburgh; 92 percent drop in burglaries in Minneapolis; and in Cleveland, a one-third decline in assaults and 17 percent reduction in purse snatching are made in Don Murray, "How Bright Lights Reduce Crime, "Coronet," February 1960. Also see, "Crusade for Light," "United States Review," Jan. 22, 1966, 196:3.

noted. States like Massachusetts, without a requirement of proof of ownership before a car can be transferred, presumably make it easier for the thief to sell the stolen car. More far-reaching legislation, probably on the Federal level, has been suggested to compel auto manufacturers to include locating ignition systems in less accessible places than under the hood; making the ignition system connection cable impossible to remove from the ignition lock; increasing the number of ignition key combinations; putting in sturdier housing to enclose the ignition terminals; surrounding ignition wires with heavier metal cables; and providing steering wheel locking devices. The safest control over car theft or unauthorized use seems to be (1) a steering column and/or transmission lock that would render a car motionless when the transmission lever was in proper position and the key removed, so that shorting the wires would not make the car move, coupled with (2) an ignition system which would force the owner to remove the key either by a spring loaded ejection lock, or an engine that will not stop until the key is removed, or a buzzer system that goes off if the key is left in the ignition when the engine is stopped. Compulsory welding of identification serial numbers into the chassis has also been proposed to deter thieves who can now easily unscrew numbers from some expensive models.

Oakland has attacked used car lot thefts and auto thefts from parking lots by a regulation making it compulsory for lot operators to construct sturdy barriers around the parking space. Passage of the ordinance followed a discovery that of all lots from which cars were stolen, 81 percent had no protective barriers. The auto theft inspection service checks the applications and renewals of all parking lot owners for compliance, and has so far reported universal cooperation.

PROPERTY SECURITY CODES

Experience with building security codes has been very limited in this country. Yet they appear to hold a substantial potential for reducing housebreakings and burglaries.[18] The only ordinance now in effect is in Oakland and it relates solely to exterior openings of commercial buildings, prescribing minimum security measures for all such accessible vents. The security code is integrated with fire code requirements for easy exit, and the chief of police can require the installation of photoelectric, ultrasonic or other intrusion detection devices in buildings that have been burglarized frequently or that contain inventory of especially high value.

The Oakland police depend exclusively on voluntary adherence to the code even though the ordinance includes penalty provisions. But no prosecution has yet been instituted for its violation. The code was drawn up after concerted educational efforts by the police with the business community on preventive measures. The police there had found that of the 2,325 commercial burglaries in 1962, 52 percent of the victims had been burglarized more than once in a single year; in 141 cases, 3 or more times. The business community was convinced that basic security provisions should be enacted into law.

The ordinance is now enforced in the following manner: a security section in the police department receives reports on all burglaries and analyzes them to see if security defects are involved. It then sends an officer to talk with the owners and to recommend better security procedures. The case is followed up for compliance. As continuing procedure, patrol officers who spot commercial building security defects also report them to the security section.

The department believes that its burglary prevention approach has been successful. It reports that in 1965 the increase in commercial burglaries was only 3.4 percent as compared to 17.5 and 16.7 percent increases in 1964 and 1963. During 1966, commercial burglaries increased only 2.3 percent over 1965. Since the code was adopted decreases of up to 75 percent in burglaries are reported among complying businesses. Only 15 out of 1,092 businesses contacted for security defects have refused to cooperate.

A successful property security code should ideally include provisions relative to residential as well as commercial property, and deal with lighting and internal security devices as well as with exterior openings. It would have to provide for administrative appeals and for ongoing enforcement checks by local officials familiar with building design, materials, and possible conflicts with other municipal codes relating to such matters as fire, safety, and sanitation. The insurance industry should be intimately involved in its formulation so as to encourage compliance by lowering premiums. New construction should be reviewed and building permits and site inspections should be made to insure compliance. A model code developed for national use by construction experts, architects, municipal planners, fire prevention inspection personnel, police, and insurance representatives would be an extremely worthwhile venture.

Short of legislation, it seems that reasonable security standards could be laid down by Federal loan agencies as a requirement of new building financing. Federal banking agencies could insist on security features and up-to-date systems in all federally insured banks. Security requirements could also be made a standard feature of all public housing or urban renewal projects, Federal or local. Limited experimentation would provide valuable experience for evaluating the efficiency and cost effectiveness of various types of security requirements and devices before they are translated into a universal legal requirement.

FIREARMS CONTROL LEGISLATION

As chapter 10 of the "General Report" indicated, the majority of the American public favors reasonable firearms control legislation. Since laws, as they now stand, do not effectively control the supply of firearms, legislative bodies at Federal, State, and local levels should act to strengthen controls. Any legislative scheme should maximize the possibility of keeping firearms out of the hands of potential criminal offenders while at the same

---

[18] On pages 80–88, the "Report of the President's Commission on Crime in the District of Columbia" noted that commercial buildings accounted for 43.7 percent housebreakings, and almost one-half of the commercial firms victimized had been entered through unlocked windows, another 6 percent through unlocked doors; 30 percent through forcing the locks; one third through breaking windows. One-third of the commercicial victims had "burglar resistant" locks.

time affording citizens ample opportunity to purchase such weapons for legitimate purposes.

It is appropriate to ban absolutely the sale of those weapons that no citizen has a justifiable reason for owning. And in addition, dangerous or potentially dangerous persons should be prohibited from purchasing firearms.

Finally, prevention of crime and apprehension of criminals would be enhanced if each firearm were registered with a governmental jurisdiction. A record of ownership would aid the police in tracing and locating those who have committed or who threaten to commit violent crime. Law enforcement officers should know where each gun is and who owns it.

CITIZEN CRIME COMMISSIONS

Direct citizen action to improve law enforcement has become an absolute necessity. In a number of instances, citizen crime commissions have provided forceful vehicles for proper and sustained citizen action.[19]

Citizen crime commissions can perform the essential function of coordinating the efforts of private groups within a community. They can work with the police to pinpoint problem areas where public education is most needed. They can see that the message reaches the groups most concerned. Such commissions can also serve as consulting agencies for individual groups or persons with specialized prevention problems.

Crime prevention education must also be sustained. Too often a crash campaign produces short term reductions in certain kinds of crime and then loses momentum. Citizen efforts in this field can be extremely effective but they also need to be coordinated to insure complete coverage and continuing vigor.

It has also been suggested that citizen crime prevention is sufficiently important in community life to justify an official agency, such as a mayor's committee or a crime prevention council, to spearhead citizen efforts. These local councils could then be coordinated on the State level by an official who would maintain a central depository of prevention material and experiences, run a clearing house for the local councils, and evaluate local programs. Former California Attorney General Stanley Mosk made such a suggestion in 1962: [20]

> We have considered and discussed, for some time, the possibility of a statewide crime prevention coordinator. * * * A formal statewide bureau in the Department of Justice for the dissemination of information and educational materials on crime prevention and to assist in establishing local crime prevention councils could be most advantageous. Right now several agencies are handling this problem. A central depository and clearing house of such information would be most useful, not just for statistics, but for programmatic data, too.

CONCLUSION

To reduce crime in their communities citizens must be prepared to back up their police forces with more than slogans. They need to keep in mind, but in perspective, the possibilities of crime in their daily lives and take reasonable steps to limit criminal opportunities. In emergency situations they must assume the responsibilities of summoning aid for victims or police in distress; they cannot stay free of involvement and yet expect others to protect them. In groups and even as individuals they can supply desperately needed auxiliary resources to the police, the courts, and correctional officers. Much work remains to be done in developing effective and lasting public education campaigns to get citizens to take the few extra precautions that can deter large numbers of crimes. Citizen crime commissions might well take on this new and important task. Compulsory laws to require cars, homes, and business to be adequately protected against invasion offer a promising, if complex, area for further study and experimentation.

Municipal government also needs to adopt a more integrated approach toward crime control; to provide the mechanism for coordination of all the local agencies whose activities and policies can have an effect on crime prevention and on opportunities for the detection and apprehension of criminals after crimes have been committed. The combination of alert and cooperative citizens, prevention-conscious police and crime-conscious local government can become a significant force against the menace of urban crime.

---

[19] For an authoritative, interesting description of the American crime commission movement and an account of its organization, mission, and history, see: Ralph G. Murdy, "Crime Commission Handbook" (Baltimore: The Criminal Justice Commission, 1965), 119 pp. mimeo.

[20] Stanley Mosk, "The Crime Prevention Problem in California," "Crime Prevention in California" (Los Angeles: Digest of a conference sponsored by Town Hall in cooperation with the California State Department of Justice, Mar. 24, 1962), p. 8.

Index

A

Advisory Commission on Inter-Governmental Relations, 70, 111
Advisory Council on Police Training and Education, 219
Agencies, police
  costs, 11
  decentralization, 7
  distribution, 7
  Federal, 8
  local
    county sheriff, 8
    responsibilities, 8
    special forces, 8
  metropolitan, 8
    see also metropolitan police force, U.S.
  personnel, *see* personnel, police
  reform, 7
  State
    creation, 6
    delegation of responsibilities, 8
    police, 8
    services provided, 8
Agent, police
  as a career position, 122
  assignment, 122
  educational level, 122
  establishment of position, 122
  minimum supervision needed, 122
  replacement of detective, 122
  scope of responsibility, 122
Alarm systems, 223
American Association of Federated Women's Clubs, 223
American Bar Association
  arrests, study, 186, 187
  need for State Councils, 219
  protection in minority communities, study, 185
  recruit standards, recommendations, 131

American Bar Foundation, police legal advisor, 50
American Civil Liberties Union, firearms, 189
American Friends Service Committee, 225
American Law Institute, 18
American Law Institute Model Pre-Arraignment Code Project, 184
Annexation
  growth, 105
  law enforcement, 105–106
  obstacles, 105
  techniques, 105
Annual Institutes on Police Community Relations, Michigan State University, 76
Applicant success rates for police positions, 9, 134
Applicant Success Rates—Regional Replies—1956–61, 9
Apprehension process, police
  rates, 1
  response time, 58
  survey, 58
  typical, 58
  see also arrests
Arlington County Police Department, Virginia, 137
Arrests
  community demands, 188
  contributing factors, 58
  demonstrators, 192–193
  harrassment of alleged law-breakers, 187
  investigative detention, 186
  minor crimes
    hostility resulting from enforcement of, 188
    misuse of statutes, 187–188
    police quotas, 188–189
    reexamination of statutes, 188

Arrests—Continued
  power of police, 186–187
  use of firearms
    fatalities, 189
    guidelines for control of, 189–190
    incidents, 189
    lack of policy, 189
Assault, aggravated, 22–23
Assault on police officers, 145
Association of Bay Area Government (ABAG), 110, 111, 112
Atlanta Police Department, community relations, 162
Automobile theft, *see* theft, automobile

B

Baltimore Police Department
  dragnet search incident, 186
  investigative arrests, 186
  survey, 49, 55
Bay Area Law Enforcement Information Control Study Committee, 85
Bay Area Police Information Network (PIN), 57, 85, 110
Bedford-Stuyvesant area, N.Y., on Negro complaints about police, 148
Berkeley Junior Traffic Police, 225
Berkeley Police Department, 126, 132
"Big Brothers," 225
Bloomington and Burnsville, Minn., joint recruitment, 74
Boston Police Department
  community relations, 160
  survey, 136
Bow Street Horse and Foot Patrol, 4
Bribery, mutual consent, 210
British Home Office, 37
British metropolitan police force, *see* metropolitan police force, British
British Royal Commission on Police, 121–122, 134

Titles of books, articles, tables, charts and names of law cases appear in italics.

Bureau of the Census, 10
Bureau of Social Science Research (BSSR), survey on public opinion of police, 145, 146, 147, 181, 192

C

Cadets
 financial aid, 137
 full-time college attendance, 137
 programs, 137
 use of, 137
California Bureau of Criminal Identification and Investigation (CII), 78, 79, 83, 84
California Commission on Peace Officers Standards and Training, 74, 77, 141, 217
California Department of Justice, 42, 82, 84, 87
California Disaster Act, 98
California Highway Patrol, Autostatis, 85
California, Independent Insurance Association, 224
California Joint Exercise of Powers Act of 1921, provisions, 110, 112
California Law Enforcement Standards and Training Act, 75
California Mental Maturity Test, 128
California Peace Officers Association, 212
California State College at Los Angeles, 43
California training program
 financial aid, 218
 requirements, 218
Chicago Police Department
 budget, 121
 cadets, 137
 laboratory, 91
 "Operation Crime Stop," 224
 police-community coordination, 155, 172
 policy on treatment of citizens, 181
 reduction in precincts, 123
 review of citizen complaints, 198
 Superintendent, 125, 172, 181
 technological application, 57, 78, 87
Chicago Police Training Academy, 76
Chief of police,
 mayoral appointment, 127
 role, 62
 selection from police ranks, 127
Cincinnati, Ohio
 citizen complaint review, 198
 police advisory committee, 156
 survey on junior high school students' opinion of police, 147, 148, 149
Citizen advisory committees, 33
Citizen complaints
 as a check on police procedures, 194
 civilian review boards
  example of operation, 200–201
  success, 202
  weaknesses, 200, 201

Citizen complaints—Continued
 court review
  civil remedies, 199
  exclusion of evidence, 200
  Federal civil statute, 199
  Federal criminal statute, 199
 disciplinary policies on police misconduct
  actions taken, survey, 197
  ensuring internal discipline, 193
  reassessment of need, 197
  reporting misconduct, 194
 general approach to external review, 197–198
 human relation commissions, local, 204–205
 investigation of complaints
  caliber of investigations, 196
  investigative units, survey, 195
  need for internal investigative units, 196
 Michigan Civil Rights Commission, 205
 Ombudsman
  evolution, 202
  examples of functions, 202–204
 publicizing complaint decision, 197
 reception of complaints
  practices discouraging complaints, 195
  proper handling, 195
 resolution of complaints
  disposition, survey, 196
  reassessment of hearing procedures, 196–197
 review by civilian officials, 198
Citizen crime commissions, see crime commissions, citizen
Citizen's associations, early law enforcement, 3
Civil Rights Commission
 Negro complaints, report, 148
 Negro representation on police forces, survey, 166, 171, 173, 174
 police brutality, 181
Civil service, 127, 132, 141, 169, 210
Civilian Review Boards, Organization and Procedures, 200
Cleveland Police Department, harassment arrests, 187
Colleges and universities, training programs, 218
 see also training programs
Command and control system, 58
Commission on Community Relations, Detroit, investigation of applicant failure, 169
Commission on Peace Officer Standards and Training, 218
Commissions on police standards, 61, 217–221
Communications
 apprehension process, 58
 computer-assisted command and control systems, 59
 Police Communication Centers, 58–59

Communications—Continued
 problems, 87–88
 radio, *see* radio equipment
 technology, 57
 teletype
  county, 87
  interjurisdictional, 87
  State, 87
Community planning
 methods, 154, 226–227
 problems, 226, 227
Community relations
 citizen aid to law enforcement, 144, 224–225
 citizen hostility, 123, 144
 community services, 13, 14
 Community Service Officer, *see* Community Service Officer
 effect on community stability, 145
 effect on individual police officers, 144–145
 failure to understand each other's problems, 123
 importance, 144
 isolation of police, 123, 144, 166
 minority groups, 34–35, 144, 147, 148, 150, 151, 158–159, 167–169
 Negro opinion of police, 146, 147
 personnel, *see* personnel, community relations
 planning, *see* community planning
 police advisory committees, *see* police advisory committees
 police-community relations units, 150
 see also community relation units
 police policies and procedures, 25, 149
 programs, 34, 37, 150
 see also community relations programs, special
 public attitude toward police, 145–146
 see also surveys, police-community relations
 recommendations on improvement, 205
Community relations programs, special
 community service, 161
 crime prevention, 161
 public education
  civilian contact
   cruises, tours, demonstrations, 159–160
   institutes, 160
   school programs, 160–161
  public relations, 159
 recreation, 161
 social services
  police role, 162–163
  police service programs, 162–163
Community Relations Training in Representative Police Departments—1966; Hours of Separate, 176

Community relations units
  authority and jurisdiction, 152–153
  citizen contacts, 153
  civilian experts, 155
  community relations officer, 151, 152, 155, 162
  departmental training programs, 154, 155
  evaluation and research, 154
  high-tension situations, handling, 154
  need for departmental support, 152
  need for units, 150
  personnel, 155–156
  personnel decisions, 153–154
  policy formulation, 153, 155
  progress in forming, 150
  responsibility, 151
  unit command, 151, 155
Community Service Officer (CSO)
  age, 123
  duties, 53, 123, 155, 162, 166–167
  office
    establishment, 122, 123
    neighborhood, 123
    purpose, 123
    selection, 123–124, 166
Computer
  code and formats, standardized, 60
  Command and Control Systems, 59
  information systems, 57
Conduct, police
  conformity to standards, 28
  departmental regulation, 20, 28
  departmental statements, 27, 28
  see also corruption
Constable
  American colonies, 5
  early England, 3, 4
  U.S., 19th century, 5
Consultant assistance, State, 61
Corruption
  effect on slum areas, 212
  police
    appeal factors, 208
    contributing factors, 208, 210, 211, 212, 215
    departmental organization, 210
    disciplinary action, 211
    gambling, 209
    general effects, 208
    internal reporting, 211
    kickbacks, 210
    morale undermining, 209
    open prosecution, 215
    patterns, 208, 209
    public tolerance, 211
    punishment beats, 209, 212
    situations, 209
    theft, 210
    ticket fixing, 209
  political influence, see political corruption
Council of State Governments, 110
Council of the Municipality of Metropolitan Toronto, 102

County Sheriff's Department, Ventura, California, 125
Court review of police actions, 30–31, 198, 199
Crime
  analysis
    major crime reports, 77, 78
    pattern establishment, 77, 78
  planning against
    community, 226–227
      see also community planning
    European effort, 227
    lack, 226
    municipal agencies, 226
    police, 226
  prevention
    business precautions
      illumination of premises, 223, 227
      protective covering, 223
      systems
        alarm, 223
        telephone warning, 222
      campaigns, 223–224
    citizen precautions
      awareness of danger, 222
      negligence, 222
    education programs, see educational programs, crime prevention
    functions of police, 13–14, 120
    history of police responsibility, 3
    legislation control, see legislation control, crime
    patrol, see patrol
    programs, 161
    resources, public
      automobile, 226
      business, 225
      churches, 225
      citizen
        "blockmothers", 225
        interest in rehabilitation, 226
        reintegration with, 226
      civic group, 225
      clubs, 225
      school safety patrols, 225
      universities, 226
  rates
    rural, 11–12
    urban, 11–12
  reporting
    duty of citizen, 224–225
    failure to report, 224
    Good Samaritan
      duty, 225
      liability, legal, 225
      willingness, 225
    program, 225
    promptness, 224
Crime commissions, citizen
  as official agencies, 229
  functions
    coordination, 229
    education, 229
Crime in California, Delinquency and Probation in California, 84

Crime scene, evidence technicians for searching, 51
CSO, see Community Service Officer

D

Dade County, 1965, Police Manpower, 100
Dade County Junior College, 76
Dade County, metropolitan
  Board of Commissioners, 99, 100, 101
  charter
    contract power, 100–101
    minimum standards provision, 99, 100
  law enforcement, 99–101
  mergers, 101
  problems, 99
  services provided, 99, 100
Dade County Public Safety Department, 76, 86, 94, 99, 100
Dade County Public Safety Department, Services Provided, 100
Dallas Police Department, 134
Delinquency control
  cooperation responsibility
    among patrol officers, 96
    among police departments, 96
    between police and other agencies, 96
    exchange of ideas, 96
  specialization
    facilities, 96
    personnel, 96
Delinquency Control Institute of the University of Southern California, 76
Department of Health, Education, and Welfare, Office of Juvenile Delinquency, 10, 160, 218
Department of Justice, Office of Law Enforcement Assistance, 43, 75, 127, 160, 177, 223
Department of Labor, Manpower Development and Training Act, 170
Detective
  caseload, 121
  coordination with patrol, 53
  Negro personnel, 173
  replacement by police agent, 122
Detention facilities
  conclusions on operation, 90
  cost, 88, 89
  management, 88
  personnel, 88–89
    correction officer, 89
    police officer, 89
  problems, 89
  sharing, 89–90
Detroit Police Department
  applicant failure, 169
  arrests for investigation, 186
  citizen complaints against, 205
  dragnet search incident, 186
  training program, 177

Director of Public Safety of Oak Park, Michigan, 134
District of Columbia
  arrests for investigation, 186
  Board of Commissioners, review of citizen complaints, 198
  citizen complaint handling, recommendations, 196
  civilian review boards, 200–201
  community recreation program, 161, 162
  community relations units, 151, 152, 155, 162
  Council on Human Relations, promotion evaluation, 172
  crime survey
    automobile thefts, 222
    disorderly conduct arrests, 180
    housebreakings, 222
    minor crime arrests, 188
  public opinion of police, surveys, 146, 147, 148
  "Signal Ten" program, 224
  use of dogs, 191
Douglas, Justice William O., misuse of minor crimes statutes, 187, 188
Drug Arrests and Dispositions in California, publication, 84

E

Education Incentive Program, Suggested, of California Commission on Peace Officers Standards and Training, 141
Education, police personnel
  levels, 10, 126, 127
  minimum requirements, 126–127
  requirements for promotion, 140
  standards, 36, 163
Education programs
  community relations, 159
  crime prevention
    business, 223
    campaigns, 223–224
    clubs
      service, 223
      women's, 223
    exhibitions, 223
    film libraries, 223
    "Junior Posse", 223
    police, 223
    public, 223, 225, 229
    schools
      elementary, 223
      high schools, 223
  law enforcement
    accredited colleges only, 128
    college courses, 127–128
    college-police academy coordination, 128
    vocational, 128
Emergency assistance, 120
English Home Office Report, 223
Ethical standards, police, 208

F

Federal Aviation Agency, 130

Federal Bureau of Investigation
  age requirement, 132
  assistance to local authorities, 42
  centralized records, 84
  establishment, 6
  integrity, 212
  investigator deployment, 55
  laboratory services, 91, 92
  National Academy, 76, 139, 141, 212
  National Crime Information Center, 57, 84
  statement on conduct, 215
  training, 75, 128, 138, 139
  uniform crime reports, 11, 96, 186
Federal Bureau of Narcotics, 75, 76
Federal Civil Rights Act, 31
Federal Communications Commission, radio networks, 60–61
Federal Communications Commission System, 87, 88
Federal Service Entrance Examination, recruitment selection, 75
Field personnel, police
  curtailment of unimportant tasks, 56
  distribution of patrols, 52
  investigator deployment, 55–56
  patrol techniques, *see* patrol, techniques
  patrol-detective coordination
    lack of unity, 53
    rivalry between forces, 53
    team policing, 53
  report preparation, 56
  saturation techniques, 52
  supervisory control, 52
  utilization, 51–56
Field practices
  arrests, 186
    see also arrests
  contact with citizens
    difficulty in maintaining composure, 179
    discrimination
      juvenile court referrals, 183
      minority groups, 183
    gangs, 179
    interrogation
      juveniles, 184
      legislation defining use, 185
      manner of conducting, 185
      minority groups, 183, 184
      misuse, 184
      police authority, 184
    physical misconduct
      earlier police brutality, 181
      examples of incidents, 182
      excessive use of force, 181, 182
      preventive measures, 183
      reasons offered by policemen, 182
      youths, 182
    verbal abuse and discourtesy
      citizen disrespect, 181
      citizen treatment study, 180
      department regulations on citizen treatment, 181

Films, training aid, 140
Firearms control
  registration, 228–229
  sale, 228–229
Food and Drug Administration, 91
Ford Foundation, 219
Fosdick, Raymond, police patrol distribution, 52
Fraternal Order of Police, 212
Fresno, California, police force, budget restrictions, 48

G

Gallup poll, public rating of police, 145, 147, 149
Gambling, police policy, 22
Gaslights, introduction on London streets, 4
General Federation of Women's Clubs, 223
Goldberg, Justice, on crime scene searching, 51
Goldstein, Professor Herman, University of Wisconsin Law School, 89
Government Expenditure Patterns, Per Capita Local, Within and Outside Metropolitan Areas in the United States, 1962, 12
Governmental units in U.S., breakdown, 68
Grants, government, training, 218
Graper, Elmer, police patrol distribution, 52

H

Ham radios, use of in crime prevention, 224
Harlem, N.Y., survey on public opinion of police, 147, 148
Harvard Business School, 43, 141
Harvard Law Review, study on citizen complaint hearings, 196
Hoover, J. Edgar, 6, 128, 212, 215
Housebreaking, survey, 222
Houston Police Department, 131
Humphrey, Vice President Hubert, statement on social problems, 163

I

IACP, *see* International Association of Chiefs of Police
Identification, persons
  missing, 225
  wanted, 225
Illinois State Police Emergency Radio Net (ISPERN), 87
Independent Insurance Agents Association of California, 224
Industrial Revolution, English, influence on police history, 4
Information systems, computerized, 57
Insurance Institute, 223
Internal Revenue Service, 209

233

International Association of Chiefs of Police
  administration, 127
  consolidation of precincts, 123
  integrity, 212
  internal investigation units, 50, 196
  library, 43
  survey
    age of personnel, 131-132
    community relations programs, 150, 155
    emotional fitness, 129
    field recruit placement prior to training, 138
    motor patrols, 55
    physical standards, 130
    resident requirements, 130
    staff inspection units, 49
    training films, 140
International Association of Chiefs of Police and Public Administration Service, 78
International Association of Chiefs of Police, Professional Standards Division, 219
International City Managers Association, 138
International Conference of Police Associations, 212
Inter-Religious Committee on Race Relations, statement on community relations unit in Washington, D.C., 152
Investigation, criminal
  consolidation, partial, 94-95
    benefits, 95
    problems, 95
  consolidation, total
    advantages, 94
    cons, 93
    geographical areas, 94
    pros, 93
  defined, 1
  field interrogation, 23
  interval units, 31, 214-215
  stopping and questioning, 38-40
Investigators, deployment, 55-56

J

Jacobs, Jane, 2
Judicial consolidation, police service
  annexation, 105-106
    see also annexation
  contract law enforcement, 106-108
    see also law enforcement, contract
  metropolitan government, 99-103
    see also Dade County, metropolitan; metropolitan Toronto Police Department; Nashville-Davidson County, metropolitan
  special districts, police, 108-109
    see also police special districts
  subordinate service district, 103-105
    see also Suffolk County; Nassau County

Justice of the peace, early England, 4, 5
Juveniles, survey on respect for police, 149

K

Kalamazoo, Michigan, study on teen-ager opinion of police, 147
Kansas City Metropolitan Squad, 95
Kansas City Police Department, 121, 133
Katzenbach, Attorney General Nicholas deB., 43
"Knock-Knock" Law, 38, 40-41

L

Laboratory services
  activities, 90
  conclusion on providing, 92
  current practices, 90-91
  problems
    duplication of facilities, 90-91
    personnel, 90-91
    proximity, 91
    quality, 91
    timeliness, 91
  States
    establishment of facilities, 91-92
    role, 91-92
Law enforcement
  citizen aid, 2, 224-225
  conclusions of Commission, 37-38
  contract, 42
  costs, 7, 11, 12, 86, 87, 106, 107, 108
  crime reporting programs, 224-225
  effectiveness, see law enforcement, effectiveness
  FBI assistance, 42
  fundamental problems, 68
  improper, 209-210
  limitations, 1, 2
  origins
    in American colonies, 5
    in England, 3
  police programs, 224
  police role, 2, 120
  pooling, 42
  public demands, 1, 2, 209
  State role, 42
Law Enforcement Agencies, a Profile of Federal, State, and Local, 7
Law enforcement agencies, growth, U.S.
  Federal
    Bureau of Investigation, 6
    Revenue Cutter Service, 6
    Secret Service, 6
  improvement, 16
  State
    departments, 6
    police, 6
    Texas Rangers, 6
    see also agencies, police
Law Enforcement Code of Ethics, 179, 212

Law Enforcement Committee of the New York Metropolitan Council, intelligence files, 79
Law enforcement contract
  areas of employment, 106
  city to county
    cost, 107
    improvement, plan, 107
    conclusions, 108
  county to city
    advantages, 106
    cost, 106
    disadvantages, 106
  description, 106
  objections, 106-107
  State to local, cost, 108
Law Enforcement Intelligence Unit (LIEU)
  membership, 79
  zones, 79
Law Enforcement Officers Training Council, designated training obligations, 76
Law enforcement policy
  advantages of formulating, 20
  articulation, 214
  aggravated assault, 22-23
  community role in establishing, 33
  court review, 32-33
  court role in establishing, 18, 33
  demonstrations, 25
  departmental statements, 27, 28
  deviations, 27
  dissemination, 26
  exclusionary rule, 31, 33
  failure to articulate, 17, 21, 209
  flexibility, 19, 27
  gambling, 22
  identification of issues
    analysis of complaints, 25
    court decisions, 26
    observation of field procedures, 25
  implementation, 29, 32
  in corrupting situations, 214
  juvenile offenders, 18
  lack of guidelines, 16, 17, 18
  legislative role in establishing, 18, 32, 33
  New York law, 17
  police role in establishing, 19, 21
  prosecutor role in establishing, 19, 33
  settling disputes, 24-25
  staff consultation, 26
  statement, 16
  street gatherings, 24
  traffic control, 17
  training for decisionmaking, 215
Law Enforcement Teletype System (LETS), 87
League of California Cities, administrative test, 75
Legal adviser, police
  civilian, 65
  need, 50, 51, 63 66
  qualifications, 51, 63

234

Legal adviser, police—Continued
  role in policy planning, 50, 64
  services, 50, 63
  training programs, 51, 63–64, 66
Legislation control, crime
  automobile theft, *see* theft, automobile
  firearms, *see* firearms
  security standards, property, *see* security standards, property
Leonard, Donald S., 43
Leonard, Glenford S., 134
Lindsay, Mayor John, 43, 48
Los Angeles County Sheriff's Department, 138
Los Angeles Police Department
  applicant rejection, 129, 134
  appointments, women, 125
  community relations officer, 151
  manpower problem, 9
  salaries, 135
  technological application, 57, 83
  training, 140, 141
Louis Harris poll, public
  opinion on bribery of police, 146, 148
  rating of Federal agents, 145

M

MacNamara, Donal E. J., 43
Major Case Squad of the Greater St. Louis Area
  accomplishments, 95
  reasons for existence, 95
Manpower reserve
  assessment of needs, 134
  countywide, 77
  Statewide, 77
Mayor's Committee on City-Citizen Relationships, Denver, Colo., 204
Metropolitan Atlanta Council of Local Governments, Metropol, establishment, 112
Metropolitan Fund, Inc., Detroit, studies, 76, 80
Metropolitan Police Academy of Michigan, Inc., 76
Metropolitan Police Department of Nashville-Davidson County, 94
Metropolitan Police Department of Washington, D.C., 121, 123, 128
Metropolitan police force, British
  effectiveness, 5
  patrol techniques, report, 190
  problems encountered, 4
  responsibilities of Home Secretary, 4
  structure, 4
Metropolitan police force, U.S.
  administrative boards, 6
  development, 5
  political control, 5
  problems encountered, 5
  reform attempts, 6
  State control, 6
  unification, 5
Metropolitan Police of London, 125

Metropolitan Toronto Police Department
  centralization
    communications, 103
    records, 103
  criticisms, 103
  effectiveness, 103
  financing, 102
  recruit-training program, 103
  size, 99, 102
Metropolitan Washington Council of Governments, 112
Mexican-American, U.S., survey on police-community relations, 149
Michigan Association of Chiefs of Police, recommendation on equal opportunity, 163
Michigan Law Enforcement Information Network (LEIN), 85
Michigan State Police Department, 78, 85
Michigan State University
  career development programs, 141
  Federal agency affiliation, 76
  Institute for Community Development and Services, 43, 178
Minnesota Multiphasic Personal Inventory (MMPI), 129
Minority groups, relation with police, 34–35, 144, 147, 148, 150, 151, 158, 167
Miranda v. *Arizona*, decision, 19, 23, 27
Misconduct, *see* corruption; field practices; political corruption
Misner, Professor Gordon E., 68, 86, 93
Missouri Crime Commission, 7
Missouri Crime Survey
  patrol-detective rivalry, 53
  police patrol distribution, 52
Model Penal Code, 18
Model Police Standards Council Act, 219, 220–221
Modus operandi analysis
  case reports, 78
  felony reports, 78
Multnomah County Police, Oregon
  personnel exchange, 45
  support unit, 49
Multnomah County Sheriff's Department, Oregon 126, 133
Municipal Police Training Council, 218
Mutual pledge system, 3, 4, 5

N

Nashville-Davidson County, metropolitan
  charter
    district division, 101, 102
    urban service expansion, 101, 102
  law enforcement
    division of charges, 102
    personnel responsibility, police, 101–102
    private police services, 102
  problems, 101–102

Nassau County
  community relations units, 151
  division of charges, 105
  internal organization, 105
  law enforcement
    cost, 104
    financing, 104
    personnel, police, 104
Nassau County Police Department, 104
National Automobile Theft Bureau, 223
National Commission on Law Observance and Enforcement, 181
National Conference of Commissioners on Uniform State Laws, 219
National Council on Crime and Delinquency Survey, 139
National Crime Information Center (NCIC), FBI, 57, 84
National Defense Education Act, 137
National League of Cities
  "National Municipal Policy," 75
  police training, 75
  survey, 50, 129, 131, 133, 138, 195
National Opinion Research Center (NORC), surveys on public opinion of police, 145, 146, 148, 149
National Symposium on Science and Criminal Justice, 57
New England Citizens Crime Commission, 209
New England State Police Compact
  development, 79
  provisions, 79
New England State Police Staff College, training program, 76
New York City Institute for Public Administration, 43
New York Committee for Economic Development, 44–45
New York District Attorney's Office, 17
New York Municipal Police Training Council Act, 76
New York Office for Local Government, 78
New York Police Department
  budget
    civilian review board, 202
    community relations, 160, 161
    community relations council, 151, 156
  Division of Police Administration Services, function, 219
  intelligence file, 79
  management, 62
  personnel
    guidelines, 121
    salaries, 135
  technological application, 57
  training program, 131, 170
New York Police Task Force, report on police departments, 48
New York State Combined Council of Law Enforcement Officials, June 1, 1964, policy statement, 38–41

New York State Intelligence and Identification System (NYSIIS), 42
New York State, training program
  financial aid, 218
  requirements, 218
New York Training Council, 77
Newark Police Department, community relations program, 160
Nightwatch system
  American colonies, 5
  in early England, 4
Northwestern University, law school training programs, 51
Northwestern University Traffic Institute, 141

O

Oakland Police Department, 96, 214
O'Connor, Sheriff J. C., of San Diego County, 224
Offenders, release, 24
Officer, police
  activities, 15–16
  assignment in minority group neighborhoods, 173
  authority to invoke criminal process, 13–14, 22
  civil liability, 31
  discretion, 14, 18, 19, 20, 22, 33
  duties, 122–123
  establishment of position, 122–123
  expertise, 20
  guidelines needed, 15
  improvised responses, 19–20
  need for, 123
  part of police teams, 123
  routine responses, 16
Oglesby, Thomas W., 129
Ombudsman, 203
Ombudsman, Swedish: Administrative Scope of Cases, 1960–63, 202
Ontario Municipal Board, 102
Ontario Police College, 77
Ontario Provincial Legislature, 102
"Operation Barrier", 225
"Operation Crimestop", 224
Operation, police
  community service, 13, 14
  definition, 14
  division of duties, 122, 124
  emergency assistance, 120
  improvement, 42
  policing demonstrations, 25
  policymaking, 18, 32
  role in juvenile process, 14
Oregon Association of City Police Officers, training, 76
Organization and management, police
  actions required, overall, 61–62
  centralization, 37, 123
  commission evaluation, 43
  consultant assistant, State, 61
  criteria for evaluation, 46
  deficiencies, 45
  field personnel utilization, 51
  internal operations, 16
  leadership development, 44–45

Organization and management, police—Continued
  occupational status, 134, 136
  problems, 43, 72–73
  progress, 42
  purchasing, *see* purchasing, police
  reluctance to change, 48
  research efforts, 48, 49
  standards, 219
  support units
    administrative, 48
    internal investigation, 50
    legal adviser, 50
      also see legal adviser, police
    planning, research and analysis, 49
    staff inspection, 49
  technological applications, 57
Organized crime activities, police tolerance, 208–209
Organized crime, existence, 79
Organized crime intelligence
  development, recent, 79
  needs
    coordination, 80
    file information, 79–80
    manpower, 80
    program centralization, 80
    resource pooling, 79
Otis Quick Scoring Mental Ability Tests, 128
Oyster Bay conferences, 79

P

Parent Teachers Association, crime prevention, 225
Parker, Chief William H., on law enforcement, 62
Patrol
  police
    detective coordination, 53
    distribution, 52
    lack of citizen contact, 190
    minority group neighborhood, 174
    objectives, 1
    preventive, 23, 224–225
    report preparation, 56
    segregation in assignments, 174
    techniques
      foot, 54
      motorized, 54–55, 190
      one-man motorized, 54–55, 190
      use of dogs, 191
  public
    citizen, 224–225
    defense units, 224
    ham radios, 224
    police reserve units, 224
    use of company cars, 225
    use of taxicabs, 225
    watchdog activities, 224
Patrol Car Service to Contract Cities, Rates Charged by Los Angeles County Sheriff's Department for, 106

Patrolman
  beginning of police career, 121
  nonenforcement tasks, 121
  overextension of capabilities, 121
Patterson, Albert L., 209
Peel, Sir Robert, Home Secretary of England, 4
Penal codes, revision guideline, 18
Pennekamp, John; Editor, *Miami Herald,* 94
Personnel, community relations
  general
    assignments, 165–166
    Community Service Officer, 166–167
      see also Community Service Officer
  post-employment residence, 166
  preemployment residence, 165
  promotions, 165
  selection
    education, 163–164
    psychological stability, 164
    racial attitudes, 164
  minority group
    assignment, 173
    attraction and selection
      evaluation of standards, 171
      Negro representation, 167–168
      reasons for under representation, 168–169
      recruitment improvements, 169–170
      remedies to increase representation, 169
      removal of discriminatory practices, 170–171
      representative of community, 167
  promotion
    appointment, 173
    elimination of discrimination, 172, 173
    ranking officers by race, 171
  training
    inservice, 177
    institutes, 178
    purpose, 175
    recruit, 175
    rollcall, 177
    special, 178
    supervisory and command officers, 177
    techniques, 178
    time spent, 175, 176
  see also personnel, police
Personnel in Representative Sheriff's Offices According to Race, 168
Personnel, police
  administrative and supervisory, 120–121, 172
  applicants
    rate of eligibility, 9, 169
    type, 121
    see also recruits
  assessment of manpower needs, 134

Personnel, police—Continued
  better division of assignments, 121–122
  cadets, see cadets
  chief administrator, 133, 142
  chief of police, see chief of police
  civilian role, 124
  community relations, see personnel, community relations
  detective, see detective
  dismissal, 133
  distribution breakdown, 7, 8–9
  education, see education, police personnel
  employment requirements, 10
  evidence technicians at crime scene, 51
  field, see field personnel, police
  individual characteristic requirements, 128–129
  leadership development, 35, 140
  legal adviser, see legal adviser, police
  meter maids, 124
  misconduct, see corruption; field practices
  overregimentation, 136
  patrolman, see patrolman
  physical standards, 36
  police agent, see agent, police
  police officer, see officer, police
  policewoman, see policewoman
  private, 215, 216
  professional attitude, 2, 21, 29, 136
  qualities needed, 125
  race, 10, 168
  recruitment, see recruitment; recruits
  retirement, 9, 142
  salaries, see salaries
  selection, 36, 163, 215
  shortage, 9, 133
  Statewide standards, 142–143
  training programs, see training programs
  turnover, 9
  workload, 56, 135–136
Philadelphia Police Department
  civilian review board, 200
  community relations program, 151, 152, 155, 166
  lowering height standard, 130
  survey on community relations, 146, 149
Philadelphia Urban League, 1965 report, Negro opinion of police, 148
PIN, see Police Information Network
Pitchess, Sheriff, Los Angeles County, 87, 88–89, 93
Pittsburgh, Pennsylvania, human-relations commission, 204
Planning, police department
  administration and organization
    corrections, 77, 78
    improvements, 77, 78
  analysis
    crime, 77, 78
    see also crime analysis

Planning, police department—Con.
  analysis—Continued
    modus operandi, 77, 78
    see also modus operandi analysis
    see also community planning
Police administration
  functions, 78
  disciplinary action, 28
  opposition to Supreme Court decisions, 27
  political control, 209, 210
  popular control, 29–33
  see also organization and management, police
Police advisory committees
  citywide committees
    functions, 158
    representation, 158
  form variations
    Cincinnati, 156
    New York City, 156
    San Francisco, 156
    St. Louis, 156
  minority group leaders, committtees, 158
  need, 156
  neighborhood committees
    composition, 157
    organization, 158
    purpose of meetings, 157
  structure, general, 156
Police agencies, see agencies, police
Police and Detective Personnel, Public Employed, by Age and Sex, 1960, 10
Police Boys Club, Washington, D.C., 161
Police Communications Center, 58–59
Police-community relations, see community planning; community relations
Police functions, see operation, police
Police, General Services and Expenditures Per Capita by City Population, 1963–64, 12
Police history
  change requirement pace, 3
  Industrial Revolution in England, 4
  law enforcement
    American colonies, 5
    early England, 3, 4
    Federal agencies, 6
    State agencies, 6
  modernization, 7
  urbanization in U.S., 5
Police Information Network (PIN), 57, 85, 110
Police integrity
  example set by FBI, 212
  internal group influence, 212
  methods of ensuring
    articulation of policy, 214
    internal investigation units, 214–215
    personnel selection, 215
    political accountability, 214
    training, 215

Police leadership
  development, 44
  exchange and rotation programs, 45
  standards, 44
  Wickersham Commission, 44
Police legal adviser, see legal adviser, police
Police Manpower, Full-Time Local, by Character of Jurisdiction, 9
Police Manpower, Full-Time Local, Per 1,000 Population, 8
Police officer, see officer, police
Police Officers, Ranking, in Representative Cities According to Race, 172
Police offices, early England, 4
Police organization, see organization, police
Police patrol, see patrol, police
Police Patrol Cars in Cities Over 10,000 Population, Manning, 54
Police Personnel in Representative Cities Outside the South According to Race, 168
Police Personnel in Representative Southern Cities According to Race, 168
Police procedures
  citizen complaints, 194
    see also citizen complaints
  court review, 31, 199
  external review of citizen grievances, 197
  internal, 192–194
  investigation of procedures
    government, 34
    legislature, 34
    universities, 34
    unofficial, 34
  lack of guidelines, 16, 17, 18
  policy, see law enforcement policy, police
  prosecutor influence, 30
  Supreme Court decision, 19, 23, 27, 199
  tactical
    patrol, 190
      see also patrol
    riots, crowds and demonstrators, 192
      see also riots
    special units
      citizen hostility, 191
      guidelines for community acceptance, 191
      training, 191
    use of dogs, 191
      citizen hostility, 191
      community acceptance, 192
      general, 191
Police promotion, see promotion, police
Police recruitment, see recruitment, police
Police recruits, see recruits, police
Police salaries, see salaries

237

Police training programs, *see* training programs
Police service, coordination and consolidation
  auxiliary services
    buildings
      city-county, 93
      location, 93
    communication, police, *see* communication, police
    detention facilities, *see* detention facilities
    equipment
      needs, 92–93
      operation, joint, 93
    laboratories, *see* laboratory services
    records, *see* records, criminal
  definition of terms, 68, 71, 72, 73
  factors involved, 68, 70
  field services, selected
    control of delinquency, *see* delinquency, control
    criminal investigation, *see* investigation, criminal
    task force operations, *see* task force operations
    vice control, *see* vice
  goal desired, 70
  jurisdictional consolidation, *see* jurisdictional consolidation, police service
  local government involvement, 68, 70
  metropolitan government control, 99
    see also Metropolitan Toronto Police Department
  mutual aid agreement, 93, 98
  obstacles
    economic, 112
    government reorganization, 111
    legal
      agreements, interlocal across State lines, 110–111
      amendments, 109
      challenges, 109
      constitutional, 109–112
      exercise of powers acts, 109–110
      objections, 109–110
      statutory, 109–112
    political and social pressures, 72–73
    relinquishment of responsibilities, 111
  solution
    cooperative agreements, 112
    council of governments, 111–112
  research methods for study, 70–71
  staff services, *see* staff services, coordination and consolidation
  working examples, 95
Police service, technological applications
  communications, *see* communications

Police service, technological applications—Continued
  computer codes and formats, standardized, 60
  information systems, 57
  radio spectrum limitations, 60
  rate of progress, 57
  research groups, 61
Police Services, Mean Per Capita Expenditures of Cities on, 1951, 12
Police special districts
  advantages, 108
  cost, 109
  criticism, 109
  disadvantages, 108
  financing, 108–109
Police Standards Council Act, Model, 219–220, 221
Police Task Force of Mayor John Lindsay, 43
Policewoman
  broadening of role, 125
  duties, 125
  number, 125
Political corruption
  alliance with organized crime, 209
  control of police, 209, 210
  effect on police, 208
President's Commission on Crime in the District of Columbia, 52, 54, 125, 138, 169, 181, 191, 202
President's Commission on Law Enforcement and Administration of Justice
  civilian role in police work, 124
  crime reduction responsibility
    citizen, 229
    local government, 229
    police, 229
  evaluation of police organization
    advisory panels, 43
    study, 43
    surveys, 43
  investigation of scientific contribution to police service, 57
  law enforcement improvement, conclusions, 37–38
  police treatment of citizens, study, 180, 182, 183, 184
  recommendations
    police organization, 43–44
    preemployment residence, 165
Professional Standards Division of International Association of Chiefs of Police, 219
Promotion, police
  leadership potential, 142
  merit system, 141
  open competition, 141, 142
  past performance, 142
  present criteria, 141, 142
  restrictions, 142
  revision of current procedures, 142
  seniority, 141
  standards, 217–218
  written examination, 142
Prostitute, harrassment arrests, 187

Public Administration Service of Chicago, 43, 219
Public Safety Department of Dade County, Florida, 130, 132
Puerto Ricans, U.S., survey on police-community relations, 149
Purchasing, police
  agent, 80
  centralized
    advantages, 80
    responsibility, 80
  departmental, 80
  intergovernmental, 80–81
  joint, 80–81

R

Radio equipment
  cars, 60
  channels, 60
  costs, 86
  cross-monitoring, 86
  digital data links, 60
  frequency space, 61
  "ham" radios, 224
  intersystem networks, 86–87
  intrajurisdictional agreements, 86
  mobile, 59–60
  point-to-point systems, 87
  portable, 60
  spectrum limitations, 60
Rattlewatch, 5
Records, criminal
  central, areawide
    advantages
      personnel reduction, 83
      time saving element, 82
    scope of services
      administrative information, 83
      operational information, 83
      reports and statistics, 83
  conclusions, 85–86
  systems
    areawide organization, 84
    criterion, 83–84
    metropolitan 85
    State, 84–85
  value, 82
Recruit Training by Program Length, Percent of Departments Providing, 1965, 11
Recruitment, police
  attracting college graduates, 126–127, 135, 136, 142
  coordination of efforts, 73, 136–137
  effect of raising standards, 133, 163
  Federal loans to students, 137
  financial incentives, 137
  flexible standards, 130
  minority groups, 123, 169
  Statewide standards, 142–143
Recruits, police
  age restrictions
    maximum, 131
    minimum, 131
    reduction, 131
    waivering, 131
  character investigation, 129

Recruits, police—Continued
  disqualification, 128, 129, 130
  emotional fitness, 129–130
  evaluation, 132
  oral interviews, 129–130
  physical requirements, 130
  probation, 132–133
  psychological testing, 129
  records, 129
  residency requirements, 130–131, 136
  screening, 10, 128, 129, 130
  training, 10, 11
    see also personnel; community relations; training
  written examination, 128
Reddin, Chief Thomas, report on police research, 57
Reforms, police
  bills, early England, 5
  problems, U.S., 7
Rehabilitation, community, 226
Reintegration, community, 226
Report on Metropolitan Police Department of President's Commission on Crime in the District of Columbia, 125
Report preparation and duplication, 56
Research
  methods, 26
  staff, 26
  technical operations, 61
  units, 26
"Resident trooper plan," 107
Revenue Cutter Service, 6
Riots
  advanced planning for handling, 193
  incidents, 193
  preventive measures
    community relations program, 145, 192
    crowd control, 192
    demonstrations control
      arrest technique, 193
      problems, 192
      special training, 193
      success of techniques, 192
Rochester, New York, civilian review board, 200
Roschach test, 129
Royal Commission on Metropolitan Toronto, 103

S

Salaries
  administrators, 135
  fringe benefits comparable to industry, 135
  increase, 134–135
  maximum, 134
  minimum, 134
  relationship with other salaries, 135
San Diego, Calif., police-community relations, 146, 149, 159, 166, 182
San Diego Police Department, 139
San Francisco, California
  gang study, 179
  interrogation study, 184

San Francisco Police Department
  community relation program, 151, 154, 155, 156, 162
  salaries, 135
San Jose Police Department, educational requirement, 126
Sauk-Prairie Police Department, 91
"Science of Law Enforcement and Citizen Responsibility, The," 223
Scotland Yard, 37
Secret Service
  investigator deployment, 55
  responsibilities, 6
Security standards, property
  buildings
    commercial, 228
    residential, 228
  effecting new construction, 228
  insurance agency involvement, 228
  reports, police, 228
  responsibility
    Federal bank agencies, 228
    Federal loan agencies, 228
    public housing, 228
    urban renewal projects, 228
  voluntary adherence, 228
Sentencing Council of the Eastern District of Michigan, 32
Services, Distributions Between those Financed by Police District Tax and Countywide Revenue, 104
Sharp, W. S., police chief in San Diego, 224
Sheriff
  American colonies, 5
  early England, 3
Shire-reeve, 3
"Signal Ten" program, 224
Smith, Bruce, Jr., 43
Smith, Bruce, Sr., 43, 52
Southeastern Michigan Chiefs of Police recruit program, 76
Southern Police Institute, 141
Southern Police Institute of the University of Louisville, 76
St. Louis police department
  community relations program, 151, 156, 159, 160
  Curriculum for Recruit Officers, Community Relations, 176
  police honesty, survey, 148
  program to aid patrol distribution, 52
  technological application, 57
  use of dogs, 192
Staff services, coordination and consolidation
  description, 73
  internal investigation
    outside assistance, 81
    units, 81, 82
  purchasing, *see* purchasing, police
  public information
    activities, 81
    programs, 81

Staff services, coordination and consolidation—Continued
  recruitment and selection
    coordination of efforts, 73
    joint activities, State level, 74–75
    other considerations, 74
    programs, 74–75
    standards, 73
  staff inspections
    coordination, 82
    purpose, 82
  study results, general, 71
  training, 75–77
Standards, State
  management, 219
  organization, 219
  programs, 218–219
  promotion, 217–218
  retention, 218
  selection, 217–218
  training, 218–219
  see also State Commission on Police Standards
State Commission on Police Standards
  findings, 217
  legislation for, 219
  operation, 219
  organization, 219–220
  power, 217
  role, 217, 220
  see also standards, State
State Crime Bureau
  benefits, 92
  requisites, 92
  use of technicians, 92
State of Washington, jail survey, 88
State police, *see* law enforcement agencies, growth, U.S. State
Stern, Mort, newspaperman, report on burglary indictments, 53
"Stop-and-Frisk" Law, 38–40
Suffolk County
  budget, 104
  charter provisions, 103
  growth, 103
Suffolk County (N.Y.) Police Department, 94, 104
Surveys, police-community relations
  general public, 145
  juveniles, 148, 149
  low income group, 149
  Negroes, 146
  other minority groups, 149
Syndicate crime, 79

T

Task force operations
  concept, 97, 98
  financing, 98
  manpower, 98
  need, 97
  powers
    municipal, multijurisdictional, 97–98
    State, 97

Teaching techniques, 139
Technology applied to police service, see police service, technological applications
Tennessee Supreme Court, 102
Texas Rangers, 6
Theft, automobile prevention
  Federal, 228
  ignition system, 228
  locking, 228
  fines, 227
  ownership proof, 228
  protective barriers, 228
  serial identification, 228
  survey, 222
Traffic Institute of Northwestern University, 76
Training aids, 140
Training programs
  California, 218
  career development, 141
  causes of inaction, 75
  central city assistance, 76
  civilian instructors, 139, 177
  community relations, 154, 175
    see also personnel, community relations, training
  content, 138–139
  continuing, 139–140
  conventional, 131
  deficiencies, 36, 75, 138, 139
  ethics, instruction, 215
  for Community Service Officers, 131
  improvement, 36
  institutes and academies, 76
  inservice, 26, 76, 140–141, 177
  length, 132, 139
  methods of instruction, 139
  need, 75, 137, 218

Training programs—Continued
  New York, 170, 218
  on policy, 27, 29
  problems
    core concept, 76–77
    manpower, 77
      see also manpower reserve
    multijurisdictional, State support, 77
  State agency
    duties, 77
    recommendations, 77
  qualifications for instructors, 139
  recruits, 10, 11, 76
  regional, 76
  return-to-school, 140
  specialized, 218
  standards, 218–219
  State, 42, 75, 76
  university and colleges, 75, 76, 141, 218
Training schools, 6
Tucson Police Department, Arizona, 139

U

"Uniform Crime Reports", FBI, 11, 96, 186
United States Conference of Mayors, survey on community relations programs, 150, 156
United States Department of Justice, 127, 141
United States Post Office Department, 42
United States Treasury Department, 42
University of Indiana, 141

University of Iowa Institute of Public Affairs, 43
University of Wisconsin Law School, 51, 89
U.S. Employment Service, community relations, 162
U.S. Supreme Court decisions
  police procedures
    Miranda v. *Arizona*, 19, 23, 27
    Screws v. *U.S.*, 199
  prisoner interrogation, 89

V

Vice
  control of problems
    areawide level
      Federal, 97
      State, 97
    local
      investigation, 96–97
      manpower, 97
      training, 97
    types and classes, 96–97
Virginia Department of Education, 140
Vollmer, Chief August, Berkeley, Calif., 43, 52, 56, 225

W X Y Z

Watts area of Los Angeles, survey on public opinion of police, 147, 148
Wickersham Commission
  police brutality, 181
  report on police, 127
Yerby, Richard D., 107
YMCA, crime prevention, 225

POLICE IN AMERICA
An Arno Press/New York Times Collection

The American Institute of Law and Criminology.
Journal of the American Institute of Law and Criminology: Selected Articles. Chicago, 1910–1929.

The Boston Police Strike: Two Reports. Boston, 1919–1920.

Boston Police Debates: Selected Arguments. Boston, 1863–1869.

Chamber of Commerce of the State of New York.
Papers and Proceedings of Committee on the Police Problem, City of New York. New York, 1905.

Chicago Police Investigations: Three Reports. Illinois, 1898–1912.

Control of the Baltimore Police: Collected Reports. Baltimore, 1860–1866.

Crime and Law Enforcement in the District of Columbia: Report and Hearings. Washington, D. C., 1952.

Crime in the District of Columbia: Reports and Hearings. Washington, D. C., 1935.

Flinn, John J. and John E. Wilkie.
History of the Chicago Police. Chicago, 1887.

Hamilton, Mary E.
The Policewoman. New York, 1924.

Harrison, Leonard Vance.
Police Administration in Boston. Cambridge, Mass., 1934.

International Association of Chiefs of Police.
Police Unions. Washington, D. C., 1944.

The Joint Special Committee.
Reports of the Special Committee Appointed to Investigate the Official Conduct of the Members of the Board of Police Commissioners. Boston, 1882.

Justice in Jackson, Mississippi: U.S. Civil Rights Commission Hearings. Washington, D. C., 1965.

McAdoo, William.
Guarding a Great City. New York, 1906.

Mayo, Katherine.
Justice to All. New York, 1917.

Missouri Joint Committee of the General Assembly.
Report of the Joint Committee of the General Assembly Appointed to Investigate the Police Department of the City of St. Louis. St. Louis, Missouri, 1868.

National Commission on Law Observance and Enforcement.
Report on the Police. Washington, D. C., 1931.

National Prison Association.
Proceedings of the Annual Congress of the National Prison Association of the United States: Selected Articles. 1874–1902.

New York City Common Council.
Report of the Special Committee of the New York City Board of Aldermen on the New York City Police Department. New York, 1844.

National Police Convention.
Official Proceedings of the National Prison Convention. St. Louis, 1871.

Pennsylvania Federation of Labor.
The American Cossack. Washington, D. C., 1915.

Police and the Blacks: U.S. Civil Rights Commission Hearings. 1960–1966.

Police in New York City: An Investigation. New York, 1912–1931.

The President's Commission on Law Enforcement and Administration of Justice.
Task Force Report: The Police. Washington, D. C., 1967.

Sellin, Thorsten, editor.
The Police and the Crime Problem. Philadelphia, 1929.

Smith, Bruce, editor.
New Goals in Police Management. Philadelphia, 1954.

Sprogle, Howard O.
The Philadelphia Police, Past and Present. Philadelphia, 1887.

U.S. Committee on Education and Labor.
The Chicago Memorial Day Incident: Hearings and Report. Washington, D. C., 1937.

U.S. Committee on Education and Labor.
Documents Relating to Intelligence Bureau or Red Squad of Los Angeles Police Department. Washington, D. C., 1940.

U.S. Committee on Education and Labor.
Private Police Systems. Washington, D. C., 1939.

Urban Police: Selected Surveys. 1926–1946.

Women's Suffrage and the Police: Three Senate Documents. Washington, D. C., 1913.

Woods, Arthur.
Crime Prevention. Princeton, New Jersey, 1918.

Woods, Arthur.
Policeman and Public. New Haven, Conn., 1919.

AMERICAN POLICE SUPPLEMENT

International Association of Chiefs of Police.
Proceedings of the Annual Conventions of the International Association of Chiefs of Police. 1893–1930. 5 vols.

New York State Senate.
Report and Proceedings of the Senate Committee Appointed to Investigate the Police Department of the City of New York. (Lexow Committee Report). New York, 1895. 6 vols.

THE POLICE IN GREAT BRITAIN

Committee on Police Conditions of Service.
Report of the Committee on Police Conditions of Service. London, 1949.

Committee on the Police Service.
Minutes of Evidence and Report: England, Wales, Scotland. London, 1919–1920.

Royal Commission on Police Powers and Procedures.
Report of the Royal Commission on Police Powers and Procedure. London, 1929.

Select Committee on Police.
Report of Select Committee on Police with the Minutes of Evidence. London, 1853.

Royal Commission Upon the Duties of the Metropolitan Police.
Minutes of Evidence Taken Before the Royal Commission Upon the Duties of the Metropolitan Police Together With Appendices and Index. London, 1908.

Committee on Police.
Report from the Select Committee on Police of the Metropolis. London, 1828.